CONTEMPORARY POLITICAL PHILOSOPHY

CONTEMPORARY POLITICAL PHILOSOPHY

AN INTRODUCTION

Second edition

———

WILL KYMLICKA

OXFORD
UNIVERSITY PRESS

OXFORD

UNIVERSITY PRESS

Great Clarendon Street, Oxford OX2 6DP

Oxford University Press is a department of the University of Oxford.
It furthers the University's objective of excellence in research, scholarship,
and education by publishing worldwide in

Oxford New York

Auckland Cape Town Dar es Salaam Hong Kong Karachi
Kuala Lumpur Madrid Melbourne Mexico City Nairobi
New Delhi Shanghai Taipei Toronto

With offices in

Argentina Austria Brazil Chile Czech Republic France Greece
Guatemala Hungary Italy Japan South Korea Poland Portugal
Singapore Switzerland Thailand Turkey Ukraine Vietnam

Oxford is a registered trade mark of Oxford University Press
in the UK and in certain other countries

Published in the United States
by Oxford University Press Inc., New York

© Will Kymlicka 2002

The moral rights of the author have been asserted

Database right Oxford University Press (maker)

First published 2002

All rights reserved. No part of this publication may be reproduced,
stored in a retrieval system, or transmitted, in any form or by any means,
without the prior permission in writing of Oxford University Press,
or as expressly permitted by law, or under terms agreed with the appropriate
reprographics rights organization. Enquiries concerning reproduction
outside the scope of the above should be sent to the Rights Department,
Oxford University Press, at the address above.

You must not circulate this book in any other binding or cover
and you must impose this same condition on any acquirer.

British Library Cataloguing in Publication Data

Data available

Library of Congress Cataloging in Publication Data

Data available

ISBN-13: 978-0-19-878274-2

16

Typeset in Minion and Trajan
by RefineCatch Limited, Bungay, Suffolk
Printed and bound in Great Britain by
Clays Ltd, St Ives plc

For Sue

CONTENTS

PREFACE TO THE SECOND EDITION

The original edition of this book was written shortly after I finished graduate school. At the time, I thought it was puzzling that there were not more political philosophy textbooks written by older colleagues who presumably had many years of lecture notes to work from, and who had much more experience both teaching and researching these topics.

Twelve years later, it seems to me that only an eager postgraduate, overly confident of his new-found knowledge and convictions, would even have the idea of writing such an ambitious book. I actually had two ambitions for the book. The first was to provide a reasonably comprehensive overview of the most important theories in contemporary Anglo-American political philosophy. The second was to show the interconnections between the various theories. I wanted to show that each theory could be seen as addressing some common questions, and as responding to the weaknesses or limitations in the way previous theories answered them, so that we could see progress over time as the field developed.

Both of these now seem somewhat overambitious. The first task, of providing a comprehensive overview, was probably unrealistic at the time, but has become even more difficult in the last decade, due to the explosion of writing in the field. One indication of this is the exponential growth in journals devoted to the field. When John Rawls wrote *Theory of Justice* in 1971, which I take as ground zero for our debates, there was only one journal (*Ethics*) devoted to the field of political philosophy, and it was more or less moribund. When I wrote the first edition of this book, the revitalized *Ethics* had been joined by a few newcomers like *Philosophy and Public Affairs* and *Political Theory*. Today, we have seen another wave of new journals, including *Journal of Political Philosophy*, *Critical Review of International Social and Political Philosophy*, and *Journal of Political Ideologies*. We have also seen the birth of new book series devoted to the field—most prominently the 'Oxford Political Theory' series from Oxford University Press, and the 'Contemporary Political Theory' series from Cambridge University Press.

In short, there are more people working in the field, publishing more articles and books, than ever before. And these publications are not simply refining old approaches, but are addressing entirely new topics that were almost invisible in the 1970s and 1980s—topics such as multiculturalism, or deliberative democracy.

So there is simply too much material for me to keep up with, and it is impossible to maintain even the pretence of a fully comprehensive introduction. Indeed, I sometimes think we need an entirely new kind of introduction to our field: one that picks a few examples to study rather than surveys the field, or one that focuses more on method and less on substantive theories.

However, I confess I have a soft spot in my heart for this book, and enjoy the thought that it has helped introduce what I believe are some very important ideas to new audiences. I think there is still a need for something which at least approximates a survey of the field.

To keep things manageable, I have had to make difficult choices about what material from the past decade to include in this new edition. In my own work, I have focused on issues of citizenship, and I think this has been one of the most fruitful areas of debate in the 1990s. Indeed, some commentators have said that 'citizenship' was the buzzword of the 1990s, like 'justice' in the 1970s, and 'community' in the 1980s. So I have added two new chapters on citizenship. The first focuses on the sorts of skills, virtues, and activities that citizens must exhibit if a democratic polity is to be effective, stable, and just. This is an issue that has been raised most forcefully by civic republicans, although it has been addressed by many schools of thought, and underlies recent accounts of civic virtues, citizenship education, public reason, and deliberative democracy.

The second chapter focuses on the relationship between citizenship and group differences. Citizenship is often assumed to be a status that we should all hold in common, but many groups seek legal and political recognition of their distinct identities, through some form of 'politics of difference' or 'politics of recognition'. This is an issue raised most forcefully by theorists of multiculturalism, but it also raises more general issues of individual versus group rights, nationalism, racism, immigration, and group representation.

These are not the only important new issues raised in the 1990s. In particular, I regret not having a chapter addressing the growing debate concerning our moral obligations to the environment and to animals—a debate which goes to the core of our basic assumptions about the nature of political morality and political community.[1] But I hope that these two new chapters on citizenship, combined with extensive updates to the previous chapters, will give readers a good, if not fully comprehensive, introduction to the field as it stands today.

As I noted earlier, one of my ambitions in the first edition was to identify the ways in which new theories can be seen as relating to older theories, building on their strengths and remedying their weaknesses. This task too is more complicated today, given the growing diversity of topics and approaches in the field. It is more difficult to see a consistent logic or narrative which explains or encompasses all the assorted developments in the field, or to find ways of measuring 'progress' in the literature.

Indeed, confronted with a growing diversity of approaches, each with its own vocabulary and preoccupations, it may seem that contemporary political philosophy is simply a disconnected series of discrete arguments or debates, each developing according to its own inner logic, unrelated to the rest of the field. The dizzying array of new theories in the last decade only increases this sense of fragmentation and dislocation.

In my view, however, this multiplication of theories and vocabularies can obscure the fact that political philosophers must all grapple with some common problems, and must do so in light of the same realities of modern life, with its characteristic needs, aspirations, and complexities. Theorists disagree about how to interpret these problems and realities, but we miss the point and purpose of these different theories if we do not keep sight of the common issues they are dealing with. And once we see these common objectives, we can also start to form judgements about whether we are making progress towards achieving them.

Indeed, it is difficult for me to understand why anyone would get involved in the project of political philosophy if they did not think we could make progress on these issues. Since this promise of progress seems to me essential to the project, I have not shied away from identifying cases where I think new theories offer not only different, but also better, answers to these common problems.

What are these common themes or problems which the various theories are trying to address? One theme which I emphasized in the first edition was the way each theory could be seen as trying to interpret what it means for governments to show 'equal concern and respect' to their citizens. I discuss this idea at length in the Introduction, and how it enables us to evaluate competing theories, so will not repeat it here.

But there are two other common themes which were implicit in the first edition, and which I have tried to highlight more strongly in this new edition. The first is the centrality of liberal democracy to contemporary political philosophy. To oversimplify, we can say that contemporary political philosophers fall into two camps. On the one hand, we have those who endorse the basic tenets of liberal democracy, and who are concerned to provide the best philosophical defence of these values. To date, there have been three main approaches to defending liberal democracy: utilitarianism, liberal equality, and libertarianism. Taken together, they have come to define the language of political debate in Anglo-American liberal democracies. The cluster of concepts associated with these three approaches—'rights', 'liberty', 'the greatest good of the greatest number', 'equal opportunity', etc.—dominates political discourse at both the theoretical and practical level. Indeed, the hegemony of these theories is so great that, to some people, they provide 'the only political language that can sound a convincing moral note in our public realms' (Grant 1974: 5).

The first three chapters of this book evaluate these three influential defences of liberal democracy. We can describe these three theories as forming the 'mainstream' of contemporary political philosophy. But there have always been those who reject liberal democracy, in whole or in part, and who offer an alternative set of concepts and principles to supplement or replace the liberal-democratic vocabulary. Chapters 4–9 look at five such schools of criticism: Marxism, communitarianism, feminism, civic republicanism, and multiculturalism. We can describe these theories as forming 'critiques and alternatives' to the mainstream liberal-democratic theories.

However, as we will see, each of these five approaches exhibits an ambivalent relationship to the idea of liberal democracy. On the one hand, they criticize mainstream theories, which they see as operating to justify or obscure fundamental problems with society, such as the exploitation and alienation of wage-labourers (Marxism), social atomism (communitarianism), the subordination of women (feminism), cultural marginalization or assimilation (multiculturalism), or political apathy (civic republicanism). But on the other hand, they often suggest that the problem is not so much with the principles of liberal democracy, but rather with their imperfect implementation, or the lack of appropriate preconditions for implementing them. To solve these problems, do we need to abandon liberal-democratic principles, or better fulfil them? Are these principles sufficient, or do they need to be supplemented?

Viewing each of these theories as offering a different defence or critique of liberal democracy helps us, I think, to see better precisely what they have in common, and where they differ.

A second, more specific, theme which emerges throughout the book concerns ideas of responsibility. The idea that 'responsibility' should be a central category of political thought is sometimes associated with feminism and civic republicanism, both of which chastise liberals for their supposed preoccupation with 'rights'. But as we will see, the idea of responsibility is central to all of these theories. Indeed they can be rephrased as an account of who is responsible for meeting which needs or costs or choices. They differ, not over the centrality of responsibility per se, but over more specific questions about personal responsibility and collective responsibility. For example, are we responsible for our own choices, in the sense that we should pay for the costs of our choices, and not expect others to subsidize our voluntarily incurred expenses? Are we responsible for remedying the involuntary disadvantages that others find themselves in, such that no one is disadvantaged by undeserved and unchosen inequalities in life-chances? Responsibility for self and responsibility for others are basic to all the theories, and thinking of the theories in these terms helps to clarify their points of agreement and disagreement.

Treating people with equal concern and respect; defences and critiques of liberal democracy; responsibility for self and other—these are some of the common themes which I have tried to weave throughout the text, and which I think provide a useful skeleton framework for understanding and evaluating the diverse and growing range of theories in the field.

My hope is that when the reader has finished this book, he or she will be able to pick up one of the journals I mentioned earlier and feel at home with the articles in it. My book will not have defined or explained all the terminology encountered in these journals, but I hope it will explain the major topics and approaches discussed in today's journals. Moreover, I hope it will explain why these topics and approaches have become matters of debate. I hope the reader will know why some topics are seen as a weakness for certain approaches, and how other approaches have emerged to remedy these weaknesses.[2]

I should emphasize that this book is not a light read. It is an introduction, but my goal is to introduce people to the cutting-edge work being done in the field. As I said in the introduction to the first edition, I believe that some truly great work has been done in the field, and I want to tell people about it.

This cutting-edge work is often quite sophisticated: the concepts are multifaceted, and the arguments rest on subtle distinctions or examples. I have tried to explain these concepts and distinctions as clearly as possible for those who are new to the material, but I have not tried to avoid the complexity or subtlety.

Put another way, this is not just an introduction to the main questions addressed in contemporary political philosophy, but also an introduction to the best answers we have to those questions. Understanding the arguments may require some concentration, but I hope you will agree the payoff is worth the effort.

NOTES

1. Consider, for example, the important Great Ape Project, an international movement to extend certain basic 'human' rights to the great apes (Cavalieri and Singer 1993). For more general issues of the extension of the moral community to include non-human animals, see DeGrazia 1995; Regan 2001. For debates about the moral status of the environment, see Eckersley 1992; Dobson 1990; Zimmerman 1993; Goodin 1992a, De-Shalit 2000.

2. Needless to say, there is a great deal of interesting work in political philosophy outside the Anglo-American tradition, often with very different preoccupations. For an account of 'the return of political philosophy' in post-war Europe, see Manent 2000.

ACKNOWLEDGEMENTS FOR THE
SECOND EDITION

For helpful comments on the first edition, and/or suggestions for the second, I would like to thank Ingrid Robeyns, Veit Bader, David Schmidtz, Matt Matravers, Paul Warren, Steven Reiber, Samuel Freeman, Shelley Tremain, Cindy Stark, and six anonymous referees for OUP.

Special thanks to Colin Macleod and Jacob Levy for their extensive comments, including answering some emergency calls for help on topics where I was out of my depth, and to Sue Donaldson who has, once again, reviewed the new material with me line by line.

I would also like to thank Idil Boran for excellent research assistance, Sarah O'Leary for bibliographic help, and Tim Barton and Angela Griffin at OUP for their enthusiasm and patience.

ACKNOWLEDGEMENTS FOR THE
FIRST EDITION

I would like to thank Richard Arneson, Ian Carter, James Griffin, Sally Haslanger, Brad Hooker, Andrew Kernohan, David Knott, Henry Laycock, Colin Macleod, Susan Moller Okin, Arthur Ripstein, Wayne Sumner, and Peter Vallentyne for helpful comments on parts or all of this book. I owe a special debt to G. A. Cohen, who taught me most of what I know about the aims and methods of political philosophy. He has generously and patiently commented on many of the arguments in this book. My greatest debt is to Sue Donaldson, who has gone over the book with me, line by line, on more than one occasion.

1

INTRODUCTION

1. THE PROJECT

This book is intended to provide an introduction to, and critical appraisal of, the major schools of thought which dominate contemporary debates in political philosophy. The material covered is almost entirely comprised of recent works in normative political philosophy and, more particularly, recent theories of a just or free or good society. It does not cover, except incidentally, the major historical figures, nor does it cover many other subjects that were once considered the focal point of political philosophy—e.g. the conceptual analysis of the meaning of power, or sovereignty, or of the nature of law. These were popular topics thirty-five years ago, but the recent emphasis has been on the ideals of justice, freedom, and community which are invoked when evaluating political institutions and policies. I will not, of course, attempt to cover all the recent developments in these areas, but will concentrate on those theories which have attracted a certain allegiance, and which offer a more or less comprehensive vision of the ideals of politics.

One reason for writing this book is my belief that there is a remarkable amount of interesting and important work being done in the field. To put it simply, the intellectual landscape in political philosophy today is quite different from what it was twenty, or even ten years, ago. The arguments being advanced are often genuinely original, not only in developing new variations on old themes (e.g. Nozick's development of Lockean natural rights theory), but also in the development of new perspectives (e.g. feminism). One result of these developments is that the traditional categories within which political theories are discussed and evaluated are increasingly inadequate.

Our traditional picture of the political landscape views political principles as falling somewhere on a single line, stretching from left to right. According to this traditional picture, people on the left believe in equality, and hence endorse some form of socialism, while those on the right believe in freedom, and hence endorse some form of free-market capitalism. In the middle are the liberals, who believe in a wishy-washy mixture of equality and freedom, and hence endorse some form of welfare state capitalism. There are, of course, many positions in between these three points, and many people accept different parts of different theories. But it is often thought that the best way to understand or describe someone's political principles is to try to locate them somewhere on that line.

There is some truth to this way of thinking about Western political theory. But it is increasingly inadequate. First, it ignores a number of important issues. For example, left and right are distinguished by their views of freedom and justice in the traditionally male-dominated spheres of government and economy. But what about the fairness or freedom of the traditionally female spheres of home and family? Mainstream political theorists from left to right have tended to either neglect these other spheres, or to claim that they do not raise questions of justice and freedom. An adequate theory of sexual equality will involve considerations that simply are not addressed in traditional left–right debates. The traditional picture has also been criticized for ignoring issues of historical context. Theories on both the left and right seek to provide us with principles we can use to test and criticize our historical traditions and cultural practices. But communitarians believe that evaluating political institutions cannot be a matter of judging them against some independent ahistorical standard. They believe that political judgement is a matter of interpreting the traditions and practices we already find ourselves in. So there are issues of our historical and communal 'embeddedness' which are not addressed in traditional left–right disputes. We cannot begin to understand feminism or communitarianism if we insist on locating them somewhere on a single left–right continuum.

So one problem concerns the narrowness of the traditional picture. This objection is a fairly common one now, and most commentators in the field have tried to bring out the greater range of principles that get invoked in political debate. But there is another feature of the traditional picture which I believe is equally in need of revision. The traditional picture suggests that different theories have different foundational values: the reason that right and left disagree over capitalism is that the left believes in equality while the right believes in freedom. Since they disagree over fundamental values, their differences are not rationally resolvable. The left can argue that if you believe in equality, then you should support socialism; and the right can argue that if you believe in freedom, you should support capitalism. But there is no way to argue for equality over freedom, or freedom over equality, since these are foundational values, with no higher value or premiss that both sides can jointly appeal to. The deeper we probe these political debates, the more intractable they become, for we are left with nothing but conflicting appeals to ultimate, and ultimately opposed, values.

This feature of the traditional picture has remained largely unquestioned, even by those commentators who reject the traditional left–right classifications. Each of the new theories is also assumed to appeal to a different ultimate value. Thus we are told that alongside the older appeal to 'equality' (socialism) and 'liberty' (libertarianism), political theories now appeal to the ultimate values of 'contractual agreement' (Rawls), 'the common good' (communitarianism), 'utility' (utilitarianism), 'rights' (Dworkin), 'identity' (multiculturalism), or 'androgyny' (feminism).[1] So we now have an even greater number of ultimate values between which there can be no rational arguments. But this explosion of potential ultimate values raises an obvious problem for the whole project of developing a single comprehensive theory of justice. If there are so many potential ultimate values, why should we continue to think that an adequate political theory can be based on just one of them? Surely the only sensible response to this plurality of proposed ultimate values is to give up the idea of developing a 'monistic' theory of justice. To subordinate all other values to one overriding value seems almost fanatical.

A successful theory of justice, therefore, will have to accept bits and pieces from most of the existing theories. But if the disagreements between these values really are foundational, how can they be integrated into a single theory? One traditional aim of political philosophy was to find coherent and comprehensive rules for deciding between conflicting political values. But how can we have such comprehensive criteria unless there is some deeper value in terms of which the conflicting values are judged? Without such a deeper value, there could only be ad hoc and localized resolutions of conflicts. We would have to accept the inevitable compromises that are required between theories, rather than hope for any one theory to provide comprehensive guidance. And indeed this is what many commentators believe is the fate of contemporary theorizing about justice. Political philosophy is, on this view, drowning in its own success. There has been an explosion of interest in the traditional aim of finding the one true theory of justice, but the result of this explosion has been to make that traditional aim seem wholly implausible.

Is this an accurate picture of the political landscape? Do contemporary political theories appeal to conflicting ultimate values? I want to explore a suggestion, advanced by Ronald Dworkin, that modern political theories do not have different foundational values. On Dworkin's view, every plausible political theory has the same ultimate value, which is equality. They are all 'egalitarian' theories (Dworkin: 1977 179–83; 1983: 24; 1986: 296–301; 1987: 7–8; cf. Nagel 1979: 111). That suggestion is clearly false if by 'egalitarian theory' we mean a theory which supports an equal distribution of income. But there is another, more abstract and more fundamental, idea of equality in political theory—namely, the idea of treating people 'as equals'. There are various ways to express this more basic idea of equality. A theory is egalitarian in this sense if it accepts that the interests of each member of the community matter, and matter equally. Put another way, egalitarian theories require that the government treat its citizens with equal consideration; each citizen is entitled to equal concern and respect. This more basic notion of equality is found in Nozick's libertarianism as much as in Marx's communism. While leftists believe that equality of income or wealth is a precondition for treating people as equals, those on the right believe that equal rights over one's labour and property are a precondition for treating people as equals.

So the abstract idea of equality can be interpreted in various ways, without necessarily favouring equality in any particular area, be it income, wealth, opportunities, or liberties. It is a matter of debate between these theories which specific kind of equality is required by the more abstract idea of treating people as equals. Not every political theory ever invented is egalitarian in· this broad sense. But if a theory claimed that some people were not entitled to equal consideration from the government, if it claimed that certain kinds of people just do not matter as much as others, then most people in the modern world would reject that theory immediately. Dworkin's suggestion is that the idea that each person matters equally is at the heart of all plausible political theories.

This is the suggestion I want to explore in this book, for I believe it is as important as any of the particular theories which it attempts to interpret. (One of its advantages is that it makes the quest for a single comprehensive theory of justice seem more intelligible.) Not everyone agrees that each of these theories is based on a principle of equality, and I will be looking at other ways of interpreting them. For example, I will be discussing what it might mean for libertarianism to have freedom as its foundational value, or for utilitarianism to have utility as its foundational value. In each case, I will compare the different interpretations to see which presents the most coherent and attractive account of the theory in question.

If Dworkin's suggestion is correct, then the scepticism many people feel about the possibility of rationally resolving debates between theories of justice may be misplaced, or, at any rate, too hasty. If each theory shares the same 'egalitarian plateau'—that is, if each theory is attempting to define the social, economic, and political conditions under which the members of the community are treated as equals—then we might be able to show that one of the theories does a better job living up to the standard that they all recognize. Whereas the traditional view tells us that the fundamental argument in political theory is whether to accept equality as a value, this revised view tells us that the fundamental argument is not whether to accept equality, but how best to interpret it. And that means people would be arguing on the same wavelength, so to speak, even those who do not fit on the traditional left–right continuum. Thus the idea of an egalitarian plateau for political argument is potentially better able to accommodate both the diversity and unity of contemporary political philosophy.

2. A NOTE ON METHOD

It is common in a book of this sort to say something about one's methodology, about how one understands the enterprise of political philosophy, what distinguishes it from other intellectual enterprises, such as moral philosophy, and how one goes about judging its success. I will not say much about these questions here, partly because I do not think there is much that can be said at a general level. Each of the theories examined below answers these questions in a different way—each offers its own account of the division between moral and political philosophy, and its own account of the criteria of successful argument. Evaluating a particular account of the nature of political philosophy, therefore, cannot be separated out from, or done in advance of, evaluating substantive theories of justice.

However, it may be helpful to foreshadow some of the points discussed in later chapters. I believe there is a fundamental continuity between moral and political philosophy, in at least two respects. First, as Robert Nozick puts it, 'moral philosophy sets the background for, and boundaries of, political philosophy. What persons may and may not do to one another limits what they may do through the apparatus of a state, or do to establish such an apparatus. The moral prohibitions it is permissible to enforce are the source of whatever legitimacy the state's fundamental coercive power has' (Nozick 1974: 6). We have moral obligations towards each other, some of which are matters of public responsibility, enforced through public institutions, others of which are matters of personal responsibility, involving rules of personal conduct. Political philosophy focuses on those obligations which justify the use of public institutions. Different theories distinguish public and private responsibility in different ways, but I agree with Nozick that the content of these responsibilities, and the line between them, must be determined by appeal to deeper moral principles.

Secondly, and relatedly, any account of our public responsibilities must fit into a broader moral framework that makes room for, and makes sense of, our private responsibilities. Even where a political theory makes a sharp distinction between public and private responsibility, so that the political principles it endorses have little immediate bearing on rules of personal conduct, it still must not crowd out (in theory or practice) our sense of personal responsibility for helping friends, keeping promises, pursuing projects. This is a problem, I believe, for utilitarian accounts of justice (Chapter 2). On the other hand, it is equally true that any account of our personal obligations must make room for what Rawls calls 'the very great values applying to political institutions', such as democracy, equality, and tolerance. For example, it is an important criticism of the 'ethic of care' that it leaves no room for these political values to operate—they are crowded out by the dynamics of ethical caring (Chapter 9).

This leaves us with many unanswered questions about the relationship between moral and political philosophy, and about the sorts of convergence and conflict we can expect or tolerate between personal and political values. But these are issues that can only be discussed within the context of particular theories.

As for the criteria by which we judge success in the enterprise of political philosophy, I believe that the ultimate test of a theory of justice is that it cohere with, and help illuminate, our considered convictions of justice. If on reflection we share the intuition that slavery is unjust, then it is a powerful objection to a proposed theory of justice that it supports slavery. Conversely, if a theory of justice matches our considered intuitions, and structures them so as to bring out their internal logic, then we have a powerful argument in favour of that theory. It is of course possible that these intuitions are baseless, and the history of philosophy is full of attempts to defend theories without any appeal to our intuitive sense of right and wrong. But I do not believe there is any other plausible way of proceeding. In any event, the fact is that we have an intuitive sense of right and wrong, and it is natural, indeed unavoidable, that we try to work out its implications—that we seek to do 'what we can to render coherent and to justify our convictions of social justice' (Rawls 1971: 21).[2]

Different theories appeal to our considered convictions in different ways. Utilitarians and libertarians, for example, answer to them in a more indirect way than liberals or feminists do, and communitarians give our intuitions a quite different status from Marxists. But, again, these are all matters to be discussed in the context of particular theories.

So political philosophy, as I understand it, is a matter of moral argument, and moral argument is a matter of appeal to our considered convictions. In saying this, I am drawing on what I take to be the everyday view of moral and political argument; that is, we all have moral beliefs, these beliefs can be right or wrong, we have reasons for thinking they are either right or wrong, and these reasons and beliefs can be organized into systematic moral principles and theories of justice. A central aim of political philosophy, therefore, is to evaluate competing theories of justice to assess the strength and coherence of their arguments for the rightness of their views.

This will seem a hopeless aim to many people. Some people believe that moral values do not really exist, and hence our 'beliefs' about these values are really just statements of personal preference. As such they cannot be right or wrong, and there is no room for rationally evaluating them. Others believe that while moral beliefs may be right or wrong, there is no way to organize them into systematic principles. Our judgements of justice come from a tacit understanding or sense of appropriateness which tells us how to respond to particular circumstances. Any attempt to formalize these judgements into abstract rules or principles distorts them and produces empty formulas. Still others believe that while we have reasons for our beliefs about justice, and while these reasons may be organized into systematic principles, the only intelligible kinds of reasons and principles are those that appeal to our historical traditions. Justice is a matter of cultural interpretation rather than philosophical argument.

I will consider some of these alternative ways of understanding the enterprise in later chapters. However, I do not believe that these (or other) critiques of the traditional aims of political philosophy are successful. I will not attempt to establish the possibility of rationally defending a comprehensive theory of justice, or refute the various objections to it. In fact, I doubt there is any way to defend that possibility, other than by providing particular arguments for a particular theory. The only way to show that it is possible to advance compelling arguments for the rightness or wrongness of principles of justice is actually to advance some compelling arguments. The rest of this book is, therefore, the only argument I have for the usefulness of my methodological assumptions. Whether it is a good argument or not is for the reader to decide.

GUIDE TO FURTHER READING

There are several other introductions to political philosophy, although most offer a much broader historical sweep than my book, introducing the major historical figures such as Aristotle, Hobbes, and Kant, as well as contemporary debates. Four helpful introductions along this line are Jean Hampton, *Political Philosophy* (Westview, 1997); Jonathan Wolff, *An Introduction to Political Philosophy* (Oxford University Press, 1996); Raymond Plant, *Modern Political Thought* (Blackwell, 1991); Dudley Knowles, *Political Philosophy* (McGill-Queen's University Press, 2001).

For introductory surveys which, like mine, are focused on contemporary debates, see Lesley Jacobs, *An Introduction to Modern Political Philosophy: The Democratic Vision of Politics* (Prentice-Hall, 1997); and Tom Campbell, *Justice*, 2nd edn. (Palgrave, 2000).

As its name suggests, the field of political philosophy constitutes an area of overlap between the disciplines of philosophy and political science. For surveys of contemporary political theory in relation to other fields of political science, see Iris Young, 'Political Theory: An Overview' and Bhikhu Parekh, 'Political Theory: Traditions in Political Philosophy', both in Robert Goodin and Hans-Dieter Klingeman (eds.), *A New Handbook of Political Science* (Oxford University Press, 1997), and William

Galston, 'Political Theory in the 1980s', in Ada Finifter (ed.), *Political Science: The State of the Discipline 2* (American Political Science Association, 1993).

An invaluable reference volume, useful to both students and scholars, is Robert Goodin and Philip Pettit (eds.), *A Companion to Contemporary Political Philosophy* (Blackwell, 1993). This volume contains forty-one entries exploring the main concepts and schools of thought in contemporary political philosophy, each accompanied by a selective bibliography. Another entry in the Blackwell Companion series—Peter Singer (ed.), *A Companion to Ethics* (Blackwell, 1991)—also has many relevant entries.

There are several anthologies available containing excerpts from the most important writings in contemporary political philosophy. Two of the best are Robert Goodin and Philip Pettit (eds.), *Contemporary Political Philosophy: An Anthology* (Blackwell, 1997), and George Sher and Baruch Brody (eds.), *Social and Political Philosophy: Contemporary Readings* (Harcourt Brace, 1999). I have also edited a two-volume anthology entitled *Justice in Political Philosophy* (Edward Elgar, 1992), which collects fifty-five of the most influential articles from 1971 to 1990.

For those who wish to keep abreast of new developments, there are several journals which publish extensively in the field of Anglo-American political philosophy. The best known and most established are *Ethics*; *Political Theory*; and *Philosophy and Public Affairs*. Other relevant journals, some of which are quite recent, include *Journal of Political Philosophy*; *Critical Review of International Social and Political Philosophy*; *Social Theory and Practice*; *Public Affairs Quarterly*; *Journal of Political Ideologies*; *Journal of Applied Philosophy*; *Ethical Theory and Moral Practice*; *Philosophy, Politics and Economics*. For a helpful survey, see David McCabe's 'New Journals in Political Philosophy and Related Fields', *Ethics*, 106/4 (1996): 800–16.

Although they generally fall beyond the scope of this book, other important political philosophy journals include *Review of Politics*; *Interpretation*; *Constellations*; and *Philosophy and Social Criticism*. The former two specialize in the history of political thought, the latter two in continental political philosophy.

Compared to other fields, political philosophy is still under-represented on the Internet. The most important website is the homepage of the 'Foundations of Political Theory' section of the American Political Science Association (**www.political-theory.org**). It contains lists of recent publications, relevant conferences, sample course syllabuses, on-line texts, and links to the webpages of other relevant associations. One such link is to the American Society for Political and Legal Philosophy (**www.political-theory.org/asplp.html**), which produces the important series of annual NOMOS volumes, focusing on particular topics in political philosophy.

Another helpful website is Lawrence Hinman's Ethics webpage (**www.ethics. sandiego.edu/index.html**). It contains many resources (annotated bibliographies, on-line texts, sample questions) for both students and professors regarding courses in ethics and political philosophy.

A third website worth checking is the Brown Electronic Article Review Service (BEARS), which provides short electronic reviews of recently published articles in ethics and political philosophy (**www.brown.edu/Departments/Philosophy/bears/ homepage.html**).

Many countries have their own professional associations for people working in the field of political philosophy. One truly international organization, however, is the Conference for the Study of Political Thought, which has chapters in many countries in North America, Europe, and Asia, and which publishes a helpful newsletter. Its website is: **www.cspt.tulane.edu**

NOTES

1. Versions of this list of 'ultimate values' can be found, with minor variations, in most recent surveys of theories of justice (e.g. Brown 1986; Pettit 1980; Sterba 1988; Campbell 1988; Miller 1976).

2. For a helpful account of this sort of 'methodological Rawlsianism', and its hegemony within contemporary Anglo-American political philosophy, see Norman 1998.

2

UTILITARIANISM

It is generally accepted that the recent rebirth of normative political philosophy began with the publication of John Rawls's *A Theory of Justice* in 1971, and his theory would be a natural place to begin a survey of contemporary theories of justice. His theory dominates contemporary debates, not because everyone accepts it, but because alternative views are often presented as responses to it. But just as these alternative views are best understood in terms of their relationship to Rawls, so understanding Rawls requires understanding the theory to which he was responding—namely, utilitarianism. Rawls believes, rightly I think, that in our society utilitarianism operates as a kind of tacit background against which other theories have to assert and defend themselves. So that is where I too will begin.

Utilitarianism, in its simplest formulation, claims that the morally right act or policy is that which produces the greatest happiness for the members of society. While this is sometimes offered as a comprehensive moral theory, I will focus on utilitarianism as a specifically political morality. On this view, utilitarian principles apply to what Rawls calls 'the basic structure' of society, not to the personal conduct of individuals. However, since much of the attraction of utilitarianism as a political morality stems from the belief that it is the only coherent and systematic moral philosophy, I will briefly discuss some features of comprehensive utilitarianism in section 3. In either its narrow or comprehensive version, utilitarianism has both devoted adherents and fierce opponents. Those who reject it say that the flaws of utilitarianism are so numerous that it cannot help but disappear from the landscape (e.g. Williams 1973). But there are others who find it hard to understand what else morality could be about than maximizing human happiness (e.g. Hare 1984).

1. TWO ATTRACTIONS

I will start with utilitarianism's attractions. There are two features of utilitarianism that make it an attractive theory of political morality. First, the goal which utilitarians seek to promote does not depend on the existence of God, or a soul, or any other dubious metaphysical entity. Some moral theories say that what matters is the condition of one's soul, or that one should live according to God's Divine Will, or that one's life goes best by having everlasting life in another realm of being. Many people have thought that morality is incoherent without these religious notions. Without God, all we are left with is a set of rules—'do this', 'do not do that'—which lack any point or purpose.

It is not clear why anyone would think this of utilitarianism. The good it seeks to promote—happiness, or welfare, or well-being—is something that we all pursue in our own lives, and in the lives of those we love. Utilitarians just demand that the pursuit of human welfare or utility (I will be using these terms interchangeably) be done impartially, for everyone in society. Whether or not we are God's children, or have a soul, or free will, we can suffer or be happy, we can all be better or worse-off. No matter how secular we are, we cannot deny that happiness is valuable, since it is something we value in our own lives.

A distinct but related attraction is utilitarianism's 'consequentialism'. I will discuss what exactly that means later on, but for the moment its importance is that it requires that we check to see whether the act or policy in question actually does some identifiable good or not. We have all had to deal with people who say that something—homosexuality, for example (or gambling, dancing, drinking, swearing, etc.)—is morally wrong, and yet are incapable of pointing to any bad consequences that arise from it. Consequentialism prohibits such apparently arbitrary moral prohibitions. It demands of anyone who condemns something as morally wrong that they show *who is wronged*, i.e. they must show how someone's life is made worse off. Likewise, consequentialism says that something is morally good only if it makes someone's life better off. Many other moral theories, even those motivated by a concern for human welfare, seem to consist in a set of rules to be followed, whatever the consequences. But utilitarianism is not just another set of rules, another set of 'dos' and 'don'ts'. Utilitarianism provides a test to ensure that such rules serve some useful function.

Consequentialism is also attractive because it conforms to our intuitions about the difference between morality and other spheres. If someone calls certain kinds of consensual sexual activity morally wrong because they are 'improper', and yet cannot point to anyone who suffers from them, then we might respond that the idea of 'proper' behaviour being employed is not a *moral* one. Such claims about proper behaviour are more like aesthetic claims, or an appeal to etiquette or convention. Someone might say that punk rock is 'improper', not legitimate music at all. But that would be an aesthetic criticism, not a moral one. To say that homosexual sex is 'improper', without being able to point to any bad consequences, is like saying that Bob Dylan sings improperly—it may be true, but it is not a moral criticism. There are standards of propriety that are not consequentialist, but we think that morality is more important than mere etiquette, and consequentialism helps account for that difference.

Consequentialism also seems to provide a straightforward method for resolving moral questions. Finding the morally right answer becomes a matter of measuring changes in human welfare, not of consulting spiritual leaders, or relying on obscure traditions. Utilitarianism, historically, was therefore quite progressive. It demanded that customs and authorities which had oppressed people for centuries be tested against the standard of human improvement ('man is the measure of all things'). At its best, utilitarianism is a strong weapon against prejudice and superstition, providing a standard and a procedure that challenge those who claim authority over us in the name of morality.

Utilitarianism's two attractions, then, are that it conforms to our intuition that human well-being matters, and to our intuition that moral rules must be tested for their consequences on human well-being. And if we accept those two points then utilitarianism seems to follow almost inevitably. If human welfare is the good which morality is concerned with, then surely the morally best act is the one which maximizes human welfare, giving equal weight to each person's welfare. Those who believe that utilitarianism has to be true are convinced that any theory which denies either of these two intuitions must be false.

I agree with the two core intuitions. If there is a way to challenge utilitarianism, it will not take the form of denying these intuitions. A successful challenge will have to show that some other theory does a better job of spelling them out. I will argue later that there are other theories which do just this. But first we need a closer look at what utilitarianism amounts to. Utilitarianism can be broken down into two parts:

1. an account of human welfare, or 'utility', and
2. an instruction to maximize utility, so defined, giving equal weight to each person's utility.

It is the second claim which is the distinctive feature of utilitarianism, and it can be combined with various answers to the first question. So our final judgement of utilitarianism will depend on our evaluation of the second claim. But it is necessary to begin by considering various answers to the first question.

2. DEFINING UTILITY

How should we define human welfare or utility? Utilitarians have traditionally defined utility in terms of happiness—hence the common but misleading slogan 'the greatest happiness of the greatest number'.[1] But not every utilitarian has accepted such a 'hedonistic' account of human welfare. In fact, there are at least four identifiable positions taken on this question.

(a) Welfare hedonism

The first view, and perhaps the most influential in the utilitarian tradition, is the view that the experience or sensation of pleasure is the chief human good. It is the one good which is an end-in-itself, to which all other goods are means. Bentham, one of the founders of utilitarianism, said, in a famous quote, that 'pushpin is as good as poetry' if it gives the same intensity and duration of pleasure. If we prefer poetry to pushpin, if we think it a more valuable thing to do with our time, it must be because it gives us more pleasure.

This is a dubious account of why we prefer some activities over others. It is a cliché, but perhaps a true one, that poets often find writing to be painful and frustrating, yet they think it is valuable. This goes for reading poetry as well—we often find poetry disturbing rather than pleasurable. Bentham might respond that the writer's happiness, like the masochist's, lies precisely in these apparently unpleasant sensations. Perhaps the poet really finds pleasure in being tortured and frustrated.

I doubt it. But we do not have to settle that question, for Robert Nozick has developed an even stronger argument against welfare hedonism (Nozick 1974: 42–5; cf. Smart 1973: 18–21). He asks us to imagine that neuropsychologists can hook us up to a machine which injects drugs into us. These drugs create the most pleasurable conscious states imaginable. Now if pleasure were our greatest good, then we would all volunteer to be hooked for life to this machine, perpetually drugged, feeling nothing but happiness. But surely very few people would volunteer. Far from being the best life we can lead, it hardly counts as leading a life at all. Far from being the life most worth leading, many people would say that it is a wasted life, devoid of value.

In fact, some people would prefer to be dead than to have that sort of life. Many people in the United States sign 'living wills' which demand that they be taken off life support systems if there is no hope of recovery, even if those systems can remove pain and induce pleasure. Whether or not we would be better off dead, we would surely be better off undrugged, doing the things we think worth doing in life. And while we hope we will be happy in doing them, we would not give them up, even for guaranteed happiness.

(b) Non-hedonistic mental-state utility

The hedonistic account of utility is wrong, for the things worth doing and having in life are not all reducible to one mental state like happiness. One response is to say that many different kinds of experiences are valuable, and that we should promote the entire range of valuable mental states. Utilitarians who adopt this account accept that the experience of writing poetry, the mental state accompanying it, can be rewarding without being pleasurable. Utilitarianism is concerned with all valuable experiences, whatever form they take.

But this does not avoid Nozick's objection. Nozick's invention is in fact called an 'experience machine', and the drugs can produce any mental state desired—the ecstasy of love, the sense of accomplishment from writing poetry, the sense of peace from religious contemplation, etc. Any of these experiences can be duplicated by the machine. Would we now volunteer to get hooked up? The answer is still, surely, no.

What we want in life is something more than, or other than, the acquisition of any kind of mental state, any kind of 'inner glow', enjoyable or otherwise. We do not just want the experience of writing poetry, we want to write poetry; we do not just want the experience of falling in love, we want to fall in love; we do not just want the feeling of accomplishing something, we want to accomplish something. It is true that when we fall in love, or accomplish something, we also want to experience it. And we hope that some of those experiences will be happy. But we would not give up the opportunity to fall in love, or accomplish something, even for the guaranteed experience of those things inside an experience machine (Lomasky 1987: 231–3; Larmore 1987: 48–9; Griffin 1986: 13–23; Finnis 1981: 85–8).

It is true that we sometimes just want certain experiences. That is one reason people take drugs. But our activities while undrugged are not just poor substitutes for getting what drugs can give us directly. No one would accept that mental states are all that matter, such that being hooked up to an experience machine would be the fulfilment of their every goal in life.

(c) Preference satisfaction

Human well-being is something more than, or other than, getting the right sequence of mental states. A third option is the 'preference-satisfaction' account of utility. On this view, increasing people's utility means satisfying their preferences, whatever they are. People may want to experience writing poetry, a preference which can be satisfied in the experience machine. But they may also want to write poetry, and so forgo the machine. Utilitarians who adopt this account tell us to satisfy all kinds of preferences equally, for they equate welfare with the satisfaction of preferences.

However, if the first two views leave too much out of their account of well-being, this third view leaves too much in. Satisfying our preferences does not always contribute to our well-being. Suppose that we are ordering food for lunch, but some of us want pizza, while others want Chinese food. If the way to satisfy the most preferences is to order pizza, then this sort of utilitarianism tells us to order it. But what if, unbeknownst to us, the pizza we ordered is poisoned, or just rancid? Ordering it now would not promote our welfare. When we lack adequate information, or have made mistakes in calculating the costs and benefits of a particular action, then what is good for us can be different from the preferences we currently have.

Preferences, therefore, do not define our good. It is more accurate to say that our preferences are predictions about our good. We want to have those things which are worth having, and our current preferences reflect our current beliefs about what those worthwhile things are. But it is not always easy to tell what is worth having, and we could be wrong in our beliefs. We might act on a preference about what to buy or do, and then come to realize that it was not worth it. We often make these sort of mistakes, both in specific decisions, like what food to order, and in 'global preferences' about what sort of life to lead. Someone who has planned for years to be a lawyer may get to law school and realize that they have made a mistake. Perhaps they had a romantic view of the profession, ignoring the competitiveness and drudgery involved. Someone who had planned to remain in their hometown may come to realize that it is a parochial way to live, narrow and unchallenging. Such people may regret the years they spent preparing for a certain way of life, or leading that life. They regret what they have done, because people want to have or do the things which are *worth* having or doing, and this may be different from what they *currently prefer* to have or do. The first is what matters to us, not the second (Dworkin 1983: 24–30; 2000: 242–54).

Utilitarianism of the preference-satisfaction variety says that something is made valuable by the fact that lots of people desire it. But that is wrong, and indeed backwards. Having the preference does not make it valuable—on the contrary, its being valuable is a good reason for preferring it. And if it is not valuable, then satisfying my mistaken preference for it will not contribute to my well-being. My utility is increased, then, not by satisfying whatever preferences I have, but by satisfying those preferences which are not based on mistaken beliefs.

A related problem with the preference-satisfaction approach is the phenomenon of 'adaptive preferences', in which people who cannot achieve some desired goal gradually lose their desire for it. This is known as the 'sour grapes' problem, after Aesop's fable about the fox who, after repeated failed attempts to reach the grapes overhead, declares that he does not want them anyway since they are probably sour. It is difficult to live with the disappointment of unsatisfied preferences, and one way to deal with this disappointment is to persuade oneself that the unattainable goal was not in fact worth seeking. The extreme version of this phenomenon is the case of the 'contented slave', who adapts to her enslavement by claiming she does not want freedom. There is some debate whether there really were such contented slaves, but the general phenomenon of adaptive preferences is well established in psychological and social science studies (Elster 1982b; 1983a). It also arises, for example, in accounts of attitudes towards traditional gender roles. The more difficult it is for people to imagine changing these roles, the more likely they will adapt their preferences so as to desire only those things which are consistent with these roles.[2]

This raises a serious problem for evaluating political institutions in terms of their ability to satisfy people's preferences. If people adapt their preferences to what they can realistically hope to achieve, then even a repressive society that denies important opportunities for fulfilment to large numbers of people may nonetheless do well in satisfying people's (adapted) preferences. In fact, it may do better than an open and democratic society which prides itself on giving freedom and opportunity to all citizens. It is quite possible that there are more unsatisfied preferences in a free society than in a repressive society that teaches people from birth not to desire certain things.

(d) Informed preferences

The fourth account of utility tries to accommodate the problem of mistaken and adaptive preferences by defining welfare as the satisfaction of 'rational' or 'informed' preferences. Utilitarianism, on this view, aims at satisfying those preferences which are based on full information and correct judgements, while filtering out those which are mistaken and irrational. We seek to provide those things which people have good reason to prefer, that really make their life better off.

This fourth account seems right—the chief human good is the satisfaction of rational preferences.[3] But while this view is unobjectionable, it is extremely vague and difficult to apply or measure. Happiness at least had the merit of being in principle measurable. We all have a rough idea of what would increase happiness, what would increase the ratio of pleasurable to painful sensations. A pleasure machine would do that best. But once we view utility in terms of satisfying informed preferences, we have little guidance.

For one thing, how do we know what preferences people would have if they were informed and rational? Which religious beliefs, for example, would informed people hold? How do we know when a desire to follow a traditional gender role is an authentic expression of the person's good, as opposed to a merely adaptive preference? What sort of 'time-discounting' is rational—i.e. is it irrational to care more about what happens to me today than about what will happen to me tomorrow? The issues involved are complex, yet we need an answer in order to begin the utilitarian calculations.

Moreover, even if we know which preferences are rational, there are many different *kinds* of informed preferences, with no obvious way to aggregate them. How do we weigh career accomplishment against romantic love, if there is no single overarching value like happiness to measure them by? The two goods may be 'incommensurable'—not measurable on any single scale.[4]

More puzzling yet is the fact that we have dropped the 'experience requirement'—i.e. informed preferences can be satisfied, and hence our utility increased on this fourth account, without it ever affecting our conscious experiences. Richard Hare, for example, argues that my life goes worse if my spouse commits adultery, even if I never come to know of it. My life is made worse because something that I wanted not to happen has happened. This is a perfectly rational and informed preference, yet my conscious experience may not change whether it is satisfied or left unsatisfied (Hare 1971: 131).

I agree with Hare that 'unexperienced' preferences should count in deter- mining well-being. It really does make my life worse when my preferences are violated without my knowing it. For example, if I continue to act towards my spouse on the belief that she has not committed adultery, then I am now acting on a falsehood. I am living a lie, and we do not want to live such a life (Raz 1986: 300–1). We often say of others that what they do not know will not hurt them. But it is hard to think that way of our own good. I do not want to go on thinking I am a good philosopher if I am not, or that I have a loving family if I do not. Someone who keeps the truth from me may spare me some uncomfortable conscious experiences, but the cost may be to undermine the whole point of my activities. I do philosophy because I think I do it well. If I am not doing it well, then I would rather do something else. I do not want to continue on the mistaken belief that I am doing it well, for I would be wasting my time, and living a lie, which are not things I want to do. If I were to discover that my belief is false, then my activity would have lost its point. And it would have lost its point, not when I discovered that the belief was not true, but when it ceased to be true. At that point, my life became worse off, for at that point I could no longer achieve the goals I was concerned to pursue.

Or consider the desires of parents regarding their children. As James Griffin notes, 'if a father wants his children to be happy, what he wants, what is valuable to him, is a state of the world, not a state of his mind; merely to delude him into thinking that his children flourish, therefore, does not give him what he values' (Griffin 1986: 13). His life is worse off if his children are suffering, even if he is blissfully unaware of this suffering.

We must accept the possibility that our lives can go worse even when our conscious experiences are unaffected. But this leads to some strange results. For example, Hare extends the notion of utility to include the preferences of dead people. I may have a rational preference that my reputation not be libelled when I am dead, or that my body not be left to rot. It seems bizarre to include the preferences of dead people in utility calculations, but what distinguishes them from the preference that one's spouse not commit unknown adultery? In both cases, we have rational preferences for things which do not affect our conscious states. Not every action which goes against a dead person's preferences makes their life worse off, but where will we draw the line? And how can we weigh the preferences of the dead against the preferences of the living?[5]

In short, the 'informed preference' account is plausible in principle, but very difficult to apply in practice. There are difficulties both in determining which preferences increase welfare when satisfied (i.e. which preferences are 'rational' or 'informed'), and in measuring levels of welfare even when we do know which preferences are rational (i.e. comparing 'incommensurable' forms of utility). As a result, we may find ourselves in a situation where it is impossible to know which act maximizes utility, either for a given individual or for society at large.

Some people have concluded from this that utilitarianism must be rejected. If we accept the fourth view of welfare as the satisfaction of informed preferences, and if welfare cannot be clearly identified or aggregated on that view, then there is no way to know which act maximizes welfare, and we need some other account of the morally right act.

But this argument is, if anything, too strong. After all, these difficulties of identifying and balancing informed preferences arise not only in utilitarian moral reasoning, but in any form of prudential reasoning about how to lead our lives (Bailey 1997: 18–19). We constantly need to make decisions about how to balance different kinds of goods, over different time-frames, and to make judgements about how our life can go better or worse. If we have no rational basis for making these judgements, due to our lack of information or the incommensurability of goods, then it is the entire structure of prudential reasoning, not just utilitarianism, which is at risk. In reality, however, we do make these decisions, more or less successfully, even if we have no procedure for guaranteeing that our preferences are truly informed, and no mathematical formula for adding up all the different kinds of goods that are in our life.

To be sure, utilitarianism as a political philosophy requires that we be able to compare utility gains and losses across lives, not just within a particular life. In order to decide who should be given scarce resources, we may need to judge whether A's potential fulfilment outweighs B's disappointment. This is the problem of the 'interpersonal comparability' of utility, and some people think that, even if we can make rational judgements about how to maximize utility within a single life, we cannot do so across lives. We cannot get inside other people's heads to know whether our fulfilments and disappointments are greater or lesser than theirs.[6]

But here again, this is too quick. If we were unable to make utility comparisons across lives, then we would be unable to make rational decisions about whether or when to help our friends, neighbours, or even our children. Yet parents continually make judgements about whether the benefits to one child outweigh the burdens or disappointments imposed on another child or the parents themselves. It would require an extreme form of solipsism to assume that we cannot make rational judgements comparing utility across lives.

Moreover, there are various indirect ways to overcome these difficulties. For example, the informed preference approach tells us to filter out those preferences which are adaptive or irrational. In practice, however, there is no realistic way for the government to make this determination directly; it would require vast amounts of information about each person's background, capacities, emotional make-up, and so on. Indeed few people would want the government to be collecting this sort of information about them. The government can, however, deal with the problem of irrational or adaptive preferences in a more indirect manner: not by examining specific preferences of individuals, but rather by trying to ensure the appropriate conditions for the *genesis* of those preferences. We may not be able to identify which specific preferences are distorted by false beliefs or adaptive preferences but we can examine the social and cultural conditions under which people form and revise their preferences, to make sure that people have access to appropriate information, and/or opportunities to test alternative ways of life, and/or protection from false or distorting images or propaganda. We deal with the problem of false or adaptive preferences, not by directly filtering them out, but by eliminating the background conditions which generate such preferences. As we will see in later chapters, particularly the chapters on communitarianism and feminism, many debates in contemporary political philosophy revolve precisely around these questions about the appropriate background conditions for the genesis of our preferences.

Similarly, there may be indirect ways of resolving the problem of interpersonal comparability. In theory, utilitarianism says that we should directly compare the welfare gains and losses of different people. In reality, this is impossible—the government cannot get inside the heads of citizens to weigh the relative strength of their joys and disappointments. However, for public policy purposes, we can adopt a more indirect strategy. We can ignore the details of individuals' preferences and focus instead on the all-purpose goods like liberties and resources which are useful to people whatever their more specific preferences. We can then use the distribution of these all-purpose goods as a reasonable proxy for the distribution of preference satisfaction (Goodin 1995: 13, 20–1). We measure gains and losses to individuals, not by examining increases or decreases in their level of preference satisfaction, but by measuring increases or decreases in the level of all-purpose means they can use to satisfy their preferences.

Utilitarianism, on this view, would not aim at maximizing the satisfaction of people's preferences directly, but rather indirectly, by maximizing the over-all amount of all-purpose goods available to people to satisfy their prefer-ences. As we will see, this 'resourcist' solution to the problem of interpersonal comparability is adopted by most liberal theories of justice, and indeed is preferable not only on grounds of convenience and feasibility, but also on grounds of responsibility (see Ch. 3, pp. 72–4 below).

So the logistical problems confronting utilitarianism are serious, but not fatal. No doubt there will be some cases where we simply cannot determine which act maximizes utility, and hence cannot determine which act is morally right, on utilitarian principles. But as we will see, this is a problem that arises for most political theories. There is no reason to exclude the possibility that humans may not always be able to determine the morally right act. In any event, even if there is an inherent incommensurability of different kinds of value, such that we cannot say that one of a range of value-increasing acts maximizes value, we can still make some less fine-grained rankings, and so make judgements about better or worse acts (Griffin 1986: 75–92).

So utilitarianism, despite its traditional ties to welfare hedonism, is compat-ible with any of the four accounts of utility. Of course, utilitarianism loses one of its attractions when it leaves hedonism behind. Once we reject the simple accounts of welfare as happiness or preference satisfaction, there is no straightforward method for measuring utility. Utilitarianism does not provide a uniquely simple criterion or scientific method to determine what is right and wrong. But while utilitarianism has no advantage over other theories in measuring human welfare, neither is it disadvantaged. Every plausible political theory has to confront these difficult questions about the proper account of human welfare, and nothing prevents utilitarianism from adopting whatever account its critics favour.[7] If we are to reject utilitarianism, then, it will have to be because of the second part of the theory—i.e. the instruction that we should maximize utility, whichever definition of utility we finally adopt.

3. MAXIMIZING UTILITY

Assuming that we have agreed on an account of utility, should we accept the utilitarian commitment to maximizing utility? Is this the best interpretation of our intuitive commitment to 'consequentialism'? Consequentialism tells us to be concerned with promoting people's utility, and, ideally, we would satisfy all the informed preferences of all people. Unfortunately, that is impossible.

There are limited resources available to satisfy people's preferences. Moreover people's preferences may conflict. So whose preferences should we satisfy? Consequentialism tells us to be concerned with consequences for human welfare, but what if the promotion of one person's welfare conflicts with that of another? Consequentialism needs to be spelled out if we are to answer that question.

How does utilitarianism spell out the idea that we should promote people's utility? Utilitarians say that the right action is the one that maximizes utility—e.g. that satisfies as many informed preferences as possible. Some people's preferences will go unsatisfied, if their preferences conflict with what maximizes utility overall. That is unfortunate. But since winners necessarily outnumber the losers, there is no reason why the preferences of the losers should take precedence over the more numerous (or more intense) preferences of the winners. For the utilitarian, equal amounts of utility matter equally, regardless of whose utility it is. No one stands in a privileged position in the calculations, no one has a greater claim to benefit from an act than any other. Hence we should bring about consequences which satisfy the greatest number of (informed) preferences amongst people in the society. (This, of course, is the barest sketch of the utilitarian account of consequentialism—I discuss two ways to flesh it out in the next section.)

This commitment to examining the consequences for human well-being is one of the attractions of utilitarianism, as compared to theories which say that we should follow tradition or divine law regardless of the human consequences. But the particular kind of consequentialism in utilitarianism is, I think, unattractive. Where it is impossible to satisfy all preferences, our intuitions do not tell us that equal amounts of utility should always have the same weight. Utilitarianism provides an oversimplified account of our commitment to consequentialism.

Before exploring these issues, however, there are some important differences within utilitarianism that need to be laid out. I have just said that, as utilitarians, we should seek to satisfy the greatest number of preferences. But as I mentioned earlier, there are two different accounts within utilitarianism of who the relevant 'we' is—on one view, all of us are obliged to act according to utilitarian principles, even in our personal conduct (comprehensive moral utilitarianism); on the other view, it is the major social institutions which are specifically obliged to act according to utilitarian principles (political utilitarianism). There are also two different accounts of what it means to 'act according to utilitarian principles'. On one view, this means that the agent should decide how to act by consciously making utilitarian calculations, by trying to assess how different actions would affect the satisfaction of informed preferences (direct utilitarianism); on the other view, the idea of maximizing utility enters only indirectly (if at all) into the agent's decision-making.

Morally right actions are those that maximize utility, but agents are more likely to maximize utility by following non-utilitarian rules or habits than by following utilitarian reasoning (indirect utilitarianism).

These two distinctions can be combined to generate different versions of utilitarianism. Utilitarian principles can be applied more or less comprehensively, and more or less directly. Much of the recent work on utilitarianism has been concerned with exploring these variations, and it seems clear that each version will generate different results. However, I believe that all versions share the same fundamental flaw. I will argue that there is something inherently unattractive about the utilitarian commitment to maximizing utility, and that this flaw is not substantially affected by how (directly or indirectly) or where (comprehensively or to politics) that commitment is applied.[8]

I will begin by considering some problems with utilitarianism as a comprehensive decision-procedure. If we view utilitarianism in this way, then the morally responsible agent will be what David Brink calls a 'U-agent'— someone who decides how to spend her time and resources by calculating the effects on overall utility of the various actions available to her (Brink 1986: 425). This sort of utilitarianism has few contemporary defenders, and many utilitarians would agree with the criticisms I am about to make. But I start with utilitarianism as a comprehensive decision-procedure because it raises in a particularly clear form problems that are also present in the more indirect and political versions of utilitarianism (s. 5). Moreover, the issues raised in this section, concerning the proper scope of personal relationships, will reappear in later chapters.

Imagine then that we are U-agents, and that we can calculate which act produces the most utility.[9] Should we base our actions on these utilitarian calculations? There are two main objections to utilitarian decision-making— it excludes the special obligations we have to particular people, and it includes preferences which should not be counted. These two problems stem from the same basic flaw, but I will examine them separately.

(a) Special relationships

U-agents who base their actions on utilitarian calculations assume that each person stands in the same moral relationship to them. But this does not allow for the possibility that I could have special moral relationships to my friends, family, lenders, etc., that I could be under a greater obligation to them than to other possible beneficiaries of my actions. Our intuitions tell us that there are such special obligations, and that they should be fulfilled even if those to whom I am not especially obligated would benefit more.

Consider a loan. It is part of our everyday morality that people come to have differential entitlements in virtue of having loaned money in the past. If someone lends me $10, then she is entitled to receive $10 back from me, even if someone else could make better use of the money. Utilitarian reasoning disregards such backward-looking entitlements, for it says that only forward-looking consequences matter. For the U-agent, the moral value of an act lies solely in its causal properties of producing desirable states of affairs. Hence what I ought to do is pull on the causal lever which will produce the maximal amount of utility for the system as a whole. In deciding how to spend my $10, I must look at all the potential preference satisfactions of people (including myself) and determine which action will maximize them. It is of no interest to the U-agent, in and of itself, that one of those people loaned me the $10, or that someone else performed some service for me on the understanding that she would receive the money. It may be that if the utilities work out in a certain way, I ought to repay the loan, or fulfil my contract. But the process of deciding what to do will go on in exactly the same way as if I had not borrowed or promised the money.

This is counter-intuitive, for most of us would say that the 'past circumstances or actions of people can create differential entitlements or differential deserts to things' (Nozick 1974: 155). The person who lent me $10 has, by that very act, acquired an entitlement to the $10 I am now considering spending, even if some other use of the money would maximize happiness. Does this conflict with our view that morality should be about consequences for human welfare? No, for in saying that I should repay the loan, I am simply saying that I have a greater obligation, at this point in time, to promote my lender's welfare than to help others. We should repay the loan, not because we do not care about the harms and benefits which arise from that act, but because one benefit in particular has special weight.

Unlike the hard-line non-consequentialist, we need not say that these entitlements are indefeasible by any calculation of overall social consequences. If repaying the loan would somehow lead to nuclear destruction, then we clearly ought not to repay the loan. But we can say that there is a duty to repay loans and fulfil contracts which has some independent weight, to be considered alongside the moral weight of overall social benefits. The existence of past entitlements on the part of particular people partially pre-empts, or constrains, the utilitarian quest to maximize the general good. Averting a disastrous drop in welfare is a good reason for using the money in a different way, but the mere fact that repaying the loan does not maximally increase welfare is not a good reason. Not to repay the loan simply because it does not maximally increase utility is to ignore the special nature of our obligation to the lender.

This is so firmly entrenched in our moral consciousness that many utilitarians have tried to give a utilitarian account of the weight we attach to promises. They point out the many by-products of breaking a promise. For example, while someone other than the lender may be able to make better use of the money, the lender will feel resentment at being deprived of a promised benefit, a disutility so great that it outweighs the increased utility achieved by giving the money to someone else (Hare 1971: 134). But this gets things backwards. We do not feel that breaking promises is wrong because it produces feelings of resentment. Rather, cheating on promises produces feelings of resentment because it is wrong (cf. Williams 1973: 143). Another utilitarian tactic is to point out that promises create expectations which people depend on. Moreover, failing to repay the loan will jeopardize the lender's willingness to lend in the future, and thereby jeopardize a valuable social institution. So utilitarians respond by pointing out that repaying loans is more likely to maximize utility than one might initially think (Sartorius 1969: 79–80).

This may be true, but it does not solve the problem. It still implies, for example, that 'if you have employed a boy to mow your lawn and he has finished the job and asks for his pay, you should pay him what you promised only if you cannot find a better use for your money' (Sartorius 1969: 79). The U-agent's reasoning, while more complex than one might initially think, still fails to recognize any special relationship between employer and employee, or lender and borrower. Some utilitarians are prepared to accept this result. Rolf Sartorius, for example, says that if the usual factors do not ensure that payment maximizes utility, i.e. if the boy 'is not likely to publicize my breaking my promise to him too loudly, appears to have a reservoir of trust in mankind generally, and any sum I could give him really would do more good if contributed to UNICEF, then the conclusion on act-utilitarian grounds must be that I should give the money to UNICEF. But is this really absurd?' (Sartorius 1969: 80). Yes, this is absurd. What is absurd here is not necessarily the conclusion but the fact that the boy's having actually performed the job, or that I had actually promised him the money, never enters into the decision as such. Notice that the consequences Sartorius mentions would be exactly the same even if the boy hadn't actually mowed the lawn, but simply (falsely) believed that he had done so, or falsely believed that I had promised him the money. The fact that the boy actually mowed the lawn, or that I had promised him the money, does not matter to the U-agent because nothing we could do or say could ever put us in a special moral relationship such that my obligation to him is greater than my obligation to others. No matter what the boy has done or I have said, he can never have a greater claim on my actions than anyone else.

In our everyday view, the existence of a promise creates a special obligation between two people. The U-agent, however, treats promises and contracts, not as creating special moral ties to one person, but as simply adding new factors into the calculation of overall utility. The everyday view says that I should repay loans *regardless* of whether it maximizes utility. The U-agent says that I should repay the loan *because* it maximizes utility. The boy has no greater claim on me than others, he just is likely to benefit more than they are, and so repayment is the best way to fulfil my utilitarian obligation.

But that is not what a promise is—'to make a promise is not merely to adopt an ingenious device for promoting the general well-being, it is to put oneself in a new relation to one person in particular, a relation which creates a specifically new prima facie duty to him, not reducible to the duty of promoting the general well-being of society' (Ross 1930: 38). For U-agents, everyone (including oneself) stands in exactly the same moral position—i.e. everyone is an equally deserving possible beneficiary of one's actions. But this is too flat a picture of the moral landscape, for some people 'may also stand to [one] in the relation of promisee to promisor, of creditor to debtor, of wife to husband, of child to parent, of friend to friend, of fellow countryman to fellow countryman, and the like, and each of these relations is the foundation of a prima facie duty' (Ross 1930: 19).

The problem here goes deeper than an inadequate account of promises. The U-agent cannot accommodate the importance of any of our commitments. We all have commitments—to family, political causes, work—which form the focal point of our lives and give some identity to our existence. But if I am to act as a U-agent, then in each of my decisions, my commitments must be simply added in with all the projects of other people, and be sacrificed when I can produce more utility by promoting someone else's projects. That may sound admirably unselfish. But it is in fact absurd. For it is impossible to be genuinely committed to something and yet be willing to sacrifice that commitment whenever something else happens to maximize utility. Utilitarian decision-making asks that I consider my projects and attachments as no more worthy of my help than anyone else's. It asks, in effect, that I be no more attached to my commitments than to other people's. But that is no different from saying that I should not really be attached to my projects at all. As Bernard Williams puts it,

if you are a person who whole-heartedly and genuinely possesses some of these admirable [projects, affections, and commitments], you cannot also be someone in whose thought and action the requirements of utilitarianism are unfailingly mirrored, nor could you wish to be such a person. . . . utilitarianism must reject or hopelessly dilute the value of these other dispositions, regressing to that picture of man which early utilitarianism frankly offered, in which he has, ideally, only private or otherwise sacrificable projects, together with the one moral disposition of utilitarian benevolence. (Williams 1981: 51, 53)

Utilitarianism is therefore often said to be 'alienating', in the sense that it forces us to distance ourselves from the commitments and projects that give meaning to our lives.[10]

Of course, our projects and commitments should respect the legitimate commitments of others. But the way to do this is not to consider them as having an equal claim on my time and energy to that of my own projects. Such an attitude is psychologically impossible, and undesirable even if possible. A valuable human life, on just about anyone's account of it, is one filled with attachments that structure one's life, that give some direction to it. It is the prospect of subsequent achievement or progress in such a commitment that makes our current actions meaningful. As a U-agent, however, one's actions will be determined almost wholly independently of one's commitments. The U-agent's decisions will be 'a function of all the satisfactions which he can affect from where he is: and this means that the projects of others, to an indeterminately great extent, determine his decision' (Williams 1973: 115). The U-agent will have few choices about how to lead his life, few opportunities to act on considerations of the kind of person he is, or wants to become. He will thus have little room for the things we associate with the very idea of 'leading a life'. These will all be submerged beneath the question of which causal levers are optimific.

If I am to lead my own life, there must be room in which I am free to form my own commitments, including the sorts of contracts and promises discussed above. The problem of not allowing people to create special obligations to others through promises is just one aspect of the broader problem of not allowing people to set and pursue their own goals. The problem in all of these cases is the U-agent's assumption that each person has an equal claim to benefit from all of his actions.

Does our intuition in favour of meaningful commitments violate the idea that morality concerns consequences? No, for our intuitive commitment to the general idea of consequentialism never included a commitment to the continuous impartial determination of our actions by the preferences of others, to the exclusion of special relationships and projects. This is simply too crude an interpretation of our belief in consequentialism.

(b) Illegitimate preferences

A second problem with utilitarianism as a decision-procedure concerns its demand, not that each person be given equal weight in our decision-making, but that each source of utility (e.g. each kind of preference) be given equal weight. Consider racial discrimination in a mainly white society. A government health care policy might plan to build one hospital for every 100,000 people, regardless of their race. But a number of whites prefer that blacks do not have equal health care, and when the utility calculations are done, it turns out that utility is maximized by depriving blacks of an equal share of health care (or school facilities etc.). Or what if the very sight of known homosexuals deeply offends the heterosexual majority? Perhaps utility is maximized if openly homosexual people are publicly punished and thrown in jail. Or what about an alcoholic on skid row who has no friends, is offensive to many people, and a nuisance to everyone, begging for money and cluttering up public parks? Perhaps utility would be maximized if we quietly took such people and killed them, so they would not be seen, and would not be a drain on social resources in jail.

Some of these preferences are of course uninformed, and so satisfying them would not actually yield any utility (assuming we have abandoned the crude hedonistic accounts of utility). But the desire to deny the rights of others is not always uninformed, and even on the best account of utility, the satisfaction of these preferences can be a genuine source of utility for some people. As Rawls puts it, such preferences are 'unreasonable' from the point of view of justice, but are not necessarily 'irrational', from the point of view of an individual's utility (Rawls 1980: 528–30). If this sort of utility is counted, it may lead to discrimination against unpopular minorities.

Our everyday morality tells us that such preferences are unfair, and should not be counted. That racists want a group of people mistreated is no reason at all to give that group less health care. The racists' desire is illegitimate, so whatever utility would come from satisfying that preference has no moral weight. Even where there is no direct prejudice, there may be unfair preferences which should not count. Someone may wish that blacks do not move into their neighbourhood, not because they actively dislike blacks—they may not care one way or the other—but because others dislike blacks, and so the property value of their home will decrease. Such a preference that blacks be excluded from a neighbourhood is not prejudiced in the same way a racist's is. But it is still an illegitimate preference, since it requires that something be wrongfully taken from blacks. In all these cases, utility is maximized by discriminatory treatment, but only as a result of preferences for benefits which are wrongfully taken from others. Preferences like that, preferences for what rightfully belongs to others, have little or no weight in our everyday moral view.

Utilitarians do not accept the claim that preferences for what 'rightfully' belongs to others are illegitimate. For the U-agent there is no standard of what 'rightfully' belongs to anyone prior to the calculation of utility. What is rightfully mine is whatever distribution maximizes utility, so utility-maximizing acts by definition cannot deprive me of my rightful share. But this violates an important component of our everyday morality. Our commitment to the idea of consequentialism does not include a commitment to the idea that each source of utility should have moral weight, that each kind of preference must be counted.

It seems, then, that the U-agent, in trying to maximize utility, is violating, rather than spelling out, our intuitive idea of consequentialism. Some people deny that utilitarian decision-making has these counter-intuitive results. They admit that utilitarian reasoning seems to allow, or even require, acts which violate special relationships or basic rights, whenever such acts would maximize utility. But they claim that these acts would be disallowed if we shifted to a more sophisticated form of utilitarian decision-making. I have been assuming that U-agents apply the test of utility maximization to particular acts. But 'rule utilitarians' argue that we should apply the test of utility to rules, and then perform whichever act is endorsed by the best rules, even if another act might produce more utility. Social cooperation requires rule-following, so we should assess the consequences, not simply of acting in a particular way on this occasion, but of making it a rule that we act in that way.[11]

The issue for U-agents, then, is to determine which set of rules is utility-maximizing. Are we better off in utilitarian terms following a rule that instructs us to keep promises, maintain special relationships, and respect rights, or following a rule that subordinates these principles to calculations of utility? The latter, utilitarians argue, would paradoxically decrease utility. It would make social cooperation difficult, create fear and insecurity, and cheapen the value of human life and liberty (Goodin 1995: 22; Singer 1977). Moreover, people are likely to abuse the power to break promises or discriminate in the name of the public good (Bailey 1997). Everyone is worse off if we adopt a rule to break promises or discriminate against unpopular groups whenever we think it would maximize utility.

Some commentators argue that rule-utilitarianism collapses into act-utilitarianism, since we can describe rules in such a detailed and narrow way as to make them equivalent to acts (Lyons 1965: ch. 4; Hare 1963: 130–6). Others dispute this (Harsanyi 1977b). But even if the distinction is valid, it seems unduly optimistic to assume that utility-maximizing rules will always protect the rights of weak and unpopular minorities. As Williams puts it, the assurance that justice will prevail is 'a tribute to the decency and imagination of those utilitarians but not to their consistency or their utilitarianism' (Williams 1972: 103).

In any event, this response does not really answer the objection, for even if it gets the right answer, it does so for the wrong reasons. On the rule-utilitarian view, the wrong done in discriminating against a minority group is the increased fear caused to others by having a rule allowing discrimination. The wrong done in not paying the boy who mowed my lawn is the increased doubts caused in others concerning the institution of promising. But surely that is a misinterpretation. The wrong is done to the person who should not have suffered from the dislike of others, and to the boy who had a special claim to the promised money. This wrong is present whatever the long-term effects on others.

The rule-utilitarian response misses the real issue. The objection to utilitarian decision-making was that certain special obligations should be included, and that certain illegitimate preferences should be excluded. These are moral requirements which take precedence over the maximization of utility (whereas the U-agent sees them merely as devices for maximizing utility). But if that was our objection, then it is irrelevant to say, as rule utilitarians do, that obeying promises and discounting prejudices often maximizes long-term utility, or that promises and human rights are even more ingenious devices for maximizing utility than we initially thought. That response confirms, rather than refutes, the criticism that U-agents treat the recognition of special obligations as subject to, rather than prior to, the maximization of utility. Our objection was not that promises are bad devices for maximizing utility, but that they are not such devices at all. This problem cannot be avoided by changing the level at which we apply the principle of utility from acts to rules. The problem, from the point of view of our everyday morality, is in applying the principle of utility itself.

We can make the same point another way. Shifting to rule-utilitarianism may change the *outcome* of the utility calculations, but it does not change the *inputs* into the calculations. The rule utilitarian is still committed to including all preferences, no matter how morally illegitimate they may appear. Focusing on rules rather than acts may make it less likely for illegitimate preferences to win the day, but they still count on a par with all other preferences. Moreover, this has the perverse consequence that the more people enjoy harming others or violating their rights, the less evil is their action. For example, while rule-utilitarianism is unlikely to endorse a lifestyle involving raping and pillaging, it does imply that the enjoyment people take in raping and pillaging counts in the calculus, and the more enjoyment they get, the less the overall wrongness of their action. As Geoffrey Scarre puts it, their enjoyment

seems to *offset some of their evil*: it is a positive quantity in the balance sheet which compensates for some of the suffering of the victims. But it conflicts radically with our ordinary moral convictions to assert that the greater the pleasure a murderous maniac derives from abusing his victim, the smaller the net amount of evil produced by his actions . . . To enjoy the killing makes the killing worse, not better. (Scarre 1996: 155)

Similarly, sadists can offset some of their evil by *sharing* the pleasure involved with other sadists. Rule-utilitarianism is unlikely to condone torturing a child, but it does imply that the torturing of a child is less evil if the torturer shares his pleasure with other sadists—perhaps by inviting an audience, or broadcasting it on the Internet. Such actions may be wrong on rule-utilitarian grounds, but less wrong than if the torturer is the only person who gains pleasure from it.

Or consider the games held in the ancient Roman Colosseum, in which a prisoner of war was torn to shreds by wild animals in front of 50,000 wildly cheering spectators. A clever rule utilitarian can no doubt find reasons why it would have maximized utility in the long run to give precedence to the rights of a handful of prisoners of war over the blood-lust of the 50,000 spectators.[12] One can reasonably ask whether these clever arguments will still work if we increase the size of the Colosseum to include more people, or if we imagine broadcasting the games on satellite TV so that millions of people around the world can enjoy the spectacle. But again, the real issue here is not the ultimate conclusion utilitarians reach, but the process by which they reach it. On the rule-utilitarian view, the larger the audience for the games, and the more each spectator enjoys it, the less evil it is. On our everyday moral view, by contrast, torturing others becomes more evil, not less, the more people enjoy it.

Some utilitarians would agree with what I have said so far. It is right and proper, they say, to view our attachments and our rights as taking precedence over the pursuit of overall utility. We should accept the everyday view that the harm done to the particular individuals who are cheated or discriminated against is sufficient grounds for demanding that people keep promises and respect rights. We should not be U-agents who decide how to act by making utilitarian calculations, and who view promises as devices for maximizing utility. Instead we should view promises, and other people's rights, as of such towering importance that they are basically invulnerable to the calculus of social interests. In short, we should be non-utilitarians in our moral reasoning. But, they argue, this does not mean that utilitarianism is wrong. On the contrary, the reason why we should be non-utilitarians in our decision-making is precisely that we are more likely to maximize utility that way. A society of non-utilitarians who believe in the intrinsic importance of promises and rights will do better, in terms of maximizing utility, than a society of act or rule utilitarians who view promises and rights as devices for maximizing utility.

This may sound paradoxical. But it raises a true and important point. Utilitarianism is essentially a 'standard of rightness', not a 'decision-procedure' (Brink 1986: 421–7; Railton 1984: 140–6). What defines utilitarianism is the claim that the right act is the one that maximizes utility, not the claim that we should deliberately seek to maximize utility. It is an open question whether we should employ a utilitarian decision-procedure in assessing acts or rules—indeed, this question is itself to be answered by examining the consequences on overall utility of different decision-procedures. And it is quite possible that we would do better in terms of the utilitarian standard of rightness by employing a non-utilitarian decision-procedure. This certainly seems true in regards to our personal attachments—everyone's life is less valuable if we are unable to make commitments in the sort of wholehearted and unconditional way precluded by direct utilitarianism. Hence, it is argued, we should be 'indirect utilitarians' who do not in fact apply utilitarian decision-procedures in our everyday decisions about either acts or rules.

While the distinction between standards of rightness and decision-procedures is sound, if we put too much weight on it, it is not clear why utilitarianism as a standard of rightness should not disappear entirely from our conscious beliefs. Taken to its extreme, indirect utilitarianism could be 'self-defeating'—it might argue for its own elimination from people's thoughts and beliefs (Williams 1973: 135). The world most likely to maximize utility may be one in which no one believes in utilitarianism. A less extreme form of indirect utilitarianism is what Williams calls 'Government House' utilitarianism (Williams and Sen 1982: 16, Williams 1973: 138–40). On this view, a small elite would know that utilitarianism was the right moral theory, and they would employ utilitarian decision-procedures to design utility-maximizing rules or institutions. The vast bulk of the population, however, would not be taught to believe in utilitarianism. They would be taught to view social rules and conventions as intrinsically justified. (This is called 'Government House' utilitarianism since it seems to have been the view of some British colonial officials in India and other British colonies: the British officials would understand that rights are simply ingenious devices for maximizing utility; the natives would be taught to think of rights as intrinsically justified and inviolable.)

This idea of Government House utilitarianism has been widely criticized as elitist, and as violating the democratic norm of 'publicity', according to which the state should be able to publicly justify its actions to its citizens.[13] Most indirect utilitarians, therefore, prefer a model in which everyone shares the same two-level moral outlook. Most of the time, we use non-utilitarian decision-procedures, and view rights and justice as invulnerable to the calculus of utility maximization, but every once in a while (perhaps only in moments of crisis), we all engage in a collective and democratic process of utilitarian decision-making to revise our everyday rules and institutions.

One can question whether this is really a psychologically plausible picture.[14] In any event, it does not yet answer the objections raised above. Consider our everyday view that certain kinds of preferences are unfair, and so should not be given any weight in our moral decision-procedures. It is possible that the utilitarian standard of rightness can justify our adopting such a non-utilitarian decision-procedure. If so, then both sides agree that certain preferences should not be counted. But on our everyday view, the reason why unfair preferences should not be given any weight in our decision-procedure is that they are morally illegitimate—they do not deserve to be counted. For the indirect utilitarian, on the other hand, the reason we do not count unfair preferences is simply that it is counter-productive to do so. Unfair preferences (if rational and informed) are as legitimate as any other preference according to the utilitarian standard of rightness, but we do better in terms of that standard by treating them as illegitimate in our decision-making.

So we have two conflicting explanations for treating certain preferences as illegitimate. To defend utilitarianism, therefore, it is not enough to show that the utilitarian standard of rightness can justify using non-utilitarian decision-procedures. One also must show that this is the right justification. The utilitarian says that the reason why we use non-utilitarian procedures is that they happen to maximize utility. But isn't it more plausible to say that the reason why we use non-utilitarian procedures is simply that we accept a non-utilitarian standard of rightness? Why think there has to be some indirect utilitarian explanation for our non-utilitarian commitments?

Some utilitarians seem to think that if a utilitarian explanation is available for our moral convictions then there is no need to consider any non-utilitarian explanations. But this begs the question. We need some argument for endorsing the utilitarian standard of rightness over alternative standards. Is there any such argument in utilitarian writings? There are in fact two distinct arguments, but I will argue that neither works on its own, and that the plausibility of utilitarianism depends on conflating the two. Once we have examined these arguments, we will see that the problems discussed above stem directly from the utilitarian standard of rightness, and are not substantially affected by how directly or indirectly that standard is applied.

4. TWO ARGUMENTS FOR UTILITY MAXIMIZATION

In this section, I will consider the two main arguments for viewing utility maximization as the standard of moral rightness. As we will see, they generate two entirely different interpretations of what utilitarianism is.

(a) Equal consideration of interests

On one interpretation, utilitarianism is a standard for aggregating individual interests and desires. Individuals have distinct and potentially conflicting preferences, and we need a standard that specifies which trade-offs amongst those preferences are morally acceptable, which trade-offs are fair to the people whose welfare is at stake. That is the question which this first interpretation of utilitarianism attempts to answer. One popular answer, found in many different theories, is that each person's interests should be given equal consideration. Each person's life matters equally, from the moral point of view, and hence their interests should be given equal consideration.

Utilitarianism, on this first view of it, accepts this general egalitarian principle. However, the idea of treating people with equal consideration is imprecise, and it needs to be spelled out in more detail if it is to provide a determinate standard of rightness. One obvious, and perhaps initially appealing, way to spell out that idea is to give equal weight to each person's preferences, regardless of the content of the preferences or the material situation of the person. As Bentham put it, we count everyone for one, no one for more than one. On the first account of utilitarianism, then, the reason that we should give equal weight to each person's preferences is that that treats people as equals, with equal concern and respect.

If we accept this as our standard of rightness, then we will conclude that morally right actions are those that maximize utility. But it is important to note that maximization is not the direct goal of the standard. Maximization arises as a by-product of a standard that is intended to aggregate people's preferences fairly. The requirement that we maximize utility is entirely derived from the prior requirement to treat people with equal consideration. So the first argument for utilitarianism is this:

1. people matter, and matter equally; therefore
2. each person's interests should be given equal weight; therefore
3. morally right acts will maximize utility.

This equal consideration argument is implicit in Mill's claim that 'In the golden rule of Jesus of Nazareth, we read the complete spirit of the ethics of utility. To do as you would be done by, and to love your neighbour as yourself, constitute the ideal perfection of utilitarian morality' (Mill 1968: 16). The argument is more explicitly affirmed by contemporary utilitarians like Harsanyi, Griffin, Singer, and Hare (Harsanyi 1976: 13–14, 19–20, 45–6, 65–7; Griffin 1986: 208–15, 295–301; Hare 1984: 106–12; Singer 1979: 12–23; Haslett 1987: 40–3, 220–2). Hare, in fact, finds it difficult to imagine any other way of showing equal consideration for each person (Hare 1984: 107; cf. Harsanyi: 1976: 35).

(b) Teleological utilitarianism

There is, however, another interpretation of utilitarianism. Here maximizing the good is primary, not derivative, and we count individuals equally only because that is the way to maximize value. Our primary duty is not to treat people as equals, but to bring about valuable states of affairs. People, as Williams puts it, are just viewed as *locations* of utilities, or as causal levers for the 'utility network'. The 'basic bearer of value for Utilitarianism is the *state of affairs*' (Williams 1981: 4). Utilitarianism, on this view, is primarily concerned not with persons, but with states of affairs. Rawls calls this a 'teleological' theory, which means that the right act is defined in terms of maximizing the good, rather than in terms of equal consideration for individuals (Rawls 1971: 24).

This second interpretation is a genuinely distinct form of utilitarianism, not simply a different way of describing the same theory. Its distinctiveness becomes clear if we look at utilitarian discussions of population policy. Derek Parfit asks whether we morally ought to double the world's population, even if it means reducing each person's welfare by almost half (since that will still increase overall utility). He thinks that a policy of doubling the population is a genuine, if somewhat repugnant, conclusion of utilitarianism.

Indeed, we should not stop with simply doubling the population. A world with 100 billion people, each of whom has a life barely worth leading, might well contain more overall utility than a world of 5 billion people, each of whom has a very high quality of life. Compare two possible worlds: world A, our world, containing 5 billion people each of whom has an average utility of 18 units, and world B, containing 100 billion, each of whose well-being has been reduced to one unit (see Fig. 1).

In World B, each person's life has become miserable—barely better than being dead—yet the overall amount of utility has increased from 90 to 100 billion units. Utilitarians, according to Parfit, should seek to maximize the total amount of utility in the world, no matter what its impact on the utility of existing individuals, and hence prefer World B (Parfit 1984: 388).

But this need not be the conclusion if we view utilitarianism as a theory of treating people as equals. Non-existent people do not have claims—we do not have a moral duty *to them* to bring them into the world. As John Broome

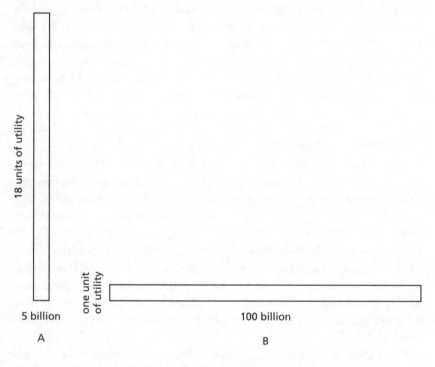

Figure 1 Parfit's repugnant conclusion

notes, 'one cannot owe anyone a duty to bring her into existence, because failing in such a duty would not be failing anyone' (Broome 1991: 92). So what is the duty here, on the second interpretation? The duty is to maximize value, to bring about valuable states of affairs, even if the effect is to make all existing persons worse off than they otherwise would have been.

The distinctness of this second interpretation is also apparent in Thomas Nagel's discussion. He demands that we add a 'deontological' constraint of equal treatment onto utilitarianism, which he thinks is concerned with selecting the 'impersonally best outcome' (Nagel 1986: 176). Nagel says we must qualify our obligation to maximize the good with the obligation to treat people as equals. Obviously his demand only makes sense with reference to the second interpretation of utilitarianism, according to which the fundamental duty is not to aggregate individual preferences fairly, but to bring about the most value in the world. For on the first interpretation, utilitarianism is already a principle of moral equality; if it fails as a principle of equal consideration, then the whole theory fails, for there is no independent commitment to the idea of maximizing utility.

This second interpretation stands the first interpretation on its head. The first defines the right in terms of treating people as equals, which leads to the utilitarian aggregation standard, which happens to maximize the good. The second defines the right in terms of maximizing the good, which leads to the utilitarian aggregation standard, which as a mere consequence treats people's interests equally. As we have seen, this inversion has important theoretical and practical consequences.

So we have two independent, and indeed conflicting, paths to the claim that utility ought to be maximized. Which is the fundamental argument for utilitarianism? Up to this point, I have implicitly relied on the first view—that is, utilitarianism is best viewed as a theory of how to respect the moral claim of each individual to be treated as an equal. Rawls, however, says that utilitarianism is fundamentally a theory of the second sort—i.e. one which defines the right in terms of maximizing the good (Rawls 1971: 27). But there is something bizarre about that second interpretation. For it is entirely unclear why maximizing utility, as our direct goal, should be considered a *moral* duty. To whom is it a duty? Morality, in our everyday view, is a matter of interpersonal obligations—the obligations we owe to each other. But to whom do we owe the duty of maximizing utility? It cannot be to the maximally valuable state of affairs itself, for states of affairs do not have moral claims. Perhaps we have a duty to those people who would benefit from the maximization of utility. But if that duty is, as seems most plausible, the duty to treat people with equal consideration, then we are back to the first interpretation of utilitarianism as a way of treating people as equals. Maximizing utility is now just a by-product, not the ultimate ground of the theory. And then we need not double the population, since we have no obligation to conceive those who would constitute the increased population.[15]

If we nonetheless accept that maximizing utility is itself the goal, then it is best seen as a non-moral ideal, akin in some ways to an aesthetic ideal. The appropriateness of this characterization can be seen by looking at the other example Rawls gives of a teleologist, namely Nietzsche (Rawls 1971: 25). The good which Neitzsche's theory seeks to maximize (e.g. creativity) is available only to the special few. Others are useful only in so far as they promote the good of the special few. In utilitarianism, the value being maximized is more mundane, something that every individual is capable of partaking in or contributing to (although the maximizing policy may result in the sacrifice of some people). This means that in utilitarian teleology, unlike Nietzsche's, every person's preferences must be given some weight. But in neither case is the fundamental principle to treat people as equals. Rather it is to maximize the good. And in both cases, it is difficult to see how this can be viewed as a moral principle. The goal is not to respect *people*, for whom certain things are needed or wanted, but rather to respect the *good*, to which certain people may or may not be useful contributors. If people have become the means for the maximization of the good, morality has dropped out of the picture, and a no-moral ideal is at work. A Nietzschean society may be aesthetically better, more beautiful, but it is not morally better (Nietzsche himself would not have rejected this description—his theory was 'beyond good and evil'). If utilitarianism is interpreted in this teleological way then it too has ceased to be a moral theory.

I said earlier that one of utilitarianism's attractions was its secular nature—for utilitarians, morality matters because human beings matter. But that attractive idea is absent from this second interpretation, whose moral point is quite obscure. Humans are viewed as potential producers or consumers of a good, and our duties are to that good, not to other people. That violates our core intuition that morality matters because humans matter. In fact, few people have endorsed utilitarianism as a purely teleological theory, without appealing at all to the ideal of equal respect for persons (G. E. Moore's *Ethics* is one prominent exception). Utilitarianism simply ceases to have any attraction if it is cut off from that core intuition.

If utilitarianism is best seen as an egalitarian doctrine, then there is no independent commitment to the idea of maximizing welfare. The utilitarian has to admit that we should use the maximizing standard only if that is the best account of treating people as equals. This is important, because much of the attraction of utilitarianism depends on a tacit mixing of the two justifications.[16] Utilitarianism's intuitive unfairness would quickly disqualify it as an adequate account of equal consideration, were it not that many people take its maximizing feature as an additional, independent reason to endorse it.

Utilitarians tacitly appeal to the good-maximization standard to deflect intuitive objections to their account of equal consideration. Indeed, it may seem to be a unique strength of utilitarianism that it can mix these two justifications. Unfortunately, it is incoherent to employ both standards in the same theory. One cannot say that morality is fundamentally about maximizing the good, while also saying that it is fundamentally about respecting the claim of individuals to equal consideration. If utilitarians were held to one or other of the standards, then their theory would lose much of its attractiveness. Viewed as a maximizing-teleological theory, it ceases to meet our core intuitions about the point of morality; viewed as an egalitarian theory, it leads to a number of results which conflict with our sense of what it is to treat people as equals, as I now hope to show in a more systematic way.

5. INADEQUATE CONCEPTION OF EQUALITY

If we are to treat utilitarianism as a plausible political morality, then we must interpret it as a theory of equal consideration. That may seem strange, given the inegalitarian acts utilitarianism might justify—e.g. depriving disliked people of their liberty. But we need to distinguish different levels at which equality can be a value. While utilitarianism may have unequal effects on people, it can nonetheless claim to be motivated by a concern for treating people as equals. Indeed, Hare asks, if we believe that people's essential interest is the satisfaction of their informed preferences, and that everyone is to be given equal consideration, then what else can we do except give equal weight to each person's preferences, everyone counting for one, no one for more than one (Hare 1984: 106)?

But while utilitarianism seeks to treat people as equals, it violates many of our intuitions about what it genuinely means to treat people with equal consideration. It is possible that our anti-utilitarian intuitions are unreliable. I will argue, however, that utilitarianism has misinterpreted the ideal of equal consideration for each person's interests, and, as a result, it allows some people to be treated as less than equals, as means to other people's ends.

Why is utilitarianism inadequate as an account of equal consideration? Utilitarians assume that every source of happiness, or every kind of preference, should be given the same weight, if it yields equal utility. I will argue that an adequate account of equal consideration must distinguish different kinds of preferences, only some of which have legitimate moral weight.

(a) External preferences

One important distinction amongst kinds of preferences is that between 'personal' and 'external' preferences (Dworkin 1977: 234). Personal preferences are preferences about the goods, resources, and opportunities etc. one wants available to oneself. External preferences concern the goods, resources, and opportunities one wants available to others. External preferences are sometimes prejudiced. Someone may want blacks to have fewer resources because he thinks them less worthy of respect. Should this sort of external preference be counted in the utilitarian calculus? Does the existence of such preferences count as a moral reason for denying blacks those resources?

As we have seen, indirect utilitarians argue that there are circumstances where we would be better off, in utilitarian terms, by excluding such preferences from our everyday decision-procedures. But the question I want to consider here is whether these preferences should be excluded more systematically, by excluding them from our standard of rightness. And I want to consider whether utilitarianism's own deepest principle provides grounds for not according external preferences any moral weight in its standard of rightness. The deepest principle, as we have seen, is an egalitarian one. Each person has an equal moral standing, each person matters as much as any other—that is why each person's preferences should count in the calculus. But if that is why we are attracted to utilitarianism, then it seems inconsistent to count external preferences. For if external preferences are counted, then what I am rightfully owed depends on how others think of me. If they think I am unworthy of equal concern, then I will do less well in the utilitarian aggregation. But utilitarians cannot accept that result, because utilitarianism is premised on the view that everyone ought to be treated as equals.

If we believe that everyone is to be treated as equals, then it offends our deepest principles to allow some people to suffer because others do not want them treated as equals. As Dworkin puts it, inegalitarian external preferences 'are on the same level—purport to occupy the same space—as the utilitarian theory'. Hence utilitarianism 'cannot accept at once a duty to defeat the false theory that some people's preferences should count for more than other people's and a duty to strive to fulfill the [external] preferences of those who passionately accept that false theory, as energetically as it strives for any other preferences' (Dworkin 1985: 363). The very principle that tells us to count equally every person's preferences in our standard of rightness also tells us to exclude those preferences which deny that people's preferences are to count equally. To paraphrase Harsanyi, utilitarians should be 'conscientious objectors' when faced with such preferences (Harsanyi 1977a: 62; Goodin 1982: 93–4).

(b) Selfish preferences

A second kind of illegitimate preference involves the desire for more than one's own fair share of resources. I will call these 'selfish preferences', since they ignore the fact that other people need the resources, and have legitimate claims to them. As with inegalitarian external preferences, selfish preferences are often irrational and uninformed. But satisfying selfish preferences will sometimes generate genuine utility. Should such preferences, if rational, be included in the utilitarian standard of rightness?

Utilitarians will object to the way I have phrased the question. As we have seen, utilitarians deny that there is such a thing as a fair share (and hence a selfish preference) independently of utilitarian calculations. For utilitarians, a fair distribution just is one that maximizes utility, and so no preference can be identified as selfish prior to utility calculations. So it begs the question against utilitarianism to assume that we can identify such things as selfish preferences prior to utilitarian calculations. But we can ask whether the utilitarian's own deepest principle provides grounds for adopting a theory of fair shares that enables us to identify and exclude selfish preferences from our standard of rightness.

This issue is discussed in a recent debate between Hare and John Mackie. Hare, like most utilitarians, believes that all rational preferences should be included in utility aggregation, even those that seem unfair. Even if I have a massive amount of resources, while my neighbour has very little, if I covet my neighbour's resources, then my desire must be included in the calculation. And if the calculations work out in my favour, perhaps because I have many friends who would share in my enjoyment, then I should get those resources. No matter how much I already have, my desire for more resources continues to count equally, even when the resources I want must come from someone with very little.

Why should utilitarians count such preferences? Hare believes that the principle of equal consideration requires it. According to Hare, the best way to interpret that egalitarian principle is to use the following mental test: we put ourselves in other people's shoes, and try to imagine how our actions affect them. And we should do this for everyone affected by our actions. We take the viewpoint of each person and treat it as being equally important as our own viewpoint, equally worthy of concern. Indeed, Hare says, we should treat these other viewpoints *as* our own viewpoint. This ensures that we are showing equal consideration for each person. If we have, in this way, put ourselves in everyone else's shoes, then we should choose that action which is best for 'me', where 'me' here means all of the 'me's', i.e. all of the different viewpoints I am now considering as equally my own. If I try to choose what is best for all my different selves, I will choose that action which maximizes the preference satisfaction of all these 'selves'. So, Hare claims, the utilitarian aggregation criterion follows naturally from this intuitive model of equal consideration. If I treat each person's interests as mattering equally, by imagining that their viewpoint is in fact one of my own, then I will adopt utilitarian principles (Hare 1984: 109–10; cf. 1982: 25–7).

Hare thinks that this is the only rational way of showing equal concern for people. But as Mackie notes, there are other possibilities, even if we accept Hare's claim that we treat people as equals by putting ourselves in their shoes, and treating each of these different selves as equally important. Rather than maximize preference satisfaction amongst all these selves, we might show our concern for them by guaranteeing each 'a fair go' in life, i.e. guarantee each an adequate level of resources and liberties. Or we might, when successively occupying these different positions, do what is best for the least well off, or provide each an equal share of the available resources and liberties. These are all different conceptions of what the abstract notion of equal consideration requires (Mackie 1984: 92).

How can we decide between these different ways of showing equal consideration? Utilitarians point out that their view may also lead to an egalitarian distribution of resources. People who lack resources will, in general, get more utility out of each additional resource than those who already have many resources. Someone who is starving is sure to get more utility from a piece of food than someone who is already well supplied with food (Hare 1978: 124–6; Brandt 1959: 415–20; Goodin 1995: 23). We can represent this graphically (see Fig. 2). If we take $10 from a rich person at point R (moving them down to point R1), and give it to a poor person at point P (moving them up to point P1), we will increase overall utility—P gains much more in utility than R loses.

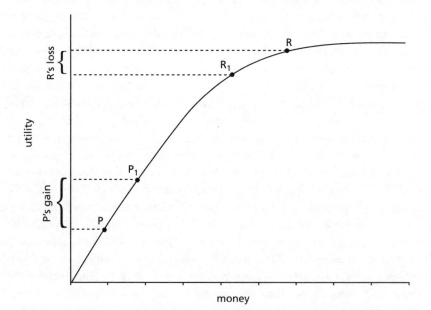

Figure 2 Declining marginal utility

So both sides can agree to start with a roughly equal distribution of resources. However, Hare and Mackie conceive this initially equal distribution in very different ways. For Mackie, so long as everyone else has their fair share of resources, then the resources initially allotted to me are mine—i.e. no one else has any legitimate claim of justice over them. Some people who already have their fair share may also want some of my share. But that is not important, morally speaking. Their preferences have no moral weight. They are selfish preferences, since they fail to respect my claim to a fair share. On Mackie's view, the state should secure each person's share of resources, and not allow them to be taken away just because other people have selfish preferences for what is rightfully someone else's. The best conception of equal consideration would exclude such selfish preferences.

For Hare, on the other hand, the resources initially distributed to me are not really mine in the same way. They are mine unless or until someone else can make better use of them, where 'better' means more productive of overall utility. Hare thinks this proviso for taking away my share is required by the same value that led the government initially to give it to me, i.e. an equal concern for each person's goals. If we care equally about people's goals, then it is right to redistribute resources whenever we can satisfy more goals by so doing.

Do we have any reason to choose one of these conceptions of equal consideration over the other? We need to look more closely at the kinds of preferences that would be involved in Hare's redistribution. Let us assume that I have my fair share, as does everyone else, and that we are in an affluent society, so that this share includes a house and lawn. Everyone else on my block plants a flower garden, but they would like my lawn left open as a public space for children to play on, or to walk dogs on. I, however, want my own garden. The desires of others to use my lawn as a public space may well outweigh, in terms of overall utility, my desire to have a garden. Hare thinks it is right, therefore, to sacrifice my desire for the greater desires of others.

If it is morally wrong for me to insist on having a garden, we need to know *who is wronged*. If my sacrifice is required to treat people as equals, who is treated as less than an equal if I disallow the sacrifice? Hare's answer is that the other members of the block are not treated as equals if their preferences are not allowed to outweigh my desire. But surely that is implausible, since they already have their own yard, their own fair share of resources. According to Hare, my neighbours' desire to decide how to use my resources, as well as their own, is a legitimate preference which grounds a moral claim. But isn't it more accurate to describe such a preference as simply selfish? Why should my neighbours suppose that the idea of equal concern gives them any claim over my share of resources? If they already have their own lawn, then I am not treating them unjustly in saying that my preference concerning my lawn outweighs or pre-empts their preferences. I still respect them as equals since I make no claim on the resources they have to lead their lives. But they do not respect me as an equal when they expect or demand that I give up my share of resources to satisfy their selfish desire to have more than their fair share.

This points to an important component of our everyday sense of what it means to treat people as equals—namely, we should not expect others to subsidize our projects at the expense of their own. Perhaps my friends and I have expensive tastes—we like to eat caviar and play tennis all day. To expect others to give up their fair share of resources to support our taste, no matter how happy it makes us, is selfish. If I already have my share of resources, then to suppose that I have a legitimate moral claim to someone else's resources, just because it will make me happier, is a failure to show equal concern for others. If we believe that others should be treated as equals, then we will exclude such selfish preferences from the utilitarian calculus.

So the very principle which supported an initially equal distribution of resources also argues for securing that distribution. Hare's proviso—that the initial distribution be subject to utility-maximizing redistribution—undermines, rather than extends, the point of the initial distribution. Hare's idea of treating other people's interests as my own when engaged in moral reasoning is not necessarily a bad one. It is one way of rendering vivid the idea of moral equality (we will look at other such devices in the next chapter). But the equal concern he seeks to promote is not achieved by treating other people's preferences as constituting equal claims on all of our actions and resources. Rather, equality teaches us how much by way of resources we have to pursue our projects, and how much is rightfully left for others. Equal concern is shown by ensuring that others can claim their own fair share, not by ensuring that they have equal weight in determining the use of my share. Securing people's fair shares, rather than leaving them subject to selfish preferences, is the better spelling out of the equal concern that Hare seeks.

This, according to Rawls, is a fundamental difference between his account of justice and the utilitarians'. For Rawls, it is a defining feature of our sense of justice that 'interests requiring the violation of justice have no value', and so the presence of illegitimate preferences 'cannot distort our claims upon one another' (Rawls 1971: 31, 450, 564). Justice 'limits the admissible conceptions of the good, so that those conceptions the pursuit of which violate the principles of justice are ruled out absolutely: the claims to pursue inadmissible conceptions have no weight at all'. Because unfair preferences 'never, so to speak, enter into the social calculus', people's claims 'are made secure from the unreasonable demands of others'. For utilitarians, on the other hand, 'no restrictions founded on right and justice are imposed on the ends through which satisfaction is to be achieved' (Rawls 1982b: 184, 171 n., 170, 182).

We can now see why utilitarianism fails to recognize special relationships, or to exclude illegitimate preferences. In each case, utilitarianism is interpreting equal consideration in terms of the aggregation of pre-existing preferences, whatever they are for, even if they invade the rights or commitments of others. But our intuitions tell us that equality should enter into the very formation of our preferences. Part of what it means to show equal consideration for others is taking into account what rightfully belongs to them in deciding on one's own goals in life.[17] Hence prejudiced and selfish preferences are excluded from the start, for they already reflect a failure to show equal consideration. However, if my goals do respect other people's rightful claims, then I am free to pursue special relationships, even if some other act maximizes utility. If my plans respect the teachings of equality, then there is nothing wrong with giving priority to my family or career. This means that my day-to-day activities will show unequal concern—I will care more about helping my friends, or the causes I am committed to, than about helping the goals of other people. That is part of what it means to have friends and causes. And that is entirely acceptable, so long as I respect the claims of others concerning the pursuit of their projects.

If we think about the values that motivate utilitarianism, the values which give it its initial plausibility, we will see that it must be modified. Utilitarianism is initially attractive because human beings matter and matter equally. But the goal of equal consideration that utilitarians seek to implement is best implemented by an approach that includes a theory of fair shares. Such a theory would exclude prejudiced or selfish preferences that ignore the rightful claims of others, but would allow for the kinds of special commitments that are part of our very idea of leading a life. These modifications do not conflict with the general principle of consequentialism, but rather stem from it. They are refinements of the general idea that morality should be about the welfare of human beings. Utilitarianism has simply oversimplified the way in which we intuitively believe that the welfare of others is worthy of moral concern.

In defending the importance of rights which protect people from utilitarian aggregation, Rawls and Mackie do not dispute the moral importance of consequences. As Rawls notes, 'all ethical doctrines worth our attention take consequences into account in judging rightness. One which did not would simply be irrational, crazy' (Rawls 1971: 30). Rawls, Mackie, and other 'rights-based' theorists simply build concern for consequences into their theories at a different and indeed earlier stage than utilitarianism. They argue that morality requires us to take the consequences for others into account in the very formation of our preferences, not just in the aggregation of those preferences.

As we have seen, indirect utilitarians claim that our intuitive commitment to non-utilitarian decision-procedures does not undermine utilitarianism as a standard of rightness, since we can give a utilitarian justification for adopting non-utilitarian procedures. But that response will not work here, for my argument concerns utilitarianism as a standard of rightness. My claim is that the very reason utilitarians give for basing their standard of rightness on the satisfaction of people's preferences is also a reason to exclude external and selfish preferences from that standard. This is an objection to the theory's principles, not to the way those principles get applied in decision-procedures.

Commentators who endorse these sorts of modifications of utilitarianism often describe the resulting theory as a balance between the values of utility and equality, or a compromise between consequentialism and deontology (e.g. Raphael 1981: 47–56; Brandt 1959: ch. 16; Hospers 1961: 426; Rescher 1966: 59). That is not what I have argued. Rather, the modifications are needed to provide a better spelling out of the ideal of equal consideration which utilitarianism itself appeals to.

It is worth pausing to consider the kind of argument that I have just presented, since it expresses, I believe, one basic form of political argument. As I mentioned in the Introduction, the idea of equality is often said to be the basis of political morality. Both Hare's utilitarianism and Mackie's 'right to a fair go' appeal to the idea that each person is entitled to equal consideration. But they do not give an equally compelling account of that idea. Our intuitions tell us that utilitarianism fails to ensure that people are treated as equals, since it lacks a theory of fair shares.

✳ This might suggest that political theorizing is a matter of correctly deducing specific principles from this shared premiss of moral equality. Political argument, then, would primarily be a matter of identifying mistaken deductions. But political philosophy is not like logic, where the conclusion is meant to be already fully present in the premises. The idea of moral equality is too abstract for us to be able to deduce anything very specific from it. There are many different and conflicting kinds of equal treatment. Equality of opportunity, for example, may produce unequal income (since some people have greater talents), and equal income may produce unequal welfare (since some people have greater needs). All of these particular forms of equal treatment are logically compatible with the idea of moral equality. The question is which form of equal treatment best captures that deeper ideal of treating people as equals. That is not a question of logic. It is a moral question, whose answer depends on complex issues about the nature of human beings and their interests and relationships. In deciding which particular form of equal treatment best captures the idea of treating people as equals, we do not want a logician, who is versed in the art of logical deductions. We want someone who has an understanding of what it is about humans that deserves respect and concern, and of what kinds of activities best manifest that respect and concern.

The idea of moral equality, while fundamental, is too abstract to serve as a premiss from which we deduce a theory of justice. What we have in political argument is not a single premiss and then competing deductions, but rather a single concept and then competing conceptions or interpretations of it. Each theory of justice is not *deduced from* the ideal of equality, but rather *aspires to* it, and each theory can be judged by how well it succeeds in that aspiration. As Dworkin puts it, when we instruct public officials to act in accordance with the concept of equality, we 'charge those whom [we] instruct with the responsibility of developing and applying their own conception . . . That is not the same thing, of course, as granting them a discretion to act as they like; it sets a standard which they must try—and may fail—to meet, because it assumes that one conception is superior to another' (Dworkin 1977: 135).[18] However confident we are in a particular conception of equality, it must be tested against competing conceptions to see which best expresses or captures the concept of equality.

This is the kind of argument I have tried to give against utilitarianism. We can see the weakness in utilitarianism as a conception of equality by comparing it to a conception which guarantees certain rights and fair shares of resources. When we compare these two conceptions, utilitarianism seems implausible as an account of moral equality, at odds with our intuitions about that basic concept. But its implausibility is not a matter of logical error, and the strength of a theory of fair shares isn't a matter of logical proof. This may be unsatisfying to those accustomed to more rigorous forms of argument. But if the egalitarian suggestion is correct—if each of these theories is aspiring to live up to the ideal of treating people as equals—then this is the form that political argument must take. To demand that it achieve logical proof simply misunderstands the nature of the exercise. Any attempt to spell out and defend our beliefs about the principles which should govern the political community will take this form of comparing different conceptions of the concept of equality.

6. THE POLITICS OF UTILITARIANISM

What are the practical implications of utilitarianism as a political morality? I have noted the danger that utilitarianism could justify sacrificing the weak and unpopular members of the community for the benefit of the majority. But utilitarianism has also been used to attack those who hold unjust privileges at the expense of the majority. Indeed, utilitarianism, as a self-conscious political and philosophical movement, arose as a radical critique of English society. The original utilitarians were 'Philosophical Radicals' who believed in a complete rethinking of English society, a society whose practices they believed were the product not of reason, but of feudal superstition. Utilitarianism, at that time, was identified with a progressive and reform-minded political programme—the extension of democracy, penal reform, welfare provisions, etc.

Contemporary utilitarians, on the other hand, are 'surprisingly conformist'—in fact they seem keen to show that utilitarianism leaves everything as it is (Williams 1972: 102). As Stuart Hampshire noted, British utilitarianism 'set out to do good in the world', and

> succeeded in large part over many years in this aim. . . . The utilitarian philosophy, before the First World War and for many years after it . . . was still a bold, innovative, even a subversive doctrine, with a record of successful social criticism behind it. I believe that it is losing this role, and that it is now an obstruction. (Quoted in Goodin 1995: 3)

To be sure, some utilitarians continue to claim that utilitarianism requires a radical critique of the arbitrary and irrational aspects of everyday morality (e.g. Singer 1979). But utilitarianism no longer forms a coherent political movement, and tends if anything to defend the status quo.

What explains this increasing conservatism? I think there are two main reasons. The first is the increasing recognition of the difficulty in actually applying utilitarian principles. Whereas the original utilitarians were willing to judge existing social codes at the altar of human well-being, many contemporary utilitarians argue there are good utilitarian reasons to defer to everyday morality. It may seem that we can increase utility by making exceptions to a rule of everyday morality, but there are utilitarian reasons for sticking to good rules under all circumstances. The gains of new rules are uncertain, whereas existing conventions have proven value (having survived the test of cultural evolution), and people have formed expectations around them. And even if it seems that the everyday rule is not a good one in utilitarian terms, there are utilitarian reasons for not evaluating rules in terms of utility. Acting directly on utilitarian grounds is counter-productive, for it encourages a contingent and detached attitude towards what should be wholehearted personal and political commitments. Moreover, it is difficult to predict the consequences of our actions, or to measure these consequences even when known. Hence our judgements about what maximizes utility are imperfect, and attempts to rationalize social institutions are likely to cause more harm than good.

As a result, modern utilitarians downplay the extent to which utilitarianism should be used as a critical principle, or as a principle of political evaluation at all.[19] Some utilitarians say we should only resort to utilitarian reasoning when our everyday precepts lead to conflicting results; others say that the best world, from a utilitarian point of view, is one in which no one ever reasons in an explictly utilitarian manner. Williams claims that this sort of utilitarianism is self-defeating—it argues for its own disappearance. This is not self-defeating in the technical sense, for it does not show that the morally right action is not, after all, the one that maximizes utility. But it does show that utilitarianism is no longer being offered as the correct language for political debate. Politics should be debated in the non-utilitarian language of everyday morality—the language of rights, personal responsibilities, the public interest, distributive justice, etc. Utilitarianism, on some modern views of it, leaves everything as it is—it stands above, rather than competes with, everyday political decision-making.

There is another reason why utilitarianism has become more conservative. Utilitarianism arose in Britain at a time when much of society was still organ-ized to benefit a small, privileged elite at the expense of the (rural and working-class) *majority*. This elitist social structure was often justified in terms of some ideologically biased conception of tradition, nature, or religion. The fundamental political disputes were about whether or not to reform the system to enhance the rights of the majority. In these circumstances, utilitari-anism's commitment to secularism and maximization meant that it sided clearly with the historically oppressed majority against the privileged elite.

In contemporary liberal democracies, however, the fundamental political questions are different. The majority (or at least its male members) has long since acquired its basic civil and political rights. Starting with the civil rights movements in the 1950s and 1960s, many of the burning political questions have centred on the rights of historically oppressed *minorities*—such as African-Americans, gays, indigenous peoples, or people with disabilities. Moreover, these rights are typically asserted against the majority—i.e. they are intended to force the majority to accept policies that are not desired by, or in the interests of, the majority. In these cases, utilitarianism no longer offers such clear or unambiguous direction. The minority in question may be both small—perhaps only 2–5 per cent of the population—and unpopular. Many members of the majority are prejudiced against such minorities, and even if not, the majority has historically supported and benefited from the oppres-sion of various minorities. The majority has enriched itself by dispossessing indigenous peoples, for example. According land rights to indigenous peoples, or accessibility rights to the disabled, may involve significant financial costs to members of the majority, and force them to give up cherished traditions and practices that excluded the minority.

In these circumstances, it is far from clear what utilitarianism recommends. If we simply count up votes or measure public opinion, we may well find that opponents of gay rights outnumber the supporters. Or if we count up who gains or loses from indigenous land rights, we may well find that more people lose than gain from these rights. A simple application of utilitarianism would seem to side with the majority against the minority seeking its rights. Of course, as we have seen, utilitarians have various reasons for saying that in the long term, everyone benefits when the rights of even small and unpopular minorities are protected against the prejudices or economic interests of the majority. We need to weigh the short-term desire or interest of the majority in oppressing or neglecting a particular minority against the long-term interests of maintaining stable and functioning institutions. But these are complex and speculative questions on which utilitarians themselves disagree.

In short, when the question is whether to defend an oppressed majority against a small privileged elite, utilitarianism gives us a clear and progressive answer. But when the question is whether to defend an oppressed minority against a large privileged majority, utilitarianism gives us vague and conflicting answers, depending on how we identify and weigh short-term and long-term effects. The problem is that 'the winds of utilitarian argumentation blow in too many directions' (Sher 1975: 159). This problem applies in virtually all areas of public policy. For example, while some utilitarians argue that utility is maximized by massive redistribution of wealth, due to the declining marginal utility of money, others defend laissez-faire capitalism because it creates more wealth. This is not just a question of predicting how different economic policies fare in terms of an agreed-upon scale of utility. It is also a question about how to define the scale—what is the relationship between economic goods and other components of the human good (leisure, community, etc.)? It is also a question of the role of utility calculations themselves—how reliably can we determine overall utility, and how important are established conventions? Given these disagreements about how and when to measure utility, utilitarianism is bound to yield fundamentally opposed judgements.

I do not mean to suggest that all these positions are equally plausible (or that these problems are not also found in non-utilitarian theories). The confidence and unanimity that the original utilitarians had in their political judgements was often the result of an oversimplified view of the issues, and a certain amount of indeterminacy is unavoidable in any theory once we recognize the complexity of the empirical and moral issues involved. Modern utilitarians are right to insist that utility is not reducible to pleasure, and that not all kinds of utility are measurable or commensurable, and that it is not always appropriate even to try to measure these utilities. However, the price of this added sophistication is that utilitarianism does not immediately identify any set of policies as distinctly superior. Modern utilitarianism, despite its radical heritage, no longer defines a distinctive political position.

GUIDE TO FURTHER READING

The most famous statements of utilitarianism remain those of its nineteenth-century founders, particularly Jeremy Bentham, John Stuart Mill, and Henry Sidgwick. Indeed, much of the literature on utilitarianism even today consists of commentaries on these authors. For these classical statements, see Jeremy Bentham, *An Introduction to the Principles of Morals and Legislation*, ed. J. H. Burns and H. L. A. Hart (Athlone Press, 1970, 1st pub. 1823); J. S. Mill, *Utilitarianism, Liberty, Representative Government*, ed. A. D. Lindsay (J. M. Dent and Sons, 1968, 1st pub. 1863); and Henry Sidgwick, *The Methods of Ethics* (Hackett, 1981, 1st pub. 1874). For contemporary commentaries, see David Lyons (ed.), *Mill's Utilitarianism: Critical Essays* (Rowman and Littlefield, 1997), Roger Crisp (ed.), *Routledge Philosophy Guidebook to Mill on Utilitarianism* (Routledge, 1997); Ross Harrison (ed.), *Bentham* (Routledge, 1999); Bart Schultz (ed.), *Essays on Sidgwick* (Cambridge University Press, 1992).

Much of the literature for and against utilitarianism treats it as a general theory of ethics or personal morality, intended to guide or evaluate our personal conduct and choices. For influential contemporary defences of utilitarian ethics, see James Griffin, *Well-Being: Its Meaning, Measurement, and Moral Importance* (Oxford University Press, 1986); David Lyons, *Forms and Limits of Utilitarianism* (Oxford University Press, 1965); Richard Brandt, *A Theory of the Right and the Good* (Oxford University Press, 1979), and *Morality, Utilitarianism and Rights* (Cambridge University Press, 1992); R. M. Hare, *Moral Thinking* (Oxford University Press, 1981). For an attempt to apply utilitarianism to a wide range of practical problems, from euthanasia to Third World poverty to animal rights, see Peter Singer, *Practical Ethics* (Cambridge University Press, 1993).

Relatively less has been written defending utilitarianism as a specifically *political* morality for the evaluation of political institutions and public policies. For two important exceptions, see Robert Goodin, *Utilitarianism as a Public Philosophy* (Cambridge University Press, 1995); and James Bailey, *Utilitarianism, Institutions, and Justice* (Oxford University Press, 1997).

Whether offered as a doctrine of personal ethics or political institutions, utilitarianism has been subject to withering critiques. One of the earliest, and still powerful, critiques is by Bernard Williams in J. J. C. Smart and B. Williams (eds.), *Utilitarianism: For and Against* (Cambridge University Press, 1973). Other important critiques (and replies) can be found in Amartya Sen and Bernard Williams (eds.), *Utilitarianism and Beyond* (Cambridge University Press, 1982); Raymond Frey (ed.), *Utility and Rights* (University of Minnesota Press, 1984); and Lincoln Allison (ed.), *The Utilitarian Response: The Contemporary Viability of Utilitarian Political Philosophy* (Sage, 1990).

Two introductory surveys of these debates are Geoffrey Scarre, *Utilitarianism* (Routledge, 1996) in the Routledge 'Problems of Philosophy' series; and William Shaw, *Contemporary Ethics: Taking Account of Utilitarianism* (Blackwell, 1998). Many of the most important readings are excerpted in Jonathan Glover (ed.), *Utilitarianism and its Critics* (Macmillan, 1990).

For those wishing to keep up with new developments in the field, the journal *Utilitas* specializes in the study of utilitarianism, and *Economics and Philosophy* often contains debates between utilitarians and their critics. There are also a couple of helpful websites devoted to utilitarianism. The first is the website of the 'Bentham Project' at University College London, which includes the site for *Utilitas* and the International Society for Utilitarian Studies (**www.ucl.ac.uk/Bentham-Project/**). The second is 'Utilitarian Resources' (www.utilitarianism.com). Both include extensive bibliographies and on-line texts.

NOTES

1. This common slogan is misleading because it is contains two distinct maximands—'greatest happiness' and 'greatest number'. It is impossible for any theory to contain a double maximand, and any attempt to implement it quickly leads to an impasse (e.g. if the two possible distributions are 10:10:10 and 20:20:0, then we cannot produce both the greatest happiness and the happiness of the greatest number). See Griffin 1986: 151–4; Rescher 1966: 25–8.

2. For discussions of adaptive preferences, see Elster 1982b; 1983b; Barry 1989b; Sunstein 1991; Sunstein 1997: chs. 1–2. For applications to gender issues, see Sunstein 1999; Okin 1999; Nussbaum 2000. This is related, of course, to the Marxist theory of false consciousness, according to which workers have been socialized in such a way as to be unable to see their real interest in socialism.

3. Of course, while I might prefer A if informed, it does not follow that A provides me with any benefit in my current uninformed state. This complicates the informed preference account of utility, but does not subvert it. What promotes my well-being is distinct from satisfying my existing preferences, even if it is also distinct from satisfying my ideally informed preferences (Griffin 1986: 11–12; 32–3). It is possible, however, that a full development of this account would bring it close to what is sometimes called an 'Objective List' theory (Parfit 1984: 493–502).

4. For discussions of 'incommensurability', and the problems it poses for utilitarianism, see Finnis 1983: 86–93; Raz 1986: 321–68; George 1993: 88–90.

5. I do not believe that the preferences of the dead are always without moral weight. What happens after our death can affect how well our life went, and our desire for certain things after our death can be an important focus for our activities in life. Indeed, if the preferences of the dead did not sometimes have moral weight, it would be impossible to make sense of the way we treat wills. See the discussion in Lomasky (1987: 212–21), Hanser (1990), and Feinberg (1980: 173–6). On the 'experience requirement' more generally, see Scanlon (1991: 22–3), Larmore (1987: 48–9), Lomasky (1987: 231–3), Griffin (1986: 13–23), Parfit (1984: 149–53).

6. For a detailed exploration of this problem, see the essays in Elster and Roemer 1991.

7. Political theories which are concerned with the distribution of resources, without determining the effect these resources have on each person's welfare, may seem an exception to this general claim. But, as I will discuss in Chapter 3, this is a misleading perception, and even resource-based theories must have some theory of people's 'essential interests, most comprehensively construed' (Dworkin 1983: 24).

8. It is not clear whether utilitarianism can in fact limit itself to the basic structure of society, or to political decision-making. Even if utilitarianism applies in the first instance to political decisions or social institutions, and not to the personal conduct of individuals, one of the decisions governments face is to determine the legitimate scope of private attachments. If people are not maximizing utility in their private lives, then reorganizing the basic structure so as to leave less room for private life could increase utility. If comprehensive moral utilitarianism cannot accommodate our sense of the value of personal attachments, then political utilitarianism will have no reason to preserve a robust private realm. In any event, the predominance of utilitarianism in political philosophy stems mostly from the belief that it is the only coherent or systematic moral philosophy (Rawls 1971: pp. vii–viii), and so the motivation

for political utilitarianism is reduced if comprehensive moral utilitarianism can be shown to be indefensible.

9. The U-agent is often described as an 'act utilitarian', because he acts directly on the basis of utility calculations. But this is misleading in so far as 'act utilitarian' is commonly contrasted with 'rule utilitarian'. What defines the U-agent is that he uses utility maximization *directly* as a decision-procedure, and, as we will see, he could do this while focusing on rules rather than acts. The distinction between direct and indirect utilitarianism cuts across the distinction between act- and rule-utilitarianism (Railton 1984: 156–7). The first contrast is whether the principle of utility maximization is viewed as a decision-procedure or a standard of rightness, not whether the principle of utility maximization (as either a standard of rightness or a decision-procedure) applies to acts or rules.

10. For other influential statements of this 'alienation' objection, see Kagan 1989: 1–2; Railton 1984; Jackson 1991.

11. Two of the most influential recent defences of rule-utilitarianism are Harsanyi 1985 and Hardin 1988; cf. Ball 1990. There are in fact several different versions of rule-utilitarianism, each with its own strengths and weaknesses. For a helpful overview, see Scarre 1996: 122–32.

12. Bailey, for example, argues that while allowing Roman-style games may increase utility on a rule-utilitarian view, it is suboptimal, in the sense that we could do even better if we socialized people to get pleasure in other ways that do not involve harming others (Bailey 1997: 21, 144–5). In other words, Roman games are good, from a utilitarian point of view, in the sense of increasing overall utility compared to the status quo, but we could do even better, and so utilitarians should prefer some alternative. Bailey thinks this argument helps bring utilitarianism in line with our everyday intuitions. In reality, however, most people think the Roman games were evil, rather than merely suboptimal, and that whatever pleasure they gave to spectators should be accorded no moral weight. For Bailey, as for Hare (1982: 30) and Smart (1973: 25–6), there is no basis in utilitarianism for excluding such illegitimate preferences from the calculus.

13. For discussions of Government House utilitarianism, see Wolff 1996a: 131: Goodin 1995: ch. 4; Bailey 1997: 26, 152–3.

14. Unlike the rule utilitarian, who views promises as ingenious devices to maximize utility, the indirect utilitarian views our *beliefs about promises* as ingenious devices for maximizing utility. But people do not, and arguably cannot, view their moral beliefs this way (Smith 1988).

15. In defence of the teleological interpretation, Parfit gives the following sort of hypothetical example: imagine a woman who can choose whether to delay her pregnancy. If she gets pregnant now, the child will have a life worth living, but will not have a very happy life. If she delays the pregnancy for two months, the resulting child will have a happy and fulfilling life. Parfit argues that most people would view it as immoral not to delay the pregnancy, unless there were some urgent reason for proceeding immediately. Yet this judgement cannot be explained on the equal consideration interpretation, since no one would be harmed or wronged by not delaying the pregnancy. (The child resulting from the immediate pregnancy is not harmed by being born, since he prefers to be alive than never to have been born; the potential child of the delayed pregnancy is not harmed, because she does not exist.) So if it is morally wrong not to delay the pregnancy, as Parfit thinks, then it must be because we have an obligation to increase the overall amount of utility in the world, an obligation independent of our obligation to treat particular people with equal concern or respect (Parfit 1984: 358–61). And if the woman has an obligation to increase the overall amount of utility in the world by conceiving the happier child, then why wouldn't all of us have an obligation to increase overall utility by bringing additional children into the world? A couple who only wanted one child should instead have two or more children, even if this reduces the average utility of themselves

and their first child, so long as the utility of each additional child outweighs the loss to the existing family members.

I will let readers judge for themselves whether this is a plausible argument for teleological utilitarianism. In so far as people think the woman should delay her pregnancy, I suspect this is partly for prudential rather than moral reasons (i.e. we think she herself will be better off if she delays the pregnancy), and also partly because people wrongly think that it would be the same child born two months later, and hence that that particular child is harmed by being brought into the world 'too early'. Once we filter out the prudential reasons, and clarify that it would be an entirely different child born (i.e. the product of a different egg and sperm), then it is far from clear that there is anything morally wrong in consciously choosing to have a child who will be less happy than some other child one could have conceived.

16. Critics of utilitarianism also conflate the two versions. This is true, for example, of Rawls's claim that utilitarians ignore the separateness of persons. According to Rawls, utilitarians endorse the principle of maximizing utility because they generalize from the one-person case (it is rational for each individual to maximize her happiness), to the many-person case (it is rational for society to maximize its happiness). Rawls objects to this generalization because it treats society as if it were a single person, and so ignores the difference between trade-offs within one person's life and trade-offs across lives (Rawls 1971: 27; cf. Nozick 1974: 32–3; Gordon 1980: 40; Mackie 1984: 86–7). However, neither the egalitarian nor the teleological version of utilitarianism makes this generalization, and Rawls's claim rests on a conflation of the two. On this, see Kymlicka 1988b: 182–5; Freeman 1994; Cumminsky 1990; Quinn 1993.

17. This is only part of what equality requires, for there are obligations to those who are unable to help themselves, and Good Samaritan obligations to those who are in dire need. In these cases, we have obligations that are not tied to respecting people's rightful claims. I return to these issues in Chapter 9.

18. This shows why it is wrong to claim that Dworkin's egalitarian plateau is 'purely formal' or 'empty' since it is compatible with many different kinds of distributions (Hart 1979: 95–6; Goodin 1982: 89–90; Mapel 1989: 54; Larmore 1987: 62; Raz 1986: ch. 9). As Dworkin notes, this objection 'misunderstands the role of abstract concepts in political theory and debate' (Dworkin 1977: 368). The idea of treating people as equals is abstract, but not formal—on the contrary, it is a substantive ideal that excludes some theories (e.g. racist ones), and that sets a standard to which other theories aspire. The fact that an abstract concept needs to be interpreted, and that different theories interpret it in different ways, does not show that the concept is empty, or that one interpretation of that concept is as good as any other.

19. For example, Bailey defends a form of utilitarianism, but suggests that it is only appropriate for 'marginal' rather than 'global' analysis—i.e. we should not attempt to design institutions *de novo* on the basis of utilitarian principles, but should only invoke utilitarianism to make marginal changes to existing institutions if and when they start to fail due to changed circumstances (Bailey 1997: 15).

3

LIBERAL EQUALITY

1. RAWLS'S PROJECT

(a) Intuitionism and utilitarianism

In the last chapter I argued that we need some or other theory of fair shares prior to the calculation of utility, for there are limits to the way individuals can be legitimately sacrificed for the benefit of others. If we are to treat people as equals, we must protect them in their possession of certain rights and liberties. But which rights and liberties?

Most of the political philosophy written in the last thirty years has been on this question. There are some people, as we have seen, who continue to defend utilitarianism. But there has been a marked shift away from the 'once widely-accepted old faith that some form of utilitarianism, if only we could discover the right form, *must* capture the essence of political morality' (Hart 1979: 77), and most contemporary political philosophers have hoped to find a systematic alternative to utilitarianism. John Rawls was one of the first to present such an alternative in his 1971 book *A Theory of Justice*. Many others had written about the counter-intuitive nature of utilitarianism. But Rawls starts his book by complaining that political theory was caught between two extremes: utilitarianism on the one side, and an incoherent jumble of ideas and principles on the other. Rawls calls this second option 'intuitionism', an approach which is little more than a series of anecdotes based on particular intuitions about particular issues.

Intuitionism is an unsatisfying alternative to utilitarianism, for while we do indeed have anti-utilitarian intuitions on particular issues, we also want an alternative theory which makes sense of those intuitions. We want a theory which shows why these particular examples elicit disapproval in us. But 'intuitionism' never gets beyond, or underneath, these initial intuitions to show how they are related, or to provide principles that underlie and give structure to them.

Rawls describes intuitionist theories as having two features:

first, they consist of a plurality of first principles which may conflict to give contrary directives in particular types of cases; and second, they include no explicit method, no priority rules, for weighing these principles against one another: we are simply to strike a balance by intuition, by what seems to us most nearly right. Or if there are priority rules, these are thought to be more or less trivial and of no substantial assistance in reaching a judgment. (1971: 34)

There are many kinds of intuitionism, which can be distinguished by the level of generality of their principles.

Common sense intuitionism takes the form of groups of rather specific precepts, each group applying to a particular problem of justice. There is a group of precepts which applies to the question of fair wages, another to that of taxation, still another to punishment, and so on. In arriving at the notion of a fair wage, say, we are to balance somehow various competing criteria, for example, the claims of skill, training, effort, responsibility, and the hazards of the job, as well as to make some allowance for need. No one presumably would decide by any one of these precepts alone, and some compromise between them must be struck. (1971: 35)

But the various principles can also be of a much more general nature. Thus it is common for people to talk about intuitively balancing equality and liberty, or equality and efficiency, and these principles would apply to the entire range of a theory of justice (1971: 36–7). These intuitionist approaches, whether at the level of specific precepts or general principles, are not only theoretically unsatisfying, but are also quite unhelpful in practical matters. For they give us no guidance when these specific and irreducible precepts conflict. Yet it is precisely when they conflict that we look to political theory for guidance.

It is important, therefore, to try to establish some priority amongst these conflicting precepts. This is the task Rawls sets himself—to develop a systematic political theory that structures our different intuitions. He does not assume that there is such a theory, but only that it is worth trying to find one:

Now there is nothing intrinsically irrational about this intuitionist doctrine. Indeed, it may be true. We cannot take for granted that there must be a complete derivation of our judgments of social justice from recognizable ethical principles. The intuitionist believes to the contrary that the complexity of the moral facts defies our efforts to give a full account of our judgments and necessitates a plurality of competing principles. He contends that attempts to go beyond these principles either reduce to triviality, as when it is said that social justice is to give every man his due, or else lead to falsehood and oversimplification, as when one settles everything by the principle of utility. The only way therefore to dispute intuitionism is to set forth the recognizably ethical criteria that account for the weights which, in our considered judgments, we think appropriate to give to the plurality of principles. A refutation of intuitionism consists in presenting the sort of constructive criteria that are said not to exist. (1971: 39)

Rawls, then, has a certain historical importance in breaking the intuitionism–utilitarianism deadlock. But his theory is important for another reason. His theory dominates the field, not in the sense of commanding agreement, for very few people agree with all of it, but in the sense that later theorists have defined themselves in opposition to Rawls. They explain what their theory is by contrasting it with Rawls's theory. We will not be able to make sense of later work on justice if we do not understand Rawls.

(b) The principles of justice

In presenting Rawls's ideas, I will first give his answer to the question of justice, and then discuss the two arguments he gives for that answer. His 'general conception of justice' consists of one central idea: 'all social primary goods—liberty and opportunity, income and wealth, and the bases of self-respect—are to be distributed equally unless an unequal distribution of any or all of these goods is to the advantage of the least favored' (1971: 303). In this 'general conception', Rawls ties the idea of justice to an equal share of social goods, but he adds an important twist. We treat people as equals not by removing all inequalities, but only those which disadvantage someone. If certain inequalities benefit everyone, by drawing out socially useful talents and energies, then they will be acceptable to everyone. If giving someone else more money than I have promotes my interests, then equal concern for my interests suggests that we allow, rather than prohibit, that inequality. Inequalities are allowed if they *improve* my initially equal share, but are not allowed if, as in utilitarianism, they *invade* my fair share. We can think of this, Rawls says, as giving the less well off a kind of veto over inequalities, which they would exercise to reject any inequalities which sacrifice, rather than promote, their interests (Rawls 1978: 64). That is the single, simple idea at the heart of Rawls's theory.

However, this general conception is not yet a full theory of justice, for the various goods being distributed according to that principle may conflict. For example, we might be able to increase someone's income by depriving them of one of their basic liberties. This unequal distribution of liberty favours the least well off in one way (income) but not in another (liberty). Or what if an unequal distribution of income benefits everyone in terms of income, but creates an inequality in opportunity which disadvantages those with less income? Do these improvements in income outweigh disadvantages in liberty or opportunity? The general conception leaves these questions unresolved, and so does not solve the problem which made intuitionist theories unhelpful.

We need a system of priority amongst the different elements in the theory. Rawls's solution is to break down the general conception into three parts, which are arranged according to a principle of 'lexical priority'.

First Principle—Each person is to have an equal right to the most extensive total system of equal basic liberties compatible with a similar system of liberty for all.

Second Principle—Social and economic inequalities are to be arranged so that they are both:

(a) to the greatest benefit of the least advantaged, and

(b) attached to offices and positions open to all under conditions of fair equality of opportunity.

First Priority Rule (The Priority of Liberty)—The principles of justice are to be ranked in lexical order and therefore liberty can be restricted only for the sake of liberty.

Second Priority Rule (The Priority of Justice over Efficiency and Welfare)—The second principle of justice is lexically prior to the principle of efficiency and to that of maximizing the sum of advantages; and fair opportunity is prior to the difference principle. (1971: 302–3)

These principles form the 'special conception' of justice, and they seek to provide the systematic guidance that intuitionism could not give us. According to these principles, some social goods are more important than others, and so cannot be sacrificed for improvements in those other goods. Equal liberties take precedence over equal opportunity which takes precedence over equal resources. But within each category Rawls's simple idea remains—an inequality is only allowed if it benefits the least well off. So the priority rules do not affect the basic principle of fair shares that remains within each category.

These two principles are Rawls's answer to the question of justice. But we have not yet seen his argument for them. In fact he has two different arguments, which I will examine in turn. I will focus on Rawls's arguments for the second principle—which he calls the 'difference principle'—governing the distribution of economic resources. I will not discuss the liberty principle, or why Rawls gives priority to it, until later chapters. However, it is important to note that Rawls is not endorsing a general principle of liberty, such that anything that can plausibly be called a liberty is to be given overriding priority. Rather, he is giving special protection to what he calls the 'basic liberties', by which he means the standard civil and political rights recognized in liberal democracies—the right to vote, to run for office, due process, free speech, mobility etc. (1971: 61). These rights are very important to liberalism—indeed, one way of differentiating liberalism just is that it gives priority to the basic liberties.

However, the assumption that civil and political rights should have priority is widely shared in our society. As a result, the disputes between Rawls and his critics have tended to be on other issues. The idea that people should have their basic liberties protected is the least contentious part of his theory. But my rejection of utilitarianism was based on the need for a theory of fair shares in economic resources as well, and that is more controversial. Some people reject the idea of a theory of fair shares of economic resources, and those who accept it have very different views about what form such a theory should take. This question of resource distribution is central to the shift from utilitarianism to the other theories of justice we will be examining. So I will concentrate for now on Rawls's account of the difference principle.

Rawls has two arguments for his principles of justice. One is to contrast his theory with what he takes to be the prevailing ideology concerning distributive justice—namely, the ideal of equality of opportunity. He argues that his theory better fits our considered intuitions concerning justice, and that it gives a better spelling-out of the very ideals of fairness that the prevailing ideology appeals to. The second argument is quite different. Rawls argues that his principles of justice are superior because they are the outcome of a hypothetical social contract. He claims that if people in a certain kind of pre-social state had to decide which principles should govern their society, they would choose his principles. Each person in what Rawls calls the 'original position' has a rational interest in adopting Rawlsian principles for the governing of social cooperation. This second argument has received the most critical attention, and is the one which Rawls is most famous for. But it is not an easy argument to interpret, and we can get a better handle on it if we begin with the first argument.[1]

2. THE INTUITIVE EQUALITY OF OPPORTUNITY ARGUMENT

The prevailing justification for economic distribution in our society is based on the idea of 'equality of opportunity'. Inequalities of income and prestige etc. are assumed to be justified if and only if there was fair competition in the awarding of the offices and positions that yield those benefits. It is acceptable to pay someone $100,000 when the national average is $20,000 if there was fair equality of opportunity—that is, if no one was disadvantaged by their race, or sex, or social background. Such an unequal income is just regardless of whether or not the less well off benefit from that inequality. (This is what Mackie meant by a 'right to a fair go'—see Ch. 2, p. 40 above).

This conflicts with Rawls's theory, for while Rawls also requires equality of opportunity in allotting positions, he denies that the people who fill the positions are thereby entitled to a greater share of society's resources. A Rawlsian society may pay such people more than average, but only if it benefits all members of society to do so. Under the difference principle, people only have a claim to a greater share of resources if they can show that it benefits those who have lesser shares. Under the prevailing idea of equality of opportunity, by contrast, the less well off have no veto over these inequalities, and no right to expect to benefit from them.

Why does the ideology of equal opportunity seem fair to many people in our society? Because it ensures that people's fate is determined by their choices, rather than their circumstances. If I am pursuing some personal ambition in a society that has equality of opportunity, then my success or failure will be determined by my performance, not by my race or class or sex. If I fail, it will not be because I happened to be born into the 'wrong' group. Our fate should not be privileged or disadvantaged by such morally arbitrary factors as the racial or ethnic group we were born into. In a society where no one is disadvantaged by their social circumstances, then people's fate is in their own hands. Success (or failure) will be the result of our own choices and efforts. Hence whatever success we achieve is 'earned', rather than merely endowed on us. In a society that has equality of opportunity, unequal income is fair, because success is 'merited', it goes to those who 'deserve' it.

People disagree about what is needed to ensure fair equality of opportunity. Some people believe that legal non-discrimination in education and employment is sufficient. Others argue that affirmative action programmes are required for economically and culturally disadvantaged groups, if their members are to have a genuinely equal opportunity to acquire the qualifications necessary for economic success. But the central motivating idea in each case is this: it is fair for individuals to have unequal shares of social goods if those inequalities are earned and deserved by the individual, that is, if they are the product of the individual's actions and choices. But it is unfair for individuals to be disadvantaged or privileged by arbitrary and undeserved differences in their social circumstances.

Rawls recognizes the attraction of this view. But there is another source of undeserved inequality which it ignores. It is true that social inequalities are undeserved, and hence it is unfair for one's fate to be made worse by that undeserved inequality. But the same thing can be said about inequalities in natural talents. No one deserves to be born handicapped, or with an IQ of 140, any more than they deserve to be born into a certain class or sex or race. If it is unjust for people's fate to be influenced by the latter factors, then it is unclear why the same injustice is not equally involved when people's fate is determined by the former factors. The injustice in each case is the same— distributive shares should not be influenced by factors which are arbitrary from the moral point of view. Natural talents and social circumstances are both matters of brute luck, and people's moral claims should not depend on brute luck.

Hence the prevailing ideal of equality of opportunity is 'unstable', for 'once we are troubled by the influence of either social contingencies or natural chance on the determination of distributive shares, we are bound, on reflection, to be bothered by the influence of the other. From a moral standpoint the two seem to be equally arbitrary' (1971: 74–5). In fact, Dworkin says that the undeserved character of natural assets makes the prevailing view not so much unstable as 'fraudulent' (Dworkin 1985: 207). The prevailing view suggests that removing social inequalities gives each person an equal opportunity to acquire social benefits, and hence suggests that any differences in income between individuals are earned, the product of people's effort or choices. But the naturally handicapped do not have an equal opportunity to acquire social benefits, and their lack of success has nothing to do with their choices or effort. If we are genuinely interested in removing undeserved inequalities, then the prevailing view of equality of opportunity is inadequate.

The attractive idea at the base of the prevailing view is that people's fate should be determined by their *choices*—by the decisions they make about how to lead their lives—not by the *circumstances* which they happen to find themselves in. But the prevailing view only recognizes differences in social circumstances, while ignoring differences in natural talents (or treating them as if they were one of our choices). This is an arbitrary limit on the application of its own central intuition.

How should we treat differences in natural talents? Some people, having considered the parallels between social and natural inequality, assume that no one should benefit from their natural inequalities. But as Rawls says, while

no one deserves his greater natural capacity nor merits a more favourable starting place in society . . . it does not follow that one should eliminate these distinctions. There is another way to deal with them. The basic structure can be arranged so that these contingencies work for the good of the least fortunate. Thus we are led to the difference principle if we wish to set up the social system so that no one gains or loses from his arbitrary place in the distribution of natural assets or his initial position in society without giving or receiving compensating advantages in return. (1971: 102)

While no one should suffer from the influence of undeserved natural inequalities, there may be cases where everyone benefits from allowing such an influence. No one deserves to benefit from their natural talents, but it is not unfair to allow such benefits when they work to the advantage of those who were less fortunate in the 'natural lottery'. And this is precisely what the difference principle says.

This is Rawls's first argument for his theory of fair shares. Under the prevailing view, talented people can naturally expect greater income. But since those who are talented do not deserve their advantages, their higher expectations 'are just if and only if they work as part of a scheme which improves the expectations of the least advantaged members of society' (1971: 75). So we get to the difference principle from an examination of the prevailing view of equality of opportunity. As Rawls puts it, 'once we try to find a rendering of [the idea of equality of opportunity] which treats everyone equally as a moral person, and which does not weight men's share in the benefits and burdens of social cooperation according to their social fortune or their luck in the natural lottery, it is clear that the [difference principle] is the best choice among the ... alternatives' (1971: 75).

That is the first argument. I think the basic premiss of the argument is correct. The prevailing view of equality of opportunity is unstable, and we should recognize that our place in the distribution of natural talents is morally arbitrary. But the conclusion is not quite right. From the fact that natural and social inequalities are arbitrary, it might follow that those kinds of inequalities should only influence distribution when it would benefit the least well off. But the difference principle says that *all* inequalities must work to the benefit of the least well off. What if I was not born into a privileged social group, and was not born with any special talents, and yet by my own choices and effort have managed to secure a larger income than others? Nothing in this argument explains why the difference principle applies to all inequalities, rather than just to those inequalities which stem from morally arbitrary factors. I will return to this point after examining the second argument.

3. THE SOCIAL CONTRACT ARGUMENT

Rawls considers the first argument for his principles of justice less important than the second. His main argument is a 'social contract' argument, an argument about what sort of political morality people would choose were they setting up society from an 'original position'. As Rawls says of the argument we have just looked at:

none of the preceding remarks [about equality of opportunity] are an argument for this conception [of justice], since in a contract theory all arguments, strictly speaking, are to be made in terms of what it would be rational to choose in the original position. But I am concerned here to prepare the way for the favoured interpretation of the two principles of justice, so that these criteria, especially the [difference principle], will not strike the reader as too eccentric or bizarre. (1971: 75)

So Rawls conceives his first intuitive argument as simply preparing the ground for the real argument, which is based on the idea of a social contract. This is an unusual strategy, for social contract arguments are usually thought of as being weak, and Rawls seems to be relegating a fairly strong argument into a back-up role behind the weaker social contract argument.

Why are social contract arguments thought to be weak? Because they seem to rely on very implausible assumptions. They ask us to imagine a state of nature before there is any political authority. Each person is on their own, in the sense that there is no higher authority with the power to command their obedience, or with the responsibility of protecting their interests or possessions. The question is, what kind of contract would such individuals, in the state of nature, agree to concerning the establishing of a political authority which would have these powers and responsibilities? Once we know what the terms of the contract are, we know what the government is obligated to do, and what the citizens are obliged to obey.

Different theorists have used this technique—Hobbes, Locke, Kant, Rousseau—and come up with different answers. But they have all been subject to the same criticism—namely, there never was such a state of nature, or such a contract. Hence neither citizens nor government are bound by it. Contracts only create obligations if they are actually agreed to. We can say that a certain agreement is the contract that people would have signed in some state of nature, and so is a hypothetical contract. But as Dworkin says, 'a hypothetical agreement is not simply a pale form of an actual contract; it is no contract at all' (Dworkin 1977: 151). The idea that we are bound by the contract we would have accepted in a state of nature implies

that because a man would have consented to certain principles if asked in advance, it is fair to apply those principles to him later, under different circumstances, when he does not consent. But that is a bad argument. Suppose I did not know the value of my painting on Monday; if you had offered me $100 for it then I would have accepted. On Tuesday I discovered it was valuable. You cannot argue that it would be fair for the courts to make me sell it to you for $100 on Wednesday. It may be my good fortune that you did not ask me on Monday, but that does not justify coercion against me later. (Dworkin 1977: 152)

Thus the idea of a social contract seems either historically absurd (if it is based on actual agreement) or morally insignificant (if it is based on hypothetical agreement).

But, as Dworkin notes, there is another way to interpret social contract arguments. We should think of the contract not primarily as an agreement, actual or hypothetical, but as a device for teasing out the implications of certain moral premises concerning people's moral equality. We invoke the idea of a state of nature not to work out the historical origins of society, or the historical obligations of governments and individuals, but to model the idea of the moral equality of individuals.

Part of the idea of being moral equals is the claim that none of us is inherently subordinate to the will of others, none of us comes into the world as the property of another, or as their subject. We are all born free and equal. Throughout most of history, many groups have been denied this equality—in feudal societies, for example, peasants were viewed as naturally subordinate to aristocrats. It was the historical mission of classical liberals like Locke to deny this feudal premiss. And the way that they made clear their denial that some people were naturally subordinate to others was to imagine a state of nature in which people were equal in status. As Rousseau said, 'man is born free, and yet everywhere is in chains'. The idea of a state of nature does not, therefore, represent an anthropological claim about the pre-social existence of human beings, but a moral claim about the absence of natural subordination amongst human beings.

Classical liberals were not anarchists, however, who believe that governments are never acceptable. Anarchists believe that people can never come to have legitimate authority over others, and that people can never be legitimately compelled to obey such authority. Since these liberals were not anarchists, the pressing question was to explain how people born free and equal can come to be governed. Their answer was roughly this: due to the uncertainties and scarcities of social life, individuals, without giving up their moral equality, would endorse ceding certain powers to the state, but only if the state used these powers *in trust* to protect individuals from those uncertainties and scarcities. If the government betrayed that trust and abused its powers, then the citizens were no longer under an obligation to obey, and indeed had the right to rebel. Having some people with the power to govern others is compatible with respecting moral equality because the rulers only hold this power in trust, to protect and promote the interests of the governed.

This is the kind of theory that Rawls is adapting. As he puts it, 'my aim is to present a conception of justice which generalizes and carries to a higher level of abstraction the familiar theory of the social contract as found, say, in Locke, Rousseau and Kant' (1971: 11). The point of the contract is to determine principles of justice from a position of equality: in Rawls's theory

the original position of equality corresponds to the state of nature in the traditional theory of the social contract. The original position is not, of course, thought of as an actual historical state of affairs, much less as a primitive condition of culture. It is understood as a purely hypothetical situation characterized so as to lead to a certain conception of justice. (1971: 12)

While Rawls's original position 'corresponds' to the idea of state of nature, it also differs from it, for Rawls believes that the usual state of nature is not really an 'initial position of equality' (1971: 11). This is where the contract argument joins up with his intuitive argument. The usual account of the state of nature is unfair because some people have more bargaining power than others—more natural talents, initial resources, or sheer physical strength—and they are able to hold out longer for a better deal, while those who are less strong or talented have to make concessions. The uncertainties of nature affect everyone, but some people can deal better with them, and they will not agree to a social contract unless it entrenches their natural advantages. This, we know, is unfair in Rawls's eyes. Since these natural advantages are undeserved, they should not privilege or disadvantage people in determining principles of justice.[2]

So a new device is needed to tease out the implications of moral equality, a device that prevents people from exploiting their arbitrary advantages in the selection of principles of justice. This is why Rawls develops the otherwise peculiar construction known as the 'original position'. In this revised original position, people are behind a 'veil of ignorance' so that

no one knows his place in society, his class position or social status, nor does any one know his fortune in the distribution of natural assets and abilities, his intelligence, strength, and the like. I shall even assume that the parties do not know their concep-tions of the good or their special psychological propensities. The principles of justice are chosen behind a veil of ignorance. This ensures that no one is advantaged or disadvantaged in the choice of principles by the outcome of natural chance or the contingency of social circumstances. Since all are similarly situated and no one is able to design principles to favor his particular condition, the principles of justice are the result of a fair agreement or bargain. (1971: 12)

Many critics have viewed this demand that people distance themselves from knowledge of their social background and individual desires as evidence of a bizarre theory of personal identity. What is left of one's self when all that knowledge is excluded? It is difficult to imagine oneself behind such a veil of ignorance, much more difficult than imagining oneself in the traditional state of nature, where the fictional people were at least relatively whole in mind and body.

But the veil of ignorance is not an expression of a theory of personal identity. It is an intuitive test of fairness, in the same way that we try ensure a fair division of cake by making sure that the person who cuts it does not know which piece she will get.[3] The veil of ignorance similarly ensures that those who might be able to influence the selection process in their favour, due to their better position, are unable to do so. As Rawls says

One should not be misled, then, by the somewhat unusual conditions which charac-terize the original position. The idea here is simply to make vivid to ourselves the restrictions that it seems reasonable to impose on arguments for principles of justice, and therefore on these principles themselves. Thus it seems reasonable and generally accepted that no one should be advantaged or disadvantaged by natural fortune or social circumstance in the choice of principles. It also seems widely agreed that it should be impossible to tailor principles to the circumstances of one's own case ... In this manner the veil of ignorance is arrived at in a natural way. (1971: 18–19)

The original position is intended 'to represent equality between human beings as moral persons', and the resulting principles of justice are those which people 'would consent to as equals when none are known to be advantaged by social and natural contingencies'. We should look at the original position as 'an expository device' which 'sums up the meaning' of our notions of fairness and 'helps us to extract their consequences' (1971: 19, 21, 586).

Rawls's argument is not, then, that a certain conception of equality is derived from the idea of a hypothetical contract. That would be subject to all the criticisms that Dworkin mentions. Rather, the hypothetical contract is a way of embodying a certain conception of equality, and a way of extracting the consequences of that conception for the just regulation of social institutions. By removing sources of bias and requiring unanimity, Rawls hopes to find a solution that is acceptable to everyone from a position of equality—i.e. that respects each person's claim to be treated as a free and equal being.

Since the premise of the argument is equality, not contract, to criticize it we need to show that it fails to embody an adequate account of equality. It is not enough—indeed, it is irrelevant—to say that the contract is historically inaccurate, or that the veil of ignorance is psychologically impossible, or that the original position is in some other way unrealistic. The question is not whether the original position could ever really exist, but whether the principles which would be chosen in it are likely to be fair, given the nature of the selection process.

Even if we accept Rawls's idea of the social contract as a device for embodying a conception of equality, it is far from clear what principles would actually be chosen in the original position. Rawls, of course, thinks that the difference principle would be chosen. But his argument here is supposed to be independent of the first intuitive argument concerning equality of opportunity. As we have seen, he does not consider that kind of argument to be relevant, 'strictly speaking', within a contract theory. So the difference principle is just one of many possible choices which parties in the original position could make.

How do the principles of justice get chosen? The basic idea is this: while we do not know what position we will occupy in society, or what goals we will have, there are certain things we will want or need to enable us to lead a good life. Whatever the differences between individuals' plans of life, they all share one thing—they all involve *leading a life*. As Waldron puts it, 'there is something like *pursuing a conception of the good life* that all people, even those with the most diverse commitments, can be said to be engaged in ... although people do not share one another's ideals, they can at least abstract from their experience a sense of *what it is like to be committed to an ideal of the good life*' (Waldron 1987: 145; cf. Rawls 1971: 92–5, 407–16). We are all committed to an ideal of the good life, and certain things are needed in order to pursue these commitments, whatever their more particular content. In Rawls's theory, these things are called 'primary goods'. There are two kinds of primary goods:

1. social primary goods: goods that are directly distributed by social institutions, like income and wealth, opportunities and powers, rights and liberties.
2. natural primary goods: goods like health, intelligence, vigour, imagination, and natural talents, which are affected by social institutions, but are not directly distributed by them.

In choosing principles of justice, people behind the veil of ignorance seek to ensure that they will have the best possible access to those primary goods distributed by social institutions (i.e. the social primary goods). This does not mean that egoism underlies our sense of justice. Since no one knows what position they will occupy, asking people to decide what is best for themselves has the same consequence as asking them to decide what is best for everyone considered impartially. In order to decide from behind a veil of ignorance which principles will promote my good, I must put myself in the shoes of every person in society and see what promotes their good, since I may end up being any one of those people. When combined with the veil of ignorance, therefore, the assumption of rational self-interest 'achieves the same purpose as benevolence' (1971: 148), for I must sympathetically identify with every person in society and take their good into account as if my own. In this way, agreements made in the original position give equal consideration to each person.

So the parties in the original position are trying to ensure the best possible access to the primary goods that enable them to lead a worthwhile life, without knowing where they will end up in society. There are still many different principles they could choose. They might choose an equal distribution of social primary goods for all social positions. But Rawls says that this is irrational when certain kinds of inequalities—e.g. those sponsored by the difference principle—improve everyone's access to primary goods. They might choose a utilitarian principle that instructs social institutions to distribute primary goods in such a way as to maximize utility in society. This would maximize the average utility that parties in the original position could expect to have in the real world, and, on some accounts of rationality, that makes it a rational choice. But it also involves the risk that you will be one of those who is endlessly sacrificed for the greater good of others. It leaves your liberties, possessions, and even your life vulnerable to the selfish and illegitimate preferences of others. Indeed, it leaves you unprotected precisely in those situations where you are most likely to need protection—e.g when your beliefs, skin-colour, sex, or natural abilities make you unpopular, or simply dispensable, to the majority. This makes utilitarianism an irrational choice, on some accounts of rationality, for it is rational to ensure your basic rights and resources are protected, even if you thereby lessen your chance of receiving benefits above and beyond the basic goods that you seek to protect.

So there are conflicting accounts of what it is rational to do in such a situation—the rationality of gambling versus the rationality of playing it safe. If we knew what the odds were of having our basic rights violated in a utilitarian society, then we would have a better idea of how rational it is to take the gamble. But the veil of ignorance excludes that information. The rationality of gambling also depends on whether one is personally risk averse or not—some people do not mind taking risks, others prefer security. But the veil of ignorance excludes knowledge of personal tastes as well. What then is the rational choice? Rawls says that it is rational to adopt a 'maximin' strategy—that is, you *maximize* what you would get if you wound up in the *minimum*, or worst-off, position. As Rawls says, this is like proceeding on the assumption that your worst enemy will decide what place in society you will occupy (1971: 152–3). As a result, you select a scheme that maximizes the minimum share allocated under the scheme.

For example, imagine that the following are the possible distributive schemes in a three-person world:

(*a*) 10:8:1
(*b*) 7:6:2
(*c*) 5:4:4

Rawls's strategy tells you to pick (*c*). If you do not know how likely it is that you will be in the best or worst position, the rational choice according to Rawls is the third scheme. For even if you end up in the worst position, it gives you more than you would get if you were in the bottom of the other schemes.

Notice that you should pick the third scheme even though the first two schemes have a higher average utility. The problem with the first two schemes is that there is some chance, unknown in size, that your life will be completely unsatisfactory. And since each of us has only one life to lead, it is irrational to accept the chance that your only life will be so unsatisfactory. So, Rawls concludes, people in the original position would select the difference principle. And this result happily matches what the first intuitive argument told us. People using a fair decision-procedure for selecting principles of justice come up with the same principles that our intuitions tell us is fair.

Many people have criticized Rawls's claim that 'maximin' is the rational strategy. Some claim that it is equally rational, if not more rational, to gamble on utilitarianism (Hare 1975: 88–107; Bailey 1997: 44–6; Barry 1989a: 333–40). Others argue that the rational strategy is some form of 'prioritarianism', which would attach greater weight to the interests of the less well off, but would still allow major gains to the affluent to outweigh minor losses to the poor (e.g. Parfit 1998; McKerlie 1994; 1996; Arneson 2000a). Yet others claim that it is impossible to assess the rationality of gambling without knowing something about the odds, or about one's risk-aversion. These critics allege that Rawls only comes up with the difference principle because he rigs the description of the veil of ignorance so as to yield it, or because he makes gratuitous psychological assumptions which he is not entitled to make (e.g. Barry 1973: ch. 9).[4]

(a) The convergence of the two arguments

There is some truth in these criticisms, but it is a misguided line of criticism. For Rawls admits that he rigs the description of the original position to yield the difference principle. He recognizes that 'for each traditional conception of justice there exists an interpretation of the initial situation in which its principles are the preferred solution', and that some interpretations will lead to utilitarianism (1971: 121). There are many descriptions of the original position that are compatible with the goal of creating a fair decision-procedure, and the difference principle would not be chosen in all of them. So before we can determine which principles would be chosen in the original position, we need to know which description of the original position to accept. And, Rawls says, one of the grounds on which we choose a description of the original position is that it yields the principles we find intuitively acceptable.

Thus, after saying that the original position should model the idea that people are moral equals, Rawls goes on to say that 'there is, however, another side to justifying a particular description of the original position. This is to see if the principles which would be chosen match our considered convictions of justice or extend them in an acceptable way' (1971: 19). Hence, in deciding on the preferred description of the original position we 'work from both ends'. If the principles chosen in one version do not match our convictions of justice, then

we have a choice. We can either modify the account of the initial situation or we can revise our existing judgments, for even the judgments we take provisionally as fixed points are liable to revision. By going back and forth, sometimes altering the conditions of the contractual circumstances, at others withdrawing our judgments and conforming them to principle, I assume that eventually we shall find a description of the initial situation that both expresses reasonable conditions and yields principles which match our considered judgments duly pruned and adjusted. (1971: 20)

So the intuitive argument and the contract argument are not independent after all. Rawls admits to modifying the original position in order to make sure that it yields principles which match our intuitions (at least those intuitions that we continue to hold after having engaged in this two-way process of harmonizing theory and intuitions). This may sound like cheating. But it only appears so if we take Rawls to be claiming that the two arguments provide entirely independent support for one another. And while he sometimes makes that claim, in other places he admits that the two arguments are interdependent, both drawing on the same set of considered intuitions.

But then why bother with the contract device? Why not just use the first intuitive argument? This is a good question. While the contract argument is not as bad as critics suggest, it is also not as good as Rawls suggests. If each theory of justice has its own account of the contracting situation, then we have to decide beforehand which theory of justice we accept, in order to know which description of the original position is suitable. Rawls's opposition to gambling away one life for the benefit of others, or to penalizing those with undeserved natural handicaps, leads him to describe the original position in one way; those who disagree with him on these issues will describe it another way. This dispute cannot be resolved by appeal to contractual agreement. It would beg the question for either side to invoke its account of the contracting situation in defence of its theory of justice, since the contracting situation presupposes the theory. All the major issues of justice, therefore, have to be decided beforehand, in order to decide which description of the original position to accept. But then the contract is redundant.

This is not to say that the contract device is entirely useless. First, the original position provides a way to render vivid our intuitions, in the same way that earlier theorists invoked the state of nature to render vivid the idea of natural equality. Secondly, while the intuitions appealed to in the equal opportunity argument show that fair equality of opportunity is not enough, they do not tell us what more is required, and the contract device may help us render our intuitions more precise. This is what Rawls means by saying the device can help 'extract the consequences' of our intuitions. Thirdly, it provides a perspective from which we can test opposing intuitions. Someone who is naturally talented might sincerely object to the idea that talents are arbitrary. We would then have a clash of intuitions. But if that same person would no longer object were she ignorant of where she was going to end up in the natural lottery, then we can say with some confidence that our intuition was the right one, and that her opposing intuition was the result of opposing personal interests. Certain intuitions might seem less compelling when they are viewed from a perspective detached from one's own position in society. The contract argument supports our intuitions by showing that they would be chosen from an unbiased perspective. The contract thus renders vivid certain general intuitions, and provides an impartial perspective from which we can consider more specific intuitions (1971: 21–2, 586).

So there are benefits in employing the contract device. On the other hand, the contract device is not required for these purposes. As we saw last chapter, some theorists (e.g. Hare) invoke 'ideal sympathizers', rather than impartial contractors, to express the idea of equal consideration (Ch. 2, p. 39 above).

Both theories instruct the moral agent to adopt the impartial point of view, but whereas impartial contractors view each person in society as one of the possible future locations of their own good, ideal sympathizers view each person in society as one of the components of their own good, since they sympathize with and so share each person's fate. The two theories use different devices, but the difference is relatively superficial, for the key move in each theory is to force agents to adopt a perspective which denies them knowledge of, or any ability to promote, their own particular good. Indeed, it is often difficult to distinguish impartial contractors from ideal sympathizers (Gauthier 1986: 237–8; Diggs 1981: 277; Barry 1989a: 77, 196).[5]

Equal consideration can also be generated without any special devices at all, just by asking agents to give equal consideration to others notwithstanding their knowledge of, and ability to promote, their own good (e.g. Scanlon 1982; Barry 1989a: 340–8). Indeed, there is a curious sort of perversity in using either the contractarian or ideal sympathizer device to express the idea of moral equality. The concept of a veil of ignorance attempts to render vivid the idea that other people matter in and of themselves, not simply as a component of our own good. But it does so by imposing a perspective from which the good of others is simply a component of our own (actual or possible) good. The idea that people are ends in themselves gets obscured when we invoke 'the idea of a choice which advances the interests of a single rational individual for whom the various individual lives in a society are just so many different possibilities' (Scanlon 1982: 127; cf. Barry 1989a: 214–15, 336, 370). Rawls tries to downplay the extent to which people in the original position view the various individual lives in society as just so many possible outcomes of a self-interested choice, but the contract device encourages that view, and so obscures the true meaning of equal concern.

So the contract device adds little to Rawls's theory. The intuitive argument is the primary argument, whatever Rawls says to the contrary, and the contract argument (at best) just helps express it. But it is not clear that Rawls needs an independent contract argument. Rawls had initially complained about the way people were forced to choose between utilitarianism, a systematic but counter-intuitive theory, and intuitionism, a collection of miscellaneous intuitions with no theoretical structure. If he has found a systematic alternative to utilitarianism which is in harmony with our intuitions, then his theory is a powerful one, in no way weakened by the interdependence of the intuitive and contract arguments. As Rawls says, 'a conception of justice cannot be deduced from self-evident premises or conditions on principles; instead, its justification is a matter of the mutual support of many considerations, of everything fitting together into one coherent view' (1971: 21). He calls this 'reflective equilibrium', and that is his aim.[6] His principles of justice are mutually supported by reflecting on the intuitions we appeal to in our everyday practices, and by reflecting on the nature of justice from an impartial perspective that is detached from our everyday positions. Because Rawls is seeking such a reflective equilibrium, criticisms like those of Hare and Barry are overstated. For even if they are right that the difference principle would not be chosen in the original position as Rawls describes it, he could redefine the original position so as to yield the difference principle. That sounds like cheating, but it is useful and legitimate if in fact it leads us to a reflective equilibrium—if it means that 'we have done what we can to render coherent and to justify our convictions of social justice' (1971: 21).

A really successful criticism of Rawls is going to have to either challenge his fundamental intuitions, or show why the difference principle is not the best spelling out of these intuitions (and hence why a different description of the original position should be part of our reflective equilibrium). I will look at theories which challenge the basic intuitions in later chapters. But first I want to look at this second option. Can we find any problems internal to Rawls's theory, criticisms not of his intuitions, but of the way he develops them?

(b) Internal problems

One of Rawls's central intuitions, as we have seen, concerns the distinction between choices and circumstances. His argument against the prevailing view of equality of opportunity depends heavily on the claim that it gives too much room for the influence of our undeserved natural endowments. I agreed with Rawls here. But Rawls himself leaves too much room for the influence of natural inequalities, and at the same time leaves too little room for the influence of our choices.

(i) Compensating for natural inequalities

I will look at the question of natural talents first. Rawls says that people's claim to social goods should not be dependent on their natural endowments. The talented do not deserve any greater income, and they should only receive more income if it benefits the less well off. So, according to Rawls, the difference principle is the best principle for ensuring that natural assets do not have an unfair influence.

But Rawls's suggestion also allows too much room for people's fate to be influenced by arbitrary factors. This is because Rawls defines the worst-off position entirely in terms of people's possession of *social* primary goods—i.e. rights, opportunities, wealth, etc. He does not look at people's possession of *natural* primary goods in determining who is worst off. Two people are equally well off for Rawls (in this context) if they have the same bundle of social primary goods, even though one person may be untalented, physically handicapped, or mentally disabled. Likewise, if someone has even a small advantage in social goods over others, then she is better off on Rawls's scale, even if the extra income is not enough to pay for extra costs she faces due to some natural disadvantage—e.g. the costs of medication for an illness, or of special equipment for some handicap.

But why should the benchmark for assessing the justice of social institutions be the prospects of the least well off in terms of social goods? This stipulation conflicts with both the intuitive and contract arguments. In the contract argument, the stipulation is unmotivated in terms of the rationality of the parties in the original position. If, as Rawls says, health is as important as money in being able to lead a successful life, and if the parties seek to find a social arrangement that guarantees them the greatest amount of primary goods in the worst possible outcome (the maximin reasoning), then why wouldn't they treat lack of health and lack of money as equally cases of being less well off for the purposes of social distribution? Every person recognizes that she would be less well off if she suddenly became disabled, even if her bundle of social goods remained the same. Why wouldn't she want society also to recognize her disadvantage?

The intuitive argument points in the same direction. Not only are natural primary goods equally necessary for leading a good life, people do not deserve their place in the distribution of natural assets, and so it is wrong for people to be privileged or disadvantaged because of that place. As we have seen, Rawls thinks this intuition leads to the difference principle, under which people only receive extra rewards for their talents if doing so is to the benefit of the less well off: 'we are led to the difference principle if we wish to set up the social system so that no one gains or loses from his arbitrary place in the distribution of natural assets or his initial position in society without giving or receiving compensating advantages in return' (1971: 102). But that is wrong, or at least misleading. We are only led to the difference principle if by 'gains or loses' we mean gains or loses in terms of *social* goods. The difference principle ensures that the well endowed do not get more social goods just because of their arbitrary place in the distribution of natural assets, and that the handicapped are not deprived of social goods just because of their place. But this does not entirely 'mitigate the effects of natural accident and social circumstance' (1971: 100). For the well endowed still get the natural good of their endowment, which the handicapped undeservedly lack. The difference principle may ensure that I have the same bundle of social goods as a handicapped person. But the handicapped person faces extra medical and transportation costs. She faces an undeserved burden in her ability to lead a satisfactory life, a burden caused by her circumstances, not her choices. The difference principle does not remove that burden.[7]

Rawls seems not to have realized the full implications of his own argument against the prevailing view of equality of opportunity. The position he was criticizing is this:

1. Social inequalities are undeserved, and should be rectified or compensated, but natural inequalities can influence distribution in accordance with equality of opportunity.

Rawls claims that natural and social inequalities are equally undeserved, so (1) is 'unstable'. Instead, he endorses:

2. Social inequalities should be compensated, and natural inequalities should not influence distribution.

But if natural and social inequalities really are equally undeserved, then (2) is also unstable. We should instead endorse:

3. Natural and social inequalities should be compensated.

According to Rawls, people born into a disadvantaged class or race not only should not be denied social benefits, but also have a claim to compensation because of that disadvantage. Why treat people born with natural handicaps any differently? Why should not they also have a claim to compensation for their disadvantage (e.g. subsidized medicine, transportation, job training, etc.), in addition to their claim to non-discrimination?

So there are both intuitive and contract reasons for recognizing natural handicaps as grounds for compensation, and for including natural primary goods in the index which determines who is in the least well off position. There are difficulties in trying to compensate for natural inequalities, as we will see in section 5. It may be impossible to do what our intuitions tell us is most fair. But Rawls does not even recognize the desirability of trying to compensate such inequalities.

(ii) Subsidizing people's choices

The second problem concerns the flip side of that intuition. People do not deserve to bear the burden of unchosen costs, but how should we respond to people who choose to do costly things? We normally feel that unchosen costs have a greater claim on us than voluntarily chosen costs. We feel differently about someone who spends $100 a week on expensive medicine to control an unchosen illness, compared with someone who spends $100 a week on expensive wine because they enjoy its taste. Rawls appeals to this intuition when criticizing the prevailing view for being insensitive to the unchosen nature of natural inequalities. But how should we be sensitive to people's choices?

Imagine that we have succeeded in equalizing people's social and natural circumstances. To take the simplest case, imagine two people of equal natural talent who share the same social background. One wants to play tennis all day, and so only works long enough at a nearby farm to earn enough money to buy a tennis court, and to sustain his desired lifestyle (i.e. food, clothing, equipment). The other person wants a similar amount of land to plant a garden, in order to produce and sell vegetables for herself and others. Furthermore, let's imagine, with Rawls, that we have started with an equal distribution of resources, which is enough for each person to get their desired land, and start their tennis and gardening. The gardener will quickly come to have more resources than the tennis-player, if we allow the market to work freely. While they began with equal shares of resources, he will rapidly use up his initial share, and his occasional farm work only brings in enough to sustain his tennis-playing. The gardener, however, uses her initial share in such a way as to generate a larger income through longer hours of work. The difference principle would only allow this inequality if it benefits the least well off—i.e. if it benefits the tennis-player who now lacks much of an income. If the tennis-player does not benefit from the inequality, then the government should transfer some of her income to him in order to equalize income.

But there is something peculiar about saying that such a tax is needed to enforce equality, where that is understood to mean treating both people as equals. Remember that the tennis-player has the same talents as the gardener, the same social background, and started with the same equal allotment of resources. As a result, he could have chosen income-producing gardening if he wished, just as she could have chosen non-income-producing tennis. They both faced a range of options which offered varying amounts and kinds of work, leisure, and income. Both chose that option which they preferred. The reason he did not choose gardening, therefore, is that he preferred playing tennis to earning money by gardening. People have different preferences about when it is worth giving up potential leisure to earn more income, and he preferred leisure while she preferred income.

Given that these differences in lifestyle are freely chosen, how is he treated unequally by allowing her to have the income and lifestyle that he did not want? Rawls defends the difference principle by saying that it counteracts the inequalities of natural and social contingencies. But these are not relevant here. Rather than removing a disadvantage, the difference principle simply makes her subsidize his expensive desire for leisure. She has to pay for the costs of her choices—i.e. she forgoes leisure in order to get more income. But he does not have to pay for the costs of his choice—i.e. he does not forgo income in order to get more leisure. He expects and Rawls's theory requires that she pay for the costs of her own choices, and also subsidize his choice. That does not promote equality, it undermines it. He gets his preferred life-style (leisureful tennis), plus some income from her taxes, while she gets her preferred lifestyle (income-producing gardening) minus some income that is taxed from her. She has to give up part of what makes her life valuable in order that he can have more of what he finds valuable. They are treated unequally in this sense, for no legitimate reason.

When inequalities in income are the result of choices, not circumstances, the difference principle creates, rather than removes, unfairness. Treating people with equal concern requires that people pay for the costs of their own choices. Paying for choices is the flip side of our intuition about not paying for unequal circumstances. It is unjust if people are disadvantaged by inequalities in their circumstances, but it is equally unjust for me to demand that someone else pay for the costs of my choices. In more technical language, a distributive scheme should be 'endowment-insensitive' and 'ambition-sensitive' (Dworkin 1981: 311). People's fate should depend on their ambitions (in the broad sense of goals and projects about life), but should not depend on their natural and social endowment (the circumstances in which they pursue their ambitions).

Rawls himself emphasizes that we are responsible for the costs of our choices. This in fact is why his account of justice is based on the distribution of primary goods, not welfare. Those who have expensive desires will get less welfare from an equal bundle of primary goods than those with more modest tastes. But, Rawls says, it does not follow that those with modest tastes should subsidize the extravagant, for we have 'a capacity to assume responsibility for our ends'. Hence 'those with less expensive tastes have presumably adjusted their likes and dislikes over the course of their lives to the income and wealth they could reasonably expect; and it is regarded as unfair that they now should have less in order to spare others from the consequences' of their extravagance (Rawls 1982b: 168–9; cf. 1975: 553; 1980: 545; 1974: 643; 1978: 63; 1985: 243–4). So Rawls does not wish to make the gardener subsidize the tennis-player. Indeed he often says that his conception of justice is concerned with regulating inequalities that affect people's life-chances, not the inequalities that arise from people's life-choices, which are the individual's own responsibility (1971: 7, 96; 1978: 56; 1979: 14–15; 1982b: 170). Unfortunately, the difference principle does not make any such distinction between chosen and unchosen inequalities. Hence one possible result of the difference principle is to make some people pay for other's choices, should it be the case that those with the least income are, like the tennis-player, in that position by choice. Rawls wants the difference principle to mitigate the unjust effects of natural and social disadvantage, but it also mitigates the legitimate effects of personal choice and effort.

So while Rawls appeals to this choices–circumstances distinction, his difference principle violates it in two important ways. It is supposed to mitigate the effect of one's place in the distribution of natural assets. But because Rawls excludes natural primary goods from the index which determines who is least well off, there is in fact no compensation for those who suffer undeserved natural disadvantages. Conversely, people are supposed to be responsible for the costs of their choices. But the difference principle requires that some people subsidize the costs of other people's choices. Can we do a better job

being 'ambition-sensitive' and 'endowment-insensitive'? This i
Dworkin's theory.

4. DWORKIN ON EQUALITY OF RESOURCES

Dworkin accepts the 'ambition-sensitive' and 'endowment-insensitive' goal
that motivated Rawls's difference principle. But he thinks that a different
distributive scheme can do a better job living up to that ideal. His theory is a
complicated one—involving the use of auctions, insurance schemes, free markets, and taxation—and it is impossible to lay out the whole theory. But I will
present some of its central intuitive ideas.

(a) Paying for one's choices: the ambition-sensitive auction

I will start with Dworkin's account of an ambition-sensitive distributive
scheme. For simplicity's sake, I will assume again that everyone has the same
natural talents (I examine Dworkin's answer to the problem of unequal
natural endowments later). Dworkin asks us to imagine that all of society's
resources are up for sale in an auction, to which everyone is a participant.
Everyone starts with an equal amount of purchasing power—100 clamshells,
in his example—and people use their clamshells to bid for those resources
that best suit their plan of life.

If the auction works out—and it can always be rerun if it does not—
everyone will be happy with the result, in the sense that they do not prefer
anyone else's bundle of goods to their own. If they did prefer a different
bundle, they could have bid for it, rather than the goods they did bid for. This
generalizes the case of the tennis-player and gardener who, starting with the
same amount of money, acquire the land they need for their desired activities.
If the auction works, this will be true of everyone—i.e. each person will prefer
their own bundle of goods to anyone else's. Dworkin calls this the 'envy test',
and if it is met, then people are treated with equal consideration, for differences between them simply reflect their different ambitions, their different
beliefs about what gives value to life. A successful auction meets the envy test,
and makes each person pay for the costs of their own choices (Dworkin 1981:
285).[8]

This idea of the envy test expresses the liberal egalitarian view of justice in
its most defensible form. If it could be perfectly enforced, the three main aims
of Rawls's theory would be fulfilled, i.e. respecting the moral equality of
persons, mitigating the arbitrariness of natural and social contingencies, and
accepting responsibility for our choices. Such a distributive scheme would be
just, even though it allows some inequality in income. The gardener and
tennis-player have unequal income, but there is no inequality in respect and

concern, since each of them is able to lead the life they choose, each has an equal ability to bid for that bundle of social goods that best serves their beliefs about what gives value to life. To put it another way, no one can claim to be treated with less consideration than another in the distribution of resources, for if someone had preferred another person's bundle of social goods, she could have bid for it as well. It is difficult to see how I could have a legitimate complaint against anyone else, or they against me.[9]

(b) Compensating natural disadvantages: the insurance scheme

Unfortunately, the auction will only meet the envy test if we assume that no one is disadvantaged in terms of natural assets. In the real world, the auction will fail the envy test, for some of the differences between people will not be chosen. Someone with handicaps may be able to bid for the same bundle of social goods as others, but she has special needs, and so her 100 clamshells will leave her less well off than others. She would prefer to be in their circumstances, without the handicap.

What should we do with natural disadvantages? Dworkin has a complex answer to that question, but we can prepare the way for it by looking at a simpler answer. The handicapped person faces extra burdens in leading a good life, burdens that cut into her 100 clamshells. Why not pay for all those extra costs before the auction, out of the general stock of social resources, and then divide up the remaining resources equally through the auction? Before the auction, we give the disadvantaged enough social goods to compensate for their unchosen inequality in natural assets. Once that is done, we give each person an equal share of the remaining resources to use in accordance with their choices in the auction. The auction results would now meet the envy test. Compensation *before* the auction would ensure that each person is equally able to choose and pursue a valuable life-plan; equal division of resources *within* the auction ensures that those choices are fairly treated. Hence the distribution would be both endowment-insensitive and ambition-sensitive.

This simple answer will not work. Extra money can compensate for some natural disadvantages—some physically handicapped people can be as mobile as able-bodied people if we provide the best technology available (which may be expensive). But that goal is impossible to achieve in other cases, for no amount of social goods will fully compensate for certain natural disadvantages. Imagine someone who is severely mentally retarded. Providing extra money can buy medical equipment, or assistance from skilled personnel, things which ensure there is no unnecessary pain in his life. And more money can always help a little more. But none of this can ever put him in a situation where his circumstances are genuinely equalized. No amount of money can make the severely retarded person as able to lead a good life as other people.

Full equality of circumstances is impossible. We could try to equalize circumstances as much as possible. But that too seems unacceptable. Since each additional bit of money can help the severely retarded person, yet is never enough to fully equalize circumstances, we would be required to give all our resources to people with such handicaps, leaving nothing for everyone else (Dworkin 1981: 242, 300; cf. Fried 1978: 120–8). If resources had to be used to equalize circumstances first (before the auction starts), there would be none left for us to act on our choices (bidding for goods in the auction). But one of our goals in equalizing circumstances was precisely to allow each person to act on their chosen life-plans. Our circumstances affect our ability to pursue our ambitions. That is why they are morally important, why inequalities in them matter. Our concern for people's circumstances is a concern to promote their ability to pursue their ends. If in trying to equalize the *means* we prevent anyone from achieving their *ends*, then we have failed completely.

If we cannot achieve full equality of circumstance, and we should not always try to achieve it, what should we do? Given these difficulties, Rawls's refusal to compensate for natural disadvantages makes sense. Including natural disadvantages in the index which determines the least well off seems to create an insoluble problem. We do not want to ignore such disadvantages, but nor can we equalize them, and what could be in between, other than ad hoc acts of compassion or mercy?

Dworkin's proposal is similar to Rawls's idea of an original position. We are to imagine people behind a modified veil of ignorance. They do not know their place in the distribution of natural talents, and are to assume that they are equally susceptible to the various natural disadvantages which might arise.[10] We give each person an equal share of resources—the 100 clamshells—and ask them how much of their share they are willing to spend on insurance against being handicapped, or otherwise disadvantaged in the distribution of natural talents. People might be willing to spend 30 per cent of their bundle of resources, for example, on such insurance, which would buy them a certain level of coverage for the different disadvantages they may suffer. If we can make sense of this hypothetical insurance market, and find a determinate answer to the question of what insurance people would buy in it, then we could use the tax system to duplicate the results. Income tax would be a way of collecting the premiums that people hypothetically agreed to pay, and the various welfare, medicare, and unemployment schemes would be ways of paying out the coverage to those who turned out to suffer from the natural disadvantages covered by the insurance.

This provides the middle ground between ignoring unequal natural assets and trying in vain to equalize circumstances. It would not lead to ignoring the problem, for everyone would buy some insurance. It is irrational to not provide any protection against the calamities that may befall you. But no one would spend all of their clamshells on insurance, since they would have nothing left to pursue their goals with, should they turn out not to have any natural disadvantages. The amount of society's resources that we dedicate to compensating for natural disadvantages is limited to the coverage people would buy through premiums paid out of their initial bundle (Dworkin 1981: 296–9). This provides a principled basis to decide how much of society's resources should be devoted to helping those who are disadvantaged by the 'natural lottery'.

Some people are still disadvantaged in undeserved ways under this scheme, so we have not found the pure ambition-sensitive and endowment-insensitive distribution we were looking for. But we cannot achieve that goal no matter what we do, so we need a theory of the 'second-best'. Dworkin claims that his insurance scheme is fair as a second-best theory, because it is the result of a decision procedure which is fair. It is generated by a procedure which treats everyone as equals, and excludes obvious sources of unfairness, so that no one is in a privileged position in buying the insurance. Hopefully everyone can recognize and accept the fairness of letting their compensation be determined by what they would have chosen in such a hypothetical position of equality.

It might seem that Dworkin's unwillingness to try as best we can to mitigate the effects of natural handicaps shows an inadequate regard for the well-being of the handicapped. After all, they did not choose to be handicapped rather than talented. But if we attempt to provide the highest possible coverage to those who turn out to be handicapped, the result would be the 'slavery of the talented'. Consider the situation of those able-bodied people who must pay for the insurance without receiving any compensation:

Someone who 'loses' in this sense must work hard enough to cover his premium before he is free to make the trade-offs between work and consumption he would have been free to make if he had not insured. If the level of coverage is high then this will enslave the insured, not simply because the premium is high, but because it is extremely unlikely that his talents will much surpass the level that he has chosen, which means that he must indeed work at full stretch, and that he will not have much choice about what kind of work to do. (Dworkin 1981: 322)

Those who were fortunate in the natural lottery would be forced to be as productive as possible in order to pay the high premiums they hypothetically bought against natural disadvantage. The insurance scheme would cease to be a constraint that the talented can reasonably be expected to recognize in deciding how to lead their lives, but would rather become the determining factor in their lives. Their talents would be a liability that restricts their options, rather than a resource that expands their options. The insurance scheme would have the effect that those with greater talents would have less freedom to choose their preferred leisure-consumption mix than those with lesser talents. Hence, equal concern for both the handicapped and the talented requires something other than maximal redistribution to the handicapped, even though it will leave the handicapped envying the talented.[11]

Jan Narveson says that this failure to ensure a real-world fulfilment of the envy test undermines Dworkin's theory. Suppose Smith is born with natural disadvantages relative to Jones, so that Jones is able to earn a larger income. Even if we tax Jones to fulfil the insurance obligations arising out of this hypothetical auction, Jones will still have more income than Smith, an undeserved inequality. As Narveson puts it, 'the *fact* is that Smith is, in every measure that matters to him or to Jones, way behind Jones in the actual world. Can we hold with a straight face that the bundle of counterfactuals added to his bundle of de facto resources sufficiently "compensates" him in the terms of a substantial theory of equality?' (Narveson 1983: 18). The envy test fails in the world, and, as Narveson says, it seems peculiar to say we have compensated for that by satisfying the envy test in some hypothetical situation.

But this objection begs the question. If we cannot fully equalize real-world circumstances, then what else can we do to live up to our convictions about the arbitrariness of one's place in the distribution of natural and social circumstances? Dworkin does not say that his scheme fully compensates for undeserved inequalities, just that it is the best we can do to live up to our convictions of justice. To criticize him, we need to show either how we can do better living up to those beliefs, or why we should not try to live up to them.

(c) The real-world equivalents: taxes and redistribution

This, then, is the core of Dworkin's theory: we identify a just distribution of resources by imagining an equal initial share of resources which is then modified over time as a result of people's hypothetical auction choices (which are choice-sensitive) and hypothetical insurance policies (to protect against unequal circumstances). This, he claims, is superior to traditional theories of equality, which provide no room for choice-sensitivity, and which provide no principled criteria for dealing with unequal natural endowments. And, he argues, it is also superior to right-wing libertarian theories—discussed next chapter—which focus exclusively on being sensitive to choices, while ignoring the need to equalize circumstances.

But what would such a theory require in practice? Assuming that the insurance model is a legitimate, albeit second-best, response to the problem of equalizing circumstances, how can we apply it to the real world? It cannot be a matter of enforcing real insurance contracts, for the insurance market was purely hypothetical. So what in the world corresponds to the buying of premiums and the giving out of coverage benefits? I said earlier that we can use the tax system to collect premiums from the naturally advantaged, and use welfare schemes as a way of paying out the coverage to those who are disadvantaged. But the tax system can only approximate the results of the insurance scheme, for two reasons (Dworkin 1981: 312–14).

First, there is no way of measuring, in the real world, what people's relative advantages and disadvantages are. One reason is that one of the things people choose to do with their lives is develop their talents. People who started with equal natural talents could come later to have differing skill levels. Those sorts of differences do not deserve compensation, since they reflect differences in choices. People who start off with greater skills may also develop them further, and then differences in talents will partially reflect different natural talents, and partially reflect different choices. In such cases, some but not all of the differences in talents deserve compensation. This will be extremely difficult to measure.

Indeed, as Richard Arneson notes, it would be 'preposterous' to even try to measure the extent to which people are responsible for their income:

the idea that we might adjust our distributive-justice system based on our estimation of persons' overall deservingness or responsibility seems entirely chimerical. Individuals do not display responsibility scores on their foreheads, and the attempt by institutions or individuals to guess at the scores of people they are dealing with would surely dissolve in practice into giving vent to one's prejudices and piques. (Arneson 2000a: 97)

It would be impossible to make these determinations, and would involve a gross violation of privacy to even try.[12]

Moreover, it is impossible to determine in advance of the auction what counts as a natural advantage. That depends on what sorts of skills people value, which depends in turn on the goals they have in life. Certain skills (e.g. physical strength) are less important now than before, while others (e.g. abstract mathematical thought) are far more valuable. There is no way to know definitively, in advance of people's choices, which natural capacities are advantages and which are disadvantages. This criterion changes continuously (if not radically), and it would be impossible to monitor these shifting criteria.

How then can we fairly implement this insurance scheme, given the impossibility of identifying those rewards which accrue from talents rather than ambitions? Dworkin's answer is perhaps rather disappointing: we tax the rich, even though some got there purely by effort with no natural advantage, and support the poor, even though some, like the tennis-player, are there by choice without any natural disadvantage. Hence some people will get less coverage than they hypothetically bought, just because they are now, by dint of effort, in the upper income categories. And some people will get more coverage than they deserve, just because they have expensive lifestyles.

A second problem with applying the model is that natural handicaps are not the only source of unequal circumstances (even in a society with equality of opportunity for different races, classes, or sexes). In the real world we lack full information and cannot rerun the auction, so that the envy test can be violated when unexpected things occur. A blight may ruin our gardener's crop for a number of years, leaving her with little income. But, unlike the tennis-player, she did not choose to lead an unproductive lifestyle. That was a wholly unforeseen natural contingency, and it would be wrong to make her pay for all the costs of her chosen lifestyle. If she had known it would be so costly, she would have chosen a different life-plan (unlike the tennis-player, who was aware of the costs of his lifestyle). These sorts of unexpected costs need to be fairly dealt with. But if we try to compensate for them through an insurance scheme similar to the one for natural talents, the result will have all the shortcomings of that other insurance scheme.

We now have two sources of deviation from the ideal of an ambition-sensitive, endowment-insensitive distribution. We want people's fate to be determined by the choices they make from a fair and equitable starting point. But the idea of an equal starting point includes not only an unachievable compensation for unequal endowment, but also an unachievable knowledge of future events. The former is needed to equalize circumstances, the latter is needed to know the costs of our choices, and hence be held responsible for them. The insurance scheme is a second-best response to these problems, and the taxation scheme is a second-best response to the problem of applying the insurance scheme. Given this distance between the ideal and the practice, it is inevitable that some people are undeservedly penalized for their unfortunate circumstances, while others are undeservedly subsidized for the costs of their choices.

Can we not do any better in achieving an ambition-sensitive, endowment-insensitive distribution? Dworkin concedes that we could achieve one or other of the aims more completely. However, the two aims pull in opposite directions—the more we try to make the distribution sensitive to people's ambitions, the more likely it is that some people disadvantaged by circumstances will be undeservedly penalized, and vice versa. These are both deviations from the ideal, and equally important deviations, so a proposal which concentrates on one to the exclusion of the other is unacceptable. We must employ both criteria, even if the effect is that neither is fully satisfied (Dworkin 1981: 327–8, 333–4).

This is a rather disappointing conclusion. Dworkin argues persuasively that a just distribution must identify 'which aspects of any persons's economic position flow from his choices and which from advantages and disadvantages that were not matters of choice' (Dworkin 1985: 208). But it seems that in practice his ideal is 'indistinguishable in its strategic implications' from theories, like Rawls's difference principle, which do not mark this distinction (Carens 1985: 67; cf. Dworkin 1981: 338–44). The hypothetical calculations

Dworkin's theory requires are so complex, and their institutional implementation so difficult, that its theoretical advantages cannot be translated into practice (Mapel 1989: 39–56; Carens 1985: 65–7; cf. Varian 1985: 115–19; Roemer 1985a).

Dworkin admits that his is a very abstract theory, but insists it can be used to evaluate real-world distributions, and to design public policies. The theory is not precise enough to single out any particular distribution as *the* correct distribution. But it can be used to rule out certain distributions as clearly unjust. For example, Dworkin argues that on any plausible account of the sort of hypothetical insurance people would buy against natural misfortunes, the coverage would be 'well above' what is offered to the disabled, sick, or unskilled in the United States or Britain today (Dworkin 1981: 321).

He also argues that his model shows the superiority of a 'third-way' between traditional socialism and free-market libertarianism (Dworkin 2000: 7; cf. Giddens 1998; White 1998). For example, he argues that his theory explains why we need both a system of public health care and also the option to buy private health insurance. The hypothetical insurance scheme shows that the former is needed to equalize circumstances; the hypothetical auction scheme shows that the latter is needed to be choice-sensitive (Dworkin 1993; 2000: ch. 8). Similarly, he says that his theory shows the necessity of combining generous welfare provisions (to equalize circumstances for those with lesser natural talents) with certain workfare requirements (to ensure that talented but lazy people pay for the costs of their choices) (Dworkin 2000: ch. 9).

Still, Dworkin's policy suggestions are surprisingly modest. They are primarily focused on *ex post* corrections to the inequalities generated by the market—i.e. they take the existing level of inequality in market income as a given, and ask how best to tax some of the unequal income of the advantaged and transfer it to the disadvantaged. But these proposals leave unaddressed an important plank in his theory—namely, that people should have equal *ex ante* endowments when they enter the market. The policy implementation of his theory should presumably include some real-world equivalent of the 100 clamshells that individuals start with in life, and use to make choices about investment, savings, risk, training, and so on. This is surely as important (if not more so) to achieving genuine equality of resources as *ex post* transfers of market income. Indeed, if there were greater equality in people's *ex ante* endowments—i.e. in their capacity to invest in productive assets or in developing their own skills and talent—there would be less need for *ex post* redistribution, since there would be fewer involuntary inequalities in market income to correct after the fact.

Of course, any attempt to achieve this sort of *ex ante* equality would require a major attack on entrenched economic divisions in our society. Dworkin himself offers no concrete policy suggestions about how to achieve this. In this respect, his policy prescriptions are 'surprisingly conservative' (Macleod 1998: 151). Can we imagine more innovative ways to implement Dworkin's theory? Several theorists have offered more radical measures to achieve liberal equality. Let me briefly mention four:

(a) 'stakeholder society': Bruce Ackerman has proposed giving everyone a one-time lump-sum 'stake' of $80,000 when they graduate from high school, financed by a 2 per cent wealth tax (Ackerman and Alstott 1999). People could use this stake as they see fit—to pay for more education or training, to help buy a house, to set up a small business, to buy stocks or bonds, or simply to spend on their preferred forms of consumption or leisure. This is actually a relatively old idea—going back at least to Thomas Paine in the eighteenth century—and would seem to fit very comfortably with Dworkin's theory. By reducing existing inequalities in young people's capacity to acquire productive assets or to develop their marketable talents, it would help ensure that distributions more truly reflect choices rather than circumstances.[13]

(b) 'basic income': Philippe Van Parijs has defended a guaranteed and unconditional basic income—say, $5,000 per year—that is given to everyone, whether employed or not (Van Parijs 1991; 1995). Liberal egalitarians have sometimes objected to such an unconditional basic income on the grounds that it might tax hard-working citizens to subsidize indolent citizens who do not want to work, such as the 'Malibu surfer'. But in fact it can be seen as simply a version of the previous stakeholder proposal.[14] The basic income can be seen as the yearly interest on one's 'stake'. The basic income proposal differs from Ackerman's proposal primarily in not allowing people to cash out their stake: they can only draw on the interest, rather than the capital. This would alleviate worries that some young people might 'blow' their stake in one go. But since having a guaranteed income makes it easier to borrow money, this proposal would still help equalize people's ability to invest in productive assets, or in their own education and training.[15]

A proposal that combines the 'stake' and 'basic income' models has been developed by John Roemer, under the label of 'coupon capitalism' (Roemer 1994; 1999: 65–8). Each young adult would receive a portfolio of stocks in the nation's firms, intended to give her a per capita share of the nation's profits. She could trade these stocks at prices quoted on a competitive stock market, but could not cash out her portfolio. At death, each person's portfolio would revert to the Treasury, to be recirculated to the next generation of young adults. Roemer calculates that one's 'stake' of stocks could generate an annual income of $8,000 per family in the United States. Roemer is not optimistic that this sort of programme could be adopted in the USA, although he points to the growing numbers of Employee-Share-Ownership Programs (ESOPs) as a possible precursor.

(c) 'compensatory education': John Roemer has defended a programme of 'compensatory' investment in the education of children from poorer families and communities (Roemer 1999: 69–70). As he notes, it is a significant egalitarian achievement that most Western countries now invest more or less equally in the education of all children, whatever their race or class. A century ago, it was often only the male children of the wealthy who received an education. However, equal public spending per child does not create equal opportunities, because children from wealthy families typically receive many advantages in their education and opportunities. Wealthy parents are themselves likely to be better educated, and to value education, and are willing and able to invest more time and resources in the education of their children. If we want to genuinely equalize opportunities, we need compensatory spending on the education of disadvantaged children. For example, Roemer estimates that to equalize future earning opportunities for white and black children in the USA would involve spending ten times as much on the education of blacks, per capita, than on whites.

(d) the 'egalitarian planner': Roemer has also suggested another approach for implementing Dworkin's theory, which he calls the 'egalitarian planner' (Roemer 1993a; 1995). As we have seen, one of the main barriers to implementing Dworkin's theory is that we have no realistic way of determining the extent to which any individual's disadvantages are due to her choices or her circumstances. Roemer agrees that this is impossible at the level of particular individuals, but argues that we can try to neutralize the effects of certain circumstantial factors at the social level. On his proposal, society would decide on a list of factors which everyone agrees are matters of circumstance rather than choice: e.g. age, gender, race, disability, and the economic class or education level of one's parents. We then divide society into groups or 'types' based on these factors. For example, one type would be 60-year-old able-bodied white males whose parents were college educated; another type would consist of 60-year-old able-bodied black women whose parents received only primary education.

Now within each type, people will vary considerably in their income or wealth. Within the group of 60-year-old able-bodied white males whose parents were college educated (call them type A), most persons might earn around $60,000, with the top 10 per cent earning over $100,000 and the bottom 10 per cent earning under $40,000. We assume that such inequalities *within* type A are due primarily to the choices people make. Since all members of type A share the same basic socio-economic and demographic circumstances, the inequalities we see within this group are likely to reflect different choices about work, leisure, training, consumption, risk, and so on. So we will not seek to redistribute resources within type A: we assume that the distributions within types are broadly ambition-sensitive. Hard-working and prudent white males of educated parents should not be forced to subsidize the choices of comparable white males with expensive tastes for leisure, or irresponsible habits.

Similarly, there will be considerable variation in income within the group of 60-year-old black women from less-educated parents (call them type B). Perhaps the average income in this group is around $20,000, with the top 10 per cent group earning $33,000, and the bottom 10 per cent earning $10,000. As before, we will assume that such inequalities within type B are due primarily to people's choices, since members of the group share most of the same social circumstances. Hence we will not expect hard-working and prudent black women to subsidize the expensive or imprudent tastes of other black women.

So on Roemer's view, inequalities within types are generally accepted as ambition-sensitive. However, notice that there are enormous inequalities *between* types A and B, and these, *ex hypothesi*, are due to circumstances not choices. Hard-working and prudent members at the 90th percentile of type A earn three times as much as hard-working and prudent members at the 90th percentile of type B. That inequality cannot be explained or justified in terms of choices. People should be rewarded for above-average levels of work or prudence, but there is no reason why members of type A who exhibit these characteristics should be rewarded three times more than members of type B who exhibit the same characteristics.

Similarly, compare the reckless and indolent white male at the 10th percentile of type A who earns four times as much as the reckless and indolent black female at the 10th percentile of type B. People should pay for their choices, and so reckless and indolent people should accept that they will do less well than others who are prudent and hard-working. But there is no reason why the costs of these imprudent decisions should be four times harsher for members of type B than for members of type A.

The goal of an 'egalitarian planner', therefore, is to accept inequality within types, but to equalize across types. Thus everyone at the 90th percentile of their type should have the same income, no matter what type they belong to; similarly at the 50th or 10th percentile (see Fig. 3). This will still ensure that people are held responsible for their choices: hard-working and prudent members of each type will do much better than members with expensive or imprudent tastes. But we will have neutralized the impact of the most important unchosen circumstances.[16]

Of course, as Roemer acknowledges, this model can only neutralize the effect of the most blatant and systematic forms of involuntary disadvantage. It wil not deal with the case of children raised by affluent and well-educated but uncaring parents who neglect them. Some members of type A will not get the advantages that are enjoyed by most members of their type, and may indeed

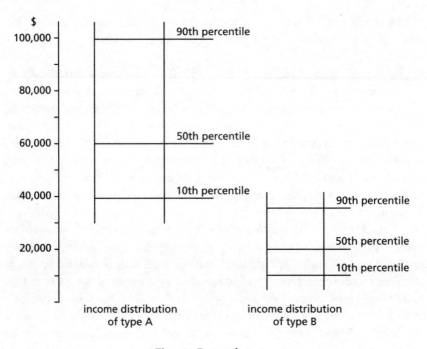

Figure 3 Roemer's types

face some of the same disadvantages suffered by most members of type B. Such people will be unfairly penalized by Roemer's scheme, which only identifies and remedies the most socially salient forms of circumstances. Still, as I noted earlier, this sort of unfairness was present in Dworkin's own account. Roemer's account does not eliminate this unfairness, but arguably would do a better job in reducing it, by better achieving the twin goals of endowment-insensitivity and ambition-sensitivity.

These are just a few examples of the interesting work being done on the practical implementation of Dworkin's theory, and are a testament to the influence his theory has had. Dworkin's idea of the envy test describes, and makes vivid, what it would be for a distribution scheme to fulfil the basic aims of Rawls's theory: a distributive scheme that respects the moral equality of persons by compensating for unequal circumstances while holding individuals responsible for their choices. There may be a more appropriate apparatus for implementing these ideas than the mixture of auctions, insurance schemes, and taxes that Dworkin employs. But if we accept these fundamental premisses, Dworkin has helped us clarify their consequences for distributive justice. Indeed, much of the most interesting work on distributive justice in the last twenty years has started from Dworkin's basic premisses and attempted to refine our ideas of ambition-sensitivity and endowment-insensitivity.[17]

It is worth pausing for a moment and reviewing the arguments presented so far. I started by examining utilitarianism, which is attractive for its insistence on interpreting morality in terms of a concern for the welfare of human beings. But that concern, which we saw was an egalitarian one, need not require the *maximization* of welfare. The utilitarian idea of giving equal weight to each person's preferences has some initial plausibility as a way of showing equal concern for people's welfare. But, on inspection, utilitarianism often violates our sense of what it is to treat people as equals, especially in its lack of a theory of fair shares. This was Rawls's motivation for developing a conception of justice that provides a systematic alternative to utilitarianism. When we examined prevailing ideas about fair shares, we encountered the belief that it is unfair for people to be penalized for matters of brute luck, for circumstances which are morally arbitrary and beyond their control. This is why we demand equal opportunity for people from different racial and class backgrounds. But the same intuition should also tell us to recognize the arbitrary nature of people's place in the distribution of natural assets. This is the motivation for Rawls's difference principle, under which the more fortunate only receive extra resources if it benefits the unfortunate.

But the difference principle is both an overreaction and also an insufficient reaction to the problem of undeserved inequalities. It is insufficient in not providing any compensation for natural disadvantages; and it is an overreaction in precluding inequalities that reflect different choices, rather than different circumstances. We want a theory to be more ambition-sensitive and less endowment-sensitive than Rawls's difference principle. Dworkin's theory aspires to these twin goals. But we saw that these goals are unreachable in their pure form. Any theory of fair shares will have to be a theory of the second-best. Dworkin's scheme of auctions and insurance is one suggestion for fairly resolving the tension between these two core goals of the liberal conception of equality.

So Dworkin's theory was a response to problems in Rawls's conception of equality, just as Rawls's theory was a response to problems in the utilitarian conception of equality. Each can be seen as attempting to refine, rather than reject, the basic intuitions which motivated the previous one. Rawls's egalitarianism is a reaction against utilitarianism, but is also partly a development from utilitarianism's core intuitions, and the same is true of Dworkin's relation to Rawls. Each theory defends its own principles by appealing to the very intuitions that led people to adopt the previous theory.

5. THE POLITICS OF LIBERAL EQUALITY

Most people view liberal egalitarianism as providing a philosophical justification for the post-war liberal-democratic welfare state. Indeed, this linkage to
the welfare state helps explain the remarkable influence of liberal egalitarian
political theories. The 1950s and 1960s saw a significant extension of the welfare state in most Western democracies, but there was no satisfactory political
philosophy at the time which could make sense of this phenomenon. The
appearance of Rawls and Dworkin's work in the 1970s provided people with
an intellectually satisfying framework in which to make sense of political
debates around the welfare state.

Prior to Rawls's work, the most common way of describing the welfare state
was to view it as an ad hoc compromise between competing ideals. Libertarians on the right believe in liberty, and hence endorse the free market,
Marxists on the left believe in equality, and hence endorse state planning,
and liberals in the middle believe in a wishy-washy compromise of liberty and
equality. This is supposed to explain why liberals endorse the welfare state,
which is an ad hoc combination of capitalist freedoms and inequalities on the
one hand with various egalitarian welfare policies on the other.

But Rawls and Dworkin have offered us a more sophisticated way to think
of the welfare state. If their theories allow some kinds of inequality-producing
economic freedoms, it is not because they believe in liberty as opposed to
equality. Rather, they believe that such economic freedoms are needed to
enforce their more general idea of equality itself. The same principle that tells
liberals to allow market freedom—i.e. that it holds people responsible for
their choices—also tells them to limit the market where it penalizes people for
their unchosen circumstances. The same conception of equality underlies
both market freedom and its constraint. Hence the liberal favours a mixed
economy and welfare state not in order to compromise conflicting ideals, 'but
to achieve the best practical realization of the demands of equality itself'
(Dworkin 1978: 133; 1981: 313, 338).

This link between the philosophy of liberal equality and the politics of the
welfare state is so strong that many people call liberal egalitarianism 'welfare
state liberalism' (e.g. Sterba 1988), and describe Rawls as offering 'a philosophical apologia for an egalitarian brand of welfare-state capitalism' (Wolff
1977: 195; cf. Doppelt 1981: 262; Clark and Gintis 1978: 311–14). But this
link is now being seriously questioned. It is no longer clear whether the
implementation of liberal egalitarianism would lead to the welfare state in any
recognizable sense.

For one thing, liberal equality requires each person to start their life with an
equal share of society's resources, and the sorts of policies needed to achieve

this go far beyond the traditional welfare state approach. As we have seen, the welfare state is primarily concerned with the *post factum* correction of market inequalities, through tax and transfer schemes. But as Mill recognized a long time ago, to focus solely on *post factum* income redistribution is to make 'the great error of reformers and philanthropists . . . to nibble at the consequences of unjust power, instead of redressing the injustice itself' (Mill 1965: 953). If our goal is to achieve greater *ex ante* equality in endowments, we need to directly attack the entrenched economic hierarchies of modern societies which disadvantage the poor, women, or racial minorities. This might involve quite radical policies, such as affirmative action, basic income, employee self-ownership, 'stakeholding', payment to homemakers, compensatory education investment, and so on. We would have to look at these one by one to see if they move us closer to the results of Dworkin's hypothetical auction, and that answer will often depend on the particular circumstances. Perhaps liberal equality would favour something like our existing schemes for ongoing income redistribution, but only after a radical one-time redistribution of wealth and property-ownership (Krouse and McPherson 1988: 103).

It is interesting to note that Rawls himself recognizes that the principles of liberal equality cannot be met by the welfare state. He endorses the quite different idea of a 'property-owning democracy' (Rawls 1971: 274). The difference has been described this way:

welfare state capitalism (as commonly understood) accepts severe class inequality in the distribution of physical and human capital, and seeks to reduce the consequent disparities in market outcomes through redistributive tax and transfer programs. Property-owning democracy, by contrast, aims at sharply reduced inequality in the underlying distribution of property and wealth, and greater equality of opportunity to invest in human capital, so that the operation of the market generates smaller inequalities to begin with. Thus, the two alternative regimes exemplify two alternative strategies for providing justice in political economy: Welfare-state capitalism accepts as given substantial inequality in the initial distribution of property and skill endowments, and then seeks to redistribute income ex post; property-owning democracy seeks greater equality in the ex ante distribution of property and skill endowments, with correspondingly less emphasis upon subsequent redistributive measures. (Krouse and McPherson 1988: 84)[18]

Rawls argues that a property-owning democracy would be superior to the welfare state, not only in reducing the need for *ex post* redistribution, but also in preventing relations of domination and degradation within the division of labour. If *ex ante* endowments are more equal, then 'no one need be servilely dependent on others and made to choose between monotonous and routine occupations which are deadening to human thought and sensibility' (Rawls 1971: 529, 281; cf. Krouse and McPherson 1988: 91–2; DiQuattro 1983: 62–3).

This raises an important point about the implications of liberal equality.

Dworkin often writes as if the most obvious or likely result of implementing his conception of justice would be to increase the level of transfer payments between occupants of existing social roles (e.g. Dworkin 1981: 321; 1985: 208). But as Rawls notes, liberal egalitarians should also be concerned with the way these existing roles are defined. An important component of the resources available to a person include opportunities for skill development, personal accomplishment, and the exercise of responsibility. These are predominantly matters, not of the income associated with a given job, but of the social relations entailed by the job. People would not generally choose to enter social relations that deny these opportunities, or that put them in relations of domination or degradation. From a position of equality, women would not have agreed to a system of social roles that defines 'male' jobs as superior to, and dominating of, 'female' jobs. And workers would not have agreed to the exaggerated distinction between 'mental' and 'manual' labour. We know that people in a position of initial equality would not have chosen these roles, for they were created without the consent of women and workers, and in fact often required their legal and political suppression. For example, the division between doctors and nurses was opposed by women health care practitioners (Ehrenreich and English 1973: 19–39), and the 'scientific management' system was opposed by workers (Braverman 1974). Both changes would have taken a substantially different form if women and workers had the same power as men and capitalists. The result would probably be not only greater equality in market income between these social roles, but also greater equality in opportunities for training, self-development, and the exercise of responsibility.

Dworkin says that increased transfer payments are justified because we can assume that the poor would be willing to do the work in higher-paying jobs if they entered the market on an equal footing (Dworkin 1985: 207). But we can also assume that if the poor entered the market on an equal footing, they would not accept jobs that, in Rawls's words, make them 'servilely dependent on others' or that are 'deadening to human thought and sensibility'. We have as good evidence for the latter as for the former. Liberal egalitarians, therefore, should be concerned not only to redistribute income from the advantaged to disadvantaged, but also to ensure that the advantaged do not have the power to define relationships of dominance and servility in the workplace. And here again, this cannot be achieved through the traditional tax and transfer schemes of the welfare state, but requires instead increasing the *ex ante* endowments people bring to the market.

It is to Rawls's credit that he recognizes the limitations of the welfare state in achieving liberal equality. Unfortunately, he does not provide much of a description of his property-owning democracy—as one critic puts it, 'these points never find their way into the substance of his theory of justice'

(Doppelt 1981: 276). Other than a rather modest proposal to limit inheritances, Rawls gives us no idea of how to implement such a property-owning democracy, or how to eliminate the entrenched class inequalities in our society. Similarly, Dworkin offers no suggestions about how to equalize *ex ante* endowments.

In short, liberal egalitarianism's institutional commitments have not kept pace with its theoretical commitments. This has led to a tension, perhaps even a crisis, in the politics of liberal egalitarianism. William Connolly says that liberalism's theoretical premises can be united with its traditional institutions 'as long as it is possible to believe that the welfare state in the privately incorporated economy of growth can be the vehicle of liberty and justice' (Connolly 1984: 233). He claims, however, that the demands of the private economy conflict with the principles of justice that underlie the welfare state. The welfare state needs a growing economy to support its redistributive programmes, but the structure of the economy is such that growth can only be secured by policies inconsistent with the principles of justice that underlie those welfare programmes (Connolly 1984: 227–31).

According to Connolly, this has led to a 'bifurcation of liberalism'. One stream clings to the traditional institutions of liberal practice, and exhorts people to lower their expectations concerning justice and freedom. The other stream (in which he includes Dworkin) reaffirms the principles, but 'the commitment to liberal principles is increasingly matched by the disengagement from practical issues . . . this principled liberalism is neither at home in the civilization of productivity nor prepared to challenge its hegemony' (Connolly 1984: 234). I think this accurately describes the condition of contemporary liberalism. The ideals of liberal equality are compelling, but they require reforms that are more extensive than Rawls or Dworkin have explicitly allowed. Neither has challenged the 'civilization of productivity' whose maintenance has involved the perpetuation of entrenched inequalities of race, class, and gender.

Part of the reason for this disengagement, I think, is that liberal egalitarians have gradually lost confidence in the ability of the state to achieve justice. When Rawls wrote his book in 1971, the welfare state was seen by many people as essentially successful, and indeed as having more or less 'solved' the problem of poverty and class division. In the past thirty years, however, that faith has been deeply shaken. The recession in the early 1970s triggered by the OPEC oil crisis, and the subsequent ballooning of government deficits, led many to think that perhaps the welfare state was not in fact affordable or sustainable. And increasing economic globalization has persuaded many people that cuts to taxes and government spending are needed for businesses to remain competitive with those in foreign countries.

Moreover, there was increasing evidence that the welfare state was not as successful as people had hoped or assumed. To be sure, some welfare programmes have worked well. Public pensions have largely eliminated the problem of poverty amongst the elderly in many countries. However, other programmes that were intended to promote equality have often ended up either perpetuating the dependence and stigmatization of the poor (e.g. the 'poverty trap' created by means-tested benefits), or have disproportionately benefited the well off (e.g. universal health care and education). Moreover, the 'new economy' seems to be producing ever-growing inequalities in market income; the gap between executives and workers, or between college educated and uneducated, has been steadily increasing. There is widespread concern that large sectors of the population will simply be excluded from this new knowledge-based economy. In short, the need for active state policies to combat inequalities in people's endowments and income is growing, yet most liberal egalitarians feel less and less confidence in the welfare state's ability to achieve this.[19]

And of course all of this has taken place in the context of a major backlash against the welfare state by the New Right in the 1980s, spearheaded by Reagan and Thatcher, who argued that the welfare state denied individual responsibility, stifled creativity, and reduced efficiency. The result has been a cutback in many welfare programmes, and a resulting dramatic increase in inequality in many Western democracies, particularly Britain and the United States. Growing market inequalities are no longer checked by any significant level of redistribution.

This has put liberal egalitarians in a bind, both intellectually and politically. Intellectually, their theories require going beyond the traditional tax/transfer welfare state to some form of 'property-owning democracy' or 'stakeholder society'. Yet politically, such ideas have seemed utopian in the difficult political and economic environment of the 1980s and 1990s. Rather than trying to extend the welfare state, liberal egalitarians have been on the defensive, trying to preserve what is left of the welfare state against New Right attacks, so as to maintain at least minimal levels of redistribution to reduce poverty and provide basic public services.

This may help explain the 'surprisingly conservative' tenor of many of Rawls's and Dworkin's works (Macleod 1998: 151). Faced with the New Right, liberal egalitarians have indeed been concerned to conserve what is left of the welfare state. Rather than emphasizing how inadequate the welfare state is, in comparison with some ideal of a property-owning democracy, liberal egalitarians have instead emphasized how necessary and justified the welfare state is, in comparison with a New Right vision of unrestricted property rights.

And yet one can ask whether this intellectual timidity has actually served the goals of liberal egalitarianism, even from a purely political perspective.

One could argue that liberal egalitarians have unintentionally played into the hands of the New Right. Partly as a response to New Right critiques that the welfare state penalizes the hard-working and rewards indolence and irresponsibility, Dworkin has tried to emphasize that the welfare state can be made more choice-sensitive. His policy recommendations focus on enabling those with resources to have more choices (e.g. allowing supplementary private health insurance), and on ensuring that the lazy or imprudent do not impose the costs of their choices on others (e.g. workfare). As we have seen, he has not invested the same time or effort in thinking how the system can be made more circumstance-insensitive.

This is understandable, in one sense, since Dworkin's main departure from traditional theories of equality is his concern for choice-sensitivity. And philosophically speaking, I agree that justice requires that people have choices, and pay for the costs of their choices. Moreover, the prospects for serious reforms aimed at remedying unequal circumstances have appeared non-existent for much of the last twenty years.

Nonetheless, by focusing on ambition-sensitivity, liberal egalitarians may have unintentionally reinforced the New Right's agenda, which is obsessed with identifying and punishing the irresponsible and indolent. According to the New Right, the welfare state wrongly limits the choices of the well off in order to subsidize the irresponsible behaviour of welfare dependants. In an odd way, Dworkin's own proposals for private health insurance and workfare fit into this framework. These policies do nothing to remedy unequal circumstances, and may indeed make it harder to generate public support for such remedies. Allowing private health insurance might erode middle-class support for public health care; and making welfare more conditional might further stigmatize the needy. That of course is not Dworkin's intention. He wants our policies to be *both* more choice-sensitive *and* more circumstance-insensitive. But he does not consider the possibility that, in our current political climate, emphasizing choice-sensitivity simply reinforces stereotypes of the 'undeserving poor' who are seeking public subsidies for their irresponsible lifestyles.

Of course, liberal egalitarians can and do challenge these stereotypes by showing that many inequalities cannot plausibly be traced to people's choices (like those between types A and B in Roemer's example). Moreover, liberal egalitarians rightly insist that society can only legitimately hold people responsible for their choices if their preferences and capacities have been formed under conditions of justice. To hold people responsible for their choices when society has not provided them with a decent education, for example, would be 'a massive piece of bad faith' (Elster 1992: 240; cf. Rawls 1979: 14–15; Arneson 1981: 205; 1997a; Scanlon 1988: 185–201).[20] So we cannot invoke people's allegedly 'irresponsible' behaviour as a reason not to remedy their unequal circumstances: the latter is a condition for being able to judge the former.

In these and other ways, liberal egalitarians have tried to fight the New Right's tendency to 'blame the victim'—i.e. the tendency to accuse the disadvantaged of being responsible for their own plight. Nonetheless, the liberal egalitarian emphasis on ambition-sensitivity may have unintentionally reinforced this popular perception that the main problem with the welfare state is that it coddles the irresponsible.[21]

Jonathan Wolff has argued that this problem points to an interesting dilemma for theorists of justice. He suggests that liberal egalitarianism may indeed be the best *theory* of justice, from a purely philosophical point of view. But politically, it promotes the wrong *ethos* of equality (Wolff 1998). It encourages the state to view its disadvantaged citizens with distrust, as potential cheaters. And in order to overcome this distrust, the disadvantaged must engage in what Wolff calls 'shameful revelation'—i.e. they have to prove they do indeed suffer from some involuntary disadvantage, whether in their natural talents or childhood upbringing. The inevitable result, he argues, is to erode, rather than to strengthen, the bonds of solidarity and mutual concern between citizens. Philosophically, it may be true that the fairest scheme of distribution would distinguish voluntary from involuntary inequalities, but any attempt to implement this distinction in practice creates distrust, shame, and stigmatization. It may identify who has the fairest claims, but only through a process that undermines the civility and solidarity that leads people to care about justice in the first place.

Elizabeth Anderson has raised a similar objection to liberal egalitarians (or what she calls 'luck egalitarians'). She argues that liberal egalitarianism's emphasis on distinguishing voluntary from involuntary inequality leads to a disrespectful pity towards the 'deserving' poor, and paternalistic hectoring of the 'undeserving' poor (Anderson 1999). Here again, the philosophical argument for liberal egalitarianism may be defensible, but the politics involved may not be.[22]

Wolff and Anderson suggest that these problems of 'ethos' are a reason for abandoning liberal egalitarianism for some other form of equality. (I will look at their preferred alternative in Chapter 5.) However, these ethos problems may instead suggest that we need to separate the two pillars of liberal egalitarianism and locate them in different places. Perhaps from the first-person point of view, when thinking about our own claims, we should make a conscientious effort to accept responsibility for our own choices, and to not ask others to subsidize our choices. Internalizing this requirement of choice-sensitivity should indeed be seen as an important part of the 'ethos' of democratic citizenship. A good citizen would apply the choices/circumstances distinction to his or her own claims. The problem arises, however, when we attempt to apply this distinction to others, and try to ascertain the extent to which they are responsible for their plight. This can lead to the pernicious dynamic of distrust and shameful revelation that Wolff discusses. So it might be part of the 'ethos' of a good citizen that we do not pry into the (ir)responsibility of others, but rather trust that they are trying to be as responsible in their choices and demands as we are in ours. Of course, this means we may be taken advantage of by some of our less scrupulous co-citizens. But if we are successful in inculcating an ethos of good citizenship that emphasizes the importance of voluntarily accepting personal responsibility for our own choices, there may be few such cheaters. (I return to the question of whether or how liberals can promote an ethos of good citizenship in Chapter 8.) In any event, a scheme of justice that encourages everyone to view their co-citizens as putative cheats is not a promising basis for developing trust and solidarity.

This suggests that the main focus for the politics of liberal egalitarianism should be to remedy (the growing) inequality in people's circumstances, perhaps through the sorts of reforms proposed by Ackerman, Roemer, and Van Parijs. This will almost certainly require radical reforms that go beyond the boundaries of the traditional welfare state. According to Dworkin, the egalitarian premiss underlying Rawls's (and his own) theory 'cannot be denied in the name of any more radical concept of equality, because none exists' (Dworkin 1977: 182). In fact, this premiss seems to have more radical implications than either Dworkin or Rawls recognizes, implications that traditional liberal institutions are unable to accommodate.

It might be that a full implementation of Rawlsian or Dworkinian justice would require substantial changes in the way we define and allocate property rights (Buchanan 1982: 124–31, 150–2; DiQuattro 1983). It might also move us closer to radical changes in gender relations. The current maldistribution in resources between men and women does not match the results of freely made choices in either Rawls's original position or Dworkin's auction. Yet neither theorist has anything to say about how this systematic devaluation of the work and contribution of women can be removed. Indeed, Rawls defines his original position (as an assembly of 'heads of families'), and his principles of distribution (as measuring 'household income'), in such a way that questions about the justice of arrangements within the family are ruled out of court by definition (Okin 1987: 49). Of all the issues from which contemporary liberals have become disengaged, gender inequality is the most glaring omission, and the one which liberal institutions seem least able to deal with (see Ch. 9, s. 1 below).

So the relationship between contemporary liberal theory and traditional liberal political practice is unclear. The two have become disengaged in a number of ways. Liberalism is often called 'mainstream' political theory, as opposed to radical or critical theory. That label is accurate in one sense, for Rawls and Dworkin are trying to articulate and defend the ideals that they believe are at the moral base of our liberal-democratic culture. But it is inaccurate in another sense, if it implies that liberal theories are committed to defending all aspects of mainstream liberal politics, or to rejecting all aspects of the political programmes of other traditions. It would be wrong to assume that the account of liberal equality I have presented is necessarily tied to any particular liberal institution, or is necessarily opposed to any particular social-ist, feminist, or multiculturalist proposal. We will have to wait until we examine these other theories before we can determine the extent of their differences with liberal equality.

Some people argue that if liberals endorse these more radical reforms, they have abandoned their liberalism, or entered into a new phase of 'post-liberalism', since the focus is no longer just on protecting individuals against the state, but also on protecting individuals from oppressive social roles and practices that developed under conditions of inequality (e.g. Hampton 1997: 191–209).[23] That seems unduly restrictive, given the historical ties between liberalism and radicalism (Gutmann 1980). It is also misleading, for however far liberal principles take us from traditional liberal practices, they are still distinctively liberal principles. I have argued in this section that liberals need to think seriously about adopting more radical politics.[24] In subsequent chapters, I will argue that radical theorists need to think seriously about adopting liberal principles. Just as liberal practice often does a disservice to liberal principles, I will argue that radical principles often do a disservice to radical politics. But before considering these theories, I will look first in the next chapter at a school of thought which argues that liberal egalitarians have gone too far in the direction of social and economic equality.

GUIDE TO FURTHER READING

The most influential statement of liberal egalitarianism is, of course, John Rawls's *A Theory of Justice* (Oxford University Press, 1971). Early discussions of Rawls's argument can be found in Brian Barry, *The Liberal Theory of Justice* (Oxford University Press, 1973), Norman Daniels (ed.), *Reading Rawls* (Basic Books, 1975), and Robert Paul Wolff, *Understanding Rawls* (Princeton University Press, 1977). Thirty years later, Rawls's book remains a topic of undiminished interest. More recent discussions include Chandran Kukathas and Philip Pettit, *Rawls: A Theory of Justice and its Critics* (Polity, 1990), and Robert Talisse, *On Rawls* (Wadsworth, 2000). For a comprehensive overview of reactions to Rawls, see the five-volume (!) set entitled *The Philosophy of Rawls*, edited by Henry Richardson and Paul Weithman (Garland, 1999).

Rawls himself has continued to develop his ideas, particularly in *Political Liberalism* (Columbia University Press, 1993), *The Law of Peoples* (Harvard University Press, 1999), and *Collected Papers*, ed. Samuel Freeman (Harvard University Press, 1999). I will discuss his more recent work on 'political liberalism' in the chapter on communitarianism, since it was written after, and offers one line of response to, the communitarian critique of his original theory.

The second most influential version of liberal egalitarianism is that developed by Ronald Dworkin, particularly in his 'What is Equality?' series of articles. These articles have now been collected together in Dworkin's *Sovereign Virtue: The Theory and Practice of Equality* (Harvard University Press, 2000). For a detailed critique of Dworkin's theory of justice, see Colin Macleod, *Liberalism, Justice and Markets: A Critique of Liberal Equality* (Oxford University Press, 1998).

Other influential statements of liberal egalitarianism include Amy Gutmann, *Liberal Equality* (Cambridge University Press, 1980); Bruce Ackerman, *Social Justice in the Liberal State* (Yale University Press, 1980); Brian Barry, *Theories of Justice* (University of California Press, 1989); Richard Arneson, 'Equality and Equal Opportunity for Welfare', *Philosophical Studies*, 56 (1989): 77–93; G. A. Cohen, 'On the Currency of Egalitarian Justice', *Ethics*, 99 (1989): 906–44; Amartya Sen, 'Equality of What?', in S. McMurrin, (ed.), *The Tanner Lectures on Human Values*, vol. i (University of Utah Press, 1980); Martha Nussbaum and Amartya Sen (eds.), *The Quality of Life* (Oxford University Press, 1993); Thomas Scanlon, *What We Owe to Each Other* (Harvard University Press, 1998); Eric Rakowski, *Equal Justice* (Oxford University Press, 1993); Philippe Van Parijs, *Real Freedom for All* (Oxford University Press, 1995); and John Roemer, 'A Pragmatic Theory of Responsibility for the Egalitarian Planner', *Philosophy and Public Affairs*, 22 (1993): 146–66. All share the underlying intuition about eliminating unchosen inequalities, while providing space for inequalities due to choices for which individuals are responsible.

A useful collection of liberal egalitarian writings can be found in Stephen Darwall (ed.), *Equal Freedom: Selected Tanner Lectures on Human Values* (University of Michigan Press, 1995).

There are no academic journals which are specifically devoted to liberal egalitarianism. However, it is arguably the dominant approach in contemporary Anglo-American political philosophy, and so is well represented in the major political philosophy journals, particularly *Ethics* and *Philosophy and Public Affairs*.

There is much debate within liberal egalitarianism about how best to implement the norms of equality of resources. The *Boston Review* has had several symposia debating the practical and philosophical merits of various proposals, including Roemer's idea of an egalitarian planner (vol. 20/2, Apr. 1995), and Van Parijs's idea of a basic income (vol. 25/5, Oct. 2000). Both symposia include commentaries from several prominent political philosophers (Scanlon, Rosenblum, Barry, Goodin etc). These symposia can be accessed on the web at: **www.bostonreview.mit.edu**

Additional information on the guaranteed basic income scheme can be found on the website of the 'Basic Income European Network', at: **www.econ.ucl.be/ETES/ BEIN/bein.html**

NOTES

1. Rawls has a number of subsidiary arguments for his two principles of justice. For example, Rawls says that his principles meet the requirements of 'publicity' (1971: 133) and 'stability' (1971: 176–82) more fully than alternative accounts of justice. Principles of justice must be publicly known and easily applied, and the corresponding sense of justice must be stable and self-reinforcing (e.g. the 'strains of commitment' must not be too great). Rawls sometimes puts considerable weight on such arguments in defending his theory, but they do not by themselves generate a determinate theory of justice, and hence are subsidiary to the two main arguments I discuss. For a summary of the subsidiary arguments, see Parekh 1982: 161–2; Raikka 1998.

2. It is this condemnation of the unfairness inherent in the traditional state of nature which sets Rawls apart from another contract tradition—a tradition which runs from Hobbes to recent theorists like David Gauthier and James Buchanan. Like Rawls, they hope to generate principles for regulating social life from the idea of an agreement in an initial position. But unlike Rawls, the agreement aims at mutual advantage, not justice, and so it is permissible, and indeed essential, that the initial situation reflect the differences in bargaining power that occur in the real world. I will discuss this second contractarian approach in Chapter 4, and ask whether theories of mutual advantage should be considered as theories of *justice* at all.

3. Rawls says that the case of choosing principles of justice in the original position is importantly different from cutting a cake without knowing which piece you will get. He calls the first case an example of 'pure procedural justice', while the second is 'perfect procedural justice'. In each case, a procedure is supposed to yield just results. But in the former case there is no 'independent and already given criterion of what is just', while in the latter case there is (Rawls 1980: 523). But the contrast is overdrawn in this case, since, as we will see, there are some 'independent and already given criterion' for assessing the results of the original position. In any event, the two cases share the feature I am drawing attention to—the use of ignorance to ensure unbiased decisions.

4. Frolich and Oppenheimer have conducted a series of experiments designed to test this question. Subjects ignorant of their own place in a reward schedule were asked to choose amongst various principles of distribution, including Rawls's maximin, utilitarianism, and a hybrid model which maximized average utility subject to some minimum floor. The latter was the dominant choice (Frolich and Oppenheimer 1992).

5. Rawls denies that there is any essential similarity between his contractualism and Hare's impartial sympathizer. But, as Barry puts it, this denial 'seems to me simply a flailing of the air' (Barry 1989a: 410 n. 30). It is unfortunate that Rawls exaggerates the distance between his theory and Hare's, for the exaggeration works to Rawls's disadvantage. See the discussion of feminist critiques of Rawls in Ch. 9, s. 3c below.

6. For the canonical account of this idea of 'reflective equilibrium', see Daniels 1979; cf. Nielsen 1993; Norman 1998.

7. This objection is raised by Barry and Sen, although they mistakenly blame the problem on Rawls's commitment to using primary goods to define the least well off position (Barry 1973: 55–7; Sen 1980: 215–16). The problem actually lies in Rawls's incomplete use of primary goods—i.e. his arbitrary exclusion of natural primary goods from the index. Rawls does discuss the idea of compensating natural disadvantages, but only in terms of a 'principle of redress' under which compensation is made in order to remove the direct effects of the handicap and thereby create equality of opportunity (Rawls 1971: 100–2). Rawls rightly rejects this view as both impossible and undesirable. But why not view compensation as a way of

eliminating an undeserved inequality in overall primary goods? Compensating people for the unchosen costs of their natural disadvantages should be done, not so that they can compete with others on an equal footing, but so they can have the same ability to lead a satisfying life. For more on this, compare Michelman (1975: 330–9), Gutmann (1980: 126–7), and Daniels (1985: ch. 3), with Pogge (1989: 183–8), and Mapel (1989: 101–6).

Some commentators argue that Rawls does support compensating natural disadvantages, but not as a matter of justice. Instead he views our obligations to the naturally disadvantaged as 'duties of public benevolence' (Martin 1985: 189–91), or 'claims of morality' (Pogge 1989: 186–91, 275). These obligations to the disadvantaged are not matters of mere charity, for they should be compulsorily enforced through the state, but nor are they claims of justice. According to Pogge and Martin, Rawls's theory of justice is about 'fundamental justice', whereas compensation for the naturally disadvantaged is about 'the overall fairness of the universe' (Martin 1985: 180; Pogge 1989: 189). Unfortunately, neither author explains this contrast, nor how it is consistent with Rawls's emphasis on 'mitigating the effects of natural accident and social fortune' (1971: 585). Martin, for example, seems to say that mitigating the effects of differential natural *assets* is a matter of fundamental justice, whereas mitigating the effects of differential natural *handicaps* is a matter of benevolence (Martin 1985: 178). It is hard to see what, within a Rawlsian approach, justifies this distinction. (Brian Barry argues that this restriction is only legitimate if Rawls is abandoning the whole idea of justice as equal consideration and adopting instead the Hobbesian idea of justice as mutual advantage—Barry 1989a 243–6; cf. n. 2 above.)

8. For further discussions of the idea of envy-freeness, and its use as a criterion of distributive justice, see Fleurbaey 1994; Arnsperger 1994.

9. It is not impossible to imagine people who will object even when the envy test is met. Since the envy test says nothing about people's welfare, it is possible that, of two equally talented people, one will be miserable while the other is elated. All the envy test tells us is that the miserable person would be even more miserable if he had the resource bundle that the elated person possesses. Imagine someone who is congenitally moody and taciturn, regardless of the sort of resources he has and the sort of success he has in his projects. In this case, satisfying the envy test will not yield equal benefits to each person. Since the miserable person cannot control his congenital grumpiness, we might think that he therefore has some extra claim on resources. (On the other hand, since the person's misery is *ex hypothesi* not due to the bundle of resources he has, it is not clear how any redistribution will change his misery.)

This example suggests that the simple typology Dworkin works with is inadequate. He tends to view everything as either *ambitions* (which he sees as coterminous with our personality-manifesting choices), or *resources* (which he sees as matters of unchosen circumstance). But there are personal attributes or psychological propensities (like grumpiness) which do not fit easily in either category, yet which affect how much benefit people get from social resources. For a critique of Dworkin's categories, see Cohen 1989: 916–34; Arneson 1989; Alexander and Schwarzschild 1987: 99; Roemer 1985a. While I cannot discuss these cases in depth, I believe that they (and other difficult cases such as uncontrollable cravings) complicate, rather than undermine, the aims and methods of Dworkin's theory. (As Dworkin notes, cravings or congenital moodiness can be viewed as a kind of natural disadvantage which could be insured against, along with other mental and physical disabilities—Dworkin 1981: 301–4.)

10. I am oversimplifying here. Dworkin in fact proposes two separate insurance schemes to deal with two different kinds of natural disadvantage: one for disabilities, one for unequal natural talents. For the details of these two insurance schemes, see Dworkin 1981. For a critique of the way he develops these two schemes, and the way he distinguishes them, see Tremain 1996; Macleod 1998: chs. 4–5; Van Parijs 1995: ch. 3; Roemer 1985a; Varian 1985.

11. There may be a better middle ground between ignoring and equalizing circumstances than Dworkin's insurance scheme. Amartya Sen's 'equality of capacities' scheme is one possibility, which Rawls himself seems to endorse for the handicapped (Rawls 1982b: 168; cf. Sen 1980: 218–19). Sen aims at a kind of equalization for those with natural disadvantage, but he limits it to the equalization of 'basic capacities', rather than the full-fledged equalization of circumstances which Dworkin rejects as impossible. The extent to which this is possible, or different from the results of Dworkin's insurance scheme, is difficult to tell (Cohen 1989: 942; cf. Sen 1985: 143–4; 1990: 115 n. 12; Dworkin 2000: ch. 7).

12. On the potential conflicts between liberal egalitarian justice and a right to privacy, see Arneson 2000a.

13. Other authors have made similar proposals, but put restrictions on how people can use their stakes—e.g. they can be used for education or investment, not for consumption and leisure (e.g. Tobin, Unger, Haveman 1988). Ackerman and Alstott consider a number of ways of financing such a scheme, in addition to the wealth tax. For some of the normative issues involved in wealth taxes, see Rakowski 2000.

14. I should note that Van Parijs himself also defends the basic income proposal as a kind of 'rent' that the employed owe to the unemployed in conditions of high unemployment.

15. For critiques and defences of the basic income proposal, see Van Parijs 1992, 2001; Groot and van der Veen 2000; White 2000; and the symposium on 'Basic Income? A Symposium on Van Parijs', in *Analyse und Kritik*, 22 (2000). For a variation on Van Parijs's proposal, which would tie the basic income to performing some socially useful activity, though not necessarily paid employment, see Atkinson 1996.

16. Of course, this approach can be combined with the others: one way to try to equalize types would be through granting stakes, or compensatory education, or basic income. For a debate about Roemer's proposal, see the symposia in *Boston Review*, 20/2 (1995).

17. For developments and refinements of Dworkin's scheme, see Richard Arneson's account of 'equality of opportunity for welfare' (1989; 1990), and his later account of 'responsibility-catering prioritarianism' (2000a; 2000b); G. A. Cohen's account of 'equality of access to advantage' (Cohen 1989; 1992; 1993); Erik Rakowski's account of 'equality of fortune' (Rakowski 1993); John Roemer's account of 'equality of access/opportunity' (Roemer 1993a; 1996). While they all use different terminology, and disagree about how precisely to define or distinguish voluntary and involuntary disadvantages, they share Dworkin's underlying intuition about eliminating unchosen inequalities, while providing space for inequalities due to choices for which individuals are responsible. Elizabeth Anderson calls all of these theorists 'luck egalitarians', since they are concerned to eliminate inequalities which are involuntary (or unlucky) (Anderson 1999). For related discussions of this general approach, see Lippert-Rasmussen 1999; Schaller 1997.

18. Note that whereas Dworkin argues that a just distribution would require *more* welfare redistribution than is currently provided, Rawls argues that a just distribution would involve *less*. He seems to think that market incomes in such a property-owning democracy will naturally satisfy the difference principle (Rawls 1971: 87), and indeed will correspond to Dworkin's idea of an ambition-sensitive, endowment-insensitive distribution (Rawls 1971: 305; cf. DiQuattro 1983: 62–3). Hence he opposes progressive income tax, and the extensive redistribution of market income (Rawls 1971: 278–9). Like Mill, Rawls seems to think that welfare provision would be 'of very minor importance' were 'the diffusion of property satisfactory' (Mill 1965: 960). But if Dworkin neglects the need to distribute property equally, Rawls neglects the need to redistribute incomes fairly. For even in his property-owning democracy there will be undeserved differences in market income due to differential natural talents, and undeserved differences in needs due to natural disadvantages and

other forms of misfortune (Krouse and McPherson 1988: 94–9; Carens 1985: 49–59; 1986: 40–1).

This points to another interesting difference between Rawls and Dworkin. Rawls thinks that the difference principle will, in practice, be similar to Dworkin's ambition-sensitive, endowment-insensitive distributive ideal, since the market naturally generates such a distribution. Dworkin thinks that the ambition-sensitive, endowment-insensitive ideal will, in practice, be similar to Rawls's difference principle, since neither markets nor governments can distinguish endowments and ambitions. Hence they both claim that their theory will, in practice, be similar to the other's, but for opposite reasons.

19. This shows the crucial importance, for any credible theory of justice, of having some theory of *state capacity*. As Bo Rothstein has argued, this is one of the major limitations of contemporary liberal egalitarian theorizing of justice (Rothstein 1992; 1998).

20. In other words, people's capacity to accept responsibility is affected by the good or bad luck of their upbringing. People raised in oppressive conditions—say, in conditions of parental neglect or sexual abuse—are less likely to develop capacities for responsibility or moral goodness. For an interesting discussion of how responsibility judgements can be made under such conditions, see Card 1996.

21. For an analysis of how illiberal welfare reforms have been justified 'in the name of liberalism', see King 1999.

22. It is unclear whether Anderson does or does not accept the Rawlsian/Dworkinian argument that involuntary disadvantages are unjust: she only says they 'might' not be unjust. For responses to Wolff and Anderson, see Arneson 2000*a*; and the electronic symposium in BEARS 1999. A related issue about the appropriate 'ethos' of liberal justice has been raised in the context of Rawls's theory. As we have seen, Rawls allows for incentives to be given to the naturally advantaged to develop their talents for the benefit of all. But why are the incentives needed in the first place? Why aren't the talented willing to develop and exercise their talents to help the less well off without demanding additional income? In some cases, the incentives may be needed to compensate for unequal burdens involved in the development or exercise of these talents (e.g. extra training, extra stress, extra risk). But Rawls clearly thinks that incentives may be needed in other cases, simply because the talented will refuse to develop and exercise their talents without greater rewards. Under these circumstances, Cohen argues, incentives are simply a form of economic blackmail by the talented. And the reason why inequalities between executives and workers is lower in Sweden or Japan than in the United States is because there is an 'ethos' of equality which discourages this sort of economic blackmail. Cohen argues that anyone who cares about justice has to be concerned with instilling such an ethos in society (see G. A. Cohen 1993; 1997; Murphy 1999; and the responses in Smith 1998; Pogge 2000; Estlund 1998; A. Williams 1998).

23. Hampton describes post-liberals as theorists who seek 'a more sophisticated way of ensuring the freedom and equality of all citizens in the face not only of governmental threats to these values but also oppressive social practices that persist despite the government's moral commitment to freedom and equality for all' (Hampton 1997: 203). For a similar argument about the need for liberals to take seriously social and cultural oppression, see Kernohan 1998.

24. I have primarily been concerned to show that the liberal-egalitarian view of an ideally just society endorses some fairly radical goals. It is a further question whether liberals should adopt radical means to achieve such goals. On this question, Rawls and Dworkin are explicitly reformist rather than revolutionary. They both argue that respect for people's liberty takes precedence over, and puts limits on, the pursuit of a just distribution of material resources (Rawls 1971: 303; 1982*b*: 11; Dworkin 1987: 48–9). I cannot discuss this issue here, although these stipulations seem unjustified in terms of the motivations of Rawls's contractors (see Pogge 1989: 127–48).

4

LIBERTARIANISM

1. THE DIVERSITY OF RIGHT-WING POLITICAL THEORY

Libertarians defend market freedoms, and oppose the use of redistributive taxation schemes to implement a liberal theory of equality. But not everyone who favours the free market is a libertarian, for they do not all share the libertarian view that the free market is *inherently* just. For example, one common argument for unrestricted capitalism is its productivity, its claim to be maximally efficient at increasing social wealth. Many utilitarians, convinced of the truth of that claim, favour the free market, since its efficiency allows for the greatest overall satisfaction of preferences.[1] But the utilitarian commitment to capitalism is necessarily a contingent one. If, as most economists agree, there are circumstances where the free market is not maximally productive—e.g. cases of natural monopolies—then utilitarians would support government restrictions on property rights. Moreover, as we saw in Chapter 2, some utilitarians argue that redistribution can increase overall utility even when it decreases productivity. Because of declining marginal utility, those at the bottom gain more from redistribution than those at the top lose, even when redistribution lessens productivity.

Others defend capitalism not on the grounds of maximizing utility, but of minimizing the danger of tyranny. Giving governments the power to regulate economic exchanges centralizes power, and since power corrupts, market regulations are the first step on 'the road to serfdom', in Hayek's memorable phrase. The more governments are able to control economic life, the more able (and willing) they will be to control all aspects of our lives. Hence capitalist freedoms are needed to preserve our civil and political liberties (Hayek 1960: 121; Gray 1986a: 62–8; 1986b: 180–5). But this defence of market freedom must also be a contingent one, for history does not reveal any invariable link between capitalism and civil liberties. Countries with essentially unrestricted capitalism have sometimes had poor human rights records (e.g. military dictatorships in capitalist Chile or Argentina; McCarthyism in the United States), while countries with an extensive welfare state have sometimes had excellent records in defending civil and political rights (e.g. Sweden).

So these two defences of the free market are contingent ones. More importantly, they are *instrumental* defences of the free market. They tell us that market freedoms are a means for promoting maximal utility, or for protecting political and civil liberties. On these accounts, we do not favour the free market because people have rights to property. Rather we give people property rights as a way of increasing utility or stabilizing democracy, and if we could promote utility or stability some other way, then we could legitimately restrict property rights.

Libertarianism differs from other right-wing theories in its claim that redistributive taxation is inherently wrong, a violation of people's rights.[2] People have a *right* to dispose freely of their goods and services, and they have this right whether or not it is the best way to ensure productivity. Put another way, government has no right to interfere in the market, even in order to increase efficiency. As Robert Nozick puts it, 'Individuals have rights, and there are things which no person or group may do to them (without violating their rights). So strong and far-reaching are these rights that they raise the question of what, if anything, the state and its officials may do' (Nozick 1974: p. ix). Because people have a right to dispose of their holdings as they see fit, government interference is equivalent to forced labour—a violation, not of efficiency, but of our basic moral rights.

(a) Nozick's 'Entitlement Theory'

How do libertarians relate justice and the market? I will focus on Nozick's 'entitlement theory'. The central claim in Nozick's theory, as in most other libertarian theories, is this: if we assume that everyone is entitled to the goods they currently possess (their 'holdings'), then a just distribution is simply whatever distribution results from people's free exchanges. Any distribution that arises by free transfers from a just situation is itself just. For the government to coercively tax these exchanges against anyone's will is unjust, even if the taxes are used to compensate for the extra costs of someone's undeserved natural handicaps. The only legitimate taxation is to raise revenues for maintaining the background institutions needed to protect the system of free exchange—e.g. the police and justice system needed to enforce people's free exchanges.

More precisely, there are three main principles of Nozick's 'entitlement theory':

1. a principle of transfer—whatever is justly acquired can be freely transferred.
2. a principle of just initial acquisition—an account of how people come

initially to own the things which can be transferred in accordance with (1).

3. a principle of rectification of injustice—how to deal with holdings if they were unjustly acquired or transferred.

If I own a plot of land, then (1) says that I am free to engage in any transfers I wish to make concerning that land. Principle (2) tells us how the land initially came to be owned. Principle (3) tells us what to do in the event that (1) or (2) is violated. Taken together, they imply that if people's current holdings are justly acquired, then the formula for a just distribution is 'from each as they choose, to each as they are chosen' (Nozick 1974: 160).

The conclusion of Nozick's entitlement theory is that 'a minimal state, limited to the narrow functions of protection against force, theft, fraud, enforcement of contracts, and so on, is justified; any more extensive state will violate persons' rights not to be forced to do certain things, and is unjustified' (Nozick 1974: p. ix).[3] Hence there is no public education, no public health care, transportation, roads, or parks. All of these involve the coercive taxation of some people against their will, violating the principle 'from each as they choose, to each as they are chosen'.

As we have seen, Rawls and Dworkin also emphasize that a just distribution must be sensitive to people's choices. But they believe that this is just half of the story. A just distribution must be ambition-sensitive, as Nozick's is, but it must also be endowment-insensitive, as Nozick's is not. It is unfair for the naturally disadvantaged to starve just because they have nothing to offer others in free exchange, or for children to go without health care or education just because they were born into a poor family. Hence liberal egalitarians favour taxing free exchanges in order to compensate the naturally and socially disadvantaged.

Nozick says this is unjust, because people are entitled to their holdings (if justly acquired), where 'entitled' means 'having an absolute right to freely dispose of it as one sees fit, so long as it does not involve force or fraud'. There are some limits on what I can do—my entitlement to my knife does not include the right to deposit it in your back, since you are entitled to your back. But otherwise I am free to do what I want with my resources. I can spend them on acquiring the goods and services of others, or I can simply give them away to others if I wish. Nozick does not object to this sort of voluntary private philanthropy—on the contrary, he says it is an excellent way to exercise one's property rights (Nozick 1974: 265–8). But I can also decide to withhold my resources from others (including the government). No one has the right to take them from me, even if it is to keep the disabled from starving.

Why should we accept Nozick's claim that people's property entitlements are such as to preclude a liberal redistributive scheme? Some critics argue that

Nozick has no argument—he gives us 'libertarianism without foundations' (Nagel 1981). But a more generous reading will detect two different arguments. As with Rawls, the first argument is an intuitive one, trying to draw out the attractive features of the free exercise of property rights. The second is a more philosophical argument which attempts to derive property rights from the premiss of 'self-ownership'. In line with my general approach, and I think with Nozick's intentions, I will interpret this self-ownership argument as an appeal to the idea of treating people as equals.

Other writers defend libertarianism by quite different arguments. Some libertarians argue that Nozick's entitlement theory is best defended by an appeal to liberty, rather than equality, while others attempt to defend it by an appeal to mutual advantage, as expressed in a contractarian theory of rational choice. So, in addition to Nozick's arguments, I will examine the idea of a right to liberty (s. 4), and the contractarian idea of mutual advantage (s. 3).

(c) The intuitive argument: the Wilt Chamberlain example

First, then, Nozick's intuitive argument. As we have seen, his 'principle of transfer' says that if we have legitimately acquired something, we have absolute property rights over it. We can freely dispose of it as we see fit, even though the effect of these transfers is likely to be a massively unequal distribution of income and opportunity. Given that people are born with different natural talents, some people will be amply rewarded, while those who lack marketable skills will get few rewards. Due to these undeserved differences in natural talents, some people will flourish while others starve. And these inequalities will then affect the opportunities of children, some of whom are born into privileged circumstances, while others are born into poverty. These inequalities, which Nozick concedes are possible results of unrestrained capitalism, are the source of our intuitive objections to libertarianism.

How then can Nozick hope to provide an intuitive defence of these rights? He asks us to specify an initial distribution which we feel is legitimate, and then argues that we intuitively prefer his principle of transfer to liberal principles of redistribution as an account of what people can legitimately do with their resources. Let me quote his argument at length:

It is not clear how those holding alternative conceptions of distributive justice can reject the [entitlement theory]. For suppose a distribution favored by one of these non-entitlement conceptions is realized. Let us suppose it is your favorite one and let us call this distribution D1; perhaps everyone has an equal share, perhaps shares vary in accordance with some dimension you treasure. Now suppose that Wilt Chamberlain is greatly in demand by basketball teams, being a great gate attraction. . . . He signs the following sort of contract with a team: In each home game, twenty-five cents from the price of each ticket of admission goes to him. . . . The season starts, and people cheerfully attend his team's games; they buy their tickets, each time dropping a separate twenty-five cents of their admission price into a special box with Chamberlain's name on it. They are excited about seeing him play; it is worth the total admission price to them. Let us suppose that in one season one million persons attend his home games, and Wilt Chamberlain winds up with $250,000, a much larger sum than the average income and larger even than anyone else has. Is he entitled to this income? Is this new distribution D2, unjust? If so, why? There is *no* question about whether each of the people was entitled to the control over the resources they held in D1; because that was the distribution (your favorite) that (for the purposes of argument) we assumed was acceptable. Each of these persons *chose* to give twenty-five cents of their money to Chamberlain. They could have spent it on going to the movies, or on candy bars, or on copies of *Dissent* magazine, or of *Monthly Review*. But they all, at least one million of them, converged on giving it to Wilt Chamberlain in exchange for watching him play basketball. If D1 was a just distribution, and people voluntarily moved from it to D2, transferring parts of their shares they were given under D1 (what was it for if not to do something with?), isn't D2 also just? If the people were entitled to dispose of the resources to which they were entitled (under D1), didn't this include their being entitled to give it to, or exchange it with, Wilt Chamberlain? Can anyone else complain on grounds of justice? Each other person already has his legitimate share under D1. Under D1, there is nothing that anyone has that anyone else has a claim of justice against. After someone transfers something to Wilt Chamberlain, third parties *still* have their legitimate shares; *their* shares are not changed. By what process could such a transfer among two persons give rise to a legitimate claim of distributive justice on a portion of what was transferred, by a third party, who had no claim of justice on any holding of the others *before* the transfer? (Nozick 1974: 160–2)

Because D2 seems legitimate, Nozick argues, his principle of transfer is more in line with our intuitions than redistributive principles like Rawls's difference principle.

What are we to make of this argument? It has some initial attraction because it emphasizes that the whole point of having a theory of fair shares is that it allows people to *do* certain things with them. It is perverse to say that it is very important that people get their fair share, but then prevent people from using that share in the way they desire. But does this confront our intuition about undeserved inequalities? Let us assume that I specified an initial distribution D1 that was in line with Rawls's difference principle. Hence each person starts with an equal share of resources, regardless of their natural talents. But at the end of the basketball season, Chamberlain will have earned $250,000, while the handicapped person, who may have no earning power, will have exhausted her resources, and will be on the verge of starvation. Surely our intuitions still tell us that we can tax Chamberlain's income to prevent that starvation. Nozick has persuasively drawn on our intuition about acting on our choices, but his example ignores our intuition about dealing fairly with unequal circumstances.

Indeed when Nozick does confront the question of unequal circumstances, he concedes the intuitive strength of the liberal position. He admits that it seems unfair for people to suffer undeserved inequalities in their access to the benefits of social cooperation. He 'feels the power' of this objection. However,

The major objection to speaking of everyone's having a right *to* various things such as equality of opportunity, life, and so on, and enforcing this right, is that these 'rights' require a substructure of things and materials and actions; and *other* people may have rights and entitlements over these. No one has a right to something whose realization requires certain uses of things and activities that other people have rights and entitlements over. (Nozick 1974: 237–8).

In other words, we can not tax Wilt Chamberlain to pay for the costs of people's handicaps because he has absolute rights over his income. But Nozick concedes that our intuitions do not uniformly favour this account of property rights. On the contrary, he accepts that some of our most powerful intuitions favour compensating undeserved inequalities. The problem with fulfilling that intuitively attractive idea, however, is that people have rights over their income. While Mackie's idea of a general right to 'a fair go' in life is intuitively attractive, 'the particular rights over things fill the space of rights, leaving no room for general rights to be in a certain material condition' (Nozick 1974: 238).

But why should we think that 'particular rights over things fill the space of rights', leaving no room for a right to a fair go in life? As Nozick acknowledges, this is not part of our everyday understanding of property rights, and is not intuitively attractive. However, he argues that this conception of absolute property rights is the unavoidable consequence of a deeper principle that we are strongly committed to: namely, the principle of self-ownership.

2. THE SELF-OWNERSHIP ARGUMENT

Nozick presents the principle of 'self-ownership' as an interpretation of the principle of treating people as 'ends in themselves'. This principle of treating people as ends in themselves, which was Kant's formula for expressing our moral equality, is also invoked by Rawls, and by utilitarians. It is indeed a principle to which we are strongly committed, and if Nozick can show that it yields self-ownership, and that self-ownership yields libertarianism, then he would have provided a strong defence of libertarianism. I will argue, however, that Nozick fails to derive either self-ownership or property-ownership from the idea of treating people as equals, or as ends in themselves.[4]

The heart of Nozick's theory, laid out in the first sentence of his book, is that 'individuals have rights, and there are things which no individual or group can do to them (without violating these rights)' (Nozick 1974: p. ix).

Society must respect these rights because they 'reflect the underlying Kantian principle that individuals are ends and not merely means; they may not be sacrificed or used for the achieving of other ends without their consent' (Nozick 1974: 30–1). This 'Kantian principle' requires a strong theory of rights, for rights affirm our 'separate existences', and so take seriously 'the existence of distinct individuals who are not resources for others' (Nozick 1974: 33). Because we are distinct individuals each with our own distinct claims, there are limits to the sacrifices that can be asked of one person for the benefit of others, limits that are expressed by a theory of rights. This is why utilitarianism, which denies the existence of such limits, is unacceptable to Nozick. Respecting these rights is a necessary aspect of respecting people's claim to be treated as ends in themselves, not means for others. According to Nozick, a libertarian society treats individuals, not as 'instruments or resources', but as 'persons having individual rights with the dignity this constitutes. Treating us with respect by respecting our rights, it allows us, individually or with whom we choose, to choose our life and to realize our ends and our conception of ourselves, insofar as we can, aided by the voluntary cooperation of other individuals possessing the same dignity' (Nozick 1974: 334).

There are important continuities here between Nozick and Rawls, not only in Nozick's appeal to the abstract principle of equality, but also in his more specific arguments against utilitarianism. It was an important part of Rawls's argument that utilitarianism fails to treat people as ends in themselves, since it allows some people to be sacrificed endlessly for the greater benefit of others. So both Rawls and Nozick agree that treating people as equals requires limits on the ways that one person can be used for the benefit of others, or for the benefit of society generally. Individuals have rights which a just society will respect, rights which are not subject to, or the product of, utilitarian calculations.

Rawls and Nozick differ, however, on the question of which rights are most important in treating people as ends in themselves. To oversimplify, we can say that for Rawls, one of the most important rights is a right to a certain share of society's resources. For Nozick, on the other hand, the most important rights are rights over oneself—the rights which constitute 'self-ownership'. The idea of having ownership rights over oneself may seem bizarre, as it suggests that there is a distinct thing, the self, which one owns. But the term 'self' in self-ownership has a 'purely reflexive significance. It signifies that what owns and what is owned are one and the same, namely, the whole person' (Cohen 1986a: 110). The basic idea of self-ownership can be understood by comparison with slavery—to have self-ownership is to have the rights over one's person that a slaveholder has over a chattel slave.

It is not immediately apparent what this difference amounts to. Why can't we accept both positions? After all, the claim that we own ourselves does not yet say anything about owning external resources. And the claim that we have rights to a fair share of society's resources does not seem to preclude the possibility that we own ourselves. Nozick believes, however, that the two are not compatible. According to Nozick, Rawls's demand that goods produced by the talented be used to improve the well-being of the disadvantaged is incompatible with recognizing self-ownership. If I own my self, then I own my talents. And if I own my talents, then I own whatever I produce with my self-owned talents. Just as owning a piece of land means that I own what is produced by the land, so owning my talents means that I own what is produced by my talents. Hence the demand for redistributive taxation from the talented to the disadvantaged violates self-ownership.

The problem is not that Rawls and Dworkin believe that other people can own me or my talents, the way that a slave is owned by another person. On the contrary, as I have tried to show, their hypothetical positions are intended to model the claim that no one is the possession of any other (Ch. 3, pp. 61–4 above). There are many ways in which liberals respect individuals' claims over their own talents. Liberals accept that I am the legitimate possessor of my talents, and that I am free to use them in accordance with my chosen projects. So the liberal denial of self-ownership is a limited one. Liberals say that because it is a matter of brute luck that people have the talents they do, their rights over their talents do not include the right to accrue unequal rewards from the exercise of those talents. Because talents are undeserved, it is not a denial of moral equality for the government to consider people's talents as part of their circumstances, and hence as a possible ground for claims to compensation. People who are born with a natural disadvantage have a legitimate claim on those with advantages, and the naturally advantaged have a moral obligation to the disadvantaged. Thus, in Dworkin's theory, the talented owe insurance premiums that get paid out to the disadvantaged, while in Rawls's theory, the talented only benefit from their talents if it also benefits the disadvantaged.

For Nozick, this constitutes a denial of self-ownership. I cannot be said to own my talents if others have a legitimate claim on the fruits of those talents. Rawls's principles 'institute (partial) ownership by others of people and their actions and labor. These principles involve a shift from the classical liberals' idea of self-ownership to a notion of (partial) property-rights in *other* people' (Nozick 1974: 172). According to Nozick, this liberal egalitarian view fails to treat people as equals, as ends in themselves. Like utilitarianism, it makes some people mere resources for the lives of others, since it makes part of them (i.e. their natural attributes) a resource for all. Since I have rights of self-ownership, the naturally disadvantaged have no legitimate claim over me or my talents. The same is true of all other interventions in free market exchanges. Only unrestricted capitalism can fully recognize my self-ownership.

We can summarize Nozick's argument in two claims:

1. Rawlsian redistribution (or other coercive government interventions in market exchanges) is incompatible with recognizing people as self-owners. Only unrestricted capitalism recognizes self-ownership.
2. recognizing people as self-owners is crucial to treating people as equals.

Nozick's conception of equality begins with rights over one's self, but he believes that these rights have implications for our rights to external resources, implications that conflict with liberal redistribution.

Two major objections to this position have been raised. First, many critics argue that Nozick is mistaken in believing that self-ownership necessarily yields absolute property rights. Self-ownership may be compatible with various regimes of property-ownership, including a Rawlsian one. Secondly, critics argue that the principle of self-ownership is an inadequate account of treating people as equals, even on Nozick's own view of what is important in our lives. If we try to reinterpret the idea of self-ownership to make it a more adequate conception of equality, and select an economic regime on that basis, we will be led towards, rather than away from, the liberal view of justice. I will examine these two objections in turn.

(a) Self-ownership and property-ownership

First, then, how does self-ownership yield property-ownership? Nozick claims that market exchanges involve the exercise of individuals' powers, and since individuals own their powers, they also own whatever comes from the exercise of those powers in the marketplace.

But, as Nozick acknowledges, this is too quick. Market exchanges involve more than the exercise of self-owned powers. They also involve legal rights over *things*, over external goods, and these things are not just created out of nothing by our self-owned powers. If I own some land, I may have improved the land, through the use of my self-owned powers. But I did not create the land, and so my title to the land (and hence my right to use the land in market exchanges) cannot be grounded solely in the exercise of my self-owned powers.

Nozick recognizes that market transactions involve more than the exercise of self-owned powers. In his theory, my title to external goods like land comes from the fact that others have transferred the title to me, in accordance with the principle of transfer. This assumes, of course, that the earlier owner had legitimate title. If someone sells me some land, my title to the land is only as good as her title, and her title was only as good as the one before her, and so on. But if the validity of my property rights depends on the validity of previous property rights, then determining the validity of my title over external goods requires going back down the chain of transfers to the beginning. But what is the beginning? Is it the point where someone created the land with their self-owned powers? No, for no one created the land. It existed before human beings existed.

The beginning of the series of transfers is not when the land was created, but rather when it was first appropriated by an individual as her private property. On Nozick's theory, we must go down the chain of transfers to see if the initial acquisition was legitimate. And nothing in the fact, if it is a fact, that we own our talents ensures that anyone can legitimately appropriate for themselves something they did not create with their talents. If the first person who took it did so illegitimately, then she has no legitimate title over it, and hence no legitimate right to transfer it to someone else, who would then have no legitimate right to transfer it to me. Hence, if I am to be entitled to all of the rewards which accrue to me from market exchanges, as Nozick believes I am, I must be the legitimate owner not only of my powers, but also of initially unowned external resources.

This question about the initial acquisition of external resources is prior to any question about legitimate transfer. If there was no legitimate initial acquisition, then there can be no legitimate transfer, on Nozick's theory. So Nozick owes us an account of how external resources come to be initially acquired by one individual for their own use. Nozick is aware that he needs such an account. There are times when he says that 'things come into the world attached to people, who have entitlements over them' (Nozick 1974: 160). But he realizes that everything which is owned today includes an element which did not come into the world as private property, legally or morally. Everything that is now owned has some element of nature in it. How then did these natural resources, which were not initially owned by anyone, come to be part of someone's private property?

(i) Initial acquisition

The historical answer is often that natural resources came to be someone's property by force. This is a rather embarrassing fact for those who hope Nozick's theory will defend existing inequalities. Either the use of force made the initial acquisition illegitimate, in which case current title is illegitimate, and there is no moral reason why government should not confiscate the wealth and redistribute it. Or the initial use of force did not necessarily render the acquisition illegitimate, in which case using force to take property away from its current owners and redistribute is also not necessarily illegitimate. Either way, the fact that initial acquisition often involved force means that there is no moral objection within Nozick's framework to redistributing existing wealth (Cohen 1988: 253–4).[5]

Nozick's response to this problem is the first one. The use of force makes acquisition illegitimate, so current title is illegitimate (Nozick 1974: 230–1). Hence those who currently possess scarce resources have no right to deprive others of access to them—e.g. capitalists are not entitled to deprive workers of access to the products or profits of the existing means of production. Ideally, the effects of the illegitimate acquisition should be rectified, and the resources restored to their rightful owner. However, it is often impossible to know who the rightful owners are—we do not know from whom the resources were illegitimately taken. Nozick suggests that we could rectify the illegitimacy of existing title by a one-time general redistribution of resources in accordance with Rawls's difference principle. Only after this redistribution will the libertarian principle of transfer hold. Where we do know the rightful owners, however, we should restore the resources to them. For example, David Lyons argues that Nozick's view supports returning much of New England to the American Indians, whose initial title was unjustly taken away (Lyons 1981). Others have argued that Nozick's principle of rectification entails reparations for African-Americans, and that these reparations are best paid in the form of affirmative action programmes (Valls 1999).

This rejection of the legitimacy of current title is not a curiosity of Nozick's presentation that can be detached from the rest of his theory. If one really believes in Nozick's entitlement theory, then current title is only as legitimate as previous titles. If previous title was legitimate, then any new distribution which results from market exchanges is just. That is what libertarians propose as their theory of justice. But the corollary of that theory is that if previous title was illegitimate, so is the new distribution. The fact that the new distribution arose from market transactions is irrelevant, since no one had any right to transfer those resources through market exchanges. This, as much as the first case, is an essential part of Nozick's theory. They are two sides of the same coin.

Many defenders of property rights would like to avoid looking too deeply into the historical origins of their property. As Blackstone noted, 'there are very few that will give themselves the trouble to consider the origin and foundation of this [property] right. Pleased as we are with the possession, we seem afraid to look back to the means by which it was acquired, as if fearful of some defect in our title.'[6] This sort of amnesia about history has much to say for it—trying to rectify past injustices in appropriation opens up a Pandora's Box (Waldron 1992). Common sense suggests that what really matters is whether the current distribution promotes people's freedom and fulfils their needs, and that we should just ignore any 'original sin' involved in the historic appropriation of resources (Sanders 1987). What matters, common sense suggests, is the end result, not the historic origins. But Nozick cannot invoke this common-sense reason for setting aside history, for his entire theory is premised on the idea that justice is a matter of 'history' not 'end states'. He rejects liberal and socialist theories precisely because they define justice in terms of 'end states' like the satisfaction of needs, the promotion of utility, or the rewarding of desert, whereas he insists there is no standard for assessing justice other than that of history. This indeed is why he calls his theory a 'historical' conception of justice (Nozick 1974: 153–4).

Because most initial acquisition was in fact illegitimate, Nozick's theory cannot protect existing holdings from redistribution. But we still need to know how acquisition could have arisen legitimately. If we cannot answer that question, then we should not only postpone the implementation of Nozick's principle of transfer until historical titles are ascertained or rectified, we should reject it entirely. If there is no way that people can appropriate unowned resources for themselves without denying other people's claim to equal consideration, then Nozick's right of transfer never gets off the ground.

What sort of initial acquisition of absolute rights over unowned resources is consistent with the idea of treating people as equals? This is an old problem for libertarians. Nozick draws on John Locke's answer to it. In seventeenth-century England there was a movement towards the 'enclosure' (private appropriation) of land which had previously been held in common for general use. This land ('the commons') had been available to all for the grazing of animals, or for gathering wood, etc. As a result of this private appropriation, some people became wealthy while others lost their access to resources, and so lost their ability to sustain themselves. Locke wished to defend this process, and so needed to give an account of how people come, in a morally legitimate way, to have full ownership rights over the initially unowned world.

Locke's answer, or at any rate one of his answers, was that we are entitled to appropriate bits of the external world if we leave 'enough and as good' for others. An act of appropriation that meets this criterion is consistent with the equality of other individuals since they are not disadvantaged by that appropriation.[7]

Locke realized that most acts of appropriation do not leave enough and as good of the object being appropriated. Those who enclosed the land in seventeenth-century England clearly did not leave enough and as good land for others. But Locke says that appropriation is acceptable if it leaves people as well or better off *overall*. And he believed that enclosing the commons would indeed make everyone better off overall, even those left without any land available to them.

Why would this be? Part of the answer lies in the 'tragedy of the commons'. When land is held in common for general use, there is little incentive for any particular person to invest their time and effort in developing the land to improve its productivity. Since the land is common, there is no way for such an individual to ensure that she will benefit from her investment. Why invest my labour growing corn on the commons when anyone else has the right to come along and pick the corn? It is only rational to invest in improving the land if I can exclude those free-riders who would reap the rewards without contributing to the labour. But this requires taking the land out of the commons, and assigning someone control over it including the right to exclude others from accessing or benefiting from it—i.e. it requires giving someone property rights over the land.

Indeed, the situation is even worse than that. Not only is it irrational for individuals to invest in improving land in the commons, but it may be rational to *deplete* the resources, once the population using the commons exceeds its carrying capacity. Consider overfishing in the oceans, which remain a kind of 'commons'. Fishing trawlers from various countries are taking so many fish from the ocean, or taking them so young (before they reproduce), that several species are endangered. This may seem irrational—people involved in the fishery are undermining their own living, and that of their children. But from the point of view of each fishing captain, or even each country, it is perfectly rational. If Canadian boats do not take the fish, the Spanish or Icelandic boats will. There is no point being environmentally responsible when no one else is: you would simply be leaving the resources in the commons unprotected for other less scrupulous people to take them. So we all rush in to be the first to take the fish, and to take them ever younger. The result is that the commons are not only left undeveloped, but in fact tend towards ruin. They are overfished, overharvested, overexploited.

So enclosing the commons is needed to avoid ruin, and to promote productive investments in the land. And if we do allow enclosure, we can safely predict that even those who are left without land will actually be better off than before. They lose the right to access the commons, but they did not in fact get much benefit from this. At best, they could only take small amounts of (undeveloped) resources from the (rapidly depleting) commons. In return, however, they are likely to be offered a job by the new landowner working on the enclosed land, and can use their wages to buy a new range of goods that were not produced before, because no one had the incentive to invest in their production before. Before they had to scramble to get a few apples from the (untended) apple trees on the commons before everyone else took them; now there are lots of apples and other foods produced on cultivated land available for a fraction of their wages. The propertyless have lost access to land, but have gained access to more of the goods that they used to get from that land.

The moral of the story is that, given the tragedy of the commons, enclosing the land is likely to make everyone, even the propertyless, better off overall than before. And this, Nozick argues, is the proper test of a legitimate appropriation: that it does not worsen anyone's overall condition. Nozick calls this the 'Lockean proviso', and he adopts it as his test of legitimate acquisition: 'a process normally giving rise to a permanent bequeathable property right in a previously unowned thing will not do so if the position of others no longer at liberty to use the thing is thereby worsened' (Nozick 1974: 178).[8] Indeed,

David Schmidtz argues that it is not only *permissible* for people to enclose the commons, but is in fact morally *obligatory*. To leave resources in the commons, knowing that they will tend to be depleted, is itself to fail to ensure that 'enough and as good' is left for others. The only way to ensure that we leave enough and as good for our children is to prevent tragedies of the commons by allocating property rights over resources (Schmidtz 1990a).

So far, so good. Libertarians make a powerful case that there must be some way for particular people, or groups of people, to acquire control over particular bits of the natural world, and exclude others from it. And it seems plausible that the right test for the legitimacy of such appropriations is whether the condition of others is worsened. This enforces the principle of equal consideration of people's interests. Acquisition does not violate equal consideration if it does not worsen anyone's situation.

But what exactly does it mean to make someone worse off? Worse off in what ways, compared to what alternative? How we answer these questions will determine which sorts of appropriation pass the Lockean proviso. Nozick's answer is that appropriation of a particular object is legitimate if its withdrawal from general use does not make people worse off *in material terms* than they had been when it was *in general use*. For example, consider Amy and Ben, who both live off land which is initially under general use. Amy now appropriates so much of the land that Ben cannot live off the remaining land. That might seem to make Ben worse off. But Amy offers Ben a wage to work on her land which exceeds what he was originally producing on his own. Amy also gets more resources than she initially produced, due to the increased productivity arising from a division of labour, and the increase in her share is larger than the increase in his share. Ben must accept this, since there is not enough land left for him to live as he used to. He needs access to the land that she appropriated, and she is able to dictate the terms of that access, so that he gets less than half of the benefits of the division of labour. Amy's act of appropriation satisfies Nozick's proviso, since the situation after her appropriation is better than general use in terms of material resources, for both Amy and Ben. (Actually, it needn't be *better* for Ben, so long as it is not worse.)

In this way, the unowned world comes to be appropriated, with full property rights, by self-owning people. Nozick believes that the proviso is easily met, and so most of the world will quickly come to be privately appropriated. Hence, self-ownership yields absolute ownership of the external world. Since initial appropriation includes the right of transfer, we will soon have a fully developed market for productive resources (i.e. the land). And since this appropriation excludes some people from access to those productive resources, we will soon have a fully developed market in labour as well. And since people will then legitimately own both the powers and the property which are involved in market exchange, they will be legitimately entitled to all the rewards which accrue from those exchanges. And since people will be entitled to all their market rewards, government redistribution to help the disadvantaged would be a violation of people's rights. It would be using some people as a resource for others.

(ii) The Lockean proviso

Has Nozick given us an acceptable account of fair initial acquisition? We can summarize it this way (cf. Cohen 1986a).

1. People own themselves.
2. The world is initially unowned.
3. You can acquire absolute rights over a disproportionate share of the world, if you do not worsen the condition of others.
4. It is relatively easy to acquire absolute rights over a disproportionate share of the world.

Therefore:

5. Once people have appropriated private property, a free market in capital and labour is morally required.

I will concentrate on Nozick's interpretation of (3), his account of what it is to worsen the conditions of others. His account has two relevant features: (a) it defines 'worse off' in terms of material welfare; (b) it defines pre-appropriation common usage as the standard of comparison. Critics have argued that both of these features are inadequate, and that any plausible revised test of initial acquisition will yield only limited property rights.

Material Welfare. The reason that Nozick emphasizes self-ownership, as we have seen, is that we are separate individuals, each with our own life to live (p. 108 above). Self-ownership protects our ability to pursue our own goals, our 'conceptions of ourselves', since it allows us to resist attempts by others to use us merely as means to their ends. One would expect Nozick's account of what it is for an act of appropriation to worsen the condition of others similarly to emphasize people's ability to act on their conception of themselves, and to object to any appropriation that puts someone in an unnecessary and undesirable position of subordination and dependence on the will of others.

But notice that the fact that Ben is now subject to Amy's decisions is not considered by Nozick in assessing the fairness of the appropriation. In fact, Amy's appropriation deprives Ben of two important freedoms: (a) he has no say over the status of the land he had been utilizing—Amy unilaterally appropriates it without asking or receiving Ben's consent; (b) Ben has no say over how his labour will be expended. He must accept Amy's conditions of employment, since he will die otherwise, and so he must relinquish control over how he spends much of his time. Before the appropriation, he may have had a conception of himself as a shepherd living in harmony with nature. Now he must abandon those pursuits, and instead obey Amy's commands, which might involve activities that exploit nature. Given these effects, Ben may be made worse off by Amy's appropriating the land, even though it leads to a small increase in his material income.

Shouldn't Nozick consider these effects, on his own account of why self-ownership is important? He says that the freedom to lead our lives in accordance with our own conception of the good is the ultimate value, so important that it cannot be sacrificed for other social ideals (e.g. equality of opportunity). He claims that a concern for people's freedom to lead their own lives underlies his theory of unrestricted property rights. But his justification of the initial appropriation of property treats Ben's autonomy as irrelevant.

It is interesting that although Nozick claims that Ben is not made worse off by the appropriation, he does not require that Ben *consent* to the appropriation. If consent were required, Ben might well refuse. If Ben is right to refuse, since it really would make him worse off according to his own (non-materialistic) conception of the good, then the appropriation should not be allowed. Perhaps Ben would be mistaken in refusing, since the gain in material welfare outweighs the loss of autonomy. In that case, we might allow Amy's appropriation as an act of paternalism. But Nozick claims to be against such paternalism. For example, he is against mandatory health insurance or pension plans that are instituted for people's own benefit. But the private appropriation of common resources can contradict a person's will as much as levying a tax on him. If we exclude paternalism, and emphasize autonomy, as Nozick himself does elsewhere in his theory, then presumably Ben should have a veto over appropriations that exclude him from the commons. Given the tragedy of the commons, Ben is almost certainly going to accept some scheme for enclosing the commons, but he would be able to ensure that the agreement regarding enclosure enables him to continue to pursue his conception of himself.[9]

Arbitrary Narrowing of the Options. Nozick's proviso says that an act of appropriation must not make others worse off than they were when the land was in common use. But this ignores many relevant alternatives. Let's say that Ben, worried about the possibility of Amy unilaterally appropriating the land, decides to appropriate it for himself, and then offers Amy a wage to work on what is now his land, keeping to himself the bulk of the benefits of the increased productivity. This too passes Nozick's test. Nozick considers it irrelevant who does the appropriating, and who gets the profits, so long as the non-appropriator is not worsened by it. Nozick is, in effect, accepting a first-come, first-served doctrine of appropriation. But why should we accept this as a fair procedure for appropriation, rather than, for example, a system which equalizes chances for appropriation? Should the most important value—our ability to lead our own lives—be dependent on the arbitrariness of a first-come, first-served doctrine?

Consider another alternative. This time Ben, who is a better organizer of labour, appropriates the land, and organizes an even greater increase in productivity, allowing both to get more than they got when Amy appropriated the land. They are both worse off when Amy appropriates than they would be when Ben appropriates. Yet Nozick allows Amy to appropriate, and denies that Ben is thereby made worse off, since he does better under Amy's appropriation than he did under common use of the land, which is the only alternative Nozick considers relevant.

Finally, what if Amy and Ben appropriate the land collectively, exercising ownership rights jointly, and dividing the labour consensually? If appropriation is going to take place amongst a community of self-owners, then why should Ben not have the option of collective ownership, rather than having Amy unilaterally deprive him of his ability to pursue his own conception of the good?

According to Nozick's proviso, all these alternatives are irrelevant. It does not matter to the legitimacy of an appropriation that some other appropriation is fairer or more efficient, or better serves people's material interests or their autonomy. Yet each of these alternatives spares somebody a harm that will occur under Nozick's scheme. Why are these harms not relevant in determining whether someone is made worse off by initial appropriations?

These problems with Nozick's proviso are made clearer if we move to the level of capitalism as an ongoing system. The acts of initial appropriation which Nozick allows will quickly lead to a situation in which there are no more accessible useful unowned things. Those who were able to appropriate may have vast wealth, while others are entirely without property. These differences will be passed on to the next generation, some of whom will be forced to work at an early age, while others have all the privileges in life. This is acceptable to Nozick, so long as the system of appropriation and transfer continues to meet the Lockean proviso—i.e. capitalism as an ongoing system is just if no one is worse off than they would have been in the commons, prior to the privatization of the external world.

Nozick assures us capitalism passes this test of not worsening people compared to their fate in the commons (Nozick 1974: 177). Of course, given the tragedy of the commons, virtually any system of property-ownership would pass this test, including state ownership, worker self-ownership, kibbutz-like communal ownership. Or consider various forms of limited rather than absolute individual property rights, such as use rights rather than ownership rights, or limited ownership rights that do not include the right to bequeath property. All of these property regimes grant some set of people sufficient control over resources to ensure that free-riders are excluded, and hence provide incentives to develop resources and to avoid depleting them. Virtually every human society that has gone beyond the hunter-gatherer stage has developed some form of property-system that avoids the tragedy of the commons—humans would have not survived otherwise—but few of them (if any) have been purely capitalist. So the mere fact that capitalism does better than the commons is not saying much, and is not a reason to prefer it over any other system for establishing property rights.[10]

Notice, moreover, that capitalism passes that test even though the property-less are dependent for their survival on those with property wanting to buy their labour, and even though some people may starve because no one does want to buy their labour. This is acceptable to Nozick since untalented people would have starved anyway had the land remained unowned. The propertyless lack a just grievance because 'those who do manage to sell their labour power will get at least as much and probably more in exchange for it than they could have hoped to get by applying it in a rude state of nature; and those proletarians whose labour power is not worth buying, although they will therefore, in Nozick's non-welfare state, die (in the absence of charity), would have died in a state of nature anyway' (Cohen 1986b: 85 n. 11).

This is a very weak requirement. It is odd to say that a person who starves to death is not made worse off by Nozick's system of appropriation when there are other systems in which that person would not have died. A more plausible test of legitimate appropriation would consider all the relevant alternatives, keeping in mind people's interest in both material goods and autonomy. Can we modify the Lockean proviso to include these considerations, while retaining its intuitive point that the test of appropriation is whether it worsens someone's condition? We might say that a system of appropriation worsens someone's condition if there is another possible scheme in which they would do better. Unfortunately, every system of property allocation will fail that test. The untalented person would be worse off in Nozick's pure capitalism than he would be under Rawls's difference principle; the talented person would be worse off under Rawls's regime than under Nozick's. In any given system, there will be someone who would do better in another system. That test is unreasonable anyway, for no one has a legitimate claim that the world be maximally adapted to suit their preferences. The fact that there is a possible arrangement in which I would be better off does not show that the existing system has harmed me in any morally significant sense. We want to know whether a system of appropriation makes people worse off, not compared to a world which is maximally adapted to their particular interests, but compared to a world in which their interests are fairly attended to.

It is an insufficient test of justice that people benefit relative to the initial state of common holdings. But nor can people demand that they have whatever system benefits them the most. The proviso requires a middle ground. It is difficult to say what that middle ground is, or how different it would be from the principles of Rawls and Dworkin. John Arthur argues that the appropriate test is an egalitarian one—appropriation worsens someone's condition if, as a result, they get less than an equal share of the value of the world's natural resources. This is the only decision that makes sense, he argues, 'in light of the fact that [each person] is as entitled to the resources as anyone else. He wasn't born deserving a smaller share of the earth's wealth, nor is anybody else naturally entitled to a larger than average share' (Arthur 1987: 344; cf. Steiner 1977: 49). Cohen argues that Rawls's difference principle might provide a fair standard of legitimate appropriation (Cohen 1986a: 133–4). Van Parijs argues that appropriators should be required to fund a basic income scheme as a condition of legitimate appropriation, as compensation for those who are left propertyless (Van Parijs 1992: 9–11). There is in fact a voluminous literature offering various models of fair initial acquisition, each of which produces somewhat different results. But virtually no one thinks that a plausible test of fair acquisition would generate Nozick's view that people can appropriate unrestricted property rights over unequal amounts of resources.[11] If the proviso recognizes the full range of interests and alternatives that self-owners have, then it will probably not generate unrestricted rights over substantially unequal amounts of resources. Some people will be made worse off in important ways, compared to morally relevant alternatives, by a system which allows people to appropriate unequal amounts of the external world. And if, as Nozick himself says, 'each owner's title to his holding includes the historical shadow of the Lockean proviso on appropriation' (Nozick 1974: 180), then it is quite possible that 'the shadow thrown by [the proviso] so entirely envelops such titles as to render them indiscernible'—i.e. any title that self-owning people acquire over unequal resources will be heavily qualified by the claims of the propertyless (Steiner 1977: 48).

Initial Ownership of the World. There is another problem with Nozick's proviso that blocks the move from self-ownership to unrestricted capitalism. Recall my summary of Nozick's argument:

1. People own themselves.
2. The world is initially unowned.
3. You can acquire absolute rights over a disproportionate share of the world, if you do not worsen the conditions of others.
4. It is relatively easy to acquire absolute rights over a disproportionate share of the world.

Therefore:

5. Once private property has been appropriated, a free market in capital and labour is morally required.

We have just examined Nozick's interpretation of (3), which seems too weak, so that (4) is false. But there is a second problem. Why accept (2), the claim that the world is initially unowned, and hence up for grabs? Why not suppose that the world is jointly owned, such that each person has an equal veto over the disposal of the land (Exdell 1977: 146–9; Cohen 1986b: 80–7)? Nozick never considers this option, but others, including some libertarians, claim that it is the most defensible account of world-ownership (Locke himself believed that the world initially belonged to everyone, not no one, for God 'hath given to men the world in common'—cf. Christman 1986b: 159–64).

What would happen if the world were jointly owned, and hence not subject to unilateral privatization? There are a variety of possible outcomes, but in general they will negate the inegalitarian implications of self-ownership. For example, the disadvantaged might be able to use their veto to bargain for a distributive scheme like Rawls's difference principle. We might end up in this way with a Rawlsian distribution, not because we deny self-ownership (such that the disadvantaged have a direct claim on the advantaged), but because we are joint owners of the external world (such that the untalented can veto uses of the land that benefit the talented without also benefiting them). A similar result might also arise if we view the external world as neither up for grabs, nor jointly owned, but as divided equally amongst all the members of the human community (Cohen 1986b: 87–90).

All of these accounts of the moral status of the external world are compatible with the principle of self-ownership, since self-ownership says nothing about what kind of ownership we have over external resources. And indeed various libertarians have endorsed these other options. There is a long tradition of 'left-libertarianism', going back to Thomas Paine, Henry George, and Léon Walras in the eighteenth and nineteenth centuries, and defended today by Hillel Steiner and Peter Vallentyne, which starts from the premiss of self-ownership, but recognizes the insurmountable difficulties in justifying unequal appropriation of the initially unowned world, and so accepts nationalization or equalization of natural resources, or compensation for those left propertyless.[12] Each of these options would have to be evaluated in terms of the underlying values that Nozick appeals to. Nozick does not undertake this sort of evaluation, but it seems clear that absolute property rights over unequal bits of the world are only secured if we invoke weak and arbitrary premisses about appropriation and the status of the external world.

(b) Self-ownership and equality

I have tried to show that the principle of self-ownership does not by itself generate a moral defence of capitalism, since a capitalist requires not only ownership of her self, but also ownership of resources. Nozick believes that self-ownership inevitably leads to unrestricted property rights, but we are in fact confronted by a variety of economic regimes that are compatible with self-ownership, depending on our theory of legitimate appropriation, and our assumptions about the status of the external world.[13] Nozick believes that self-ownership requires that people be entitled to all the rewards of their market exchanges, but different regimes vary in the extent to which they allow self-owning individuals to retain their market rewards. Some will allow the naturally talented to parlay their talents into unequal ownership of the external world (although not necessarily to the extent allowed by Nozick), others will redistribute market income so as to ensure that the naturally disadvantaged have equal access to resources (as in Rawls or Dworkin). Self-ownership is compatible with all these options.

Is there any reason for self-owners to prefer libertarian regimes over liberal egalitarian ones? I can think of three possible arguments that draw on aspects of, but also go beyond, the idea of self-ownership, since that idea by itself is insufficient to identify a just distribution. One argument concerns consent, the second concerns the idea of self-determination, the third concerns dignity.

Nozick might say that the choice of economic regime should be decided, if possible, by the consent of self-owning people. And, he might claim, self-owning people would all choose a libertarian regime, were it up to them. But that is dubious. As we have seen, Nozick's own scheme of acquisition depended on Ben not having to give his consent to Amy's appropriation. Different people would do best in different economic regimes, and so would consent to different regimes. One could try to ensure unanimous consent by seeking agreement behind a veil of ignorance, as Rawls does. But as we have seen, that leads to liberal, not libertarian, results.

Secondly, Nozick might claim that the assumptions which lead to liberal results, while formally compatible with self-ownership, in fact undermine the value of self-ownership. For example, the assumption that the world is jointly owned, or that it should be collectively appropriated, would nullify the value of self-ownership. For how can I be said to own myself if I may do nothing without the permission of others? In a world of joint ownership, don't Amy and Ben jointly own not only the world but also *in effect* each other? Amy and Ben may have legal rights over themselves (unlike the chattel slave), but they lack independent access to resources. Their legal rights of self-ownership are therefore purely formal, since they require each other's permission whenever they wish to use resources in the pursuit of their goals. We should select a regime that contains not only formal self-ownership, but also a more substantive self-ownership that provides one with effective control over one's life.

Following Charles Fried, I will use the term 'self-determination' to describe this more substantive conception of self-ownership. He says that it requires a 'determinate domain ... free of the claims of others' (Fried 1983: 55).

Similarly, Jon Elster says that substantive self-ownership involves 'the right to choose which of one's abilities to develop' (Elster 1986: 101). Common to both these interpretations of substantive self-ownership is the idea that in the central areas of one's life, in our most important projects, we should be free to act on our own conceptions of the good. Both argue that respecting self-determination is an important part of treating people as ends not means, as distinct individuals each with their own life to lead.

I think that Nozick appeals to both the formal and substantive conceptions of self-ownership. He explictly defends the formal conception, dealing with legal rights over one's physical being. But at least part of Nozick's defence of formal self-ownership is that it promotes substantive self-ownership—it promotes our ability to act effectively on our conception of ourselves. Indeed, he says it is precisely this capacity for substantive self-ownership—the 'ability to form a picture of one's whole life . . . and to act in terms of some overall conception of the life one wishes to lead'—which is the fundamental basis of his theory of rights. It is this ability to form and pursue a conception of the good which gives life meaning, and it is because we can lead meaningful lives that we should be treated as ends in ourselves (Nozick 1974: 51).

So it seems plausible that Nozick would endorse selecting the regime which best promotes substantive self-ownership (within the constraints imposed by formal self-ownership). While different economic regimes are compatible with formal self-ownership, he might argue that liberal regimes render self-ownership purely formal, whereas the more libertarian regimes ensure substantive self-ownership, since libertarian property rights leave people free to act without others' permission.

The difficulty, of course, is that in a libertarian regime not everyone can parlay their formal self-ownership into substantive self-determination. Libertarians cannot guarantee each person substantive control over their lives, and indeed, Nozick explicitly says that formal self-ownership is all that people can legitimately claim. He says that the worker who lacks any property, and who must sell her labour on adverse terms to the capitalist, has 'full' self-ownership (Nozick 1974: 262–4). She has full self-ownership even though, Nozick concedes, she may be forced to agree to whatever terms the capitalist is offering her in order to survive. The resulting 'agreement' might well, as in Victorian England, be essentially equivalent to the enslavement of the worker. The fact that the worker has formal rights of self-ownership means that she cannot be the legal possession of another person (unlike the chattel slave), but economic necessity may force her to agree to terms which are almost as adverse.

Lack of property can be just as oppressive as lack of legal rights. As Mill put it:

No longer enslaved or made dependent by force of law, the great majority are so by force of poverty; they are chained to a place, to an occupation, and to conformity with the will of an employer, and debarred by the accident of birth both from the enjoyments, and from the mental and moral advantages, which others inherit without exertion and independently of desert. That this is an evil equal to almost any of those against which mankind have hitherto struggled, the poor are not wrong in believing. (Mill 1967: 710)

The 'full' self-ownership of the propertyless worker is no more substantive than the self-ownership of Amy or Ben in a world of collective ownership. Amy has no access to productive resources without Ben's permission, but the same is true of the worker who is dependent on the agreement of the capitalist. In fact, people in a situation of collective ownership have more real control over their lives, since Amy and Ben must strike a deal in order to use their resources, whereas a capitalist need not strike an agreement with any particular worker in order to survive, especially if the worker is untalented, or if there is a large pool of unemployed.

Libertarianism not only restricts the self-determination of the propertyless worker, it makes her a resource for others. Those who enter the market after others have appropriated all the available property are 'limited to gifts and jobs others are willing to bestow on them', and so 'if they are compelled to cooperate in the scheme of holdings, they are forced to benefit others. This forced compliance with the property system constitutes a form of exploitation and is inconsistent with the most basic of [Nozick's] root ideas, rendering as it does the latecomers mere resources for others' (Bogart 1985: 833–4).

What regime best promotes substantive self-ownership? Self-determination requires resources as well as rights over one's physical being. We are only able to pursue our most important projects, free from the demands of others, if we are not forced by economic necessity to accept whatever conditions others impose on us in return for access to needed resources. Since meaningful self-determination requires both resources and liberties, and since each of us has a separate existence, each person should have an equal claim to these resources and liberties.

But, if so, then the concern for self-determination leads us towards liberal regimes, not libertarian ones. Libertarians claim that liberal welfare programmes, by limiting property rights, unduly limit people's self-determination. Hence the removal of welfare redistribution programmes (Nozick), or their limitation to an absolute minimum (Fried), would be an improvement in terms of self-determination. But while redistributive programmes do restrict the self-determination of the well-off to a limited degree, they also give real control over their lives to people who previously lacked it. Liberal redistribution doesn't sacrifice self-determination for some other goal. Rather, it aims at a fairer distribution of the means required for self-determination. Libertarianism, by contrast, allows undeserved inequalities in that distribution—its concern with self-determination does not extend to ensuring the fair distribution of the conditions required for self-determination.

A liberal regime which taxes the unequal rewards of undeserved talents does limit some people's self-determination. But is this a serious or unacceptable limitation? Being free to choose one's own career is crucial to self-determination, but being subject to taxation on the rewards which accrue from undeserved natural talents does not seriously impair one's self-determination. Even if one's income is taxed in accordance with Rawlsian principles, one still has a fair share of resources and liberties with which to control the essential features of one's life. Taxing income from the exercise of natural talents does not unfairly disadvantage anyone in their substantive self-ownership—i.e. in their ability to act according to their conception of themselves.[14]

Finally, Nozick might argue that welfare redistribution denies people's dignity, and this dignity is crucial to treating people as equals (e.g. Nozick 1974: 334). Indeed Nozick often writes as if the idea that other people have claims on the fruits of my talents is an assault on my dignity. But why is taxation an assault on my dignity? Nozick often ties dignity to self-determination, but if so, then one could argue that it is liberal regimes, not libertarian ones, which best promote each person's dignity, since they ensure that everyone has the capacity for self-determination. In any event, dignity is predicated on, or a by-product of, other moral beliefs. We only feel something to be an attack on our dignity if we are already convinced that it is wrong. Redistribution will feel like an assault on dignity only if we believe it is morally wrong. If we believe instead that redistribution is a required part of treating people as equals, then it will serve to promote, rather than attack, people's sense of equal dignity.

So there are serious difficulties confronting any attempt to defend libertarianism in terms of self-ownership, consent, self-determination, or dignity. All of these are either indeterminate or support liberal egalitarianism. Self-ownership does not preclude redistributive taxation, since many different economic regimes are formally compatible with self-ownership. And if we look beyond formal self-ownership to those regimes which best ensure substantive self-ownership, then Nozick has not given us any reason to prefer libertarian inequalities to liberal equality.

But why should we be concerned with formal self-ownership at all? In the above argument, I used the idea of substantive self-ownership as a test for deciding between those regimes that are compatible with formal self-ownership. But if we contrast these two conceptions, surely substantive self-determination is more fundamental. We do not endorse self-determination because it promotes formal self-ownership. Rather, we will endorse formal self-ownership in so far as it promotes self-determination. Indeed, as I mentioned earlier, Nozick himself sometimes treats the substantive conception as the more fundamental. So why not just start with self-determination as our preferred conception of treating people as equals? Rather than ask which of the regimes that are compatible with formal self-ownership best promotes self-determination, why not just ask which regime best promotes self-determination? It may be that the best regime, assessed in terms of self-determination, not only goes beyond formal self-ownership, but also limits it. In that case, formal self-ownership should give way to the substantive self-determination that really matters to us (Cohen 1986b: 86; Kernohan 1990).

This seems so obviously preferable that an explanation is needed for Nozick's emphasis on formal self-ownership. Nozick, like the classical liberals, wants to articulate a conception of equality which denies that anyone is by nature or by right subordinate to another. No one is merely a resource for others, the way a slave is the resource of his owner. If slavery is the paradigm case of a denial of equality, it might seem that the best way to affirm equality is to give each person the legal rights over himself that slave-owners have over their slave; the best way to prevent the enslavement of one person to another is to give each person ownership over himself. Unfortunately, the fact that I have legal rights of self-ownership does not mean that I have the ability to avoid what is in effect enslavement to another. Even if the capitalist does not have the same legal rights over me that slave-owners had over slaves, I may not have any real ability to decide on the nature and terms of my living. The best way to prevent the sort of denial of equality that occurs in slavery is not to reverse the legal rights involved, but rather to equalize the substantive control each person possesses, in the form of equal liberties and resources.

Indeed, Susan Okin argues that Nozick's principle of self-ownership actually leads back to a form of 'matriarchal slavery'. Nozick talks about people's claim to the products of their labour, but he ignores the fact that people are themselves the product of someone else's labour—namely, their mother's. Why then does the mother not own her baby? As Okin notes, a woman who buys or is given sperm, and who buys or is given all the food involved in sustaining the fetus, meets all of Nozick's criteria for legitimate ownership of the resulting product. If we own whatever we produce with our talents, using only goods that were freely transferred to us, then mothers would seem to own their children (or perhaps co-own them with the father, if he made co-ownership a condition for the sale or gift of the sperm). She concludes that Nozick's entire theory rests on the implicit exclusion of women, and on the assumption that the work of bearing and raising children operates according to some other set of principles that he ignores (Okin 1989b: ch. 4). To avoid this problem, the principle of self-ownership will need serious reformulation. (For one attempt, see Jeske 1996.)

Nozick's emphasis on the idea of formal self-ownership may also be due to the undifferentiated nature of that concept. The idea of self-ownership mis-leadingly suggests that we either have or lack self-ownership, as if the various rights and powers which constitute self-ownership must be accepted or rejected as a package. If that was indeed our choice, then it would make sense to emphasize self-ownership. But in reality there is a range of options, involving different kinds of control over one's choices and one's circum-stances. The idea of self-ownership tends to prevent people from considering all the relevant options, as Nozick's own discussion reveals. The claim that undifferentiated self-ownership is crucial to treating each person as an end in herself is only plausible if it is being compared with the single option of the undifferentiated denial of self-ownership.

We need to distinguish different elements involved in controlling one's self, and see how they relate to the different elements involved in controlling external resources. We should consider each of these rights and powers on its own terms, to see in what ways it promotes each person's essential interests. Which combination of rights and resources contributes to each person's ability to act on their goals and projects, their conception of themselves? The best mix will involve more than formal self-ownership (e.g. access to resources), but it may also involve less, for it may be worth giving up some formal self-ownership for the sake of substantive self-determination.

To summarize this section, I have argued that Rawlsian redistribution is compatible with formal self-ownership, and that it does a better job than libertarianism in fairly promoting substantive self-ownership. I have also argued that formal self-ownership is a red herring, for substantive self-determination is the more fundamental value. But there is a deeper problem with Nozick's self-ownership argument. Nozick has not adequately con-fronted Rawls's claim that people do not have a legitimate claim to the rewards of the exercise of their undeserved talents. I've tried to show that we can get a Rawlsian distributive scheme even without denying self-ownership, since redistribution could arise from the requirements of a fair theory of access to external resources. But I still think that Rawls's denial of self-ownership was perfectly sound. I think that we can treat people's talents as part of their circumstances, and hence as possible grounds, in and of them-selves, for compensation. People have rights to the possession and exercise of their talents, but the disadvantaged may also have rights to some compensa-tion for their disadvantage. It is wrong for people to suffer from undeserved inequalities in circumstances, and the disadvantaged have direct claims on the more fortunate, quite independently of the question of access to external resources. As I said in discussing his Wilt Chamberlain example, Nozick has not given us any reason to reject that Rawlsian intuition.

3. LIBERTARIANISM AS MUTUAL ADVANTAGE

Many libertarians acknowledge that Nozick's argument fails. The problem, they say, is not with Nozick's conclusions, but with his attempt to defend them by appeal to Kant's egalitarian idea of treating people as ends in themselves. If we start with the idea that each person matters equally, then justice will require something other than Nozickian self-ownership. But, they claim, that just shows that libertarianism is not properly viewed as a theory of treating people as equals. What then is it a theory of? There are two main possibilities: in this section, I will consider libertarianism as a theory of mutual advantage; in the next section, I will consider it as a theory of freedom.

Mutual advantage theories of libertarianism are often presented in contractarian terms. This can be confusing, since liberal egalitarian theories have also been presented in contractarian terms, and the shared use of the contract device can obscure the fundamental differences between them. Before evaluating the mutual advantage defence of libertarianism, therefore, I will lay out some of the differences between the Rawlsian and mutual advantage versions of contractarianism.

For Rawls, the contract device is tied to our 'natural duty of justice'. We have a natural duty to treat others fairly, for they are 'self-originating sources of valid claims'. People matter, from the moral point of view, not because they can harm or benefit us, but because they are 'ends in themselves' (Rawls 1971: 179–80), and so are entitled to equal consideration. This is a 'natural' duty because it is not derived from consent or mutual advantage, but simply owed to persons as such (Rawls 1971: 115–16). The contract device helps us determine the content of this natural duty, for it requires that each party take into consideration the needs of others 'as free and equal beings'. To ensure that the contract gives equal consideration to each of the contractors, Rawls's original position abstracts from differences in talent and strength that might create unequal bargaining power. By removing these arbitrary differences, the contract device 'substitutes a moral equality for a physical inequality' (Diggs 1981: 277), and thereby 'represents equality between human beings as moral persons' (Rawls 1971: 19). For Rawls, then, the contract is a useful device for determining the content of our natural duty of justice, because it properly represents our moral equality (Ch. 3, s. 3 above).

Mutual advantage theorists also use a contract device, but for opposite reasons. For them, there are no natural duties or self-originating moral claims. There is no moral equality underneath our natural physical inequality. The modern world view, they say, rules out the traditional idea that people and actions have any inherent moral status. What people take to be objective moral values are just the subjective preferences of individuals (J. Buchanan 1975: 1; Gauthier 1986: 55–8; Narveson 1988: 110–21).

So there is nothing naturally 'right' or 'wrong' about one's actions, even if they involve harming others. However, while there is nothing inherently wrong in harming you, I would be better off by refraining from doing so if every other person refrains from harming me. Adopting a convention against injury is mutually advantageous—we do not have to waste resources defending our own person and property, and it enables us to enter into stable cooperation. It may be in our short-term self-interest to violate such an agreement on occasion, but acting on short-term self-interest makes mutual cooperation and constraint unstable, and thereby harms our long-term self-interest (it eventually leads to Hobbes's 'war of all against all'). While injury is not inherently wrong, each person gains in the long run by accepting conventions that define it as 'wrong' and 'unjust'.

The content of such conventions will be the subject of bargaining—each person will want the convention to protect their own interests as much as possible while constraining them as little as possible. While conventions are not really contracts, we can view this bargaining over mutually advantageous conventions as the process by which a community establishes its 'social contract'. While this contract, unlike Rawls's, is not an elaboration of our traditional notions of moral and political obligation, it will include some of the constraints that Rawls and others take to be 'natural duties'—for example, the duty not to steal, or the duty to share the benefits of cooperation fairly amongst the contributors. Mutually advantageous conventions occupy some of the place of traditional morality, and, for that reason, can be seen as providing a 'moral' code, even though it is 'generated as a rational constraint from the non-moral premises of rational choice' (Gauthier 1986: 4).

This sort of theory is aptly described by David Gauthier, its best-known proponent, as 'moral artifice', for it is an artificial way of identifying constraints on what people are naturally entitled to do. It involves 'artifice' in another sense as well: it requires society to establish complex mechanisms to actually enforce these self-interested agreements against individuals, coercively if necessary. The need for such coercive enforcement may not immediately be clear: if the agreements are in everyone's self-interest, why cannot we rely on everyone to voluntarily comply with them? Why would we need some artificial social mechanism to enforce the agreements?

The difficulty is that while it is in everyone's interests to *agree* to the contract or convention, it may not be in everyone's interests actually to *comply* with it. Consider the case of overfishing in the oceans I discussed earlier. It is clearly in everyone's interests to agree to a set of rules limiting fishing to an environmentally sustainable level. Each person's livelihood is in jeopardy if the species is fished to extinction. But it is not in my interest actually to stop overfishing unless I am confident that everyone else will do so as well. If others continue to overfish, then my abstinence will make little or no difference—I cannot save the species on my own. I am simply letting others benefit from the plundering of the seas. In the language of game theory, I have no reason to 'cooperate' if I suspect that others will 'defect'.

Even if I do trust others to cooperate, we then face another problem. It may be rational for me to defect precisely because I can trust others to cooperate. If I can assume that everyone else will abide by environmentally responsible harvesting rules, then why shouldn't I go out and do some extra fishing over my limit? So long as others abide by the rules, my small amount of overfishing will not harm the species. If others do not overfish, my defection will make little difference—I cannot destroy the species on my own. This may seem 'unfair', from a moral point of view, but on a mutual advantage approach, this is irrelevant, since there is no such thing as a 'moral point of view' independent of self-interest. Yet if everyone reasons that their individual defection will make no difference, then everyone will defect, and the system breaks down.

In short, while it is in my self-interest to agree to a set of environmentally responsible rules, there may be circumstances when it is not in my self-interest actually to abide by the rules. Each person, rationally pursuing their own self-interest, will make choices that lead to collectively irrational outcomes. This is an example of what is called a 'collective action' problem. Another classic example is the so-called 'Prisoner's Dilemma'. Imagine that you and your partner-in-crime are jailed (in separate rooms) on suspicion of robbery, and the prosecutor gives each of you the following offer:[15]

'I don't have enough evidence to convict you or your partner of robbery, but I can convict you both of breaking and entering, which carries a sentence of one year. However, if you will confess to robbery, and give evidence against your partner, then, if she doesn't confess, you will go free without penalty. If she also confesses, you will both get five years. And if you do not confess, and your partner does, then you will get twenty years and she will go free.'

Let's assume that both prisoners are motivated solely by self-interest (i.e. they want to minimize their time in jail), and do not know what the other prisoner is doing. The options facing each prisoner can be put this way:

1st-best outcome: I confess, partner doesn't confess
(I go free, she gets twenty years)
2nd-best outcome: I don't confess; partner doesn't confess
(we both get one year)
3rd-best outcome: I confess; partner confesses
(we both get five years)
4th-best outcome: I don't confess, my partner confesses
(I get twenty years, my partner goes free)

It would obviously be rational for the prisoners to agree in advance—perhaps before they even commit the crime—not to confess. Let's imagine that they have indeed made such an advance agreement. Yet when the time comes actually to decide whether to confess, each prisoner now faces a dilemma. Let's assume that what my partner does is not affected by what I do: she will confess or not regardless of what I do. If so, then it is rational for me to confess, since whatever my partner does, I am better off by confessing. If she confesses, then I will get my third-best outcome by also confessing, rather than my fourth-best outcome. If she does not confess, then I will get my first-best outcome by confessing, rather than my second-best outcome. So I will do better by confessing, no matter what my partner does.

And of course my partner is in precisely the same situation. She is better off confessing no matter what I do. So she will confess. The result, then, is that we end up in the third-best option: we both get five years. If we had both stayed silent, we could have got the second-best outcome—one year each. Not confessing is the collectively rational outcome. But confessing is the individually rational choice. To achieve the collectively rational outcome, we need somehow to prevent people from acting on their rational self-interest.

Scholars disagree about how widespread these sorts of collective action problems are, and how people overcome them. For example, confessing may not be rational if it precludes future opportunities for cooperation with my partner. Confessing may be rational in a 'single-play' Prisoner's Dilemma, but not in an 'iterated' or multi-play PD, where the two prisoners will meet again.[16]

But the central point remains: to ensure collectively rational outcomes, it is not enough to agree to certain conventions. It is also necessary to establish some mechanism to compel compliance with them: i.e. some mechanism to prevent people from defecting (by overfishing or confessing) even when it is individually rational to do so.[17] The usual Hobbesian response is to give the state the power to punish us for defecting, thereby increasing the costs of not cooperating with the rules. We have to add the risk of fines or jail into our calculations, and this may tip the balance in favour of cooperating rather than defecting. (Similarly, gangs and organized crime syndicates attempt to prevent their members from confessing to the police by threatening to punish them or their family. The fear of punishment discourages many criminals from 'defecting' from the rules of the gang or syndicate.)

Gauthier himself, however, thinks that this reliance on coercive enforcement is an inadequate response to the problem. For example, I will not fear punishment if I know that the state lacks the personnel or resources to monitor my behaviour properly, or if I know that the police or judges can be bribed. But to establish a comprehensive system of policing and justice that avoids these problems would be very expensive, and perhaps even unworkable.[18]

Gauthier instead suggests that people can overcome collective action problems without the threat of punishment from a coercive state, if they adopt the principle of 'constrained maximization'. Constrained maximization is a disposition to comply with mutually advantageous conventions, without calculating whether it might be rational to defect, so long as one is sure that others will cooperate as well. Gauthier assumes that people are ultimately motivated by self-interest, but argues that they will only in fact maximize their well-being if they accept that their pursuit of self-interest should be constrained by principles of 'morality', as defined by mutually advantageous conventions. People must agree that they 'ought' to follow these conventions, so long as others can be trusted to follow them as well, even when it is rational to defect. Indeed, people should be socialized to think of defection as 'wrong' or 'unfair' under these circumstances. If the social convention itself is 'just' (i.e. mutually advantageous), and if others can be trusted to cooperate, then people should view cooperation as a 'moral' obligation that precludes the possibility of defecting for self-interested reasons. It is rational, from a self-interested point of view, to commit oneself to being a 'constrained maximizer' rather than a 'straightforward maximizer'—i.e. to commit oneself to *not* acting on self-interest in deciding whether to cooperate with other constrained maximizers in following mutually advantageous conventions.[19]

On Gauthier's view, then, mutual advantage theories mimic traditional morality not only in establishing rules which limit what we are naturally free to do, but also in requiring that we view these rules as taking precedence over the unconstrained pursuit of self-interest. The rules may themselves be grounded in mutual advantage, but to achieve the mutually advantageous outcome, we need to view these rules as 'obligations' which partially pre-empt self-interested decision-making.

Many critics have questioned whether Gauthier's notion of 'constrained maximization' is coherent or psychologically feasible, and argue that in the end mutual advantage theories must rely heavily on coercive enforcement to overcome collective action problems.[20] I will set those concerns aside, and focus instead on whether these mutually advantageous conventions, however enforced, are a plausible basis for defending libertarianism. These conventions will certainly incorporate some of the duties and obligations we traditionally associate with morality. However, the overlap between mutual advantage and morality as traditionally understood is far from complete. Whether it is advantageous to follow a particular convention depends on one's preferences and powers. Those who are strong and talented will do better than those who are weak and infirm, since they have much greater bargaining power. The infirm produce little of benefit to others, and what little they do produce may be simply expropriated by others without fear of retaliation. Since there is little to gain from cooperation with the infirm, and nothing to fear from retaliation, the strong do not gain from accepting conventions which recognize or protect the interests of the infirm.

This is precisely what Rawls objected to in traditional state of nature arguments—they allow differences in bargaining power that should be irrelevant when determining principles of justice. He devised his 'original position' to eliminate differences in bargaining power. Gauthier, however, is using the contract device to determine principles of mutual advantage, rather than principles of impartial morality, and so differences in bargaining power are central to his enterprise. The resulting conventions will accord rights to various people, but since these rights depend on one's bargaining power, mutual advantage contractarianism does 'not afford each individual an inherent moral status in relation to her fellows' (Gauthier 1986: 222).

It is hard to exaggerate the difference between these two versions of contractarianism. Rawls uses the device of a contract to develop our traditional notions of moral obligation, whereas Gauthier uses it to replace them; Rawls uses the idea of the contract to express the inherent moral standing of persons, whereas Gauthier uses it to generate an artificial moral standing; Rawls uses the device of the contract to negate differences in bargaining power, whereas Gauthier uses it to reflect them. In both premises and conclusions, these two strands of contract theory are, morally speaking, a world apart.

I will question the plausibility of the mutual advantage approach momentarily. But, even if we accept it, how does it justify a libertarian regime in which each person has unfettered freedom of individual contract over her self and her holdings? It cannot, of course, yield self-ownership as a natural right. As Gauthier says, mutual advantage theories do not offer people an 'inherent moral status', and if there are no natural duties to respect others, then obviously there is no natural duty to respect their self-ownership, and hence no duty to treat them in ways they would voluntarily consent or contract to. But libertarians argue that respecting self-ownership is mutually advantageous—it is in each person's interest to accord self-ownership rights to others, and not try to coerce them into promoting our good, so long as they reciprocate. The costs of coercing others are too high, and the payoffs too low, to be worth the risk of being coerced oneself. Mutual advantage does not, however, justify any further rights—rights to a certain share of resources under Rawls's difference principle, for example. The poor would gain from such a right, but the rich have an interest in protecting their resources, and the poor lack sufficient power to take the resources, or to make the costs of protection exceed its benefits. Mutual advantage yields libertarianism, therefore, because everyone has both the interest and the ability to insist on self-ownership, but only some people have an interest in redistribution, and they do not have the ability to insist on it (Harman 1983: 321–2; cf. Barry 1986: ch. 5).

Does mutual advantage justify granting each person rights of self-ownership? Since people lack inherent moral status, whether one has the unfettered right of contract over one's talents and holdings depends on whether one has the power to defend one's talents and holdings against coercion by others. Mutual advantage libertarians claim that everyone does, in fact, have this power. They claim that humans are by nature equal, not in Rawls's sense of sharing a fundamental equality of natural right—rather, equality of rights 'is derivative from a fundamental *factual* equality of condition, in fact an equal vulnerability to the invasions of others' (Lessnoff 1986: 107). As Hobbes put it, 'as to strength of body, the weakest hath enough to kill the strongest'. People are, by nature, more or less equal in their ability to harm others and their vulnerability to being harmed—and this factual equality grounds equal respect for self-ownership.

But this is unrealistic. Many people lack the power to defend themselves, and so cannot claim the right of self-ownership on mutual advantage grounds. As James Buchanan says, 'if personal differences are sufficiently great', then the strong may have the capacity to 'eliminate' the weak, or perhaps to seize any goods produced by the weak, and thereby set up 'something similar to the slave contract' (J. Buchanan 1975: 59–60). These are not abstract possibilities—personal differences *are* that great. It is an inescapable consequence of mutual advantage theories that the congenitally infirm 'fall beyond the pale' of justice (Gauthier 1986: 268), as do young children since 'there is little the child can do to retaliate against those jeopardizing its well-being' (Lomasky 1987: 161; Grice 1967: 147–8).

It is doubtful that many mutual advantage theorists really believe in this assumption of a natural equality in bargaining power. Their claim in the end is not that people are in fact equals by nature, but rather that *justice is only possible in so far as this is so*. By nature, everyone is entitled to use whatever means are available to them, and the only way moral constraints will arise is if people are more or less equal in their powers and vulnerabilities. For only then does each person gain more from the protection of their own person and property than they lose by refraining from using other people's bodies or resources. Natural equality is not sufficient, however, for people of similar physical capacities may find themselves with radically unequal technological capacities, and 'those with a more advanced technology are in a position to dictate the terms of interaction to their fellows' (Gauthier 1986: 231; Hampton 1986: 255). Indeed, technology may get us to the point where, as Hobbes put it, there is a 'power irresistible' on earth, and for Hobbes and his contemporary followers, such power 'justifieth all actions really and properly, in whomsoever it is found'. No one could claim rights of self-ownership against such power.[21]

Mutual advantage, therefore, subordinates individual self-ownership to the power of others. This is why Nozick made self-ownership a matter of our natural rights. Coercing others is wrong for Nozick, not because it is too costly for the coercer, but because people are ends in themselves, and coercion violates people's inherent moral status by treating them as a means. Nozick's defence of libertarianism, therefore, relies precisely on the premiss that Gauthier denies—namely, that people have inherent moral status. But neither approach actually yields libertarianism. Nozick's approach explains why everyone has equal rights, regardless of their bargaining power, but cannot explain why people's rights do not include some claim on social resources. Gauthier's approach explains why the vulnerable and weak do not have a claim on resources, but can't explain why they have an equal claim to self-ownership, despite their unequal bargianing power. Treating people as ends in themselves requires more than (or other than) respecting their self-ownership (contra Nozick); treating people according to mutual advantage often requires less than respect for self-ownership (contra Gauthier).[22]

Let's assume, however, that mutual advantage does lead to libertarianism. Perhaps Lomasky is right that it costs too much to determine who one can enslave and who one must treat as an equal, so that the strong would agree to conventions that accord self-ownership to even the weakest person (Lomasky 1987: 77). How would this constitute a *defence* of libertarianism? On our everyday view, mutually advantageous activities are only legitimate if they respect the rights of others (including the rights of those too weak to defend their interests). It may not be advantageous for the strong to refrain from killing or enslaving the weak, but the weak have prior claims of justice against the strong. To deny this is 'a hollow mockery of the idea of justice—adding insult to injury. Justice is normally thought of not as ceasing to be relevant in conditions of extreme inequality in power but, rather, as being especially relevant in such conditions' (Barry 1989a: 163). Exploiting the defenceless is, on our everyday view, the worst injustice, whereas mutual advantage theorists say we have no obligations at all to the defenceless.

This appeal to everyday morality begs the question, since the whole point of the mutual advantage approach is that there are no natural duties to others—it challenges those who believe there is 'a real moral difference between right and wrong which all men [have] a duty to respect' (Gough 1957: 118). As Buchanan puts it, there simply is no such thing as a natural moral equality underlying our natural physical inequality, and so everyday morality is 'highly vulnerable' to empirical 'refutation' (J. Buchanan 1975: 54; cf. Gauthier 1986: 55–8). To say that Gauthier ignores our duty to protect the vulnerable is not to give an argument against his theory, for the existence of such duties is the very issue in question.

But, precisely because it abandons the idea that people have inherent moral status, the mutual advantage approach is not an alternative account *of* justice, but rather an alternative *to* justice. While mutual advantage may generate just outcomes under conditions of natural and technological equality, it licences exploitation wherever 'personal differences are sufficiently great', and there are no grounds within the theory to prefer justice to exploitation. If people act justly, it is not because they see justice as a value, but only because they lack 'power irresistible' and so must settle for justice. From the point of view of everyday morality, therefore, mutual advantage contractarianism may provide a useful analysis of rational self-interest or of realpolitik, 'but why we should regard it as a method of moral justification remains utterly mysterious' (Sumner 1987: 158; cf. Barry 1989*a*: 284). As Rawls says, 'to each according to his threat advantage' simply does not count as a conception of justice (Rawls 1971: 134).

None of this will perturb the mutual advantage theorist. If one rejects the idea that people or actions have inherent moral status, then moral constraints must be artificial, not natural, resting on mutually advantageous conventions. And if mutually advantageous conventions conflict with everyday morality, then 'so much the worse for morality' (Morris 1988: 120). Mutual advantage may be the best we can hope for in a world without natural duties or objective moral values.

The mutual advantage approach will be attractive to those who share its scepticism about moral claims. Most political philosophy in the Western tradition, however, shares the opposite view that there are obligation-generating rights and wrongs which all persons have a duty to respect. I share this assumption. It is true that our claims about natural duties are not observable or testable, but different kinds of objectivity apply to different areas of knowledge, and there is no reason to expect or desire that moral duties have the same kind of objectivity as the physical sciences. As Nagel says, 'if any values are objective, they are objective *values*, not objective anything else' (Nagel 1980: 98).

Even if we can identify such norms of justice, there remains the difficult question of *motivation*: why should I care about what I morally ought to do? Mutual advantage theorists argue that I only have a reason to do something if the action satisfies some desire of mine, so that 'if something's being just is to count as a good reason for doing it, justice must be shown to be in the interest of the agent' (Barry 1989*a*: 363). If moral actions do not increase my desire satisfaction, I have no reason to perform them. This theory of rationality may be true even if there are objective moral values or natural duties. Rawls's approach may give a true account of justice, and yet 'be only an intellectual activity, a way of looking at the world that can have no motivational effect on human action' (Hampton 1986: 32).[23]

Why should people who possess unequal power refrain from using it in their own interests? Buchanan argues that the powerful will treat others as moral equals only if they are 'artificially' motivated to do so 'through general adherence to internal ethical norms' (J. Buchanan 1975: 175–6). And indeed Rawls does invoke 'adherence to internal ethical norms'—namely a pre-existing disposition to act justly—in explaining the rationality of moral action (Rawls 1971: 487–9). Similarly, Brian Barry argues that the desire to behave in ways that respect others as moral equals 'must be admitted as an irreducible motive' (Barry 1989a: 167). In calling this appeal to internal ethical norms 'artificial', Buchanan implies that Rawls and Barry have failed to find a 'real' motivation for acting justly. But why shouldn't our motivation for acting justly be a moral motivation? Why shouldn't we say, with Kant, that morality 'is a sufficient and *original* source of determination within us' that does not need 'a ground of determination external to itself'? (Kant, quoted in Riley 1982: 251 n. 47). Why cannot people be motivated to act morally simply by coming to understand the moral reasons for doing so?

This may seem 'artificial' to those who accept a mutual advantage view of rationality, but the acceptability of that view is precisely what is at issue. As Barry notes, the Hobbesian equation of rationality with the efficient pursuit of self-interest is 'pure assertion'. While 'it is not possible to refute egoism in the literal sense of showing it to be logically inconsistent', the recognition that others are fundamentally like ourselves in having needs and goals gives us 'powerful reasons for accepting the claims of impartial morality' (Barry 1989a: 285, 273). The 'proof' of moral equality, therefore, is based on 'what we might call human consistency', and the 'virtually unanimous concurrence of the human race in caring about the defensibility of actions in a way that does not simply appeal to power' suggests that this 'human consistency' is indeed a powerful motivation (Barry 1989a: 288, 285, 174–5).[24]

Of course, even if we accept the possible existence of irreducibly moral motivations, this does not yet tell us anything about how effective these moral motivations are. Is the recognition that other people are like ourselves sufficient to motivate us to accept the sorts of sacrifices or burdens which moral equality may require? Are liberal theories of justice unrealistic in the extent to which they expect people to give precedence to moral reasons over self-interested reasons? I will return to this question in subsequent chapters, since one of the major concerns of communitarians, civic republicans, and feminists has been that liberals offer an inadequate account of our moral motivation.

These are difficult issues, and some people will remain sceptical about the existence of moral duties and/or moral motivations. If so, then mutual advantage may be all we have with which to construct social rules. But none of this helps the libertarian, for mutually advantageous conventions may often be non-libertarian. Some people will have the ability to coerce others, violating their self-ownership, and some people will have the ability to take other's property, violating their property-ownership. Mutual advantage, therefore, provides only a very limited defence of property rights, and what little defence it does provide is not a recognizably moral defence.

4. LIBERTARIANISM AS LIBERTY

Some people argue that libertarianism is not a theory of equality or mutual advantage. Rather, as the name suggests, it is a theory of *liberty*. On this view, equality and liberty are rivals for our moral allegiance, and what defines libertarianism is precisely its avowal of liberty as a foundational moral premiss, and its refusal to compromise liberty with equality (unlike the welfare state liberal).

This is not a plausible interpretation of Nozick's theory. Nozick does say that we are free, morally speaking, to use our powers as we wish. But this self-ownership is not derived from any principle of liberty. He does not say that freedom comes first, and that, in order to be free, we need self-ownership. He gives us no purchase on the idea of freedom as something prior to self-ownership from which we might derive self-ownership. His view, rather, is that the scope and nature of the freedom we ought to enjoy is a function of our self-ownership.

Other libertarians, however, say that libertarianism is based on a principle of liberty. What does it mean for a theory to be based on a principle of liberty, and how does such a principle serve to defend capitalism? One obvious answer is this:

1. an unrestricted market involves more freedom;
2. freedom is the fundamental value;
3. therefore, the free market is morally required.

This view, while very common in popular discourse, is not widely found in the philosophical literature, perhaps because it is very difficult to sustain. Attempts to measure freedom are notoriously complicated, as are attempts to assign an intrinsic value to freedom as such. We value different kinds of freedoms for different reasons, and the idea that we should maximize freedom as such is neither clear nor obviously desirable.

(a) The value of liberty

(i) The role of liberty in egalitarian theories
Let's start with premiss (2), concerning the value of liberty. Before examining the claim that liberty is a fundamental value, it is important to clarify the role of liberty in the theories we have examined so far. I have argued that utili-

tarianism, liberalism, and Nozick's libertarianism are all egalitarian theories in the sense of being premised on moral equality. While liberty is not the fundamental value in these theories, that does not mean that they are unconcerned with liberty. On the contrary, the protection of certain liberties was of great importance in each theory. This is obvious in the case of Nozick, who emphasizes the formal liberties of self-ownership, and Rawls, who assigns lexical priority to the basic civil and political liberties. But it is also true of most utilitarians, like Mill, who felt that utility was maximized by according people the freedom to choose their own way of life.

In deciding which liberties should be protected, theorists of moral equality situate these liberties within an account of equal concern for people's interests. They ask whether a particular liberty promotes people's interests; if so, then it should be promoted because people's interests should be promoted. For example, if each person has an important interest in the freedom to choose their marital partner, then denying someone that liberty denies her the respect and concern she is entitled to, denies her equal standing as a human being whose well-being is a matter of equal concern. Defending a particular liberty, therefore, involves answering the following two questions:

(a) which liberties are important, given our account of people's interests?
(b) what distribution of important liberties gives equal consideration to each person's interests?

In other words, egalitarian theorists ask how a particular liberty fits into a theory of people's interests, and then ask how a distribution of that liberty fits into a theory of equal concern for people's interests. In Rawls's case, for example, we ask what scheme of liberties would be chosen from a contracting position that represents impartial concern for people's interests. In this way, particular liberties can come to play an important role in theories of moral equality. I will call this the 'Rawlsian approach' to assessing liberties.

Mutual advantage theories assess liberty in a similar way. Like Rawls, they ask which particular liberties promote people's interests, and then ask what distribution of these liberties follows from a proper weighing of people's interests. The only difference is that in mutual advantage theories people's interests are weighed according to their bargaining power, not according to impartial concern. In Gauthier's case, for example, we ask what scheme of liberties would be agreed to by contractors negotiating for mutual advantage on the basis of their interests.

As we have seen, many libertarians defend their preferred liberties (e.g. the freedom to exercise one's talents in the market) in one of these two ways. Indeed, some of the libertarians who say that their theory is 'liberty-based' also defend their preferred liberties in terms of consideration for people's interests, weighed according to the criteria of equality or mutual advantage.

They call that a liberty-based argument, to emphasize their belief that our essential interest is an interest in certain kinds of liberty, but this new label does not affect the underlying argument. And, regardless of the label, assessing liberties in terms of either moral equality or mutual advantage will not yield libertarianism, for reasons I have discussed.

Can the defence of libertarianism be liberty-based in a way that is genuinely different from a defence based on equality or mutual advantage? What would it mean for libertarians to defend their preferred freedoms by appealing to a principle of liberty? There are two possibilities. One principle of liberty is that freedom should be maximized in society. Libertarians who appeal to this principle defend their preferred liberties by claiming that the recognition of these particular liberties maximizes freedom in society. The second principle of liberty is that people have a right to the most extensive liberty compatible with a like liberty for all. Libertarians who appeal to this principle defend their preferred liberties by claiming that recognizing these particular liberties increases each person's overall freedom. I will argue that the first principle is absurd, and has no attraction to anyone, including libertarians; and the second principle is either a confused way of restating the egalitarian argument, or it rests on an indeterminate and unattractive conception of freedom. Moreover, even if we accept the absurd or unattractive interpretations of the principle of liberty, they still will not defend libertarianism.

(ii) Teleological liberty

The first candidate for a foundational principle of liberty says that we should aim to maximize the amount of freedom in society. If freedom is the ultimate value, why not have as much of it as possible? This is the way teleological utilitarians argue for the maximization of utility, so I will call this the 'teleological' liberty principle. But, as we saw in Chapter 2, this sort of theory loses touch with our most basic understanding of morality. Because teleological theories take concern for the good (e.g. freedom or utility) as fundamental, and concern for people as derivative, promoting the good becomes detached from promoting people's interests. For example, we could increase the amount of freedom in society by increasing the number of people, even if each person's freedom is unchanged. Yet a more populous country is not, for that reason alone, more free in any morally relevant sense.

Indeed, it may be possible to promote the good by sacrificing people. For example, a teleological principle could require that we coerce people to bear and raise children and thereby increase the population. This deprives existing people of a freedom, but the result would increase the overall amount of freedom, since the many freedoms of the new population outweigh the loss of one freedom amongst the earlier population. The principle could also justify unequally distributing liberties. If five people enslave me, there is no reason to assume that the loss of my freedom outweighs the increased freedom of the five slave-owners. They may gain more options or choices collectively from the freedom to dispose of my labour than I lose (assuming that it is possible to measure such things—see pp. 143-5 below). No libertarian supports such policies, for they violate fundamental rights.

Whatever libertarians mean by saying their theory is liberty-based, it cannot be this. Yet this is a natural interpretation of the claim that freedom is the fundamental value, and it is encouraged by the libertarian's rhetorical rejection of equality. Libertarians believe in equal rights of self-ownership, but many of them do not want to defend this by appeal to any principle of equality. They try to find a liberty-based reason for equally distributing liberties. Thus some libertarians say that they favour equal liberties because they believe in freedom, and since each individual can be free, each individual should be free.[25] But if this really was the explanation of the libertarian commitment to equal liberty, then they should increase the population, since future people too can be free. Libertarians reject increasing the overall amount of freedom through increasing the population, and they reject it for the same reason they reject increasing the overall amount of freedom by unequally distributing liberties—namely, their theory is equality-based. As Peter Jones puts it, 'to prefer equal liberty to unequal liberty is to prefer equality to inequality, rather than freedom to unfreedom' (Jones 1982: 233). So long as libertarians are committed to equal liberty for each person, they are adopting an equality-based theory.

(iii) Neutral liberty

The second, and more promising, candidate for a foundational principle of liberty says that each person is entitled to the most extensive liberty compatible with a like liberty for all. I will call this the 'greatest equal liberty' principle. This principle works within the general framework of an egalitarian theory, since now equal liberty cannot be sacrificed for a greater overall liberty, but it is importantly different from the Rawlsian approach (p. 139 above). The Rawlsian approach assessed particular liberties by asking how they promote our interests. The greatest equal liberty approach assesses particular liberties by asking how much freedom they give us, on the assumption that we have an interest in freedom as such, in maximizing our overall freedom. Both approaches connect the value of particular liberties to an account of our interests. But the Rawlsian approach did not say that we have an interest in freedom as such, or that our interest in any particular liberty corresponds to how much freedom it contains, or that it even makes sense to compare the amount of freedom contained in different liberties. Different liberties promote different interests for many different reasons, and there is no reason to assume that the liberties which are most valuable to us are the ones with the most freedom. The greatest equal liberty approach, however, says that the value of any particular liberty just is how much freedom it contains, for our interest in particular liberties stems from our interest in freedom as such. Unlike the Rawlsian approach, judgements of the value of different liberties require, and are derived from, judgements of greater or lesser freedom.

If libertarianism appeals to this greatest equal liberty principle, then it is not a 'liberty-based' theory in the strict sense, for (unlike a teleological liberty-based theory) rights to liberty are derived from the claims of people to equal consideration. But it is liberty-based in a looser sense, for (unlike the Rawlsian approach to liberty) it derives judgements of the value of particular liberties from judgements of greater or lesser freedom. Can the libertarian defend his preferred liberties by appeal to the greatest equal liberty principle? Before we can answer that question, we need some way of measuring freedom, so that we can determine whether the free market, for example, maximizes each individual's freedom.

In order to measure freedom, we need to define it. There are many definitions of freedom in the literature, but some of these definitions can be excluded for our purposes. For example, some people define freedom in terms of the exercise of our *rights*. Whether or not a restriction decreases our freedom depends on whether or not we had a right to do the restricted thing. For example, preventing someone from stealing is not a restriction on their liberty, on this view, since they had no right to steal. This is a 'moralized' definition of liberty, since it presupposes a prior theory of rights. This sort of moralized definition reflects a very common way of talking about freedom in everyday discourse. However, it cannot be used here. If the greatest equal liberty principle is to be foundational, such 'moralized' definitions must be excluded. If we are trying to derive rights from judgements of greater or lesser liberty, our definition of liberty cannot presuppose some principle of rights. Libertarians who appeal to the greatest equal liberty principle believe that whether we have a right to appropriate unowned resources, for example, depends on whether that right increases each person's freedom. But on a moralized definition of freedom, we first need to know whether people have a right to appropriate unowned resources in order to know whether a restriction on appropriation is a restriction on their freedom.

So if the greatest equal liberty principle is to do any work, we need to define liberty in a non-moralized way—as the presence of options or choices, for example—without assuming that we have a right to exercise those options. We can then assign rights so as to maximize each individual's freedom, compatible with a like freedom for all. Hence whether people have a right to appropriate previously unowned natural resources depends on whether according that right increases or decreases each person's freedom (cf. Sterba 1988: 11–15).

However, there are two different ways to give a non-moralized definition of liberty, which offer two different criteria for determining whether a particular liberty increases someone's overall freedom. The first 'neutral' view offers a purely quantitative measure of freedom, based on a simple counting up of possible actions or choices. The second 'purposive' view offers a more qualitative measure of freedom, based on some assessment of the value or importance of these different options.

Let's start with the 'neutral' view. On this view, we are free in so far as no one prevents us from acting on our (actual or potential) desires. This is a non-moralized definition since it does not presuppose that we have a right to act on these desires. Using this definition we may be able to make comparative judgements about the quantity of one's freedom. One can be more or less free, on this definition, since one can be free to act on some but not other desires. If we can make such quantitative judgements about the amount of freedom provided by different rights, then we can determine which rights are most valuable. If the principle of greatest equal liberty employs this definition of freedom, then each person is entitled to the greatest amount of neutral freedom compatible with a like freedom for all.

Does this provide a plausible standard for assessing the value of different liberties? There are two potential problems here. First, our intuitive judgements about the value of different liberties do not seem to be based on quantitative judgements of neutral freedom. Compare the inhabitants of London with citizens of an underdeveloped communist country like Albania (prior to 1989). We normally think of the average Londoner as better off in terms of freedom. After all, she has the right to vote, and practise her religion, as well as other civil and democratic liberties. The Albanian lacks these. On the other hand, Albania does not have many traffic lights, and those people who own cars face few if any legal restrictions on where or how they drive. The fact that Albania has fewer traffic restrictions does not change our sense that Albanians are worse off, in terms of freedom. But can we explain that fact by appealing to a quantitative judgement of neutral freedom?

If freedom can be neutrally quantified, so that we can measure the number of times each day that traffic lights legally prevent Londoners from acting in a certain way, there is no reason to assume that these will outnumber the times that Albanians are legally prevented from practising religion in public. As Charles Taylor (from whom I have taken the example) puts it, 'only a minority of Londoners practice some religion in public places, but all have to negotiate through traffic. Those who do practice a religion generally do so on one day of the week, while they are held up at traffic lights every day. In sheer quantitative terms, the number of acts restricted by traffic lights must be greater than that restricted by a ban on public religious practice' (Taylor 1985a: 219).

Why do we not accept Taylor's 'diabolical defence' of Albanian freedom—

why do we think that the Londoner is better off in terms of freedom? The answer, presumably, is that restrictions on civil and political liberty are more important than restrictions on traffic mobility. They are more important, not because they involve *more freedom*, neutrally defined, but because they involve *more important freedoms*. They are more important because, for example, they allow us to have greater control over the central projects in our lives, and so give us a greater degree of self-determination, in a way that traffic freedoms do not, whether or not they involve a smaller quantity of neutral freedom.

The neutral view of liberty says that each neutral freedom is as important as any other. But when we think about the value of different liberties in relation to people's interests, we see that some liberties are more important than others, and indeed some liberties are without value entirely—e.g. the freedom to libel others (Hart 1975: 245). Our theory must be able to explain the distinctions we make amongst different kinds of liberty.

The problems for neutral freedom go still deeper. The required judgements of greater or lesser freedom may be impossible to make, for there is no scale on which to measure quantities of neutral freedom. I said earlier that if we could count the number of free acts restricted by traffic laws and political censorship, traffic laws would probably restrict more free acts. But the idea of a 'free act' is an elusive one. How many free acts are involved in the simple waving of a hand? If a country outlaws such waving, how many acts has it forbidden? How do we compare that to a restriction on religious ceremonies? In each case, we could, with equally much or little justification, say that the laws have outlawed one act (waving a hand, celebrating religious belief), or that they have outlawed an infinite number of acts, which could have been performed an infinite number of times. But the principle of greatest equal liberty requires the ability to discriminate between these two cases. We need to be able to say, for example, that denying religious ceremonies takes away five units of free acts, whereas denying waving of one's hand takes away three. But how we could go about making such judgements is quite mysterious. As O'Neill puts it, 'We can, if we want to, take any liberty—e.g. the liberty to seek public office or the liberty to form a family—and divide it up into however many component liberties we find useful to distinguish—or for that matter into more than we find it useful to distinguish' (O'Neill 1980: 50). There is no non-arbitrary way of dividing up the world into actions and possible actions which would allow us to say that more neutral freedom is involved in denying free traffic movement than denying free speech. (The one exception involves comparing two essentially identical sets of rights, where the second set contains all the neutral freedoms in the first set, plus at least one more free act—see Arneson 1985: 442–5.)

Traffic laws and political oppression both restrict free acts. But any attempt to weigh the two on a single scale of neutral freedom, based on some individuation and measurement of free acts, is implausible. There may be such a scale, but those libertarians who endorse a neutral version of the greatest equal liberty principle have not made many strenuous attempts to develop such a scale.[26] Moreover, as I discuss below in section 4b, there is no reason to assume that such a scale, if it could be defined, would support libertarianism.

(iv) Purposive liberty

Our most valued liberties (the ones that make us attracted to a principle of greatest equal liberty) do not seem to involve the greatest neutral freedom. The obvious move, for advocates of the greatest equal liberty principle, is to adopt a 'purposive' definition of liberty. On such a definition, the amount of freedom contained in a particular liberty depends on how important that liberty is to us, given our interests and purposes. As Taylor puts it, 'Freedom is important to us because we are purposive beings. But then there must be distinctions in the significance of different kinds of freedom based on the distinction in the significance of different purposes' (Taylor 1985a: 219). For example, religious liberty gives us more freedom than traffic liberty because it serves more important interests, even if it does not contain quantitatively more neutral freedom.[27]

A purposive definition of freedom requires some standard for assessing the importance of a liberty, in order to measure the amount of freedom it contains. There are two basic standards—a 'subjective' standard says the value of a particular liberty depends on how much an individual desires it; an 'objective' standard says that certain liberties are important whether or not a particular person desires them. The latter is often thought to be preferable because it avoids the problem of the 'contented slave' who does not desire legal rights, and hence, on a subjective standard, does not lack any important freedoms.

On either view, we assess someone's freedom by determining how valuable (subjectively or objectively) her specific liberties are. Those liberties that are more highly valued contain, for that reason, more purposive freedom. On the purposive version of the greatest equal liberty principle, therefore, each person is entitled to the greatest possible amount of purposive liberty compatible with a like liberty for all. Like the Rawlsian approach to assessing liberties, this allows for qualitative judgements of the value of particular liberties, but it differs from the Rawlsian approach in supposing that these liberties must be assessed in terms of a single scale of freedom.

This is more attractive than the neutral version, for it corresponds with our everyday view that some neutral freedoms are more valuable than others. The problem, however, is that the whole language of greater and lesser freedom is no longer doing any work in the argument. The purposive version of the greatest equal liberty principle is in fact just a confused way of restating the

Rawlsian approach. It seems to differ in saying that the reason we are entitled to important liberties is that we are entitled to the greatest amount of equal liberty, a step that is absent in the Rawlsian approach. But that step does no work in the argument, and indeed simply confuses the real issues.

The principle of greatest equal liberty provides the following argument for protecting a particular liberty:

1. each person's interests matter and matter equally.
2. people have an interest in the greatest amount of freedom.
3. therefore, people should have the greatest amount of freedom, consistent with the equal freedom of others.
4. the liberty to x is important, given our interests.
5. therefore, the liberty to x increases our freedom.
6. therefore, each person ought (*ceteris paribus*) to have the right to x, consistent with everyone else's right to x.

Contrast that with the Rawlsian argument:

1. each person's interests matter and matter equally.
4. the liberty to x is important, given our interests.
6. therefore, each person ought (*ceteris paribus*) to have the right to x, consistent with everyone else's right to x.

The first argument is a needlessly complex way of stating the second argument. The step from (4) to (5) adds nothing (and, as a result, steps (2) and (3) also add nothing). Libertarians, on this view, say that because a particular liberty is important, therefore it increases our freedom, and we should have as much freedom as possible. But, in fact, the argument for the liberty is completed with the assessment of its importance.

Consider Loevinsohn's theory of measuring freedom, which uses a subjective standard for measuring purposive freedom. He says that 'when force or the threat of penalties is used to prevent someone from pursuing some possible course of action, the degree to which his liberty is thereby curtailed depends . . . on how important the course of action in question is to him' (Loevinsohn 1977: 343; cf. Arneson 1985: 428). Hence the more I desire a liberty, the more freedom it provides me. If I desire religious liberty more than traffic liberty, because it promotes important spiritual interests, then it gives me more freedom than traffic liberty. But Loevinsohn does not explain what is gained by shifting from the language of 'a more desired liberty' to 'more freedom'. This redescription (the move from (4) to (5) in the above argument) adds nothing, and so the principle of greatest equal liberty ((2) and (3) above) is doing no work. I do not mean that it is impossible or illegitimate to redescribe more desired liberties as more extensive freedom, but the fact that we can redescribe them in this way does not mean that we have said anything of moral significance, or that we have found a distinctly liberty-based way of assessing the value of particular liberties.

The greatest equal liberty premiss is not only unnecessary, it is confusing, for a number of reasons. For one thing, it falsely suggests that we have just one interest in liberty. Saying that we evaluate different liberties in terms of how much purposive freedom they provide suggests that these different liberties are important to us for the same reason, that they all promote the same interest. But in fact different liberties promote different interests in different ways. Religious liberties are important for self-determination—i.e. for acting on my deepest values and beliefs. Democratic liberties often serve a more symbolic interest—denying me the vote is an assault on my dignity, but may have no effect on my ability to pursue my goals. Some economic liberties have a purely instrumental value—I may desire free trade between countries because it reduces the price of consumer goods, but I would support restrictions on international trade if doing so lowered prices. I do not desire these different liberties for the same reason, and the strength of my desire is not based on the extent to which they promote a single interest.[28] Again, it is possible to redescribe these different interests as an interest in a more extensive purposive freedom, but it is needlessly confusing.

Moreover, talking about our interest in more extensive freedom, as opposed to our different interests in different liberties, obscures the relationship between freedom and other values. Whatever interest we have in a particular liberty—be it intrinsic or instrumental, symbolic or substantive—it is likely that we have the same interest in other things. For example, if the freedom to vote is important for its effect on our dignity, then anything else that promotes our dignity is also important (e.g. meeting basic needs, or preventing libel), and it is important for the very same reason. The defender of purposive freedom says that our concern is with important liberties, not just any old neutral liberty. But if we look at what makes liberties important to us, then freedom no longer systematically competes with other values like dignity, or material security, or autonomy, for these often are the very values which make particular liberties important. Describing more important liberties as more extensive freedom, however, invites this false contrast, for it pretends that the importance of particular liberties stems from the amount of freedom they contain.

So neither version of the greatest equal liberty principle offers a viable alternative to the Rawlsian approach to assessing liberties. It is worth noting that Rawls himself once endorsed a right to the most extensive equal liberty, and it was only in the final version of his theory that he adopted what I have called the Rawlsian approach. He now defends a principle of equal rights to 'basic liberties', while disavowing any claims about the possibility, or significance, of measurements of overall freedom (Rawls 1982a: 5–6; Hart 1975:

233–9). He recognized that in determining which are the basic liberties, we do not ask which liberties maximize our possession of a single commodity called 'freedom'. His earlier claim that people should be maximally free was 'merely elliptical for the claim that they [should be] free in every important respect, or in most important respects' (MacCallum 1967: 329). But as Rawls now recognizes, once we say this, then the principle of greatest equal liberty does no work. For the reason it is important to be free in a particular respect is not the amount of freedom it provides, but the importance of the various interests it serves. As Dworkin puts it,

if we have a right to basic liberties not because they are cases in which the commodity of liberty is somehow especially at stake, but because an assault on basic liberties injures us or demeans us in some way that goes beyond its impact on liberty, then what we have a right to is not liberty at all, but to the values or interests or standing that this particular constraint defeats. (Dworkin 1977: 271)

In making liberty-claims, therefore, we are entitled, not to the greatest equal amount of this single commodity of freedom, but to equal consideration for the interests that make particular liberties important.[29]

(b) Freedom and capitalism

It is often thought that libertarianism can best be understood and defended in terms of some principle of liberty. So far, I have considered three possible definitions of liberty that could be used in this defence. Moralized definitions will not work, because they presuppose a theory of rights. The neutral definition is not promising, because quantitative measurements of neutral freedom lead to indeterminate or implausible results. And the purposive definition simply obscures the real basis of our assessment of the value of liberties.

Some readers may feel a certain impatience at this point. Whatever the conceptual niceties, they might think, surely there is some important connection between freedom and the free market, or between liberty and libertarianism. Surely, in the end, is it not true that what distinguishes left-liberals from libertarians is that the former favour more government restrictions on individual freedom? This assumption is deeply ingrained in both academic and popular discourse. Anthony Flew, for example, claims that whereas liberals and socialists favour government restrictions, libertarianism is 'opposed to any social and legal constraints on individual freedom' (Flew 1979: 188; cf. Rothbard 1982: p. v). Flew thus identifies the welfare state with restrictions on freedom, and capitalism with the absence of restrictions on freedom.

This equation of capitalism with unrestricted freedom is even shared by some defenders of the welfare state, who agree that redistributive policies are a compromise between freedom and equality, and acknowledge that anyone who believed only in freedom should endorse capitalism.

But is it true that the free market involves more freedom than the welfare state? In order to assess this claim, we need first to define freedom. Flew seems to be assuming a non-moralized neutral definition of freedom. By eliminating welfare state redistribution, the free market eliminates some legal constraints on the disposal of one's resources, and thereby creates some neutral freedoms. For example, if government funds a welfare programme by an 80 per cent tax on inheritance and capital gains, then it prevents people from giving their property to others. Flew does not tell us how much neutral freedom would be gained by removing this tax, but it clearly would allow someone to act in a way they otherwise could not. This expansion of neutral freedom is the most obvious sense in which capitalism increases freedom, but many of these neutral freedoms will also be valuable purposive freedoms, for there are important reasons why people might give their property to others. So capitalism does provide certain neutral and purposive freedoms unavailable under the welfare state.

However, we need to be more specific about this increased liberty. Every claim about freedom, to be meaningful, must have a triadic structure—it must be of the form 'X is free from Y to do Z', where X specifies the agent, Y specifies the preventing conditions, and Z specifies the action. Every freedom claim must have these three elements: it must specify who is free to do what from what obstacle (MacCallum 1967: 314). Flew has told us the last two elements—his claim concerns the freedom to dispose of property without legal constraint. But he has not told us the first—i.e. who has this freedom? As soon as we ask that question, Flew's equation of capitalism with freedom is rendered problematic. For it is the owners of the resource who are made free to dispose of it, while non-owners are deprived of that freedom. Suppose that a large estate you would have inherited (in the absence of an inheritance tax), now becomes a public park or a low-income housing project (as a result of the tax). The inheritance tax does not *eliminate* the freedom to use the property, rather it *redistributes* that freedom. If you inherit the estate, then you are free to dispose of it as you see fit, but if I use your backyard for my picnic or garden without your permission, then I am breaking the law, and the government will intervene and coercively deprive me of the freedom to continue. On the other hand, my freedom to use and enjoy the property is increased when the welfare state taxes your inheritance to provide me with affordable housing or a public park. So the free market legally restrains my freedom, while the welfare state increases it. Again, this is most obvious on a neutral definition of freedom, but many of the neutral freedoms I gain from the inheritance tax are also important purposive ones.[30]

That property rights increase some people's freedom by restricting others' is obvious when we think of the origin of private property. When Amy unilaterally appropriated land that had previously been held in common, Ben was legally deprived of his freedom to use the land. Since private ownership by one person presupposes non-ownership by others, the 'free market' restricts as well as creates liberties, just as welfare state redistribution both creates and restricts liberties. Hence, as Cohen puts it, 'private property is a distribution of freedom *and* unfreedom' (Cohen 1981: 227). As a result, 'the sentence "free enterprise constitutes economic liberty" is demonstrably false' (Cohen 1979: 12; cf. Gibbard 1985: 25; Goodin 1988: 312–13).

This undermines an important claim Nozick makes about the superiority of his theory of justice to liberal redistributive theories. He says that Rawls's theory cannot be 'continuously realized without continuous interference in people's lives' (Nozick 1974: 163). This is because people, left to their own devices, will engage in free exchanges that violate the difference principle, so that preserving the difference principle requires continually intervening in people's exchanges. Nozick claims that his theory avoids continuous interference in people's lives, for it does not require that people's free exchanges conform to a particular pattern, and hence does not require intervening in those exchanges.[31] Unfortunately, the system of exchanges which Nozick protects *itself* requires continuous interference in people's lives. It is only continuous state intervention that prevents people from violating Nozick's principles of justice. Nozick's property rights, therefore, just as much as Rawls's difference principle, can only be preserved by continuous interference in people's lives.

Since property rights entail legal restrictions on individual freedom, anyone like Flew who claims to oppose 'any social or legal constraints on individual freedom' should presumably reject state-enforced property rights, and endorse anarchism instead. But libertarians are not anarchists: they strongly believe that the state should impose constraints on individual freedom to uphold property rights.

Some libertarians might argue that the freedom acquired by the property-owner is greater than the freedom lost to others. But it is not clear how we would make such a measurement. And even if we could make this measurement, it is not clear how this would relate to the 'greatest equal liberty' principle. Increasing overall freedom by granting freedom to some at the expense of others seems to violate, not uphold, the greatest equal liberty principle, which says that people should have the greatest amount of freedom *consistent with the equal freedom of others*. Even if upholding property rights creates more freedom for property-owners than is lost to others, this is hardly a way of increasing equal liberty, unless there is some provision to ensure that everyone owns equal amounts of property.[32]

In any event, most libertarians do not claim that the free market creates more freedom than it takes away. They argue, with Flew, that it does not create any unfreedom at all: that capitalism involves no restrictions on individual freedom. How can libertarians say this? The answer is that they have shifted to a moralized definition of freedom, which defines freedom in terms of the exercise of one's rights. The freedom of non-owners is not lessened in any way when they are prevented from trespassing on my property because they had no right to trespass. Since they had no right to trespass on my property, their (moralized) freedom is not diminished by the enforcement of my property rights.

Much of the popular rhetoric about how the free market increases freedom is dependent on this moralized definition of freedom. On any non-moralized definition of freedom, private property creates both freedom and non-freedom. On a moralized definition, however, we can say that the free market imposes no restrictions on anyone's freedom, since it only prevents people from doing what they have no right to do (i.e. make use of other people's property).

Of course, once libertarians adopt this moralized definition, the claim that the free market increases people's freedom requires a prior argument for the existence of property rights, an argument which cannot itself be liberty-based. To defend the claim that the free market increases freedom, morally defined, libertarians must show that people have a right to property. But this is not an argument from liberty to property rights. On the contrary, the liberty claim presupposes the existence of property rights—property rights only increase freedom if we have some prior and independent reason to view such rights as morally legitimate. And I have suggested that existing attempts to defend such rights by appeal to self-ownership or mutual advantage have failed.

In any event, once we define liberty as the freedom to do what one has a moral right to do, then liberty can no longer play a role in deciding between competing theories of rights. Every theory can argue that a government which acts on its conception of people's moral rights is not restricting (moralized) liberty. If one accepts the libertarian claim that people have a moral right to acquire absolute property rights over unequal amounts of the world, then capitalism involves no restriction on (moralized) freedom. But if we accept instead the liberal egalitarian view that people have no moral right to the benefits which accrue from their undeserved talents, then it is the welfare state which involves no restrictions on (moralized) freedom. If people do not have a moral right to benefit from their undeserved natural advantages, then the welfare state does not restrict any (moralized) freedom when it redistributes resources from the advantaged to the disadvantaged. Saying that people should be free to do what they have a right to do is of no help in resolving this dispute between liberals and libertarians. We can only choose between their accounts of moralized freedom by first choosing between their accounts of our moral rights.

We can now see the flaw in standard libertarian claims that equate the welfare state with restrictions on freedom, and capitalism with the absence of restrictions on freedom. This claim trades on inconsistent definitions of freedom. Libertarians invoke the non-moralized definition of freedom when arguing that the welfare state restricts the freedom of property-owners. This claim is true, but capitalism equally restricts people's freedom on the non-moralized definition. To avoid this problem, libertarians shift to the moralized definition when arguing that capitalism does not restrict the freedom of non-owners.[33] That claim would be true if we accepted Nozick's or Gauthier's arguments in defence of property rights, but is not itself a reason to accept those arguments. So the usual claim that the welfare state restricts freedom whereas capitalism does not restrict freedom depends on shifting definitions of freedom halfway through the argument.

To properly sort out the relationship between capitalism and freedom, we need to pick one definiton of freedom and stick to it. Can any definition of liberty, used consistently, support the claim that libertarianism provides greater equal freedom than a liberal redistributive regime?

What if libertarians stick consistently to the neutral definition of liberty, and claim that the free market increases one's overall amount of neutral freedom? First, one must show that the gains in neutral liberty from allowing private property outweigh the losses. It is not clear that this is true, or even that it is possible to carry out the required measurements. Moreover, even if capitalism did increase one's neutral freedom, we would still want to know how important these neutral freedoms are. If our attachment to the free market is only as strong as our attachment to the freedom to libel others, or to run through red lights, then we would not have a very strong defence of capitalism.

What if libertarians adopt the purposive definition, and claim that the free market provides us with the most important liberties? It is certainly true that control of property is essential to pursuing our purposes in life, and helps us achieve some measure of autonomy and privacy in our lives.[34] But unrestricted property rights only promote one's most important purposes if one actually has property. Being free to bequeath property can promote your most important purposes, but only if you have property to bequeath. So whatever the relationship between property and purposive freedom, the aim of providing the greatest equal freedom suggests an equal distribution of property, not unrestricted capitalism. Nozick denies this, by saying that formal rights of self-ownership are the most important liberties even to those who lack property. But, as we have seen, the notion of dignity and agency that Nozick relies on, based on the idea of acting on one's conception of oneself, requires control of resources as well as one's person. Having independent access to resources is important for our purposes, and hence our purposive freedom, and that argues for liberal equality not libertarianism.

What if libertarians stick to the moralized definition of liberty, and claim that the free market provides the freedom we have a right to? On a moralized definition, we can only say that respecting a certain liberty increases our freedom if we already know that we have a right to that liberty. I do not believe that libertarians have given us a plausible argument that there is such a moral right to unrestricted property-ownership. Such a right is unlikely to come out of a plausible theory of moral equality (because it allows undeserved inequalities to have too much influence), nor will it come out of a plausible theory of mutual advantage (because it allows undeserved inequalities to have too little influence). It is difficult to see how any other argument can avoid these objections. But even if we come up with a plausible conception of equality or mutual advantage which includes capitalist property rights, it is confusing to then say that it is an argument about freedom.

So it seems to me that none of the three definitions of liberty supports the view that libertarianism increases freedom. The failure of these three approaches suggests that the very idea of a liberty-based theory is confused. Our commitment to certain liberties does not derive from any general right to liberty, but from their role in the best theory of moral equality (or mutual advantage). The question we should ask is which specific liberties are most valuable to people, given their essential interests, and which distribution of those liberties is legitimate, given the demands of equality or mutual advantage. The idea of freedom as such, and lesser or greater amounts of it, does no work in political argument.

Scott Gordon objects to this elimination of 'freedom' as a category of political evalution, and its replacement with the evaluation of specific freedoms: 'If one is driven ... to greater and greater degrees of specification, freedom as a philosophical and political problem would disappear, obscured altogether by the innumerable specific "freedoms"' (Gordon 1980: 134). But, of course, this is just the point. There is no philosophical and political problem of freedom as such, only the real problem of assessing specific freedoms. Whenever someone says that we should have more freedom, we must ask who ought to be more free to do what from what obstacle? Contrary to Gordon, it's not the specification of these things, but the failure to specify them, that obscures the real issues.[35] Whenever someone tries to defend the free market, or anything else, on the grounds of freedom, we must demand that they specify which people are free to do which sorts of acts—and then ask why those people have a legitimate claim to those liberties—i.e. which interests are promoted by these liberties, and which account of equality or mutual advantage tells us that we ought to attend to those interests in that way. We cannot pre-empt these specific disputes by appealing to any principle or category of freedom as such.

5. THE POLITICS OF LIBERTARIANISM

Libertarianism shares with liberal equality a commitment to the principle of respect for people's choices, but rejects the principle of rectifying unequal circumstances. Taken to the extreme, this is not only intuitively unacceptable, but self-defeating as well, for the failure to rectify disadvantageous circumstances can undermine the very values (e.g. self-determination) that the principle of respect for choices is intended to promote. The libertarian denial that undeserved inequalities in circumstances give rise to moral claims suggests a failure to recognize the profound consequences of such differences for people's capacity for choices, agency, and dignity.

In practice, however, libertarianism may have a slightly different complexion. Libertarianism gains much of its popularity from a kind of 'slippery-slope' argument which draws attention to the ever-increasing costs of trying to meet the principle of equalizing circumstances. Like Rawls, the libertarian sees the popular conception of equality of opportunity as unstable. If we think social disadvantages should be rectified, then there is no reason not to rectify natural disadvantages. But, libertarians say, while unequal circumstances may *in principle* give rise to legitimate claims, the attempt to implement that principle inevitably leads *in practice* down a slippery slope to oppressive social intervention, centralized planning, and even human engineering. It leads down the road to serfdom, where the principle of respect for choices gets swallowed up by the requirement to equalize circumstances.

Why might this be? Liberals hope to balance the twin demands of respecting choices and rectifying circumstances. In some cases, this seems unproblematic. The attempt to equalize educational facilities—e.g. to ensure that state schools in predominantly black neighbourhoods are as good as predominantly white schools—does not impinge in an oppressive way on individual choice. Removing well-entrenched inequalities between different social groups requires little intervention in, or even attention to, discrete individual choices. The inequalities are so systematic that no one could suppose that they are traceable to different choices of individuals. But the principle of equalizing circumstances applies to disparities not only between social groups, but also between individuals, and it is less obvious whether those differences are due to choices or circumstances. Consider the problem of effort. In defending the principle of ambition-sensitivity, I used the example of the gardener and the tennis-player, who legitimately come to have differential income due to differential effort. It was important for the success of that example that the two people are similarly situated—i.e. there are no inequalities in skill or education which could prejudice one person's ability to make the relevant effort. But in the real world there are always some differences in people's background which could be said to be the cause of their different choices.

For example, differences in effort are sometimes related to differences in self-respect, which are in turn often related to people's social environment. Some children have more supportive parents or friends, or simply benefit from the contingencies of social life (e.g. not being sick for a test). These different influences will not be obvious, and any serious attempt to establish their presence will be severely invasive. Rawls says that the 'social bases of self-respect' are perhaps the most important primary good (Rawls 1971: 440), but do we want governments measuring how supportive parents are?

Moreover, rather than compensate for the effect of unequal circumstances on effort, why not ensure that there are no differential influences on effort to begin with, by bringing up children identically?[36] Liberals regard that as an unacceptable restriction on choice. But the libertarian fears it is a logical culmination of the liberal egalitarian commitment to equalize circumstances. The liberal wants to equalize circumstances in order to more fully respect choices, but how do we ensure that the former will not swallow the latter?

And why not extend the principle of equalizing circumstances to genetic engineering, manipulating embryos to be more equal in their endowments (Reinders 2000; Brown 2001)? Or consider biological transfers: if one person is born blind and another person is born with two good eyes, why not require the transfer of one good eye to the blind man (Nozick 1974: 207–8; Flew 1989: 159)? Dworkin points out that there is a difference between changing things so that people are treated as equals, and changing people so that they are, as changed, equal. The principle of equalizing circumstances requires the former, for it is part of the more general requirement that we treat people as equals (Dworkin 1983: 39; Williams 1971: 133–4). That is a valid distinction, but it does not avoid all the problems, for on Dworkin's own theory, people's natural talents are part of their circumstances ('things used in pursuing the good'), not part of the person ('beliefs which define what a good life is about'). So why should eye transfers count as changing people, rather than simply changing their circumstances? Dworkin says that some features of our human embodiment can be both part of the person (in the sense of a constitutive part of our identity) and part of a person's circumstances (a resource). Again that seems sensible. But the lines will not be easy to draw. Where does blood fit in? Would we be changing people if we required healthy people to give blood to haemophiliacs? I do not think so. But what then about kidneys? Like blood, the presence of a second kidney is not an important part of our self-identity, but we are reluctant to view such transfers as a legitimate demand of justice.

Again we find a slippery slope problem. Once we start down the road of equalizing natural endowments, where do we stop? Dworkin recognizes this slippery slope, and says that we might decide to draw an inviolable line around the body, regardless of how little any particular part of it is important to us, in order to ensure that the principle of equalizing circumstances does not violate our person. Libertarians, in practice, simply extend this strategy. If we can draw a line around the person, in order to ensure respect for individual personality, why not draw a line around her circumstances as well? In order to ensure that we do not end up with identical personalities due to identical upbringing, why not say that differential circumstances do not give rise to enforceable moral claims?[37]

If we view libertarianism in this way, its popularity becomes more understandable. It is inhumane to deny that unequal circumstances can create unfairness, but until we can find a clear and acceptable line between choices and circumstances, there will be some discomfort at making these forms of unfairness the basis of enforceable claims. Libertarianism capitalizes on that discomfort, by suggesting that we can avoid having to draw that line.

Having said that, it is important not to exaggerate the popularity of libertarianism, or its political influence. There has undoubtedly been a shift to the right in the 1980s and 1990s in many countries, with a retrenchment of the welfare state, a backlash against 'tax and spend liberals', and the election of 'conservative' or 'New Right' parties. But it would be a mistake, I think, to suppose that these changes are motivated by distinctly libertarian beliefs. Most supporters of this shift to the right acknowledge some obligation to redress unequal opportunities, and to protect the vulnerable. Their opposition to the welfare state is not necessarily rooted in any rejection of the liberal-egalitarian goal of an ambition-sensitive, endowment-sensitive distribution. Rather, they think that the welfare state has simply failed in practice to achieve either of these goals.

On the one hand, the welfare state is widely seen as taxing hard-working citizens to subsidize the lazy or indolent who simply do not want to work—a violation of the norm of ambition-sensitivity, and of the principle that people should be responsible for their choices. Public opinion polls suggest that people today are more likely than twenty years ago to say that people on unemployment insurance or welfare benefits are responsible for their condition, rather than being the victim of misfortune or unequal opportunities.

On the other hand, the welfare state is also seen as having failed to actually remedy the disadvantages facing the poor. Whereas liberal egalitarians have traditionally assumed that redistributive policies would enable the disadvantaged to enter the mainstream of society and effectively exercise their civil and political rights, the New Right argues that the welfare state has promoted passivity amongst the poor, without actually improving their life-chances, and created a culture of dependency. Far from being the solution, the welfare state has itself perpetuated the problem, by reducing citizens to passive dependants who are under bureaucratic tutelage. Hence the welfare state has failed in practice to remedy unequal circumstances, and may instead have entrenched the poor in their disadvantaged position.

To overcome these failings of the welfare state, the New Right suggests that we must go 'beyond entitlement', and focus instead on people's responsibility to earn a living.[38] Since the welfare state discourages people from becoming self-reliant, the safety net should be cut back, and any remaining welfare benefits should have obligations tied to them. This is the idea behind one of the principal reforms of the welfare system in the 1980s: 'workfare' programmes, which require welfare recipients to work for their benefits, so as to reinforce the idea that citizens should be self-supporting. This approach, it is said, would do better than the welfare state in promoting responsibility and enabling people to escape from poverty or unemployment.

In so far as these are the ideas and beliefs which underlie popular disenchantment with the welfare state, and popular support for right-wing policies, it has very little to do with libertarianism in the philosophical sense. Citizens in Western democracies have not en masse rejected the principles of liberal equality, but many no longer believe that the welfare state achieves these principles. And so the debate between right-wing and left-wing parties is not over the principle of protecting the vulnerable—that is not disputed by either side—but over empirical questions about who really is involuntarily disadvantaged, and about whether redistributive policies actually help them overcome these disadvantages.

This suggests that people who currently support right-wing parties would endorse redistributive policies if they were confident these policies would work to remedy involuntary disadvantages without subsidizing the indolent.[39] Unfortunately, the perceived failings of the welfare state have not only contributed to a dissatisfaction with traditional redistributive policies, but have also generated widespread distrust of the government's capacity to actually achieve social justice. As Hugh Heclo notes, 'There is now a deeply embedded cynicism about the ability of government programs to produce desired social changes. This is the result, not only of conservative rhetoric, but of hard experience as well-meaning efforts have collided with the unforgiving complexity of social reality' (quoted in King 1999: 45). Many people have come to believe that the problem does not lie in the details of particular social policies, but in the very capacity of the state to 'engineer' society. And so many people assume that any new proposals for social policy will fail, and will just be a waste of taxpayers' money.[40]

This decline in 'managerial optimism' is widespread throughout the Western democracies, but has proceeded much further in some countries than others. Indeed, this is one of the crucial factors in explaining variations in social policy. It is often assumed that the reason why some countries have a more modest welfare state than others is that their citizens hold distinctively individualistic or libertarian conceptions of justice. In fact, there are only minor differences between Western countries in popular beliefs about fairness, and/or the desirability of public policies that remedy involuntary disadvantage. The more significant difference is in the extent to which citizens trust the state to successfully implement such policies and/or trust their co-citizens to cooperate with them. According to Rothstein, it is differing levels of trust, not differing principles of justice, which primarily explain the variations in support for the welfare state across the Western democracies.[41]

There are various reasons, then, why many citizens have supported right-wing parties which seek to retrench the welfare state. (Of course, many people simply do not like paying high taxes, but that was always true, and hence does not explain why people today have become less willing to support the welfare state than twenty years ago.) But note that none of these reasons is rooted in libertarian arguments about the sanctity of self-ownership or property rights. The major arguments between the 'left' and the 'right' today are not about the importance of either holding people responsible for their choices or remedying unequal circumstances, but about several essentially empirical questions:

(a) to what extent are people poor because of misfortune and unequal opportunities, or because of their own choices? If we redistribute money to the poor are we helping the victims of unequal circumstances (as the left tends to believe) or subsidizing expensive tastes and irresponsible choices (as the right tends to believe)?

(b) has the welfare state helped the poor overcome their disadvantage and participate in society (as the left tends to believe), or has it created a class of welfare dependants caught in a poverty trap who are marginalized (as the right tends to believe)?

(c) in cases where the condition of the poor is partly due to their own choices and partly due to unequal circumstances, which comes first? Should we insist that the poor prove they are capable of acting responsibly before they are eligible for assistance (as the right tends to believe), or should we equalize their circumstances before we hold them responsible for their choices (as the left tends to believe)?

(d) does the state have the capacity to remedy involuntary disadvantages (as the left tends to believe), or are the sources of social ills like poverty, homelessness, high school drop-out rates, and so on so complex that state attempts to solve them will generally fail, and often worsen the problem (as the right tends to believe)?

These are all complex issues, not easy to resolve.[42] But none of the right-wing positions appeals to libertarian principles. Most right-wing arguments accept the desirability, in principle, of remedying unequal circumstances, but dispute the size of these inequalities, and the success of the welfare state in remedying them. For libertarians, by contrast, the state has no obligation to remedy unequal circumstances. Indeed, libertarians insist that the state is *prohibited* from even trying to remedy such circumstances, since these attempts would violate sacred property rights. That sort of libertarian position is not widespread even in 'right-wing' circles, a fact acknowledged and bemoaned by many libertarians.[43]

GUIDE TO FURTHER READING

For collections of recent libertarian thought, see Tibor Machan and Douglas Rasmussen (eds.), *Liberty for the Twenty-First Century: Contemporary Libertarian Thought* (Rowman and Littlefield, 1995), and David Boaz (ed.), *The Libertarian Reader: Classic and Contemporary Writings from Lao-tzu to Milton Friedman* (Free Press, 1997). The latter volume contains an extensive annotated bibliography to libertarian thought. Norman Barry provides an overview of contemporary libertarianism in his *Libertarianism in Philosophy and Politics* (Cambridge University Press, 1991). For a comprehensive critique, see Alan Haworth, *Anti-Libertarianism: Markets, Philosophy and Myth* (Routledge, 1994).

Although my focus in this chapter is on contemporary libertarian thought, the works of Friedrich Hayek remain profoundly influential, particularly his *Road to Serfdom* (University of Chicago Press, 1944) and *The Constitution of Liberty* (University of Chicago Press, 1960). For commentary, see Chandran Kukathas, *Hayek and Modern Liberalism* (Oxford University Press, 1989); and Roland Kley, *Hayek's Social and Political Thought* (Oxford University Press, 1994).

As noted in the chapter, the arguments for libertarianism have tended to fall into three main clusters: (*a*) self-ownership; (*b*) mutual advantage; (*c*) maximizing liberty. The most influential account of the *self-ownership* argument is Robert Nozick's *Anarchy, State, and Utopia* (Basic Books, 1974). The most powerful critique is G. A. Cohen's *Self-Ownership, Freedom and Equality* (Cambridge University Press, 1995). Cohen's critique of Nozick has been the subject of (at least) three symposia: in *Critical Review*, 12/3 (1998); *Journal of Ethics*, 2/1 (1998); and *Proceedings of the Aristotelian Society*, supplementary volume (1990). For more general overviews of the debate around Nozick's defence of libertarianism, see Jeffrey Paul (ed.), *Reading Nozick* (Rowman and Littlefield, 1981); and Jonathan Wolff, *Robert Nozick: Property, Justice, and the Minimal State* (Stanford University Press, 1991).

While the idea of self-ownership has typically been invoked as a defence of right-wing libertarianism, there is in fact a long tradition of 'left-wing libertarianism', which seeks to combine a strong principle of self-ownership with an equally strong commitment to the principle of the equal ownership of external resources. For a comprehensive overview of this tradition, see the two-volume set edited by Peter Vallentyne and Hillel Steiner (*The Origins of Left-Libertarianism: An Anthology of Historical Writings* and *Left-Libertarianism and its Critics: The Contemporary Debate*, both published by Palgrave, 2000).

For clear statements of the *mutual advantage* argument for libertarianism, see David

Gauthier, *Morals by Agreement* (Oxford University Press, 1986), and Jan Narveson's *The Libertarian Idea* (Temple University Press, 1988). Gauthier's argument is evaluated by the contributors to *Contractarianism and Rational Choice: Essays on Gauthier*, edited by Peter Vallentyne (Cambridge University Press, 1991). For the definitive account of the social contract tradition Gauthier draws upon, see Jean Hampton, *Hobbes and the Social Contract Tradition* (Cambridge University Press, 1986).

Although the *maximizing liberty* argument is perhaps the one most commonly invoked in popular discussions of libertarianism, there have been surprisingly few attempts by academics to provide a theoretical elucidation of what it means to maximize liberty, or how we would try to measure amounts of liberty. For an influential attempt to show that the very idea is meaningless, see Charles Taylor, 'On Negative Freedom', in his *Philosophy and the Human Sciences: Philosophical Papers*, vol. ii (Cambridge University Press, 1985). For a heroic effort to meet this challenge, see Ian Carter, *A Measure of Freedom* (Oxford University Press, 1999).

In addition to these arguments, there is also a long-standing tradition which defends libertarianism and minimal government on purely *utilitarian* grounds, as ensuring the most efficient use of resources, and the greatest overall welfare. For influential statements of this efficiency/utilitarian defence of libertarianism, see Richard Epstein, *Takings* (Harvard University Press, 1985); *Bargaining with the State* (Princeton University Press, 1995); *Simple Rules for a Complex World* (Harvard University Press, 1995); James Buchanan and Gordon Tullock, *The Calculus of Consent* (University of Michigan Press, 1962); James Buchanan and Richard Congleton, *Politics by Principle, Not Interest* (Cambridge University Press, 1998); Richard Posner, *The Economics of Justice* (Harvard University Press, 1983); *Overcoming Law* (Harvard University Press, 1996). The claim that libertarian political arrangements maximize utility is, of course, controversial. For doubts, see Rick Tilman, *Ideology and Utopia in the Social Philosophy of the Libertarian Economists* (Greenwood, 2001). In any event, the basic philosophical issues raised by this utilitarian-libertarian position are the same as those raised by other forms of utilitarianism, discussed in Chapter 2.

There are several journals which specialize in libertarian philosophy, including *Critical Review*; *Social Philosophy and Policy*; *Journal of Libertarian Studies*; *Independent Review*.

Useful websites include:

(a) Libertarian.org, which offers 'an introduction to libertarianism' and 'an overview of the libertarian philosophy and the libertarian movement'. It is affiliated with the larger Free-Market.Net: The Freedom Network (**www.libertarian.org; www.free-market.net**).

(b) The Foundation for Economic Freedom, which publishes the magazine *Ideas on Liberty*. Its website contains lesson plans, bibliographies, and discussion forums on 'the economic and ethical advantages of free markets' (**www.fee.org**).

(c) The Libertarian Party (the 'party of principle'), perhaps the only school of thought discussed in this book with its own political party (**www.lp.org**).

(d) 'Critiques of Libertarianism', a website with an extensive set of links critiquing libertarian theories and policy proposals (**www.world.std.com/~mhuben/ libindex.html**).

NOTES

1. There is in fact a voluminous literature which aims to show that libertarianism ensures the maximally efficient use of resources, sometimes described as the 'law and economics' and 'public choice' literature. See, e.g., Posner 1983; 1996; Epstein 1985; 1995*a*; Buchanan and Tullock 1962; Buchanan and Congleton 1998; cf. N. Barry 1986: chs. 2–4.

2. It is particularly important to distinguish libertarians from 'neo-conservatives', even though both were part of the movement for free-market policies under Thatcher and Reagan, and so are sometimes lumped together under the label the 'New Right'. As we will see, libertarianism defends its commitment to the market by appeal to a broader notion of per-sonal freedom—the right of each individual to decide freely how to employ their powers and possessions as they see fit. Libertarians therefore support the liberalization of laws concerning homosexuality, divorce, drugs, abortion, etc., and see this as continuous with their defence of the market. Neo-conservatives, on the other hand, 'are mainly interested in restoring trad-itional values, strengthening patriotic and family feelings, pursuing a strong nationalistic or anti-Communist foreign policy and reinforcing respect for authority', all of which may involve limiting 'disapproved lifestyles' (Brittan 1988: 213). The neo-conservative endorses market forces 'more because of the disciplines they impose than the freedom they provide. He or she may regard the welfare state, permissive morality, and 'inadequate' military spending, or preparedness to fight, as different examples of the excessive self-indulgence that is supposed to be sapping the West'. From the libertarian point of view, therefore, neo-conservatives are the 'New Spartans', and the chauvinistic foreign policy and moralistic social policy adopted by Reagan and Thatcher stand opposite to their commitment to personal freedom (Brittan 1988: 240–2; cf. Carey 1984).

3. In this passage, Nozick (like most libertarians) includes 'fraud' as one of the activities which a minimal state can and should prohibit. But can a libertarian theory consistently prohibit fraud? Fraud is not a violation of anyone's self-ownership, and on libertarian theories, the responsibility for determining the veracity of a seller's promises typically rests with the buyer, not the state ('caveat emptor': let the buyer beware). If the state can paternalistically protect people from fraud, why not also insist on mandatory labelling laws, or health and safety requirements, or mandatory testing of new foods or drugs? See Child 1994 for a detailed critique of the inconsistencies in libertarian discussions of the fraud standard. Cf. Katz 1999.

4. It is unclear whether Nozick himself would accept the claim that treating people as 'ends in themselves' is equivalent to treating them 'as equals', or whether he would accept Dworkin's egalitarian plateau. Rawls ties the idea of treating people as ends in themselves to a principle of equality (Rawls 1971: 251–7), and Kai Nielsen argues that Dworkin's egalitarian plateau 'is as much a part of Nozick's moral repertoire' as Rawls's (Nielsen 1985: 307). However, even if there is some distance between Nozick's 'Kantian principle' of treating people as ends in themselves and Dworkin's principle of treating people as equals, they are clearly related notions, and nothing in my subsequent arguments requires any tighter connection. All that matters, for my purposes, is that Nozick defends libertarianism by reference to some principle of respect for the moral status and intrinsic worth of each person.

5. Of course, there may be non-Nozickean reasons for respecting property rights even when initially acquired illegitimately—reasons of utility, or reasonable expectations. But these 'teleological' justifications for property rights conflict with Nozick's 'historical' or 'emergent' conception of justification (see Schmidtz 1990*b*).

6. Blackstone, *Commentaries on the Law of England*, book 2.

7. Locke also gave other answers—e.g. that we can appropriate that with which we have mixed our labour. But Nozick rightly rejects this answer as unworkable. If I add some home-made tomato juice to the ocean, how much of the ocean do I now own? If I put a fence around a plot of land, do I own the land *inside* the fence, or just the land *under* the fence—it is only the latter I have actually mixed my labour with (Nozick 1974: 174).

8. Nozick's claim is ambiguous here. He does not tell us what the 'normal process' of appropriation is. Hence it is unclear whether 'not worsening' is merely a necessary condition for legitimate appropriation (in addition to the 'normal process'), or whether it is a sufficient condition (any process which does not worsen the conditions of others is legitimate). If it is not a sufficient condition, he does not tell us what is (Cohen 1986a: 123).

9. For the need to include autonomy, not just material well-being, in our account of 'not worsening', see Kernohan 1988: 70; Cohen 1986a: 127, 135. Milde 1999 argues that this same problem undermines Gauthier's mutual advantage account of property rights, discussed in the next section of the chapter.

10. See Schmidtz 1994, who emphasizes that public or communal ownership can also avoid the tragedy of the commons, and may indeed be better in certain circumstances at avoiding free-rider and externality problems, although he thinks this is true only in limited circumstances.

11. For a sample of this enormous literature, see Arneson 1991; Arthur 1987; Bogart 1985; Christman 1986; 1991; G. A. Cohen 1986a; 1986b; 1990b; 1998; Epstein 1998; Exdell 1977; Feallsanach 1998; Fox-Decent 1998; Gorr 1995; Ingram 1993; Kernohan 1988; 1990; 1993; Mack 1990; 1995; Michael 1997; Otsuka 1998b; Ryan 1994; Sanders 1987; Schmidtz 1990a; 1994; Schwartz 1992; Shapiro 1991; Vallentyne 1997; 1998; Weinberg 1997; 1998; Wenar 1998. For a courageous defender of Nozick's view, see Palmer 1998.

12. For a comprehensive overview of this tradition, see Vallentyne and Steiner 2000; cf. Steiner 1981: 561–2; Vogel 1988. Even Locke seemed to think that unequal property-ownership could not arise from any right of individual appropriation. It required collective consent, in the form of an acceptance of money (Christman 1986: 163). In his survey of contemporary libertarianism, Norman Barry argues that none of the different versions of libertarianism (utilitarian, contractarian, natural rights, egoistic) has an adequate account of original title (Barry 1986: 90–3, 100–1, 127–8, 158, 178).

13. This is not to say that self-ownership has no implications for property-ownership. Andrew Kernohan argues that some of the rights entailed in self-ownership logically entail access to resources. Owning one's powers, in the fullest legal sense, entails owning the exercise of these powers, and this requires the right to exercise those powers oneself, the managerial right to decide who else may exercise them, and the income right to any benefit which flows from their exercise. None of these rights can be fulfilled without some rights over external resources (Kernohan 1988: 66–7). However, this logical connection between self-ownership and property-ownership still leaves a wide range of legitimate property regimes. Indeed, the only regime it excludes is precisely the one Nozick wishes to defend—i.e. a regime where some people lack any access to resources. According to Kernohan, this lack of property-ownership is a denial of their self-ownership.

14. As Andrew Kernohan notes, the right to keep all of one's market income is not the only, or even the primary, component of self-ownership, and limiting it can strengthen other more important components of substantive self-ownership (Kernohan 1990).

15. I am taking this version of the PD from Darwall 1998: 58; cf. Gauthier 1986: 79–80.

16. For a comprehensive discussion of Prisoner's Dilemmas, and the various circumstances in which it is rational to cooperate or defect, see Campbell and Sowden 1985.

17. See Gauthier's helpful discussion of the difference between the 'bargaining problem'

(what is the mutually advantageous rule), and the 'compliance problem' (how to constrain people from defecting from mutually advantageous rules) (Gauthier 1991).

18. A self-interested fisherman will overfish unless monitored and punished by police officers. But a self-interested police officer would accept a bribe from the fisherman, unless monitored and punished by some superiors. And a self-interested superior would accept a bribe from the police officer, unless subject to some system of monitoring and punishment from an even higher-up authority. And so on . . .

19. This has interesting parallels with the problem facing utilitarians. As we saw in Chapter 2, attempting to decide how to act on the basis of utilitarian reasoning may be counter-productive and actually impede our ability to maximize overall utility in society. Similarly, deciding how to act on the basis of egoistic reasoning may be counter-productive and impede our ability to maximize our individual utility. And the solution offered in each case is similar: Gauthier's solution of 'constrained maximization' parallels the utilitarian solution of rule-utilitarianism. In each case, we are told to follow the rules, without calculating whether our decision to follow the rule maximizes overall utility or individual self-interest. Kavka calls Gauthier's solution 'rule-egoism', to bring out this parallel with rule-utilitarianism (Kavka 1986: ch. 9).

20. See the essays in Vallentyne 1991.

21. For futile attempts to show that mutual advantage is compatible with, and indeed requires, compulsory aid to the defenceless, see Voice 1993; Lomasky 1987: 161–2, 204–8; Waldron 1986: 481–2; Narveson 1988: 269–74; Grice 1967: 149. For a discussion of their futility, see D. Phillips 1999; Goodin 1988: 163; Copp 1991; Gauthier 1986: 286–7.

22. I have treated equality and mutual advantage approaches as mutually exclusive options, based on diametrically opposed assumptions about morality. But it is worth noting that some people have argued for a hybrid theory which would integrate the two perspectives. Such a hybrid approach is sometimes called a 'Humean' approach, since Hume is said to have combined elements of Kantian equality with Hobbesian mutual advantage (e.g. Sayre-McCord 1994). Barry argues, however, that Hume's theory, and its subsequent descendants, simply waver inconsistently between the two approaches, rather than coherently integrating them (Barry 1989a: 145–78). In any event, it is doubtful that such a third model would lead to libertarianism. For more on the distinction between these two approaches, see Barry 1989a; Kymlicka 1990; A. Buchanan 1990.

23. Or as Kant put it, we may recognize certain moral truths or moral reasons, and yet this recognition may 'be attended only with a cold and lifeless approbation and not with any moving force' (quoted in Riley 1982: 251 n. 47).

24. As Elster notes, there is ample empirical evidence for the salience of these moral motivations: 'The main political reforms of the last century have not been supported by instrumental considerations. Rather, they have been carried by social movements anchored in a conception of justice' (Elster 1987: 89). See also J. Cohen 1997 on the irreducible role of moral reasons in explaining the anti-slavery movement.

25. Left-wing theorists often make the same mistake. George Brenkert, for example, argues that Marx's commitment to freedom is not tied to any principle of equality (Brenkert 1983: 124, 158; but cf. Arneson 1981: 220–1; Geras 1989: 247–51).

26. For interesting attempts to define and measure neutral liberty, see Steiner 1983; 1994; Carter 1992; 1995a; 1995b; 1999. Carter tries to overcome some of the problems of individuating acts by distinguishing between 'act-types' (e.g. living in a house) and 'act-tokens' (e.g. living in this particular house at this particular time), and argues that we can measure the 'extents of action' involved in each act-token by references to its spatio-temporal dimensions. He suggests that using this framework allows us to refute Taylor's 'diabolical defence' of Albania as a free

country (Carter 1992: 45), although I confess I do not myself see how it shows that Britain is freer than Albania.

27. Proponents of this 'purposive' view of the definition of freedom include Loevinsohn 1977; Norman 1981; Raz 1986: 13–16; Sen 1990*b*; 1991; Arneson 1985; Connolly 1993: 171–2.

28. As these examples show, our interest in the freedom to do *x* is not simply our interest in doing *x*. I may care about the freedom to choose my own clothes, for example, even though I don't particularly care about choosing clothes. While my wardrobe is a matter of almost complete indifference, I would find any attempt by others to dictate my clothing to be an intolerable invasion of privacy. On the other hand, I may care about other freedoms, like the freedom to buy foreign goods without tariffs, only in so far they enable me to buy more goods. In yet other cases, our being free to do something, like religious worship, may be constitutive of the very value of that act. That we freely choose to celebrate religious belief is crucial to the value of religious celebration. So our interest in the freedom to do *x* may be instrumental to, intrinsic to, or quite independent of, our interest in x. Hence our interest in different freedoms varies, not only with our interest in each particular act, but also with the range of instrumental, intrinsic, and symbolic interests promoted by having the freedom to do that particular act. Needless to say, it is hopelessly confusing to say that all these different interests are really a single interest in a more extensive freedom.

29. For a more in-depth discussion, see Norman 1991*a*; 1991*b*, where he discusses the problem of 'Taking "Free Action" Too Seriously'.

30. Steven Reiber argues that while a redistributive inheritance tax may simply redistribute the freedom to use the taxed resources, it does unilaterally reduce the freedom to bequeath property (Rieber 1996).

31. Nozick's claim here is not actually true. His theory does require that people's free exchanges preserve a particular pattern—namely, the Lockean proviso—and so it too requires continuously intervening in free exchanges to preserve a patterned distribution. This undermines Nozick's famous contrast between 'patterned theories', like Rawls's, and 'historical theories', like his own. All theories include both patterned and historical elements. Rawls, for example, allows people to come to have legitimate entitlements in virtue of their past actions and choices in conformity with the difference principle (a historical element), and Nozick requires that the pattern of distribution resulting from people's actions make no one worse off than they would have been in the state of nature (a patterned element). Nozick claims that the Lockean proviso is not a patterned requirement (Nozick 1974: 181), but if so, then nor is Rawls's difference principle (Bogart 1985: 828–32; Steiner 1977: 45–6). In any event, even if this contrast can be sustained, it is not a contrast between theories which interfere in people's lives and those which do not.

32. For a related discussion of some of the tensions in libertarianism between respecting each person's liberty and promoting overall liberty, see Kagan 1994.

33. To be fair, one can find liberal egalitarians using definitions of liberty in the same inconsistent way. They invoke the moralized definition to argue that the welfare state involves no restriction on freedom (since it only taxes resources that the advantaged had no moral right to), but invoked the non-moralized definition to argue that capitalism does restrict freedom (since it limits the freedom of non-owners to use resources owned by others).

34. For the importance of controlling property for these values, see Waldron 1991; Michelman 1996.

35. Gordon's subsequent discussion manifests these dangers. For example, he says that the free market increases people's freedom, but must be constrained in the name of justice. But he does not specify which people acquire which freedoms in the free market (specifying these things, he says, would obscure the problem of 'freedom as such'). As a result, he ignores the

loss of freedom caused by private property, and hence creates a false conflict between justice and freedom. For a similarly confused attempt to preserve the idea of 'freedom' as a separate value, see Raphael 1970: 140–1. He notes that a redistribution of property could be seen as redistributing freedom in the name of justice, rather than as sacrificing freedom for justice. But, he says, this would eliminate freedom as a separate value, and so 'it is more sensible to acknowledge the complexity of moral objectives to be pursued by the State, and to say that justice and the common good are not identical with freedom, although they are all closely related', and hence 'the State ought *not* to intervene in social life to the utmost extent in order to serve the objectives of justice and the common good' (Raphael 1970: 140–1). In order to preserve the alleged contrast between freedom and justice or equality, both Gordon and Raphael distort or ignore the actual freedom and unfreedoms involved. Other discussions of what it might mean for liberty to be 'accorded priority over other political goods or values' rest on similar confusions—e.g. invoking criteria to measure freedom that appeal to these other values, thus rendering the priority claim unintelligible (e.g. Gray 1989: 140–60; Loevinsohn 1977).

36. For responses to the worry that Rawlsian liberalism, taken to its logical conclusion, requires abolishing the family and replacing it with some form of equalized state child-raising, see Mallon 1999; Lloyd 1994; Fishkin 1983.

37. For an interesting comparison of liberal and libertarian (and feminist) approaches to disability, see Silvers, Wasserman, and Mahowald 1998.

38. *Beyond Entitlement* is the title of Lawrence Mead's influential New Right critique of the welfare state as promoting passivity and exclusion, see Mead 1986; cf. N. Barry 1990: 43–53.

39. For clear evidence to this effect, see Bowles and Gintis 1998; 1999; Gilens 1999.

40. Some people have argued that the infirmities of the welfare state are so great that even a strict Rawlsian, whose only concern is to maximally benefit the least well off, should reject policies such as public pensions and public health care and endorse free-market capitalism—e.g. D. Shapiro 1997; 1998. For empirical evidence to the contrary, see Sterba 2000: 471–4.

41. Rothstein 1998: 164–5. For empirical evidence on popular beliefs about justice in the Western democracies, and its relationship to philosophical theories of justice, see Miller 1992; 1999: ch. 4; Swift et al. 1995; Skitka and Tetlock 1993.

42. Consider the question of state capacity. It seems clear that liberal-egalitarian theories have operated with over-optimistic assumptions about state capacity. For example, in developing his theory of liberal equality, Bruce Ackerman explicitly appeals to the idea of a 'perfect technology of justice' (Ackerman 1980: 21; for similar assumptions, see Arneson 1990: 158; Roemer 1985a: 154). Of course, Ackerman knows that this is not available in the real world. But he does not tell us which parts of the resulting theory can be implemented, given our actually existing 'technology of justice'. The inherent limitations in the capacity of the state to achieve social objectives have been theorized by social scientists, both on the right (Glazer 1988) and the left (Rothstein 1998). But this literature has not yet permeated the philosophical debates. One looks in vain in the corpus of the major left-liberal political philosophers (Rawls, Dworkin, Cohen, Roemer, Arneson, Ackerman) for a discussion of the extent to which the state can or cannot fulfil the principles of justice they endorse.

43. Loren Lomasky, a prominent American defender of the (mutual advantage version of) libertarians, has written an article entitled 'Libertarianism as if (the Other 99 Percent of) People Mattered' (Lomasky 1998), which acknowledged that only a tiny fraction of Americans endorse libertarian ideals. His article addresses the question of how libertarians should act politically in a democracy, given that the vast majority of people do not agree with their principles.

5

MARXISM

The standard left-wing critique of liberal justice is that it endorses formal equality, in the form of equal opportunity or equal civil and political rights, while ignoring material inequalities, in the form of unequal access to resources. This is a valid criticism of libertarianism, given its commitment to formal rights of self-ownership rather than substantive self-determination. But contemporary liberal egalitarian theories, like those of Rawls and Dworkin, do not seem vulnerable to the same criticism. Rawls does believe that material inequalities (under the difference principle) are compatible with equal rights (under the liberty principle), and some critics take this as evidence of a lingering commitment to formal equality (e.g. Daniels 1975a: 279; Nielson 1978: 231; Macpherson 1973: 87–94). But the inequalities licensed by the difference principle are intended to promote the material circumstances of the less favoured. Far from neglecting substantive self-determination in the name of formal equality, the difference principle is justified precisely because 'the capacity of the less fortunate members of society to achieve their aims would be even less' were they to reject inequalities which satisfy the difference principle (Rawls 1971: 204). To oppose these inequalities in the name of people's substantive self-determination is therefore quite misleading.[1]

Given this shared commitment to material equality, do socialists and liberal egalitarians share the same account of justice? For some strands of socialist thought, the answer is yes. There seems to be no deep difference between Dworkin's liberal theory of equality of resources and various socialist theories of 'compensatory justice', which also aim at an ambition-sensitive, endowment-insensitive distribution (e.g. Dick 1975; DiQuattro 1983; cf. Carens 1985).[2] Similarly, there seem to be no deep differences between liberal accounts of a 'property-owning democracy' or 'stakeholder society' and various models of 'market socialism', which also aim at greater equalization of ownership of productive assets while still relying on markets for the distribution of goods and services.[3]

However, there are other strands of socialist thought which move in a different direction. I will discuss a few such strands in this chapter, drawn from recent Marxist writings. With the discrediting and eventual dissolution of communist regimes in Eastern Europe, it is often said that Marxism is now 'dead', relegated to the dustbin of history, like older theories of theocracy, feudalism, or absolutist monarchies. Surprisingly, however, the death of communist regimes in the East has gone hand in hand with a rebirth of Marxist theorizing in the West. Marx and Marxism were more or less entirely ignored by Anglo-American philosophers for most of the twentieth century (Ware 1989: 1–2). In the last twenty years, however, there has been an outpouring of writings on Marxism, and attempts to reformulate Marxian theories. This movement is often known as 'analytical Marxism', since its proponents aim to reformulate Marx's insights using the tools and methods of contemporary Anglo-American analytic philosophy and social science.

This process of 'reformulating' Marx has of course been a selective project. Many of Marx's beliefs and predictions have been soundly refuted, and very few people would want to defend his corpus *tout court*. In particular, few analytic Marxists wish to defend Marx's theory of history, known as 'historical materialism'. According to this theory, the development of human societies is determined by class struggle, which is itself determined by the development of the means of economic production, and the inevitable result of this development is the revolutionary overthrow of capitalism by the proleteriat. Capitalism would be replaced first with socialism, and eventually, once abundance has been achieved, with full-blown communism.

Few analytic Marxists today believe in the inevitability of proletarian revolution. Precisely for this reason, however, it has become more important for Marxists to clarify the normative basis of their commitments to socialism or communism. When Marxists believed that socialism was *inevitable*, there was no need to explain why it was *desirable*. It was simply the end point of a predetermined sequence of historical developments. Capitalism would self-destruct, due to its inner contradictions, and the increasingly immiserated workers would have no choice but to overthrow it. Economic contradictions, not moral arguments, would underlie the revolution.

Marx and Engels were in fact quite scathing about theorists who tried to give moral arguments in favour of socialism. Moral arguments were seen as both unnecessary, since workers had no rational alternative to revolution, and strategically divisive, since the idea of justice is endlessly contestable. Moreover, defenders of capitalism had already crafted elaborate ideological justifications for the freedom and equality of capitalism. Shifting the debate onto the terrain of moral argument would allow these ideologists of capitalism to distract the workers from their task of revolution.

Today, however, Marxists realize that if socialist or communist ideals are to be implemented, it will require persuading people that these ideals are morally legitimate, and worth pursuing. Far from being increasingly immiserated, many workers have experienced an increasing standard of living, and often vote for political parties committed to capitalism. If socialist parties are to succeed, arguments must be given why a socialist society would be more desirable—more free, just, or democratic—than the sort of welfare state capitalism we see today. And indeed much of the work in contemporary analytic Marxism has been concerned precisely with developing these sorts of normative arguments.

In other words, the death of 'scientific' Marxism as a theory of historical inevitability has helped give birth to Marxism as a normative political theory.[4] A fundamental goal of the new analytical Marxism is to offer a critique of, and alternative to, liberal theories of justice.

In this chapter, I will look at two strands of critique. One strand objects to the very idea of justice. Justice, on this view, is a remedial virtue, a response to some flaw in social life. Justice seeks to mediate conflicts between individuals, whereas communism overcomes those conflicts, and hence overcomes the need for justice. The second strand shares liberalism's emphasis on justice, but rejects the liberal belief that justice is compatible with private ownership of the means of production. Within this second strand, there is a division between those who criticize private property on the grounds of exploitation, and those who criticize it on the grounds of alienation. In either case, however, Marxist justice requires socializing the means of production, so that productive assets are the property of the community as a whole, or of the workers within each firm. Where liberal-egalitarian theories of justice try to employ private property while negating its inequalities, Marxists appeal to a more radical theory of justice that views private property as inherently unjust.

1. COMMUNISM AS BEYOND JUSTICE

One of the most striking features of Rawls's theory is its claim that 'justice is the first virtue of social institutions' (Rawls 1971: 3). Justice, according to Rawls, is not one amongst a number of other political values, like freedom, community, and efficiency. Rather, justice is the standard by which we weigh the importance of these other values. If a policy is unjust, there is no separate set of values one can appeal to in the hope of overriding justice, for the legitimate weight attached to these other values is established by their location within the best theory of justice. (Conversely, one of the tests of a theory of justice is that it gives due weight to these other values. As Rawls says, if a theory of justice does not give adequate scope to community and freedom, then it will not be attractive to us.)

Liberals emphasize justice because they see a tight connection between it and the basic idea of moral equality. Liberals promote the *moral* equality of people by formulating a theory of *juridical* equality, which articulates each individual's claims to the conditions which promote their well-being. Many Marxists, on the other hand, do not emphasize justice, and indeed object to the idea that communism is based on a principle of justice. In this regard, they are following Marx himself, who attacked the ideas of 'equal right' and 'fair distribution' as 'obsolete verbal rubbish' (Marx and Engels 1968: 321). This is the conclusion Marx draws from his analysis of the 'contribution principle'— i.e. the claim that labourers have a right to the products of their labour. While many socialists in his day viewed the contribution principle as an important argument for socialism, Marx says that it has many 'defects' which make it, at best, a transitional principle between capitalism and communism. The contribution principle gives people an 'equal right', since everyone is measured by an equal standard (i.e. labour). However, some people have greater natural talents, so this equal right becomes an 'unequal right for unequal labour':

it tacitly recognizes unequal individual endowment and thus productive activity as natural privileges. *It is, therefore, a right of inequality, in its content, like every right.* Right by its very nature can consist only in the application of an equal standard; but unequal individuals (and they would not be different individuals if they were not unequal) are measurable only by an equal standard in so far as they are brought under an equal point of view, are taken from one *definite* side only, for instance, in the present case, are regarded *only as workers* and nothing more is seen in them, everything else being ignored. (Marx and Engels 1968: 320)

According to Allen Wood, this passage shows that Marx was averse, not only to the idea of justice, but to the concept of moral equality underlying it. On Wood's view, Marx was 'no friend to the idea that "equality" is something good in itself', and he was not 'a believer in a society of equals' (Wood 1979: 281; 1981: 195; cf. Miller 1984: ch. 1).

But Marx's argument here does not reject the view that the community should treat its members as equals. What he denies is that the community should do so through implementing a theory of juridical equality. In this passage, Marx endorses a principle of equal regard, but denies that any 'equal right' ever captures it because rights work by defining one limited viewpoint by which individuals are to be regarded equally. For example, the contribution principle views people as workers only, but ignores the fact that different workers vary both in their talents and in their needs—for example, 'one worker is married, another not; one has more children than another, and so on' (Marx and Engels 1968: 320). In reality, the number of viewpoints relevant to determining the true meaning of equal regard is indefinite, or, in any event, cannot be specified in advance. But notice that this description of the effect of 'equal rights' is only a criticism if people are owed equal concern and respect—that is why these inequalities are 'defects'. Marx rejected the idea of equal rights, not because he was not a friend to the idea of treating people as equals, but precisely because he thought rights failed to live up to that ideal. In fact, the idea of moral equality is basic to Marx's thought (Arneson 1981: 214–16; Reiman 1981: 320–2; 1983: 158; Geras 1989: 231, 258–61; Elster 1983a: 296; 1985: ch. 4).[5]

Marxists have a number of objections to the idea of juridical equality. The first one, as we have seen, is that equal rights have unequal effects, since they only specify a limited number of the morally relevant standpoints. But that argument is weak, for even if it is true that we cannot define in advance all the relevant standpoints, it does not follow that the best way of treating people with equal regard is by not specifying any viewpoints at all. Even if a schedule of rights cannot fully model equal regard, it may do so better than any other alternative. In fact, what else can we do except try to specify the standpoints we think morally relevant? We can only avoid this difficult task by avoiding having to make distributive decisions at all. This is indeed what some Marxists have hoped to do, by assuming that there will be an abundance of resources under communism, but, as we will see, this is an unrealistic hope.

A second objection is that theories of 'just distribution' concentrate too much on *distribution*, rather than on the more fundamental questions of *production* (Young 1981; Wood 1972: 268; Buchanan 1982: 56–7, 122–6; Wolff 1977: 199–208; Holmstrom 1977: 361; cf. Marx and Engels 1968: 321). If all we do is redistribute income from those who own productive assets to those who do not, then we will still have classes, exploitation, and hence the kind of contradictory interests that make justice necessary in the first place. We should instead be concerned with transferring ownership of the means of production themselves. When this is accomplished, questions of fair distribution become obsolete.

This raises an important point. We should be concerned with ownership, for ownership allows people not only to accrue greater income, but also to gain a measure of control over other people's lives. A scheme of redistributive taxation may leave a capitalist and a worker with equal incomes, but it would still leave the capitalist with the power to decide how the worker spends much of her time, a power that the worker lacks in relation to the capitalist. As an objection to the idea of justice, however, this complaint fails. Nothing in the idea of justice limits it to questions of income. On the contrary, as we have seen, both Rawls and Dworkin include productive assets as one of society's resources to be distributed in accordance with a theory of justice. Indeed, Rawls argues that a more egalitarian pattern of property-ownership is required for his ideal of a 'property-owning democracy'. And if Dworkin tends, when discussing the practical implementation of his theory, to look solely at schemes of income redistribution, rather than a fundamental redistribution of wealth, that is incompatible with his own theory of justice

(Ch. 3, s. 5). The Marxist objection to the class structure of capitalist relations of production is, above all, a distributive objection, and so fits comfortably within the normal scope of theories of justice (as Marx himself sometimes noted—Marx and Engels 1968: 321; Marx 1973: 832; cf. Arneson 1981: 222–5; Geras 1989: 228–9; Cohen 1988: 299–300).

At best, these two objections point to limitations in the way that some people have developed their conceptions of justice. The heart of the Marxist critique, however, is an objection to the very idea of a juridical community. Many Marxists believe that justice, far from being the first virtue of social institutions, is something that the truly good community has no need for. Justice is appropriate only if we are in the 'circumstances of justice', circumstances which create the kinds of conflicts that can only be solved by principles of justice. These circumstances are usually said to be of two main kinds: conflicting goals, and limited material resources. If people disagree over goals, and are faced with scarce resources, then they will inevitably make conflicting claims. If, however, we could eliminate either the conflicts between people's goals, or the scarcity of resources, then we would have no need for a theory of juridical equality, and would be better off without it (Buchanan 1982: 57; Lukes 1985: ch. 3).

According to some Marxists, the circumstance of justice which communism seeks to overcome is conflicting conceptions of the good. They take the family as an example of an institution which is non-juridical, where there is an identity of interests, in which people respond spontaneously to the needs of others out of love, rather than responding on the basis of rightful duties or calculations of personal advantage (cf. Buchanan 1982: 13). If the community as a whole also had an identity of interests and affective ties, then justice would not be needed, because to conceive of oneself as a bearer of rights is to 'view oneself as a potential party to interpersonal conflicts in which it is *necessary* to assert claims and to "stand up" for what one claims as one's due' (Buchanan 1982: 76). If we fulfilled each other's needs out of love, or out of a harmony of interests, then there would be no occasion for such a concept of rights to appear.

I have argued elsewhere that Marx did not believe in this vision of an affectively integrated community with an identity of interests. For Marx, communist relations are free of antagonism 'not in the sense of individual antagonism, but of one arising from the social conditions of life of the individuals' (Marx and Engels 1968: 182).[6] The 'harmony of ends' solution to the circumstances of justice is, in fact, more of a communitarian ideal than a Marxian one (cf. Ch. 6, s. 8c below). Moreover, it is doubtful whether this is a possible solution to the circumstances of justice. For even if we share a set of goals, we may still have conflicting personal interests (e.g. two music-lovers wanting the only available opera ticket). And even where we lack conflicting personal interests, we may disagree about how to achieve a shared project, or about how much support it deserves. You and I may both believe that experiencing music is a valuable part of a good life, and that music should be supported with one's time and money. But you may wish to support music in such a way as to allow the greatest number of people to experience it, even if that means that they experience lower-quality music, whereas I want to support the highest-quality music, even if that means some people never experience it. So long as there are scarce resources, we will disagree over how much support should go to which musical projects. Shared ends only eliminate conflicts over the use of scarce resources when people share means and priorities as well. But the only people who share identical ends for the identical reasons with identical intensity are identical people. And this raises the question of whether conflicting ends are best seen as a 'problem' which needs to be 'remedied' or overcome. It is perhaps true that conflicts are not, in and of themselves, something to be valued. But the diversity of ends which makes such conflicts inevitable may be something to be valued.

The other solution to the circumstances of justice is to eliminate material scarcity. As Marx puts it:

In a higher phase of communist society, after the enslaving subordination of the individual to the division of labour . . . has vanished; after labour has become not only a means to life but life's prime want; after the productive forces have also increased with the all-round development of the individual, and all the springs of co-operative wealth flow more abundantly—only then can the narrow horizon of bourgeois right be crossed in its entirety and society inscribe on its banners: From each according to his ability, to each according to his needs! (Marx and Engels 1968: 320–1)

Marx was emphatic about the need for abundance, for he thought that scarcity made conflicts unresolvable. The highest development of the productive forces 'is an absolutely necessary practical premise [of communism] because without it *want* is merely made general, and with *destitution* the struggle for necessities and all the old filthy business would necessarily be reproduced' (Marx and Engels 1970: 56). It was perhaps because he was so pessimistic about the social effects of scarcity that he became so optimistic about the possibility of abundance (Cohen 1990*b*).

However, this solution to the circumstances of justice is also implausible (Lukes 1985: 63–6; Buchanan 1982: 165–9; Nove 1983: 15–20). Certain resources (e.g. space) are inherently limited, and the recent wave of environmental crises has revealed the empirical limits to other resources we depend on (e.g. clean drinking water; oil reserves). Moreover, certain kinds of conflicts and harms can arise even with an abundance of certain resources. One example that arises *because* of an ability and desire to help others is the potential conflicts involved in paternalism. So even if justice is appropriate only as a response to problems in society, it may not be possible to overcome these problems.

But is justice best viewed as a remedial virtue that should be superseded? Marxists argue that while justice helps mediate conflicts, it also tends to create conflicts, or, at any rate, to decrease the natural expression of sociability. Hence justice is a regrettable necessity at present, but a barrier to a higher form of community under conditions of abundance. It is better if people act spontaneously out of love for each other, rather than viewing themselves and others as bearers of just entitlements.

But why are these two opposed, why must we choose either love or justice? After all, some people argue that a sense of justice is a precondition of, and indeed partly constitutive of, love for others. The concern seems to be that if we give people rights they will automatically claim them, regardless of the effects on others, including the ones they love. For example, Buchanan says that justice involves 'casting the parties to conflict in the narrow and unyielding roles of rights-bearers' (Buchanan 1982: 178). Similar complaints about 'rights-talk' have been raised by communitarians, who argue that the language of rights and justice encourages an antagonistic, zero-sum conception of social life, and displaces more noble sentiments of love or affection.[7]

But why can't I choose to waive my rights whenever their exercise would harm the people I love? Consider the family. Does the fact that women in France now have the right to move to another town and work there without their spouse's permission mean that they will exercise that right rather than keep their families together? (Similarly, have men, who have always had that right, never forgone a career move for the sake of their families?) Buchanan says that 'for those who find the bonds of mutual respect among right-bearers too rigid and cold to capture some of what is best in human relationships, Marx's vision of genuine community—*rather than* a mere juridical association—will remain attractive' (Buchanan 1982: 178, my emphasis). But if the family is an example of what is best in human relationships, then the contrast is spurious. The family has always been a juridical association, in which spouses and children are all rights-bearers (though not equally so). Does that mean that marriage is after all not a sphere of mutual affection, but, as Kant put it, an agreement between two people for 'reciprocal use of each other's sexual organs'? Of course not. Families can have loving relationships, and the juridical nature of marriage does nothing to prevent them. Surely no one believes that people will only act out of love if they are denied the opportunity to do otherwise.[8]

Rawls's claim about the priority of justice is not a claim 'about whether a person will, or should, push to the limit their rightful claims to various advantages' (Baker 1985: 918). While the priority of justice ensures that individuals are able to claim certain advantages, it equally ensures that they are able to share these advantages with those they love. Generous and loving people will be generous and loving with their just entitlements—far from inhibiting this, the priority of justice makes it possible. What justice excludes is not love or affection, but injustice—the subordination of some people's good to others', through the denial of their just entitlements (Baker 1985: 920). And this, of course, is the opposite of genuine love and affection.

Justice is not only compatible with a concern for others, it is itself an important form of concern for others. It is often said that a concern for rights involves a self-understanding that is grounded in egoism and a concern to protect oneself against the likely antagonism of others in a zero-sum social world. Buchanan, for example, says that to think of oneself as a rights-bearer is to 'view oneself as a potential party to interpersonal conflicts in which it is *necessary* to assert claims' (Buchanan 1982: 76). To claim a right, on this view, is to have a certain pessimistic view of how others will *respond* to our requests. But Buchanan himself suggests another reason for valuing the recognition of rights. He says that for someone to think of himself as a rights-bearer is to 'think of himself as being able to demand what he has a right to as his due, rather than as something he may merely request as being desirable' (Buchanan 1982: 75–6). These are two very different self-understandings, although they are often conflated. The second self-understanding concerns not the probability of getting something I want or need, but the grounds on which I think of myself as properly (e.g. not selfishly) having it. I may want to avoid taking advantage of the (potentially self-sacrificing) love of others. If so, then justice can serve as a standard for determining what I am non-selfishly entitled to, even when others are prepared to give me more than I am entitled to.

Justice can also serve as a standard for determining how to respond to the needs of others, even where the reason I want to help is simply my love for them. I may desire to help several people, all of whom are in need, because I love them, not because I owe them my help. But what if their needs conflict? As Rawls points out, it is no good to say I should act benevolently rather than justly, for 'benevolence is at sea as long as its many loves are in opposition in the persons of its many objects' (Rawls 1971: 190). While love is my motivation, justice may be the standard I appeal to, given that love yields conflicting imperatives. Hence, 'while friendship may render justice unnecessary as a *motive*, it may still require some aspects of justice as a *standard*. Friends do not automatically know what to do for one another' (Galston 1980: 289 n. 11). Justice, therefore, serves two important purposes. When making claims, I may wish to know what I am properly entitled to, even when others will fulfil my requests without concern for my entitlements. When responding to the claims of others, I may wish to know what their entitlements are, even when love is the motivation for my response. In neither case is my interest in the teachings of justice a matter of 'standing up for my due'.

The public recognition of rights can be valuable in another way. A person may be sure of getting what she wants, by virtue of her participation in a highly respected social practice (e.g. as a teacher). She has no need for rights, on Buchanan's first account of them, because others value her contribution to that practice, and reward her generously for it. Yet she may want to know that people would accord her rights even if they did not share her commitments. And she may want to know this even if she has no desire to leave that practice, for this recognizes that she is a source of value in and of herself, not just qua occupant of a social role.

Justice is more than a remedial virtue. Justice does remedy defects in social coordination, and these defects are ineradicable, but it also expresses the respect individuals are owed as ends in themselves, not as means to someone's good, or even to the common good. Justice recognizes the equal standing of the members of the community, through an account of the rights and entitlements we can justly claim. But it does not force people to exercise these entitlements at the expense of the people or projects they care about. Justice constitutes a form of concern that we should have for the members of our community, and enables us to pursue all the other forms of love and affection which are consistent with that underlying moral equality. The view that we could create a community of equals by abandoning these notions of fairness, rights, and duties is untenable.[9]

Marx's dismissive approach to justice is part of a broader pattern. He believed that communism would eliminate the need for most of the basic concepts and categories of liberal thought, including rights, toleration, representative democracy, opposition political parties, the rule of law, and markets. All of these, Marx believed, were 'merely remedial, palliatives for dealing with material, social, cultural and epistemological problems that can be overcome, thereby rendering the remedies unnecessary' (Lukes 1995: 3). Marx envisaged a future society without scarcity, conflicting economic interests, ethnic or religious divisions, or imperfect rationality. Such a society would not need the sorts of practices and institutions which liberal states have developed to remedy these problems. Moreover, as I noted at the beginning of the chapter, Marx thought that engaging in moral debates about these practices and institutions was simply a distraction from the real business of the inevitable proletarian revolution. As a result, until quite recently, few Marxists have shown an interest in developing a normative theory of justice, rights, toleration, or democracy.

Today, however, virtually all analytic Marxists accept that scarcity, conflict, pluralism, and imperfect rationality are permanent features of the human condition, and that any plausible normative political theory must explain how political institutions will deal with these facts. And the first step in this direction is to develop a Marxist theory of justice.[10]

2. COMMUNIST JUSTICE

If justice is both ineradicable and desirable, what would Marxist justice look like? It is standardly supposed that Marxism is egalitarian, indeed more egalitarian than liberalism, further to the left. This is certainly true in regard to mainstream liberalism and its ideology of equal opportunity, according to which unlimited inequalities are legitimate so long as there is fair competition for higher-paying positions (Ch. 3, s. 2 above). But it is not immmediately obvious what room there is to the left of Rawls's version of liberal egalitarian justice, since it too rejects the prevailing ideology, and accepts inequalities only if they work to the benefit of the least well off. What distinguishes Marxist from Rawlsian justice is not the extent to which resources should be equalized, but rather the form in which such equalization should occur. Rawls believes that equality of resources should take the form of equalizing the amount of private property available to each person. For Marx, on the other hand, 'the theory of the Communists may be summed up in a single phrase: Abolition of private property.' Private ownership is permissible in areas of 'personal property', like the clothes, furnishings, and leisure goods we use at home and at play. But it is 'fundamental' to Marxism that 'there is no moral right to the private ownership of and control of productive resources' (Geras 1989: 255; cf. Cohen 1988: 298). Equalization of productive resources should take the form of socializing the means of production, so that each person has equal participation in collective decisions about the deployment of productive assets, made at the level of either individual firms or national economic planning.

Why should equality take the form of equal access to public resources, rather than an equal distribution of private resources? One reason is simply that Rawls's idea of a 'property-owning democracy' may not be empirically viable. It may be impossible to equalize productive resources in modern economies except through socializing ownership. As Engels put it, 'the bourgeoisie . . . could not transform these puny means of production into mighty productive forces without transforming them, at the same time, from means of production of the individual into *social* means of production workable only by a collectivity of men'. Under capitalism, however, these 'socialized means of production' are still treated 'just as they had been before, i.e. as the means of production of individuals'. The solution to this contradiction 'can only come about by society openly and directly taking possession of the productive forces which have outgrown all control except that of society as a whole' (Marx and Engels 1968: 413, 414, 423).

For Engels, the need to socialize ownership is not based on any distinctive theory of justice, but simply on an inability to conceive of any other device for equalizing resources in a modern industrial economy. Some Marxists also object on empirical grounds to Rawls's assumption that the inequalities arising from market transactions in a well-ordered society would tend to benefit the less well off. If they would not, and if redistributive mechanisms are inherently vulnerable to political pressure, then we might adopt socialism on the basis of a 'greater-likelihood principle' (Schweickart 1978: 11, 23; DiQuattro 1983: 68–9; Clark and Gintis 1978: 322).

For these and other reasons, some critics conclude that Rawls's idea of a property-owning democracy is 'at best fanciful' (Nielsen 1978: 228), and that the whole idea of a property-owning democracy only makes sense in its original Jeffersonian context of an agrarian society composed of independent landholders (Macpherson 1973: 135–6; Weale 1982: 57). If so, then socializing the means of production may be the only viable way of implementing the difference principle. On the other hand, as I noted in Chapter 3, liberal egalitarians have advanced various proposals for increasing *ex ante* equality in endowments—such as the stakeholder society, compensatory education, basic income, coupon capitalism, and the pragmatic egalitarian planner—which have simply never been tried. It may be premature to declare that greater equality in productive assets in unfeasible.

While these objections to the viability of an egalitarian private property regime account for much of the left-wing criticism of Rawls's theory—and for much of the day-to-day debate between liberal egalitarians and socialists—there are also more theoretical objections to the very idea of private property. According to many Marxists, private ownership of the means of production should be abolished because it gives rise to the wage-labour relationship, which is inherently unjust. Some Marxists claim that wage-labour is inherently exploitative, others claim that it is inherently alienating. On either view, justice is only secured by abolishing private property, even if a Rawlsian property-owning democracy is empirically viable.

(a) Exploitation

The paradigm of injustice for Marxists is exploitation, and, in our society, the exploitation of the worker by the capitalist. The fundamental flaw of liberal justice, Marxists claim, is that it licenses the continuation of this exploitation, since it licenses the buying and selling of labour. Does liberal justice allow some to exploit others? It depends, of course, on how we define exploitation. In its everyday usage, exploitation (when applied to persons rather than natural resources) means 'taking unfair advantage of someone'. Every theory of justice, therefore, has its own theory of exploitation, since every theory has an account of the ways it is permissible and impermissible to benefit from others. On Rawls's theory, for example, a talented person takes unfair advantage of the untalented if he uses their weak bargaining position to command an unequal share of resources not justified by the difference principle. It is not exploitative, however, for someone to benefit from employing others if this works to the maximal benefit of the least well off. If we are convinced of the fairness of Rawls's theory, then we will deny that it licenses exploitation, since part of what it means to accept a theory of justice just is to accept its standard for judging when others are unfairly taken advantage of.

Marxists, however, operate with a more technical definition of exploitation. In this technical usage, exploitation refers to the specific phenomenon of the capitalist extracting more value from the worker's labour (in the form of produced goods) than is paid back to the worker in return for that labour (in the form of wages). According to classical Marxist theory, capitalists only hire workers when they can extract this 'surplus value', and so this exploitative transfer of surplus value from the worker to the capitalist is found in all wage relationships. This technical definition of exploitation is sometimes said to be of scientific rather than moral interest. For example, the fact that capitalists extract surplus value is said to explain how profits are possible in a competitive economy, and this claim does not by itself entail that it is wrong to extract surplus value. Most Marxists, however, have taken the extraction of surplus value as evidence of an injustice—indeed, as the paradigm of injustice.

Does Marxist exploitation have moral significance, i.e. does it involve taking unfair advantage of someone? The traditional argument that technical exploitation is unjust goes like this (from Cohen 1988: 214):

1. Labour and labour alone creates value.
2. The capitalist receives some of the value of the product.

Therefore:

3. The labourer receives less value than he creates.
4. The capitalist receives some of the value the labourer creates.

Therefore:

5. The labourer is exploited by the capitalist.

There are a number of gaps in this argument. Premiss (1) is controversial, to say the least. Many Marxists have tried to defend it by appeal to 'the labour theory of value', according to which the value of a produced object is determined by the amount of labour required to produce it. But as Cohen points out, the labour theory of value actually contradicts (1), for the labour theory says that the value of an object is determined by the amount of labour *currently* required to produce it, not how much labour was actually involved in producing it. If technology changes in such a way that an object can now be produced with half the labour previously required, the labour theory of value says that the value of the object is cut in half, even though the amount of labour embodied in the already produced object is unaffected. The actual labour expended by the worker is irrelevant, if the labour theory of value is true.

What matters, morally speaking, is not that the workers create value, but that 'they create *what has value* . . . What raises a charge of exploitation is not that the capitalist appropriates some of the value the worker produces, but that he appropriates some of the value *of what* the worker produces' (Cohen 1988: 226–7). Creating products that have value is different from creating the value of those products, and it is the former that really matters for the charge of exploitation. Even if someone other than the worker creates the value of the product—if, for example, its value is determined by the desires of its consumers—then Marxists would still say that the worker is exploited by the capitalist, for it is the worker, not the capitalist or the consumers, who created the product. Hence the proper argument is this (Cohen 1988: 228):

1. The labourer is the only person who creates the product, that which has value.
2. The capitalist receives some of the value of the product.

Therefore:

3. The labourer receives less value than the value of what he creates.
4. The capitalist receives some of the value of what the labourer creates.

Therefore:

5. The labourer is exploited by the capitalist.

This modified version of the Marxist argument yields the conclusion that wage relationships are inherently exploitative. But it is not clear that the exploitation involved here is an injustice. In the first place, there is nothing unjust about volunteering to contribute one's labour to others. Most Marxists, therefore, add the proviso that the worker must be forced to work for the capitalist. Since workers do not in general own any productive assets, and can only earn a living by working for a propertied capitalist (though not necessarily for any particular capitalist), most wage relationships fall under this proviso (Reiman 1987: 3; Holmstrom 1977: 358).

Is the forced transfer of surplus value exploitative in the everyday sense? This is both too weak and too strong. It is too weak in excluding from the purview of exploitation wage-labour which is not, strictly speaking, forced. If, for example, a safety net is in place, guaranteeing a minimal income to all, then the propertyless can acquire a subsistence living through the welfare state, without having to work for a capitalist. But we might still want to say that workers are exploited. While the propertyless are not forced to work for a capitalist in order to survive, that may be the only way for them to earn a decent standard of living, and we might think it is unfair that they should have to yield surplus labour to capitalists in order to secure a comfortable living. One can say that such people are 'forced' to work for the capitalist, since the alternatives are in some way unacceptable or unreasonable. But, as we will see, the important question is not whether workers are forced to work for capitalists, but whether the unequal access to resources which 'forces' workers to accept that surplus transfer is unfair.

Defining exploitation as forced transfer of surplus labour is also too strong, for there are many legitimate instances of forced transfer of surplus value. What if workers are like apprentices who must work for others for a period of five years, but then are able to become capitalists themselves (or masters)? According to Jeffrey Reiman, this is exploitative: 'we care about workers being forced to sell their labour power, because we understand this as forcing them to work without pay. And we care about how long workers are forced to work without pay, because of how we feel about people being forced to work without pay for any period of time' (Reiman 1987: 36). But this is implausible. If all workers can become capitalists, and if all capitalists begin as workers, then there is no inequality over the course of people's lifetimes. Like apprentices, there is simply a period where workers have to pay their dues (Cohen 1988: 261 n. 9). To insist that it is exploitative to forcibly transfer surplus value, regardless of how this fits into a larger pattern of distributive justice, guts the charge of exploitation of all its moral force. It manifests a kind of fetishism about owning one's labour. Indeed, it manifests a libertarian concern with self-ownership:

Marxists say that capitalists steal labour time from working people. But you can only steal from someone that which properly belongs to him. The Marxist critique of capitalist injustice therefore implies that the worker is the proper owner of his labour time: he, no one else, has the right to decide what will be done with it . . . Hence the Marxist contention that the capitalist exploits the worker depends on the proposition that people are the rightful owners of their own powers. [Indeed], if, as Marxists do, you take appropriation of labour time as such, that is, in its fully general form, as a paradigm of injustice, then you *cannot* eschew affirmation of something like the self-ownership principle. (Cohen 1990a: 366, 369)

That this is a libertarian assumption is shown by the fact that compulsory taxation to support children or the infirm also counts as exploitation, according to Reiman's definition. If we force workers to pay taxes to support the infirm, then we are forcing them to work without pay.[11]

In his initial presentation of the Marxist exploitation argument, Cohen denied that it presupposes that people own the products of their labour: 'One can hold that the capitalist exploits the worker by appropriating part of the value of what the worker produces without holding that all of that value should go to the worker. One can affirm a principle of distribution according to need, and add that the capitalist exploits the worker because his need is not the basis on which he receives part of the value of what the worker produces' (Cohen 1988: 230 n. 37). But what then is the justification for saying that the capitalist is exploiting the *worker*? Assuming that the capitalist does not need the object, and hence has no legitimate claim to it, it does not follow that the worker has any claim under the needs principle. The person most in need may be some third party (e.g. a child), and then the child has the only legitimate claim to the object. If the capitalist nonetheless appropriates the object, then he is unjustly treating the child, not the worker. Indeed, if the worker appropriates the object, then she too is unjustly treating the child. When the needs principle is violated, the people who are unjustly treated are the needy, not the producers.

Moreover, what if the capitalist does need the surplus value? Let's say that the capitalist is infirm, and has had the good fortune to have inherited a large number of shares in a company. Cohen implies that this is still exploitation, for 'his need is not the basis on which he receives part of the value of what the worker produces'. Rather, it is his ownership of the means of production. But the worker's need is not the basis on which she receives the product either. Rather, it is her production of the object. So who then is the capitalist exploiting? No one, for under the needs principle, no one else had any legitimate claim to the resources. Moreover, why can't need be the basis on which a capitalist receives surplus value? What if the government, in order to avoid leaving support for the infirm subject to the vagaries of day-to-day politics, endows the infirm with capital from which they can derive a steady stream of financial support? Distributing capital to the infirm might, in fact, be a very good way of meeting the needs principle (cf. Cohen 1990a: 369–71; Arneson 1981: 206–8). Once we drop the self-ownership claim, then the appropriation of surplus labour is not, as such, inherently exploitative—it all depends on how the particular transaction fits into a larger pattern of distributive justice.

There is another problem with the exploitation argument. What about those who are forced *not* to sell their labour? Married women have been legally precluded from taking wage employment in many countries. Hence they are not exploited. On the contrary, they are being protected from exploitation, which is indeed how many people defend sexual discrimination. But if married women in these countries are given a small income from government taxes, then they become exploiters, on the Marxian exploitation argument, since part of each worker's income is forcibly taken away and put at their disposal. But it would be perverse to view women under these circumstances as beneficiaries of exploitation. They suffer from an injustice worse than exploitation by capitalists, and one of the first tasks of feminist movements has been to gain equal access for women to wage-labour markets.[12] Or consider the unemployed, who are legally able to accept wage employment, but can find none. They too are not exploited, under the Marxist definition, since they do not produce any surplus value for the capitalist to appropriate. And if the government taxes workers to pay them a benefit, then they too become exploiters. Yet they are worse off than those who are able to find a wage relationship (Roemer 1982b: 297; 1988: 134–5).

These examples suggest that there is a deeper injustice underlying exploitation—namely, unequal access to the means of production. Disenfranchised women, the unemployed, and wage-workers in our society all suffer from this injustice, while capitalists benefit from it. The exploitation of workers by capitalists is just one form this distributive inequality can take. The subordinate position of women and the unemployed are other forms, and judging by people's struggles to gain wage employment, these may be more damaging forms. For those who lack access to property, being forced to sell one's labour may be better than being forced not to (women), or being unable to (unemployed), or eking out a marginal existence from crime, begging, or living off whatever land remains common property (Marx's 'lumpenproletariat').

Something has gone wrong here. Exploitation theory was supposed to provide a radical critique of capitalism. Yet, in its standard form, it neglects many of those who are worst off under capitalism, and actually precludes the action needed to help them (e.g. welfare support for children, the unemployed, and the infirm). If exploitation theory is to take due account of these groups, it must abandon the narrow focus on surplus transfer, and instead examine the broader pattern of distribution in which these transfers occur. This is the main aim of John Roemer's work on exploitation. He defines exploitation, not in terms of surplus transfer, but in terms of unequal access to the means of production. Whether one is exploited or not, on his view, depends on whether one would be better off in a hypothetical situation of distributive equality—namely, where one withdrew with one's labour and per capita share of external resources. If we view the different groups in the economy as players in a game whose rules are defined by existing property relations, then a group is exploited if its members would do better if they stopped playing the game, and withdrew with their per capita share of external resources and started playing their own game. According to Roemer, both employed and unemployed workers would be better off by withdrawing from the capitalist game, and so are exploited.

Exploitation in the technical sense—the transfer of surplus value—plays only a limited role in Roemer's theory. It is one of the most common results of distributive injustice under capitalism, but it has no ethical interest apart from that inequality. It is 'a bad thing only when it is the consequence of an *unjust* unequal distribution in the means of production' (Roemer 1988: 130). Surplus transfer is legitimate when it is untainted by distributive inequality, or when it helps compensate for that inequality. For example, state-mandated support for the unemployed and for disenfranchised women reduces, rather than creates, exploitation, for it helps rectify 'the loss suffered by [them] as a result of the unequal initial distribution of property' (Roemer 1988: 134). For Roemer, the 'ethical imperative' of exploitation theory, therefore, is not to eliminate surplus transfers, but to 'abolish differential ownership of the alienable means of production' (Roemer 1982*b*: 305; 1982*c*: 280).

Cohen says that Roemer's theory makes Marxists 'more consistent egalitarians' (Cohen 1990*a*: 382). But Roemer's account of exploitation still views compulsory support of the infirm (or children) as exploitation, for it gives them more than they would be able to secure for themselves with their per capita share of resources.[13] Inequalities due to unequal natural talents are not a matter of exploitation, and so Roemer's 'ethical imperative' is still less egalitarian than those theories which attempt to compensate for natural disadvantages. By defining exploitation in terms of the results of an unequal distribution of external resources, Roemer works 'without recourse to the radical egalitarian premise of denying self-ownership' (Roemer 1988: 168).

Roemer expresses sympathy with theories which take this radical step, like those of Rawls and Dworkin. And he himself says that the shift from socialism to communism should involve eliminating differential entitlement to resources due to differences in natural talents. He says that inequalities due to differences in natural talents can be seen as a form of 'socialist exploitation'— i.e. a form of exploitation that continues to exist under socialism, but which would be abolished under communism. But while he personally endorses the legitimacy of restricting self-ownership to remedy inequalities due to natural talents, he says that this is a separate issue from the traditional Marxist conception of the way workers are exploited under capitalism, which presupposes that people are entitled to the fruits of their labour (Roemer 1982*c*: 282–3; 1982*b*: 301–2). Marxist exploitation theory works with the 'more conservative' premiss that people have rights of self-ownership, so that equality of resources does not include any requirement that unequal talents be compensated for (Roemer 1988: 160; cf. 1982*a*: chs. 7–8).

Arneson gives a similar account of exploitation. Like Roemer, he says that judgements of 'wrongful exploitation' require a comparison with a hypothetical egalitarian distribution, although his account of equal distribution precludes differences that arise from unequal natural talents as well as unequal external resources. Arneson believes that most workers under capitalism are exploited according to this test, for they suffer from undeserved inequalities in either wealth or talent which enable others to take advantage of them (Arneson 1981: 208). As with Roemer, surplus transfer plays a derivative role in Arneson's theory. Surplus transfer is wrong if it is the result of an unequal distribution, but is legitimate if it arises independently of, or if it is used to compensate for, undeserved differences in wealth or natural talents. Hence compulsory support for the unemployed is legitimate, as is support for the infirm. Most of the surplus taken from workers under capitalism, however, is not of the legitimate kind, since it winds up in the hands of those who benefit from the unequal distribution of talents and wealth. Hence capitalism is exploitative, albeit for more complex reasons than suggested by the initial Marxian exploitation argument.

This is a more plausible account of exploitation. By focusing on the broader pattern of distribution, not just the exchange that occurs within the wage relationship, Roemer and Arneson avoid both of the problems that plagued Reiman's account. Their accounts allow us to say that workers in a welfare state can be exploited, whether or not they are 'forced' to work for capitalists, since they are denied fair access to the means of production. Their accounts also allow us to deal with cases of distributive injustice that occur outside the wage relationship, like the injustice of being unable or unfree to find employment, since these too involve a denial of fair access to resources.[14]

Unfortunately, this is a more attractive approach precisely because it has left behind all that was distinctive about the original Marxist approach to exploitation. This new approach differs in three important ways from that original approach. First, the idea of exploitation is now derived from a prior and broader principle of distributive inequality. In order to know what counts as exploitation, we need first to know what people are entitled to by way of rights over themselves and external resources. And once we make these underlying principles explicit, it is clear that exploitation is simply one of many forms of distributive injustice, not the paradigm of injustice. Unfortunately, Marxists remain prone to exaggerating the moral centrality of exploitation. Roemer, for example, expands the ambit of exploitation to cover all forms of distributive inequality.[15] As we have seen, this enables him to consider the fate of the unemployed as well as the wage-worker. But it is confusing to call both of these cases of exploitation. Our everyday sense tells us that exploitation requires some direct interaction between exploiter and exploited in which the former takes unfair advantage of the latter, and this is not generally true of the unemployed. They are unfairly neglected or excluded, but not necessarily unfairly taken advantage of, for capitalists may gain no benefit from their plight. To say that all forms of injustice are forms of exploitation is not to gain an insight but to lose a word.[16]

Moreover, Roemer's attempted assimilation obscures the relationship between equality and exploitation. He says that different forms of inequality (unfair advantage, exclusion, neglect) are all cases of the broader category of exploitation. But the opposite is more accurate—exploitation is one of the many forms of inequality, all of which are assessed by a deeper and broader principle of equality. On Roemer's theory, this deeper principle of equality is expressed in the 'ethical imperative' to equalize access to resources. Exploitation is no longer at the moral heart of the theory.

Secondly, the broader theory of justice in which exploitation is situated has become progressively closer to a Rawlsian theory of justice. The original Marxist argument said that workers are entitled to the product of their labour, and it is the forced denial of that entitlement which renders capitalism unjust. But most contemporary Marxists have tried to avoid that libertarian premiss, since (among other reasons) it makes aid to the dependent morally suspect. And the more they try to accommodate our everyday sense that not all technical exploitation is unjust, the more they have appealed to Rawlsian principles of equality. While the Marxist rhetoric of exploitation is taken to be more radical than liberal egalitarian views of justice, 'the Marxist condemnation of the injustice of capitalism is not so different from the conclusion that other apparently less radical contemporary theories of political philosophy reach, albeit in language less flamboyant than Marxism's' (Roemer 1988: 5). Arneson's theory of Marxist exploitation, for example, appeals to the same principle of an ambition-sensitive, endowment-insensitive distribution that underlies Dworkin's theory. In its new forms, Marxist exploitation theory seems to apply liberal-egalitarian principles, rather than compete with them.

Finally, this new account of exploitation abandons what was the *raison d'être* of the original Marxist exploitation argument—namely, the claim that there is an inherent injustice in wage-labour. For if the test of wrongful exploitation is whether there are undeserved inequalities, then some wage relationships are not exploitative. There are two 'clean routes' to wage-labour. First, as we have seen, endowing the infirm with ownership of capital can compensate for unequal natural talents, and so bring us closer to an endowment-insensitive distribution. Secondly, differential ownership of the means of production can arise amongst people with equal endowments, if they have different preferences concerning investment or risk. In the gardener/tennis-player example I used in Chapter 3, the tennis-player wanted to use his resources immediately in consumption, in the form of a tennis court, whereas the gardener invested her resources in production, in the form of a vegetable garden (Ch. 3, s. 4). This was legitimate, I argued, even though the tennis-player ended up working for the gardener (or some other owner of productive assets), because it met the 'envy test'. Each party was free to make the same choices as the other, but neither party desired the other's lifestyle, since they had different preferences about work and leisure. Similarly, the gardener might have acquired more assets by taking a large risk, while the tennis-player, who could have taken the same risk, preferred to have a smaller but risk-free income. Different choices about leisure and risk can lead, in a legitimate and envy-free way, to unequal ownership of productive assets.

Where people's preferences do not differ in these ways, or where any such differences are less important to people than a shared desire to have a democratic say in one's workplace, then we are likely to maintain a system of equal ownership of productive assets. But to enforce a blanket prohibition on wage-labour would be an arbitrary violation of the ambition-sensitivity requirement of a just distribution.[17]

None of this justifies existing inequalities in ownership of the means of production. Marx scorned those who argued that capitalists acquired their property through conscientious savings, and he went on to show that 'conquest, enslavement, robbery, murder, briefly force, play the great part' in capital accumulation (Marx 1977c: 873–6, 926; cf. Roemer 1988: 58–9). This unjust initial acquisition undermines the risk argument, for even if capitalists are willing to take risks with their capital, it is not (morally speaking) their capital to take risks with. Workers might be willing to take the same risks as capitalists if they had any capital to take risks with. In any event, 'it cannot seriously be maintained that a worker's life involves less risk than a capitalist's. Workers face the risk of occupational disease, unemployment, and impoverished retirement, which capitalists and managers do not face' (Roemer 1988: 66). So neither effort nor risk aversion can justify existing inequalities (Roemer 1982b: 308; contra Nozick 1974: 254–5). But the fact that capitalism historically arose out of undeserved inequalities does not show that wage-labour could not arise legitimately within a regime such as Rawls's 'property-owning democracy'. Indeed, if people are well informed about the consequences of their choices, and if their different preferences were formed under conditions of justice, then 'the argument appears almost irrefutable' (Elster 1983a: 294).[18]

So private property need not be exploitative. Conversely, socialization of the means of production may be exploitative. Marxists are fond of saying that exploitation is impossible within socialism, since producers control their product (e.g. Holmstrom 1977: 353). But on the new approach to exploitation, it is not enough that people have equal access to social resources, in the form of a vote in a democratically run, worker-owned firm. It all depends on what people democratically decide to do with their resources. Consider a firm that is permanently divided into two groups—a majority which, like the gardener, prefers income to leisure, and a minority which, like the tennis-player, prefers leisure to income. If the majority wins all the decisions, and if the minority are not allowed to convert their socialist right of equal access to social resources into a liberal entitlement of equal individual resources (e.g. by selling their share of the firm), they will be unfairly taken advantage of. They will be exploited, on the Roemer–Arneson approach, since they would be better off by withdrawing with their per capita share of resources (Arneson 1981: 226; Geras 1989: 257).

Concern for exploitation, therefore, does not justify a general preference in favour of socializing, rather than equalizing, the means of production. Equalizing resources may be non-exploitative, even if some people work for others, and socializing resources may be exploitative, even if everyone works for each other. It depends on the preferences people have, and the circumstances they find themselves in. What matters is that people have the sort of access to resources that enables them to make whatever decisions concerning work, leisure, and risk best suit their goals in life. That kind of self-determination may be best achieved through a mix of private property, public ownership, and worker democracy, since each form of ownership creates certain options while blocking others (Lindblom 1977: ch. 24; Goodin 1982: 91–2; Weale 1982: 61–2). These are largely empirical questions, and they cannot be pre-empted by blanket charges of exploitation.

(b) Needs

So far, I have not said much about Marx's claim that distribution under communism will be based on the principle 'to each according to his needs'. I did say that this principle is incompatible with the traditional Marxist conception of exploitation, which excludes the compulsory transfer of surplus labour from workers to others. But what can be said of it on its own, as a principle of justice? As we have seen, it is possible that Marx himself did not think of it as a principle of justice. Given his prediction of abundance, 'to each according to his needs' is not a principle under which scarce resources are distributed, but simply a description of what happens under communism—people take what they need from the stock of abundant resources (Wood 1979: 291–2; Cohen 1990b; but cf. Geras 1989: 263).

Most contemporary Marxists, however, do not share Marx's optimism concerning abundance, and instead invoke the needs principle as a distributive principle. Viewed in this way, it is most plausibly understood as a principle of equal need satisfaction, since Marx offers it as a solution to the 'defects' of the contribution principle, which, as we have seen, are the inequalities created by people's different needs (Elster 1983a: 296; 1985: 231–2). Is this an attractive principle? It is not very attractive if needs are interpreted in terms of bare material necessities. A socialist government that only provided for people's bare material needs would hardly constitute an advance on the welfare state programmes of some Western democracies. Marxists, however, interpret 'needs' in a much more expansive way. Indeed for Marx, human needs are distinguished by their 'limitless and flexible nature', so that people's needs include 'a rich individuality which is as all-sided in its production as in its consumption' (Marx 1977c: 1068; 1973: 325). Hence 'needs' is being used as a synonym for 'interests', which include both material necessities and the various goods that people feel worth having in their lives. So construed, needs encompass such things as important desires and ambitions, and so the needs principle 'is most plausibly understood as a principle of equal welfare' (Elster 1983a: 296), rather than a principle of equal need satisfaction in any more limited sense.

Unfortunately, once we adopt this expansive interpretation of the needs principle, it no longer gives us much guidance on how to distribute resources. Marxists seem to think that the needs principle is an answer to the question of what it means to give equal consideration to people's interests. But once we expand 'needs' to encompass all our interests, and drop the assumption of abundance, saying that distribution ought to be by need is not an answer to that question, but simply another way of asking it. It tells us nothing about how to attend to the different sorts of interests we have. For example, while needs in the minimal sense are not matters of choice, needs in the Marxist sense fall on both sides of the choices–circumstances line. Whether a given share of resources satisfies one's needs, therefore, depends on how expensive one's needs are, which depends both on one's circumstances and one's choices. Should we provide extra resources for those with expensive needs? And if so, should we spend all our resources on the severely handicapped? Should we distinguish between expensive needs that are chosen and those that are not? These are the questions that Rawls and Dworkin focus on, for without an answer to them, a theory of justice is incomplete. But Marxists have not, in general, explained how the needs principle assigns weight to people's interests.

In so far as Marxists have given some content to the needs principle, the most common area of disagreement with liberal egalitarianism concerns the claim that people are responsible for the costs of their choices, and hence that distributions should be ambition-sensitive. Some Marxists reject the claim outright, on the grounds that people's choices are the product of their material or cultural circumstances, so that people are not responsible for their choices (e.g. Roemer 1985a: 178–9; 1986a: 107, 109; 1988: 62–3). Levine says that this denial that individuals are responsible for their choices 'suggests a far more radical conception of what it is to treat people as equals' than is found in Dworkin's theory (Levine 1989: 51 n. 25). But it is not clear what is particularly radical (or attractive) about denying responsibility. For one thing, there is a tension between the denial of individual responsibility and our commitment to democracy. If people are not responsible for their preferences, why should we respect these preferences as legitimate inputs into the democratic process, and why should we view people as capable of rational argumentation and deliberation? There is a 'pragmatic incoherence' in treating people as responsible agents in our democratic theory, but not as responsible agents in our theory of justice (Elster 1992: 239).

Moreover, requiring some people to subsidize other people's expensive tastes is simply unfair, as many Marxists would agree. As Arneson puts it, 'Consider two persons, both with artistic need, one of whom is cost-conscious and learns to satisfy this need through media that are cheap (watercolours, pen-and-ink drawings), while the other is not mindful of cost and develops talents that can be exercised only at extravagant cost (huge marble sculptures, deep-sea photography). It is not obvious that 'to each according to his need' is the appropriate principle for distributing scarce resources to these artists' (Arneson 1981: 215). In order to deal with expensive choices, the needs principle requires some guidelines regarding what counts as 'reasonable' needs, so that 'people could be told at the early stages of preference formation that society will not underwrite all sorts of expensive tastes' (Elster 1983a: 298; Geras 1989: 264). According to Arneson, the need for such a social norm reflects 'the vagueness of Marx's slogan' but does not 'call in question its basic moral thrust' (Arneson 1981: 215). But this is in fact a very different understanding of the needs principle, since it tells people to adjust their needs to a pre-existing standard of distribution, whereas the needs principle is usually interpreted as requiring that we adjust distribution to people's pre-existing needs (Elster 1983a: 298).

Whether this ambition-sensitivity requirement is best seen as an abridgement of the needs principle or as an elaboration of it, the net effect is to make Marxist equality more or less identical to Dworkin's theory of equality of resources (Elster 1983a: 298 n. 65).[19] Or, if it is different, Marxists do not tell us how it differs, for they do not tell us how to measure the costs of people's choices. What, for example, plays the role of Dworkin's auction? Marxists have traditionally opposed market mechanisms. But if people are to be held responsible for the costs of their choices, then something like a market is required to measure that opportunity cost. (See Nove 1983: ch. 1 on how the Marxist hostility to markets, combined with the assumption of abundance, has prevented Marxists from coming up with any coherent notion of opportunity costs.)

There is less dispute over the claim that a just distribution be endowment-insensitive. The needs principle 'severs all connections between the amount of benefits one receives from the economy and the "morally arbitrary" genetic and social factors that determine one's ability to contribute to that economy' (Arneson 1981: 215–16). The requirements of the needs principle are clearer here, for it was 'designed precisely to take care of such instances' (Elster 1983a: 298). But even here the needs principle is incomplete, for it does not tell us what to do when it is impossible to compensate fully for natural disadvantages. As we saw in Chapter 3, it is impossible to equalize the circumstances of a severely retarded person, and undesirable to devote all our resources to that task. This led Dworkin to devise his hypothetical insurance scheme. But there is no similar solution to this problem in the contemporary Marxist literature, and indeed no similar recognition that it is a problem. It is not enough to say that the needs principle compensates for unequal circumstances. We need to know how to do so, and at what price. Until these questions are answered. it is impossible to tell whether or how the needs principle compares with liberal theories of equality.

(c) Alienation

With respect to both the exploitation principle and the needs principle, then, we see a gradual convergence between Marxist and liberal-egalitarian theories of justice. As Roemer puts it, 'the lines drawn between contemporary ana-lytical Marxism and contemporary left-liberal political philosophy are fuzzy. This indicates there is a common core' (Roemer 1986b: 200). However, there is a quite different strand of Marxist thinking which is more clearly distinct from that of liberal egalitarianism. According to Steven Lukes, Marx's critique of capitalism appeals not only to a 'Kantian' concern with exploitation, but also to a 'perfectionist' concern with alienation (Lukes 1985: 87; cf. Miller 1989: 52–4).[20] Whereas the Kantian strand emphasizes the way private property reduces some people (the workers) to a means for the benefit of others (capitalists), the perfectionist strand emphasizes the way private property inhibits the development of our most important capacities. The problem with private property, on this perfectionist view, is not simply that it is exploitative, for even those who benefit from exploitation are alienated from their essential human powers. This alienation argument seems a more promising route for defending a prohibition on private property, for while equalizing private property eliminates exploitation, it may just universalize the alienation.

Perfectionist arguments, of which Marx's alienation argument is one example, say that resources should be distributed in such a way as to encour-age the 'realization of distinctively human potentialities and excellences', and to discourage ways of life which lack these excellences (Lukes 1985: 87). Such theories are 'perfectionist' because they claim that certain ways of life consti-tute human 'perfection' (or 'excellence'), and that such ways of life should be promoted, while less worthy ways of life should be penalized. This is unlike liberal or libertarian theories, which do not try to encourage any particular way of life, but rather leave individuals free to use their resources in whatever ways they themselves find most valuable. I will consider the general contrast between liberal and perfectionist theories in the next chapter, but I will look briefly at how Marxist perfectionism might defend a prohibition on private property.

Any perfectionist argument must explain what the 'distinctive human excel-lences' are, and how the distribution of resources should be arranged so as to promote them. In Marx's case, our distinctive excellence is said to be our capacity for freely creative cooperative production. To produce in a way that stunts this capacity is to be 'alienated' from our true 'species-nature'. Hence, Marxist perfectionists argue, resources in a communist society should be distributed so as to encourage people to achieve self-realization through cooperative production. Distribution might still be governed by the needs principle, but for perfectionists the needs principle is not concerned with all needs. Rather, it would involve 'some selection of those forms of human interest and concerns which most fully express the ideal of co-operative, creative, and productive activities and enjoyments' (Campbell 1983: 138; cf. Elster 1985: 522).

How should this ideal be promoted? Marxists argue it is best promoted by abolishing wage-labour and socializing the means of production. Wage-labour alienates us from our most important capacity, because it turns the worker's labour-power into a mere commodity the disposition of which is under someone else's control. Moreover, for many workers under capitalism, this exercise of labour-power tends to be mindless and devoid of any intrinsic satisfaction. Socializing the means of production ensures that each person has an effective say in how her work life is organized, and enables her to organize production so as to increase its intrinsic satisfaction, rather than to increase the profits of the capitalist. Capitalism reduces our life's activity to a means which we endure in order to secure a decent living, but socialism will restore work to its rightful place as an end in itself, as 'life's prime want' (or, more accurately, socialism will make it possible for the first time in history for labour to assume this rightful place).

This, then, is the perfectionist argument for abolishing private property in the means of production. What are we to make of it? Phrased as a choice between intrinsically satisfying and intrinsically unsatisfying work, most people will favour creative and cooperative work. The evidence is overwhelming that most workers in capitalism wish that their jobs were more satisfying. The 'degradation of labour' which capitalism has imposed on many people is abhorrent, an unconscionable restriction on their ability to develop their human potential (Schwartz 1982: 636–8; Doppelt 1981). Liberals try to deal with this by distinguishing legitimate and illegitimate ways that people can come to be employed by others. But on the Marxist view, any wage relationship is alienating, since the worker gives up control over her labour-power, and over the products of her labour. Wage-labour may not be exploitative, if both parties started with an equal share of resources, but it is alienating, and we can eliminate the alienation by socializing productive resources rather than equalizing private property.

However, while unalienated labour is surely better than alienated labour, these are not the only values involved. I may value unalienated labour, yet value other things even more, such as my leisure. I may prefer playing tennis to unalienated production. I must engage in some productive work to secure the resources necessary for my tennis, and all else being equal, I would prefer it to be unalienated work. But all else is not always equal. The most efficient way to produce goods may leave little room for creativity or cooperation (e.g. assembly-line production). If so, then engaging in non-alienated work may require a greater investment in time than I am willing to make. For example, if I can acquire the resources I need by doing either two hours a day of alienated work or four hours a day of unalienated work, the extra two hours of tennis may outweigh the two hours of alienation. The question, then, is not whether I prefer unalienated labour to alienated labour, but whether I prefer leisure so much that I would accept alienated labour in order to acquire it. Opportunities for unalienated work 'are not so much manna from the sky. Resources must be used to make these opportunities available, which means lesser availability of some other goods', like leisure (Arneson 1987: 544 n. 38).[21]

Consumption is another good that may conflict with non-alienated production. Some people enjoy consuming a wide variety of goods and services, from food to opera to computers. Agreeing to perform alienated labour in return for higher wages may enable them to expand their range of desired consumption. If we prohibit alienated labour, we eliminate their alienation, but we also make it more difficult for them to pursue forms of consumption they truly value. Marxist perfectionists tend not to be concerned with possible decreases in material consumption. They consider people's concern with consumption as a symptom of the pathology of materialism created by capitalism, so that the transition to socialism 'will involve a large shift in cultural emphasis from consumption to production as the primary sphere of human fulfillment' (Arneson 1987: 525, 528). But is it pathological to be concerned with expanding one's consumption? The 'keeping up with the Joneses' syndrome may be, for the pursuit of such status goods is often irrational. But that is not true of many desires for increased consumption. There is nothing pathological about a music-lover wanting expensive stereo equipment, and being willing to perform alienated labour to acquire it. Hence there is no reason for communism to 'exclude or stigmatize those who prefer the passive pleasures of consumption' over the active pleasures of production (Elster 1985: 522).

The pursuit of unalienated labour can also conflict with relationships to family and friends. I may want a part-time job that allows me as much time as possible with my children, or perhaps seasonal work, so that I can spend part of each year with friends or relatives. As Elster notes, the Marxist emphasis on self-realization in work can compete with spontaneous personal relationships, for there is a 'tendency for self-realization to expand into all available time . . . [and this] is a threat to both consumption and to friendship' (Elster 1986: 101).

The issue is not whether unalienated labour is a good, but whether it is an overriding good, a good which is necessary to any decent life, and which outweighs in value all competing goods. I see no reason to think unalienated labour is such a good. Marx's own argument for this claim is quite implausible. He argued that freely cooperative production is our distinctive human excellence because this is what differentiates us from other species—it is what defines us *as humans*. But this 'differentia' argument is a non sequitur. Asking what is best in a human life is not a question 'about biological classification. It is a question in moral philosophy. And we do not help ourselves at all in answering it if we decide in advance that the answer ought to be a single, simple characteristic, unshared by other species, such as the differentia is meant to be' (Midgley 1978: 204). Exaltation of cooperative productive activity 'is a particular moral position and must be defended as such against others; it cannot ride into acceptance on the back of a crude method of taxonomy' (Midgley 1978: 204). Whether or not other animals have the same capacity for productive labour as humans has no bearing on the question of the value of that capacity in our lives. There is no reason to think that our most important capacities are those that are most different from other animals.

This focus on productive labour is also sexist. Consider Marx's claim that because workers are alienated from their 'species-life' (i.e. 'labour, life activity, productive life itself'), therefore 'man (the worker) only feels himself freely active in his animal functions—eating, drinking, procreating, or at most in his dwelling and in dressing up, etc.; and in his human functions he no longer feels himself to be anything but an animal' (Marx 1977a: 66). But why is production a more 'human function' than reproduction (e.g. raising children)? It may be less *distinctively* human, in the sense that other animals also reproduce. But this just shows how irrelevant that criterion is, for family life is surely as important to our humanity as production. Marx combined a profound sensitivity to historical variations in the predominantly male sphere of productive life with an almost total insensitivity to historical variations in the predominantly female sphere of reproductive life, which he viewed as essentially natural, not distinctively human (Jaggar 1983: ch. 4; O'Brien 1981: 168–84). Any theory which hopes to incorporate the experience of women will have to question the elevation of productive labour.

There are many values that may compete with unalienated production, such as 'bodily and mental health, the development of cognitive facilities, of certain character traits and emotional responses, play, sex, friendship, love, art, religion' (Brown 1986: 126; cf. Cohen 1988: 137–46). Some people will view productive labour as 'life's prime want', but others will not. A prohibition on alienated labour, therefore, would unfairly privilege some people over others. As Arneson puts it, the identification of socialism with a particular vision of the good life 'elevates one particular category of good, intrinsic job satisfaction, and arbitrarily privileges that good and those people who favor it over other equally desirable goods and equally wise fans of those other goods' (Arneson 1987: 525; cf. Arneson 1993a: 292–6). Given that people differ in the value they attach to labour, 'differential alienation of labor, from an initial position of equal opportunity and fair division of assets, can vastly increase the welfare and life quality of people'. Hence 'a perfectionist defense of nonalienation seems remote' (Roemer 1985*b*: 52).

Not all Marxists who emphasize the flourishing of unalienated production under communism are perfectionists. Some Marxists who proclaim the end of alienation are simply making a prediction about what people will do with their equal resources, not giving a perfectionist instruction about how to distribute those resources. They predict that people will value unalienated labour so highly that they will never accept improved leisure or family life as compensation for alienation. Should this prediction turn out to be false, however, there would be no reason to interfere with people's choices by prohibiting alienation. It is unclear whether Marx's comments on alienation are predictions or perfectionist instructions (Arneson 1987: 521). Engels, however, was anti-perfectionist, at least in the case of sexual relations. When discussing the nature of sexual relations in communism, he says that the old patriarchal relations will end, but

what will there be new? That will be answered when a new generation has grown up: a generation of men who never in their lives have known what it is to buy a woman's surrender with money or any other social instrument of power, a generation of women who have never known what it is to give themselves to a man from any other considerations than real love or to refuse to give themselves to their lover from fear of the economic consequences. When these people are in the world, they will care precious little what anybody today thinks they ought to do; they will make their own practice and their corresponding public opinion about the practice of each individual—and that will be the end of it. (Engels 1972: 145)

The equal distribution of resources ensures that exploitative relations will not arise, but there is no correct socialist model of personal relations which is to be encouraged or imposed. But why shouldn't economic relations likewise be left to the free choices of people from a position of material equality? We should wait and see what that 'new generation' will choose to do with their lives and talents, and while they may systematically favour unalienated labour, there is no reason for perfectionist intervention to encourage that result.

Again, none of this will justify the existing distribution of meaningful work. I have argued that people should be free to sacrifice the quality of work life for other values, like better leisure. Under capitalism, however, those with the best jobs typically also have the best consumption and leisure, while those with poor jobs often get no compensating increase in leisure or consumption. But the solution is not to give everyone the best possible work, at the expense of improved leisure, since some people would rather have better leisure. As Arneson puts it, 'The core socialist objection to a capitalist market is that people who have fewer resources than others through no fault of their own do not have a fair chance to satisfy their preferences. The solution to this problem is not to privilege anybody's preferences [e.g. those for work over leisure], but to tinker with the distribution of resources that individuals bring to market trading.' Hence Dworkin's aim of an envy-free market distribution 'is one aspect of socialist aspiration, not a rival doctrine' (Arneson 1987: 537, 533).

This returns us to the 'Kantian' strand of Marxist thought, which leaves individuals free to decide for themselves what is worth doing with their fair share of resources. And, as we have seen, this leads to a series of questions about fair distribution which Marxists have not addressed. Until they do, it is difficult to tell whether Marxism provides a distinctive account of justice from those of other political traditions.

3. SOCIAL DEMOCRACY AND SOCIAL JUSTICE

So far in this chapter, I have examined whether contemporary analytic Marxism provides an alternative approach to liberal egalitarianism. But there are other non-Marxist conceptions of socialism. In Marx's own day, these were often associated with various Christian sects, whose promotion of equality and collective ownership was tied up with specifically Christian views of fellowship, piety, and material renunciation. Marx tended to dismiss such groups as 'utopian socialists'.

In the twentieth century, however, the strongest proponents of socialist ideals in the West have been neither Marxist nor Christian, but rather secular social-democratic parties, often closely affiliated with labour movements. And it is sometimes said that the sort of 'social democracy' endorsed by these parties is fundamentally different from the sort of 'liberal democracy' favoured by liberal egalitarians.

Not everyone agrees that there is any significant distinction between 'social democracy' and 'left-liberal democracy'. Indeed, Rawls himself has said that his conception of justice can be described as either 'left liberal' or 'social democratic' (Rawls 1993a: 416). Conversely, many social-democratic parties in Western Europe have explicitly cited Rawls in developing and defending their platforms. In many cases, it seems that 'social democracy' and 'liberal equality' are simply different terms for the same core set of ideas, with European theorists preferring the former term, and North American theorists preferring the latter.

However, some commentators insist that social democrats have a more 'social' conception of justice, unlike the 'individualistic' conception of justice found in Rawls or Dworkin. David Miller, for example, distinguishes 'distributive equality', which he describes as individualistic and rooted in the liberal tradition, from 'social equality', which is more holistic or communitarian and rooted in the socialist tradition. The former is concerned with the claims of individuals to their equal share of resources; the latter is concerned with constructing the right sort of egalitarian social relationships. The former is concerned with ensuring greater equality in people's private share of resources, the latter with ensuring people's equal standing in public life (Miller 1993; 1997).

Michael Walzer captures this 'social' aspect of equality with his image of a 'society of misters'. In a social democracy, people meet and greet each other on equal terms. We address each other as 'Mr' or 'Ms', rather than addressing upper-class people as 'sir' or 'madam', and lower-class people as 'Jones'. This ideal has also historically been phrased as the ideal of a 'classless' society, not in the Marxist sense of abolishing wage-labour, but rather in the sense that class position should not determine's one's social relationships. As Miller puts it, a society of social equals is 'a community in which people's dealings with and emotional attachment to others are not inhibited by the barriers of class' (Miller 1993: 302). Similarly, the great English socialist Anthony Crosland argued that the goal of social justice is to 'weaken the existing deep-seated stratification, with its concomitant feelings of envy and inferiority, and its barriers to uninhibited mingling between the classes' (Crosland 1964: 77). Or as R. H. Tawney put it:

What is repulsive is not that one man should earn more than others, for where community of environment, and a common education and habit of life, have bred a common tradition of respect and consideration, these details of the counting-house are forgotten or ignored. It is that some classes should be excluded from the heritage of civilization which others enjoy, and that the fact of human fellowship, which is ultimate and profound, should be obscured by economic contrasts, which are trivial and superficial. (Tawney 1964: 113)

This idea of a more social conception of equality is often connected to the idea that there are different 'spheres' of justice. According to Walzer, for example, one sphere of justice concerns money and commodities, exchanged in the market. Goods and services available in the market should be distributed according to people's ability to pay, and Walzer thinks it is both impossible and unnecessary to try to eliminate involuntary inequalities in people's ability to pay for such goods. What matters is that these inevitable market-based inequalities do not cross the boundary and contaminate other spheres of justice, such as democratic citizenship, education, health care, or public honour, whose goods should be distributed without reference to one's ability to pay. Involuntary inequalities in people's ability to earn money and to buy private commodities, like boats or fancy stereos, are permissible, but these market inequalities must not enable people to buy political influence, basic public services, or public recognition, and thereby undermine equality in the public sphere (Walzer 1983).

This idea of developing a more social conception of equality, focused on the texture of people's social relationships rather than the 'details of the counting-house', is an important and attractive one. And it is not limited to the social democratic tradition. We find similar attempts to develop a more social or civic model of equality within utilitarianism, communitarianism and feminism.[22] By contrast, most of the analytic Marxists we have examined in this chapter share the same 'distributive' focus as liberal egalitarians. The conceptions of justice advanced by Roemer, Elster, Arneson, and Cohen, like those of Rawls and Dworkin, are focused on determining the just claims of individuals.[23]

But why should these be viewed as competing, rather than complementary, views of justice? One might think that the pernicious social consequences of material inequalities simply give us a further strong reason for wanting to achieve distributive justice. After all, one way to ensure that social relationships are egalitarian is to ensure that individuals have roughly equal shares of resources, and hence enter society on a roughly equal footing. If so, then liberal egalitarianism will help achieve both a just distribution to individuals, and egalitarian social relations between individuals.

Why then do some people think that 'social equality' is an alternative to, rather than supplement to, liberal equality? Why think that the only or best way to achieve social equality is to sacrifice distributive justice for individuals? There are at least three different answers here, I think.

The first is that some social democrats, like David Miller and Michael Walzer, simply do not accept the liberal-egalitarian argument that undeserved inequalities are unfair. On Miller's view, it is not unjust that the gifted have substantially more resources than the less talented. The fact that natural talents are morally arbitrary is not, for Miller, a reason to say that people do not deserve their market income (Miller 1999: ch. 7; cf. Walzer 1983: ch. 4). So we cannot justify redistributing resources on the grounds that the talented affluent have more than their fair share, or that the less well off have less than their fair share. On Miller's view, inequalities in market income may well be fair if they are broadly proportionate to people's contributions. However, these inequalities, while fair in and of themselves, may undermine the desired sense of 'fellowship' underlying a society of equals, and so must be limited and contained. A classless society is not necessarily more just, in the sense of distributing resources more fairly, but is attractive for reasons other than distributive justice, such as community.

Other social democrats, however, agree with liberal egalitarians that undeserved inequalities are unfair, but do not believe that the state is capable of identifying or remedying the growing inequalities in market income. Trying to fight these inequalities directly is a futile exercise. What the state can do, however, is to try to minimize the social consequences of these unjust inequalities. It can try to ensure that these unjust inequalities only affect people's private lives—i.e. people's private consumption or leisure—without undermining social equality (Kaus 1992). On this view, social-democratic equality is a kind of fall-back position. If we cannot achieve distributive justice, we should at least protect social equality.

Yet others argue that even if we could remedy involuntary disadvantages in people's resources, this could only be achieved through means that would themselves erode social equality. As I discussed in the conclusion to Chapter 3, some theorists argue that liberal egalitarianism, even if defensible in theory, promotes the wrong *ethos* of equality (Wolff 1998; Anderson 1999). Trying to distinguish voluntary from involuntary disadvantages requires the state to view its disadvantaged citizens with distrust, as potential cheaters. And in order to overcome this distrust, the disadvantaged must engage in what Wolff calls 'shameful revelation'—i.e. they have to prove they do indeed suffer from some involuntary disadvantage, whether in their natural talents or childhood upbringing. The inevitable result, he argues, is to erode the sense of social equality between citizens. To avoid this problem, we should abandon the attempt to distinguish voluntary from involuntary inequalities, and instead focus on the question of which material inequalities undermine social equality (or what Anderson calls 'democratic equality'). If material inequalities do not violate social equality, we will allow them, no matter how undeserved. But if material inequalities do undermine social equality, we will remedy them, even if these inequalities are the result of voluntary choices (Anderson 1999).

So there are various reasons for thinking there is a potential conflict between the social-democratic pursuit of social equality and the liberal-egalitarian pursuit of distributive equality. It's worth noting that on all of these arguments, the social-democratic conception of equality is actually less demanding than liberal distributive equality. Whereas the liberal egalitarians seek to remedy a wide range of undeserved disadvantages in people's standard of living and access to goods and services, social democrats only seek to remedy these inequalities that erode people's standing as equals in public life. Liberal equality aims to ensure that people have an equal share of resources to pursue their conception of the good; social-democratic equality aims to ensure that people are respected as equals in society even though they may have a very unequal ability to pursue their conception of the good.

All of these arguments for social equality rightly stress the importance of people's social status or public standing. It is surely correct that the harm of poverty is not just the shortage of particular goods or services, but the shame, pity, condescension, or invisibility which poisons relations between the poor and other members of society. Contemporary liberal egalitarians and analytic Marxists have largely ignored this profound aspect of inequality. And there is some evidence that people are more willing to accept redistribution if it can be seen as restoring social equality, not merely increasing someone's purchasing power.

And yet one could also argue that defenders of social equality are remarkably blasé about the importance of material resources in people's personal or private lives. There is a tendency to suggest that the 'details of the counting-house' are of no real consequence for people's lives, so long as they do not erode people's standing in the society of misters. But is it really unimportant that some people live in spacious houses while others are in cramped apartments; or that some people can afford month-long vacations overseas while others cannot afford to eat out at a local restaurant; or that some people have rewarding and fulfilling 'careers' while others have mind-numbing 'jobs', if they have a job at all? Why should we accept such large disparities in people's life-chances and standards of living when they are unchosen and undeserved? Why should we allow people's ability to pursue their conception of the good life to be dependent on such morally arbitrary factors?

It seems odd to defend the importance of social equality by denigrating the importance of individual equality. It may also be strategically unwise. For if we say that people are entitled to their unequal market incomes, then the affluent may resent having to give up some of 'their' money to ensure social equality for others, especially if no attempt is made to filter out those recipients who are responsible for their current disadvantage. People may be more willing to make sacrifices in the name of social equality than 'merely' distributive equality, but the evidence is overwhelming that people resent being taxed to support lifestyles they view as irresponsible (Bowles and Gintis 1999; Gilens 1999). So even if our aim is simply to protect social equality, we may still need to emphasize that the affluent do not deserve all of their wealth, and the less well off do not deserve their disadvantages.

Much work remains to be done in clarifying the relationship between social equality and distributive equality. It would be a mistake, I think, to suppose that these are inherently opposed ways of thinking about justice. In many cases, concerns about social equality will simply supplement and strengthen our commitment to distributive justice. But there may be other cases in which preserving social equality requires something more than, or other than, the pursuit of distributive equality.

4. THE POLITICS OF MARXISM

One of the most distinctive features of Marxism is its preoccupation with labour. This is true of both of the strands of Marxism we have examined in this chapter. The Kantian strand views work as the fundamental site of capitalist injustice (i.e. exploitation). The perfectionist strand views work as the fundamental site of the socialist goal of non-alienation. But there is a third sense in which labour is fundamental to Marxism—namely, the fact that workers are identified as the main agents of social change. According to Marxist sociology, the struggle against capitalist injustice will take the form of a struggle between two increasingly polarized classes—workers and capitalists. Capitalists must oppress workers, for their wealth comes from the exploitation of workers, and workers must oppose capitalists, since they have nothing to lose but their chains. Class conflict is endemic to the wage relationship, which is endemic to capitalism, and so the wage relationship is the linchpin around which revolutionary struggle occurs. Other groups may be unfairly treated, but Marxists have viewed them as marginal in terms of both power and motivation. Only workers are able and willing to challenge the whole edifice of capitalist injustice. To concentrate on the fate of other groups is reformist, not revolutionary, since their oppression is less, and less essential, than the workers'.

Marxist theories of justice are, in large part, attempts to give the rationale for this class struggle. As Roemer puts it, 'the purpose of a theory of exploitation is . . . to explain class struggle. As Marxists, we look at history and see poor workers fighting rich capitalists. To explain this, or to justify it, or to direct it and provide it with ideological ammunition, we construct a theory of exploitation in which the two antagonistic sides become classified as the exploiters and the exploited' (Roemer 1982c: 274–5). And since the explanation of class struggle is located directly in the wage relationship, there has been a natural tendency for Marxists to locate the justification for socialism directly in the wage relationship. Thus we get theories of the inherent exploitation or alienation of wage-labour.

It is increasingly difficult to accept this traditional Marxist view about the centrality of labour to progressive politics. Many of the most important contemporary struggles for justice involve groups which are not, or not only, oppressed by the wage relationship—e.g. racial groups, single mothers, immigrants, gays and lesbians, the disabled, the elderly. As we've seen, support for these groups may in fact conflict with the labour-emphasizing arguments for socialism. Marxists have tended in practice to support the claims of these non-proletarian groups. They have tended to support the needy, whether or not their needs are related to any labour-based principle of alienation or exploitation. But as Cohen points out, they have often justified doing so by treating 'the set of exploited producers as roughly coterminous with the set of those who needed the welfare state's benefits' (Cohen 1990a: 374). In other words, while Marxist theory has been labour based, its practice has been needs based, and the obvious inconsistencies have been papered over by assuming that the needy are also the exploited.

However, it is increasingly clear that the needy and the Marxian exploited are not always the same people. This 'forces a choice between a principle of self-ownership embedded in the doctrine of exploitation and a principle of equality of benefits and burdens that negates the self-ownership principle and which is required to defend support for very needy people who are not producers and who are, a fortiori, not exploited' (Cohen 1990*a*: 13–14; cf. Arneson 1993*a*). I have argued that it is arbitrary, at the level of theory, to endorse the 'fetishism of labour' implicit in the doctrines of exploitation and alienation (Roemer 1985*b*: 64). But it is also unhelpful at the level of practice, for it neglects forms of injustice which motivate some of the most important contemporary progressive political movements. If there is to be an effective movement for radical social change, it will have to involve a coalition of both the needy and the exploited. But the rhetoric of Marxist exploitation and alienation does not speak to the needs of non-labourers, and may indeed oppose them.

Marxists pride themselves on their unity of theory and practice. But their theory betrays their practice. Faced with the choice between self-ownership and distributive equality, Marxists have, in practice, embraced equality, and have done so in a much more committed way than liberals have. But at the level of theory, Marxists remain committed to a fetishism of labour that is in some ways less radical, and less attractive, than liberal egalitarian theories of justice, and this has hampered the quest for an effective radical movement. A genuine unity of theory and practice may require a greater unity of Marxism and liberal equality.

GUIDE TO FURTHER READING

Most of the interesting philosophical work on Marxism in the last twenty-five years has been done by a group of scholars known as 'analytical Marxists', who seek to explore and reconstruct Marxism using the tools of Anglo-American analytical philosophy. The major exponents of this school of thought include G. A. Cohen, Jon Elster, Philippe Van Parijs, and John Roemer. We have already encountered many of these names in the chapter on liberal egalitarianism, since their reconstructions of Marxism have taken them in the direction of liberal egalitarianism. For helpful overviews of this movement, see John Roemer (ed.), *Analytical Marxism* (Cambridge University Press, 1986); the special issue of the *Canadian Journal of Philosophy* on 'Analyzing Marxism: New Essays on Analytical Marxism' (supplementary vol. 15, 1989); and Lesley Jacobs, 'The Second Wave of Analytical Marxism', *Philosophy of Social Sciences*, 26/2 (1996): 279–92. For a critique, see Marcus Roberts, *Analytical Marxism: A Critique* (Verso, 1996). This approach is also sometimes called 'rational choice Marxism', since it draws in part on neoclassical models of rational choice theory. Hence Terrell Carver and Paul Thomas (eds.), *Rational Choice Marxism* (Pennsylvania State University Press, 1995).

The key texts of this school of thought include: G. A. Cohen's *History, Labour, and*

Freedom: Themes from Marx (Oxford University Press, 1988); *Self-Ownership, Freedom and Equality* (Cambridge University Press, 1995); and *If You're an Egalitarian, How Come You're So Rich?* (Harvard University Press, 2000); Jon Elster, *Making Sense of Marx* (Cambridge University Press, 1985); Philippe Van Parijs, *Marxism Recycled* (Cambridge University Press, 1993); and John Roemer's *Free to Lose: An Introduction to Marxist Economic Philosophy* (Harvard University Press, 1988); and *Theories of Distributive Justice* (Harvard University Press, 1996).

Although many analytical Marxists have embraced some form of liberal egalitarianism, there is still interest in developing some distinctly socialist or social-democratic form of egalitarianism. Some analytic Marxists seek to identify distinctive institutional mechanisms for achieving equality, such as market socialism. While there is growing recognition that any efficient and fair society must allow some room for markets, market socialism would set greater limits on either the capital or labour markets than liberal egalitarianism. For investigations of the idea of market socialism, see Pranab Bardhan and John Roemer (eds.), *Market Socialism: The Current Debate* (Oxford University Press, 1993); Roemer's *A Future for Socialism* (Verso, 1994); and Bertell Ollman (ed.), *Market Socialism: The Debate among Socialists* (Routledge, 1998).

Other theorists attempt to develop a distinctly socialist philosophical foundation for equality. Some theorists argue that the social-democratic tradition offers an alternative account of equality, emphasizing 'social equality' (or 'civic/democratic' equality), as distinct from the individual 'distributive equality' emphasized by liberalism. Important versions of this ideal include Michael Walzer, *Spheres of Justice: A Defence of Pluralism and Equality* (Blackwell, 1983); David Miller, *Principles of Social Justice* (Harvard University Press, 1999), ch. 11; Elizabeth Anderson, 'What is the Point of Equality?', *Ethics*, 99/2 (1999): 287–337; and Mickey Kaus, *The End of Equality* (Basic Books, 1992).

For other recent attempts to imagine a post-Marxist socialist conception of equality, see Andrew Levine, *Rethinking Liberal Equality from a 'Utopian' Point of View* (Cornell University Press, 1998), and Jane Franklin (ed.), *Equality* (Institute for Public Policy Research, 1997), which is an attempt by leading left intellectuals in Britain to reinterpret the meaning of socialism for 'New Labour' in Britain.

Two journals which regularly publish debates in analytical Marxism are *Politics and Society* and *New Left Review*.

Analytical Marxism has arguably departed a great deal from the views of Marx himself. For a comprehensive overview of the debate over whether Marx himself had an implicit or explicit moral theory, see Norman Geras, 'The Controversy about Marx and Justice', in A. Callinicos (ed.), *Marxist Theory* (Oxford University Press, 1989); Geras, 'Bringing Marx to Justice: An Addendum and Rejoinder', *New Left Review* (1993), 195: 37–69; and Rodney Peffer, *Marx, Morality and Social Justice* (Princeton University Press, 1990). For an excellent introduction to Marx, and his relation to contemporary analytical Marxism, see Terrell Carver (ed.), *The Cambridge Companion to Marx* (Cambridge University Press, 1991).

For a comprehensive website on all things Marxist, see the 'Marx-Engels Archive' at www.csf.colorado.edu/psn/marx/

NOTES

1. While both liberal egalitarians and Marxists share a commitment to material equality, they disagree over the means which can be used to pursue it. If a society is in violation of the difference principle, but respects civil rights, then Rawls and Dworkin deny that we can limit civil liberties in order to correct the material inequality. By contrast, some Marxists would be prepared to accept more radical means to achieve distributive justice (see Ch. 3, n. 23).

2. In fact, important aspects of Dworkin's approach were foreshadowed in James Dick's account of 'compensatory justice', which argues that inequalities in resources are legitimate if they compensate for differences in the burdens people face (Dick 1975). According to Dick, people whose work involves special risks or hardships are entitled to greater pay than those whose work is safe and enjoyable. The aim, on his view, is to achieve an equal distribution of both benefits and burdens. Under plausible market conditions, this view is likely to collapse into Dworkin's equality of resources view: the former's account of 'burdens' is really just the flip side of the latter's account of 'expensive preferences', both of which are determined by market mechanisms under conditions of equal resources (Carens 1985).

3. Compare the proposals discussed at the end of Chapter 3 with recent work on market socialism, such as Bardhan and Roemer 1993; LeGrand and Estrin 1989; Miller 1989. The clear overlap here is reflected in the fact that Roemer's proposal for equalizing share ownership is sometimes described as 'coupon capitalism' and sometimes as 'market socialism'.

4. One of the leading analytic Marxists, G. A. Cohen, provides a fascinating autobiographical discussion of this shift in his own views. He was raised to believe in the inevitability of communist equality, but having lost that faith, he now emphasizes the need to persuade people of its moral desirability (Cohen 2000).

5. The idea of moral equality often appears in Marx in the same form as it appears in Kant, Rawls, and Nozick—i.e. as the requirement that we should treat people as ends in themselves, not means. He thought that capitalism failed to treat people as ends both in the relations of production (where the capitalist labour process reduces the worker to the status of a thing, an instrument, to be exploited by the capitalist), and in the relations of exchange (where 'each views the needs and desires of the other not as needs and desires, but rather as levers to be manipulated, as weaknesses to be preyed upon'—Buchanan 1982: 39).

6. Marx says that life under communism would be a 'social life' (Marx 1977a: 90–3), and that communist individuals would be 'social individuals' (Marx 1973: 705, 832). But he did not say that there will be an inherent harmony of interests, nor that we should aim at creating such a harmony. For my view of what these claims amount to, see Kymlicka 1989a: ch. 6.

7. e.g. Sandel 1982: 30–3; Glendon 1991; Etzioni 1993; Hardwig 1990. Waldron 1993: 370–91 offers a more subtle view, arguing that while notions of rights and justice are unnecessary when affection exists, they are necessary to deal with situations where affection fades.

8. For the way good marriages (and good friendships) combine justice and love, see Okin 1989b; Kleingeld 1998; Friedman 1993. For discussions on the the way we manifest our ethical values in our decisions about whether or when to exercise our rights, see Tomasi 1991, 2001: ch. 3; Meyer 1997. For defences of the centrality of rights to any desirable conception of community, see S. Walker 1998; Ignatieff 2000; Dworkin 1989.

9. As I noted at the beginning of the chapter, Marxists have historically raised other objections to justice. For example, appeals to justice were said to be strategically divisive, due to the essential contestability of the idea of justice, and unnecessary, since the motor of history is the rational interest of the disadvantaged. Also, conceptions of justice were said to be ideological, shaped to suit existing property relations, and hence a socialist conception of justice must

follow, rather than precede, changes in property relations. Many of these supposed defects of justice are premised on Marx's now-discredited theory of historical materialism. For the ideology objection, see Wood 1981: 131–2; Brenkert 1983: 154–5; Wood 1972: 274, and the response in Geras 1989: 226–8; Nielsen 1989; Arneson 1981: 217–22; Norman 1989. For the role of moral motivation in class struggle, see Wood 1984; Miller 1984: 15–97; and the response in Geras 1989: 251–4; Nielsen 1987.

10. Compared to the voluminous literature by analytic Marxists on justice, there is still comparatively little work done on developing a Marxist theory of democracy. For a notable exception, see Gilbert 1980; 1991.

11. Reiman denies that compulsory aid to the disabled is exploitative because it can be seen as an insurance policy that everyone buys, and so is 'an indirect return to individuals of labour equal to what they contribute, and thus not altering the basic distributive principle' that no one is made to work for anyone else (Reiman 1989: 312 n. 12). But this is clearly false of many recipients of such aid—e.g. the congenitally infirm. Holmstrom, who like Reiman defines exploitation in terms of 'forced, unpaid, surplus labour' (Holmstrom 1977: 358), says that support for the infirm is not exploitative, because 'The surplus is under the control of those who produce it. There is no class of non-producers who appropriate what workers have produced. Workers do not consume it all, but they control it as a class' (363). But the fact that workers control it *as a class* does not show that *individual* workers are not forced to hand over surplus product to others. What if I, as an individual worker, object to what the working class as a whole decides to do with the surplus product? Can I insist that I get the full value of what I have produced? If not, and if I must work to earn a living, then I am exploited on her definition. Moreover, what if there is a constitutional guarantee of welfare rights, under which workers are legally required to support the infirm? Then, under her definition, the working class as a whole is exploited, since they do not legally control the entire surplus.

12. For an interesting attempt to reformulate Marx's surplus value conception of exploitation to apply to women's unpaid caring activities, see Bubeck 1995: ch. 2.

13. Roemer tries to avoid this implication by adding a 'dominance condition' (Roemer 1982a: 237), or the requirement that there be no 'consumption externalities' (i.e. the workers must not get any pleasure from helping the disabled) (Roemer 1989: 259). But these are ad hoc, since they are disconnected from the 'ethical imperative' he identifies as the basis of exploitation theory (as he admits—Roemer 1982c: 277 n.). Indeed, they seem to be question-begging attempts to disavow the libertarian content of exploitation theory, and to block libertarian claims that the welfare state is exploitative (Bertram 1988: 126–7).

14. As Arneson notes, this account of why the exploitation of an impoverished worker is wrong also explains why it is wrong for a capitalist to let his factory be idle, leaving the worker to starve (Arneson 1993a: 288). By contrast, the traditional Marxist account of exploitation would imply that the owner who closes his factory is no longer exploiting anyone.

15. Similarly, Van Parijs has extended the notion of exploitation to cover the case of inequality between rich and poor countries (what he calls 'citizenship-exploitation'), and even the case of inequality between job-holders and the jobless (what he calls 'job exploitation') (Van Parijs 1993: 143–7, 123–30).

16. Roemer has, in places, moved away from this assimilation of injustice and exploitation. In order to match our everyday sense that exploitation involves someone taking advantage of another, he adds the following proviso: not only must the exploited group fare better by withdrawing with its talents and per capita share of resources, the exploiters must fare worse if the exploited withdraw with their existing resources (Roemer 1982b: 285). Where this added condition is not met, groups that are denied equal access to resources are 'Marxian-unfairly treated', but not 'exploited', for others do not take advantage of them ('they could disappear

from the scene and the income of others would not change'—Roemer 1982*b*: 292). But, as he admits, this added condition still fails to capture our intuitive sense of 'taking unfair advantage' (Roemer 1982*b*: 304 n. 12; cf. Elster 1982*a*: 366–9). In a subsequent book, Roemer returns to his original definition of exploitation as 'the loss suffered by a person as a result of the unequal initial distribution of property' (Roemer 1988: 134), whether or not this loss comes about from being taken advantage of. Hence a person is capitalistically exploited 'if he would gain by virtue of an egalitarian redistribution of society's alienable means of production' (Roemer 1988: 135), and the unemployed are as exploited as wage-workers under this test.

17. Paul Warren argues that even if there are 'clean routes' to wage-labour relations, it would still be permissible to prohibit them as exploitative, since the employer both exercises unequal power over the relationship, and gains disproportionately from the relationship. Even if the inequality in resources between employer and employee is legitimate (i.e. due to voluntary choices), it would be wrong to allow the employer to take advantage of the legitimate inequality in this illegitimate way (Warren 1997). Warren's article makes it sound as though the need to gain employment is an unexpected and unwelcome consequence of the (voluntary) inequality in resources, from which the would-be worker needs protection. This is misleading. *Ex hypothesi*, both parties faced the same set of options, including the opportunity to become an employer or co-owner by making the necessary choices regarding savings, investment, and risk. The would-be worker made different choices, since she had other goals in life, perhaps involving greater leisure, consumption, or security, knowing that this would require her to work for others. The decision to become a worker was part of the option she chose, in preference to other options, including the option to become an employer. In other words, decisions about employment are already factored into the envy test. In any event, people in a liberal society are free to enter into relations of unequal power and unequal rewards—indeed, many (most?) forms of human association involve this to some degree. There is no requirement that organizations in a liberal society (churches, charitable organizations, political parties) be organized so as to either equalize the power of all members, or reward people according to their labour expended. What matters is that people make these choices about what kinds of relationships to enter from a position of equal resources, and that is present in the 'clean route' to wage-labour.

18. For Roemer's attempt to refute the argument, see Roemer 1988: 149–56. His main objection is that even if we equalize resources, the differential ownership of capital which would arise from people's choices would largely reflect the lingering influence of earlier injustice. Those people who were born into poor families will not be taught the habits of risk-taking and deferred gratification which are passed on within rich families. Different preferences concerning work and leisure do not justify differential ownership of the means of production, because the preferences themselves were formed under conditions of injustice (Roemer 1988: 62–3, 152–3; 1985*b*: 52). This is a valid point—people are fully responsible for their choices only when their preferences are formed under conditions of justice (cf. Rawls 1979: 14; Arneson 1981: 205; Scanlon 1988: 185–201). But this hardly defends a blanket prohibition on private property. It suggests that, for a generation or two, we must attend to, and perhaps compensate for, this influence. Perhaps we could implement an affirmative action programme to encourage previously disadvantaged groups to acquire and pass on the relevant dispositions. This does not undermine the general principle that different ambitions can legitimately give rise to differential ownership of the means of production.

19. Some socialists who accept the principle that distributions should be ambition-sensitive are nonetheless concerned to limit the kinds of inequalities it generates. For example, some say that extensive differences in income would violate self-respect (Nielsen 1978: 230; Daniels 1975*a*: 273–7; Doppelt 1981: 259–307; Keat 1982: 68–70; but cf. Rawls 1971: 107; DiQuattro 1983:

59–60; Gutmann 1980: 135–8), or would undermine the conditions necessary for developing a sense of justice (Clark and Gintis 1978: 315–16), or a sense of solidarity (Crocker 1977: 263). I doubt that these problems would arise for income differences which pass the envy test (how can the greater resources of others violate my self-respect when they accompany a lifestyle that I did not want and freely rejected?). Some say that extensive income inequality would undermine the equality of political power necessary for democracy (Daniels 1975a: 256–8), or would create unequal opportunities for children (Nielsen 1985: 297–8). These are serious worries, but they are recognized by Rawls and Dworkin, who agree that they impose constraints on legitimate inequalities (re political equality, see Rawls 1971: 225–6; Dworkin 1988; re unequal opportunity, see Rawls 1971: 73). For further socialist views on ambition-sensitivity, see Nielsen 1985: 293–302; Elster 1985: 231–2, 524; 1992: 237–40; Levine 1988: 53; 1999.

Carens argues that the central difference between socialists and liberals involves, not the needs principle, but the other half of Marx's famous slogan ('from each according to his abilities, to each according to his needs'). Carens takes this as imposing a duty on people to contribute, a duty to make 'good use' of their talents, whereas liberals think this could enslave the talented by forcing them to do something they are good at but do not enjoy (Carens 1986: 41–5). I do not believe that most Marxists actually share Carens's duty-imposing interpretation of Marx's slogan, but it is an important issue that deserves more discussion.

20. Lukes also distinguishes a 'utilitarian' strand in Marx's thought, but I will leave this aside, partly because we have already examined utilitarianism, and partly because this strand of Marx's thought has had less influence on contemporary Marxists than the Kantian and perfectionist strands. Moreover, I doubt there was a utilitarian strand in Marx's thought. He rejected the idea that a person can be harmed just because that would increase the overall good (Murphy 1973: 217–20; but cf. Allen 1973; Brenkert 1981).

21. Marx himself once claimed that 'the realm of freedom really begins only where labour determined by necessity and external expediency ends; it lies by its very nature beyond the sphere of material production proper' (Marx 1981: 958–9). This is not his usual view of the matter, nor is it shared by most contemporary Marxists (e.g. Cohen 1978: 323–5), but it is surely true that the 'development of human powers as an end in itself' can occur outside production, and that 'nothing in the nature of things prevents the sphere of leisure from becoming the main arena for that free many-sided development of the individual that Marx prized' (Arneson 1987: 526).

Even if we accept the emphasis on production as the arena of self-fulfilment, there are other values besides non-alienation at stake. Marxists say that the value of production lies in 'the development of human powers as an end in itself'. But some people think that the value of productive labour lies in contributing to an organization that efficiently serves vital needs. For such 'service-oriented' workers, workplace democracy may be a 'wasteful self-indulgence' which places the welfare of the worker above that of the recipients (Arneson 1987: 525). Perfectionists argue that work is only meaningful if there is worker democracy (Nielsen 1978: 239; Schwartz 1982: 644). But what is wrong with caring more about what gets done than about how it gets done? There is a plurality of goods to be gained from labour—Arneson lists seventeen of them—of which the free development of one's talents is just one, and different goods flourish best under different systems of work organization and property-ownership (Arneson 1987: 527). So there is no simple correlation between socializing productive assets and increasing the value of our productive activities.

22. Similar distinctions between 'social/civic' equality and 'individualistic/distributive' equality are made by utilitarians (Temkin 1993: chs. 9–10; Broome 1991: ch. 9); communitarians (Sandel 1996); and feminists (Young 1990; Tronto 1993).

23. However, there are also some liberals and Marxists who have argued for a more 'social'

conception of justice and equality. For example, Mickey Kaus argues that liberals should abandon what he calls 'money liberalism' (or distributive equality) for what he calls 'civic liberalism' (or social equality) (Kaus 1992). Similarly, Reiman argues that analytic Marxism should 'take as its ideal not some distribution of things but a certain social relation among persons' (Reiman 1991: 158; cf. Reiman 1989).

6

COMMUNITARIANISM

1. INTRODUCTION

The rallying cry of the French Revolution—'liberté, egalité, et fraternité'—
lists the three basic ideals of the modern democratic age. The great ideologies
of the eighteenth and nineteenth centuries—socialism, conservatism, liberalism, nationalism, and republicanism—each offered its own conception of the
ideals of liberty, equality, and community. The ideal of community took many
different forms, from class solidarity or shared citizenship to a common
ethnic descent or cultural identity. But for all of these theories, and for the
philosophers who helped defend them, community was one of the basic
conceptual building blocks to be shaped and defined.

After the Second World War, however, community seemed to drop out of the
picture. For example, in *Theory of Justice*, Rawls says that his work is intended to
provide an interpretation of the concepts of liberty and equality. It is not that
Rawls explicitly rejected the value of community; he simply paid little attention
to it. Perhaps he thought that community was no longer a subject of ideological
dispute, or that recent history had revealed that the ideal of community was
too liable to manipulation by fascist, racist, or totalitarian regimes.

Rawls was not unique in this regard. Until recently, most contemporary liberal philosophers have said little about the ideal of community. If community is discussed at all, it is often seen as derivative of liberty and equality—
i.e. a society lives up to the ideal of community if its members are treated as
free and equal persons. Liberal visions of politics do not include any
independent principle of community, such as shared nationality, language,
identity, culture, religion, history, or way of life.

In the last twenty years, community has resurfaced. An entire school of
thought has arisen in political philosophy, known as 'communitarianism',
whose central claim is precisely the necessity of attending to community
alongside, if not prior to, liberty and equality. Communitarians believe that
the value of community is not sufficiently recognized in liberal theories of
justice, or in the public culture of liberal societies.

This emphasis on community can be found in Marxism as well, and is of course a defining feature of the communist ideal. However, the kind of communitarianism which has recently come to prominence with the writings of Michael Sandel, Michael Walzer, Alasdair MacIntyre, Daniel A. Bell, and Charles Taylor is quite different from traditional Marxism. Marxists see community as something that can only be achieved by a revolutionary change in society, by the overthrow of capitalism and the building of a socialist society. The new communitarians, on the other hand, believe that community already exists, in the form of common social practices, cultural traditions, and shared social understandings. Community does not need to be built *de novo*, but rather needs to be respected and protected. To some extent, communitarians see community in the very social practices that Marxists see as exploitative and alienating. As Amy Gutmann puts it, whereas the 'old' communitarians looked to Marx, and his desire to remake the world, the 'new' communitarians look to Hegel, and his desire to reconcile people to their world (Gutmann 1985).[1]

Indeed, there are many similarities between communitarian critiques of modern liberalism and Hegel's critique of classical liberal theory. Classical liberals like Locke and Kant attempted to identify a universal conception of human needs or human rationality, and then invoked this ahistorical conception of the human being to evaluate existing social and political arrangements. According to Hegel, this sort of approach—which he called *Moralität*—is too abstract to provide much guidance, and too individualistic, since it neglects the way that humans are inevitably embedded in particular historical practices and relationships. The alternative (which Hegel calls *Sittlichkeit*) emphasizes the way that the good of individuals—indeed, their very identity and capacity for moral agency—is bound up with the communities they belong to, and the particular social and political roles they occupy.[2]

Echoes of this contrast between *Moralität* and *Sittlichkeit* can be found in many contemporary communitarian writings. Like Hegel, communitarians charge modern liberals with adopting an abstract and individualistic approach, and propose instead a more contextual and community-sensitive approach. However, while the broader themes in the liberal-communitarian debate are familiar, the specific issues and perspectives are new, reflecting distinctly modern concerns about the nature of community in contemporary Western democracies.

The new communitarians are united by the belief that political philosophy must pay more attention to the shared practices and understandings within each society. They also agree that this requires modification of traditional liberal principles of justice and rights. They differ, however, on how these principles should be modified.

We can distinguish three distinct, sometimes conflicting, strands of communitarian thought. Some communitarians believe that community *replaces* the need for principles of justice. Others see justice and community as perfectly consistent, but think that a proper appreciation of the value of community requires us to modify our conception of what justice is. These latter communitarians fall into two camps. One camp argues that community should be seen as the *source* of principles of justice (i.e. justice should be based on the shared understandings of society, not on universal and ahistorical principles); the other camp argues that community should play a greater role in the *content* of principles of justice (i.e. justice should give more weight to the common good, and less weight to individual rights). I will briefly consider the first two strands, before focusing on the third.

2. COMMUNITY AND THE LIMITS OF JUSTICE

Some communitarians argue that principles of justice are not needed in true community. This is related to the Marxist idea that justice is only a 'remedial' virtue, although Marxists tend to think that the flaw which justice remedies is material scarcity, whereas communitarians suggest that the flaw is the absence of the 'more noble' virtues of benevolence or solidarity. According to Sandel, for example, if people responded spontaneously to the needs of others out of love or shared goals, then there would be no need to claim one's rights. Hence an increased concern with justice can, in some circumstances, reflect a worsening of the moral situation, rather than a moral improvement. Sandel suggests that the family is a social institution where justice is not needed, and where a preoccupation with justice may diminish the sense of love, and thereby lead to more conflict (1982: 28–35; cf. Hegel 1949: paras. 154–64).

I have already suggested in the previous chapter why this view of justice as a remedial virtue is mistaken (pp. 173–5). Justice does not displace love or solidarity, and nothing in the idea of justice precludes people from choosing to forgo their rightful claims in order to help others. Justice simply ensures that these decisions are genuinely voluntary, and that no one can force others to accept a subordinate position. Justice enables loving relationships, but ensures that they are not corrupted by domination or subordination.

3. JUSTICE AND SHARED MEANINGS

Many communitarians agree with Rawls about the importance of justice. However, they claim that liberals misinterpret justice as an ahistorical and external criterion for criticizing the ways of life of every society. Utilitarians, liberal egalitarians, and libertarians may disagree about the content of justice, but they all seem to think that their preferred theory provides a standard that every society should live up to. They do not regard it as a decisive objection that their theory may be in conflict with local beliefs.

Indeed, this potential for conflict with local beliefs is sometimes seen by liberals as the *point* of discussing justice. Theories of justice provide a standpoint for questioning our beliefs, and for ensuring that they are not merely local prejudices. As Ronald Dworkin puts it, 'In the end, political theory can make no contribution to how we govern ourselves except by struggling, against all the impulses that drag us back into our own culture, towards generality and some reflective basis for deciding which of our traditional distinctions and discriminations are genuine and which spurious.' For Dworkin, justice should be our critic, not our mirror (1985: 219).

Michael Walzer argues that this quest for a universal theory of justice is misguided. There is no such thing as a perspective external to the community, no way to step outside our history and culture. The only way to identify the requirements of justice, he claims, is to see how each particular community understands the value of social goods. A society is just if it acts in accordance with the shared understandings of its members, as embodied in its characteristic practices and institutions. Hence identifying principles of justice is more a matter of cultural interpretation than of philosophical argument (Walzer 1983; cf. Bell 1993: 55–89).

According to Walzer, as I noted in Ch. 5, p. 196, the shared understandings in our society require 'complex equality'—i.e. a system of distribution that does not try to equalize all goods, but rather seeks to ensure that inequalities in one 'sphere' (e.g. wealth) do not permeate other spheres (e.g. health care; political power). However, he admits that other societies do not share this understanding of justice, and for some societies (e.g. caste societies) justice may involve virtually unlimited inequality in rights and goods (Walzer 1983).

Walzer's theory is, of course, a form of cultural relativism, and it is beyond the scope of this book to discuss that age-old philosophical debate. However, there are two common objections to communitarian attempts to define justice in terms of a community's shared understandings. First, and paradoxically, cultural relativism violates one of our deepest shared understandings. According to cultural relativism, slavery is wrong if our society disapproves of it. But that is not how most people understand claims of justice. They put the causal arrow the other way around—i.e. we disapprove of slavery because it is wrong. Its wrongness is a reason for, not the product of, our shared understanding.[3] Secondly, it may be difficult to identify shared understandings about justice, especially if we attend not only to the voices of the vocal and powerful, but also to the weak and marginalized. People disagree about issues such as the proper role of government in the provision of health care (which Walzer endorses) or affirmative action (which Walzer opposes). In order to resolve these disagreements, we need to assess competing understandings in the light of a more general conception of justice. So even if we start with local understandings, as Walzer suggests, we are driven by the existence of disagreement, and our own critical reflection, towards a more general and less parochial standpoint.

4. INDIVIDUAL RIGHTS AND THE COMMON GOOD

For many communitarians, the problem with liberalism is not its emphasis on justice, nor its universalism, but rather its 'individualism'. According to this criticism, liberals base their theories on notions of individual rights and personal freedom, but neglect the extent to which individual freedom and well-being are only possible within community. Once we recognize the dependence of human beings on society, then our obligations to sustain the common good of society are as weighty as our rights to individual liberty. Hence, communitarians argue, the liberal 'politics of rights' should be abandoned for, or at least supplemented by, a 'politics of the common good'.

This, I believe, is the most important issue raised by the new communitarians. It challenges an important assumption which has been shared by all of the theories we have examined so far, with the exception of the perfectionist strand of Marxism. While utilitarianism, liberals, libertarians, and (Kantian) Marxists disagree on how to show equal concern for people's interests, they agree on a central feature of how to characterize those interests. They all believe that we promote people's interests by letting them choose for themselves what sort of life they want to lead. They disagree about what package of rights or resources best enables people to pursue their own conceptions of the good. But they agree that to deny people this self-determination is to fail to treat them as equals.

I have not yet discussed or defended the importance of self-determination (it was one of the issues I set aside in Chapter 3 by postponing discussion of Rawls's liberty principle). I have simply taken it for granted that we have an intuitive understanding of what it means to be self-determining, and of why that is thought to be an important value. But we need to examine this issue more closely, for communitarians challenge many of the standard assumptions about the nature and value of self-determination. In particular, communitarians argue that liberals both misconstrue our capacity for self-determination, and neglect the social preconditions under which that capacity can be meaningfully exercised. I will look at these two objections in turn, after first laying out the liberal account of the value of self-determination.

Many liberals think that the value of self-determination is so obvious that it does not require any defence. Allowing people to be self-determining is, they say, the only way to respect them as fully moral beings. To deny self-determination is to treat someone like a child or an animal, rather than a full member of the community.

But this is too quick. We know that some people are not well equipped to deal with the difficult decisions life requires. They make mistakes about their lives, choosing to do trivial, degrading, even harmful, things. If we are supposed to show concern for people, why should we not stop people from making such mistakes? When people are unable to deal effectively with life, respecting their self-determination may amount in practice to abandoning them to an unhappy fate. Saying that we ought to respect people's self-determination under these circumstances becomes an expression of indifference rather than concern. Dworkin says that it is 'the final evil of a genuinely unequal distribution of resources' that some people 'have been cheated of the chance others have had to make something valuable of their lives' (Dworkin 1981: 219). But what about those who are unable to make something valuable of their lives even when they have the chance? Do we not have obligations here too?

Liberals do leave room in their theory for acts of paternalism—for example, in our relations with children, the demented, and the otherwise temporarily incapacitated.[4] But liberals insist that every competent adult be provided with a sphere of self-determination which must be respected by others. As Mill put it, it is the right and prerogative of each person, once they have reached the maturity of their years, to interpret for themselves the meaning and value of their experiences. For those who pass the threshold of age and mental competence, the right to be self-determining in the major decisions in life is inviolate.

But why should we view self-determination in terms of such a threshold? Some of the people who have reached the 'age of reason', and who have a mental competence above the agreed-upon minimum, still make poor choices about how to lead their lives. Being a 'competent adult', in the sense that one is not mentally handicapped, is no guarantee that one is good at making something valuable of one's life. So why should government not decide what sort of lives are best for its citizens?

Marxist perfectionism is one example of such a policy, for it prohibits people from making what it views as a bad choice—i.e. choosing to engage in alienated labour. I argued that this policy is unattractive, for it relies on too narrow an account of the good. It identifies our good with a single activity—productive labour—on the grounds that it alone makes us distinctively human. But not all paternalist or perfectionist policies are based on such an implausible account of the good life. Consider a policy which subsidizes theatre while taxing professional wrestling. Defenders of such a policy need not say that theatre is the only, or even the most important, good in life. They simply claim that of these two options, as they currently exist, theatre is the more valuable. They may have a number of different arguments for this claim. Studies may reveal that theatre is stimulating, whereas wrestling produces frustration and docility; or that wrestling fans often come to regret their past activities, whereas theatre-goers rarely regret theirs; or that the majority of people who have tried both forms of entertainment prefer theatre. Under these circumstances, the claim that theatre is better entertainment than wrestling has some plausibility. Why then should the government not encourage people to attend the theatre, and save them from wasting their lives on wrestling?

Liberals view such policies, no matter how plausible the underlying theory of the good, as an illegitimate restriction on self-determination. If there are willing participants and spectators for wrestling, then the anti-wrestling policy is an unjustified restriction on people's freely chosen leisure. How can liberals defend the importance of people being free to choose their own leisure? Since the argument for perfectionism depends on the assumption that people can make mistakes about the value of their activities, one possible line of defence is to deny that people can be mistaken in their judgements of what is valuable in life. Defenders of self-determination might argue that judgements of value, unlike judgements of fact, are simply the expressions of our subjective likes and dislikes. These choices are ultimately arbitrary, incapable of rational justification or criticism. All such choices are equally rational, and so the state has no reason to interfere in them. Many perfectionists have assumed that this sort of scepticism about value judgements has to be the liberal position, for if we concede the possibility of people making mistakes, then surely the government must encourage the right ways of life, and discourage or prohibit mistaken ones (Unger 1984: 52, 66–7; Jaggar 1983: 194, 174; Sullivan 1982: 38–40).

But liberals do not endorse scepticism (see Nagel 1986; ch. 8; Dworkin 2000: ch. 6; Rawls 1993a: 62–4; Scanlon 1993). One reason is that scepticism does not in fact support self-determination. If people cannot make mistakes in their choices, then neither can governments. If all ways of life are equally valuable, then no one can complain when the government chooses a particular way of life for the community. Hence scepticism leaves the issue unresolved.

How do liberals defend the importance of self-determination? We need to look more closely at this idea. Self-determination involves deciding what to do with our lives. How do we make such decisions? At the most general level, our aim is to lead a good life, to have those things that a good life contains. Put at such a general level, that claim may seem quite uninformative. But it has important consequences. For, as we saw in Chapter 2, leading a good life is different from leading the life we currently believe to be good (Ch. 2, pp. 15–16 above). We recognize that we may be mistaken about the value of our current activities. We may come to see that we have been wasting our lives, pursuing trivial goals that we had mistakenly considered of great importance. This is the stuff of great novels—the crisis in faith. But the assumption that this could happen to all of us, and not just to the tragic heroine, is needed to make sense of the way we deliberate about important decisions in our life. We deliberate carefully because we know we could make wrong decisions. And not just in the sense of predicting wrongly, or of calculating uncertainties. For we deliberate even when we know what will happen, and we may regret our decisions even when things went as planned. I may succeed in becoming the best push-pin player in the world, but then come to realize that pushpin is not as valuable as poetry, and regret that I had ever embarked on that project.

Deliberation, then, does not only take the form of asking which course of action maximizes a particular value that is held unquestioned. We also question, and worry about, whether that value is really worth pursuing. As Rawls puts it,

As free persons, citizens recognize one another as having the moral power to have a conception of the good. This means that they do not view themselves as inevitably tied to the pursuit of the particular conception of the good and its final ends which they espouse at any given time. Instead, as citizens, they are regarded as, in general, capable of revising and changing this conception on reasonable and rational grounds. Thus it is held to be permissible for citizens to stand apart from conceptions of the good and to survey and assess their various final ends. (Rawls 1980: 544)

We can 'stand apart' or 'step back' from our current ends, and question their value to us. The concern with which we make these judgements, at certain points in our lives, only makes sense on the assumption that our essential interest is in living a good life, not the life we currently believe to be good. We do not just make such judgements, we worry, sometimes agonize, over them—it is important to us that we do not lead our lives on the basis of false beliefs about the value of our activities (Raz 1986: 300–2).

The idea that some things really are worth doing, and others are not, goes very deep in our self-understanding.[5] We take seriously the distinction between worthwhile and trivial activities, even if we are not always sure which things are which. Self-determination is, to a large extent, the task of making these difficult, and potentially fallible, judgements, and our political theory should take this difficulty and fallibility into account.

Should we therefore be perfectionists, supporting state policies which discourage trivial activities to which people are mistakenly attached? Not necessarily. For one thing, no one may be in a better position than I am to know my own good (Goodin 1990). Even if I am not always right, I may be more likely to be right than anyone else. Mill defended a version of this argument by claiming that each person contained a unique personality whose good was different from that of anyone else. The experience of others, therefore, provides no grounds for overriding my judgement. This is the opposite of Marxist perfectionism—where Marxists say that each person's good lies in a capacity she shares with all other humans. Mill says it lies in something she shares with no one else. But surely both extremes are wrong. Our good is neither universal nor unique, but tied in important ways to the cultural practices we share with others in our community. We share enough with others around us that a well-intentioned perfectionist government could, by drawing on the wisdom and experience of others, arrive at a reasonable set of beliefs about its citizens' good. Of course, we might doubt that governments have either the right intentions or abilities to execute such a programme. But nothing in principle excludes the possibility that governments can identify mistakes in people's conceptions of the good.

Why then do liberals oppose state paternalism? Because, they argue, no life goes better by being led from the outside according to values the person does not endorse. My life only goes better if I am leading it from the inside, according to my beliefs about value. Praying to God may be a valuable activity, but I have to believe that it is a worthwhile thing to do—that it has some worthwhile point. We can coerce someone into going to church and making the right physical movements, but we will not make her life better that way. It will not work, even if the coerced person is mistaken in her belief that praying to God is a waste of time, because a valuable life has to be led from the inside.[6] A perfectionist policy that violates this 'endorsement constraint', by trying to bypass or override people's beliefs about values, is self-defeating (Dworkin 1989: 486–7). It may succeed in getting people to pursue valuable activities, but it does so under conditions in which the activities cease to have value for the individuals involved. If I do not see the point of an activity, then I will gain nothing from it. Hence paternalism creates the very sort of pointless activity that it was designed to prevent.

So we have two preconditions for the fulfilment of our essential interest in leading a life that is good. One is that we lead our life from the inside, in accordance with our beliefs about what gives value to life; the other is that we be free to question those beliefs, to examine them in the light of whatever information, examples, and arguments our culture can provide. People must therefore have the resources and liberties needed to lead their lives in accordance with their beliefs about value, without being penalized for unorthodox religious or sexual practices, etc. Hence the traditional liberal concern for civil and personal liberties. And individuals must have the cultural conditions necessary to acquire an awareness of different views about the good life, and to acquire an ability to examine these views intelligently. Hence the traditional liberal concern for education, freedom of expression, freedom of the press, artistic freedom, etc. These liberties enable us to judge what is valuable in life in the only way we can judge such things—i.e. by exploring different aspects of our shared cultural heritage.

This account of the value of self-determination forms the basis of Rawls's original argument for his liberty principle. According to Rawls, freedom of choice is needed precisely to find out what is valuable in life—to form, examine, and revise our beliefs about value.[7] Liberty helps us come to know our good, to 'track bestness', in Nozick's phrase (Nozick 1981: 314, 410–11, 436–40, 498–504; cf. Dworkin 1983: 24–30). Since we have an essential interest in getting these beliefs right and acting on them, government treats people with equal concern and respect by providing each person with the liberties and resources needed to examine and act on these beliefs.

Rawls argues that this account of self-determination should lead us to endorse a 'neutral state'—i.e. a state which does not justify its actions on the basis of the intrinsic superiority or inferiority of conceptions of the good life, and which does not deliberately attempt to influence people's judgements of the value of these different conceptions.[8] He contrasts this idea of state neutrality with perfectionist theories which include a particular view, or range of views, as to what ways of life are most worthy or fulfilling. Perfectionists demand that resources should be distributed so as to encourage the development of such ways of life. One's share of resources depends on how much one needs to pursue, or how much one contributes to, this preferred view of the good life. People are not, therefore, free to choose their own conception of the good life, at least not without being penalized by society. People make mistakes about the good life, and the state has the responsibility to teach its citizens about a worthwhile life. It abandons that responsibility to its citizens if it funds, or perhaps even tolerates, life-plans that have misconceived views about human excellence.

For Rawls, on the other hand, our essential interests are harmed by attempts to enforce a particular view of the good life on people, and so the state should remain neutral regarding the good life. 'Neutrality' may not be the best word to describe the issue at stake here. After all, liberal egalitarianism is not based on any general idea of moral neutrality. On the contrary, as we have seen throughout this book, liberal egalitarianism is a deeply moral theory, premised on fundamental principles of the intrinsic moral worth of individuals, racial and gender equality, justice as fairness, equality of opportunity, individual rights and responsibilities, and so on. Liberal egalitarianism is not only committed to these principles, but also seeks to use state power to uphold and enforce them, and to prohibit any actions or practices which violate them.

So the sort of 'neutrality' endorsed by Rawls and Dworkin is a more limited one, focused solely on the intrinsic merits of different (justice-respecting) conceptions of the good life. The role of the state is to protect the capacity of individuals to judge for themselves the worth of different conceptions of the good life, and to provide a fair distribution of the rights and resources to enable people to pursue their conception of the good. The state tells people what is rightfully theirs, and what rightfully belongs to others, and insists that people adjust their conceptions of the good to respect the rightful claims of others. But if someone's conception of the good life does respect these principles of justice, then liberals say that the state should not be assessing the intrinsic merits of her (justice-respecting) way of life. The liberal state does not justify its actions by reference to some public ranking of the intrinsic worth of different ways of life, for there is no public ranking to refer to. As Rawls puts it, the state is neutral towards different conceptions of the good 'not in the sense that there is an agreed public measure of intrinsic value or satisfaction with respect to which all these conceptions come out equal, but in the sense that they are not evaluated at all from a [public] standpoint' (Rawls 1982*b*: 172).

So the sort of 'neutrality' endorsed by liberals is limited in scope to (justice-respecting) conceptions of the good. Moreover, even with respect to conceptions of the good, the term 'neutrality' may still be misleading. Neutrality in its everyday usage often refers to the consequences of actions, rather than the justifications for them. A 'neutral' policy, in this everyday sense, would be one that ensured that all conceptions of the good fared equally well in society, no matter how expensive and unattractive they were. Some critics have taken Rawls to defend neutrality in this everyday sense (e.g. Raz 1986: 117). However, this sort of neutrality is quite illiberal, since it would both restrict freedom of choice, and violate the requirement that people accept responsibility for the costs of their choices. Any society which allows different ways of life to compete for people's free allegiance, and which requires people to pay for the costs of their choices, will seriously disadvantage expensive and unattractive ways of life. Liberals accept, and indeed value, these unequal consequences of civil liberties and individual responsibility. Hence liberal neutrality is neutrality in the justification of state policies, not in their consequences. State neutrality is simply the idea that there is no public ranking of the value of different (justice-respecting) ways of life (Rawls 1988: 260, 265; 1993*a*: 192–4; Nagel 1991: 116; Kymlicka 1989*b*: 883–6).[9]

Given these potential confusions over the term 'neutrality', it might be preferable to talk of 'state anti-perfectionism' rather than 'state neutrality'. The term 'state anti-perfectionism' highlights the real issue—the role of perfectionist ideals in state decision-making—and clarifies that the relevant alternative is some form of state perfectionism.

Of course, even a liberal state must make *some* assumptions about people's interests or well-being. After all, when a liberal state tries to guarantee certain liberties, opportunities, or resources for people, it assumes that people's lives will go better by having these things. Some critics have argued that this shows the inevitability of appealing to perfectionist ideals when developing any political theory. But for liberals, there is an important difference between determining what sorts of *means* or resources people need, and what sorts of *ends* they should pursue with those means. As we saw in Chapter 3, Rawls's theory involves the distribution of certain 'all-purpose means' or 'primary goods' which he claims will be useful whatever people's (justice-respecting) conception of the good turns out to be. According to Rawls, people who do not yet know their particular conception of the good (e.g. the parties in the original position under the veil of ignorance) could nonetheless agree that there are certain things that are essential or useful for virtually all ways of life, such as material resources and individual liberties. These all-purpose means will then be used by individuals to help form, revise, and pursue their own particular conception of the good (see Ch. 3, pp. 64–5 above).

One can question whether the rights and resources on Rawls's list of 'primary goods' really are useful for all ways of life, such as those of, say, monks who take a vow of poverty. Actually, I believe that would-be monks do need access to Rawls's primary goods, and that Rawls's list does as good a job as possible in identifying those means that will be useful for the widest possible range of (justice-respecting) lifestyles.[10] But in any event, this is not the fundamental issue for most critics of state neutrality. For most defenders of state perfectionism, the problem with Rawls's account is not that it disadvantages some unusual but worthy lifestyles, but rather that it tolerates too many common but worthless lifestyles. Perfectionists would like the state to distribute resources, not so as to enable as wide a range of lifestyles as possible, but rather so as to serve the specific ends deemed most worthy by the state. State perfectionists want to use the distribution of resources to shape people's ends, not only to provide them with all-purpose means.

For Rawls and Dworkin, however, if the resources distributed by the state are only useful for one plan of life, then we will be unable to act on our beliefs about value, should we come to believe that the one preferred conception of the good life is misguided. (Or, at any rate, we will be unable to do so without suffering some penalty in social benefits.) Since lives have to be led from the inside, someone's essential interest in leading a life that is good is not advanced when society penalizes, or discriminates against, the projects that she, on reflection, feels are most valuable for her. Distributing resources according to a 'thin theory of the good', or what Dworkin calls 'resources in the widest sense', best enables people to act on and examine their beliefs about value, and that is the most appropriate way to promote people's essential interest in leading a good life.

5. COMMUNITARIANISM AND THE COMMON GOOD

Communitarians object to the neutral state. They believe it should be abandoned for a 'politics of the common good' (Sandel 1984b: 16–17; Taylor 1985b). This contrast between the 'politics of neutrality' and communitarianism's 'politics of the common good' can be misleading. There is a 'common good' present in liberal politics as well, since the policies of a liberal state aim at promoting the interests of the members of the community. The political and economic processes by which individual preferences are combined into a social choice function are liberal modes of determining the common good. To affirm state neutrality, therefore, is not to reject the idea of a common good, but rather to provide an interpretation of it (Holmes 1989: 239–40). In a liberal society, the common good is the result of a process of combining preferences, all of which are counted equally (if consistent with the principles of justice). All preferences have equal weight not because they have been judged by the state as having equal intrinsic value, but because 'they are not evaluated at all from a [public] standpoint' (Rawls 1982b: 172). As we have seen, this anti-perfectionist insistence on state neutrality reflects the belief that people's interest in leading a good life is not advanced when society discriminates against the projects that they believe are most valuable for them. Hence the common good in a liberal society is adjusted to fit the pattern of preferences and conceptions of the good held by individuals.

In a communitarian society, however, the common good is conceived of as a substantive conception of the good life which defines the community's 'way of life'. This common good, rather than adjusting itself to the pattern of people's preferences, provides a standard by which those preferences are evaluated. The community's way of life forms the basis for a public ranking of conceptions of the good, and the weight given to an individual's preferences depends on how much she conforms or contributes to this common good. The public pursuit of the shared ends which define the community's way of life is not, therefore, constrained by the requirement of neutrality. It takes precedence over the claim of individuals to the resources and liberties needed to pursue their own conceptions of the good. A communitarian state can and should encourage people to adopt conceptions of the good that conform to the community's way of life, while discouraging conceptions of the good that conflict with it. A communitarian state is, therefore, a perfectionist state, since it involves a public ranking of the value of different ways of life. But whereas Marxist perfectionism ranks ways of life according to a trans-historical account of the human good, communitarianism ranks them according to their conformity to existing practices.

Why should we prefer this 'politics of the common good' over liberal neutrality? Liberals say that state neutrality is required to respect people's self-determination. Communitarians, however, object both to the liberal idea of self-determination, and to the supposed connection between self-determination and neutrality. I will consider these two objections in turn.

6. THE UNENCUMBERED SELF

On the liberal view of the self, individuals are considered free to question their participation in existing social practices, and opt out of them, should those practices seem no longer worth pursuing. As a result, individuals are not defined by their membership in any particular economic, religious, sexual, or recreational relationship, since they are free to question and reject any particular relationship. Rawls summarizes this liberal view by saying that 'the self is prior to the ends which are affirmed by it' (Rawls 1971: 560), by which he means that we can always step back from any particular project and question whether we want to continue pursuing it. No end is exempt from possible revision by the self. This is often called the 'Kantian' view of the self, for Kant was one of the strongest defenders of the view that the self is prior to its socially given roles and relationships, and is free only if it is capable of holding these features of its social situation at a distance and judging them according to the dictates of reason (Taylor 1979: 75–8, 132–3).

Communitarians believe that this is a false view of the self. It ignores the fact that the self is 'embedded' or 'situated' in existing social practices, that we cannot always stand back and opt out of them. Our social roles and relationships, or at least some of them, must be taken as givens for the purposes of personal deliberation. As MacIntyre puts it, in deciding how to lead our lives, we 'all approach our own circumstances as bearers of a particular social identity. . . . Hence what is good for me has to be the good for one who inhabits these roles' (MacIntyre 1981: 204–5). Self-determination, therefore, is exercised within these social roles, rather than by standing outside them. And so the state respects our self-determination not by enabling us to stand back from our social roles, but by encouraging a deeper immersion in and understanding of them, as the politics of the common good seeks to accomplish.

Communitarians have a number of different arguments against the liberal account of the self and its ends. I will consider three, which can be summarized this way: the liberal view of the self (1) is empty; (2) violates our self-perceptions; and (3) ignores our embeddedness in communal practices.[11]

First, the emptiness argument. Being free to question all our social roles is self-defeating, Charles Taylor says, because 'complete freedom would be a void in which nothing would be worth doing, nothing would deserve to count for anything. The self which has arrived at freedom by setting aside all external obstacles and impingements is characterless, and hence without defined purpose' (Taylor 1979: 157). True freedom must be 'situated', Taylor argues. The desire to subject all aspects of our social situation to our rational self-determination is empty, because the demand to be self-determining is indeterminate. It 'cannot specify any content to our action outside of a situation which sets goals for us, which thus imparts a shape to rationality and provides an inspiration for creativity' (Taylor 1979: 157). We must accept the goal that our situation 'sets for us'. If we do not, then the quest for self-determination leads to Nietzschean nihilism, the rejection of all communal values as ultimately arbitrary: 'One after the other, the authoritative horizons of life, Christian and humanist, are cast off as shackles on the will. Only the will to power remains' (Taylor 1979: 159). If we deny that communal values are 'authoritative horizons', then they will appear as arbitrary limits on our will, and hence our freedom will require rejecting them all (MacIntyre 1981: ch. 9).

But this misconstrues the role that freedom plays in liberal theories. According to Taylor, liberals claim that the freedom to choose our projects is inherently valuable, something to be pursued for its own sake, a claim that Taylor rejects as empty. Instead, he says, there has to be some project that is worth pursuing, some task that is worth fulfilling. But the concern for freedom within liberalism does not take the place of these tasks and projects. On the contrary, the liberal defence of freedom rests precisely on the importance of those projects. Liberals do not say that we should have the freedom to select our projects for its own sake, because freedom is the most valuable thing in the world. Rather, our projects and tasks are the most important things in our lives, and it is because they are so important that we should be free to revise them, should we come to believe that they are not worthwhile. Our projects are the most important things in our lives, but since our lives have to be led from the inside, in accordance with our beliefs about value, we should be free to form, revise, and act on our plans of life. Freedom of choice is not pursued for its own sake, but as a precondition for pursuing those projects that are valued for their own sake.

Some liberals have endorsed the position Taylor rightly criticizes as empty. Isaiah Berlin attributes it to Mill, for example (Berlin 1969: 192; but cf. Ladenson 1983: 149–53). Claiming that freedom of choice is intrinsically valuable may seem like an effective way of defending a broad range of liberal freedoms. But the implications of that claim conflict with the way we understand the value in our lives in at least two important ways: (1) Saying that freedom of choice is intrinsically valuable suggests that the more we exercise our capacity for choice, the more free we are, and hence the more valuable our lives are. But that is false, and indeed perverse. It quickly leads to the existentialist view that we should wake up each morning and decide anew what sort of person we should be. This is perverse because a valuable life is a life filled with commitments and relationships. These give our lives depth and character. And what makes them commitments is precisely that they are not the sort of thing that we question every day. We do not suppose that someone who makes twenty marriage choices is in any way leading a more valuable life than someone who has no reason to question her original choice. A life with more marital choices is not even *ceteris paribus* better than a life with fewer such choices. (2) Saying that freedom of choice is intrinsically valuable suggests that the value we seek in our actions is freedom, not the value internal to the activity itself. This suggestion is endorsed by Carol Gould. She says that while we seem to act for the sake of the purposes internal to a given project, truly free activity has freedom itself as the ultimate end: 'Thus freedom is not only the activity that creates value but is that for the sake of which all these other values are pursued and therefore that with respect to which they become valuable' (Gould 1978: 118).

But this is doubtful. First, as Taylor notes, telling people to act freely does not tell them what particular actions are worth doing. But even if it provided determinate guidance, it still presents a false view of our motivations. If I am writing a book, for example, my motivation is not to be free, but to say something that is worth saying. Indeed, if I did not really want to say anything, except in so far as it is a way of being free, then my writing would not be fulfilling. What and how I write would become the result of arbitrary and ultimately unsatisfying choices. If writing is to be intrinsically valuable, I have to care about what I am saying, I have to believe that writing is worth doing for its own sake. If we are to understand the value people see in their projects, we have to look to the ends which are internal to them. I do not pursue my writing for the sake of my freedom. On the contrary, I pursue my writing for its own sake, because there are things which are worth saying. Freedom is valuable because it allows me to say them.

The best defence of individual freedoms is not necessarily the most direct one, but the one which best accords with the way that people on reflection understand the value of their lives. And if we look at the value of freedom in this way, then it seems that freedom of choice, while central to a valuable life, is not the value which is centrally pursued in such a life.

No one disagrees that projects have to be our primary concern—that does not distinguish the liberal and the communitarian. The real debate is not over whether we need such tasks, but over how we acquire them and judge their worth. Taylor seems to believe that we can acquire these tasks only by treating communal values as 'authoritative horizons' which 'set goals for us' (Taylor 1979: 157–9). Liberals, on the other hand, insist that we have an ability to detach ourselves from any particular social practice. No particular task is set for us by society, no particular practice has authority that is beyond individual judgement and possible rejection. We can and should acquire our tasks through freely made personal judgements about the cultural structure, the matrix of understandings and alternatives passed down to us by previous generations, which offers us possibilities we can either affirm or reject. Nothing is 'set for us'; nothing is authoritative before our judgement of its value.

Of course, in making that judgement, we must take something as a 'given'—we ask what is good for us now, given our place in school, work, or family. Someone who is nothing but a free rational being would have no reason to choose one way of life over another (Sandel 1982: 161–5; Taylor 1979: 157; Crowley 1987: 204–5). But liberals believe that what we put in 'the given' in order to make meaningful judgements can not only be different between individuals but also can change within one individual's life. If at one time we make choices about what is valuable given our commitment to a certain religious life, we could later come to question that commitment, and ask what is valuable given our commitment to our family. The question then is not whether we must take something as given in making judgements about the value of our activity. Rather, the question is whether an individual can question and possibly replace what is in 'the given', or whether the given has to be set for us by the community's values. Taylor fails to show that we must take communal values as given, that it is empty to say that such communal values should be subject to individual evaluation and possible rejection.

One can weaken the communitarian objection by arguing that even if we can get our purposes this way, unset by the community, we nonetheless should treat communal ends as authoritative. We should do this because the liberal view relies on a false account of the self. The liberal view, we have seen, is that 'the self is prior to its ends', in the sense that we reserve the right to question even our most deeply held convictions about the nature of the good life. Michael Sandel, however, argues that the self is not prior to, but rather constituted by, its ends—we cannot distinguish 'me' from 'my ends'. Our selves are at least partly constituted by ends that we do not choose, but rather discover by virtue of our being embedded in some shared social context (Sandel 1982: 55–9, 152–4). Since we have these constitutive ends, our lives go better not by having the conditions needed to select and revise our projects, but by having the conditions needed to come to an awareness of these shared constitutive ends. A politics of the common good, by expressing these shared constitutive ends, enables us to 'know a good in common that we cannot know alone' (Sandel 1982: 183).

Sandel has two arguments for this claim, which I will call the 'self-perception' and 'embedded-self' arguments. The first argument goes like this: Rawls's view of the 'unencumbered self' does not correspond with our 'deepest self-understanding' in the sense of our deepest self-perception. According to Sandel, if the self is prior to its ends, then we should, when introspecting, be able to see through our particular ends to an unencumbered self. But, Sandel notes, we do not perceive our selves as being unencumbered: Rawls's view of the self as 'given prior to its ends, a pure subject of agency and possession, ultimately thin', is 'radically at odds with our more familiar notion of ourselves as beings "thick with particular traits"' (Sandel 1982: 94, 100). On Rawls's view, 'to identify any characteristics as *my* aims, ambitions, desires, and so on, is always to imply some subject "me" standing behind them, at a certain distance' (Sandel 1984a: 86). There would have to be this thing, a self, which has some shape, albeit an ultimately thin shape, standing at some distance behind our ends. To accept Rawls, I would have to see myself as this propertyless thing, a disembodied rather ghostly object in space, or as Rorty puts it, as a kind of 'substrate' lying 'behind' my ends (Rorty 1985: 217).[12] In contrast, Sandel says that our deepest self-perceptions always include some motivations, which shows that some ends are constitutive of the self.

But the question of perception here is misleading. What is central to the liberal view is not that we can perceive a self prior to its ends, but that we understand ourselves to be prior to our ends in the sense that no end or goal is exempt from possible re-examination. For re-examination to be meaningfully conducted, I must be able to see my self encumbered with different motivations from those I now have, in order that I have some reason to choose one over another as more valuable for me. My self is, in this sense, perceived prior to its ends, i.e. I can always envisage my self without its *present* ends. But this does not require that I can ever perceive a self unencumbered by any ends—the process of practical reasoning is always one of comparing one 'encumbered' potential self with another 'encumbered' potential self. There must always be some ends given with the self when we engage in such reasoning, but it does not follow that any particular ends must always be taken as given with the self. As I said before, it seems that what is given with the self can change over the course of a lifetime. Thus there is a further claim that Sandel must establish: he must show not only that we cannot perceive a totally unencumbered self, but that we cannot perceive our self encumbered by a different set of ends. This requires a different argument, which I call the embedded-self argument.

This third argument contrasts the communitarian view of practical reasoning as self-discovery with the liberal view of practical reasoning as judgement. For liberals, the question about the good life requires us to make a judgement about what sort of a person we wish to be or become. For communitarians, however, the question requires us to discover who we already are. For communitarians, the relevant question is not 'What should I be, what sort of life should I lead?' but 'Who am I?' The self 'comes by' its ends not 'by choice' but 'by discovery', not 'by choosing that which is already given (this would be unintelligible) but by reflecting on itself and inquiring into its constituent nature, discerning its laws and imperatives, and acknowledging its purposes as its own' (Sandel 1982: 58). For example, Sandel criticizes Rawls's account of community, because 'while Rawls allows that the good of community can be internal to the extent of engaging the aims and values of the self, it cannot be so thoroughgoing as to reach beyond the motivations to the subject of motivations' (Sandel 1982: 149). On a more adequate account, Sandel claims, communal values are not just affirmed by the members of the community, but define their identity. The shared pursuit of a communal goal is 'not a relationship they choose (as in a voluntary association) but an attachment they discover, not merely an attribute but a constituent of their identity' (Sandel 1982: 150). The good for such members is found by a process of self-discovery—by achieving awareness of, and acknowledging the claims of, the various attachments they 'find'.

But surely it is Sandel here who is violating our deepest self-understandings. For we do not think that this self-discovery replaces or forecloses judgements about how to lead our life. We do not consider ourselves trapped by our present attachments, incapable of judging the worth of the goals we inherited or ourselves chose earlier. We do indeed find ourselves in various relationships, but we do not always like what we find. No matter how deeply implicated we find ourselves in a social practice, we feel capable of questioning whether the practice is a valuable one—a questioning which is not meaningful on Sandel's account. (How can it not be valuable since the good for me just is coming to a greater self-awareness of the attachments I find myself in?) The idea that deliberation is completed by this process of self-discovery (rather than by judgements of the value of the attachments we discover) is implausible.

In places, Sandel admits that practical reasoning is not just a question of self-discovery. He says that the boundaries of the self, although constituted by its ends, are nonetheless flexible and can be redrawn, incorporating new ends and excluding others. In his words, 'the subject is empowered to participate in the constitution of its identity'; on his account 'the bounds of the self [are] open and the identity of the subject [is] the product rather than the premise of its agency' (Sandel 1982: 152). The subject can, after all, make choices about which of the 'possible purposes and ends, all impinging indiscriminately on its identity' it will pursue, and which it will not (Sandel 1982: 152). The self, constituted by its ends, can be 'reconstituted' as it were, so self-discovery is not enough. But at this point it is not clear whether the distinction between the two views does not collapse.

There are apparent differences here. Sandel claims that the self is constituted by its ends, and that the boundaries of the self are fluid, whereas Rawls says that the self is prior to its ends, and its boundaries are fixed antecedently.

But these two differences hide a more fundamental identity; both accept that the *person* is prior to her ends. They disagree over where, within the person, to draw the boundaries of the self; but this question, if it is indeed a meaningful question, is one for the philosophy of mind, not political philosophy. For so long as Sandel admits that the person can re-examine her ends—even the ends constitutive of her self—then he has failed to justify communitarian politics. He has failed to show why individuals should not be given the conditions appropriate to that re-examining, as an indispensable part of leading the best possible life. And amongst these conditions should be the liberal guarantees of personal independence necessary to make the judgement freely. Sandel trades on an ambiguity in the view of the person that he uses in defending communitarian politics. The strong claim (that self-discovery replaces judgement) is implausible, and the weak claim (which allows that a self constituted by its ends can nonetheless be reconstituted), while attractive, fails to distinguish him from the liberal view.[13]

Sandel says that liberalism ignores the way we are embedded in our social roles. He emphasizes that as 'self-interpreting beings', we can interpret the meaning of these constitutive attachments (Sandel 1984a: 91). But the question is whether we can reject them entirely should we come to view them as trivial or degrading. On one interpretation of communitarianism, we cannot, or at any rate, we should not. On this view, we neither choose nor reject these attachments, rather we find ourselves in them. Our goals come not by choice, but by self-discovery. A Christian housewife in a monogamous heterosexual marriage can interpret what it means to be a Christian or a housewife—she can interpret the meaning of these shared religious, economic, and sexual practices. But she cannot stand back and decide that she does not want to be a Christian at all, or a housewife. I can interpret the meaning of the roles I find myself in, but I cannot reject the roles themselves, or the goals internal to them, as worthless. Since these goals are constitutive of me as a person, they have to be taken as given in deciding what to do with my life; the question of the good in my life can only be a question of how best to interpret their meaning. It makes no sense to say that they have no value for me, since there is no 'me' standing behind them, no self prior to these constitutive attachments.

It is unclear which if any communitarians hold this view consistently. It is not a plausible position, since we can and do make sense of questions not just about the meaning of the roles we find ourselves in, but also about their value. Perhaps communitarians do not mean to deny that; perhaps their idea of our embeddedness is not incompatible with our rejecting the attachments we find ourselves in. But then the advertised contrast with the liberal view is a deception, for the sense in which communitarians view us as embedded in communal roles incorporates the sense in which liberals view us as independent of them, and the sense in which communitarians view practical reasoning as a process of 'self-discovery' incorporates the sense in which liberals view it as a process of judgement and choice. The differences would be merely semantic. And once we agree that individuals are capable of questioning and rejecting the value of the community's way of life, then the attempt to discourage such questioning through a 'politics of the common good' seems an unjustified restriction on people's self-determination.

7. THE FIRST LIBERAL ACCOMMODATION OF COMMUNITARIANISM: POLITICAL LIBERALISM

So I think the communitarian critique of the liberal belief in rational revisability can be answered.[14] The communitarian conception of the embedded self is not a plausible conception of the self-understandings of most citizens in Western democracies. It may be surprising, therefore, that many liberals have attempted to at least partially accommodate the communitarian position, and to show that people who accept the communitarian conception of the self can still accept a (reformulated) version of liberalism. I will discuss this liberal reformulation—known as 'political liberalism'—below.

While liberals reject the communitarian critique in its broadest form, there is a narrower version of the argument which many liberals take very seriously. On this weaker version, communitarians accept that the liberal view of rational revisability, far from being inherently 'empty' or 'incoherent', is indeed compelling and attractive to many, perhaps even most citizens. However, they insist that it is not accepted by *all* citizens. Even if the communitarian idea of the embedded self is wrong as a general account of how people relate to their ends, it may nonetheless be an accurate description of the way *some* people see themselves.

Consider the members of strongly traditionalist groups, such as fundamentalist religious groups or isolated ethnocultural minorities. Such groups often feel threatened by liberalism's emphasis on autonomy. They fear that if their members are informed about other ways of life, and are given the cognitive and emotional capacities to understand and evaluate them, many will choose to reject their inherited way of life, and thereby undermine the group. To prevent this, fundamentalist or isolationist groups often wish to raise and educate their children in such a way as to minimize the opportunities for children to develop or exercise the capacity for rational revisability. They may also seek to make it very difficult for members to leave the group. Their goal is to ensure that their members are indeed 'embedded' in the group, unable to conceive of leaving it or to succeed outside of it.

For example, some minority religious or ethnic groups seek to limit the amount of education girls receive, or to remove their children from classes which teach about non-traditional ways of life. Other groups forbid the possession of private property, so that anyone who leaves the group is reduced to complete poverty. These measures limit the freedom of individual members within the group to question or revise traditional practices. As such, they seem to conflict with the liberal commitment to individual freedom or personal autonomy.

So we can formulate a narrower communitarian critique which offers an account, not of the way most people relate to their ends, but of how certain traditionalist groups conceive of themselves. This is a considerable weakening of the communitarian position, since it is now relevant to only a smaller subset of citizens. But it still raises a question which many liberals take very seriously: how should a liberal state deal with non-liberal minority groups which do not value autonomy? Even if such non-liberal groups are relatively few in number, do liberals have the right simply to impose 'our' beliefs about autonomy on them?

If a non-liberal minority is seeking forcibly to impose its traditionalist way of life on other groups, then most people would probably agree that state intervention is justified in the name of self-defence against aggression. But what if the group has no interest in ruling over others, and instead simply wants to be left alone to run its own community in accordance with its traditional non-liberal norms? In this case, it may seem wrong to impose liberal values. So long as these minorities do not want to impose their values on others, shouldn't they be allowed to organize their society as they like, even if this involves limiting the liberty of their own members? Indeed, isn't it fundamentally *intolerant* to force a peaceful ethnic minority or religious sect—which poses no threat to anyone outside the group—to reorganize their community according to 'our' liberal principles of individual liberty?

These are difficult questions, and have given rise to important disputes, not only between liberals and non-liberals, but also within liberalism itself. For tolerance is itself a fundamental liberal value. Yet promoting individual freedom or personal autonomy seems to entail intolerance towards illiberal groups.

There is a large and growing debate amongst liberals about whether autonomy or tolerance is the fundamental value within liberal theory. This contrast is described in different ways—e.g. a contrast between 'comprehensive' and 'political' liberalism (Rawls 1993*a*; Moon 1993), or between 'Enlightenment' and 'Reformation' liberalism (Galston 1995), or between 'Kantian' and 'modus vivendi' liberalism (Larmore 1987). Underneath all these contrasts is a similar concern—namely, that there are many groups within the boundaries of liberal states which do not value personal autonomy, and which restrict the ability of their members to question and dissent from traditional practices. Basing liberal theory on autonomy threatens to alienate these groups, and undermine their allegiance to liberal institutions, whereas a tolerance-based liberalism can provide a more secure and wider basis for the legitimacy of government.

These new theories of 'political liberalism' reflect a sincere attempt to accommodate 'communitarian' minority groups. However, I think they obscure, rather than remove or defuse, the potential conflicts between liberal principles and illiberal groups.

To see this, we need to examine the idea of tolerance. Liberalism and toleration are indeed closely related, both historically and conceptually. The development of religious tolerance was one of the historical roots of liberalism. Religious tolerance in the West emerged out of the interminable Wars of Religion, and the recognition by both Catholics and Protestants that a stable constitutional order cannot rest on a shared religious faith. According to Rawls, liberals have simply extended the principle of tolerance to other controversial questions about the 'meaning, value and purpose of human life' (Rawls 1987: 4; 1985: 249; 1993a: xxviii).

But if liberalism can indeed be seen as an extension of the principle of religious tolerance, it is important to recognize that religious tolerance in the West has taken a specific form—namely, the idea of individual freedom of conscience. It is now a basic individual right to worship freely, to propagate one's religion, to change one's religion, or indeed to renounce religion altogether. To restrict an individual's exercise of these liberties is seen as a violation of a fundamental human right.

There are other forms of religious toleration which are not liberal. They are based on the idea that each religious group should be free to organize its community as it sees fit, including along non-liberal lines. In the 'millet system' of the Ottoman Empire, for example, Muslims, Christians, and Jews were all recognized as self-governing units (or 'millets'), and allowed to impose restrictive religious laws on their own members. The Ottoman Turks were Muslims who conquered much of the Middle East, North Africa, Greece, and Eastern Europe during the fourteenth and fifteenth centuries, thereby acquiring many Jewish and Christian subjects. For various theological and strategic reasons, the Ottomans allowed these minorities not only the freedom to practise their religion, but a more general freedom to govern themselves in purely internal matters, with their own legal codes and courts. For about five centuries, between 1456 and the collapse of the empire in the First World War, three non-Muslim minorities had official recognition as self-governing communities—the Greek Orthodox, the Armenian Orthodox, and the Jews—each of which was further subdivided into various local administrative units, usually based on ethnicity and language. Each millet was headed by the relevant church leader (the Chief Rabbi and the two Orthodox Patriarchs), and the legal traditions and practices of each religious group, particularly in matters of family status, were respected and enforced wherever their members lived throughout the empire.

While the Christian and Jewish millets were free to run their internal affairs, their relations with the ruling Muslims were tightly regulated. In particular, non-Muslims could not proselytize. But within these limits, they enjoyed significant self-government, obeying their own laws and customs. Their collective freedom of worship was guaranteed, together with their possession of churches and synagogues, and they could run their own schools.

This system was generally humane, tolerant of group differences, and remarkably stable. But it was not a liberal society, for it did not recognize any principle of *individual* freedom of conscience. Since each religious community was self-governing, there was no external obstacle to basing this self-government on religious principles, including the enforcement of religious orthodoxy. Hence there was little or no scope for individual dissent within each religious community, and little or no freedom to change one's faith. While the Muslims did not try to suppress the Jews, or vice versa, they did suppress heretics within their own community. Heresy (questioning the orthodox interpretation of Muslim doctrine) and apostasy (abandoning one's religious faith) were punishable crimes within the Muslim community. Restrictions on individual freedom of conscience also existed in the Jewish and Christian communities.

The millet system was, in effect, a federation of theocracies. It was a deeply conservative and patriarchal society, antithetical to the ideals of personal liberty endorsed by liberals from Locke to Kant and Mill. There were significant restrictions on the freedom of individuals to question or reject church doctrine. The Ottomans accepted the principle of religious tolerance, in the sense that the dominant religion was willing to coexist with others, but did not accept the quite separate principle of individual freedom of conscience.

Variations on the millet model have been demanded by some traditionalist minorities today in the name of 'tolerance'. But this is not the sort of tolerance which liberals historically have endorsed. So it is not enough to say that liberals believe in toleration. The question is, what sort of toleration? Historically, liberals have believed in a specific notion of tolerance—one which involves freedom of individual conscience, not just collective worship. Liberal tolerance protects the right of individuals to dissent from their group, as well as the right of groups not to be persecuted by the state. It limits the power of illiberal groups to restrict the liberty of their own members, as well as the power of illiberal states to restrict the liberty of collective worship.

This shows, I think, that liberals have historically seen autonomy and tolerance as two sides of the same coin. What distinguishes *liberal* tolerance is precisely its commitment to autonomy—i.e. the idea that individuals should be free to rationally assess and potentially revise their existing ends (Mendus 1989: 56).

But is liberalism's historic commitment to autonomy an acceptable basis for government in our pluralistic society, given that some groups do not value autonomy? Should liberals try to find some alternative basis for liberal theory which can accommodate such groups—that is, find some form of tolerance that is more tolerant of illiberal groups?

Many liberals have started searching for such an alternative. Rawls himself, in his more recent work, has backed away from a commitment to autonomy, on the grounds that some people do not see their ends as potentially revisable, and to defend liberal institutions on this basis is therefore 'sectarian' (1987: 24; 1985: 246).[15] This objection is echoed by other theorists who want to reformulate liberalism in a way which will appeal even to those who reject the idea that people can stand back and assess their ends (Larmore 1987; Galston 1991; Moon 1993).

This reformulated liberalism is often known as the idea of 'political liberalism', in contrast to a 'comprehensive liberalism' which appeals to the value of autonomy. According to Rawls, this reformulation does not involve changing the fundamental conclusions of his original theory. He still endorses his two principles of justice: the liberty principle which guarantees everyone the most extensive set of equal basic liberties; and the difference principle which requires an equal distribution of resources except where inequalities work to the benefit of the least well off (see Ch. 3, s. 1).

What Rawls has changed, however, is his argument for these two principles, in particular his argument for the principle of liberty. More exactly, he now hopes to show that there are several different arguments for the protection of basic liberties, some of which appeal to the value of autonomy, but some of which do not. These different arguments will appeal to different groups in society, and the end result is an 'overlapping consensus' in which we all agree on the necessity of upholding basic liberties, albeit for different reasons.

To illustrate this idea of an 'overlapping consensus' Rawls takes the issue of freedom of conscience. He distinguishes between two important arguments for freedom of conscience. On the first argument, religious beliefs are 'seen as *subject to revision* in accordance with deliberative reason', and we need freedom of conscience because there 'is no guarantee that all aspects of our present way of life are the most rational for us and not in need of at least minor if not major revision' (Rawls 1982b: 25–9, my emphasis). This is the familiar liberal argument for basic liberties, rooted in the idea of rational revisability, which says that religious liberty is needed for us to rationally evaluate and potentially revise our conceptions of faith. On the second argument, religious beliefs are 'regarded as *given and firmly rooted*', and we need freedom of conscience because society contains 'a plurality of such conceptions, each, as it were, non-negotiable'. This second argument accepts the communitarian view of the person, but says that since we are all embedded in a variety of different and competing religious groups, we need to accept a principle of religious liberty in the form of freedom of conscience.

Rawls thinks that these two arguments 'support the same conclusion' (1982*b*: 29)—i.e. that recognizing the *plurality* of conceptions of the good within society, each of which is seen as fixed and beyond rational revision, has the same implications for individual liberty as affirming the *revisability* of each individual's conception of the good. Hence communitarians and liberals can develop an overlapping consensus on freedom of conscience. He thinks this approach can then be generalized to other basic liberties, including freedom of association, speech, sexuality, and so on.

It is important to note that for Rawls this overlapping consensus should be a principled agreement, not just a strategic compromise. The overlapping consensus is not a 'modus vivendi' that both sides accept because they lack the power to impose what they truly desire or believe in. Rather, both sides accept the resulting principles (e.g. of freedom of conscience) as morally legitimate, albeit for different reasons that appeal to their different conceptions of the self. Since both sides view it as legitimate, the agreement is stable, and does not depend on maintaining any particular balance of power between the groups. If one group gains more power in society, it will not seek to break the agreement.

That, in a nutshell, is Rawls's strategy. I do not think it works. It is true that the two arguments Rawls identifies for religious liberty support the same conclusion on some issues. In particular, both the liberal and communitarian arguments support the conclusion that the dominant religious group should not be able to impose its faith on minority religious groups. So both endorse a principle of tolerance between groups. But the two arguments do not support the same conclusion on issues of individual freedom of conscience—i.e. the freedom of individual members *within each group* to question and reject their inherited beliefs. For example, heresy, proselytization, and apostasy are essential liberties on the first liberal argument, since they enable individuals to engage in rational revisability, but futile and disruptive nuisances on the second communitarian argument, since they tempt people to question inherited beliefs which should be seen as given and fixed.

If Rawls's aim is to ensure an overlapping consensus, one might have expected him therefore to drop proselytization, heresy, and apostasy from the list of basic liberties guaranteed in a liberal society, and to allow communitarian groups to establish a millet-like system in which these activities would be legally forbidden for their members. Liberals and communitarians can agree on the need to prevent the state from imposing one way of life on everyone in a pluralistic society, and hence on the right of each religious group to pursue its own religious rituals and practices. But they may not agree on the freedom of individuals within each group to question and revise these rituals and practices—i.e. to engage in acts of heresy, apostasy, and proselytization. There is no overlapping consensus on the value of these further liberties.

Yet Rawls does not allow traditionalist communitarian groups to establish millet-like systems. His definition of freedom of conscience is the full liberal one, which protects the right of individuals to reject their inherited religion, as well as tolerance between religious groups. Indeed, he says that one essential part of the overlapping consensus is an agreement to conceive of citizens as having the 'moral power' to 'form, revise and pursue' a conception of the good. This is in fact one of our two basic moral powers, along with a sense of justice. According to Rawls, people need to agree about these two moral powers because they provide the shared framework within which questions about the interpretation of the two principles of justice are debated and resolved. Hence agreement on these two moral powers is an essential part of the overlapping consensus. This makes it explicit that communitarian groups are expected to accept that individuals have the power to revise, as well as to pursue, their conception of the good.

Why would traditionalist communitarian groups accept the principle of individual freedom of conscience, and the associated ideal of our moral power to form and revise a conception of the good? Rawls suggests two answers to this question. On the one hand, it provides certain positive benefits; on the other hand, it does not involve any costs. Positively, Rawls suggests that only a strong right of individual freedom of conscience can protect smaller religious groups (including communitarian religious groups) from the intolerance of larger religious groups. In a number of places he suggests that without guarantees of 'equal liberty of conscience', minority faiths could be persecuted by dominant religious groups (e.g. Rawls 1982b: 25–9; 1989: 251). So even if the members of a communitarian group conceive their religious views as non-revisable, they will still endorse individual freedom of conscience as the best or only way to protect themselves from persecution by other groups. Once we recognize that a diversity of religions is an inevitable part of modern plural societies—this is part of what Rawls calls 'the fact of pluralism'—then individual civil liberties are the only way to protect minority religions.

Unfortunately, this claim is incorrect. As the Ottoman millet example shows, one can ensure tolerance *between* groups without accepting tolerance of individual dissent *within* each group. And so while communitarian minorities may agree that freedom of conscience is *one* way to protect them from majority tyranny, they will not necessarily agree that it is the best or only way. They may prefer the millet model. This will depend on the costs associated with each model.

This leads to Rawls's second argument, which is more complicated.

According to Rawls, even if communitarian groups do not positively value the full liberal right to individual freedom of conscience, they can nonetheless accept it, because it does not really harm them or interfere with their way of life. Or, more exactly, accepting the liberal conception of revisability will not interfere with their way of life if we make clear that this liberal conception only applies to certain limited *political* questions. The idea that we can form and revise our conception of the good is, Rawls now says, strictly a 'political conception' of the person, adopted solely for the purposes of determining our public rights and responsibilities. It is not, he insists, intended as a general account of the relationship between the self and its ends applicable to all areas of life, or as an accurate portrayal of our deepest self-understandings. On the contrary, in private life it is quite possible that some people's personal identity will be bound to particular ends in such a way as to preclude rational revision. Accepting liberalism as a political conception in public life does not require communitarians to give up their belief in an embedded self or constitutive ends in private life. As Rawls puts it,

It is essential to stress that citizens in their personal affairs, or in the internal life of associations to which they belong, may regard their final ends and attachments in a way very different from the way the political conception involves. Citizens may have, and normally do have at any given time, affections, devotions, and loyalties that they believe they would not, and indeed could and should not, stand apart from and objectively evaluate from the standpoint of their purely rational good. They may regard it as simply unthinkable to view themselves apart from certain religious, philosophical and moral convictions, or from certain enduring attachments and loyalties. These convictions and attachments are part of what we may call their 'nonpublic identity'. (Rawls 1985: 241)

So Rawls allows that some people may, in their private life, view their religious commitments as non-revisable. He only requires that, in political contexts, people ignore the possible existence of such 'constitutive' ends. As *citizens*, everyone sees himself or herself as having a 'highest-order interest' in their capacity to form and revise a conception of the good, even though as *private individuals* some people may not see themselves as having or valuing that capacity. Rawls's conception of the autonomous person provides the language of public justification in which people discuss their rights and responsibilities as citizens, although it may not describe their 'non-public identity'.

Hence Rawls distinguishes his 'political liberalism' from the 'comprehensive liberalism' of John Stuart Mill. Mill emphasized that people should be able to assess the worth of inherited social practices in all areas of life, not just political life. People should not obey social customs simply because they are customary, but only if they are worthy of allegiance. Each person must be able to determine for himself whether these customs are 'properly applicable to his own circumstances and character' (Mill 1982: 122). Mill's insistence on people's right to question and revise social practices was not limited to the political sphere. Indeed, Mill was mostly concerned about the way people blindly followed popular trends and social customs in their everyday personal lives. Hence Mill's liberalism is based on an ideal of rational reflection that applies to human action generally, and that is intended 'to inform our thought and conduct as a whole' (Rawls 1987: 6).

Rawls worries that members of communitarian groups do not accept Mill's idea of autonomy as a principle governing human thought and action generally. However, he thinks that such people can nonetheless accept the idea of autonomy if it is restricted to political contexts, leaving them free to view their non-public identities in quite different ways. People can accept his political conception 'without being committed in other parts of their life to comprehensive moral ideals often associated with liberalism, for example, the ideals of autonomy and individuality' (Rawls 1985: 245).

Rawls's account of our non-public identity is close to the communitarian conception of the self defended by Sandel. And indeed one way to understand Rawls's 'political liberalism' is to say that, for Rawls, people can be communitarians in private life, and liberals in public life.

This is an ingenious strategy for reconciling communitarian groups to liberalism, but I do not think it is succcesful. Rawls's assumption that adopting political liberalism is cost free for communitarian groups depends on a very sharp distinction between public and private. In public, members of communitarian groups must pretend they value the capacity for autonomy, but anyone who does not in fact value this capacity can simply refrain from exercising it in private life. While political liberalism gives people the right to rationally assess and revise their ends, it does not compel that they do so. Those people who see their ends as non-revisable can continue to think and act this way in private life. The existence of a legal right to question one's ends does not by itself require or encourage the actual exercise of that right. So even if this view of autonomy conflicts with a religious minority's self-understanding, there is no cost to accepting it for political purposes. It leaves untouched a communitarian group's ability to view their traditional practices and customs as non-revisable, and to pursue them accordingly in private life.

The problem, however, is that accepting revisability even as a purely political conception has inevitable 'spillover' effects on private life, and these impose serious costs on communitarian groups (Tomasi 2001). In fact, there are two potential problems here, one concerning civil liberties, the other concerning the distribution of resources. I will look at these two problems in order.

First, while it is true that a liberal state does not require or encourage people to engage in rational revisability in private life, it does *enable* revisability in ways that communitarian groups might oppose. To begin with, as I noted earlier, some communitarian groups would like to legally prohibit apostasy, heresy, and proselytization, which they view as undermining people's constitutive ends. Rawls rules this out, but he has given such groups no reason why limiting these liberties should not be an option available to them. Moreover, these liberties do not remain merely formal rights written in some remote law. The liberal state makes various efforts to ensure that these rights are in fact available to people.

For example, as Rawls himself emphasizes, it is essential that the liberal state inform everyone of their basic liberties, including the right to revise their ends. People must know that apostasy, heresy, and proselytization are not crimes. People must also know how they can enforce their rights if someone tries to prevent them—i.e. they must know how to access the police and courts. This is in itself a major blow to those traditionalist minorities who would like to make the very idea of apostasy or heresy 'unthinkable'.

More importantly, the liberal state also takes actions to ensure that individuals actually have the personal capacity to exercise these rights. For example, a liberal state will want children to learn the cognitive and imaginative skills needed to evaluate different ways of life, and to survive outside their original community. This is one of the basic goals of education in a liberal society. Moreover, a liberal state will also want to ensure that the costs of exercising the right of revisability are not prohibitive. For example, it will want to ensure that communitarian religious groups do not place so many obstacles to exit that people are *de facto* imprisoned in their group.

Consider the Canadian case of *Hofer* v. *Hofer*, which dealt with the powers of the Hutterite Church over its members. The Hutterites live in large agricultural communities, called colonies, within which there is no private property. Two lifelong members of a Hutterite colony were expelled for apostasy. They demanded their share of the colony's assets, which they had helped create with their years of labour. When the colony refused, the two ex-members sued in court. They objected to the fact that they had 'no right at any time in their lives to leave the colony without abandoning everything, even the clothes on their backs' (Janzen 1990: 67).

The Hutterites defended this practice on the grounds that freedom of religion protects a congregation's ability to live in accordance with its religious doctrine, even if this limits individual freedom. But as Justice Pigeon of the Canadian Supreme Court noted, the usual liberal notion of freedom of religion 'includes the right of each individual to change his religion at will'. Hence churches 'cannot make rules having the effect of depriving their members of this fundamental freedom'. The proper scope of religious authority, he argued, is therefore 'limited to what is consistent with freedom of religion as properly understood, that is freedom for the individual not only to adopt a religion but also to abandon it at will'. Justice Pigeon thought that it was 'as nearly impossible as can be' for people in a Hutterite colony to reject its religious teachings, because of the high cost of changing their religion, and so they were effectively deprived of freedom of religion. On his view, the Hutterites had to provide some compensation to apostates for their years of labour in order for exit to be a meaningful option.[16]

Or consider the case of *Yoder* v. *Wisconsin* in the United States, which dealt with the power of the Amish community over its members. The Amish, like the Hutterites in Canada, tried to make it difficult for their members to leave the group, albeit in a different way. They wanted to withdraw their children from school before the age of 16, so as to limit severely the extent to which the children learn about the outside world or acquire the skills needed to succeed outside the group. And they too defended this by arguing that freedom of religion protects a group's freedom to live in accordance with its doctrine, even if this limits the individual freedom of children. They saw no value in educating their children so as to be able to question community practices, or to succeed outside the community.

In both of these cases, we see a similar conflict. Because the communitarian group sees itself as vulnerable to the liberal right of revisability, it seeks to impose as many obstacles as possible to the actual exercise of this liberty. Because the liberal state is committed to certain basic legal rights, including rights to revise one's ends, it seeks to ensure that individuals are actually able to exercise these rights, and hence tries to reduce or eliminate group-imposed obstacles that would nullify the right. This is the inevitable spillover into private life of legal rights.[17]

These cases raise difficult issues, and people are likely to disagree about the best resolution of them. In fact, the majority of justices on the Canadian Supreme Court defended the right of the Hutterites to expel apostates without any compensation (Justice Pigeon was in the minority), and the majority of justices on the American Supreme Court defended the right of the Amish to pull their children from schools before the age of 16.[18]

We might think of these two decisions in favour of communitarian groups as examples of 'political liberalism' in action. But in fact the two Supreme Court decisions do not invoke the idea of political liberalism, and it is doubtful that political liberalism could endorse these decisions. Rawls says that for the purposes of political argument and legal rights we should assume that people have a basic interest in their capacity to form and revise their conception of the good. It would seem to follow, as Justice Pigeon argued, that the power of religious communities over their own members must be such that individuals can freely and effectively exercise that capacity. Were the Hutterites or Amish to accept Rawls's conception of the person, even if only for the purposes of political debate, then they too would have to accept the view that freedom of religion must be interpreted by the courts in terms of an individual's capacity to form and revise her religious beliefs.[19] The two Supreme Courts only reached the opposite conclusion by subordinating the individual's right of freedom of conscience to the group's right to uphold religious doctrine. This indeed is what many communitarian groups want, but this desire is not defensible, or even articulable, in the framework of Rawls's political liberalism, which requires that political debate be framed in terms of our moral power to form and revise a conception of the good.

This suggests that Rawls's 'political liberalism' strategy will not succeed in accommodating many communitarian groups. Nor should this be surprising. After all, political liberalism in fact offers very little to communitarian groups. It offers them a different argument for liberal principles and liberal institutions, but it does not offer any significant change in the principles or institutions themselves. In particular, it offers no way for communitarian groups to limit the civil liberties of their members, including the right of individuals to engage in apostasy or heresy, or more generally to question and revise their inherited conception of the good.

Communitarian groups do not just object to particular arguments for basic liberties. It is the liberties themselves which communitarian groups fear and dislike. And political liberalism is as committed to the full set of basic liberties as comprehensive liberalism. Rawls says that the liberal conception of revisability is only accepted for political purposes, but communitarians can see that this will inevitably enable the exercise of revisability in private life.[20] Political liberalism not only involves giving people certain formal legal rights to revise their ends, but also the knowledge of these rights, and the educational and legal conditions needed to exercise them. None of this is desirable from the point of view of many communitarian groups.

This in turn suggests that the entire distinction between political and comprehensive liberalism is overstated. Both are committed not only to public rights, but also to ensuring the conditions in private life needed to actually exercise these rights. Both are committed, in other words, not only to the legal recognition of liberties, but also to enabling their exercise. Of course, one could imagine a form of comprehensive liberalism which goes even futher to require or pressure individuals to actually exercise their rights of rational revisability, and to teach people to be deeply sceptical of the value of traditional ways of life. At times, Rawls seems mainly concerned to avoid this sort of 'hyper-liberalism', which obviously is completely unacceptable to communitarian groups. But most comprehensive liberals do not endorse this sort of hyper-liberalism. As I noted earlier, the standard liberal view is not that people should or must revise their ends, but simply that people be legally free and practically able to do so, should new circumstances, experiences, or information raise questions about their previous commitments. Rawls's political liberalism, as much as comprehensive liberalism, is committed to enabling this sort of autonomy. And that is why political liberalism offers little to communitarian groups.

In short, Rawls has not explained why people who are communitarians in private life should be liberals in political life. Rawls may be right that 'Within different contexts we can assume diverse points of view toward our person without contradiction so long as these points of view cohere together when circumstances require' (Rawls 1980: 545). But he has not shown that these points of view do cohere. On the contrary, they clearly conflict on issues of intra-group dissent such as proselytization, apostasy, heresy, and mandatory education. Given the spillover costs to communitarian groups of endorsing political liberalism, and given that they can protect themselves from majority intolerance through a non-liberal millet system, they have no reason to be part of the overlapping consensus on liberalism.

This suggests that there is a deep tension between the communitarian conception of the self and the liberal commitment to the priority of civil rights. If, as communitarians argue, people's private identity really is tied to certain ends, such that they have no interest or ability to question and revise them, then a millet-like system which allows for internal restrictions within each group may be a superior response to religious pluralism. If individuals are incapable of revising their inherited religious commitments, or if it is appropriate to discourage individuals from exercising that capacity, then the millet system may best protect and advance those constitutive ends.

This is indeed what communitarians have claimed. They insist that once we drop the assumption that autonomy is a general value—as Rawls seems to have done—then religious and cultural groups should be allowed to protect their members' constitutive ends by restricting certain individual rights.[21] Sandel himself defends the right of the Amish to be exempted from mandatory education laws, arguing that freedom of conscience should be understood as freedom to pursue one's constitutive ends, not as freedom to rationally revise one's religion (Sandel 1990). He argues that people's religious affiliation is so profoundly constitutive of who they are that their overriding interest is in protecting and advancing that identity, and that they have no comparable interest in being able to stand back and assess that identity. Hence there is little or no value (and perhaps even positive harm) in teaching Amish children about the outside world.

This suggests that if we wish to defend full individual freedom of conscience, and not just group tolerance, we must reject the communitarian idea that people's ends are fixed and beyond rational revision. Or, conversely, if we truly wish to accommodate communitarian conceptions of the self, then we must be willing to provide some exemption for communitarian groups from the rigorous enforcement of individual liberties. Either way, Rawls's attempt to reconcile the traditional liberal commitment to basic liberties with a communitarian conception of the self seems unsuccessful.

There is another problem here for Rawls's attempt to accommodate communitarian groups. The assumption that we can assess and revise our ends is crucial not only for Rawls's principle of liberty, but also for his position about responsibility. As we saw in Chapter 3, the liberal egalitarian theory of justice denies that people can claim a greater share of primary goods on the grounds that their way of life is more expensive than others (Ch. 3, p. 74). In his earlier work, Rawls rejects such subsidies for expensive ways of life on the grounds that people have the capacity to rationally adjust their aims in the light of principles of justice, and hence to revise or moderate any projects which cannot be achieved within the constraints of their fair share of resources.[22] This view about responsibility, I believe, presupposes the capacity for rational revisability. Consider the following passage where Rawls gives his most detailed defence of the view that we should not subsidize expensive ways of life:

It is not by itself an objection to [his theory] that it does not accommodate those with expensive tastes. One must argue in addition that it is unreasonable, if not unjust, to hold such persons responsible for their preferences and to require them to make out as best they can. But to argue this seems to presuppose that citizens' preferences are beyond their control as propensities or cravings which simply happen. . . . The use of primary goods, however, relies on a capacity to assume responsibility for our ends. This capacity is part of the moral power to form, to revise, and rationally to pursue a conception of the good . . . In any particular situation, then, those with less expensive tastes have presumably adjusted their likes and dislikes over the course of their lives to the income and wealth they could reasonably expect; *and it is regarded as unfair that they now should have less in order to spare others from the consequences of their lack of foresight or self-discipline.* The idea of holding citizens responsible for their ends is plausible, however, only on certain assumptions. First, *we must assume that citizens can regulate and revise their ends and preferences in the light of their expectations of primary goods.* . . . This conception includes what we may call a social division of responsibility: society, the citizens as a collective body, accepts the responsibility for maintaining the equal basic liberties and fair equality of opportunity, and for providing a fair share of the other primary goods for everyone within this framework, while citizens (as individuals) and associations accept the responsibility for revising and adjusting their ends and aspirations in view of the all-purpose means they can expect, given their present and foreseeable situation. (Rawls 1982b: 168–9; emphasis added; cf. Rawls 1985: 243)

Because people have the capacity to rationally adjust their aims, Rawls used to claim, we have no obligation to subsidize those with expensive ways of life. It would indeed be *unfair* to expect those who responsibly exercise this capacity of moderating their aims in the light of justice to subsidize those who imprudently or unreasonably fail to moderate their expensive aims.

On Rawls's new view, however, we cannot assume that this capacity for revising our ends actually exists—it is only assumed hypothetically for political purposes. If so, why is it not unfair to refuse to subsidize those raised with more expensive aims? If (as Rawls now says) the members of traditionalist groups have ends 'that they believe they would not, and indeed could and should not, stand apart from and objectively evaluate', and 'regard it as simply unthinkable to view themselves apart from certain religious, philosophical and moral convictions', then why would they agree to pay the extra costs associated with these unrevisable convictions? Why would they accept responsibility for costs that they are unable to adjust or moderate?

Rawls is aware that his new 'political' approach seems to undercut his earlier argument about people's capacity to rationally adjust their aims. And so in his more recent work, he offers a different argument why we should not subsidize expensive ways of life. He asks whether those people whose religious beliefs impose an obligation to go on expensive pilgrimages should receive more resources than those whose religious beliefs impose more modest obligations. He responds that, while this may indeed seem to ensure greater equality in religious liberty, it is divisive:

Plainly, this kind of guarantee is socially divisive, a recipe for religious controversy if not civil strife. Similar consequences result, I believe, whenever the public conception of justice adjusts citizens' claims to social resources so that some receive more than others depending on the determinate final ends and loyalties belonging to their conception of the good ... One main reason for using an index of primary goods in assessing the strength of citizens' claims in questions of political justice is precisely to eliminate the socially divisive and irreconcilable conflicts which such principles [requiring that we adjust people's claims to their costs of their ends] would arouse. (Rawls 1982a: 44–5)

In other words, on this new account, subsidizing expensive ways of life is not unfair, per se, but rather socially divisive. The reason why people with expensive projects should not be subsidized is not that they would then be unfairly exploiting the prudence or self-discipline of others. (On this new view, presumably those with modest projects also simply inherited them as fixed and unrevisable, rather than having rationally adjusted them to fit norms of justice.) The problem, rather, is that people will dispute and resent attempts to claim extra resources, leading to conflict.

This issue of social conflict is an important one, and I will return to it below. But it is out of place here, since it begs the very question at issue. Recall that on Rawls's view (unlike the Hobbesian mutual advantage theorists), we are to assume that people are not egoistic, but rather are motivated by a sense of justice (Ch. 4 p. 137). So people will only resent giving extra resources to those with expensive ways of life if they think it is unjust to do so. But that is precisely what is in question. If people had no control over the extra costs involved in their way of life, why wouldn't fairness require compensating for these costs, just as we compensate for the extra costs created by unchosen natural handicaps or illnesses?

In fact, Rawls here is making precisely the mistake that utilitarians often make. As I noted in Chapter 2, utilitarians say that the reason it is wrong to break promises is that it causes resentment. But this is backwards: breaking promises causes resentment because we think it is wrong. So too with Rawls's claim that subsidies for expensive ways of life are wrong because they are socially divisive. This is backwards: they are socially divisive because we think they are wrong. And, as Rawls himself earlier admitted, we think they are wrong because we think people have the capacity to adjust their aims.[23] If we no longer believed people had such a capacity, we would not necessarily think it wrong or unfair to subsidize their unchosen extra costs.

In short, the attempt by 'political liberals' to avoid relying on the assumption of rational revisability fails. Rational revisability is essential to the liberal position in at least two different respects. First, it is needed to explain why liberalism protects the right of individuals to revise their way of life and to persuade others to change their way of life (and not just the right to pursue their inherited way of life). Second, it is needed to explain why liberalism holds people responsible for the costs of their way of life. Liberalism accords people both the right to rationally revise their way of life, and also the duty to do so, if it violates norms of justice.

Why is Rawls so reluctant to explicitly endorse autonomy as a general human interest? What is wrong with Mill's 'comprehensive' liberalism? The problem, Rawls says, is that not everyone accepts this ideal of autonomy, and so appealing to it in political life would be 'sectarian'. The autonomy-based defence of individual rights invokes 'ideals and values that are not generally . . . shared in a democratic society', and hence 'cannot secure sufficient agreement'. To base liberalism on a controversial value like autonomy would mean that liberalism 'becomes but another sectarian doctrine' (Rawls 1987: 6, 24; 1985: 246).

This is a legitimate point, but Rawls overstates it, and draws the wrong conclusion from it. The idea that we have an interest in being able to assess and revise our inherited conceptions of the good is very widely shared in Western democratic societies.[24] There are some insulated minorities who reject this ideal, including some indigenous groups, and religious sects (the Amish and Hutterites). These groups pose a challenge for liberal democracies, since they often demand internal restrictions that conflict with individual civil rights. We cannot simply ignore this demand, or ignore the fact that they reject the idea of autonomy.

But Rawls's strategy is no solution to the questions raised by the existence of non-liberal minorities. His strategy is to continue to enforce individual civil rights and to impose responsibility for the costs of people's way of life, but to do so on the basis of a 'political' rather than a 'comprehensive' liberalism. This obviously does not satisfy the demands of non-liberal minorities. They want internal restrictions that take precedence over individual rights, and they want their claims on resources adjusted to their pre-existing aims, rather than adjusting their aims to prior standards of justice. Rawls's political liberalism is as hostile to these demands as Mill's comprehensive liberalism. The fact that Rawls's new theory is less comprehensive does not make his theory more sympathetic to the demands of non-liberal minorities.

It seems to me, then, that this first liberal attempt to accommodate the communitarian conception of the embedded self is unsuccessful. Liberalism is committed to rational revisability, and communitarian groups which reject this principle will not accept either political or comprehensive liberalism. If we understand communitarianism as a doctrine about the 'constitutive' or non-revisable nature of certain ends, then this doctrine is at odds with some of liberalism's most basic commitments.

What then should we do when the majority in a modern society subscribes to a liberal conception of the self, but a traditionalist ethnic or religious minority subscribes to a communitarian conception? I will return to this question in Chapter 8, as it is one of the topics raised in the recent debate on 'multiculturalism'. Indeed, we could say that a concern for multiculturalism is a natural evolution of the communitarian position on the self. Communitarians originally claimed that their conception of the self was simply superior to the liberal view, and should therefore replace it in our political theory. But once the scope of the communitarian critique is narrowed to focus on those traditionalist groups which reject autonomy, then the claim is no longer that communitarianism offers the one true or best conception of the self. Rather, the claim is that we need to recognize and accommodate the existence of diverse views of the self in society. In particular, we need to enable culturally or religiously distinctive communitarian groups to coexist with a predominantly liberal society. The communitarian critique of the liberal self, once narrowed in this way, becomes a question of accommodating cultural diversity—of multiculturalism.

8. THE SOCIAL THESIS

However, communitarianism is not just a doctrine about the self and its ends. Indeed, many communitarians reject Sandel's idea of constitutive ends, and endorse the liberal belief in rational revisability. They criticize liberalism, not for its account of the self and its interests, but for neglecting the social conditions required for the effective fulfilment of those interests. Their concern is not to question the capacity for revisability and informed choice, but precisely to develop and sustain it.

For example, Taylor claims that many liberal theories are based on 'atomism', on an 'utterly facile moral pyschology' according to which individuals are self-sufficient outside of society. Individuals, according to atomistic theories, are not in need of any communal context in order to develop and exercise their capacity for self-determination. Taylor argues instead for the 'social thesis', which says that this capacity can only be exercised in a certain kind of society, with a certain kind of social environment.[25]

If this really were the debate, then we would have to agree with the communitarians, for the 'social thesis' is clearly true. The view that we might exercise the capacity for self-determination outside society is absurd. But liberals like Rawls and Dworkin do not deny the social thesis. They recognize that individual autonomy cannot exist outside a social environment that provides meaningful choices and that supports the development of the capacity to choose amongst them. They recognize and discuss the role of the family, schools, and the larger cultural environment in nurturing autonomy (e.g. Rawls 1971: 563–4; Dworkin 1985: 230–3).

Taylor believes, however, that the social thesis requires us to abandon a core liberal premiss—namely, the idea of a 'neutral state' which does not justify its actions on the basis of the intrinsic superiority or inferiority of conceptions of the good life, and which does not deliberately attempt to influence people's judgements of the value of these different conceptions. According to Taylor, a neutral state cannot adequately protect the social environment necessary for self-determination.[26] The social thesis tells us that the capacity to choose a conception of the good can only be exercised in a particular sort of community, and, Taylor argues, this sort of community can only be sustained by a (non-neutral) 'politics of the common good'. It is only possible to sustain any sort of viable community—including the sort of community committed to liberal values of freedom—if the state protects and privileges the community's traditional or dominant way of life. In other words, some limits on individual self-determination are required to preserve the social conditions which enable self-determination.

Taylor's argument raises many issues. Indeed, a major portion of political philosophy in the last twenty years can be seen as responding, implicitly or explicitly, to Taylor's challenge to work out the social preconditions of liberal freedom. To oversimplify, we could divide the debate into two broad headings. First there are questions about the social conditions for the *development* of the capacity for autonomy. This primarily concerns the raising and educating of children, and hence involves issues about the nature and role of families and schools. I will discuss these issues in Chapters 7 (schooling) and 9 (the family). But Taylor himself is more concerned with the social conditions for the *exercise* of the capacity for autonomy by adults. This primarily involves questions about a society's culture, social life, and public sphere. These are the issues I will discuss in the rest of this chapter.

There are both theoretical and practical reasons why these questions about the social conditions of freedom have become a matter of intense debate. Theoretically, it is increasingly accepted that a political theory is simply incomplete if it does not address these questions. But more importantly, there is a growing fear that these social preconditions—whether it be the family, schools, civil society, or the state—are failing. The popular press and political speeches are awash in claims about the 'decline of the family', or the decline of our schools, civic organizations, public spaces, and democratic institutions. In other words, these questions have become a major topic for political theory because many people believe there is a real and growing problem in the actual practice of liberal democracy.

In this section, then, I will consider Taylor's argument that liberal neutrality cannot sustain the social conditions for the exercise of autonomy. I will consider three versions of this claim: one about the need to sustain a cultural structure that provides people with meaningful options; a second about the need for shared forums in which to evaluate these options; and a third about the preconditions for solidarity and political legitimacy. In each case, communitarians invoke the social thesis to show how a concern for self-determination supports, rather than precludes, a communitarian politics of the common good.

(a) Duties to protect the cultural structure

Meaningful choices concerning our projects require meaningful options, and (the social thesis tells us) these options come from our culture. Liberal neutrality, however, is incapable of ensuring the existence of a rich and diverse culture which provides such options. Self-determination requires pluralism, in the sense of a diversity of possible ways of life, but

> any collective attempt by a liberal state to protect pluralism would itself be a breach of liberal principles of justice. The state is not entitled to interfere in the movement of the cultural market place except, of course, to ensure that each individual has a just share of available necessary means to exercise his or her moral powers. The welfare or demise of particular conceptions of the good and, therefore, the welfare or demise of social unions of a particular character is not the business of the state. (Cragg 1986: 47)

Liberals believe that a state which intervenes in the cultural marketplace to encourage or discourage any particular way of life restricts people's self-determination. However, if the cultural marketplace proceeds on its own it will eventually undermine the cultural structure which supports pluralism. As Joseph Raz puts it, 'Supporting valuable forms of life is a social rather than an individual matter . . . perfectionist ideals require public action for their viability. Anti-perfectionism in practice would lead not merely to a political stand-off from support for valuable conceptions of the good. It would undermine the chances of survival of many cherished aspects of our culture' (Raz 1986: 162). Liberal neutrality is therefore self-defeating.

This is an important objection. Many liberals are surprisingly silent about the possibility that 'the essential cultural activities which make a great diversity conceivable to people [could] begin to falter'. As Taylor says, 'it is as though the conditions of a creative, diversifying freedom were given by nature' (Taylor 1985a: 206 n. 7). Rawls attempts to answer this worry by claiming that good ways of life will in fact sustain themselves in the cultural marketplace without state assistance, because in conditions of freedom, people are able to recognize the worth of good ways of life, and will support them (Rawls 1971: 331–2; cf. Waldron 1989: 1138). But this is inadequate. The interests people have in a good way of life, and the forms of support they will voluntarily provide, do not necessarily involve sustaining its existence for future generations. For example, my interest in a valuable social practice may be best promoted by depleting the resources which the practice requires to survive beyond my lifetime.

Consider the preservation of historical artefacts and sites, or of natural wilderness areas. The wear and tear caused by the everyday use of these things would prevent future generations from experiencing them, were it not for state protection. So even if the cultural marketplace can be relied on to ensure that existing people can identify valuable ways of life, it cannot be relied on to ensure that future people have a valuable range of options.

So let us grant Raz's argument that state support may be needed to ensure the survival of an adequate range of options for those who have not yet formed their aims in life. Why does that require rejecting neutrality? Consider two possible cultural policies: In the first case, the government ensures an adequate range of options by providing tax credits to individuals who make culture-supporting contributions in accordance with their personal perfectionist ideals. The state acts to ensure that there is an adequate range of options, but the evaluation of these options occurs in civil society, outside the apparatus of the state (cf. Dworkin 1985: ch. 11). In the second case, the evaluation of different conceptions of the good becomes a political question, and the government intervenes, not simply to ensure an adequate range of options, but to promote particular options. Raz's argument shows that one or other of these policies must be implemented, but he has not given a reason to prefer one policy over the other.

Hence the existence of duties concerning the protection of the cultural structure is not incompatible with neutrality. In fact, Dworkin emphasizes our duty to protect the cultural structure from 'debasement or decay' (Dworkin 1985: 230). Like Taylor, he talks about how the capacity imaginatively to conceive conceptions of the good life requires specialized debate among intellectuals who attempt to define and clarify the alternatives facing us, or the presence of people who attempt to bring the culture of the past to life again in the art of the present, or who sustain the drive to cultural innovation, and about how the state can and should protect these essential cultural activities (Taylor 1985a: 204–6; Dworkin 1985: 229–32). And while Rawls does not include state support for culture in his theory of justice, since he thinks that the operation of his principles of justice would in fact protect the preconditions of a diverse culture, there is no reason why he should reject such support where this is not the case (Rawls 1971: 331, 441–2, 522–9). Like Dworkin, he would simply insist that it is not the job of the state to rank the relative value of the various options within the culture.

A communitarian state might hope to improve the quality of people's options, by encouraging the replacement of less valuable aspects of the community's ways of life by more valuable ones. But liberal neutrality also hopes to improve the range of people's options. Freedom of speech and association allows each group to pursue and advertise its way of life, and those ways of life that are unworthy will have difficulty attracting adherents. Since individuals are free to choose between competing visions of the good life, liberal neutrality creates a marketplace of ideas, as it were, and how well a way of life does in this market depends on what it offers to prospective adherents. Hence, under conditions of freedom, satisfying and valuable ways of life will tend to drive out those which are unsatisfying (or so liberals optimistically believe). Liberals endorse civil liberties in part precisely because they make it possible 'that the worth of different modes of life should be proved practically' (Mill 1982: 54).

Liberals and communitarians both aim to secure the range of options from which individuals make their autonomous choices. What they disagree on is where perfectionist ideals should be invoked. Are good ways of life more likely to establish their greater worth when they are evaluated in the cultural marketplace of civil society, or when the preferability of different ways of life is made a matter of political advocacy and state action? Hence the dispute should perhaps be seen as a choice, not between perfectionism and neutrality, but between social perfectionism and state perfectionism—for the flip side of state neutrality is support for the role of perfectionist ideals in civil society.

(b) Neutrality and collective deliberations

Some communitarians argue that the liberal preference for the cultural marketplace over the state as the appropriate arena for evaluating different ways of life stems from an atomistic belief that judgements about the good are only autonomous when they are made by isolated individuals who are protected from social pressure. Liberals think that autonomy is promoted when judgements about the good are taken out of the political realm. But in reality individual judgements require the sharing of experiences and the give and take of collective deliberation. Individual judgements about the good depend on the collective evaluation of shared practices. They become a matter of subjective and arbitrary whim if they are cut off from collective deliberations:

[S]elf-fulfillment and even the working out of personal identity and a sense of orientation in the world depend upon a communal enterprise. This shared process is the civic life, and its root is involvement with others: other generations, other sorts of persons whose differences are significant because they contribute to the whole upon which our particular sense of self depends. Thus mutual interdependency is the foundational notion of citizenship ... Outside a linguistic community of shared practices, there could be biological *homo sapiens* as logical abstraction, but there could not be human beings. This is the meaning of the Greek and medieval dictum that the political community is ontologically *prior* to the individual. The *polis* is, literally, that which makes man, as human being, possible. (Sullivan 1982: 158, 173)

Or, as Crowley puts it, state perfectionism is

an affirmation of the notion that men living in a community of shared experiences and language is the only context in which the individual and society can discover and test their values through the essentially political activities of discussion, criticism, example, and emulation. It is through the existence of organised public spaces, in which men offer and test ideas against one another ... that men come to understand a part of who they are. (Crowley 1987: 282; cf. Beiner 1983: 152)

The state is the proper arena in which to formulate our visions of the good, because these visions require shared enquiry. They cannot be pursued, or even known, by solitary individuals.

But this misconstrues the sense in which Rawls claims that the valuation of ways of life should not be a public concern. Liberal neutrality does not restrict the scope of perfectionist ideals in the collective activities of individuals and groups. Collective activity and shared experiences concerning the good are at the heart of the 'free internal life of the various communities of interests in which persons and groups seek to achieve, in modes of social union consistent with equal liberty, the ends and excellences to which they are drawn'. Rawls's argument for the priority of liberty is grounded in the importance of this 'free social union with others' (Rawls 1971: 543). He simply denies that 'the coercive apparatus of the state' is an appropriate forum for those deliberations and experiences:

While justice as fairness allows that in a well-ordered society the values of excellence are recognized, the human perfections are to be pursued within the limits of the principle of free association. ... [Persons] do not use the coercive apparatus of the state to win for themselves a greater liberty or larger distributive shares on the grounds that their activities are of more intrinsic value. (Rawls 1971: 328–9)

Unfortunately, communitarians rarely distinguish between collective activities and political activities. It is true that participation in shared linguistic and cultural practices is what enables individuals to make intelligent decisions about the good life. But why should such participation be organized through the state, rather than through the free association of individuals? It is true that we should 'create opportunities for men to give voice to what they have discovered about themselves and the world and to persuade others of its worth' (Crowley 1987: 295). But a liberal society does create opportunities for people to express these social aspects of individual deliberation. After all, freedom of assembly, speech, and association are fundamental liberal rights. The opportunities for collective enquiry simply occur within and between groups and associations below the level of the state—friends and family, in the first instance, but also churches, cultural associations, professional groups and trade unions, universities, and the mass media. Liberals do not deny that 'the public display of character and judgement and the exchange of experience and insight' are needed to make intelligent judgements about the good, or to show others that I 'hold [my] notion of the good responsibly' (Crowley 1987: 285). Indeed, these claims fit comfortably in many liberal discussions of the value of free speech and association (e.g. Scanlon 1983: 141–7). What the liberal denies is that I should have to give such an account of myself *to the state*, or that my claim to public resources should depend on justifying my way of life to the state.

A similar failure to consider the distinctive role of the state weakens radical critiques of liberal neutrality, like that of Habermas in his earlier work. Habermas wanted the evaluation of different ways of life to be a political question, but unlike communitarians, he did not hope that this political deliberation would serve to promote people's embeddedness in existing practices. Indeed, he thought that political deliberation is required precisely because in its absence people will tend to accept existing practices as givens, and thereby perpetuate the false needs and false consciousness which accompany those historical practices. Only when existing ways of life are 'the objects of discursive will-formation' can people's understanding of the good be free of deception. Neutrality does not demand the scrutiny of these practices, and hence does not recognize the emancipatory interest people have in escaping false needs and ideological distortions.[27]

But why should the evaluation of people's conceptions of the good affect their claims of justice, and why is the state the appropriate arena for this evaluation? Communities smaller than the entire political society, groups and associations of various sizes, might be more appropriate forums for those forms of 'discursive will-formation' which involve evaluating the good, and interpreting one's genuine needs. While Habermas rejects the communitarian tendency to endorse existing social practices uncritically as the basis for political deliberations about the good, he shares their tendency to assume that anything which is not politically deliberated is thereby left to an individual will incapable of rational judgement.

So liberal neutrality does not neglect the importance of a shared culture for meaningful individual options, or of the sharing of experiences for meaningful individual evaluation of those options. Liberal neutrality does not deny these social requirements of individual autonomy, but rather provides an interpretation of them, one which relies on social rather than political processes. None of this proves that neutrality should be endorsed. Neutrality requires a certain faith in the operation of non-state forums and processes for individual judgement and cultural development, and a distrust of the operation of state forums for evaluating the good. Nothing I have said shows that this optimism and distrust are warranted. Indeed, just as critics of neutrality have failed to defend their faith in politics, so liberals have failed to defend their faith in non-state forums.

In fact, it seems that each side in the neutrality debate has failed to learn the lesson taught by the other side. Despite centuries of liberal insistence on the importance of the distinction between state and society, communitarians still seem to assume that whatever is properly social must become the province of the political. They have not confronted the liberal worry that the all-embracing authority and coercive means which characterize the state make it a particularly inappropriate forum for the sort of genuinely shared deliberation and commitment that they desire. Despite centuries of communitarian insistence on the historically fragile nature of our culture, and the need to consider the conditions under which a free culture can sustain itself, liberals still tend to take the existence of a tolerant and diverse culture for granted, as something which naturally arises and sustains itself, the ongoing existence of which is therefore simply assumed in a theory of justice. Communitarians are right to insist that a culture of freedom is a historical achievement, and liberals need to explain why the cultural marketplace does not threaten that achievement either by failing to connect people in a strong enough way to their communal practices (as communitarians fear), or conversely, by failing to detach people in a strong enough way from the expectations of existing practices and ideologies (as Habermas fears). A culture which supports self-determination requires a mix of both exposure and connection to existing practices, and also distance and dissent from them. Liberal neutrality may provide that mix, but that is not obviously true, and it may be true only in some times and places. So both sides need to give us a more comprehensive comparison of the opportunities and dangers present in state and non-state forums and procedures for evaluating the good.

I have argued elsewhere that before invoking the state as the arena for evaluating conceptions of the good, we should first improve the forums in civil society for non-politicized debate, so as to ensure that all groups in society have genuinely free and equal access to the cultural marketplace that liberals value so highly.[28] But while this question remains open, it should be clear that we are not likely to get anywhere in answering it if we continue to see it as a debate between liberal 'atomism' and communitarianism's 'social thesis'. According to communitarians, liberals fail to recognize that people are naturally social beings. Liberals supposedly think that society rests on an artificial social contract, and that state power is needed to keep naturally asocial people together in society. But there is a sense in which the opposite is true: liberals believe that people naturally form and join social relations and forums in which they come to understand and pursue the good. The state is not needed to provide that communal context, and is likely to distort the normal processes of collective deliberations and cultural development. It is communitarians who seem to think that individuals will drift into anomic isolation without the state actively bringing them together to evaluate and pursue the good.[29]

(c) Solidarity and political legitimacy

There is another issue raised by the social thesis. Individual choices require a secure cultural context, but a cultural context, in turn, requires a secure political context. Whatever the proper role of the state in protecting the cultural marketplace, it can only fulfil that function if public institutions are stable, and that in turn requires that they have legitimacy in the eyes of the citizens. Taylor believes that political institutions governed by the principle of neutrality will be incapable of sustaining legitimacy, and hence incapable of sustaining the social context required for self-determination.

According to Taylor, the neutral state undermines the shared sense of the common good which is required for citizens to accept the sacrifices demanded by the welfare state. Citizens will only identify with the state, and accept its demands as legitimate, when there is a 'common form of life' which 'is seen as a supremely important good, so that its continuance and flourishing matters to the citizens for its own sake and not just instrumentally to their several individual goods or as the sum total of these individual goods' (Taylor 1985b: 213). This sense of the common good has been undermined because, in part, we now have a political culture of state neutrality in which people are free to choose their goals independently of this 'common form of life', and to trump the pursuit of this common good should it violate their rights. Whereas a communitarian state would foster an identification with the common form of life, the

rights model goes very well with a more atomist consciousness, where I understand my dignity as that of an individual bearer of rights. Indeed—and here the tension surfaces between the two—I cannot be too willing to trump the collective decision in the name of individual rights if I haven't already moved some distance from the community which makes these decisions. (Taylor 1985b: 211 cf. Sandel 1996: 3–4.)

This 'distancing' from the community's shared form of life means we become unwilling to shoulder the burdens of liberal justice. As a result, liberal democracies are undergoing a 'legitimation crisis'—citizens are asked to sacrifice more and more in the name of justice, but they share less and less with those for whom they are making sacrifices. There is no shared form of life underlying the demands of the neutral state.

Rawls and Dworkin, on the other hand, believe that citizens will accept the burdens of justice even in their relations with people who have very different conceptions of the good. A person should be free to choose any conception of the good life that does not violate the principles of justice, no matter how much it differs from other ways of life in the community. Such conflicting conceptions can be tolerated because the public recognition of principles of justice is sufficient to ensure stability even in the face of such conflicts. As Rawls puts it, 'although a well-ordered society is divided and pluralistic . . . public agreement on questions of political and social justice supports ties of civic friendship and secures the bonds of association' (Rawls 1980: 540; cf. Rawls 1985: 245). People with different conceptions of the good will respect each other's rights, not because it promotes a shared way of life, but because citizens recognize that each person has an equal claim to consideration. Hence the basis for state legitimacy is a shared sense of justice, not a shared conception of the good. Liberals seek to sustain a just society through the public adoption of principles of justice, without requiring, and indeed precluding, the public adoption of certain principles of the good life.

Taylor believes this is sociologically naive: people will not respect the claims of others unless they are bound by shared conceptions of the good, unless they can identify with a politics of the common good. He describes 'two package solutions emerging out of the mists to the problem of sustaining a viable modern polity in the late twentieth century', which correspond roughly to the communitarian and liberal model, and says there are 'severe doubts' about the long-term viability of the liberal model. By enforcing individual rights and state neutrality, a liberal state precludes the public adoption of principles of the good, but, Taylor asks, 'Could the increasing stress on rights as dominant over collective decisions come in the end to undermine the very legitimacy of the democratic order?' (Taylor 1985b: 225).

I think that Taylor is correct to say that the liberal model, as described by Dworkin and Rawls, is sociologically naive. Shared political principles may indeed be a *necessary* condition for political unity—where people disagree too deeply on questions of justice, the result may be civil war. But shared political principles are not *sufficient* for unity. The mere fact that people share similar beliefs about justice is not enough to sustain solidarity, social unity, or political legitimacy.

Notice, for example, that the liberal view does not tell us *to whom* we have obligations of justice, or with whom we should be making democratic decisions. After all, Rawls and Dworkin do not endorse the idea of a single world government. They assume that the principles of justice they endorse should be adopted and implemented within some bounded political community. It is to our co-citizens, rather than humanity at large, that we have primary obligations of justice. They both accept that we have some obligations to humanity at large, but these 'humanitarian' obligations to foreigners are weaker than our 'egalitarian' obligations to co-citizens (e.g. Rawls 1993*b*; 1999*b*).

One could imagine a form of liberalism which is not limited in this way to bounded political communities. And indeed some commentators have argued that the logic of liberalism requires, at least as our long-term goal, the creation of a single world-state, with a single scheme of liberties and distributive justice, so that all people in the world would have the same right to move freely, to earn a living, to share in collective self-government, and to receive social benefits, no matter where they live or move throughout the world.

I will discuss such 'cosmopolitan' conceptions of liberalism later in this chapter (s. 10). But this is not what most liberals, including Rawls and Dworkin, have endorsed. They take for granted that we live in a world of states, each with its own scheme of justice and democratic decision-making, and that the primary goal of a theory of justice is to figure out what citizens of these bounded political communities owe each other.

Liberalism presupposes, in other words, that nation-states form what David Miller calls 'ethical communities'—that is, communities whose citizens have special moral obligations to each other not owed to outsiders (Miller 1995). Or, as Yael Tamir puts it, Rawls's liberal egalitarianism is a 'morality of community' (Tamir 1993). Liberal justice requires a sense of community: a sense that citizens belong together in a single country, should govern themselves collectively, and should feel solidarity towards each other.

This point is often obscured within liberal theory, which hides its commitment to community in the language of universalism. As Samuel Black notes, in virtually all liberal theories, a subtle but profound shift takes place in terminology. What begins as a theory about the moral equality of *persons* typically ends up as a theory of the moral equality of *citizens* (Black 1991). The basic rights which liberalism accords to individuals turn out to be reserved for some individuals—namely, those who are citizens of the state. Only citizens have the right to move freely into a country, to earn a living, to share in collective self-government, or to receive social benefits. People outside the country, even if born just 5 miles across the border, are not entitled to the rights of citizenship, since they are not members of 'our' community.

Liberal justice, in short, operates within bounded communities, and requires that citizens see these boundaries as morally significant. Boundaries serve to distinguish 'us' from 'them' for the purposes of claims of justice and rights. But what explains or sustains this bounded sense of 'ethical community'? Why should someone in Maine feel more solidarity with a resident of Texas, 4,000 miles away, than with a resident of New Brunswick, 5 miles across the border with Canada?

Rawls and Dworkin suggest that it is a shared commitment to common principles of liberal justice which explains this sense of ethical community: we feel we belong together in a single ethical community because we share the same principles of justice. But that cannot be right. The vast majority of citizens in Western democracies do indeed share the same liberal-democratic political principles. But that is just the problem: these principles of justice are shared not only *within* states, but also *across* (Western) states. The person in New Brunswick is likely to share the same view of justice as the person in Maine. In fact, if recent elections are any indication, New Brunswickers are *more* likely to share the (centrist-liberal) views of the average Maine resident than (conservative) Texans.

The same phenomenon exists throughout the West. The boundary between Sweden and Norway does not mark a boundary in conceptions of justice, nor the boundary between Belgium and Holland, or Spain and Portugal, or Australia and New Zealand. Each of these countries thinks of itself as a distinct 'ethical community', whose citizens have stronger obligations to 'our' co-citizens than to the 'foreigners' in neighbouring states. But this sense of forming a distinct ethical community cannot be based on adherence to distinct political principles, since the foreigners in neighbouring countries share the same range of principles.[30]

In fact, given the almost universal acceptance of liberal democracy in the West, the sharing of political principles cannot explain why the Western world is divided into separate nation-states at all, or where the boundaries of these states are drawn, and hence cannot explain why citizens feel a sense of ethical community towards those inside but not outside these borders (Sandel 1996: 6–17).

Rawls and Dworkin acknowledge that adherence to liberal principles cannot explain the existence or location of boundaries between liberal democracies. They admit that their liberal theories simply take for granted the separate existence and boundaries of liberal democracies, and assume that any disputes about the existence or boundaries of states have been settled beforehand.[31] They acknowledge that, in the real world, many of these disputes were settled in an arbitrary and coercive manner. It was often a matter of historical accident, even historic injustice, that any particular piece of territory became part of any particular country. Yet Rawls and Dworkin hope that so long as citizens within these (arbitrary) boundaries come to share the same political principles, this will be sufficient to generate a sense of 'ethical community' amongst citizens, and thereby ensure solidarity, legitimacy, and stability.

Put another way, Rawls and Dworkin assume that if people share the same liberal-democratic principles, they will not question historic boundaries and jurisdiction. But this is clearly wrong. Consider the case of Canada. As a result of the liberalization of Québécois society since the 1960s, there has been a pronounced convergence in political principles between English- and French-speaking Canadians over the last thirty years (Dion 1991: 301). If agreement on principles generated agreement on boundaries, we should have witnessed a decline in support for Quebec secession over this period, yet nationalist sentiment has in fact grown consistently. The fact that anglophones and francophones in Canada increasingly share the same principles of justice has not lessened secessionist sentiment since the Québécois rightly assume that their own national state could respect the same principles. Deciding to secede would not require them to abandon their political principles, since they could implement the same principles in their own state. Separatist Québécois accept that political communities should adhere to liberal norms of justice; they simply want to form their own separate and self-governing liberal-democratic political community. In short, they want to form their own (liberal-democratic) 'ethical community'.

We see the same trend in many other countries containing substate nationalist movements, such as Britain (with the Scots) or Spain (with the Catalans). In all of these cases, an increasing convergence on liberal-democratic values between majority and minority has gone hand in hand with demands by minority groups for increased self-government, perhaps even secession. Everyone agrees that political communities should make their decisions democratically and in accordance with individual rights, but they disagree about *which* political community should make these decisions. Should decisions about immigration policy be made by the Canadian parliament or Quebec's National Assembly? Should decisions about the environment be made by the British parliament or the Scottish Assembly? Should decisions about education be made by the Spanish parliament in Madrid or the Catalan government in Barcelona? The minority group accepts liberal-democratic values, but wants to implement them within its own self-governing political institutions, and thereby create or sustain its own ethical community based on liberal justice. The growing convergence on liberal-democratic principles has done nothing to reduce the importance of these disputes, or the threat they pose to the stability of many Western states.[32]

Stability, then, requires not only agreement on the principles that political communities should implement, but also agreement on the identification of these political communities themselves—i.e. their scale or boundaries. If nation-states are to function as bounded ethical communities, then people must not only agree on the principles which govern their community, but must also agree that they in fact form a single ethical community which belongs together and should govern together. If this sense of community is lacking—if two groups simply do not want to stay together in a single state— then no amount of agreement on liberal justice will keep a state together.

This suggests social unity requires a sense of community that goes deeper than the sharing of political principles. Citizens must feel that they *belong* to the same community. They must have a desire to continue to live together and govern together, and to share the same fate, rather than seeking to form their own separate country, or seeking to be annexed to some foreign state. Social unity, in short, requires that citizens identify with each other, and view their fellow citizens as one of 'us'. This sense of shared belonging and shared identity helps sustain the relationships of trust and solidarity needed for citizens to accept the results of democratic decisions (even when they are in a minority on any particular decision), and the obligations of liberal justice (Miller 1995).

So Taylor is surely right to think that something more than shared principles of justice is required to explain political legitimacy and solidarity. What is the basis for such a sense of communal belonging? What more, or what else, is needed to sustain unity than shared political principles? This is one of the great unresolved questions of contemporary political philosophy. It has generated much speculation in the last few years. We can identify three broad approaches to the problem of social unity and political stability: (*a*) an emphasis on a common way of life; (*b*) an emphasis on common nationhood; (*c*) an emphasis on political participation. We can call the first the communitarian approach; the second the liberal nationalist approach; and the third the civic republican approach. I will look at the first two in this chapter, and the third in the next.

These labels are potentially misleading. In one sense, all three of these approaches can be considered 'communitarian', in that they all take seriously the need for liberal democracies to develop and sustain a sense of ethical community. And many theorists draw on aspects from all three approaches. Taylor himself weaves elements of all three approaches into his work, and the literature is replete with other hybrid theories which attempt to combine or integrate aspects of liberalism, republicanism, communitarianism, and nationalism in order to solve the problem of social unity. But for analytic purposes, it is worth examining each approach on its own, before seeing how they can or cannot be combined.

Let us start, then, with the communitarian idea that the basis of social unity must be a shared 'way of life'—i.e. a common conception of the good life. If citizens within a state share a way of life, then they will naturally want to live together in a single state, and hence will accept the legitimacy of the boundaries. They will also naturally want to govern together, and so will accept the legitimacy of common political decision-making. Moreover, they will also be more likely to fulfil their obligations of justice to redistribute resources to the less well off, since in helping their co-citizens they are simultaneously strengthening their shared way of life, and in that sense helping themselves. By contrast, liberalism requires us to make sacrifices for people who not only have different, but even competing, ways of life. Evangelical Christians, who believe in proselytizing for Christ, are being asked to pay taxes to support atheists, who may use that money to publicly denounce and challenge religious belief. If people share a way of life, however, then they can be confident that the people they help through the welfare state will promote, or at least not criticize, their view of the good life.

But if liberals are naive to think that solidarity rests on shared beliefs about justice, surely this communitarian answer is even more naive. It rests on a romanticized view of earlier societies in which legitimacy was based on the effective pursuit of shared ends. Communitarians imply that we could recover the sense of allegiance that was present in earlier days if we accepted a politics of the common good, and encouraged everyone to participate freely in it. Common examples of such earlier societies are the republican democracies of ancient Greece, or eighteenth-century New England town governments.

But these historical examples ignore an important fact. Early New England town governments may have had a great deal of legitimacy amongst their members in virtue of the effective pursuit of their shared ends. But that is at least partly because women, atheists, Indians, and the propertyless were all excluded from membership. Had they been allowed membership, they would not have been impressed by the pursuit of what was often a racist and sexist 'common good'. The way in which legitimacy was ensured amongst all members was to exclude some from membership.

Contemporary communitarians are not advocating that legitimacy be secured by denying membership to those groups in the community who have not historically participated in shaping the 'common way of life'. Communitarians believe that there are certain communal practices that everyone can endorse as the basis for a politics of the common good. But what are these practices? Communitarians often write as if the historical exclusion of certain groups from various social practices was just arbitrary, so that we can now include them and proceed forward. But the exclusion of women, for example, was not arbitrary. It was done for a reason—namely, that the ends being pursued were sexist, defined by men to serve their interests. Demanding that women accept an identity that men have defined for them is not a promising way to increase their sense of allegiance. We cannot avoid this problem by saying with Sandel that women's identities are constituted by existing roles. That is simply false: women can and have rejected those roles, which in many ways operate to deny their individual identities. That was also true in eighteenth-century New England, but legitimacy there was preserved by excluding women from membership. We must find some other way of securing legitimacy, one that does not continue to define excluded groups in terms of an identity that others created for them.

Sandel and Taylor say that there are shared ends that can serve as the basis for a politics of the common good which will be legitimate for all groups in society. But they give no examples of such ends—and surely part of the reason is that there are none. They say that these shared ends are to be found in our historical practices, but they do not confront the fact that those practices were defined by a small section of society—propertied white men—to serve the interests of propertied white men. These practices are gender coded, race coded, and class coded, even when women, blacks, and workers are legally allowed to participate in them. Attempts to promote these kinds of ends reduce legitimacy, and further exclude marginalized groups. Indeed, just such a loss of legitimacy seemed to be occurring amongst many elements of American society in the 1980s—blacks, gays, single mothers, non-Christians—as the right wing tried to implement its agenda based on the Christian, patriarchal family. Many communitarians undoubtedly dislike the Moral Majority's view of the common good, but the problem of the exclusion of historically marginalized groups seems endemic to the communitarian project. As Hirsch notes, 'any "renewal" or strengthening of community sentiment will accomplish nothing for these groups'. On the contrary, our historical sentiments and traditions are 'part of the problem, not part of the solution' (Hirsch 1986: 424).

Consider one of the few concrete examples of communitarian politics that Sandel offers—the regulation of pornography. Sandel argues that such regulation by a local community is permissible 'on the grounds that pornography offends its way of life' (Sandel 1984*b*: 17). To consider how exclusionary this argument can be, contrast it with recent feminist discussions of pornography. Many women's groups have demanded the regulation of pornography on the grounds that women have been excluded from the process of defining traditional views of sexuality. Pornography, some feminists argue, plays a critical role in promoting violence against women, and in perpetuating the subordination of women to male-defined ideas of sexuality and gender roles (e.g. MacKinnon 1987: chs. 13–14). This argument is controversial, but if pornography does in fact play this role in the subordination of women, it does so not because it 'offends our way of life', but precisely because it conforms to our cultural stereotypes about sexuality and the role of women. In fact, as MacKinnon notes, from a feminist point of view the problem with pornography is not that it violates community standards but that it enforces them.

Sandel's argument is in fundamental conflict with this feminist argument. The problem with Sandel's view can be seen by considering the regulation of homosexuality. Homosexuality is 'offensive to the way of life' of many Americans. Indeed, measured by any plausible standard, more people are offended by homosexuality than by pornography. Would Sandel therefore allow local communities to criminalize homosexual relations, or the public affirmation of homosexuality? If not, why not? What distinguishes the two cases, on Sandel's view? For liberals, the difference is that homosexuality does not harm others, and the fact that others are offended by it has no moral weight. The majority in a local (or national) community does not have the right to enforce its 'external preferences' concerning the practices of those people who are outside the mainstream way of life (see Ch. 2, pp. 37–8 above).[33] But this is precisely what Sandel cannot say. On his argument, members of marginalized groups must adjust their personalities and practices so as to be inoffensive to the dominant values of the community. Nothing in Sandel's argument gives members of marginalized groups the power to reject the identity that others have historically defined for them.[34]

Likewise, in the case of pornography, Sandel is not affirming the importance of giving women the ability to reject the male view of sexuality, and to define their own sexuality. On the contrary, he is saying that pornography can be regulated whenever one male-defined view of sexuality (the pornographer's) conflicts with another male-defined view of sexuality (the 'way of life' of the community). And nothing guarantees that the men who are offended by pornography will not have a different but equally oppressive view of female sexuality (e.g. the view that women's sexuality must be kept strictly repressed). However the community decides, women, like all marginalized groups, will have to adjust their aims to be inoffensive to a way of life that they had little or no role in defining. This is no way to develop feelings of legitimacy amongst members of marginalized groups.

Communitarians like to say that political theory should pay more attention to the history of each culture. But it is remarkable how rarely communitarians themselves undertake such an examination of our culture. They wish to use the ends and practices of our cultural tradition as the basis for a politics of the common good, but they do not adequately confront the fact that these practices were defined by a small segment of the population. If we look at the history of our society, surely liberal neutrality has the great advantage of its potential inclusiveness, and its denial that subordinated groups must fit into the 'way of life' that has been defined by the dominant groups.[35]

Sandel concludes his book by saying that when politics goes well 'we can know a good in common that we cannot know alone' (Sandel 1982: 183). But given the diversity of modern societies, we should say instead that politics goes well precisely when it does not adopt an ideology of the 'common good' that can only serve to exclude many groups. Increasing the level of state legitimacy may well require greater civic participation by all groups in society, but, as Dworkin notes, it only makes sense to invite people to participate in politics (or for people to accept that invitation) if they will be treated as equals (Dworkin 1983: 33). And that is incompatible with defining people in terms of roles they did not shape or endorse. If legitimacy is to be earned, it will not be by strengthening communal practices that have been defined by and for others. It will require enabling the oppressed to define their own aims. Liberalism may not do enough in this regard, but as Herzog puts it, if liberalism is the problem, how could communitarianism be the solution (Herzog 1986: 484)?[36]

9. THE SECOND LIBERAL ACCOMMODATION OF COMMUNITARIANISM: LIBERAL NATIONALISM

We do not yet have a satisfactory answer to Taylor's challenge regarding the bases of social unity and political legitimacy in a liberal state. We have considered and rejected both the traditional liberal view that solidarity is sustained by shared beliefs about universal principles of justice, and the communitarian view that solidarity is sustained by shared beliefs in a particularistic conception of the good. Both views are implausible as an account of solidarity within modern political communities. Beliefs about justice are too widely shared across states, and beliefs about the good life are not shared within states. Neither can explain why we feel a special sense of obligation to our co-citizens.

This suggests that we need a different account of social unity. Social unity requires something in between these two approaches: it requires that citizens share more than simply liberal principles, but less than a shared conception of the good life. What could this be? This is an immensely difficult theoretical question, but it is not just a theoretical question. It has been an urgent practical question for many liberal democracies. And if we examine the actual practice of liberal democracies in the West, we can see the outlines of a possible answer. States try to develop solidarity by appealing to ideals of *nationhood*. Each state tries to convince its citizens that they form a 'nation', and hence belong together in a single political community, and owe each other special obligations. Since the people who share a state are not only co-citizens, but also co-nationals, there is a natural bond of solidarity, and a natural desire to exercise self-government.

This idea that co-citizens are, or should be, co-nationals is a comparatively recent one in world history. In the past, the territorial boundaries of states had a purely legal significance: boundaries told us which laws people were subject to, and which rulers and institutions exercised authority over which territory.

But in modern democracies, the boundaries of nation-states do more than this. They also define a body of citizens—a political community—which is seen as the bearer of sovereignty, and whose will and interests form the standards of political legitimacy. Democracy is the rule of and for 'the people', and 'the people' is usually defined as all those individuals permanently residing within the state's territorial boundaries.

It is important to remember how new this idea is. In earlier periods of European history, elites tried to dissociate themselves from 'the plebs' or 'the rabble', and justified their powers and privileges precisely in terms of their alleged distance from the masses. Political boundaries specified the scope of a lord's fiefdom, but did not demarcate a single people or community. The idea that serfs and lords belonged to the same society would have been incomprehensible to people in the feudal era, when elites were not only physically segregated from peasants, but also spoke a different language. The lords were seen, not only as a different class, but as a different and superior race of people, with their own language and civilization, unrelated to the folk culture of the peasants in their midst, and this was the basis of their right to rule.

The rise of nationalism, however, valorized 'the people'. Nations are defined in terms of 'the people'—i.e. the mass of population on a territory, regardless of class or occupation—who become 'the bearer of sovereignty, the central object of loyalty, and the basis of collective solidarity' (Greenfeld 1992: 14). National identity has remained strong in the modern era in part because its emphasis on the importance of 'the people' provides a source of dignity to all individuals, whatever their class.

The use of the vernacular in modern political life is a manifestation of this shift towards a national identity. The use of the language of the people is confirmation that the political community really does belong to the people, and not to the elite. And while national communities still exhibit major economic inequalities, the different economic classes are no longer seen as separate races or cultures. It is seen as right and proper that lower-class children are exposed to the high culture of literature and the arts (which itself has become expressed in the vernacular), while upper-class children are exposed to the history and folk culture of the masses. All individuals within the territory are supposed to be exposed to a common national culture, speak the same national language in public, and participate in common educational and political institutions.

In short, nationalism has created the idea of a single national community which encompasses all classes on the territory. And within the Western democracies, this myth has gradually moved closer to reality, as the achievement of both a wider franchise and mass literacy has enabled almost all citizens to participate, however unequally, in common national cultural and political institutions operating in the vernacular.

State boundaries, then, do not just circumscribe legal jurisdictions, but also define a 'people' or 'nation' who form a common political community, and who share a common national language, culture, and identity. Of course, the boundaries of states rarely coincide exactly with people's national identities. Most states contain people who do not feel a part of the dominant national community, either because they are perceived as 'aliens' by the majority, and so have been prevented from integrating into it (e.g. illegal immigrants; Turkish guest-workers in Germany), or because they have and cherish their own distinct national identity, and so do not wish to integrate (e.g. the Québécois in Canada). I will return to these cases in Chapter 8, since they raises issues of multiculturalism.

As a general rule, however, liberal democracies have aspired to forge a common national identity amongst the people permanently residing on their territory. Moreover, they have been surprisingly effective in this 'nation-building' project.[37] Who would have known that the French language, which was not widely used in much of France at the time of the Revolution, would become a defining feature of the national identity of citizens throughout France? Who would have known that immigrants from all over the world, arriving on American shores with no knowledge of English or of American institutions, would so quickly adopt an American national identity, and accept the principle that their life-chances would be bound up with participation in common national institutions operating in the English language? The remarkable success of these nation-building efforts is reflected in the widespread use of the term 'nation-state' to refer to modern states, as if it were indeed inevitable or at least natural for states to have successfully diffused a common national language and identity amongst all citizens.

This surprising degree of coincidence of territory and national identity has been achieved in two ways. In some cases, it has been achieved by redrawing boundaries to better match people's pre-existing national identities. This is the case with the secession of Norway from Sweden in 1906, or of Slovakia from the Czech Republic in 1993. But more often, the aim has been to revise people's national identities to better fit existing boundaries. This is the aim of the classic 'nation-building' programmes undertaken by all Western democracies, in which common institutions operating in a common language are established throughout the entire territory of the state.[38] Western states have used a wide range of 'nation-building' tools—such as compulsory education, national media, official language laws, naturalization policies, national holidays and symbols, compulsory military service—to help diffuse and consolidate this sense of nationhood.

Where these nation-building policies were resisted by certain groups or regions, such as by indigenous peoples in the United States or Canada, Western states have also resorted to more drastic measures. These include conquest, ethnic cleansing, colonial rule, and large-scale settlement so as to 'swamp' the resisting group with new settlers who are more sympathetic to nation-building.

One reason why Western states have invested so much in the promotion of a sense of nationhood is that, if successfully inculcated amongst the majority of citizens, it overcomes the problems which confronted Rawls's and Dworkin's account of social unity. We saw earlier that the sharing of political principles cannot explain solidarity within states, since many people outside the state also share these principles. Indeed, Rawls and Dworkin could not account for why such boundaries exist, or where they are located. But if we base solidarity on shared nationhood, and if each state succeeds in promoting a distinct national identity within its borders, then boundaries will indeed be morally significant—they will in fact correspond with the limits of ethical communities. The location of boundaries is no longer simply the result of historical accident or injustice, but rather marks an actual change in people's loyalties and identities. People on the other side of the border are not in fact 'one of us'. Even if they are just 5 miles away, and even if they share the same principles of justice, they will have been raised with a different national identity, in a different national culture, with different national heroes and symbols, and often in a different national language.

We can call this the 'liberal-nationalist' approach to social unity, since it is the approach which most real-world liberal democracies have adopted. But is it really a 'liberal' approach? State efforts to promote a particular language or identity may seem closer to a communitarian politics of the common good than to a liberal politics of state neutrality. Should we not perhaps describe this as a form of communitarianism?[39]

The answer, I think, depends on what sort of national identity is being promoted, and why. As we have seen, communitarian accounts of a politics of the common good typically presuppose a shared conception of the good which is to be collectively promoted, even if this limits the ability of individual members to revise their ends. One can certainly imagine forms of nation-building which take this communitarian form. For example, in Greece promoting a common Greek national identity has involved promoting the Greek Orthodox religion. Anyone who is not Orthodox cannot be a true member of the Greek nation, accepting the Orthodox Church is a *de facto* criterion for gaining citizenship, and members of other religions are subject to various legal disadvantages.

But nation-building need not take the form of promoting a particular conception of the good life. The basis of a common national identity need not be a shared conception of the good, but rather a thinner and more diffuse sense of belonging to an intergenerational society, sharing a common territory, having a common past and sharing a common future. This, indeed, is how national identities typically function in modern Western democracies. Citizens think of themselves as 'American', for example, and identify with other Americans, without sharing a religion or conception of the good. They may automatically think of other Americans as 'one of us', without knowing anything about the others' conception of the good. Americans disagree with each other about the good life, but they still recognize and identify each other as Americans, because they share a sense of belonging to an intergenerational society which has some historical reference points, and a common future. They may disagree about how to interpret their past, and may have very different hopes for the future, but they recognize each other as belonging to the same society, and this sense of shared belonging underlies their national identity.

What underlies this shared national identity? In non-liberal states, shared identity is typically based on a common ethnic descent, religious faith, or conception of the good. However, these cannot provide the basis for social unity in a liberal state, since none of them is shared in modern pluralist states. What then makes citizens in a liberal state feel that they belong together, that they are members of the same nation? The answer typically involves a sense of shared history, territory, a common language, and common public institutions. Citizens share a sense of belonging to a particular historical society because they share a language and history; they participate in common social and political institutions which operate in this shared language, and which manifest and perpetuate this shared history; and they see their life-choices as bound up with the survival of this society and its institutions into the indefinite future. Citizens can share a national identity in this sense, and yet share very little in terms of ethnicity, religion, or conceptions of the good.[40]

Liberal states actively promote this sort of 'thin' national identity. And they do so, not in order to promote a particular conception of the good life, but rather to increase the likelihood that citizens will fulfil their obligations of justice. People are more likely to make sacrifices for others if these others are viewed as 'one of us', and so promoting a sense of national identity strengthens the sense of mutual obligation needed to sustain liberal justice.

Of course, liberal states have also promoted national identities for other, less praiseworthy, goals—e.g. to encourage uncritical patriotism, and the willingness to die for one's country. Indeed, prior to the Second World War, we could say that these were often the dominant motives for state nation-building policies. Moreover, these historical policies often aimed at promoting a fairly 'thick' conception of national identity, based not only on a shared language and public institutions, but also on a particular religion or way of life. This was true, for example, of the heavy-handed conception of 'Americanization' imposed on immigrants to the United States in the early part of the twentieth century, in which immigrants were pressured to conform to the customs and habits of the the dominant WASP group. But there is a widespread trend throughout the Western democracies, particularly in the post-war period, towards a considerable 'thinning' of the national identity, so as to emphasize national solidarity without requiring cultural assimilation.

If states promote such thin national identities on the grounds that possessing them will make citizens more likely to fulfil their obligations of justice, then there is no violation of liberal neutrality. The identity the state is promoting is not grounded in a particular conception of the good, and the state is not engaged in ranking the intrinsic merits of different ways of life. The liberal nationalist state remains an anti-perfectionist state, which leaves the evaluation of the merits of competing conceptions of the good life to individual choice (and revision) in civil society. There is no limitation on the rational revisability of conceptions of the good life. The liberal nationalist state simply attempts to develop and sustain the sense that citizens belong together in an ethical community, so that we are more likely to fulfil our obligations of justice to our co-citizens.

Sceptics might argue that liberal nationalism will always have a tendency to 'thicken' the content of the national identity, so as to privilege particular lifestyles, religions, or traditional customs. We can see many examples of this today in Eastern Europe, or in older conceptions of 'Americanization'. This tendency to 'thicken' notions of national identity is a permanent danger in any regime that tries to build unity through ideas of nationhood. Indeed, one way to assess the extent to which nation-building is liberal or not is precisely to gauge the thickness of the national identity being promoted, and the extent to which it imposes particular conceptions of the good on people.[41]

But liberal nationalists would insist that nation-building can be, and has been, thinned in such a way that promoting a common national identity does not involve promoting a common conception of the good. If so, then there is a fundamental difference between liberal nationalism and most communitarian conceptions of a politics of the common good. Indeed, communitarians themselves emphasize that liberal nationalism does not qualify as a form of 'politics of a common good'. As Sandel puts it, while a strong sense of nationhood has been built in the United States, 'the nation proved too vast a scale across which to cultivate the shared self-understandings necessary to community in the . . . constitutive sense' (Sandel 1984a: 93). Alasdair MacIntyre has made similar comments about the inability or inappropriateness of trying to pursue communitarian goals at the national level (MacIntyre 1981: 221; 1994: 302; cf. Miller 1989: 60–7). Co-nationals may share a common language and sense of belonging to a particular historical society, but often disagree fundamentally about the ultimate ends in life. A common national identity, therefore, is too thin a basis for communitarian politics.[42]

For this reason, most communitarians have looked to the local level for a truly communitarian politics, since there is the possibility for a consensus on questions of the good life at a local level. We could say that, for Sandel and MacIntyre, politics is regrettably but inevitably liberal at the national level, but potentially and desirably communitarian at the local level.

From a liberal point of view, however, the very fact which makes national identity so inappropriate for communitarian politics—namely, that it does not rest on shared beliefs about the good—is precisely what makes it an appropriate basis for liberal politics (Tamir 1993: 90). The common national identity provides a source of trust and solidarity that can accommodate deep disagreement over conceptions of the good life. And exposure to the common national culture provides a range of choices for people without imposing any particular conception of the good life, and without limiting people's ability to question and revise particular values or beliefs.

It would appear then that liberal nationalism is indeed a distinctly liberal approach to social unity. This may be a surprising claim, since, until recently, many people argued that the very idea of a 'liberal nationalism' was an oxymoron—that all nationalisms were by definition illiberal. But the more people have examined the actual practice of liberal democracies in trying to sustain social unity, and the more people have considered the link beween national identity and individual freedom, the more people have concluded that ideals of nationhood provide an important basis for the achievement of liberal ideals of justice and liberty. To date, nationhood has provided the best basis on which to promote communal trust and solidarity without limiting the freedom of individuals to form and revise their conceptions of the good.

Whether liberal nationalism can continue to sustain feelings of solidarity and legitimacy is a more difficult question. Some communitarians argue that, whatever its historic success, liberal nationalism is simply too thin a basis to sustain solidarity in the long term. Liberal nationalism says that solidarity is based, not only on sharing beliefs about justice, but also on sharing a national identity. This is a stronger account of solidarity than Rawls and Dworkin offer. But is it strong enough? After all, it still requires me to make sacrifices for people who are very different from me in ethnicity, religion, and way of life. Why should the mere fact that they are co-nationals motivate me to help them? Some communitarians argue that the growing feelings of apathy and discontent in Western democracies, and the backlash against the welfare state, show that liberal nationalism is failing, and can no longer sustain the bonds between citizens and the state (and the bonds between citizens themselves) (e.g. Sandel 1996).

Even if the thin bond of common nationhood was a powerful motivating force in the past, perhaps it is losing its salience in an era of multiculturalism, transnationalism, and globalization. Many commentators have started talking about 'the end of the nation-state', as political powers are moving upwards to transnational institutions (like the World Bank or European Union) or downwards to local or regional governments (Guéhenno 1995).

Whether we are really witnessing the end of the nation-state is a much-debated question, to which I will return next chapter. But it is worth emphasizing, again, that if liberal nationalism is inadequate to the tasks at hand, it is difficult to see how communitarianism could be the solution. As I noted earlier, many communitarians accept that a politics of the common good is not viable at the national level, and hence try to remedy the lack of solidarity and legitimacy at the national level by decentralizing power to local levels, which can develop and sustain stronger forms of solidarity and legitimacy based on the pursuit of a common conception of the good. I personally doubt whether such shared conceptions of the good exist even at the local level.[43] But even if they do, notice how this position—weak liberal politics at the national level; strong communitarian politics at the local level—fails to solve our original problem. After all, the challenge Taylor set us was to motivate citizens to live up to the obligations of justice imposed by the modern welfare state. The communitarian decentralist approach is no answer to this challenge. For if solidarity requires communitarian politics, and if communitarian politics can only operate at the local level, then we will be unable to deal with the most serious issues of injustice in modern states. We may be able to sustain redistribution *within* local communities or neighbourhoods that share a common conception of the good, but the most urgent injustices require redistribution *across* communities—e.g. from white surburbanites to black inner-city families, or from wealthy Silicon Valley to poor Appalachia. Local communitarian politics cannot help us here. This requires a source of solidarity which is not local, and not grounded on a shared conception of the good. It requires, in short, a common national identity.[44]

10. NATIONALISM AND COSMOPOLITANISM

Indeed, one could argue that the real flaw in liberal nationalism is not its inability to sustain distributive justice within national boundaries, but its seeming indifference to issues of global justice across national boundaries. While there may be serious inequalities within Western nation-states, these pale in comparison with the sorts of inequalities we see between the West and the developing countries in the Third World. These inequalities are not only staggering in size, but also seem the very paradigm of the sort of 'morally arbitrary' inequality which Rawls and Dworkin say should be remedied. After all, what could be more a matter of brute luck or the natural lottery than which country one is born in (Beitz 1979: 136–42)? As Carens notes, the gulf in life-chances between rich and poor countries is the modern equivalent of feudalism. People who are born on one side of the Rio Grande are born into the modern equivalent of the nobility, while those who are born a few miles across the river are born into the modern equivalent of serfdom (Carens 1987).

It would appear then that liberal egalitarianism's foundational commitment to remedying undeserved inequalities should push it in the direction of a truly global or 'cosmopolitan' conception of distributive justice. That, indeed, is what many commentators on Rawls have argued. According to these critics, Rawls's theory of justice should be applied globally, not just domestically. People in the 'original position' would not want their fate to depend so heavily on the morally arbitrary fact of which country they were born into (Pogge 1989: chs. 5–6; 1994; Beitz 1979: part 3; Barry 1989c; Tan 2000).[45]

This sort of global inequality could be reduced in two different ways. One is to redistribute resources from citizens in rich countries to citizens in poor countries. Of course, the sort of global institutions which are needed to engage in this sort of international redistribution do not yet exist. But since Rawls argues that we have a 'natural duty of justice' to create just institutions where they do not yet exist, the implication is that we should be working towards the construction of such global institutions (Shue 1988). The other option does not require new global institutions: it simply requires rich countries to open their borders to people from poor countries. We can either transfer resources to poor people, or allow poor people to come to where the resources are.[46]

Defenders of global justice argue that Western countries must adopt one or other of these strategies, or some combination of them. Some argue, for example, that Western countries are only justified in restricting immigration from poor countries if they have lived up to their obligation to transfer resources to those countries (Goodin 1992b). This, it seems, is the inescapable conclusion of liberal-egalitarian principles.[47]

Liberal nationalism, however, seems concerned only about sustaining domestic institutions of distributive justice, and takes for granted the right of Western nation-states to both hoard their unequal wealth and close their borders to immigrants. Several commentators have argued that this indifference to global justice is one of the main failings of liberal nationalism (Pogge 1998; Lichtenberg 1999; Barry 1999). They assume that to defend any notion of global or cosmopolitan justice requires abandoning liberal nationalism.

And yet some liberal nationalists are in fact defenders of a more cosmopolitan conception of justice.[48] This may seem like a contradiction in terms. But whether we see nationalism and global justice as conflicting may depend, in part, on our assumptions or predictions about people's innate moral sympathies. Cosmopolitan critics of liberal nationalism often write as if the natural or spontaneous tendency of human beings is to feel sympathy for all other humans around the world, and to be willing to make sacrifices for them.

Nationalism, on this view, artificially restricts our natural inclination to conceive of and pursue justice globally. Liberal nationalists, on the other hand, argue that people's natural or spontaneous sympathies are often very narrow, far narrower than the nation-state. Historically, the sort of redistribution that people have willingly accepted has generally been limited to their own kin group and/or co-religionists. This was an insufficient basis for justice in modern states, since citizens often differ in their ethnicity and religion. Nation-building, then, was a way of 'artificially' extending people's restricted sympathies to include all co-citizens, even those with a different ethnic background, religious confession, or way of life. If we were to reject the moral salience of nationhood, as cosmopolitan critics propose, the worry is that this would lead, not to the expansion of our moral sentiments to include foreigners, but rather to the restriction of our moral sentiments back to kin and confession, as was the historic norm.

For liberal nationalists, then, the extension of moral concern to co-nationals was an important and fragile historic achievement, and should not be abandoned on the naive expectation that people's natural sympathies are global in scope. This is not to say we should reject all concerns for global justice, but rather should move towards global justice by building upon, rather than tearing down, the achievements of liberal nationalism. How the centrality of nationhood can be maintained while simultaneously working towards a more global sense of justice is not easy to see, and much work remains to be done in sorting out the relations between liberal egalitarianism, liberal nationalism, and cosmopolitanism.[49]

11. THE POLITICS OF COMMUNITARIANISM

As we have seen, communitarianism involves two separate lines of argument, and each has a rather different political flavour. The first line of argument concerns the relationship between the self and its ends. In so far as the communitarian idea of 'constitutive ends' and the 'embedded self' is offered as an alternative to the liberal belief in rational revisability, then it is a very conservative doctrine that would limit the ability of individuals to question or reject traditions and practices they find oppressive, demeaning, and unsatisfying. The leaders of traditionalist or fundamentalist ethnic or religious groups may find this an attractive position, but it is doubtful that many communitarians really endorse such an illiberal view, and much of this debate about the self and its ends seems based on false oppositions and straw-man arguments.

As a result, most communitarians have shifted to the second line of argument, concerning the need for a social context for individual freedom. This too sometimes takes the form of straw-man arguments, as when liberals are said to believe in 'atomism' and thereby deny the 'social thesis'. But as we have seen, there are also several real political issues here, most of which are concerned, in one way or another, with the relationship between unity and diversity.

To oversimplify, we could say that liberals accept and indeed welcome the fact that citizens in modern societies have adopted an increasingly wide range of different and often competing conceptions of the good life, and view this diversity of ends as a source of cultural richness and individual autonomy. They do not fear that this diversity of ends will undermine social unity, so long as people share a commitment to liberal justice (and perhaps a thin national identity).

Communitarians, by contrast, are more anxious about the proliferating diversity of ends in modern societies, and its impact on social unity and the ability of groups to come together to accomplish shared goals. They do not believe that social unity can be sustained by such a weak bond as shared principles of justice (or a thinned-out national identity), and fear that the balance between diversity and unity has been lost.

It is this sense of anxiety which is perhaps the most characteristic feature of contemporary communitarianism, and is typically accompanied by laments about the 'decline' or 'failure' of various social institutions, whether it be the family, neighbourhood associations, the media, schools, or churches. Indeed, in popular discourse, the term 'communitarian' is used to refer to anyone who is anxious about the existing state of our social institutions. Whereas 'liberals' in popular discourse are often seen as exclusively focused on protecting individuals' civil liberties and access to economic resources, 'communitarians' are concerned about the fate of our social institutions, and their capacity to generate a sense of ethical community.

If communitarians share this anxiety that the relationship between diversity and unity is out of kilter, they disagree about how to re-establish the balance. To paraphrase Derek Phillips, we can think of communitarians as either 'looking backward' or 'looking forward' (Phillips 1993), and these two perspectives generate very different political conclusions. Those who look backward typically offer a nostalgic lament for the 'decline' of community, which presupposes that our social institutions functioned well in the 'good old days', but have been eroded by the increasingly aggressive assertion of individual and group diversity. Such movements as feminism, gay rights, and multiculturalism—as well as more general trends towards consumerism and materialism—are seen as having undermined the sense of community. It is said that we have 'gone too far' in accommodating individual choice and cultural diversity, and indeed have become a 'permissive society' that is more concerned with pursuing our individual preferences than with fulfilling our communal responsibilities. Such nostalgic communitarians seek to retrieve a balance between diversity and unity by 'retrieving' a conception of the common good, and by containing or reducing the sort of diversity that would undermine that common conception of the good (e.g. by limiting gay rights, restricting divorce, promoting prayer in schools).

This is obviously the language of traditional conservatism, wrapped up in the new vocabulary of communitarianism, and is essentially at odds with liberal values. Phillips himself thinks that most communitarians fall into this 'looking backward' category. But there is another strand of communitarianism which accepts that individual choice and cultural diversity are unavoidable and indeed desirable features of modernity. It accepts that we live in multiracial, multireligious, and multicultural societies whose members assert the right to decide for themselves whether traditional ways of life are worthy of their continued allegiance. Forward-looking communitarianism accepts these facts, but worries that our traditional sources of social unity cannot bear the weight of all of this diversity. It seeks therefore to find new stronger sources of commonality to counterbalance the new stronger forms of diversity. It seeks new ways to build bonds of community that integrate and accommodate (rather than constrict) our diverse choices and lifestyles. One popular example in the United States is the call for a new programme of 'national service' that would bring together young citizens from very different backgrounds to work together on certain common projects.

Understood in this way, the communitarian concern for social unity need not rest on illiberal values or assumptions. As I noted earlier, liberal nationalism can itself be seen as such a forward-looking form of communitarianism, since it seeks to draw upon the distinctly modern idea of nationhood as a way of bonding together people who are otherwise very different in their origins, beliefs, and ways of life. The sort of participatory democracy I discuss in the next chapter can also be seen as a form of forward-looking communitarianism which seeks to build new bonds of solidarity through the very practice of deliberating about our differences. The effectiveness of these various proposals for strengthening unity while respecting diversity and choice remains largely untested.

Forward-looking communitarianism, therefore, merges into liberal nationalism and republicanism. And in so far as it is committed to protecting the rights of women and minorities to question traditional practices and to assert their distinctive identities, it also merges into feminism and multiculturalism. Indeed, if we think of forward-looking communitarians as anyone who is concerned about sustaining bonds of ethical community in an era of individual choice and cultural diversity, then virtually all political theorists today qualify for the label. Forward-looking communitarianism is not so much a position of its own, but simply a question or challenge which all political theories must now face up to.

The distinction between forward- and backward-looking communitarianism is not hard and fast. Many communitarians attempt to integrate both elements into their theories, alternating between a nostalgic rhetoric of decline and a visionary rhetoric of building new bonds of solidarity across differences. It is therefore difficult to locate communitarianism on a simple left–right continuum: one can find elements of conservative reaction and progressive reform in most communitarian authors.

In any event, the questions raised by communitarians about the social conditions of individual freedom are important ones, and have given rise to a flourishing debate. But it is not a debate between those who do and those who do not accept the social thesis. In fact, as we have seen, it is a number of different debates—about civil society, cultural structures, political legitimacy, state boundaries—each of which should be considered on its own.[50]

GUIDE TO FURTHER READING

Although communitarianism is, in one sense, as old as political philosophy itself, it sprang into prominence in the early 1980s with the publication of four essential texts: Michael Sandel, *Liberalism and the Limits of Justice* (Cambridge University Press, 1982); Alisdair MacIntyre, *After Virtue: A Study in Moral Theory* (Duckworth, 1981); Michael Walzer, *Spheres of Justice: A Defence of Pluralism and Equality* (Blackwell, 1983); and Charles Taylor, *Philosophy and the Human Sciences: Philosophical Papers*, vol. ii (Cambridge University Press, 1985).

In retrospect, it has become clear that these four authors were advancing quite different lines of argument, and calling all of them 'communitarian' obscures as much as it reveals. However, these books did all share one feature: they all criticized the sort of liberal egalitarianism defended by Rawls and Dworkin as in some way or other insensitive to issues of community. As a result, the debate initiated by these authors quickly became labelled the 'liberal-communitarian debate'. This debate more or less dominated Anglo-American political philosophy in the 1980s, as liberals attempted to respond to the communitarian critique, and theorists in other traditions tried to figure out how this debate affected their own concerns about liberal democracy.

One line of communitarian argument critiqued liberal theories of the self, particularly their emphasis on autonomy or rational revisability. For examples of liberal responses to this line of communitarian critique, see my *Liberalism, Community and Culture* (Oxford University Press, 1989); Ronald Dworkin, 'Liberal Community', *California Law Review*, 77/3 (1989): 479–504; Allen Buchanan, 'Assessing the Communitarian Critique of Liberalism', *Ethics*, 99/4 (1989): 852–82; Joseph Raz, *The Morality of Freedom* (Oxford University Press, 1986). These authors all seek to defend the liberal ideal of autonomy as rational revisability. But other liberals have responded to the communitarian critique by weakening the commitment to rational revisability, and moving instead to a conception of 'political liberalism'. This idea was introduced in John Rawls, 'Justice as Fairness: Political not Metaphysical', *Philosophy and Public*

Affairs, 14/3 (1985): 223–51, and developed more fully in his *Political Liberalism* (Columbia University Press, 1993). Other important statements of political liberalism include Charles Larmore, *Patterns of Moral Complexity* (Cambridge University Press, 1987); and Donald Moon, *Constructing Community: Moral Pluralism and Tragic Conflicts* (Princeton University Press, 1993). For commentaries on political liberalism, see Victoria Davion and Clark Wolf (eds.), *The Idea of a Political Liberalism: Essays on Rawls* (Rowman and Littlefield, 2000).

Another line of communitarian argument critiqued liberal theories of social unity. Many liberals have responded to this critique by developing new theories of liberal nationalism. This approach was pioneered in two books which still dominate the field: Yael Tamir, *Liberal Nationalism* (Princeton University Press, 1993); and David Miller, *On Nationality* (Oxford University Press, 1995). More recent studies include Paul Gilbert, *Philosophy of Nationalism* (Westview, 1998); Gilbert, *Peoples, Cultures, and Nations in Political Philosophy* (Georgetown University Press, 2000); Margaret Canovan, *Nationhood and Political Theory* (Edward Elgar, 1996); Ross Poole, *Nation and Identity* (Routledge, 1999); Charles Blattberg, *From Pluralist to Patriotic Politics: Putting Practices First* (Oxford University Press, 2000); David Miller, *Citizenship and National Identity* (Polity Press, 2000). Commentaries on liberal nationalism can be found in Nenad Miscevic (ed.,) *Nationalism and Ethnic Conflict: Philosophical Perspectives* (Open Court, 2000); Robert McKim and Jeff McMahan (eds.), *The Morality of Nationalism* (Oxford University Press, 1997); Simon Caney, David George, and Peter Jones (eds.,) *National Rights, International Obligations* (Westview, 1996); Jocelyne Couture, Kai Nielsen, and Michel Seymour (eds.,) *Rethinking Nationalism* (University of Calgary Press, 1998); Desmond Clarke and Charles Jones (eds.), *The Rights of Nations: Nations and Nationalism in a Changing World* (Palgrave, 1999). Excerpts of many of the key writings are contained in Ronald Beiner (ed.), *Theorizing Nationalism* (State University of New York Press, 1998).

Both communitarians and liberal nationalists emphasize the importance of some notion of a cohesive political community, and typically assume that norms of justice apply within such bounded political communities. As a result, both approaches have been challenged by defenders of a more global or 'cosmopolitan' conception of justice. See, in particular, Lea Brilmayer and Ian Shapiro (eds.), *Global Justice* (New York University Press, 1999); Kok-Chor Tan, *Toleration, Diversity, and Global Justice* (Pennsylvania State University Press, 2000); Charles Jones, *Global Justice: Defending Cosmopolitanism* (Oxford University Press, 1999); Charles Beitz, *Political Theory and International Relations* (Princeton University Press, 1979); Thomas Pogge, *Realizing Rawls* (Cornell University Press, 1989). For Rawls's defence of his assumption that distributive justice applies domestically, not globally, see *The Law of Peoples* (Harvard University Press, 1999). For a review of this debate, see Charles Beitz, 'International Liberalism and Distributive Justice: A Survey of Recent Thought', *World Politics*, 51 (1999): 269–96.

Liberals were not the only people who felt compelled to respond to communitarianism. For example, both feminists and socialists in the 1980s grappled with the question of whether communitarianism supplemented or contradicted their own critiques of liberalism. For examples of feminist and socialist assessments of the communitarian critique, see Elizabeth Frazer and Nicola Lacey, *The Politics of Community: A Feminist Critique of the Liberal-Communitarian Debate* (Harvester Wheatsheaf, 1993); Penny Weiss and Marilyn Friedman (eds.), *Feminism and Community* (Temple University Press, 1995); David Miller, 'In What Sense must Socialism be Communitarian?', *Social Philosophy and Policy*, 6/2 (1989): 51–73.

For anthologies which include many of the key writings, both communitarian critiques of liberalism, and liberal and other responses, see Shlomo Avineri and Avner de-Shalit (eds.), *Communitarianism and Individualism* (Oxford University Press, 1992); Edward W. Lehman (ed.), *Autonomy and Order: A Communitarian Anthology* (Rowman and Littlefield, 2000); Michael Sandel (ed.), *Liberalism and its Critics* (Blackwell, 1984).

For diametrically opposed assessments of the liberal-communitarian debate, see Daniel A. Bell, *Communitarianism and its Critics* (Oxford University Press, 1993), who thinks communitarians won the debate, and Derek Phillips *Looking Backward: A Critical Appraisal of Communitarian Thought* (Princeton University Press, 1993), who sides with the liberals. For other assessments, see Stephen Mulhall and Adam Swift, *Liberals and Communitarians* (Blackwell, 1996), which remains perhaps the best survey of the debate; C. F. Delaney (ed.), *The Liberal-Communitarian Debate: Liberty and Community Values* (Rowman and Littlefield, 1994); Elizabeth Frazer, *The Problems of Communitarian Politics: Unity and Conflict* (Oxford University Press, 1999); Ellen Frankel Paul, Fred Miller, and Jeffrey Paul (eds.), *The Communitarian Challenge to Liberalism* (Cambridge University Press, 1996).

Needless to say, communitarians did not stop writing in the early 1980s. Indeed, all four of the leading communitarian philosophers have since produced major works that have generated yet another round of critical commentaries. However, this 'second wave' of communitarian writings has tended to move away from the critique of the liberal self, and moved either upwards to more abstract metatheoretical debates about rationality, or downwards to more practical questions about how to sustain the social and political contexts of liberal democracy, particularly concerns about social unity. For an example of the former shift to metaethical debates, see Alisdair MacIntyre's new work on the link between rationality and tradition, particularly his *Whose Justice? Which Rationality?* (University of Notre Dame Press, 1988), or Michael Walzer's work on the link between moral argument and culturally embedded 'shared understandings', particularly his *Thick and Thin: Moral Argument at Home and Abroad* (Harvard University Press, 1994). In these works, both MacIntyre and Walzer are primarily interested in the ancient question of universalism versus cultural relativism in ethics. For critiques of MacIntyre, see John Horton and Susan Mendus (eds.), *After MacIntyre: Critical Perspectives on the Work of Alisdair MacIntyre* (Polity, 1994). For assessments of Walzer's work, see David Miller and Michael Walzer (eds.), *Pluralism, Justice and Equality* (Oxford University Press, 1995); William Galston, 'Community, Democracy, Philosophy: The Political Thought of Michael Walzer', *Political Theory*, 17/1 (1989): 119–30; Brian Orend, *Michael Walzer on War and Justice* (McGill-Queen's University Press, 2001).

For an example of the shift downwards to debates about social unity and solidarity, see Michael Sandel, *Democracy's Discontent: America in Search of a Public Philosophy*

(Harvard University Press, 1996). For commentaries on Sandel's new work, see Anita Allen and Milton Regan (eds.), *Debating Democracy's Discontent: Essays on American Politics, Law, and Public Philosophy* (Oxford University Press, 1998). See also Emilios Christodoulis (ed.), *Communitarianism and Citizenship* (Ashgate, 1998).

Charles Taylor's new works span both sets of issues. See, in particular, his *Sources of the Self: The Making of the Modern Identity* (Cambridge University Press, 1989) and *A Catholic Modernity* (Oxford University Press, 1999). For critiques of Taylor, see James Tully and Daniel Weinstock (eds.), *Philosophy in an Age of Pluralism: The Philosophy of Charles Taylor in Question* (Cambridge University Press, 1994); and Ruth Abbey, *Charles Taylor* (Princeton University Press, 2001). Both Taylor and Walzer have also written important books on multiculturalism—I will discuss these works in Chapter 8.

Communitarianism has not simply remained an academic school of thought. Under the indefatigable leadership of Amitai Etzioni, an American sociologist, an official 'Communitarian Network' has been launched, with an official statement of principles, and a long list of prominent public figures who have endorsed it. For popular presentations of this 'communitarian movement', see Amitai Etzioni, *The Spirit of Community: Rights, Responsibilities and the Communitarian Agenda* (Crown Publishers, 1993); Etzioni, *Next: The Road to the Good Society* (Basic Books, 2001); and Henry Tam, *Communitarianism: A New Agenda for Politics and Citizenship* (New York University Press, 1998).

The Communitarian Network has its own journal, called *The Responsive Community*. The journal publishes popularized versions of academic arguments about communitarianism, as well as more policy-related advocacy pieces. The Network also has its own website (**www.gwu.edu/~ccps/**), associated with the Institute for Communitarian Policy Studies at George Washington University, in Washington, DC. The website contains extensive bibliographies, position papers, teaching materials and course syllabuses, and links to communitarian organizations in other countries.

NOTES

1. On Hegel's idea of 'reconciling' people to their world, see Hardimon 1992; 1994. It is interesting to note that in his more recent work, Rawls too appeals to this idea (Rawls 1999*b*: 11–12).

2. For Hegel's critique of liberalism, see Hegel 1949: paras. 141, 144. For its relevance to contemporary communitarian critiques of liberalism, see Smith 1989.

3. Walzer attempts to deal with this problem by acknowledging a small class of rights which he views as truly universal—what he calls a 'thin' universal code of political morality that all societies should respect (Walzer 1994). This would rule out slavery or genocide, no matter how much these are a part of local cultural traditions, but would not rule out caste systems or authoritarian theocracies, if these reflected local cultural understandings. For a similar attempt to distinguish a universal but thin code from a culturally relative thick code, see Bell 2000.

4. Certain acts of paternalism involving competent adults may be justified when we are faced with clear cases of weakness of will. For example, most people know that the gain in safety is well worth the effort of putting on a car seat-belt. Yet many people let momentary

inconvenience override their reason. Mandatory seat-belt legislation helps overcome this weakness of will, by giving people an extra incentive to do something that they know they already have sufficient reason to do.

5. As Dworkin notes, this does not apply to all of our preferences or interests: there is no right or wrong answer to the question of whether we should prefer chocolate or vanilla. These are just brute preferences, or what Dworkin calls 'volitional interests'. He distinguishes these from the more important category of 'critical interests', where we are making fallible judgements about what is truly worthwhile (Dworkin 2000: 242–54).

6. The case of coerced religious worship has been a favourite example of liberals from Locke to Rawls. It is not clear that religious worship can be generalized in this way, since there is an epistemic requirement to praying that is not always present elsewhere. However, I believe that the 'endorsement constraint' is applicable to most valuable and important forms of human activity (Dworkin 1989: 484–7; Raz 1986: 291–3; A. Cohen 1996; but cf. Daniels 1975a: 266). Some liberals argue that the endorsement constraint makes perfectionism necessarily self-defeating. For even if the state can encourage or force people to pursue the most valuable ways of life, it cannot get people to pursue them for the right reasons. Someone who changes their lifestyle in order to avoid state punishment, or to gain state subsidies, is not guided by an understanding of the genuine value of the new activity (Waldron 1989: 1145–6; Lomasky 1987: 253–4). This is a valid point against coercive and manipulative forms of perfectionism. But it does not rule out short-term state intervention designed to introduce people to valuable ways of life. One way to get people to pursue something for the right reasons is to get them to pursue it for the wrong reasons, and hope they will then see its true value. This is not inherently unacceptable, and it occurs often enough in the cultural marketplace. So the endorsement constraint argument, by itself, cannot rule out all forms of state perfectionism.

7. In his most recent work, Rawls has tried to downplay the importance of the revisability of our ends, and to find ways of defending the liberty principle without appeal to it. He now says that we should accept the principle of rational revisability for the purposes of determining our public rights and responsibilities, without necessarily accepting it as an accurate portrayal of our private self-understandings. I will discuss this new conception in section 7. However, I will concentrate on Rawls's original view here, because it is the one to which most communitarians have responded.

8. For other major statements of liberal neutrality, see Ackerman 1980: 11, 61; Larmore 1987: 44–7; Dworkin 1978: 127; 1985: 222; Rawls 1993a: 179ff.

9. To avoid these possible misinterpretations of the term 'neutrality', Rawls has instead used the term 'priority of the right over the good'. But that too has multiple and misleading meanings, since it is used by Rawls to describe both the affirming of neutrality over perfection-ism, and the affirming of deontology over teleology. These issues need to be kept distinct, and neither, viewed on its own, is usefully called a matter of the 'priority of the right'. See Kymlicka 1988b: 173–90 for a critique of Rawls's usage of 'priority of the right'. Given the absence of any obviously superior alternative, I will continue to use the term 'neutrality'.

10. Monks committed to personal asceticism typically belong to monastic orders that have large land holdings, revenues from which help pay for the land, buildings, and maintenance of their community, and which are used in promoting their good works. Moreover, the vow of poverty is understood as a renunciation of the monks' legitimate entitlements under a theory of fairness, not a renunciation of things which they think should not be part of a legitimate theory of fairness. Indeed the spiritual value of the renunciation is tied to the fact that it is renouncing something one is entitled to. More generally, most ways of life that are seen as non-materialistic (e.g. ecological lifestyles lived in communion with nature; spiritual lifestyles that seek to create 'sacred spaces') nonetheless require access to resources in order to be

successfully pursued—e.g. control over land, water, and air. Material resources are an essential means for such lifestyles. For the claim that Rawls's list of primary goods is biased against such ways of life, see Schwartz 1973; Nagel 1973. I discuss this objection at length in Kymlicka 1989b.

11. There is another objection that deserves mention, concerning the need for social confirmation of our individual judgements. According to some communitarians, while it may be important for individuals to endorse the value of their activities from the inside, it is equally if not more important that other people confirm that judgement from the outside. Without outside confirmation, we lose our sense of self-respect, and our confidence in the value of our own judgements. A communitarian state, therefore, would limit Dworkin's 'individual endorsement' constraint where it unduly threatens the communitarian 'social confirmation' constraint. I discuss this in Kymlicka 1988a: 195–7; cf. B. Williams 1985: 169–70; Smith 1985: 188–92; Dworkin 1987: 16–17.

12. Sharon Lloyd suggests that this objection may stem from certain misleading aspects of the metaphor of 'stepping back' from one's ends. She prefers the metaphor of 'mental squinting' to describe how people critically reflect on their ends (Lloyd 1992).

13. I have focused on Sandel's writings, but the same ambiguity in the communitarian theory of the self can also be found in MacIntyre 1981: 200–6 and Taylor 1979: 157–60. See Kymlicka 1989a: 56–7 for a discussion of these writers. Sandel's claim that Rawls's view of the self violates our self-understanding gets much of its force from being linked to the further claim that Rawls views people as being essentially disembodied. According to Sandel, the reason that Rawls denies that people are entitled to the rewards which accrue from the exercise of their natural talents is that he denies that natural talents are an essential part of our personal identity. They are mere possessions, not constituents, of the self (Sandel 1982: 72–94; Larmore 1987: 127). But this is a misinterpretation. The reason why Rawls denies that people are entitled to the fruits of the exercise of their natural talents is that no one deserves their place in the natural lottery; no one deserves greater natural talents than anyone else (Ch. 3, s. 2 above). This position is entirely consistent with the claim that natural talents are constituents of the self. The fact that natural talents are constitutive of the self does nothing to show that a gifted child deserves to be born more talented than an ordinary child. Many liberals would not accept the claim that all our natural attributes are constituents of the self (e.g. Dworkin 1983: 39), and I myself am unsure where to draw this line (Ch. 4, s. 5 above). But wherever we draw this line, the ways in which we are essentially *physically embodied* does nothing to support Sandel's conception of the ways that we are *socially embedded*.

14. I take the term 'rational revisability' from A. Buchanan 1975.

15. The fullest statement of Rawls's new approach is in his 1993 book called *Political Liberalism*. Rawls denies that this new approach was motivated by a need to respond to the communitarian critique of liberalism, but he makes clear that he thinks it does in fact respond to communitarian concerns.

16. *Hofer* v. *Hofer et al.* (1970) 13 DLR (3d) 1; cf. Janzen 1990: 65–7.

17. Rawls acknowledges the existence of such a spillover. He says that 'requiring children to understand the political conception in these ways is in effect, though not in intention, to educate them to a comprehensive liberal conception' (Rawls 1993a: 199). But if so, then accepting the political conception entails heavy costs for non-liberal groups—costs that will be perceived as unnecessary, since they can ensure (group) tolerance without accepting the protection of individual liberties. Cf. Tomasi (2001), who argues that Rawls seriously underestimates these spillover effects.

18. *Yoder* v. *Wisconsin* 406 US 205. Rawls argues that his political liberalism is more sympathetic to the demands of the Amish than Mill's comprehensive liberalism. Whereas comprehensive liberalism 'may lead to requirements designed to foster the values of autonomy and

individuality as ideas to govern much if not all of life', political liberalism 'has a different aim and requires far less', since it is only concerned with promoting a liberal ideal of *citizenship* ('the state's concern with [children's] education lies in their role as future citizens'). As a result, Rawls says, political liberalism 'honors, as far as it can, the claims of those who wish to withdraw from the modern world in accordance with the injunctions of their religion, provided only that they acknowledge the principles of the political conception of justice and appreciate its political ideals of person and society' (Rawls 1988: 267–8). However, this is misleading. For one thing, the distinction between political and comprehensive liberalism is unstable, since accepting the value of autonomy for political purposes has unavoidable implications for private life (see note 20 below). Moreover, many religious communities would object to political liberalism on its own terms, as a theory of citizenship. While Rawls would want educators to prepare children for the rights and duties of citizenship, religious sects see 'a different purpose of education . . . to prepare their children for life in their communities'. They are concerned not with preparing people for exercising political rights, but with 'the need for obedience. They argue that education should reorient the individual's self-regard and nurture a desire to abide by the will of the community'. Hence these groups have sought exemption from precisely the sort of education that Rawls's 'political liberalism' insists upon. See Janzen 1990: 143, 97; Callan 1996; Spinner-Halev 2000.

19. Rawls does emphasize that the point of protecting civil rights is not to *maximize* the development and exercise of the capacity to form and revise a conception of the good. As he rightly notes, it would be 'absurd' to try to maximize 'the number of deliberate affirmations of a conception of the good'. Rather, 'these liberties and their priority are to guarantee equally for all citizens the social conditions essential for the adequate development and the full and informed exercise of these powers' (1982b: 47–9). It seems clear, however, that the Hutterites do not provide the social conditions essential for the 'full and informed' exercise of autonomy.

20. Indeed, the connection between the political and the private is not only causal, but conceptual. Rawls accepts that exercising autonomy in the political sphere may causally promote its exercise in private life. But he insists that this is a contingent and unintended effect, and that his political conception of the person only concerns the way 'that the moral powers [of autonomy and a sense of justice] are exercised in political life and in basic institutions as citizens endeavour to maintain them and to use them to conduct public business' (1988: 272 n. 28). But what does it mean to exercise our capacity for autonomy 'in political life'? The capacity for autonomy is quite different in this respect from the capacity for a sense of justice, although Rawls treats them together in this passage. The capacity for a sense of justice is exercised by 'assessing the justice and effectiveness of laws and social policies', and hence is primarily concerned with, and exercised in, political life. The capacity to form and revise a conception of the good, on the other hand, is primarily concerned with what Rawls calls our 'non-public identity'—with our comprehensive, rather than our political, identity. As Rawls himself puts it, 'liberty of conscience and freedom of association enable us to develop and exercise our moral powers in forming, revising, and rationally pursuing our conceptions of the good that belong to our comprehensive doctrines, and affirming them as such' (1989: 254). Hence the capacity for justice is about evaluating *public* policies and institutions; while the capacity to form/revise a conception of the good is about evaluating the comprehensive religious and moral doctrines that define our *private* identity. So what then does it mean to say that the exercise of this latter capacity can be restricted to political life, without it impinging on our private identity? Since the capacity involved just is the capacity to form and revise our comprehensive ends, it seems that any exercise of it necessarily involves our private identity.

21. See, e.g. Kukathas 1992; McDonald 1991b; Karmis 1993; Mason 1993. For related discussions, see Exdell 1994.

22. Recall that this was indeed one of Rawls's main objections to utilitarianism, which accords equal weight to everyone's pre-existing desires, no matter how expensive or unreasonable, rather than holding people responsible for adjusting their desires in the light of principles of fairness (Ch. 2, p. 42).

23. In any event, denying such subsidies can be just as divisive as providing them, particularly if those with expensive costs view it as unfair, as they are likely to do if they are in fact unable to rationally adjust their aims.

24. See Nickel 1990: 214; Coser 1991. Rawls's fear that the Millian conception of autonomy is not widely shared depends on conflating this conception of autonomy with the other, more controversial, conceptions discussed in section 6. It is important to note that while Mill's conception is 'general', in applying to all areas of life, it is not 'comprehensive', since it does not define a set of final ends or intrinsic goods to be pursued by each individual. Rather, it concerns the capacity by which we deliberate and assess our final ends.

25. Taylor 1985a: 190–1; cf. Jaggar 1983: 42–3; Wolgast 1987: ch. 1. For Taylor's acceptance of the idea of the revisability of our ends, see his helpful account of 'strong evaluation' in Taylor 1985a: 220–1.

26. Taylor says that he is criticizing the 'primacy of rights' doctrine, by which he means the claim that individual rights have primacy over other moral notions, such as individual duties, the common good, virtue, etc. According to Taylor, this doctrine is found in Hobbes, Locke, and Nozick. I find this schema unhelpful, for none of these moral notions, including individual rights, is the right sort to be morally primary. (Notice, for example, that Hobbes and Nozick are both 'primacy of rights' theorists on Taylor's schema. But since Nozick affirms what Hobbes denies—i.e. that individuals have inherent moral standing—any agreement between them over individual rights must be derivative, not morally primary: cf. Ch. 4, s. 3 above.) The debate that Taylor wishes to consider is best pursued by asking not whether rights in general have primacy over duties in general, but whether there are particular rights, duties, virtues, etc. that are inadequately recognized in liberal or (as Taylor describes them) 'ultraliberal' theories. And if we look at the debate this way, one of Taylor's arguments is that state neutrality can undermine the social conditions necessary for individual autonomy. That claim, if true, has importance for liberal and libertarian theories whether or not they endorse the 'primacy of rights' doctrine. Some communitarians take the social thesis to undermine liberalism in a more fundamental way, by undermining its moral individualism. Moral individualism is the view that individuals are the basic unit of moral value, so that any moral duties to larger units (e.g. the community) must be derived from our obligations to individuals. But, communitarians argue, if we reject the atomistic view that individuals are self-originating persons, then we must also reject Rawls's claim that we are 'self-originating sources of valid claims' (Rawls 1980: 43). But this is a non sequitur. Rawls's claim that we are self-originating sources of valid claims is not a sociological claim about how we develop. It is a moral claim about the location of moral value. As Galston says, 'while the formative power of society is surely decisive, it is nevertheless *individuals* that are being shaped. I may share everything with others. But it is *I* that shares them—an independent consciousness, a separate locus of pleasure and pain, a demarcated being with interests to be advanced or suppressed' (Galston 1986: 91). While my good is socially determined, it is still my good that is affected by social life, and any plausible political theory must attend equally to the interests of each person.

27. For example, Habermas used to argue that the need for a 'discursive desolidification of the (largely externally controlled or traditionally fixed) interpretations of our needs' is the heart of his disagreement with Rawls (Habermas 1979: 198–9). However, he now rejects the idea of politically evaluating people's conceptions of the good (Habermas 1985: 214–16; cf. Benhabib 1986: 332–43; Funk 1988: 29–31).

28. Kymlicka 1989*b*. For a critique of my arguments, see Hurka 1993, and the reply in Weinstock 1998. Other important contributions to the state perfectionist–state neutrality debate include Caney 1991; 1995; Neal 1994; Dyzenhaus 1992; Sher 1997; Hurka 1993; Goodin and Reeve 1989; Wall 1998; Chan 2000.

29. The suggestion that non-political activity is inherently solitary is implicit in a number of communitarian writings. For example, Sandel claims that under communitarian politics 'we can know a good in common that we cannot know alone' (Sandel 1982: 183). And Sullivan claims that state perfectionism is needed to ensure that no one is 'cut off from collective deliberations' (Sullivan 1982: 158). Liberals make the opposite assumption that the state is not required to lead individuals into collective associations and deliberations (Macedo 1988: 127–8; Feinberg 1988: 105–13).

30. Of course, this is not to say that everyone in the Western democracies shares the same substantive theory of distributive justice. As we have seen in previous chapters, while almost everyone shares a similar conception of the 'constitutional essentials' (civil liberties, representative democracy), there are deep disagreements between the left and right about distributive justice, including notions of equality of opportunity, responsibility for choices, remedying unequal circumstances, and so on. But these left–right debates exist within every Western democracy, so that the range of conceptions of justice is similar across all countries. Whether we focus on beliefs in constitutional essentials (which are similar across Western democracies) or beliefs about distributive justice (which are debated within each country, although the range of views is similar across all countries), in neither case do national boundaries mark a change in people's beliefs about justice.

31. For example, see Dworkin's claim that in his theory 'we treat community as prior to justice and fairness in the sense that questions of justice and fairness are regarded as questions of what would be just or fair within a particular political group'—a 'political group' whose boundaries and membership are taken as givens (Dworkin 1986: 208; cf. Rawls 1993*a*: 277). See Galloway 1993 for a criticism of this tendency of liberals to take boundaries and membership as givens.

32. For a more detailed development of this argument, see Norman 1995. For a related critique of the idea that shared principles underlie social unity, see Paris 1991.

33. Dworkin 1985: 353–72; cf. Ch. 2, s. 5*a* above. More accurately, homosexuality can only be said to harm others if one invokes a controversial conception of the good which does not pass the test of 'public reason'—see Ch. 7, s. 2 below.

34. Sandel suggests that American laws against sodomy should be overturned on the ground that some homosexual relations aim at the same substantive ends as characterize heterosexual marriages, which have traditionally received Supreme Court protection (Sandel 1989: 344–5). But why should the freedom of homosexuals depend on their pursuing the same aims and aspirations as heterosexuals? Many gay rights groups would deny that they have the same (restrictive) view of intimacy and sexuality as that which characterizes traditional heterosexual marriages. What if, as the Supreme Court argued in a recent case upholding anti-sodomy laws, gay rights threaten the perceived sanctity of the heterosexual family? In any event, Sandel does not explain how his new argument that anti-sodomy laws are unconstitutional fits in with his earlier claim about the freedom of local communities to regulate activities that offend their way of life. .

35. On the exclusionary tendencies of communitarianism, see Gutmann 1985: 318–22; Herzog 1986: 481–90; Hirsch 1986: 435–8; Rosenblum 1987: 178–81; Phillips 1993. I have argued elsewhere that many of these considerations also argue against non-communitarian forms of perfectionist intervention in the cultural marketplace. Even where it is not deliberately aimed at promoting the community's way of life, state perfectionism would tend to distort the free

evaluation of ways of life, to rigidify the dominant ways of life, regardless of their intrinsic merits, and to exclude unfairly the values and aspirations of marginalized and disadvantaged groups within our society (Kymlicka 1989b: 900–2).

36. Rawls cites the need for public legitimacy as grounds for supporting rather than opposing neutrality. He claims that perfectionism threatens the public consensus, because people will not accept the legitimacy of state policies based on a conception of the good they do not share. Rawls seems to think that this will be true of any society where citizens are divided by conflicting conceptions of the good. Put at this general level, Rawls's claim is surely false. As Raz shows, it is possible for people with conflicting ends to agree nonetheless on a procedure for arriving at a public ranking of the value of different ways of life, or perhaps to accept a particular public ranking with which they disagree but which they nonetheless see as a better second-best option than neutrality (Raz 1986: 126–32). There is no inherent connection between neutrality and state legitimacy. However, the kinds of conflicting ends in modern democracies, and the history underlying them, are such that perfectionism of the communitarian variety surely is a threat to state legitimacy.

37. Nation-building has been less successful in other parts of the world, particularly sub-Saharan Africa—see Davidson 1993; Laitin 1992; Kymlicka 2002.

38. For the ubiquity of this process around the world, see Gellner 1983; Anderson 1983.

39. Indeed, Taylor himself cites state nation-building policies designed to promote a particular language as an example of communitarian politics (Taylor 1992). Conversely, Brighouse rejects nation-building on the grounds that it violates liberal neutrality (Brighouse 1998).

40. This is a thumbnail sketch of the nature of national identity in a liberal state, and its role in promoting political stability and relationships of trust and solidarity. For accounts of liberal nationalism, see Tamir 1993; Canovan 1996; Spinner 1994: ch. 7; Miller 1995; 2000; and Kymlicka 1995a.

41. I try to develop a more comprehensive set of criteria for distinguishing liberal from illiberal forms of nation-building in Kymlicka and Opalski 2001.

42. But see Bell 1993, who argues that nationhood can be a viable basis for communitarian politics.

43. Taylor is aware that there will not be unanimity over any conception of the good life, even at the local level, but argues that it is permissible for the majority to promote its conception of the common good, so long as it tolerates other ways of life (Taylor 1992).

44. See Orwin 1998: 88 on the conflict between Sandel's commitment to decentralization and his desire for redistribution. It is also difficult to see how this retreat to localism will provide any sort of response to the challenges of globalization.

45. Rawls attempts to respond to this argument by saying (*inter alia*) that the main cause of poverty in the Third World is not lack of resources, but bad government; and that rich countries do have a duty to help poor countries establish their own just schemes of domestic distribution, but do not have a duty to promote equality of life-chances across national boundaries (Rawls 1993b; 1999a). For other defences of limiting justice to nation-states, see Miller 2000: ch. 10; Walzer 1995a. For a critique, see Pogge 1994; Tan 2000; Beitz 1999.

46. For proposals to transfer resources to poor countries, see Pogge 1997a (proposing a global resources dividend) and Van Parijs 1995: 223–8 (a global universal basic income). It is important to emphasize that these proposals would involve redistributing resources to the *citizens* of poor countries, directly or indirectly, not necessarily to their governments, which might just spend the resources on military weapons or corruption. For proposals to open borders, as a way of reducing inequality, see Carens 1987; Bader 1995; Pogge 1997b. The latter option, while requiring less international coordination, is obviously insufficient since it is

often only the better off within poor countries who can afford to uproot themselves and travel to rich countries.

47. I should emphasize that the challenge of justifying closed borders does not just arise for liberal egalitarians—see Barry and Goodin 1992 for a collection of essays exploring this queston from various ethical perspectives, including libertarian, Marxist, natural law, etc. For other discussions of the ethics of open and closed borders, see Cole 2000; Schwartz 1995; Kershnar 2000.

48. See, e.g. Tamir 1993: 161; Tan 2000; Kymlicka 1995a: 224 n. 18.

49. For an interesting critique of the view that nationalism can be seen as a step in a series of 'expanding circles' of solidarity, see Miscevic 1999. He argues that while nationalist sentiments do not preclude concern for *distant* strangers, they do inhibit solidarity with *proximate* strangers—i.e. with the members of neighbouring national groups with whom there is typically a history of conflict or competition or invidious comparison.

50. For helpful attempts to break down the debate into different empirical issues, see Buchanan (1989) and Walzer (1990). For a philosophically informed attempt to provide empirical support for the communitarian position, see Bellah et al. (1985); but cf. Macedo (1988); Stout (1986).

7

CITIZENSHIP THEORY

The communitarian critique of liberalism had a dramatic impact on contemporary Anglo-American political philosophy. In the 1970s, the central concepts were justice and rights, as liberals attempted to define a coherent alternative to utilitarianism. In the 1980s, the keywords became community and membership, as communitarians attempted to show how liberal individualism was unable to account for, or to sustain, the communal sentiments, identities, and boundaries needed for any feasible political community.

It was perhaps inevitable that the next stage in the debate would be an attempt to transcend this opposition between liberal individualism and communitarianism, and to integrate the demands of liberal justice and community membership. One obvious candidate for this job is the idea of citizenship. Citizenship is intimately linked to liberal ideas of individual rights and entitlements on the one hand, and to communitarian ideas of membership in and attachment to a particular community on the other. Thus it provides a concept that can mediate the debate between liberals and communitarians.

It is not surprising, therefore, that there has been an explosion of interest in the concept of citizenship amongst political theorists. In 1978, it could be confidently stated that 'the concept of citizenship has gone out of fashion among political thinkers' (van Gunsteren 1978: 9). By 1990, citizenship was the 'buzzword' amongst thinkers on all points of the political spectrum (Heater 1990: 293; Vogel and Moran 1991: p. x).

Interest in citizenship has been sparked not only by these theoretical developments, but also by a number of recent political events and trends throughout the world—increasing voter apathy and long-term welfare dependency in the United States, the resurgence of nationalist movements in Eastern Europe, the stresses created by an increasingly multicultural and multiracial population in Western Europe, the backlash against the welfare state in Thatcher's England, the failure of environmental policies that rely on voluntary citizen cooperation, disaffection with globalization and the perceived loss of national sovereignty, etc.

These events have made clear that the health and stability of a modern democracy depends, not only on the justice of its basic institutions, but also on the qualities and attitudes of its citizens: e.g. their sense of identity, and how they view potentially competing forms of national, regional, ethnic, or religious identities; their ability to tolerate and work together with others who are different from themselves; their desire to participate in the political process in order to promote the public good and hold political authorities accountable; their willingness to show self-restraint and exercise personal responsibility in their economic demands, and in personal choices which affect their health and the environment. Without citizens who possess these qualities, democracies become difficult to govern, even unstable.[1] As Habermas notes, 'the institutions of constitutional freedom are only worth as much as a population makes of them' (Habermas 1992: 7).

Many classical liberals believed that a liberal democracy could function effectively even in the absence of an especially virtuous citizenry, by creating checks and balances. Institutional and procedural devices such as the separation of powers, a bicameral legislature, and federalism would all serve to block would-be oppressors. Even if each person pursued her own self-interest, without regard for the common good, one set of private interests would check another set of private interests. Kant, for example, thought that the problem of good government 'can be solved even for a race of devils' (quoted in Galston 1991: 215).[2] However, it has become clear that procedural-institutional mechanisms to balance self-interest are not enough, and that some level of civic virtue and public-spiritedness is required (Galston 1991: 217, 244; Macedo 1990: 138–9).

Consider the many ways that public policy relies on responsible personal lifestyle decisions: the state will be unable to provide adequate health care if citizens do not act responsibly with respect to their own health, in terms of maintaining a healthy diet, exercising regularly, and limiting their consumption of liquor and tobacco; the state will be unable to meet the needs of children, the elderly, or the disabled if citizens do not agree to share this responsibility by providing some care for their relatives; the state cannot protect the environment if citizens are unwilling to reduce, reuse, and recycle in their own consumer choices; the ability of the government to regulate the economy can be undermined if citizens borrow immoderate amounts or demand excessive salary increases; attempts to create a fairer society will flounder if citizens are chronically intolerant of difference and generally lacking in a sense of justice. Without cooperation and self-restraint in these areas, 'the ability of liberal societies to function successfully progressively diminishes' (Galston 1991: 220).

In short, we need 'a fuller, richer and yet more subtle understanding and practice of citizenship', because 'what the state needs from the citizenry cannot be secured by coercion, but only cooperation and self-restraint in the exercise of private power' (Cairns and Williams 1985: 43).

It is not surprising, therefore, that there should be increasing calls for 'a theory of citizenship'. Political theorists in the 1970s and 1980s focused primarily on what Rawls called the 'basic structure' of society: constitutional rights, political decision-making procedures, social institutions. Indeed, as I noted in Chapter 2, Rawls says that this 'basic structure' is the primary subject of a theory of justice (Rawls 1971: 7–11). Today, however, it is widely accepted that political theorists must also pay attention to the qualities and dispositions of the citizens who operate within these institutions and procedures. Hence political theorists in the 1990s have focused on the identity and conduct of individual citizens, including their responsibilities, loyalties, and roles.

The need for such a theory of citizenship received dramatic support from Robert Putnam's influential study of the performance of regional governments in Italy. He showed that these regional governments, set up in the postwar period, performed very differently, despite having more or less identical institutions. And it appears that the best explanation for the variation in performance was not differences in the income or education of the citizens, but rather in their civic virtue, what Putnam calls their 'social capital'—their ability to trust, their willingness to participate, their sense of justice (Putnam 1993).

While Putnam's particular study has been disputed (Sabetti 1996), the general point that the virtues and identities of citizens is an important and independent factor in democratic governance is now widely accepted. And it is also recognized that this requires political theorists to consider the need for what Sandel calls a 'formative project' or 'formative politics': i.e. for government policies to inculcate the appropriate sorts of qualities of character and civic virtues (Sandel 1996: 6, 305). And this in turn has led to a veritable flood of writings on issues of civic virtues and practices, civic participation, civic identities, and citizenship education.[3]

So a theory of citizenship is now widely seen as a necessary supplement to earlier theories of institutional justice. In fact, some suggest that the former eliminates or at least lessens the need for the latter. As the previous chapters make clear, there are deep and abiding disagreements over the norms of distributive justice, and over the appropriate forms of redistributive policies. This means that no single theory of justice can be expected to gain complete consensus in modern democratic societies. There is, therefore, relatively little point engaging in ever-greater refinements of these theories. What we should do instead is to develop better theories of democratic citizenship, which tell us how active, informed, and responsible citizens debate and resolve their disagreements, including disagreements over theories of instutitional justice (Fishkin 1996; Tully 2000: 469).

I am sceptical that theories of democratic citizenship can take the place of theories of justice. For one thing, as we will see, we need to appeal to principles of justice to help resolve disagreements about how to promote civic virtue and political participation. This means that disagreements about justice will spill over into disagreements about citizenship. Indeed, 'new' debates over citizenship are often 'old' debates over justice dressed up in new clothing. In any event, I will discuss theories of citizenship as an important supplement to, rather than a replacement for, theories of justice: theories of citizenship identify the virtues and practices needed to promote and maintain the sorts of institutions and policies defended within theories of justice.

In this chapter, I will examine some of the key issues relating to theories of citizenship. I will first try to clarify what sorts of virtues and practices are said to be required by democratic citizens (s. 1). In the literature, the term 'civic republican' is often used to describe anyone who takes seriously the need for civic virtue. But there are two very different forms of civic republicanism: a classical view which emphasizes the intrinsic value of political participation, and a liberal view which emphasizes its instrumental importance. I will compare these two views in sections 2 and 3, and then consider how liberal states can in fact try to promote the appropriate forms of citizenship virtues and practices (s. 4).

1. THE VIRTUES AND PRACTICES OF DEMOCRATIC CITIZENS

Before describing the new work on citizenship, it is necessary to quickly outline the view of citizenship that is implicit in much post-war political theory, and that is defined almost entirely in terms of the possession of rights. The most influential exposition of this post-war conception of citizenship-as-rights is T. H. Marshall's 'Citizenship and Social Class', written in 1949.[4] According to Marshall, citizenship is essentially a matter of ensuring that everyone is treated as a full and equal member of society. And the way to ensure this sense of membership is through according people an increasing number of citizenship rights.

Marshall divides citizenship rights into three categories which he sees as having taken hold in England in three successive centuries: civil rights, which arose in the eighteenth century; political rights, which arose in the nineteenth century; and social rights—e.g. to public education, health care, unemployment insurance, and old-age pension—which have become established in the twentieth century (Marshall 1965: 78 ff.).[5] And with the expansion of the rights of citizenship, he notes, there was also an expansion of the class of citizens. Civil and political rights that had been restricted to white property-owning Protestant men were gradually extended to women, the working class, Jews and Catholics, blacks, and other previously excluded groups.

For Marshall, the fullest expression of citizenship requires a liberal-democratic welfare state. By guaranteeing civil, political, and social rights to all, the welfare state ensures that every member of society feels like a full member of society, able to participate in and enjoy the common life of society. Where any of these rights are withheld or violated, people will be marginalized and unable to participate.

This is often called 'passive' or 'private' citizenship, because of its emphasis on passive entitlements, and the absence of any obligation to participate in public life. It is still widely supported. When asked what citizenship means to them, people are much more likely to talk about rights than responsibilities or participation. For most people, citizenship is, as the American Supreme Court once put it, 'the right to have rights'.[6]

It is quite understandable why people support this model of citizenship-as-rights. As Stephen Macedo puts it, 'the benefits of private citizenship are not to be sneezed at: they place certain basic human goods (security, prosperity, and freedom) within the grasp of nearly all, and that is nothing less than a fantastic human achievement' (Macedo 1990: 39).

Nevertheless, this orthodox post-war conception of citizenship has come increasingly under attack in the last decade. Many commentators argue that we need to supplement (or replace) the passive acceptance of citizenship rights with the active exercise of citizenship responsibilities and virtues, including economic self-reliance, political participation, and even civility. (Marshall's view has also been criticized for failing to properly recognize and accommodate the social and cultural pluralism of modern societies. I will discuss these calls for a more 'multicultural' or 'group-differentiated' model of citizenship in the next chapter on multiculturalism.)

The first task for theorists of citizenship was to specify more concretely the sorts of civic virtues required for a flourishing democracy. According to William Galston's influential account, responsible citizenship requires four types of civic virtues: (i) *general* virtues: courage; law-abidingness; loyalty; (ii) *social* virtues: independence; open-mindedness; (iii) *economic* virtues: work ethic; capacity to delay self-gratification; adaptability to economic and technological change; and (iv) *political* virtues: capacity to discern and respect the rights of others; willingness to demand only what can be paid for; ability to evaluate the performance of those in office; willingness to engage in public discourse (Galston 1991: 221–4).[7]

Many of these virtues—particularly the general and economic virtues—are needed in virtually any political order, whether it is large or small, agrarian or industrialized, democratic or authoritarian, pluralistic or homogeneous. For this reason, the concern with civic virtue is in fact a very old one in the history of Western political thought, even when political communities were much smaller and more homogeneous. But modern theories of citizenship must respond to the realities of contemporary pluralistic societies. The sorts of civic virtues required for a large, pluralistic modern society, and the appropriate means to promote them, may differ from those required for a small, homogeneous pre-modern city-state.

Thus much of the current debate has been focused on those virtues which are distinctive to modern pluralistic liberal democracies, relating to the basic principles of a liberal regime, and to the political role citizens occupy within it. These virtues include the ability and willingness to question political authority, and to engage in public discourse about matters of public policy. These are perhaps the most distinctive aspects of citizenship in a liberal democracy, since they are precisely what distinguish 'citizens' within a democracy from the 'subjects' of an authoritarian regime.

The need to question authority arises in part from the fact that citizens in a representative democracy elect representatives who govern in their name. Hence an important responsibility of citizens is to monitor those officials, and judge their conduct. The need to engage in public discourse arises from the fact that the decisions of government in a democracy should be made publicly, through free and open discussion. But the virtue of public discourse is not just the willingness to participate in politics, or to make one's views known. It also involves the willingness to engage in a conversation: to listen as well as to speak, to seek to understand what others say, and to respond respectfully to the views of others, so as to continue the conversation.[8]

As William Galston notes, this willingness to engage in public discourse is a complicated virtue. It 'includes the willingness to listen seriously to a range of views which, given the diversity of liberal societies, will include ideas the listener is bound to find strange and even obnoxious. The virtue of political discourse also includes the willingness to set forth one's own views intelligibly and candidly as the basis for a politics of persuasion rather than manipulation or coercion' (Galston 1991: 227).

This is often called the virtue of 'public reasonableness'. Liberal citizens must give reasons for their political demands, not just state preferences or make threats. Moreover, these reasons must be 'public' reasons, in the sense that they are capable of being understood and accepted by people of different faiths and cultures. Hence it is not enough to invoke Scripture or tradition. Liberal citizens must justify their political demands in terms that fellow citizens can understand and accept as consistent with their status as free and equal citizens. It requires a conscientious effort to distinguish those beliefs which are matters of private faith from those which are capable of public defence, and to see how issues look from the point of view of those with differing religious commitments and cultural backgrounds.

It is not always clear how we are to identify what qualifies as a 'public reason'—this has been a subject of great dispute.[9] And on most views, public reasons will not always be able to resolve the disputes between adherents of different religious and cultural traditions. At some point, the public reasons may simply run out, and we will be left with conflicting claims based on religious or cultural beliefs that are not publicly shareable. In these circumstances, we need to cultivate the related virtue of accommodation or compromise. For example, some commentators have suggested that public reasons may not be able to fully resolve disputes over abortion, and that the only reasonable response is therefore some sort of compromise.[10]

This particular conception of public reasonableness—one that requires citizens to consider which of their religious beliefs or cultural traditions are capable of public defence, and to seek honourable compromises when public reasons run out—is distinctly modern. Its prominence in the recent literature on citizenship is partly related to the recognition that modern societies are ethnically and religiously diverse.

But it also reflects another important shift in contemporary democratic theory, from 'vote-centric' to 'talk-centric' theories of democracy. In much of the post-war period, democracy was understood almost exclusively in terms of voting. Citizens were assumed to have a set of preferences, fixed prior to and independent of the political process, and the function of voting was simply to provide a fair decision-making procedure or aggregation mechanism for translating these pre-existing preferences into public decisions, either about who to elect (in standard elections) or about what laws to adopt (in issue-specific referenda).

But it is increasingly accepted that this 'aggregative' or 'vote-centric' conception of democracy cannot fulfil norms of democratic legitimacy. For one thing, since preferences are assumed to be formed independently of and prior to the political process, it provides no opportunity for citizens to try to persuade others of the merits of their views, or the legitimacy of their claims. Similarly, it provides no opportunity for citizens to distinguish claims based on self-interest, prejudice, ignorance, or fleeting whims from those grounded in principles of justice or fundamental needs. There is in fact no public dimension to the process at all. While citizens may need to physically leave their homes to go to the ballot box, the aggregative vote-centric model does not expect or encourage citizens to meet in public to discuss and debate their reasons for the claims they make. Indeed, with new technology, it is quite possible to have a form of aggregative democracy in which citizens never leave their home, and vote through the Internet.

As a result, the outcome of the aggregative model has only the thinnest veneer of legitimacy. It provides a mechanism for determining winners and losers, but no mechanism for developing a consensus, or shaping public opinion, or even formulating an honourable compromise. Consider citizens who believe that their claims are based on fundamental principles of justice, yet who are outvoted in an aggregative democracy. They have not been offered any reason for believing that they are mistaken about the justice of their claims. They have had no opportunity to persuade others of this claim, or to be persuaded by others that they are mistaken. They have simply been out-numbered. Many studies have shown that citizens will accept the legitimacy of collective decisions that go against them, but only if they think their arguments and reasons have been given a fair hearing, and that others have taken seriously what they have to say. But if there is no room for such a fair hearing, then people will question the legitimacy of decisions. This is particularly true for people belonging to a marginalized minority group, who know in advance that they have little hope of winning a majority vote. They may in effect be permanently excluded from exercising any real power within the system.

To overcome these shortcomings of the vote-centric approach, democratic theorists are increasingly focusing on the processes of deliberation and opinion formation that precede voting. Theorists have shifted their attention from what goes on in the voting booth to what goes on in the public deliberations of civil society. John Dryzek, one of the founders of this new model of democracy, calls this the 'deliberative turn' in democratic theory, which he dates to around 1990—not coincidentally, the same time as the turn towards theories of citizenship (Dryzek 2000: p. v).[11] A more deliberative democracy would, it is hoped, bring several benefits for society at large as well as for individuals and groups within society.[12] The collective benefits for society would include better decisions, since the decision-making process would draw forth the otherwise unarticulated knowledge and insights of citizens, and since citizens would test and discard those assumptions or beliefs which were found in public debate to be wrong or short-sighted or otherwise indefensible.[13] It would also lead to greater unity and solidarity in society. For one thing, political decision-making would be seen as more legitimate since everyone would have a fair chance to have their views heard and considered. Moreover, the very fact that people share the experience of deliberating in common provides a tangible bond that connects citizens and encourages greater mutual understanding and empathy. In a deliberative democracy, we would seek to change other people's behaviour only through non-coercive discussion of their claims, rather than through manipulation, indoctrination, propaganda, deception, or threats. This is a sign of mutual respect (Dryzek 2000: 2), or indeed of civic friendship (Blattberg 2000).

We might even hope that this shared deliberation would sometimes lead to greater agreement on various important issues, as seemingly implacable disagreements turn out to be based on misunderstandings or incomplete information, and that we would converge on a 'common ordering of individual needs and wants into a single vision of the future in which all can share'

(Barber 1984: 224). For most deliberative democrats, however, this sort of consensus is at best a happy but occasional by-product of deliberation, not its presupposition or goal—deliberating about our differences is not the same as eliminating our differences.[14]

(This means, of course, that deliberative democracy cannot entirely do away with the sorts of 'aggregative' procedures emphasized by the earlier model of democracy. At the end of the day, after the arguments are duly considered, some voting or electoral procedure is needed for resolving the remaining disagreements.)

So 'deliberative democracy' promises benefits to the larger society. But it offers particular benefits to minority or marginalized groups. If such groups are to have any real influence in a majoritarian electoral system, and any reason to accept the legitimacy of the system, it will be through participating in the formation of public opinion, rather than through winning a majority vote. As Simone Chambers puts it, 'voice rather than votes is the vehicle of empowerment' (Chambers 2001). This seems clear from the recent advances made by groups such as gays and lesbians, the deaf, or indigenous peoples, who account for less than 5 per cent of the overall electorate. Their empower-ment has largely come through participating in a public debate that has trans-formed the pre-existing assumptions held by members of the larger society about what is right and fair for these groups. If democracy is to help promote justice for these groups, rather than leaving them subject to the 'tyranny of the majority' (or the indifference and neglect of the majority), then democracy will have to be more deliberative. As a result, a wide range of theorists—liberals, communitarians, critical theorists, feminists, multiculturalists—have identified the need for greater deliberation as one of the key priorities for modern democracies.[15]

Much more could be said about this new deliberative model of democracy. In particular, what are the appropriate forums for deliberation? At what levels should these forums exist—local, national, or supranational? Should these forums be issue specific or general? How do we ensure that all groups and views are adequately represented in these forums? Is the goal to make existing mechanisms of voting, referenda, electoral representation, and judicial decision-making more deliberative, or to create new forums for deliberation, such as 'deliberative polls', 'citizen juries', town hall meetings, or constituent assemblies? Theorists have just begun to address these complex questions about the implementation of deliberative democracy. And it has become clear that the answers to these questions will depend, at least in part, on our theor-ies of justice.[16] Libertarians and liberal egalitarians will differ, for example, on whether campaign financing should be regulated to ensure an 'equal voice' in democratic deliberations.

The key point for us, however, is that this shift to a more deliberative model of democracy makes it even more urgent to attend to issues of civic virtue. On the aggregative model, citizens were assumed to act in a private and more or less self-interested way: any interaction with others was assumed to reflect strategic behaviour about how best to get one's way (e.g. through bargaining or log-rolling). On the deliberative model, however, citizens are assumed to act in public with the goal of mutual understanding, and not just to act strategically for personal benefit.[17] This is obviously a more demanding picture of the requirements of democratic citizenship. Democratic citizens must be not only active and participatory, critical of authority, and non-dogmatic, but also committed to seeking mutual understanding through deliberation rather than exclusively seeking personal benefit through bargaining or threats. Without citizens who display these virtues, liberal democracy cannot fulfil its promise of justice, and may indeed slowly succumb to undemocratic or illiberal forces.

Of course, it is not necessary that every citizen display all of these virtues to a high degree. A liberal democracy may not be possible for a society of devils, but nor does it require a society of angels. It would be more accurate to say that liberal justice requires a critical threshold: there must be a sufficient number of citizens who possess these virtues to a sufficient degree. Where to set this threshold is obviously a complicated question, which cannot be answered in the abstract.

But wherever we set the threshold, there are many people who think that we are dangerously close to falling below it. Moreover, the trends do not look good. There appears to be a general decline in people's commitment to public participation, respectful dialogue, or critical attention to government (Walzer 1992a: 90). Many people today seem to be alienated from, or simply indifferent to, the political process. According to a recent survey, for example, only 12 per cent of American teenagers said voting was important to being a good citizen. Moreover, this apathy is not just a function of youth—comparisons with similar surveys from the previous fifty years suggest that 'the current cohort knows less, cares less, votes less, and is less critical of its leaders and institutions than young people have been at any time over the past five decades' (Glendon 1991: 129). The evidence from Great Britain is similar (Heater 1990: 215).

What we see, in short, is growing awareness of the importance of civic virtues, at the same time as there is growing fear that these virtues are in decline. We see a growing emphasis on the need for people to be active citizens who participate in public deliberation, at the same time we see a trend toward greater apathy, passivity, and withdrawal into the private sphere of family, career and personal projects.

2. CIVIC REPUBLICANISM

How then can we overcome this 'syndrome of civic privatism' (Habermas 1996: 78), and encourage citizens to live up to the demands of democratic citizenship, and display the civic virtues it requires? This is the central question which has occupied the school of thought known as 'civic republicanism'. (The term 'republicanism' is not, of course, a reference to the Republican Party in the United States, but rather is intended to evoke images of the city-state republics of classical Athens and Rome or Renaissance Florence, which are widely believed to have successfully encouraged active and publicly spirited citizenship.)

However, civic republicans answer this question of how to promote active citizenship in very different ways. To oversimplify, we can say there are two camps within contemporary civic republicanism. One camp tries to persuade people to accept the burdens of democratic citizenship by persuading them that these are not in fact 'burdens'. The activities of political participation and public deliberation, on this view, should not be seen as a burdensome obligation or duty, but rather as intrinsically rewarding. People should happily embrace the call of democratic citizenship because the life of an active citizen is indeed the highest life available to us. We can call this the 'Aristotelian' interpretation of republicanism, since Aristotle was one of the first and most influential proponents of this view about the intrinsic value of political participation.

The second camp avoids making any claims about the intrinsic value of political participation, and accepts that for many people, the call of democratic citizenship may indeed be felt as a burden. It emphasizes however that there are powerful instrumental reasons why we should accept this burden, in order to maintain the functioning of our democratic institutions, and to preserve our basic liberties.[18]

I will discuss this 'instrumental' interpretation of republicanism in the next section. In this section, I will focus on the Aristotelian version. The distinguishing feature of this view is its emphasis on the intrinsic value of political participation for the participants themselves. Such participation is, in Adrian Oldfield's words, 'the highest form of human living-together that most individuals can aspire to' (Oldfield 1990b: 6). On this view, political life is superior to the merely private pleasures of family, neighbourhood, and profession, and so should occupy the centre of people's lives. Failure to participate in politics makes one a 'radically incomplete and stunted being' (Oldfield 1990a: 187; cf. Pocock 1992: 45, 53; Skinner 1992; Beiner 1992).

This is obviously another example of the sort of 'perfectionist' approach which I discussed last chapter, premised on a particular view about what makes lives truly excellent or truly human (Ch. 6, s. 4). Hence liberals will view it, like all forms of state perfectionism, as unfairly privileging one particular conception of the good life over others. I will return to this concern below. In any event, this view about the value of political participation is difficult to accept. As even its proponents admit, this view is markedly at odds with the way most people in the modern world understand the good life. Most people find the greatest happiness in their family life, work, religion, or leisure, not in politics. Some people find political participation fulfilling and satisfying, but for most people, it is seen as an occasional, and often burdensome, activity needed to ensure that government respects and supports their freedom to pursue these personal occupations and attachments. This assumption that politics is primarily a means to private life is shared by most people on all points of the political spectrum, whether the left (Ignatieff 1989: 72–3), right (Mead 1986: 254), liberals (Rawls 1971: 229–30), civil society theorists (Walzer 1989: 215), or feminists (Elshtain 1981: 327).

This in fact reflects one of the defining features of modern life, which is expressed in Benjamin Constant's famous distinction between ancient and modern freedom. The liberty of the ancients, Constant argued, was their active participation in the exercise of political power, not the peaceful enjoyment of personal independence. The Athenians were free men because they were collectively self-governing, although they lacked personal independence and civil liberties, and were expected to sacrifice their pleasures for the sake of the polis. The liberty of the moderns, on the other hand, lies in the unimpeded pursuit of happiness in their personal occupations and attachments, which requires freedom from the exercise of political power (typically through some set of constitutionally protected civil rights and liberties). Whereas the ancients sacrificed private liberty to promote political life, moderns view politics as a means (and somewhat of a sacrifice) needed to protect their private life.

Aristotelian republicans are trying, in effect, to reverse this historic shift, and to restore the primacy of the 'liberty of the ancients' to our conceptions of the good life. One can try to do this in two ways: either by celebrating the intrinsic value of political participation, or by denigrating the value of private life. Most Aristotelian republicans adopt a mixture of both strategies.

Some people have argued that the modern emphasis on 'private' life is antisocial, and a denial of our inherently social nature. According to Marx, for example, the individual rights emphasized by liberals are the freedoms of 'a man treated as an isolated monad withdrawn into himself . . . [T]he right of man to freedom is not based on the union of man with man, but on the separation of man from man. It is the right to this separation' (Marx 1977b: 53). Aristotelian republicans similarly complain that the liberal valorizing of 'private' life is a form of 'atomism', and defend political participation as a way of fulfilling our intrinsic human need for social bonds and relationships.

In fact, however, as we saw in the previous chapter, the flip side of liberalism's distrust of politics is its positive endorsement of social life and civil society. As Nancy Rosenblum notes, the liberal view of private liberty actually presupposes our natural sociability:

> Private life means life in civil society, not some presocial state of nature or antisocial condition of isolation and detachment . . . private liberty provides escape from the surveillance and interference of public officials, multiplying possibilities for private associations and combinations . . . far from inviting apathy, private liberty is supposed to encourage public discussion and the formation of groups that give individuals access to wider social contexts and access to government. (Rosenblum 1987: 61)

When the state leaves people in the 'perfect independence' of private life, it does not leave them in isolation, but rather leaves them free to form and maintain 'associations and combinations', or what Rawls calls 'free social unions'. Because we are social animals, individuals will use their freedom to join with others in the pursuit of shared ends. Modern freedom, for Constant, was indeed based on the 'union of man with man', but he believed that the union of men arising from free association in civil society was more genuine, and more free, than the coerced unity of political associations. The liberal ideal of private life was not to protect the individual from society, but to free society from political interference. It is more accurate to view liberalism, not as antisocial, but as 'the glorification of society', for liberals 'rated social life the highest form of human achievement and the vital condition for the development of morality and rationality', while the political was reduced to 'the harsh symbol of the coercion necessary to sustain orderly social transactions' (Wolin 1960: 363, 369, 291; cf. Holmes 1989: 248; Schwartz 1979: 245).

To defend Aristotelian republicanism, therefore, it is not enough to show that individuals require society to lead a truly human life—liberals do not deny this. Aristotelian republicans must go beyond this and show that individuals need to be politically active. As we saw in Chapter 6 (s. 8), this distinction between participating in society and participating in politics has often been obscured by communitarian critiques of liberal 'atomism'. But when Aristotle said that men were *zoon politikon*, he did not mean simply that men are *social* animals. On the contrary, 'the natural, merely social companionship of the human species was considered to be a limitation imposed upon us by the needs of biological life, which are the same for the human animal as for other forms of animal life' (Arendt 1959: 24). Political life, on the other hand, was different from, and higher than, our merely social life.

Aristotelian republicans have made attempts to challenge the liberal glorification of society, and to reinstate politics as a higher form of life. But the liberal view pervades the modern age. Whereas the Greeks felt that 'under no circumstances could politics be only a means to protect society', modern theorists assume that politics should serve society, although they disagree on what kind of society politics should serve. It may be 'a society of the faithful, as in the middle ages, or a society of property-owners, as in Locke, or a society relentlessly engaged in a process of acquisition, as in Hobbes, or a society of producers, as in Marx, or a society of job-holders, as in our society, or a society of labourers, as in socialist and communist countries. In all these cases, it is the freedom . . . of society which requires and justifies the restraint of political authority. Freedom is located in the realm of the social, and force or violence becomes the monopoly of government' (Arendt 1959: 31). This is one of those cases, like the commitment to moral equality, where liberalism has simply won the historical debate, and all subsequent debate occurs, in a sense, within the boundaries of basic liberal commitments.

In order to explain the modern indifference to the intrinsic value of polit-ical participation, republicans often argue that political life today has become impoverished, compared to the active citizenship of, say, ancient Greece. Polit-ical life has become too large in scale, or too manipulated by money, or too stage-managed by the media, or too dominated by 'experts', to be rewarding for most citizens. On this view, if we could create forums for political action at a more human scale (like the face-to-face politics of ancient Athens), and prevent these forums from being colonized by the imperatives of money, media entertainment, or bureaucratic expertise, then people would find polit-ics much more rewarding than they do now. And this republican argument for smaller-scale political forums nicely dovetails with the arguments of delibera-tive democrats, who also endorse such forums as the best way to put 'public talk' rather than 'private voting' at the heart of the political process.

On this view, the main problem facing Aristotelian republicanism is essen-tially a problem of *transition*. If deliberative democratic forums were already in place, then people would find it rewarding to participate in them. But how do we get from here to there? The people who currently benefit from the rule of money, expertise, and media ratings are not going to voluntarily give up their positions of power. So the needed political reforms will only occur if average citizens participate and mobilize for reforms that will strengthen their role in the political process. But since existing political institutions are frustrating and stultifying, few people are willing to participate.[19]

My own view, however, is that even if these more deliberative forums were created, there would still be many people who would find political life a sacrifice. Aristotelian republicans assume that people have turned away from political participation because they find politics unfulfilling. Our attachment to private life, I believe, is the result, not (or not only) of the impoverishment of public life, but of the enrichment of private life. We no longer seek gratification in politics because our personal and social life is so much richer than that of the ancient Greeks.

There are many reasons for this historical change, including the rise of romantic love and the nuclear family (and its emphasis on intimacy and privacy); increased prosperity (and hence richer forms of leisure and consumption); the Christian commitment to the dignity of labour (which the Greeks despised); and the growing dislike for war (which the Greeks esteemed). The Greeks viewed the private sphere as a sphere of 'privation' (this indeed is the origin of the word 'private'), and saw little of value in it (if indeed they had any comparable concept of the 'private' at all). But we 'moderns' can find immense joys in intimacy, love, leisure, consumption, and work.

Aristotelian republicans insist that those passive citizens who find greater pleasure in the joys of family and career than in politics are somehow misguided and 'stunted'. But what is the basis for such a claim? I do not believe that Aristotelian republicans have offered any plausible defence of their conception of the good life. For example, after asserting that political life is 'the highest form of human living-together that most individuals can aspire to', Oldfield goes on to say: 'I shall not argue for this moral point. It has in any case been argued many times within the corpus of civic republican writing' (1990b: 6). But as I have just noted, these historical defences of the primacy of political life emerged at a time when people saw the private sphere as a sphere of privation. As Galston puts it, Aristotelian republicans who denigrate private life as tedious and self-absorbed show no delight in real communities of people, and indeed are 'contemptuous' of everyday life (Galston 1991: 58–63).[20] (As we will see in Chapter 9, this Aristotelian republican contempt for the private sphere is also historically tied up with contempt for women—see Vogel 1991: 68; Young 1989: 253; Phillips 1991: 49; 2000).

Aristotelian republicanism is sometimes called a form of 'communitarianism', and indeed it can be seen as a kind of second-order communitarianism. On the traditional communitarian view of a 'politics of the common good', people enter politics in order to promote certain *already-existing* shared ends, based on a common faith or traditional way of life. Aristotelian republicanism, by contrast, need not assume that people have any pre-political common ends. It can accept the fact that people in their private life do not share a common set of ends, and that there will be no consensus amongst citizens about the appropriate goals of public policy. It assumes, however, that political participation itself can come to be seen as the shared good. The 'common good' to be promoted through political participation is not some pre-political cultural practice or tradition, but the intrinsic value of political participation itself.

But any such attempt to privilege a single conception of the good life is bound to fail in modern societies. Given the deep and enduring differences amongst citizens in their views of the good life, we cannot expect a consensus on the intrinsic value of political activities, or the relative importance of political activities as compared to activities in the social or personal sphere. People disagree not only about the value of pre-political practices and traditions, but also about the intrinsic value of political participation itself. The 'fact of pluralism' defeats not only traditional communitarianism, but also the revival of Aristotelian republicanism.[21]

3. INSTRUMENTAL VIRTUES

As a result, liberals cannot accept the doctrine of Aristotelian republicanism. This doctrine could only be implemented through a coercive form of state perfectionism, in which the government pre-empts and constrains individuals' own judgements about the good life. This violates liberal commitments to individual autonomy and state neutrality.

However, this does not mean that liberals can be indifferent to the quality or quantity of political participation. On the contrary, as we have seen, liberal democracy and liberal justice require a critical threshold of active and responsible participation. For liberals, however, these virtues are defended and promoted precisely in terms of their *instrumental* importance in sustaining just institutions, rather than in terms of their intrinsic value for participants.

Rawls distinguishes between republicanism and 'civic humanism'. According to republicanism, certain political virtues must be promoted amongst citizens in order to prevent the degeneration of liberal democracy into tyranny or religious/nationalist fanaticism. Rawls notes that this justification for promoting civic virtues is entirely consistent with his view of liberalism, since virtues are defended as preconditions for liberal justice. By contrast, 'civic humanism' (or what I have called Aristotelian republicanism) asserts that political virtues should be promoted because our 'essential nature' is realized in political life, which is the 'privileged locus of the good life'. As Rawls notes, there is a 'fundamental opposition' between liberal egalitarianism and civic humanism, since civic humanists defend virtues on the basis of a particular conception of the good life, not on grounds of justice.[22]

So liberals will offer a different, more modest and more instrumental, account of civic virtue. On this account, it is accepted that people will have differing views about the intrinsic value of political participation, and that some people will find their greatest joys and projects in other areas of life, including the family, work, the arts, or religion. A liberal democracy must respect such diverse conceptions of the good life, as far as possible, and should not compel people to adopt a conception of the good life which privileges political participation as the source of meaning or satisfaction.

Therefore, liberals, while concerned to ensure a critical threshold of active citizenship, will accept that many people are more or less apolitical, and will try to limit the demands of active citizenship so as to accommodate these conceptions of the good life. To be sure, liberal citizens should recognize an obligation to create just institutions where these are absent, or to uphold these institutions where they are threatened. But this obligation is, for many people, an episodic one, strongest in times of crises, constitutional change, or external threat.[23] If there are serious injustices in our society which can only be rectified by political action, then citizens should recognize an obligation to protest against that injustice. Or if our political institutions are no longer functioning, perhaps due to excessive levels of apathy, or to the abuse of power, then citizens have an obligation to protect these institutions from being undermined. To sit passively by while injustices are committed, or democratic institutions collapse, in the hope that others will step in, is to be a free-rider. Everyone should do their fair share to create and uphold just institutions.

However, the extent of injustice, and the health of political institutions, will vary from time to time, and from society to society. In some times and places, though perhaps only in fortunate circumstances, our natural duty of justice will not require us to participate actively. Where a society is basically well ordered, and its institutions healthy, then individuals should be free to follow their own conceptions of the good, even if these give little or no weight to political participation.

So there will be times and places where minimal citizenship is all that we can or should require. In one sense, this reduces the need for civic virtue. For example, the stringent demands of 'public reasonableness' will be less significant for those who do not participate politically. But in another sense, the liberal commitment to civil society as the arena for pursuing the good life generates its own issues of civic virtue. Just as the state cannot function properly without some threshold of *political* virtues amongst active citizens (such as public reasonableness, and a critical attitude to authority), so too civil society cannot function properly without some threshold of *social* virtues amongst passive citizens.

The obligations of passive or minimal citizenship are often described in purely negative terms—i.e. the obligation not to break the law, and not to harm others, or restrict their rights and liberties. Minimal citizenship, in short, is often seen as simply requiring non-interference with others (e.g. McLaughlin 1992a). But that ignores one of the most basic requirements of liberal citizenship, which is the social virtue of 'civility' or 'decency'. This is a virtue that even the most minimal citizen must learn, since it applies not only to political activity, but also—indeed, primarily—to our actions in everyday life, on the street, in neighbourhood shops, and in the diverse institutions and forums of civil society.

Civility refers to the way we treat non-intimates with whom we come into face-to-face contact. To understand civility, it is helpful to compare it with the related requirement of non-discrimination. The legal prohibition on discrimination initially only applied to government actions. Government laws and policies which discriminated against people on the basis of race or gender have gradually been struck down in Western democracies, since they violate the basic liberal commitment to equality of opportunity. But it has become clear that whether individuals have genuinely equal opportunity depends not only on government actions, but also on the actions of institutions within civil society—corporations, schools, stores, landlords, etc. If people are discriminated against by prejudiced shop-owners or real-estate agents, they will be denied equal citizenship, even if the state itself does not discriminate. Hence legal requirements of non-discrimination have increasingly been applied to 'private' firms and associations.

This extension of non-discrimination from government to civil society is not just a shift in the scale of liberal norms, it also involves a radical extension in the obligations of liberal citizenship. For the obligation to treat people as equal citizens now applies to the most common everyday decisions of individuals. It is no longer permissible for businesses to refuse to hire black employees, or serve black customers, or to segregate their black employees or customers. But not just that. The norms of non-discrimination also entail that it is impermissible for businesses to ignore their black customers, or treat them rudely, although it is not always possible to enforce this legally. Businesses must in effect make blacks feel welcome, just as if they were whites. Blacks must, in short, be treated with *civility*. The same applies to the way citizens treat each other in schools or recreational associations, even in private clubs.

This sort of civility is the logical extension of non-discrimination, since it is needed to ensure that all citizens have the same opportunity to participate within civil society. But it now extends into the very hearts and minds of citizens. Liberal citizens must learn to interact in everyday settings on an equal basis with people for whom they might harbour prejudice.

The extent to which this requirement of civility can (or should) be legally enforced is limited. It is easier to compel businesses to be non-discriminatory in hiring than to compel them to treat black customers with civility. But the recent spread of laws and regulations against sexual and racial harassment, both in society generally and within schools and businesses, can be seen as an attempt to ensure a level of civility, since they include forms of hate speech as well as physical intimidation. And while it is obviously impossible to compel civility between citizens in less formal settings—e.g. whether whites smile or scowl at an Asian family in the neighbourhood park—liberal citizenship nonetheless requires this sort of civility.

It is easy to trivialize this requirement of civility as being simply 'good manners'. Philip Rieff, for example, dismisses the insistence on civility as a superficial façade that simply hides a deeper indifference to the needs of others. As he puts it, 'We have long known what "equality" means in American culture: it means . . . a smile fixed to the face, demanding you return a smile' (quoted in Cuddihy 1978: 6). John Murray Cuddihy views civility as the imposition of a Protestant (and bourgeois) sense of 'good taste' on other religious groups. He argues that Catholics and Jews (and now Muslims) have had to abandon their conception of true faith, which required the public expression of contempt for other religions, to conform to this 'religion of civility'.

It is true that in liberal societies the moral obligation of civility is sometimes confused with an aesthetic conception of 'good manners'. For example, the expectation of civility is sometimes used to discourage the sort of forceful protest that may be needed for an oppressed group to be heard. For a disadvantaged group to 'make a scene' is often seen as 'in bad taste'. This sort of exaggerated emphasis on good manners can be used to promote servility. True civility does not mean smiling at others no matter how badly they treat you, as if oppressed groups should be nice to their oppressors. Rather, it means treating others as equals on the condition that they extend the same recognition to you. While there is some overlap between civility and a more general politeness, they are nonetheless distinct—civility involves upholding norms of equality within the public life of a society, including civil society, and thereby upholding essential liberal values.[24]

4. THE SEEDBEDS OF CIVIC VIRTUE

So even if we reject Aristotelian republicanism, any plausible political theory must still have an *instrumental* concern for civic virtues. In particular, any theory concerned with democratic legitimacy and social justice must be concerned about the virtue of public reasonableness in political life, and the virtue of civility in civil society. Both of these virtues are needed for citizens to fulfil their natural duty of justice to create and uphold just institutions. Without such virtues, liberal democracy would be unable to achieve either justice or stability.

But how can we ensure that these instrumental virtues will be present? As Baier notes, 'lists of productive virtues . . . do not tell us how to bring those virtues into being' (Baier 1994: 222). And as we have seen, many people worry that Western democracies are falling below the critical threshold for civic virtue, with declining levels of participation and civility. What can be done to reverse these trends? What sort of 'formative project' can states undertake to promote these virtues (Sandel 1996: 6)?

One approach would be to try to impose a legal duty on people to exhibit these virtues. We might pass a law requiring everyone to vote, for example, or attend monthly neighbourhood meetings to discuss political affairs. There are a few countries which have such laws: Australia has a mandatory voting law; South Korea has a mandatory neighbourhood meeting law. But these are rather heavy-handed attempts to overcome 'civic privatism', and would do nothing by themselves to ensure that people participate actively or responsibly. Indeed, forcing citizens to engage in political activities they dislike may simply increase their resentment at the political process. In any event, it is difficult to see how the more diffuse virtues of civility or public reasonableness could be legally codified.

One might hope that the very act of political participation itself will teach people responsibility and toleration. Even if initially entered into involuntarily or grudgingly, political participation will expose people to new ideas and develop new sympathies and identities. This is a familiar theme in democratic theory, going back at least to Rousseau and J. S. Mill, who believed that political participation 'enlarges the minds of individuals, familiarizes them with interests which lie beyond the immediacy of personal circumstance and environment, and encourages them to acknowledge that public concerns are the proper ones to which they should pay attention' (Oldfield 1990a: 184).

Unfortunately, this faith in the educative function of participation seems overly optimistic. Emphasizing participation does not yet explain how to ensure that citizens participate responsibly—i.e. in a public-spirited, rather than self-interested or prejudiced, way (Mulgan 1991: 40–1). Empowered citizens may use their power irresponsibly by pushing for benefits and entitlements society cannot ultimately afford; or by voting themselves tax breaks and slashing assistance to the needy; or by 'seeking scapegoats in the indolence of the poor, the strangeness of ethnic minorities, or the insolence and irresponsibility of modern women' (Fierlbeck 1991: 592).

It is true that successful political participation requires the ability to create coalitions, which encourages a partial development of the virtues of justice and public reasonableness. No one can succeed in political life if they make no effort to listen to or accommodate the needs and views of others. But in many cases, a winning coalition can be built while ignoring the claims of marginalized groups. Indeed, if a significant portion of the population is prejudiced, then ignoring or attacking such groups may be the best route to political success.

So merely compelling political participation is unlikely to be a satisfactory solution to the problem of civic virtues. Instead, most scholars working on this topic have assumed that civic virtue must be promoted indirectly. Rather than have a state-imposed duty of participation or civic virtue, the approach has been to try to locate and strengthen the 'seedbeds of civic virtue'. The goal is to identify those social institutions and practices which inculcate civic virtue, and then to see how these institutions and practices can be protected and strengthened.

What are the seedbeds of civic virtue? There are a variety of aspects of liberal society that can be seen as inculcating civic virtues, including the market, civic associations, and the family. Let me briefly look at each of these.

Theorists of the 'New Right' often praise the market as a school of civic virtue. Many Thatcher/Reagan reforms of the 1980s aimed to extend the scope of markets in people's lives—through freer trade, deregulation, tax cuts, the weakening of trade unions, and reducing welfare benefits—in part in order to teach people the virtues of initiative and self-reliance. As we saw in Chapter 4, much of the recent right-wing attack on the welfare state has been formulated precisely in terms of citizenship. The welfare state was said to promote passivity amongst the poor, creating a culture of dependency, reducing citizens to passive dependants under bureaucratic tutelage. The market, by contrast, encourages people to be self-supporting. The New Right believes that being self-supporting is not only an important civic virtue in itself, but also a precondition for being accepted as a full member of society. By failing to meet the obligation to support themselves, the long-term unemployed are a source of shame for society as well as themselves (Mead 1986: 240).[25] Failure to fulfil common obligations is as much an obstacle to full membership in society as the lack of equal rights. In these circumstances, 'To obligate the dependent as others are obligated is essential to equality, not opposed to it. An effective welfare [policy] must include recipients in the common obligations of citizens rather than exclude them' (Mead 1986: 12 f.).

According to the New Right, to promote active citizenship for all, we must go beyond Marshall's emphasis on citizenship-as-rights or entitlements, and focus instead on people's responsibility to earn a living. Since the welfare state erodes this responsibility the safety net should be cut back, and any remaining welfare benefits should have obligations tied to them, for example, through 'workfare' programmes, which require welfare recipients to work for their benefits, so as to reinforce the idea that citizens should be self-supporting.

So markets are seen as promoting a variety of important virtues: self-reliance, initiative, and full membership. Moreover, markets are said to encourage civility, since companies which refuse to hire black employees, or serve black customers, will be at a competitive disadvantage.

However, the limits of the market as a school of civic virtue are clear. Many market deregulations arguably made possible an era of unprecedented greed and economic irresponsibility, as evidenced by the savings-and-loan and junk bond scandals in America. Markets teach initiative, but not a sense of justice or social responsibility (Mulgan 1991: 39). And so long as a sizeable portion of the population harbours prejudices towards certain groups, then businesses will have an economic incentive to serve that market, by creating goods and services that exclude these groups.[26] In any event, the market cannot teach those civic virtues specific to political participation and dialogue—e.g. the virtue of public reasonableness.

'Civil-society theorists' emphasize the necessity of civility and self-restraint to a healthy democracy, but deny that either the market or political participation is sufficient to teach these virtues. Instead, it is in the voluntary organizations of civil society—churches, families, unions, ethnic associations, cooperatives, environmental groups, neighbourhood associations, support groups, charities—that we learn the virtues of mutual obligation. As Michael Walzer puts it, 'The civility that makes democratic politics possible can only be learned in the associational networks' of civil society (Walzer 1992a: 104).

Because these groups are voluntary, failure to live up to the responsibilities that come with them is usually met simply with disapproval, rather than legal punishment. Yet because the disapproval comes from family, friends, colleagues, or comrades, it is in many ways a more powerful incentive to act responsibly than punishment by an impersonal state. It is here that 'human character, competence, and capacity for citizenship are formed', for it is here that we internalize the idea of personal responsibility and mutual obligation, and learn the voluntary self-restraint which is essential to truly responsible citizenship (Glendon 1991: 109).

The claim that civil society is the 'seedbed of civic virtue' (Glendon 1991: 109; 1995) is essentially an empirical claim, for which there is little hard evidence one way or the other. It is an old and venerable view, but it is not obviously true. It may be in the neighbourhood that we learn to be good neighbours, but neighbourhood associations also teach people to operate on the 'NIMBY' (not in my backyard) principle when it comes to the location of group homes or public works.[27] Similarly, the family is often 'a school of despotism' that teaches male dominance over women (Okin 1992: 65); churches often teach deference to authority and intolerance of other faiths; ethnic groups often teach prejudice against other races, and so on.

Walzer recognizes that most people are 'trapped in one or another subordinate relationship, where the "civility" they learn is deferential rather than independent and active'. In these circumstances, he says, we have to 'reconstruct' the associational network 'under new conditions of freedom and equality'. Similarly, when the activities of some associations 'are narrowly conceived, partial and particularist', then 'they need political correction'. Walzer calls his view 'critical associationalism' to signify that the associations of civil society may need to be reformed in the light of principles of citizenship (Walzer 1992a: 106–7).

But this may go too far in the other direction. Rather than supporting voluntary associations, this approach may unintentionally license wholesale intervention in them. It is one thing for governments to intervene to protect the rights of people inside and outside the group, if these rights are threatened. But do we want governments to reconstruct churches, for example, to make them more internally democratic, or to make sure that their members learn to be critical rather than deferential? And, in any event, wouldn't reconstructing churches, families, or unions to make them more internally democratic start to undermine their essentially uncoerced and voluntary character, which is what supposedly made them the seedbeds of civic virtue?

Indeed, it would be unreasonable to expect churches to teach the virtue of public reasonableness. Public reasonableness is essential in political debate, but is unnecessary and sometimes undesirable in the private sphere. It would be absurd to ask church-goers to abstain from appealing to Scripture in deciding how to run their church.

Civil-society theorists demand too much of voluntary associations in expecting them to be the main school for, or a small-scale replica of, democratic citizenship. While these associations may teach civic virtue, that is typically not their *raison d'être*. The reason why people join churches, families, or ethnic organizations is not to learn civic virtue. It is rather to honour certain values, and enjoy certain human goods, and these motives may have little to do with the promotion of citizenship. To expect parents or priests to organize the internal life of their groups so as to maximally promote citizenship is to ignore why these groups exist in the first place. (Some associations, like the Boy Scouts, are designed to promote citizenship, but they are the exception not the rule.)[28]

A similar issue arises with theorists of 'maternal citizenship', who focus on the family, and mothering in particular, as the school of responsibility and virtue. According to Jean Elshtain and Sara Ruddick, mothering teaches women about the responsibility to conserve life and protect the vulnerable, and these lessons should become the guiding principles of political life as well. For example, mothering involves a 'metaphysical attitude' of 'holding', which gives priority to the protection of existing relationships over the acquisition of new benefits (Ruddick 1987: 242). This has obvious implications for decisions about war or the environment.

I will discuss these theories of maternal citizenship, and related accounts of 'the ethics of care', in Chapter 9. However, it is doubtful whether mothering involves the same attributes or virtues as democratic citizenship, and some critics have argued that there is no evidence that maternal attitudes such as 'holding' promote democratic values such as 'active citizenship, self-government, egalitarianism, and the exercise of freedom' (Dietz 1985: 30; Nauta 1992: 31; Mouffe 1992a). As Dietz puts it, 'An enlightened despotism, a welfare-state, a single-party bureaucracy and a democratic republic may all respect mothers, protect children's lives and show compassion for the vulnerable' (Dietz 1992: 76). Similarly, it is difficult to see how the virtues appropriate for the intimate relation between mother and child can be translated into the virtues needed in the anonymous settings of civil society or political participation, such as civility and public reasonableness.

It seems then that we cannot rely on the market, the family, or the associations of civil society to teach the full range of civic virtues. Each teaches us certain important virtues, but also certain dispositions which may be vices when exercised in the political domain. In any event, people are unlikely to learn the specifically political virtues of public reasonableness and scepticism of authority in any of these spheres, since these spheres are often held together by private discourse and respect for authority. Some publicly spirited parents or associations may deliberately take on the task of trying to promote these political virtues, but there is no guarantee they will do so, and it would clearly be inappropriate and impermissible for the government to intervene in families or churches to force them to do so.

Where then do we learn these virtues? The answer, according to many recent theorists, is the system of education. Schools must teach children how to engage in the kind of critical reasoning and moral perspective that defines public reasonableness. And indeed, promoting these sorts of virtues is one of the fundamental justifications for mandatory education. As Amy Gutmann puts it, children at school 'must learn not just to behave in accordance with authority but to think critically about authority if they are to live up to the democratic ideal of sharing political sovereignty as citizens'. People who 'are ruled only by habit and authority . . . are incapable of constituting a society of sovereign citizens' (Gutmann 1987: 51).

Of course, there is nothing intrinsic to schooling that guarantees that it will do any better than families or churches in promoting political virtues. On the contrary, schools historically have often been used to promote deference, chauvinism, xenophobia, and other illiberal and undemocratic vices. But many scholars today believe that schools can be (re)organized to be effective seedbeds of civic virtues that may not be learned elsewhere. Moreover, of all the institutions which influence young people's beliefs and dispositions— schools, media, families, churches—there are fewest objections to state regulation of schools (Weinstock 2001). Freedom of expression and the press limit state control over the media; freedom of conscience limits state control of churches, and privacy rights limit state regulation of the family. Hence there is an almost overwhelming tendency in modern liberal societies to look to the schools as the remedy for all of our behavioural social ills (e.g. teenage pregnancy; smoking; obesity; racism; and so on).

However, this idea that schools should teach children to be sceptical of political authority, and to distance themselves from their own cultural traditions when engaging in public discourse, is controversial. Traditionalists object to it on the grounds that it inevitably leads children to question tradition and parental or religious authority in private life. And that is surely correct. As Gutmann admits, education for democratic citizenship will inevitably involve 'equipping children with the intellectual skills necessary to evaluate ways of life different from that of their parents', because 'many if not all of the capacities necessary for choice among good lives are also necessary for choice among good societies' (Gutmann 1987: 30, 40).

Hence those cultural or religious groups which rely heavily for their survival on an uncritical acceptance of tradition and authority 'are bound to be discouraged by the free, open, pluralistic, progressive' attitudes which liberal education encourages (Macedo 1990: 53–4). This is why groups such as the Amish have sought to remove their children from the school system, either by seeking to establish separate religious schools or home schooling, or by seeking exemption from certain aspects of the curriculum where these liberal virtues are learned and practised (e.g. exemptions from sex education, or from integrated physical education classes).[29]

Some theorists worry that separate religious schools cannot provide an adequate education in either civility or public reasonableness, even if these virtues are included in the curriculum. For these virtues are not only, or even primarily, learned through the explicit curriculum, but rather through the 'hidden curriculum'—i.e. the general environment and infrastructure of schools (Gutmann 1987: 53). For example, common schools teach civility not just by telling students the moral value of civility, but also by insisting that students sit beside students of different races and religions, and cooperate with them on school projects or sports teams. Similarly, common schools teach public reasonableness not only by telling students that there are a plurality of religious views in the world, and that reasonable people disagree on the merits of these views. They also create the social circumstances whereby students can see the reasonableness of these disagreements. It is not enough to simply tell students that the majority of the people in the world do not share their religion. So long as one is surrounded by people who share one's faith, one may still succumb to the temptation to think that everyone who rejects one's religion is somehow illogical or depraved. To learn public reasonableness, students must come to know and understand people who are reasonable and decent and humane, but who do not share their religion. Only in this way can students learn how personal faith differs from public reasonableness, and where to draw that line. This sort of learning requires the presence within a classroom of people with varying ethnocultural and religious backgrounds.

This suggests that the ideal of liberal education involves some degree of detachment from the student's home community or culture, and interaction with people from other communities and cultures. Meira Levinson calls this the ideal of the 'detached school' (Levinson 1999). This need not involve a complete rejection of the idea of separate schooling or home schooling, but would require finding at least some room or stage in the education process for a more integrated school environment. It might involve separate schooling at an earlier age, for example, and then integrated education in secondary school. Or it might involve student or teacher exchange programmes. As Eamonn Callan puts it, 'The essential demand is that schooling properly involves at some stage sympathetic and critical engagement with beliefs and ways of life at odds with the culture of the family or religious or ethnic group into which the child was born' (Callan 1997: 133).[30]

Yet it is clear that many conservative religious groups will resist any such attempt to give their children a sympathetic engagement with other religions or lifestyles. Some groups like the Amish seek to avoid any contact with members of other faiths; other groups accept common schooling but oppose any attempt to include in the common curriculum discussion of lifestyles at odds with their own beliefs (e.g. homosexuality). This refusal to engage with other ways of life may jeopardize the development of certain civic virtues needed for the functioning of the modern state, but this argument is unlikely to persuade conservative religious groups, since many of them view the modern secular state as itself an instrument of wickedness in the world.

This creates a dilemma for liberals, many of whom wish to accommodate peaceful and law-abiding groups like the Amish. This is particularly true of the political liberals I discussed in the last chapter. To impose 'our' liberal values on groups which reject them is seen as 'sectarian' (see Ch. 6, s. 7). These political liberals will want to adjust citizenship education to minimize the impact on parental and religious authority. William Galston, for example, argues that the need to teach children how to engage in public discourse and to evaluate political leaders 'does not warrant the conclusion that the state must (or may) structure public education to foster in children sceptical reflec-tion on ways of life inherited from parents or local communities' (Galston 1991: 253; cf. Rawls 1988: 267–8). However, he admits that it is not easy for schools to promote a child's willingness to question political authority with-out undermining her 'unswerving belief in the correctness' of her parents' way of life.

Should a liberal state require some degree of integrated schooling in the name of citizenship education? In answering this, it is worth distinguishing two kinds of religious groups that might seek exemption from common schooling. Some groups, like the Amish, voluntarily isolate themselves from the larger society, and avoid participating in either politics or the mainstream institutions of civil society. They do not vote, or hire employees, or attempt to influence public policy (except where a proposed policy would jeopardize their isolation), and seek only to be left alone. Since they do not participate in either politics or civil society, it is less urgent that they learn the virtues of civility and public reasonableness. Jeff Spinner calls the Amish 'partial citizens', and he argues that because they have relinquished the right to participate, they can also be absolved of the responsibilities which accompany that right, including the responsibility to learn and practise civility and public reasonableness (Spinner 1994: 98). Hence he supports their right to withdraw their children from school at the age of 14, before they would have to learn about the larger society, or interact with non-Amish children. Assuming that such groups are small, and sincerely committed to their self-imposed isolation, they pose no threat to the practice of liberal citizenship in society generally. Such groups should not be encouraged, since they accept no responsibility to work together with other citizens to solve the country's injustices and problems. They are free-riders, in a sense, benefiting from a stable liberal order that they do nothing to help maintain.[31] But a liberal state can afford a few such free-riders.[32]

By contrast, other religious groups seeking exemption from integrated schools are active participants in both civil society and politics, and seek to influence public policy generally. This would include fundamentalist Christians in the United States, or fundamentalist Muslims in Britain. In these cases, one could argue that, having chosen to exercise their rights as full citizens, they must accept the sort of education needed to promote responsible citizenship, including the obligation to engage sympathetically with other ways of life at some point in the educational process.

There are difficult practical as well as philosophical questions here about the role of schools in inculcating virtues. On the one hand, schools could fill an important gap by teaching certain political virtues that are not guaranteed to be learned in families or private associations. But schools are part of the larger society, and it would be a mistake to think that they can function well if their goals are not supported by other social institutions. If parents and churches come to think that the education offered in schools is fundamentally at odds with their beliefs, they will not support these schools, or their children's educational achievements within them, and may seek to undercut the school's messages. A truly 'detached' school, set over and against other social institutions, is unlikely to be effective.

In any event, it seems clear that no single institution can be relied upon as the exclusive 'seedbed of civic virtue', and that citizens learn an overlapping set of virtues from an overlapping set of institutions. The liberal hope is that this rather haphazard mélange of influences will generate the critical threshold of civic virtue.

But all of this discussion of where citizens learn virtues may seem beside the point. After all, the real question for any instrumental theory of virtue is why people would choose to *exercise* these virtues when they conflict with other preferences or goals. As I emphasized earlier, the liberal view does not assume that the exercise of these virtues is intrinsically rewarding, but may instead be seen as a sacrifice or burden. Why then would citizens choose to engage in public reason when they can get what they want in the political process through threats, bargaining, or sheer numbers? Why engage in civility when one benefits from the current patterns of discrimination and prejudice against minority groups?

Of course, if too many people abandon public reason and civility, the result may be to put the very legitimacy and stability of democratic institutions in question. In so far as we all have a self-interested reason to care about the stability of democratic institutions, we also have a self-interested reason to care about the overall level of virtue in society. But this is a rather remote and long-term interest, which does not fully explain why I should engage in any particular action of public reason or civility here and now. My individual action is unlikely to have any significant impact on the overall health of the democratic system. Why should I give priority to my long-term instrumental interest in promoting civic virtue over my short-term intrinsic interest in promoting my particular conception of the good, through threats or discrimination if need be?

This raises again the challenge Taylor posed to liberalism in the last chapter. Taylor argued that liberalism offered no plausible account of why citizens would continue to vote for redistributive welfare policies, and accept a legal obligation to make sacrifices for co-citizens, given that co-citizens no longer share a common conception of the good. Why make sacrifices for co-citizens whose way of life is not only different from mine, but perhaps even in conflict with it? The same question arises here, although in the context of individual behaviour rather than support for public policy. Why would citizens accept the burdens of public reason and civility in their personal conduct in order to accommodate co-citizens who have different, and perhaps even conflicting, conceptions of the good?

Not surprisingly, liberals offer the same two-level response here that they offered in the last chapter. At one level, liberals emphasize that citizens are assumed to have a sense of justice, and this shared commitment to principles of justice provides a sense of solidarity that unites people with different conceptions of the good. At another level, liberal nationalists argue that social unity based on principles of justice is too thin, and must be further stabilized and strengthened by the development of a shared sense of nationhood, based on a common language, history, and public institutions.

As I noted last chapter, many liberals are hesitant to adopt this second nation-building level, and prefer to rely solely on people's sense of justice as a motive for accepting the demands of active and responsible citizenship. But in fact, the existence of this sort of nation-building is implicitly assumed by virtually all theorists of deliberative democracy and civic virtue. For example, most accounts of public reasonableness simply take for granted that citizens share a common language, and that democratic states form 'a community of communication'.[33] Indeed, it is difficult to imagine how deliberative democracy is possible without a shared language. But the diffusion of a shared language within each state is one of the main goals of nation-building, and in assuming the existence of such a common language, theorists are implicitly assuming the appropriateness of nation-building. Indeed, liberal nationalists argue that the shift from an aggregative to a deliberative model of democracy, and the recognition of the need for greater civic virtue, simply strengthens the argument for building a sense of common nationhood. As David Miller puts it, a common sense of national identity 'is the precondition of achieving political aims such as social justice and deliberative democracy' (Miller 1995: 162, 96; cf. Kymlicka 2001: ch. 10).

5. COSMOPOLITAN CITIZENSHIP

This attempt to link active citizenship and deliberative democracy with liberal nationalism is subject to the same objection as liberal nationalist accounts of distributive justice: namely that it ignores the need for a more 'cosmopolitan' or transnational conception of democracy. While liberal nation-building may have helped in the past to consolidate and promote democracy at a national level, what we need now is a more global conception of democratic citizenship, focused on supranational or international institutions, such as the European Union, the United Nations, or the World Bank.

One reason we may want to strengthen such international institutions is that we believe in a global conception of justice, and hence the need to transfer resources from the citizens of rich countries to the citizens of poor countries. That is, we may want cosmopolitan political institutions because we believe in a cosmopolitan conception of justice. But there are independent reasons for establishing international political institutions. It is increasingly recognized that we need such institutions to deal with issues of economic globalization, common environmental problems, and international security. As a result, we are witnessing a veritable explosion of such international organizations in the post-war period.

Yet these institutions do not fit well into existing nation-based theories of democracy. At present, these transnational organizations exhibit a major 'democratic deficit', and have little public legitimacy in the eyes of citizens. They are basically organized through intergovernmental relations, with little if any direct input from individual citizens. Moreover, these institutions have evolved in an ad hoc way, each in response to a particular need, without any underlying theory or model about the kinds of transnational institutions we want, or how they should be governed, or how they should relate to each other, or what sorts of principles should regulate their structures or actions.

In short, while we have an increasing number of transnational institutions, which exercise an increasing influence over our lives, we have no political theory of transnational institutions. We have well-developed theories about what sorts of principles of justice should be implemented by the institutions of the nation-state; well-developed theories about what sorts of political rights citizens should have vis-à-vis these national institutions; and well-developed theories about what sorts of virtues, loyalties, and commitments citizens should have to these institutions. By contrast, few people have any clear idea what principles of justice or standards of democratization or norms of virtue or loyalty should apply to transnational institutions.[34]

It is increasingly clear, therefore, that we can no longer take the nation-state as the sole or dominant context for political theory. We need a more cosmopolitan conception of democracy and governance that explicitly addresses these issues. One of the most common objections to liberal nationalism is not only that it ignores this need for a theory of transnational democracy, but also that its emphasis on common nationhood as the glue of a democracy makes it impossible to theorize democracy at a level which transcends national and linguistic boundaries (e.g. D. Held 1995; 1999; Young 2000b).

Yet many liberal nationalists agree that there is a need for transnational political institutions. The issue, as with liberal-nationalist accounts of justice, is whether we view the nation-state as a building block or an obstacle to a more cosmopolitan conception of democracy. Should we view cosmopolitan democracy as an alternative to outmoded models of nation-centred democracy, or as a supplement to, and dependent on, nation-centred democracy,

For example, consider one of the few serious attempts at developing a democratic transnational political institution: the European Union. The EU has two major centres of decision-making: the European Parliament, whose members are directly elected by citizens in Europe-wide elections; and the European Commission and Council of Ministers, whose members are appointed by national governments (which are themselves elected in country-specific national elections). Corresponding to these two centres of decision-making, there are two broad strategies for trying to remedy the EU's democratic deficit. One is to increase the power of the (directly elected) European Parliament, at the expense of the (nationally nominated) Commission and Council of Ministers, and thereby increase the extent to which the EU is directly accountable to individual citizens in pan-European elections. The alternative is to leave most of the power in the hands of the Commission and Council of Ministers, but to increase the extent to which national governments are accountable in national elections for how their delegates act in the Commission/Council.

Many defenders of cosmopolitan citizenship endorse the first approach: they think it is essential to increase the extent to which international institutions are directly accountable to individual citizens. But it seems clear that most Europeans themselves prefer the second approach. There is very little grass-roots demand for a strengthened EU Parliament. On the contrary, most people, in virtually all European states, show little interest in the affairs of the European Parliament, and little enthusiasm for increasing its powers. What they want, instead, is to strengthen the accountability of their *national* governments for how these governments act at the intergovernmental Council of Ministers. That is, citizens in each country want to debate amongst themselves, in their vernacular, what the position of their government should be on EU issues. For example, Danes wish to debate, in Danish, what the Danish position should be vis-à-vis Europe. They show little interest in starting a European-wide debate (in English?) about what the EU should do. They are keenly interested in having a democratic debate about the EU, but the debate they wish to engage in is not a debate with other Europeans about 'what should we Europeans do?' Rather, they wish to debate with each other, in Danish, about what we Danes should do.

Moreover, attempts to create a genuinely democratic form of transnational citizenship could have negative consequences for democratic citizenship at the domestic level. For example, the inevitable result of giving more power to the elected European Parliament, on the grounds that it is more 'democratic', would be to take away the veto power which national governments now have over most EU decisions. Decisions made by the EU Parliament, unlike those made by the Council, are not subject to the national veto. This means that the EU would cease to be accountable to citizens through their national legislatures. At the moment, if a Danish citizen dislikes an EU decision, she can try to mobilize other Danes to change their government's position on the issue. But if the EU is 'democratized'—i.e. if the elected Parliament replaces the nominated Council as the major decision-making body—a Danish citizen would have to try to change the opinions of the citizens of every other European country (none of which speak her language). And, for obvious and understandable reasons, few Europeans seek this sort of 'democratization'. For Danish citizens to engage in a debate with other Danes, in Danish, about the Danish position vis-à-vis the EU is a familiar and manageable task. But for Danish citizens to engage in a debate with Italians to try to develop a common European position is a daunting prospect. In what language would such a debate occur, and in what forums? Not only do they not speak the same language, or share the same territory, they also do not read the same newspapers, or watch the same television shows, or belong to the same political parties. So what would be the forum for such a trans-European debate?

Given these obstacles to a trans-European public debate, it is not surprising that neither the Danes nor the Italians have shown any enthusiasm for 'democratizing' the EU. They prefer exercising democratic accountability through their national legislatures. Paradoxically, then, the net result of increasing direct democratic accountability of the EU through the elected European Parliament might in fact be to undermine democratic citizenship. It would shift power away from the national level, where mass participation and vigorous democratic debate in a common language is possible, towards the transnational level, where democratic participation and deliberation is very difficult. As Dieter Grimm argues, given that there is no common European mass media at the moment, and given that the prospects for creating such a Europeanized media in the foreseeable future 'are absolutely non-existent', dramatically shifting power from the Council to the Parliament would 'aggravate rather than solve the problem' of the democratic deficit (Grimm 1995: 296).

This suggests that, for the foreseeable future at least, nation-states will remain the primary locus for the exercise of democratic citizenship. This is not to deny the importance, indeed necessity, of establishing international institutions whose decisions are subject to some form of democratic accountability. But given the difficulties of establishing meaningful forms of deliberative democracy and mass participation at the transnational level, we should perhaps try to develop cosmopolitan democracy by building on the achievements of the nation-state. In other words, the success of transnational democracy may be dependent on the ongoing health of national democracies: transnational political institutions will work best if their rules and decisions are debated and ratified within national democratic forums. If so, then focusing on the virtues, practices, and loyalties needed to sustain national democratic forums may not be as myopic as it first appeared (Thompson 1999).

6. THE POLITICS OF CIVIC REPUBLICANISM

In most post-war political theory, the fundamental normative concepts were democracy (for evaluating procedures) and justice (for evaluating outcomes). Citizenship, if it was discussed at all, was usually seen as derivative of democracy and justice—i.e. a citizen is someone who has democratic rights and claims of justice. There is increasing support, however, from all points of the political spectrum, for the view that citizenship must play an independent normative role in any plausible political theory, and that the promotion of responsible citizenship is an urgent aim of public policy. This concern with citizenship is found equally amongst liberals, radicals, libertarians, communitarians, and feminists.

And yet a striking feature of the current debate is the timidity with which authors apply their theories of citizenship to questions of public policy. The literature has not yielded many new proposals or recommendations on how to promote citizenship. If civic virtue is important, why not pass Good Samaritan laws, as many European countries have done? If political participation is important, why not require mandatory voting, as in Australia or Belgium? If public-spiritedness is important, why not require a period of mandatory national service, as in most European counties? If state schools help teach responsible citizenship, because they require children of different races and religions to sit together, and learn to respect each other, why not prohibit private schools?

These are the kinds of policies which are concerned specifically with promoting citizenship, rather than justice or democracy per se. Yet few authors even contemplate such proposals. Instead, most citizenship theorists either leave the question of how to promote citizenship unanswered (Glendon 1991: 138), or focus on 'modest' or 'gentle and relatively unobtrusive ways' to promote civic virtues (Macedo 1990: 234, 253).[35] While citizenship theorists bemoan the excessive focus given to rights, they seem reluctant to propose any policies that could be seen as restricting those rights.

There may be good reasons for this timidity, but it sits uneasily with the claim that we face a crisis of citizenship, and that we urgently need a theory of citizenship. As a result, much recent work on citizenship virtues seems quite hollow. In the absence of some account of legitimate and illegitimate ways to promote or enforce good citizenship, many works on citizenship reduce to a platitude: namely, society would be better if the people in it were nicer and more thoughtful.[36]

Indeed, it is not clear how urgent the need to promote good citizenship is. The literature on citizenship is full of dire predictions about the decline of virtue, but, as Galston admits, 'cultural pessimism is a pervasive theme of human history, and in nearly every generation' (Galston 1991: 237). We can find similar worries about political apathy amongst political sociologists in the 1950s, and even in Tocqueville in the 1830s. If there are worrying signs, such as decreasing voting rates, there are also many positive trends. Citizens today are more tolerant, more respectful of others' rights, and more committed to democracy and constitutionalism, than previous generations (Macedo 1990: 6–7). If there is a decline in citizen involvement in traditional party-based national politics, there has been a veritable explosion of various 'counter-publics'—new forms of public involvement in which citizens energetically debate new ideas and alternatives (Fraser 1997; Phillips 2000: 291–2).

So it remains unclear how serious the problem is, or how we should try to combat it.

This suggests that the current preoccupation with citizenship is perhaps not quite what it seems. The explicit goal is to develop a theory of citizenship that can supplement previous theories of just institutions. But in many cases, I believe, the new language of citizenship is simply being used (or misused) to camouflage older arguments about the justice of social institutions. By the end of the 1980s, we had reached a kind of impasse on theories of justice. Libertarians, liberal egalitarians, utilitarians, and communitarians disagreed about the appropriate principles of distributive justice and the appropriate scope of individual rights. They disagreed about the role of individual responsibility, choice, and community membership in determining our obligations of justice. There was no likely prospect of any one approach winning a decisive intellectual victory: it was clear that each tradition's view of justice would continue to exert an influence on public debates and public opinion.

Under these conditions, it was no longer sufficient or effective to defend one's preferred policies in terms of justice. Since our conceptions of justice are themselves controversial, arguing that a particular policy will promote liberal egalitarian justice, say, will only be persuasive to those who endorse that conception of justice. A more effective approach would be to defend policies in terms of ideals that cut across these different intellectual traditions, and that can appeal to people with different views of justice.

The ideal of democratic citizenship was the most obvious candidate to serve this function. The first to use this appeal to citizenship effectively, I think, was the New Right. When libertarians objected to the welfare state on grounds of justice—i.e. by insisting that taxation to help the needy is an unjust appropriation of people's rightful entitlements—they had little success. The libertarian claim that the state has no right or responsibility to help the vulnerable is too stark a theory of justice for most citizens to swallow. But when the New Right started criticizing the welfare state on grounds of citizenship—i.e. by insisting that the welfare state bred dependency, passivity, and permanent marginalization—it was much more successful. No one, whatever their views of justice, could endorse public policies that undermined people's potential for active and responsible citizenship.

Liberal egalitarians were in a similar position. When they objected to the growing inequality in market income on grounds of justice—i.e. by insisting that this inequality was typically the result of morally arbitrary differences in people's circumstances—they had little success. The left-liberal claim that the state should seek to remedy all inequalities in circumstance is too demanding a conception of justice for many people. But when liberal egalitarians started criticizing inequality on the grounds that it impeded citizenship—i.e. by insisting that the rich could buy elections, and the poor were effectively disenfranchised—they were more successful. No one, whatever their conception of justice, can accept public policies which turn a democracy into a plutocracy. Moreover, this growing inequality was said to undermine the 'ties that bind' us together as a nation, and thereby erode the sense of solidarity. If we are to remain a strong and united nation, there must be some common public spaces where rich and poor can meet together to discuss matters of common concern as equals, and there must be equal access to education, the media, and so on. Programmes to combat poverty and marginalization that used to be defended in terms of equalizing life-chances are now defended in terms of promoting democratic citizenship.

Similarly, cultural conservatives used to oppose reforms such as women's rights, gay rights, or multiculturalism on the grounds that they encouraged or tolerated 'unnatural' or 'ungodly' ways of life, or degrading or false conceptions of the good life. But this perfectionist argument for conservatism had little success, since it rests on a view of the good life which is controversial. We simply do not agree on what is 'natural' or 'godly'. So conservatives have instead shifted to arguments about citizenship. The traditional family is defended now, not in terms of nature or religion, but as the 'seedbed of virtue'.

In all of these cases, arguments about citizenship are, in effect, a kind of strategic retreat from earlier arguments about justice. What used to be rejected as intrinsically wrong (as unjust), is now said to be instrumentally wrong (as eroding the virtues needed to sustain a liberal-democratic order). This shift has been made in the hope that the instrumental arguments about virtue will have wider acceptance than appeals to controversial theories of justice.

Appeals to virtue are not only less controversial, but also appear more noble. For the left to defend policies on the grounds that they increase the spending power of the poor, so that they can enjoy greater equality of leisure or consumer goods, seems rather crass. It is much more inspiring if we say that these policies promote, not the private consumption of the poor, but rather their public liberty and their capacity to be active citizens. To be concerned about people's capacity to engage in private consumption seems shallow and materialistic, whereas concern about people's capacity for political participation seems noble.[37] Hence both left and right have shifted from arguments about the fair distribution of private resources to arguments about the seedbeds of active citizenship.

That these citizenship arguments are invoked strategically does not mean, of course, that they are invalid. But it does suggest that these new theories of citizenship are hardly a disinterested search for the seedbeds of civic virtue. Those on the left look for ways in which economic inequality erodes active citizenship; those on the right look for ways in which welfare policies aimed at reducing economic inequality erode civic virtue. Feminists, gays, and multiculturalists look to find ways in which traditional status hierarchies of gender, sexuality, and race erode active citizenship; conservatives look to find ways in which state policies supporting women, gays, and minorities erode civic virtue.[38] It is difficult to think of cases where people have defended policies on grounds of citizenship that they were not already committed to on grounds of justice. In this sense, it is not clear whether adopting the perspective of citizenship really leads to different policy conclusions from the more familiar perspectives of justice. It may instead be a matter of putting old wine into new bottles.

GUIDE TO FURTHER READING

For general overviews of the recent 'citizenship debates', see Gershon Shafir (ed.), *The Citizenship Debates: A Reader* (University of Minnesota Press, 1998); Ronald Beiner (ed.), *Theorizing Citizenship* (State University of New York Press, 1995); Martin Bulmer and Anthony Rees (eds.), *Citizenship Today: The Contemporary Relevance of T. H. Marshall* (University College London Press, 1996); Derek Heater, *What is Citizenship* (Blackwell, 2000); Engin Isin and Patricia Wood, *Citizenship and Identity* (Sage, 1999); Herman van Gunsteren, *A Theory of Citizenship: Organizing Plurality in Contemporary Democracies* (Westview Press, 1998).

As we have seen in this chapter, the 'citizenship debates' are really several different debates, focusing on disparate issues about virtues, democratic legitimacy, citizenship education, and civic identities. For general theories of *civic virtue*, see Richard Dagger, *Civic Virtues: Rights, Citizenship and Republican Liberalism* (Oxford University Press, 1997); Stephen Macedo, *Liberal Virtues: Citizenship, Virtue and Community* (Oxford University Press, 1990); William Galston, *Liberal Purposes: Goods, Virtues, and Duties in the Liberal State* (Cambridge University Press, 1991). For collections on this topic, see David Batstone and Eduardo Mendieta (eds.), *The Good Citizen* (Routledge, 1999); Robert Hefner (ed.), *Democratic Civility: The History and Cross-cultural Possibility of a Modern Political Ideal* (Transaction Publishers, 1998).

The emphasis on civic virtue is tied to the shift towards a more *'deliberative' conception of democracy*, which requires that citizens be able and willing to participate in an active and responsible way in political life. One influential statement of this new conception is Amy Gutmann and Dennis Thompson, *Democracy and Disagreement* (Harvard University Press, 1996). For commentaries on their theory, see Stephen Macedo (ed.), *Deliberative Politics: Essays on Democracy and Disagreement* (Oxford University Press, 1999). Other important statements of deliberative democracy include Joshua Cohen, 'Deliberation and Democratic Legitimacy', in R. Goodin and P. Pettit (eds.), *Contemporary Political Philosophy: An Anthology* (Blackwell, 1997); Jürgen Habermas, *Between Facts and Norms: Contributions to a Discourse Theory of Law and Democracy* (MIT Press, 1996); and James Bohman, *Public Deliberation: Pluralism, Complexity and Democracy* (MIT Press, 1996). Two important collections on this topic are James

Bohman and William Rehg (eds.), *Deliberative Democracy: Essays on Reason and Politics* (MIT Press, 1997); and Jon Elster (ed.), *Deliberative Democracy* (Cambridge University Press, 1998).

Some theorists use slightly different terminology to express this new model. For example, Simone Chambers talks about 'reasonable democracy' (*Reasonable Democracy: Jürgen Habermas and the Politics of Discourse*, Cornell University Press, 1996); Iris Marion Young talks about 'communicative democracy' ('Justice and Communicative Democracy', in Roger Gottlieb (ed.), *Radical Philosophy: Tradition, Counter-Tradition, Politics*, Temple University Press, 1993); John Dryzek talks about 'discursive democracy' (*Discursive Democracy*, Cambridge University Press, 1990); and Philip Pettit talks about 'contestatory democracy' ('Democracy, Electoral and Contestatory', in Ian Shapiro and Stephen Macedo (eds.), *Designing Democratic Institutions: NOMOS 42*, New York University Press, 2000). All share the idea that our conception of democracy must become more 'voice centred' and less 'vote centred', although they disagree about how to enable and evaluate different forms of 'voice'.

For useful surveys of the literature on deliberative democracy, see John Dryzek, *Deliberative Democracy and Beyond: Liberals, Critics, Contestations* (Oxford University Press, 2000); David Kahane, 'Pluralism, Deliberation and Citizen Competence: Recent Developments in Democratic Theory', *Social Theory and Practice*, 26/3 (2000): 509–35; Ricardo Blaug, 'New Theories of Discursive Democracy: A User's Guide', *Philosophy and Social Criticism*, 22/1 (1996): 49–80; James Bohman, 'The Coming of Age of Deliberative Democracy', *Journal of Political Philosophy*, 6/4 (1988): 399–423.

Other important recent contributions to democratic theory include Ian Shapiro, *Democratic Justice* (Yale University Press, 1999), and Jeremy Waldron, *Law and Disagreement* (Oxford University Press, 1999).

Much of the literature on deliberative democracy may seem rather utopian in its expectations about the sorts of deliberative capacities and dispositions citizens will have. But there have been some attempts to test the viability of this model. For experiments in how to improve the deliberative quality of democratic decision-making, see James Fishkin, *The Voice of the People* (Yale University Press, 1995), or check out the website of Fishkin's Center for Deliberative Polling (**www.la.utexas.edu/research/delpol/index.html**). For studies about whether citizens have the necessary 'competences', see Stephen Elkin and Karol Soltan (eds.), *Citizen Competence and Democratic Institutions* (Pennsylvania State University Press, 1999).

Some theorists have supposed that the only or best way to sustain these new models of civic virtue and deliberative democracy is to return to some form of *republicanism*, which privileges political participation as the highest form of life. For examples of this republican revival, see Adrian Oldfield, *Citizenship and Community: Civic Republicanism and the Modern World* (Routledge, 1990); and Quentin Skinner, *Liberty before Liberalism* (Cambridge University Press, 1998). A very different account of 'republicanism', which shares the liberal commitment to the centrality of civil liberties, is Philip Pettit, *Republicanism* (Oxford University Press, 1997). For an overview and critique of the 'republican revival', see Bill Brugger, *Republican Theory in Political Thought: Virtuous or Virtual?* (St Martin's Press, 1999); Alan Patten, 'The Republican Critique of Liberalism', *British Journal of Political Science* 26 (1996): 25–44; and the symposium in *Yale Law Review*, 97 (1988).

The need for civic virtues amongst citizens has raised the question of where citizens learn these virtues. There appear to be two broad answers. The first emphasizes the role of the organizations and institutions of *civil society* as the 'seedbed of virtue', where people learn ideas of self-discipline, cooperation, and duty. For discussions of this idea, see Thomas Janoski, *Citizenship and Civil Society: Obligations in Liberal, Traditional and Social Democratic Regimes* (Cambridge University Press, 1998); Robert Fullinwider (ed.), *Civil Society, Democracy and Civic Renewal* (Rowman and Littlefield, 1999); Nancy Rosenblum, *Membership and Morals: The Personal Uses of Pluralism in America* (Princeton University Press, 1998); Mary-Ann Glendon and D. Blankenhorn (eds.), *Seedbeds of Virtue: Sources of Competence, Character and Citizenship in American Society* (Madison Books, 1995); Michael Walzer (ed.), *Toward a Global Civil Society* (Berhahan Books, 1995).

The other broad answer focuses on the need for some form of formal *citizenship education*, to supplement and sometimes correct the lessons we learn in civil society. For discussions of the importance of citizenship education for a liberal society, see Eamonn Callan, *Creating Citizens: Political Education and Liberal Democracy* (Oxford University Press, 1997); Meira Levinson, *The Demands of Liberal Education* (Oxford University Press, 1999), David Bridges (ed.), *Education, Autonomy and Democratic Citizenship: Philosophy in a Changing World* (Routledge, 1997); Walter Feinberg, *Common Schools/Uncommon Identities: National Unity and Cultural Difference* (Yale University Press, 1998); Stephen Macedo, *Diversity and Distrust: Civic Education in a Multicultural Democracy* (Harvard University Press, 2000); Robert Fullinwider (ed.), *Public Education in a Multicultural Society* (Cambridge University Press, 1995); Harry Brighouse, *School Choice and Social Justice* (Oxford University Press, 2000), and two symposia, one on 'Citizenship, Democracy and Education', in *Ethics*, 105/3 (1995), and one on 'Democratic Education in a Multicultural State' in *Journal of Philosophy of Education*, 29/2 (1995). One of the most influential early discussions of this topic, Amy Gutmann's *Democratic Education*, first published in 1987, has been reissued in a second edition (Princeton University Press, 1999).

For *feminist* views of the new citizenship literature, see Ruth Lister (ed.), *Citizenship: Feminist Perspectives* (New York University Press, 1998); Maria Christine Bernadetta Voet and Rian Voet, *Feminism and Citizenship* (Sage, 1998), Anne Phillips, 'Feminism and Republicanism: Is This a Plausible Alliance?', *Journal of Political Philosophy*, 8/2 (2000): 279–93, and the symposia in *Feminist Review*, 57 (Autumn 1997) and *Hypatia*, 12/4 (1997).

For defences of the need for *transnational forms of democratic citizenship*, see David Held, *Democracy and the Global Order: From the Modern State to Cosmopolitan Governance* (Polity Press, 1995); Danielle Archibugi and David Held, *Cosmopolitan Democracy: An Agenda for a New World Order* (Polity Press, 1995); Derek Heater, *World Citizenship and Government: Cosmopolitan Ideas in the History of Western Political Thought* (St Martin's Press, 1996); Bruce Robbins (ed.), *Cosmopolitics: Thinking and Feeling beyond the Nation* (University of Minnesota Press, 1998); Kimberly Hutchings and Ronald Dannreuther (eds.), *Cosmopolitan Citizenship* (St Martin's

Press, 1999), and the symposium on 'Citizenship Denationalized' in *Indiana Journal of Global Legal Studies*, 7/2 (2000). Much of the work on this topic of transnational democracy has been inspired by the development of the European Union, and attempts to remedy its 'democratic deficit': see Percy Lehning and Albert Weale (eds.), *Citizenship, Democracy and Justice in the New Europe* (Routledge, 1997); Michael Nentwich and Albert Weale (eds.), *Political Theory and the European Union: Legitimacy, Constitutional Choice and Citizenship* (Routledge, 1998); Andrew Linklater, *The Transformation of Political Community: Ethical Foundations of the Post-Westphalian Era* (University of South Carolina Press, 1998).

There are many websites devoted to issues of citizenship promotion, citizenship education, and civic values. For some American examples, see the Center for Civic Education (**www.civiced.org**), focusing on democratic education; the Civic Practices Network (**www.cpn.org**), focusing on developing new approaches to enhance citizens' roles in public problem-solving and responsible democratic deliberation; and the Institute for the Study of Civic Values (**www.libertynet.org/~edcivic/iscvhome.html**). The Boston Review website has an interesting 'New Democracy Forum', which focuses on how to promote deliberative democracy (**www.bostonreview.mit.edu/ndf.html**). More international websites include the European Citizenship Education Network (**www.publiek-politiek.nl/english**), and CIVITAS, an international NGO dedicated to promoting civic education and civil society around the world (**www.civnet.org**).

The new journal *Citizenship Studies* has quickly become a leading forum for issues of citizenship theory. Since civic republicanism can be seen in many ways as a natural evolution of communitarian concerns with social unity, it is not surprising that the communitarian journal *Responsive Community*, mentioned in Chapter 6, also contains many discussions of citizenship theory.

NOTES

1. This may account for the recent interest in citizenship promotion amongst governments (e.g. Britain's Commission on Citizenship, *Encouraging Citizenship*, 1990; Senate of Australia, *Active Citizenship Revisited*, 1991; Senate of Canada, *Canadian Citizenship: Sharing the Responsibility*, 1993).

2. Other liberals, however, recognized the need for civic virtue, including Locke, Mill, and the British Idealists (see Vincent and Plant 1984: ch. 1).

3. For the pre-1994 literature, see the bibliography in Kymlicka and Norman 1994, and the collected essays in Beiner 1995. For more recent writings, see Janoski 1998; Dagger 1997; Callan 1997; van Gunsteren 1998; Shafir 1998; Hutchings and Dannreuther 1998; Lister 1998; and the bibliography in Kymlicka and Norman 2000.

4. Reprinted in Marshall 1965. For a concise introduction to the history of citizenship, see Heater 1990; Walzer 1992a.

5. It is often noted how idiosyncratically English this history is. In many European countries most of this progress occurred only in the last forty years, and often in reverse order. Even in England, the historical evidence supports an 'ebb and flow model' of citizenship rights, rather than a 'unilinear' model (Heater 1990: 271; Parry 1991: 167; Held 1989: 193).

6. *Trop v. Dulles* 356 US 86, 102 (1958). Recent studies suggest that this linking of citizenship

with rights is true in both Britain and the United States, although the British tend to emphasize social rights (e.g. to public education and health care), whereas Americans usually mention civil rights (e.g. freedom of speech and religion) (King and Waldron 1988; Conover, Crewe, and Searing 1991: 804).

7. Many of the virtues on Galston's list can be further subdivided into more specific sorts of dispositions and skills. For example, Barber suggests that the specifically political virtues can be subdivided into commonality, deliberation, inclusiveness, provisionality, listening, learning, lateral communication, imagination, and empowerment (Barber 1999: 42–5). There are now many such lists, which can be more or less refined.

8. James Bohman in particular has emphasized this idea of the importance of not just listening to others, but also of responding to them, so as to continue the conversation. He calls this the idea of 'uptake'. See Bohman 1996: 58–9, 116–18; cf. Bickford 1996.

9. There is now a voluminous literature on public reasonableness. See for example, Gutmann and Thompson 1996; d'Agostino 1996; Rawls 1993a; J. Cohen 1996; Benhabib 1996; Macedo 1990; and the essays in Macedo 1999.

10. On the importance of this sort of accommodation or compromise in any deliberative democracy, see Gutmann and Thompson 1996; Weinstock 2000.

11. For discussions of this shift from an 'aggregative' to a 'deliberative' conception of democracy, see Young 2000a: ch. 1; Dryzek 1990: ch. 1; Christiano 1996: 133–50; J. Cohen 1997a: 143–55; Miller 2000: ch. 1; Phillips 2000. Not everyone uses the labels of 'aggregative' and 'deliberative' democracy to describe these two models. Dryzek and Young object to the term 'deliberative' democracy, since they think it suggests an overly rationalist picture of the nature of political communication. Dryzek prefers the term 'discursive democracy', and Young prefers the term 'communicative democracy'. They are, however, equally committed to the 'talk-centric' conception of democracy. The older aggregative model is also sometimes known, particularly within American political science, as the 'pluralist' model—a term which dates back to the 1950s. This is potentially misleading today, since the sort of 'pluralism' it refers to concerns organized interest groups, not the sort of identity groups which underlie contemporary debates about 'pluralism'. For different senses of pluralism, see Eisenberg 1995.

12. For a list of ten such benefits, see Elster 1998a: 11; cf. Cooke 2000, who lists five benefits.

13. There is an analogy here to the problem discussed in the utilitarianism chapter about how to define utility or well-being (Ch. 2, s. 2). As we saw, utilitarians have recognized that it is necessary to define well-being not simply as the satisfaction of pre-existing preferences, whatever they are for, but rather as the satisfaction of *informed* preferences. The satisfaction of mistaken, adaptive, or uninformed preferences can in fact be harmful. This then raises the question of how to organize society to ensure that people can indeed develop informed preferences about the good life. The situation with theories of democracy is similar. The aggregative democracy model defines the desired outcome as a fair weighting or aggregating of individuals' pre-existing preferences, whatever they are for. But a democratic decision will be more legitimate and more beneficial if people's political claims and preferences are informed, and this in turn requires attention to the political preconditions which make it possible for people to form and revise their claims in an informed manner. This, in effect, is the goal of deliberative democracy.

14. There is a lively dispute about whether 'consensus' should indeed be the goal of deliberative democracy. Some theories of deliberative democracy have assumed that rational deliberation can and should lead to a convergence of views, as partial interests are reformulated into truly general interests, and as the best arguments win the day. This quest for consensus is often found in those theories of deliberative democracy influenced by Habermas (e.g. Benhabib 1992). Others have argued, more plausibly, that deliberation may sometimes

actually reveal that we are further apart than we initially expected, and that our disagreements are even deeper, and less subject to easy resolution or empirical testing (Young 1996: 126; 2000a: 40–4; Frazer and Lacey 1993). Femia asserts that deliberative democrats are committed to the idea that deliberation should result in a 'unified public will', a commitment he views as naive (Femia 1996: 378–81; cf. Ferejohn 2000). But most deliberative democrats in fact share his scepticism about the likelihood of arriving at a consensus (Dryzek 2000: 72; Mouffe 2000: 98–102).

15. For liberals, see Rawls 1999a: 574; Dworkin 2000: 364–5; Gutmann and Thompson 1996; for communitarians, see Sandel 1996; for critical theorists, see Habermas 1996; Chambers 1996; for feminists, see Fraser 1992; Phillips 1995: 145–65; for multiculturalists, see M. Williams 1998; 2000; Young 2000a.

16. For proposals, experiments, and case-studies in deliberative democracy, see Fishkin 1991; 1995 (on deliberative polls); Elster 1998b (on constituent assemblies); Chambers 1998 (on constitutional conventions); Pettit 2000 (on 'contestatory' consultative mechanisms). For discussions of how to ensure fair group representation within these deliberative forums, see M. Williams 2000; De Greiff 2000.

17. This contrast between 'communicative action' aimed at mutual understanding and 'strategic action' aimed at instrumental success is most systematically developed by Habermas (Habermas 1979). (Habermas's influence on theories of deliberative democracy is indeed one of the few areas where the continental tradition of political philosophy has strongly influenced Anglo-American theory.) The contrast between communicative action and strategic action is an important one, although not easy to apply. After all, people can engage in communicative actions for strategic reasons. Giving a principled reason for my self-interested claim may simply be a way of scaring off opposition, by implying that I will be unwilling to compromise on my 'principle' (see Elster 1995; Johnson 1998). One of the challenges for theorists of deliberative democracy is to consider not only how to promote communicative action, but how to reduce or filter out strategic communicative action. Elster argues, optimistically, that even if people originally enter into deliberation only for strategic reasons, they will eventually internalize the requirements of 'reasonableness' to which they formerly only paid lip-service. Elster calls this the 'civilizing force of hypocrisy' (Elster 1998a: 12; cf. Johnson 1998: 172).

18. For similar distinctions between the two forms of republicanism, see Patten 1996: 26; Burtt 1993: 360; Rawls 1988: 272–3.

19. For the view that a central problem facing republicanism is this transition argument, see Herzog 1986: 483–90; Burtt 1993: 363.

20. See also Habermas's discussion of the 'civic-republican ethos and its expectations of virtue that have morally overburdened citizens since time immemorial' (Habermas 1996: 487).

21. Quentin Skinner offers an interesting variant on the Aristotelian republican argument. He seems to concede that political participation will not have intrinsic value for many people. However, he argues that we must get people to view political participation as if it has intrinsic value, or else they will not fulfil their duties to protect democracy from its various internal and external threats (Skinner 1992: 219–21). We must, in other words, deliberately inculcate a view of the good life we know to be false, in order to defend democratic institutions. This is akin to the idea of 'Government House' utilitarianism discussed in Chapter 2, although Skinner suggests that all citizens would come to believe this 'noble lie', whereas Government House utilitarians think that the elite should stay cognizant of the lie they inculcate amongst the masses.

22. Rawls 1988: 272–3. For other accounts of the relationship between republicanism and liberalism, see Dworkin 1989: 499–504; Taylor 1989a: 177–81; Hill 1993: 67–84; Sinopli 1992: 163–71; Patten 1996; Berkowitz 1999; Wallach 2000.

23. For the view that deliberative democracy is episodic, see Ackerman 1991.

24. My discussion here draws extensively on Jeff Spinner's account of civility (1994: ch. 3). It also draws on Patricia White's account of civility, or what she calls 'decency' (1992), although I disagree in part with her emphasis. She seems primarily concerned with improving the overall level of 'decency' in society, rather than with eliminating glaring instances of incivility aimed at identifiable groups. For example, she compares the smiling and cooperative waiters in a Canadian café with the surly and uncooperative waiters in a Polish café (1992: 208), and argues that we should educate children to be friendly with strangers rather than surly. While I agree that it is a good thing for people to display this sort of decency, and that a minimal level of it is a precondition of a functioning democracy, I do not think this is the fundamental problem for citizenship education. From my point of view, waiters who are only minimally cheerful to all their customers are morally preferable to waiters who are generally very cheerful but who are surly to black customers. The latter may display more decency overall, but their behaviour towards an identifiable group threatens the most basic norms of liberal citizenship. However, I agree with White that it is important to be sensitive to the cultural variations in norms of civility (White 1992: 215; cf. Young 1993). For a more critical discussion of civility, see Calhoun 2000.

25. For evidence that there is a set of social expectations that Americans have of each other, and of themselves, that must be fulfilled if people are to be perceived as full members of society, see Mead 1986: 243; Shklar 1991: 413; Moon 1988: 34–5; Dworkin 1992: 131.

26. For example, real-estate agents have an economic incentive to maintain segregated housing. In any event, New Right reforms arguably violated the requirements of liberal justice. According to critics cutting welfare benefits, far from getting the disadvantaged back on their feet, has expanded the underclass. Class inequalities have been exacerbated, and the working poor and unemployed have been effectively disenfranchised, unable to participate in the social and political life of the country (Fierlbeck 1991: 579). So even if the market taught civic virtue, laissez-faire capitalism violates the principle that all members of society have an equal opportunity to be active citizens.

27. There is nothing wrong with residents opposing something which they think is intrinsically wrong, no matter where it is located (e.g. people who oppose nuclear power plants). But there is a problem when neighbours organize to avoid doing their fair share regarding necessary public programmes and services, such as housing for the disabled or lower-income people.

28. For an excellent analysis of the complex role civic associations play in inculcating civic virtue, see Rosenblum 1998. She gives a powerful critique of what she calls the 'transmission belt' theory of civic associations, according to which each association should train citizens in the virtues they need for political life.

29. For discussions of religious groups seeking separate schools as a way of avoiding autonomy-promoting liberal education, see McLaughlin 1992b; Halstead 1991; Spinner 2000.

30. For the most forceful defence of this ideal of a 'detached school', see Levinson 1999. As she puts it, 'It is difficult for children to achieve autonomy solely within the bounds of their families and home communities—or even within the bounds of schools whose norms are constituted by those from the child's home community. If we take the requirements of auton-omy seriously, we see the need for a place separate from the environment in which children are raised' (Levinson 1999: 58).

31. This is a different line of argument from those who defend the exemption for the Amish by arguing that their separate schools provide adequate citizenship education. This was the view of the American Supreme Court, which said that the Amish education system prepared Amish children to be good citizens, since they became productive and peaceful members of the Amish community (*Wisconsin* v. *Yoder* 406 US 205 (1972)). However, as I noted earlier,

liberal citizenship requires more than being law-abiding and economically self-sufficient. It requires also civility and public reasonableness. For a critique of *Yoder*'s account of civic responsibilities, see Arneson and Shapiro 1995.

32. As Spinner notes, there are unlikely to be many such groups, since the price of 'partial citizenship' is to cut oneself off from the opportunities and resources of the mainstream society (Spinner 1994: ch. 5). Of course, one could object to these exemptions for the Amish, not because they threaten liberal citizenship in general, but because they wrongly narrow the opportunities of their own children, including their opportunities for democratic citizenship (Gutmann 1980). Spinner argues that, even with the exemption from mandatory schooling, Amish children learn enough about the outside world for exit to be a meaningful option available to them.

33. For the centrality of this assumption to theories of democracy, see Wright 2000. She also emphasizes the costs this can have for linguistic minorities—an issue I will discuss in the next chapter.

34. For preliminary attempts to develop such a conception of cosmopolitan citizenship, see D. Held 1995; 1999; Archibugi and Held 1995; Heater 1996; Robbins 1998; Hutchings and Dannreuther 1999; Carter 2001.

35. For other accounts of the 'unobtrusive' promotion of citizenship, see Habermas 1992: 6–7; Hill 1993; Rawls 1993a: 216–20.

36. For example, Mouffe criticizes liberalism for reducing citizenship 'to a mere legal status, setting out the rights that the individual holds against the state' (1992c: 227), and seeks to 're-establish the lost connection between ethics and politics', by understanding citizenship as a form of 'political identity that is created through the identification with the *res publica*' (230). Yet she offers no suggestions about how to promote or compel this public-spirited participation, and insists (against civic republicans) that citizens must be free to choose not to give priority to their political activities. Her critique of liberalism, therefore, seems to reduce to the claim that the liberal conception of our citizenship rights does not tell us how a good citizen would choose to exercise her rights—a claim which liberals would readily accept. Many critiques of liberal citizenship amount to the same unenlightening claim.

37. There is obviously a deep tension in our culture on this question. On the one hand, as I noted earlier, most citizens endorse the view that we find our highest goods in the private spheres of family, work, and religion, rather than in political participation. Yet when it comes to issues about distribution, we talk as if it is unimportant how many resources people have in private life, and as if what really matters is the ability to participate politically.

38. For example, feminists argue that traditional forms of sexism undermine civility and public reasonableness; conservatives argue that the resulting forms of feminist 'political correctness' undermine civility and public reasonableness.

8

MULTICULTURALISM

The traditional model of 'citizenship-as-rights' has been challenged from two directions. The first, examined last chapter, emphasized the need to supplement the focus on rights with greater attention to civic virtues and active political participation. The second challenge, examined in this chapter, emphasizes the need to supplement the focus on common rights with greater attention to cultural pluralism and group-differentiated rights.

This second challenge reflects a broad-ranging movement not only in political philosophy, but also in real-world politics. This movement has been discussed under various labels: the 'politics of difference', 'identity politics', 'multiculturalism', 'the politics of recognition'. While each term carries slightly different connotations, the underlying idea is similar. Modern societies are said to be characterized by deep diversity and cultural pluralism. In the past, this diversity was ignored or stifled by models of the 'normal' citizen, which were typically based on the attributes of the able-bodied, heterosexual white male. Anyone who deviated from this model of normalcy was subject to exclusion, marginalization, silencing, or assimilation. Thus non-white groups were often denied entry to Western democracies, or if admitted were expected to assimilate to become citizens; indigenous peoples were either shunted into isolated reserves and/or forced to abandon their traditional lifestyles; homosexuality was often criminalized, and even if legal, gays were nonetheless expected to stay silent about their sexuality in public life; people with disabilities were hidden away in institutions; and so on.

Today, however, previously excluded groups are no longer willing to be silenced or marginalized, or to be defined as 'deviant' simply because they differ in race, culture, gender, ability or sexual orientation from the so-called 'normal' citizen. They demand a more inclusive conception of citizenship which recognizes (rather than stigmatizes) their identities, and which accommodates (rather than excludes) their differences.

It is sometimes said that what distinguishes these reform movements is that they are about 'identity', and hence forms of 'identity politics', unlike earlier class-based political movements of workers or farmers, which were about economic interests.[1] However, in reality, politics is almost always a matter of both identities and interests. The question is always *which* identities and interests are being promoted.

In the traditional model of 'citizenship-as-rights', the goal was to promote a certain sort of common national identity amongst citizens. As T. H. Marshall himself emphasized, citizenship is not just a certain legal status, defined by a set of rights and responsibilities. It is also an identity, an expression of one's membership in a political community. And his argument for extending citizenship rights to include basic social rights, such as health care and education, was precisely that it would help promote a common sense of national membership and national identity. Ensuring that people had health care and education was important for Marshall not just for humanitarian reasons—i.e. to meet basic needs. Social rights would also help integrate previously excluded groups into a common national culture, and thereby provide a source of national unity and loyalty. The goal was to include people in a 'common culture' which should be a 'common possession and heritage' (Marshall 1965: 101–2). Providing social rights would help secure 'loyalty to a civilisation that is a common possession'. He was particularly concerned to integrate the English working classes, whose lack of education and economic resources excluded them from enjoyment of this national culture—e.g. from knowing and enjoying Shakespeare, John Donne, Dickens, the King James Bible, Cromwell, the Glorious Revolution, and cricket.[2]

Marshall felt that a common set of social rights would integrate people into a common national culture, and that this was good from the point of view of both the previously excluded group and the state. Marshall assumed that cultural integration was good for the working class, since they were of course native-born English—i.e. English by ethnicity, religion, language. They ought to be co-owners of the national culture, as it were, since it is their national culture. They are not members of some other nation, with its own national culture. They are English, and have a birthright to share in its national history and culture.

And indeed the development of the welfare state has been quite successful in integrating the working classes into national cultures throughout the Western democracies. To be sure, there are still many class differences in the popular culture of the masses and the high culture of the well off. The affluent are more likely to prefer tennis to wrestling; or to read newspapers rather than tabloids. But there is a core of a common national culture which most Britons are familiar with, including the BBC, Shakespeare, historical events (Waterloo) and figures (Churchill), soccer, and contemporary politicians.

This attempt to integrate the working class into a national culture was not entirely done for altruistic reasons. There were fears that if the working class did not identify with and feel loyal to British civilization, its members might be tempted to support 'foreign' ideas, particularly communism and Soviet Bolshevism.[3] Moreover, from the point of view of the state, it is easier to govern a society when its citizens share a common national language, culture, and identity. All of the major functions of the state—communication and consultations, planning, investment, regulations, enforcement—work better if there is a certain cultural commonality amongst citizens. And as we noted in Chapter 6, integrating citizens into a common national culture also may promote mutual understanding, trust, and solidarity.

In short, extending citizenship to include common social rights was a tool of nation-building, intended in part to construct and consolidate a sense of common national identity and culture. And this helps explain *how* these social rights are implemented in practice. For example, the right to education is not a right to education in any language the children or parent choose, but rather to education in the national language, since the goal is not just to meet some abstract need for rationality, literacy, or knowledge, but also to educate people in a way that will help integrate them into the national culture. Similarly, Western countries do not provide health care in separate hospitals for each ethnic group, even though this might be an efficient way of delivering health care, since the goal is not only to meet certain basic needs in the abstract, but rather to create a common sense of citizenship, based on common entitlements and common experiences in the exercise of those entitlements. Social rights are, in general, the right to gain certain common benefits through common public institutions operating in a common national language, so as to meet basic needs while simultaneously creating a common national identity.

So the traditional model of 'citizenship-as-common-rights' was deeply connected to ideas of national integration. This link between common citizenship rights and national integration is now under attack.[4] It has become clear that many groups—blacks, women, indigenous peoples, ethnic and religious minorities, gays and lesbians—still feel marginalized or stigmatized despite possessing the common rights of citizenship. Many members of these groups feel marginalized, not (or not only) because of their socio-economic status, but also because of their socio-cultural identity—their 'difference'. They argue that the common rights of citizenship, originally defined by and for white heterosexual, able-bodied men, cannot accommodate the needs of other groups, and hence demand some form of what Iris Marion Young calls 'differentiated citizenship' (Young 1989). On this view, members of certain groups would be incorporated into the political community, not only as individuals, but also through the group, and their rights would depend, in part, on their group membership. They demand these group-specific forms of citizenship either because they reject the very idea that there should be a single common national culture or because they think that the best way to include people in such a common culture is through differentiated citizenship rights.

Some groups reject the very idea of integrating into the 'common' national culture. These include 'national minorities' like the Québécois, Catalans, or Flemish, who think of themselves as forming distinct 'nations' within the larger state, and fight to maintain themselves as distinct self-governing societies with their own public institutions, operating in their own national language and culture.[5] To achieve this goal, they need a range of differentiated rights, including some form of territorial self-government, official language status in their self-governing region, and the right to establish a full set of public institutions (legal, educational, and political) operating in their own language.

A similar story can be said about many indigenous peoples, who also reject integration in the name of maintaining themselves as distinct nations or peoples, and who claim a variety of differentiated rights to achieve this goal, including land claims, treaty rights, and self-government powers.

Other groups accept the idea of national integration, but feel that certain forms of differential treatment are required to achieve this. For example, many gay people feel wrongly excluded from their own national culture. The source of this exclusion is not any economic inequality (in fact, gays tend to be as well off as heterosexuals). Rather, they are stigmatized within their own national culture, whose official symbols are heterosexual. In Western societies, our cultural model of what it is to be a 'good' or 'normal' person is to be heterosexual. If gays are to fully integrate, those aspects of the national culture which stigmatize them must be challenged. Gays cannot participate fully in the national culture, not because of any lack of education or material resources, but because of a status hierarchy within that national culture which demeans and degrades them, and treats them as less worthy of concern or respect. This status inequality used to be reflected in discriminatory laws (some of which remain on the books in the United States and Britain), but even when those laws have been repudiated, the status inequality is still reflected in more subtle ways. For example, gays have tended to be invisible in the national media, school curricula, or public museums; they are subject to increased risks of physical attack; they face high levels of private discrimination.[6] Therefore, gays seek a range of rights and policies which attack this status hierarchy, including public recognition of gay marriages; or representation on school boards or police boards.

A similar story can be said about many religious minorities, who feel stigmatized and excluded from the national culture, and who seek various forms of recognition of their differences (e.g. public recognition of their religious holidays, exemptions from laws that interfere with religious worship, such as animal slaughtering legislation that prohibits the ritually prescribed form of slaughtering for Jews and Muslims, or dress codes which prevent Sikhs from wearing their turbans in the army or police).

Why have members of these groups mobilized for some form of differentiated citizenship, rather than (or in addition to) the common social rights demanded by the working class? Why did Marshall's strategy of integrating all citizens through common social rights fail in these cases?

Some critics of these claims argue that they are primarily the result of self-seeking group leaders (e.g. 'ethnic entrepreneurs'), who encourage feelings of resentment and inequality amongst group members in order to justify maintaining control over them, and to justify receiving government grants for their organizations. On this view, group elites have an incentive to keep group members in a (real or perceived) position of disadvantage, since their clientele and funding would dry up if group members succeeded in the larger society (e.g. Hardin 1995).

There is no doubt some truth in this story about the motivations of some group leaders. Minority group leaders can be as cynical and self-serving as political elites in the mainstream society. But this does not explain why non-elite group members have often supported demands for differentiated citizenship. Critics suggest that group elites manipulate group members by keeping them ill informed about their true opportunities. But that is contradicted by the fact that the mobilization for differentiated citizenship has tended to increase, not decrease, with the wealth and education of group members. The fact is that demands for differentiated citizenship have grown in strength throughout the West, even in the most democratic countries, where group leaders are subject to vigorous forms of public contestation and electoral accountability, and even where group members have high levels of education and knowledge.

This is not to say, of course, that *all* members of these groups support the same demands for differentiated citizenship. Most of these groups are heterogeneous, and typically exhibit the same sorts of cleavages in political views and personal lifestyles as the larger society. They are gay and straight blacks, right-wing and left-wing women, religious and secular Québécois, progressive and conservative immigrants, and so on. These differences are often reflected in internal debates within the group about what sorts of claims to make. I will discuss the relevance of some of these internal cleavages later in this chapter.

But none of this changes the fact that there is a clear trend amongst the members of many groups to demand certain forms of differentiated citizenship. What explains these demands? To oversimplify, we can say that in every Western democracy, there are two powerful hierarchies. First, there is an *economic* hierarchy. In the British case that Marshall was theorizing about, this starts at the top with the landed aristocracy through the mercantile and industrial capitalist elite to professionals, white-collar workers, and skilled craftsmen down to unskilled manual labourers. One's position in this economic hierarchy is determined by one's relationship to the market or to the means of production. Struggles against the inequalities inherent in this economic hierarchy generate a politics of redistribution. This is the traditional form of working-class mobilization, which Nancy Fraser characterizes this way (Fraser 1998; 2000):

Politics of Redistribution
— focuses on socioeconomic injustices rooted in the economic structure of society, including exploitation (having the fruits of one's labour appropriated by others), economic marginalization (being confined to undesirable work or excluded from the labour market entirely), and economic deprivation (lacking an adequate material standard of living).
— the remedy is economic restructuring, such as income redistribution, reorganizing the division of labour, or regulating investment decisions.
— the targets of public policies are classes or classlike collectivities defined economically by a distinctive relation to the market or the means of production.
— aims to reduce group differences (i.e. to reduce class differences in opportunities and culture).

Marshall's conception of citizenship rights was primarily intended to make sense of this political struggle over economic inequalities. But there was another hierarchy in British society that Marshall paid less attention to. This is a *status* hierarchy, which says that it is better to be English than Irish; better to be Protestant than Catholic (and better to be a Christian of either sort than Jewish or Muslim); better to be white than black or brown or yellow; better to be male than female; better to be heterosexual than homosexual; and better to be able-bodied than disabled. This status hierarchy is reflected in a history of discriminatory laws against lower-status groups, and in their ongoing invisibility or stereotyping in the media, schools, museums, or state symbols. All of these public institutions either discriminate against, or simply ignore, lower-status groups.

We can find similar sorts of status hierarchies in all other Western democracies, which also give a higher status to Christian, heterosexual, able-bodied white men. Struggles against these status hierarchies generate a 'politics of recognition'. This is the sort of politics underlying the current mobilization by gays, religious minorities, immigrants, and national minorities, which Fraser characterizes this way:

Politics of Recognition
— focuses on cultural injustices, rooted in social patterns of representation, interpretation and communication, including cultural domination (being subject to patterns of interpretation associated with another culture); nonrecognition (being rendered invisible in the authoritative communicative practices of one's

culture); and disrespect (being disparaged in stereotypic public cultural representations or in everyday life interactions).

— the remedy is cultural or symbolic change to upwardly revalue disrespected identities and cultural products of maligned groups, or positively value cultural diversity.
— targets are status groups, defined by relations of recognition in which they enjoy lesser esteem, honour, prestige than other groups.
— aims to affirm group differences.

Although we can distinguish the politics of redistribution and recognition for analytical purposes, they are often combined in the real world. Some groups find themselves at or near the bottom of both hierarchies, and so need to mobilize for both redistribution and recognition. Indeed many people— Marxists in particular—have supposed that the second hierarchy is purely secondary and epiphenomenal. On this view, one's place in the economic hierarchy determines one's place in the status hierarchy—a group becomes culturally stigmatized only if and because it is economically disadvantaged. If we eliminate economic inequalities, cultural inequalities would automatically fade away. Hence the traditional Marxist view that all of our effort should be devoted to the politics of redistribution. Attempting to tackle cultural stigma-tization without challenging the underlying economic inequalities is said to be futile and pointless. A surprising number of liberals have also endorsed this view about the secondary and derivative nature of cultural inequalities.

However, the evidence suggests that the status hierarchy is not reducible to the economic hierarchy. To be sure, some groups, like women, blacks, and indigenous peoples, are both disproportionately concentrated in vulnerable economic positions, and also subject to demeaning or silencing cultural repre-sentations. But there are other groups which are economically well off yet culturally stigmatized. This is true, for example, of gays in most Western democracies, who enjoy similar per capita levels of income or education as heterosexuals, but suffer from extreme homophobia. It is also true of some well-established immigrant or religious groups, like Arab- or Japanese-Americans, who enjoy higher-than-average levels of education and income, but who are culturally marginalized. Similarly, many national minorities, like the Catalans or Québécois, enjoy the same standard of living as the majority, and in some cases actually a higher than average income, yet their language and culture is seen as inferior to that of the majority. For all of these groups, achieving economic equality has not eliminated the status inequality (although it has undoubtedly helped reduce it), and hence has not eliminated the need to mobilize for a politics of recognition.

Conversely, there are groups which enjoy a privileged position in the status hierarchy, yet are economically disadvantaged. This is arguably the case of the traditional male working class in most Western countries. While the working class suffers from an unjust economic hierarchy, they often benefit from the status hierarchy. Most working-class men could gain satisfaction from the thought that their male gender, white skin, Christian religion, and hetero-sexual orientation were defined as the norm, giving them a superior status to women, blacks, Jews, or gays.

Of course, before the introduction of the welfare state, working-class men often were not able to enjoy the fruits of this status hierarchy, due to their lack of access to education, economic opportunities, and income. Therefore, the solution for the exclusion of the traditional working class was primarily to enrich common citizenship through social rights. There was no need to chal-lenge the status hierarchy. And indeed many (white, male, Christian, hetero-sexual) members of the working class have resisted attempts by women, gays, religious minorities, or immigrants to challenge the status hierarchy. As eco-nomically disadvantaged members of a high-status group, the traditional working class had an interest in challenging the economic hierarchy, but a self-interest in preserving the status hierarchy.

So there is no simple correlation between the economic and status hier-archies. And this explains why Marshall's strategy of integration through common social rights made sense for the working class but has not satis-fied other groups. The remedy for the exclusion of the traditional working class was close to a pure case of the politics of economic redistribution, without any need to engage in a politics of recognition. But for most other excluded groups, equality requires something else, or something more: namely, an attack on the status hierarchy. In some cases, like gays and Jews, the goal may be something close to a pure politics of recognition, since they already have economic equality. For other groups, like women or blacks, equality requires both a politics of redistribution and a politics of recognition.[7]

The growing realization that status inequalities are not entirely reducible to, or derivative of, economic inequalities has led to increased interest in the politics of recognition. Yet these demands for recognition through differenti-ated citizenship remain deeply controversial. Indeed, many people regard the very idea of group-differentiated citizenship as a contradiction in terms. On the orthodox view, citizenship is, by definition, a matter of treating people as individuals with equal rights under the law. This is what distinguishes demo-cratic citizenship from feudal and other pre-modern views that determined people's political status by their religious, ethnic, or class membership. Hence 'the organization of society on the basis of rights or claims that derive from group membership is sharply opposed to the concept of society based on citizenship' (Porter 1987: 128). The idea of differentiated citizenship, therefore, is a radical development in citizenship theory.

My goal in these final two chapters is to examine some of the issues which are raised by this new politics of recognition in which groups seek to challenge traditional status hierarchies through some form of differentiated citizenship that affirms previously stigmatized group differences. What are the moral arguments for or against such group-differentiated rights? In particular, how do they relate to the underlying principles of liberal democracy, such as individual freedom, social equality, and democracy? How are recognition and redistribution related?

As we have seen, the movement for recognition is a very broad one, and to answer these questions it may be helpful to separate out the different sorts of groups involved. In the next chapter, I will focus on the claims raised by women's groups, and also touch briefly on the claims of gays and people with disabilities. In this chapter, I will focus on the claims raised by ethnocultural groups, such as immigrants, national minorities, indigenous peoples, racial groups, and ethnoreligious groups. This is itself a very heterogeneous set of groups, each raising different types of claims. However, their claims have two important features in common: (*a*) they go beyond the familiar set of common civil and political rights of individual citizenship which are protected in all liberal democracies; (*b*) they are adopted with the intention of recognizing and accommodating the distinctive identities and needs of ethnocultural groups. I will use the term 'multiculturalism' as an umbrella term for the claims of these ethnocultural groups.[8] (Since these ethnocultural groups seeking recognition tend to be minorities, for reasons I explain below, I will also use the term 'minority rights'.)

The philosophical debate on multiculturalism and minority rights has changed dramatically in recent years, both in its scope and in its basic terminology. Until the mid-1980s, there were very few political philosophers or political theorists working in the area. Indeed, for most of this century, issues of ethnicity have been seen as marginal by political philosophers. (Much the same can be said about many other academic disciplines, from sociology to geography to history.)

Today, however, after decades of relative neglect, the question of multiculturalism has moved to the forefront of political theory. There are several reasons for this. Most obviously, the collapse of communism unleashed a wave of ethnic nationalisms in Eastern Europe which dramatically affected the democratization process. Optimistic assumptions that liberal democracy would emerge smoothly from the ashes of communism were derailed by issues of ethnicity and nationalism. But there were many factors within long-established democracies which also pointed to the salience of ethnicity: the nativist backlash against immigrants and refugees in many Western countries; the resurgence and political mobilization of indigenous peoples, resulting in the draft declaration of the rights of indigenous peoples at the United Nations; and the ongoing, even growing, threat of secession within several

Western democracies, from Canada (Quebec) to Britain (Scotland), Belgium (Flanders), and Spain (Catalonia).

All of these factors, which came to a head at the beginning of the 1990s, made it clear that Western democracies had not resolved or overcome the tensions raised by ethnocultural diversity. It is not surprising, therefore, that political theorists have increasingly turned their attention to this topic. The last few years have witnessed the first philosophical books in English on the normative issues involved in secession, nationalism, immigration, group representation, multiculturalism, and indigenous rights.[9]

But the debate has not only grown in size. The very terms of the debate have also dramatically changed, and this is what I would like to focus on. I will try to distinguish three distinct stages in the debate.

1. THE FIRST STAGE: MULTICULTURALISM AS COMMUNITARIANISM

The first stage was the pre-1989 debate. Those few theorists who discussed the issue in the 1970s and 1980s assumed that the debate over multiculturalism was essentially equivalent to the debate between 'liberals' and 'communitarians' (or between 'individualists' and 'collectivists'). Confronted with an unexplored topic, it was natural that political theorists would look for analogies with other more familiar topics, and the liberal-communitarian debate seemed the most relevant. After all, multiculturalism seems to involve people mobilizing as members of cultural communities, and seeking some form of 'group rights' to recognize and protect their community. All of this has a 'communitarian' sound to it.

As we have seen in Chapter 6, one version of the liberal-communitarian debate revolves around the priority of individual freedom. Liberals insist that individuals should be free to decide on their own conception of the good life, and applaud the liberation of individuals from any ascribed or inherited status. Liberal individualists argue that the individual is morally prior to the community: the community matters only because it contributes to the well-being of the individuals who compose it. If those individuals no longer find it worthwhile to maintain existing cultural practices, then the community has no independent interest in preserving those practices, and no right to prevent individuals from modifying or rejecting them.

Communitarians dispute this conception of the 'autonomous individual'. They view people as 'embedded' in particular social roles and relationships. Such embedded selves do not form and revise their own conception of the good life; instead, they inherit a way of life which defines their good for them. Rather than viewing group practices as the product of individual choices, communitarians view individuals as the product of social practices. Moreover, they often deny that the interests of communities can be reduced to the interests of their individual members. Privileging individual autonomy is therefore seen as destructive of communities. A healthy community maintains a balance between individual choice and protection of the communal way of life, and seeks to limit the extent to which the former can erode the latter.

In this first stage of the debate, the assumption was that one's position on multiculturalism was dependent on, and derivative of, one's position on the liberal-communitarian debate. If one is a liberal who cherishes individual autonomy, then one will oppose multiculturalism as an unnecessary and dangerous departure from the proper emphasis on the individual. Communitarians, by contrast, view multiculturalism as an appropriate way of protecting communities from the eroding effects of individual autonomy, and of affirming the value of community. Ethnocultural minorities in particular are worthy of such protection, partly because they are most at risk, but also because they still have a communal way of life to be protected. Unlike the majority, ethnocultural minorities have not yet succumbed to liberal individualism, and so have maintained a coherent collective way of life.

This debate over the relative priority and reducibility of individuals and groups dominated the early literature on multiculturalism.[10] Defenders of minority rights agreed that they were inconsistent with liberalism's commitment to moral individualism and individual autonomy, but argued that this just pointed out the inherent flaws of liberalism.

So defenders of multiculturalism were initially drawn to communitarianism as a possible philosophical foundation for minority rights. Conversely, as we saw in Chapter 6, the natural evolution of communitarianism was in the direction of some form of multiculturalism. Whereas the first wave of communitarians argued that the liberal conception of the self was inappropriate in general, for majorities as much as minorities, the second wave made the more modest claim that an autonomy-based liberalism was inappropriate for those distinctively 'communal' groups which exist within liberal societies. And indeed, as we have seen, both Sandel and Taylor specifically cite certain minority rights as examples of communitarianism in action, and as manifesting a form of 'politics of the common good' not possible at the majority or national level.

In short, in the first stage of the debate, defending multiculturalism involved endorsing the communitarian critique of liberalism, and viewing minority rights as defending cohesive and communally minded minority groups against the encroachment of liberal individualism.

2. THE SECOND STAGE: MULTICULTURALISM WITHIN A LIBERAL FRAMEWORK

It is increasingly recognized that this is an unhelpful way to conceptualize most multiculturalism claims in Western democracies. Assumptions about the 'striking parallel' between the communitarian attack on liberalism and the notion of minority rights have been increasingly questioned.[11]

To be sure, there are some groups which are clearly 'communitarian'. This is true of isolationist ethnoreligious groups that voluntarily distance themselves from the larger world, such as the Hutterites, Amish or Hasidic Jews. And some of the more isolated or traditionalist indigenous communities may also fit this description as 'communitarian' groups. The question of how liberal states should respond to such non-liberal groups has already been raised in Chapter 6, section 7, regarding religious freedom, and Chapter 7, section 4, in the context of issues of citizenship education.

But most ethnocultural groups within Western democracies do not want to be protected from the forces of modernity in liberal societies. On the contrary, they want to be full and equal participants in modern liberal societies. This is true, for example, of blacks in the United States, whose commitment to liberal principles is generally the same as for whites. It is also true of most immigrant groups, which seek inclusion and full participation in the mainstream of liberal-democratic societies, with access to its education, technology, literacy, mass communications, etc. And it is true of most non-immigrant national minorities, like the Québécois, Flemish, or Catalans. Some of their members may wish to secede from a liberal democracy, but if they do, it is not to create an illiberal communitarian society, but rather to create their own modern liberal democratic society (Newman 1996; Davis 1994; Keating and McGarry 2001). The Québécois wish to create a 'distinct society', but it is a modern, liberal society—with an urbanized, secular, pluralistic, industrialized, bureaucratized, consumerist mass culture.

Indeed, far from opposing liberal principles, public opinion polls show there are often no statistical differences between national minorities and majorities in their adherence to liberal principles. And immigrants also quickly absorb the basic liberal-democratic consensus, even when they come from countries with little or no experience of liberal democracy. The commitment to individual autonomy is deep and wide in modern societies, crossing ethnic, linguistic, and religious lines.[12]

In short, the overwhelming majority of debates about multiculturalism are not debates between a liberal majority and communitarian minorities, but debates amongst liberals about the meaning of liberalism. They are debates between individuals and groups who endorse the basic liberal-democratic consensus, but who disagree about the interpretation of these principles in multiethnic societies—in particular, they disagree about the proper role of language, nationality, and ethnic identities within liberal-democratic societies and institutions. Groups claiming minority rights insist that at least certain forms of public recognition and support for their language, practices, and identities are not only consistent with basic liberal-democratic principles, including the importance of individual autonomy, but may indeed be required by them.

This then has led to the second stage of the debate, in which the question becomes: what is the possible scope for multiculturalism *within* liberal theory? Framing the debate this way does not resolve the issues. On the contrary, the place of multiculturalism within liberal theory remains very controversial. But it changes the terms of the debate. The issue is no longer how to protect communitarian minorities from liberalism, but whether minorities that share basic liberal principles nonetheless need minority rights. If groups are indeed liberal, why do their members want minority rights? Why aren't they satisfied with the traditional common rights of citizenship?

This is the sort of question that Joseph Raz has tried to answer in his recent work. Raz insists that the autonomy of individuals—their ability to make good choices amongst good lives—is intimately tied up with access to their culture, with the prosperity and flourishing of their culture, and with the respect accorded their culture by others. Multiculturalism helps ensure this cultural flourishing and mutual respect (Raz 1994; 1998; Margalit and Raz 1990). Other liberal writers like David Miller, Yael Tamir, and Jeff Spinner have made similar arguments about the importance of 'cultural membership' or 'national iden- tity' to modern freedom-seeking citizens (Tamir 1993; Miller 1995; Spinner 1994). I have tried to argue this as well (Kymlicka 1989*a*; 1995*a*). The details of the argument vary, but each of us, in our own way, argues that there are compelling interests related to culture and identity which are fully consistent with liberal principles of freedom and equality, and which justify granting special rights to minorities. We can call this the 'liberal culturalist' position.

Critics of liberal culturalism have raised many objections to this entire line of argument. Some deny that we can intelligibly distinguish or individuate 'cultures' or 'cultural groups'; others deny that we can make sense of the claim that individuals are 'members' of cultures; yet others say that even if we can make sense of the claim that individuals are members of distinct cultures, we have no reason to assume that the well-being or freedom of the individual is necessarily tied up in any way with the flourishing of the culture. People may choose to form a strong bond with a particular language or culture, but that is their choice, not a need, and on a liberal view, they should be held responsible for the costs of their choices, and not expect others to subsidize this 'expensive taste'.[13]

These are important objections, but I think they can be answered. In general, the language and culture people are raised in should be seen as part of their unchosen circumstances, rather than a voluntary taste. Indeed, access to one's language and culture can sometimes be a precondition for the very capacity to make meaningful choices. Having to abandon one's language and culture for another, while obviously not impossible, is often a very difficult and costly process, and it is unreasonable to expect minorities to bear this cost, when members of the majority face no comparable sacrifice.[14]

In any event, these objections have not yet succeeded in dampening enthusiasm for liberal culturalism, which has quickly developed into the consensus position amongst liberals working in this field.[15] However, even those sympathetic to liberal culturalism face an obvious problem. It is clear that some kinds of minority rights would undermine, rather then support, individual autonomy. This would be true, for example, of minority rights that enabled a group to deny education or health care to children, or that enabled a group to forcibly confine women to the home. While most ethnocultural groups in Western societies share the same basic liberal values as the majority, we have seen that there are some exceptions, particularly some conservative ethnoreligious groups, and these illiberal groups might demand the right to restrict the freedoms of (some of) their own members. And even when a minority group has in general embraced liberal-democratic values, there still may be particular long-standing traditions or customs which are in conflict with liberal equality, and which the group may be reluctant to abandon. For example, an immigrant group may want to maintain traditional customs regarding arranged marriages, or to maintain traditional rules regarding divorce, both of which may seriously disadvantage women. Indeed, many of these potentially illiberal practices or customs revolve around issues of gender and sexuality. As a result, many feminists have expressed the concern that multiculturalism in practice will typically mean giving male members of the group the power to control the women in the group, and to maintain traditional forms of gender inequality.[16] Minority rights which take this form undermine, rather than enhance, the individual autonomy of group members.

A crucial task facing liberal defenders of multiculturalism, therefore, is to distinguish the 'bad' minority rights that involve *restricting* individual rights from the 'good' minority rights that can be seen as *supplementing* individual rights. I have proposed distinguishing two kinds of rights that a minority group might claim. The first involves the right of a group against its own members, designed to protect the group from the destabilizing impact of *internal* dissent (e.g. the decision of individual members not to follow traditional practices or customs). The second kind involves the right of a group against the larger society, designed to protect the group from the impact of *external* pressures (e.g. the economic or political decisions of the larger society). I call the first 'internal restrictions', and the second 'external protections'.

Both of these are often labelled as 'collective rights' or 'group rights', but they raise very different issues. Internal restrictions involve *intra-group* relations—the ethnocultural group may seek the use of state power to restrict the rights of its own members in the name of group solidarity. This raises the danger of individual oppression. Critics of 'collective rights' in this sense often invoke the image of theocratic and patriarchal cultures where women are oppressed and religious orthodoxy legally enforced as an example of what can happen when the alleged rights of the collectivity are given precedence over the rights of the individual.

Obviously, groups are free to require certain beliefs or actions as terms of membership in private, voluntary associations. A Catholic organization can insist that its members attend church. Everyone in a liberal society has the legal right to decide whether or not to attend church, or whether or not to criticize religious dogmas, but if someone chooses not to attend a church or to criticize its dogmas, they can be denied membership in the church and its voluntary organizations. That is simply part and parcel of the liberal right of free association, one of our most basic civil liberties. The problem of internal restrictions arises, however, when a group argues that its members should not in fact have the legal right to decide whether or not to attend church, or to question traditional beliefs. This is what occurred in the Ottoman millet system discussed in Chapter 6, where people did not have the legal right to engage in apostasy or heresy. Similarly, a group may argue that its members should not have a legal right to an education, to freedom of marriage partners, or to equality in divorce. All of these would be internal restrictions.[17]

External protections, by contrast, involve *inter*-group relations—i.e. the ethnic or national group may seek to protect its distinct existence and identity by limiting the impact of the decisions of the larger society. This too raises certain dangers—not of individual oppression within a group, but of unfairness between groups. One group may be marginalized or segregated in the name of preserving another group's distinctiveness. Critics of 'collective rights' in this sense often cite the old apartheid system in South Africa as an example of what can happen when a minority group demands special protections from the larger society.

However, external protections need not create such injustice. Granting special representation rights, land claims, or language rights to a minority need not, and often does not, put it in a position to dominate other groups. On the contrary, such rights can be seen as putting the various groups on a more equal footing, by reducing the extent to which the smaller group is vulnerable to the larger.

The two kinds of claims need not go together. Some ethnic or national groups seek external protections against the larger society without seeking to legally impose internal restrictions on their own members. Other groups do not claim any external protection against the larger community, but seek wide powers over the behaviour of their own members. Yet other groups make both kinds of claims. These variations lead to fundamentally different conceptions of minority rights, and it is important to determine what sort of claim a group is making.

Given the commitment to individual autonomy, I believe that liberals should be sceptical of claims to internal restrictions. Liberal culturalism rejects the idea that groups can legitimately restrict the basic civil or political rights of their own members in the name of preserving the purity or authenticity of the group's culture and traditions. However, a liberal conception of multiculturalism can accord groups various rights against the larger society, in order to reduce the group's vulnerability to the economic or political power of the majority. Such 'external protections' are consistent with liberal principles, although they too become illegitimate if, rather than reducing a minority's vulnerability to the power of the larger society, they instead enable a minority to exercise economic or political dominance over some other group.

To oversimplify, we can say that minority rights are consistent with liberal culturalism if (*a*) they protect the freedom of individuals within the group; and (*b*) they promote relations of equality (non-dominance) between groups (Kymlicka 1995*a*: ch. 3).[18] As I discuss below, it is not always easy to determine in advance whether a particular right being claimed by a minority will be used to impose internal restrictions or to create external protections, and some minority claims may inevitably contain elements of both. This often requires careful attention to the details of the particular case. But I believe that if we undertook such an investigation, we would find that in most cases, ethno-cultural groups in Western democracies are not in fact seeking to limit the basic liberties of their own members, and are not seeking to prevent their members from questioning and revising traditional practices and customs.[19]

For example, when blacks or indigenous peoples seek special group representation rights within the political institutions of the larger society, the goal is to ensure that their interests are considered in the decisions of the larger society, not to restrict dissent within their own group.[20] Similarly, when immigrants seek funding for mother-tongue language programmes or arts groups, or exemptions from Sunday closing legislation or dress codes that conflict with their religious beliefs, they are seeking to limit their vulnerability to the economic or political power of the majority, not trying to limit the liberty of their own members.[21]

A more complicated case concerns self-government rights for national minorities. On the one hand, these rights devolve powers to smaller political units, so that the national minority cannot be outvoted or outbid by the majority on decisions that are of particular importance to their culture, such as issues of education, immigration, resource development, language, and family law. As such they are external protections. But they also raise the prospect that the national minority will use its self-governing powers to limit the civil or political rights of its own members, and hence can potentially be used to impose internal restrictions.

Whether self-government rights can be used to impose internal restrictions will largely depend on whether the exercise of these self-government rights is subject to the same sorts of constitutional limitations that apply to the exercise of legislative power by the larger government. Is minority self-government subject to constitutional protections of individual civil and political rights? If we look at the actual examples of self-government by national minorities in the West, we find that they are indeed generally subject to the same constitutional limitations as that of the larger government. And so long as these constitutional limitations remain in place, minority self-government will primarily be a matter of external protections, and not of imposing internal restrictions.

In short, most forms of minority rights in the West serve to reduce the vulnerability of minority groups to the economic pressures and political decisions of the larger society. Such rights are intended to ensure that the larger society does not deprive the minority of the conditions necessary for its survival, not with preventing the minority's own members from engaging in untraditional or unorthodox practices.

In the second stage of the debate, therefore, the question of multiculturalism is reformulated as a question within liberal theory, and the aim is to show that some (but not all) minority rights claims enhance liberal values. In my opinion, this second stage reflects genuine progress. We now have a more accurate description of the claims being made by ethnocultural groups, and a more accurate understanding of the normative issues they raise. We have gotten beyond the sterile and misleading debate about individualism and collectivism.

However, I think this second stage also needs to be challenged. While it has a better understanding of the nature of most ethnocultural groups, and the demands they place on the liberal state, it misinterprets the nature of the liberal state, and the demands it places on minorities.

3. THE THIRD STAGE: MULTICULTURALISM AS A RESPONSE TO NATION-BUILDING

Let me explain. The assumption—generally shared by both defenders and critics of multiculturalism—is that the liberal state, in its normal operation, abides by a principle of 'benign neglect' towards ethnocultural diversity. That is, the state is indifferent to the ethnocultural identities of its citizens, and to the ability of ethnocultural groups to reproduce themselves over time. On this view, liberal states treat culture in the same way as religion—i.e. as something which people should be free to pursue in their private life, but which is not the concern of the state (so long as they respect the rights of others). Just as liberalism precludes the establishment of an official religion, so too there cannot be official cultures that have preferred status over other possible cultural allegiances.

This notion of benign neglect is different from, and stronger than, the idea of liberal neutrality discussed in Chapter 6, section 4. The idea of liberal neutrality says that the state should not rank the intrinsic merits of different conceptions of the good life, and this entails that the state should not say that speaking English is intrinsically more worthy than speaking French, or that being a Christian is intrinsically more worthy than being an atheist. However, it is consistent with liberal neutrality for the state to nonetheless promote a particular language or religion, so long as the justification for this is not their intrinsic value. It would be possible, for example, to say that everyone should speak English, not because it is a better language, but just because it is the most common language, and hence the most efficient means of communication. Similarly, one could say that the state should promote a national religion, not because it is the true religion, but because society is more harmonious if everyone shares the same religion. (This was Rousseau's view.) Or, as we saw last chapter, promoting political participation is consistent with neutrality if done to ensure just and stable institutions, but not if done on the grounds of its alleged intrinsic worth.

State neutrality, therefore, simply rules out certain kinds of arguments or justifications for public policy—namely, those which appeal to a ranking of the intrinsic merits of conceptions of the good life. It does not rule out policies which promote a particular language, culture, or religion so long as 'neutral' reasons are offered for these policies.

Obviously, state neutrality, while a necessary condition for justice for liberals, is not sufficient. The fact that there are neutral reasons for promoting a common religion does not mean it is legitimate for the state to declare and promote a national religion. On the contrary, liberals have firmly endorsed the principle that states should not only avoid promoting religion for non-neutral reasons relating to controversial conceptions of the good, they should avoid promoting it *at all*, even for neutral reasons of efficiency or social harmony. There should be a firm 'separation of church and state'.

In other words, in the sphere of religion, liberals believe not just in the idea of state neutrality, but in the stronger idea of benign neglect. There should be a strict separation of church and state which prohibits any policies to privilege one religion over another, no matter how neutral the justification.

This is the model which many people have assumed should apply also to ethnocultural diversity. After all, the benign neglect of religion seems to have worked very well in accommodating religious diversity. Following centuries of civil war between Catholics and Protestants in Europe, the principle of benign neglect has helped to ensure relative peace and tranquillity. So why should we not also apply this strict separation model to ethnocultural diversity as well?

For example, Michael Walzer argues that liberalism involves a 'sharp divorce of state and ethnicity'. The liberal state stands above all the various ethnic and national groups in the country, 'refusing to endorse or support their ways of life or to take an active interest in their social reproduction'. Instead, the state is 'neutral with reference to language, history, literature, calendar' of these groups. He says the clearest example of such a neutral liberal state is the United States, whose benign neglect of ethnocultural diversity is reflected in the fact that it has no constitutionally recognized official language (Walzer 1992d: 100–1; cf. Walzer 1992b: 9). For immigrants to become Americans, therefore, is simply a matter of affirming their allegiance to the principles of democracy and individual freedom defined in the US Constitution.

Indeed, some theorists argue that this is precisely what distinguishes liberal 'civic nations' from illiberal 'ethnic nations' (Pfaff 1993: 162; Ignatieff 1993). Ethnic nations take the reproduction of a particular ethnonational culture and identity as one of their most important goals. Civic nations, by contrast, are indifferent to the ethnocultural identities of their citizens, and define national membership purely in terms of adherence to certain principles of democracy and justice. For minorities to seek special rights, on this view, is a radical departure from the traditional operation of the liberal state. Therefore, the burden of proof lies on anyone who would wish to endorse such minority rights.

This is the burden of proof which liberal culturalists like Raz try to meet with their account of the role of cultural membership in securing freedom and self-respect. They try to show that minority rights supplement, rather than diminish, individual freedom and equality, and help to meet needs which would otherwise go unmet in a state that clung rigidly to ethnocultural neutrality.

The presumption in the second stage of the debate, therefore, has been that advocates of multiculturalism must demonstrate compelling reasons to depart from the norm of benign neglect. I believe, however, that this idea that liberal-democratic states (or 'civic nations') are indifferent to ethnocultural identities is manifestly false. The religion model is altogether misleading as an account of the relationship between the liberal-democratic state and ethnocultural groups.

Consider the actual policies of the United States. Historically, decisions about the boundaries of state governments, and the timing of their admission into the federation, were deliberately made to ensure that anglophones would be a majority within each of the fifty states of the American federation. This helped establish the dominance of English throughout the territory of the United States. And the continuing dominance of English is ensured by several ongoing policies. For example, it is a legal requirement for children to learn the English language in schools; it is a legal requirement for immigrants (under the age of 50) to learn English to acquire American citizenship; and it is a *de facto* requirement for employment within the government or to get government contract work that the applicant speak English.

These decisions are not isolated exceptions to some norm of benign neglect. On the contrary, they are tightly interrelated, and together they have shaped the very structure of the American state, and the way the state structures society. (Since governments account for 40–50 per cent of GNP in most Western countries, the language of government is not negligible.)

These policies have all been pursued with the intention of promoting integration into what I call a 'societal culture'. By a societal culture, I mean a territorially concentrated culture, centred on a shared language which is used in a wide range of societal institutions, in both public and private life (schools, media, law, economy, government, etc.). I call it a *societal* culture to emphasize that it involves a common language and social institutions, rather than common religious beliefs, family customs, or personal lifestyles. Societal cultures within a modern liberal democracy are inevitably pluralistic, containing Christians as well as Muslims, Jews, and atheists; heterosexuals as well as gays; urban professionals as well as rural farmers; conservatives as well as socialists. Such diversity is the inevitable result of the rights and freedoms guaranteed to liberal citizens, particularly when combined with an ethnically diverse population. This diversity, however, is balanced and constrained by linguistic and institutional cohesion; cohesion that has not emerged on its own, but rather is the result of deliberate state policies.

The American government has deliberately created such a societal culture, and promoted the integration of citizens into it. The government has encouraged citizens to view their life-chances as tied up with participation in common societal institutions that operate in the English language, and has nurtured a national identity defined in part by common membership in a societal culture. Nor is the United States unique in this respect. As I discussed in Chapter 6, all liberal democracies (except perhaps Switzerland) have embraced this goal of developing a common national language and culture. This is part of the 'liberal-nationalist' strategy to help secure solidarity and political legitimacy within democratic states.

Obviously, the sense in which English-speaking Americans share a common 'culture' is a very thin one, since it does not preclude differences in religion, personal values, family relationships, or lifestyle choices.[22] While thin, it is far from trivial. On the contrary, as I discuss below, attempts to integrate people into such a common societal culture have often been met with serious resistance. Although integration in this sense leaves a great deal of room for both the public and private expression of individual and collective differences, some groups have nonetheless vehemently rejected the idea that they should view their life-chances as tied up with the societal institutions conducted in the majority's language.

So we need to replace the idea of 'benign neglect' with a more accurate model which recognizes the central role of nation-building within liberal democracies. To say that states are nation-building is not to say that governments can only promote one societal culture. It is possible for government policies to encourage the sustaining of two or more societal cultures within a single country—indeed, as I discuss below, this is precisely what characterizes multination states like Canada, Switzerland, Belgium, or Spain.

However, historically, virtually all liberal democracies have, at one point or another, attempted to diffuse a single societal culture throughout all of its territory.[23] Nor should this be seen purely as a matter of cultural imperialism or ethnocentric prejudice. As we discussed in Chapters 6 and 7, this sort of nation-building serves a number of important goals: equality of opportunity, solidarity, trust, deliberative democracy (Tamir 1993; Miller 1995; Canovan 1996).[24]

So states have engaged in this process of 'nation-building'—that is, a process of promoting a common language, and a sense of common membership in, and equal access to, the social institutions operating in that language. Decisions regarding official languages, core curriculum in education, and the requirements for acquiring citizenship, all have been made with the intention of diffusing a particular culture throughout society, and of promoting a particular national identity based on participation in that societal culture.

If this nation-building model provides a more accurate account of modern liberal democratic states, how does this affect the issue of multiculturalism? I believe it gives us a very different perspective on the debate. The question is no longer how to justify departure from a norm of benign neglect, but rather, do majority efforts at nation-building create injustices for minorities? And if so, do minority rights help protect against these injustices?

This would be a third way of conceptualizing the debate. I cannot discuss all of its implications, but let me give some examples of how this new model may affect the debate over multiculturalism.

4. FIVE MODELS OF MULTICULTURALISM

How does nation-building affect minorities? As Taylor notes, the process of nation-building inescapably privileges members of the majority culture:

If a modern society has an 'official' language, in the fullest sense of the term, that is, a state-sponsored, -inculcated, and -defined language and culture, in which both economy and state function, then it is obviously an immense advantage to people if this language and culture are theirs. Speakers of other languages are at a distinct disadvantage. (Taylor 1997: 34; cf. Wright 2000: 231)

This means that members of minority cultures face a choice. If all public institutions are being run in another language, minorities face the danger of being marginalized from the major economic, academic, and political institutions of the society. Faced with this dilemma, minorities have (to oversimplify) four basic options:[25]

(i) they can emigrate en masse, particularly if they have a prosperous and friendly state nearby that will take them in. This has rarely occurred in the recent history of the West, but has happened recently in Eastern Europe (e.g. with the mass emigration of ethnic Germans from Kazakhstan to Germany, or of Jews from Russia to Israel).

(ii) they can accept integration into the majority culture, although seek to negotiate better or fairer terms of integration;

(iii) they can seek the sorts of rights and powers of self-government needed to maintain their own societal culture—i.e. to create their own economic, political, and educational institutions in their own language;

(iv) they can accept permanent marginalization, and seek only to be left alone on the margins of society.

Each of these reflects a different strategy that minorities can adopt in the face of state nation-building. To be successful, each of them (except emigration) requires certain accommodations from the state. These may take the form of multiculturalism policies, or self-government and language rights, or treaty rights and land claims, or legal exemptions. Different forms of minority rights reflect different strategies about how to respond to, and to limit, state nation-building pressures.

We can find some ethnocultural groups that fit each of these categories (and other groups that are caught between them). For example, some immigrant ethnoreligious sects choose permanent marginalization. This would seem to be true, for example, of the Hutterites in Canada, or the Amish in the United States. But the option of accepting marginalization is only likely to be attractive to ethnoreligious sects whose theology requires them to avoid all contact with the modern world. The Hutterites and Amish are unconcerned about their marginalization from universities or legislatures, since they view such 'worldly' institutions as corrupt.

Virtually all other ethnocultural minorities, however, seek to participate in the modern world, and to do so, they must either integrate or seek the self-government needed to create and sustain their own modern institutions. Faced with this choice, ethnocultural groups have responded in different ways. I will briefly discuss five types of ethnocultural groups that are found within Western democracies: national minorities, immigrants, isolationist ethno-religious groups, metics, and racial caste groups. In each case, I will discuss how they have been affected by majority nation-building, what sorts of minority rights claims they have made in response to this nation-building, and how these claims relate to underlying liberal-democratic principles.

(a) National minorities

By national minorities, I mean groups that formed complete and functioning societies in their historic homeland prior to being incorporated into a larger state. National minorities can be subdivided into two categories: 'substate nations' and 'indigenous peoples'. Substate nations are nations which do not currently have a state in which they are a majority, but which may have had such a state in the past, or which may have sought such a state. They find themselves sharing a state with other nations for a variety of reasons. They may have been conquered or annexed by a larger state or empire in the past; ceded from one empire to another; or united with another kingdom through royal marriage. In a few cases, multination states arise from a more or less voluntary agreement between two or more national groups to form a mutually beneficial federation.

Indigenous peoples are peoples whose traditional lands have been overrun by settlers, and who have then been forcibly, or through treaties, incorporated into states run by people they regard as foreigners. While other minority nations dream of a status like nation-states, with similar economic and social institutions and achievements, indigenous peoples typically seek something rather different: the ability to maintain certain traditional ways of life and beliefs while nevertheless participating on their own terms in the modern world. In addition to the autonomy needed to work out that sort of project, indigenous peoples also typically require of the larger society a respect and recognition to begin to make amends for indignities they suffered for decades or centuries as second-class citizens (or even non-citizens or slaves).

The contrast between indigenous peoples and substate nations is not precise, and there is no universally agreed definition of 'indigenous peoples'. One way to distinguish substate nations from indigenous peoples in the Western context is that the former were contenders but losers in the process of

European state formation, whereas the latter were isolated from that process until recently, and so retained a pre-modern way of life until well into this century. Substate nations would have liked to form their own states, but lost in the struggle for political power, whereas indigenous peoples existed outside this system of European states. The Catalans, Basques, Flemish, Scots, Welsh, Corsicans, Puerto Ricans, and Québécois, then, are substate nations, whereas the Sami, Inuit, Maori, and American Indians are indigenous peoples. In both North America and Europe, the consequences of incorporation have been much more catastrophic for indigenous peoples than for other national minorities.[26]

However they were incorporated, both substate nations and indigenous peoples have typically resisted state nation-building, and have fought to maintain or regain their own self-governing institutions, often operating in their own language, so as to be able to live and work in their own culture. They demand to maintain or regain their own schools, courts, media, political institutions, and so on. To achieve this, they typically demand some form of autonomy. At the extreme, this may involve claims to outright secession, but more usually it involves some form of regional autonomy. And they typically mobilize along nationalist lines, using the language of 'nationhood' to describe and justify these demands for self-government. While the ideology of nationalism has typically seen full-fledged independence as the 'normal' or 'natural' end point, economic or demographic reasons may make this infeasible for some national minorities. Moreover, it is increasingly clear that substantial forms of self-government can be achieved *within* the boundaries of a larger state, and so there is a growing interest in exploring these other forms of self-government, such as federalism.

In short, national minorities have typically responded to majority nation-building by seeking greater autonomy which they use to engage in their own competing nation-building, so as to protect and diffuse their societal culture throughout their traditional territory. Indeed, they often seek to use the same tools that the majority uses to promote this nation-building— e.g. they seek control over the language and curriculum of schooling in their region of the country, the language of government employment, the requirements of immigration and naturalization, and the drawing of internal boundaries. We can see this clearly in the case of Flemish or Québécois nationalism, which have been concerned precisely with gaining and exercising these nation-building powers, so as to maintain or rebuild their own societal culture. But it is also increasingly true of many indigenous peoples around the world, who have adopted the language of 'nationhood', and who are engaged in a major campaign of 'nation-building', which requires the exercise of much greater powers of self-government and the building of many new societal institutions.[27]

How should liberal democracies respond to such minority nationalisms? Historically, liberal democracies have tried to suppress minority nationalisms, often ruthlessly. At various points in the eighteenth and nineteenth centuries, for example, France banned the use of the Basque and Breton languages in schools or publications, and banned any political associations which aimed to promote minority nationalism; the British in Canada stripped the Québécois of their French-language rights and institutions, and redrew political boundaries so that the Québécois did not form a majority in any province; Canada also made it illegal for Aboriginals to form political associations to promote their national claims; and when the United States conquered the south-west in the war with Mexico in 1848, it stripped the long-settled Hispanics of their Spanish-language rights and institutions, imposed literacy tests to make it difficult for them to vote, and encouraged massive immigration into the area so that the Hispanics would become outnumbered.

All of these measures were intended to disempower national minorities, and to eliminate any sense of possessing a distinct national identity. This was justified on the grounds that minorities that view themselves as distinct 'nations' would be disloyal, and potentially secessionist. And it was often claimed that minorities—particularly indigenous peoples—were backward and uncivilized, and that it was in their own interests to be incorporated (even against their will) into more civilized and progressive nations. National minorities, therefore, were often the first target of majority nation-building campaigns.[28]

But the attitude of liberal democracies towards minority nationalism has changed dramatically in this century. It is increasingly recognized that the suppression of minority nationalism was mistaken, for both empirical and normative reasons. Empirically, the evidence shows that pressuring national minorities to integrate into the dominant national group simply will not work. Western states badly misjudged the durability of minority national identities. The character of a national identity can change quickly—e.g. the heroes, myths, and traditional customs. But the identity itself—the sense of being a distinct nation, with its own national culture—is much more stable. Liberal-democratic governments have, at times, used all the tools at their disposal to destroy the sense of separate identity amongst their national minorities, from the prohibition of tribal customs to the banning of minority-language schools. But despite centuries of legal discrimination, social prejudice, and indifference, national minorities have maintained their sense of forming a distinct nation, and their desire for national autonomy.

As a result, when the state attacks the minority's sense of distinct nationhood, the result is often to promote rather than reduce the threat of disloyalty and secessionist movements. Indeed, recent surveys of ethnonationalist conflict around the world show that self-government arrangements diminish the likelihood of violent conflict, while refusing or rescinding self-government rights is likely to escalate the level of conflict (Gurr 1993, 2000; Hannum 1990; Lapidoth 1996). In the experience of Western democracies, the best way to ensure the loyalty of national minorities has been to accept, not attack, their sense of distinct nationality.

Moreover, the suppression of minority nationalism is difficult to defend normatively. After all, if the majority can engage in legitimate nation-building, why not national minorities, particularly those which have been involuntarily incorporated into a larger state? To be sure, liberal principles set limits on *how* national groups go about nation-building. Liberal principles will preclude any attempts at ethnic cleansing, or stripping people of their citizenship, or the violation of human rights. These principles will also insist that any national group engaged in a project of nation-building must respect the right of other nations within its jurisdiction to protect and build their own national institutions. For example, the Québécois are entitled to assert national rights vis-à-vis the rest of Canada, but only if they respect the rights of Aboriginals within Quebec to assert national rights vis-à-vis the rest of Quebec.

These limits are important, but they still leave significant room, I believe, for legitimate forms of minority nationalism. Moreover, these limits are likely to be similar for both majority and minority nations. All else being equal, national minorities should have the same tools of nation-building available to them as the majority nation, subject to the same liberal limitations. What we need, in other words, is a consistent theory of permissible forms of nation-building within liberal democracies. I do not think that political theorists have yet developed such a theory. One of the many unfortunate side-effects of the dominance of the 'benign neglect' model is that liberal theorists have never explicitly confronted this question.[29]

I do not have the space here to defend any particular theory of permissible nation-building,[30] but simply to insist that this is the relevant question we need to address. The question is not 'have national minorities given us a compelling reason to abandon the norm of benign neglect?', but rather 'why should national minorities not have the same powers of nation-building as the majority?' This is the context within which minority nationalism must be evaluated—i.e. as a response to majority nation-building, using the same tools of nation-building. And the burden of proof surely rests on those who would deny national minorities the same powers of nation-building as those which the national majority takes for granted.

(b) Immigrant groups

By immigrant groups, I mean groups formed by the decision of individuals and families to leave their original homeland and emigrate to another society, often leaving their friends and relatives behind. This decision is typically made for economic reasons, although sometimes also for political reasons, to move to a freer or more democratic country. Over time, and with the second and subsequent generations born in the new country of residence, they give rise to ethnic communities with varying degrees of internal cohesion and organization.

But it is essential immediately to distinguish two categories of immigrants—those who have the right to become citizens, and those who do not. Much confusion in the academic literature, and the wider public debate, has arisen from conflating these two cases. I will use the term 'immigrant group' only for the former case, and will discuss the latter case, which I will call 'metics', below.

Immigrants, then, are people who arrive under an immigration policy which gives them the right to become citizens after a relatively short period of time—say, three to five years—subject only to minimal conditions (e.g. learning the official language, and knowing something about the country's history and political institutions). This has been the traditional policy governing immigration in the three major 'countries of immigration'—namely, United States, Canada, and Australia.

Historically, immigrant groups have responded very differently to majority nation-building from national minorities. Unlike national minorities, the option of engaging in competing nation-building has been neither desirable nor feasible for immigrant groups in Western democracies. They are typically too small and territorially dispersed to hope to recreate their original societal culture from scratch in a new country. Instead, they have traditionally accepted the expectation that they will integrate into the larger societal culture. Indeed, few immigrant groups have objected to the requirement that they must learn an official language as a condition of citizenship, or that their children must learn the official language in school. They have accepted the assumption that their life-chances, and even more the life-chances of their children, will be bound up with participation in mainstream institutions operating in the majority language.

Western democracies now have over 200 years of experience concerning how such groups integrate, and there is little evidence that legal immigrants with the right to become citizens pose any sort of threat to the unity or stability of a liberal democracy. There are few (if any) examples of immigrant groups mobilizing behind secessionist movements, or nationalist political parties, or supporting revolutionary movements to overthrow elected governments. Instead, they integrate into the existing political system, just as they integrate economically and socially.[31]

So immigrants have not resisted majority nation-building campaigns to integrate them into the mainstream society. However, what immigrants have tried to do is to renegotiate the terms of integration. Indeed, many recent debates over 'multiculturalism' in immigrant countries are precisely debates over renegotiating the terms of integration. Immigrants are demanding a more tolerant or 'multicultural' approach to integration that would allow and support immigrants to maintain various aspects of their ethnic heritage even as they integrate into common institutions operating in the majority language. Immigrants insist that they should be free to maintain some of their old customs regarding food, dress, recreation, religion, and to associate with each other to maintain these practices. This should not be seen as unpatriotic or 'un-American'. Moreover, the institutions of the larger society should be adapted to provide greater recognition and accommodation of these ethnic identities—e.g. schools and other public institutions should accommodate their religious holidays, dress, dietary restrictions, and so on.

How should liberal democracies respond to such demands for immigrant multiculturalism? Here again, liberal democracies have historically resisted these demands. Until the 1960s, all three of the major immigrant countries adopted an 'Anglo-conformity' model of immigration. That is, immigrants were expected to assimilate to existing cultural norms, and, over time, become indistinguishable from native-born citizens in their speech, dress, leisure activities, cuisine, family size, identities, and so on. To be too visibly 'ethnic' in one's public behaviour was seen as unpatriotic. This strongly assimilationist policy was seen as necessary to ensure that immigrants become loyal and productive members of society.

However, it is increasingly accepted that this assimilationist approach is neither necessary nor justifiable. It is unnecessary since there is no evidence that those immigrants who remain proud of their heritage are less likely to be loyal and productive citizens of their new country. And it is unjustifiable, since it imposes unfair costs on immigrants. The state imposes a range of *de jure* and *de facto* requirements for immigrants to integrate in order to succeed, and these requirements are often difficult and costly for immigrants to meet. Since immigrants cannot respond to this by adopting their own nation-building programmes, but rather must attempt to integrate as best they can, it is only fair that the state minimize the costs involved in this state-demanded integration.

Put another way, immigrants can demand fairer terms of integration. This demand typically involves two basic elements. (*a*) We need to recognize that integration does not occur overnight, but is a difficult and long-term process that operates intergenerationally. This means that special accommodations (e.g. mother-tongue services) are often required for immigrants on a transitional basis. (*b*) We need to ensure that the common institutions into which immigrants are pressured to integrate provide the same degree of respect, recognition, and accommodation of the identities and practices of immigrants as they traditionally have of the identities and practices of the majority group. This requires a systematic exploration of our social institutions to see whether their rules and symbols disadvantage immigrants. For example, we need to examine dress codes, public holidays, even height and weight restrictions, to see whether they are biased against certain immigrant groups. We also need to examine the portrayal of minorities in school curricula or the media to see if they are stereotypical, or fail to recognize the contributions of immigrants to national history or world culture. These measures are needed to ensure that liberal states are offering immigrants fair terms of integration.

Here again, I do not have the space to discuss in detail the fairness of each of these policies. The requirements of fairness are not always obvious, particularly in the context of people who have chosen to enter a country, and political theorists have done little to date to illuminate the issue. But there is growing recognition that this is the relevant question we need to address. The question is not whether immigrants have given us a compelling reason to diverge from the norm of benign neglect, but rather, how can we ensure that state policies aimed at pressuring immigrants to integrate are fair?

(c) Isolationist ethnoreligious groups

Whereas most immigrants wish to participate in the larger society, there are some small immigrant groups which voluntarily isolate themselves from the larger society, and avoid participating in politics or civil society. As I noted earlier, this option of voluntary marginalization is only likely to be attractive to ethnoreligious groups whose theology requires them to avoid all contact with the modern world, such as Hutterites, Amish, or Hasidic Jews, all of whom emigrated to escape persecution for their religious beliefs. They are unconcerned about their marginalization from the larger society and polity, since they view its 'worldly' institutions as corrupt, and seek to maintain the same isolated traditional way of life they had in their original homeland.

In order to avoid contact with the modern world, and to maintain their traditional way of life, these groups seek exemption from various laws. For example, they demand exemption from military service or jury duty, since these would implicate them in the operation of worldly governments. And they have demanded exemption from compulsory education laws, in order to ensure that their children are not exposed to corrupting influences (e.g. they seek the right to take their children out of school before the legal age of 16, and to be exempted from certain parts of the core curriculum which teach about the lifestyles of the modern world).

The response of these groups to majority nation-building is very different from that of either national minorities or immigrant groups. After all, nation-building aims to integrate citizens into a modern societal culture, with its common academic, economic, and political institutions, and this is precisely what ethnoreligious sects wish to avoid. Moreover, the sorts of laws from which these groups seek exemption are precisely the sorts of laws which lie at the heart of modern nation-building (e.g. mass education).

How should liberal democracies respond to such demands to be exempted from majority nation-building? Perhaps surprisingly, many Western democracies have historically been quite accepting of these demands. This is surprising, since by their own admission these groups often lack any loyalty to the state. Moreover, they are often organized internally in illiberal ways. They inhibit attempts by group members to question traditional practices or religious authorities (and indeed often try to prevent children from acquiring the capacity for such critical reflection), and may restrict women to the household. And they are not responsible citizens in the country as a whole, in the sense that they take no interest in trying to tackle problems in the larger society (e.g. they take no interest in how to solve the problems of urban poverty, pollution, or drug abuse).[32]

As I noted in Chapter 7, Jeff Spinner calls these groups 'partial citizens', because they voluntarily waive both the rights and responsibilities of democratic citizenship (Spinner 1994). They do not exercise their right to vote and to hold office (and their right to welfare benefits), but by the same token they also seek to evade their civic responsibility to help tackle the country's problems. Unlike most national minorities and immigrant groups, therefore, these ethnoreligious sects reject principles of state loyalty, liberal freedoms, and civic responsibility.

Why then were the demands of these groups accepted? Part of the reason, at least in the North American context, is that they arrived at a time when both the United States and Canada were desperately seeking immigrants to settle the western frontier, and were willing to make concessions to acquire large groups of immigrants with useful agricultural skills. It is not clear that liberal democracies today would be as willing to make the same concessions to newly arriving ethnoreligious sects.

And indeed it is not clear whether it is appropriate, from the point of view of liberal-democratic principles, to offer such concessions. After all, these groups deny liberty to their own members, and avoid their civic obligations to the rest of society. For this reason, various attempts have been made over the years to take away these exemptions, and to force these groups to fulfil their civic duties (e.g. military service and jury duty), and force the children to attend the usual length of compulsory schooling, with the standard core curriculum, so that they learn to be competent democratic citizens capable of participating in the outside world.

However, in general, most democratic states continue to tolerate these groups, so long as they do not egregiously harm people inside the group (e.g.

sexually abuse children), and so long as they do not attempt to impose their views on outsiders, and so long as members are legally free to leave. This toleration is typically justified either on the grounds of a communitarian conception of freedom of religion, or on the grounds that these groups were given specific promises of toleration when they entered the country— historical promises which were not given to other immigrants.[33]

These first three types of groups—national minorities, immigrants, and ethnoreligious sects—have all been the targets of majority nation-building programmes. As liberal states embarked on their projects of diffusing a common societal culture throughout the entire territory of the state, and encountered these types of groups, they sought to pressure them to integrate.

The final two types of groups I will discuss—namely, metics and racial caste groups, like the African-Americans—are very different. Not only were they not pressured to integrate into the majority culture, they were in fact prohibited from integrating. Whereas the first three types of groups were pressured to integrate, even if they wanted to remain apart, these last two groups were forcibly kept separate, even if they wanted to integrate. This history of exclusion continues to cause many difficulties for Western democracies.

(d) Metics

While isolationist groups like the Amish voluntarily waive their citizenship, there are some migrants who are never given the opportunity to become citizens. This is actually a diverse category of people, including *irregular migrants* (e.g. those who entered the country illegally or overstayed their visa, and who are therefore not legally domiciled, such as many Mexicans in California or North Africans in Italy), and *temporary migrants* (e.g. those who entered as refugees seeking temporary protection or as 'guest-workers', such as Turks in Germany). When they entered the country, these people were not conceived of as future citizens, or even as long-term residents, and indeed they would not have been allowed to enter in the first place if they were seen as permanent residents and future citizens. However, despite the official rules, they have settled more or less permanently. In principle, and to some extent in practice, many face the threat of deportation if they are detected by the authorities, or if they are convicted of a crime. But they nonetheless form sizeable communities in certain countries, engage in some form of employment, legal or illegal, and may marry and form a family. This is true, for example, of Mexicans in California, Turks in Germany, or North Africans in Italy or Spain. Borrowing a term from ancient Greece, Michael Walzer calls these groups 'metics'—that is, long-term residents who are nonetheless excluded from the polis (Walzer 1983). Since metics face enormous obstacles to integration—legal, political, economic, social, and psychological—they tend to exist in the margins of the larger society.

Generally speaking, the most basic claim of metics is to regularize their status as permanent residents, and to gain access to citizenship. They want, in effect, to be able to follow the immigrant path to integration into the mainstream society, even though they were not initially admitted as immigrants.

How should liberal democracies respond to this demand for access to citizenship? Historically, Western democracies have responded in different ways to these demands. Some countries—particularly the traditional immigrant countries—have grudgingly accepted these demands. Guest-workers who stay beyond their original contract are often able to gain permanent residence, and periodic amnesties are offered for illegal immigrants, so that over time they become similar to immigrants in their legal status and social opportunities.

But some countries—particularly those which do not think of themselves as immigrant countries—have resisted these demands. Not only did these countries not admit these particular individuals as immigrants, they do not admit any immigrants, and may have no established process or infrastructure for integrating immigrants. Moreover, many of these metics have either broken the law to enter the country (illegal immigrants), or broken their promise to return to their country of origin (guest-workers), and so are not viewed as worthy of citizenship. Moreover, countries with no tradition of accepting newcomers are often more xenophobic, and prone to view all foreigners as potential security threats, or as potentially disloyal, or simply as unalterably 'alien'. In these countries, of which Germany, Austria, and Switzerland are the best-known examples, the official policy has not been to try to integrate metics into the national community, but to get them to leave the country, either through expulsion or voluntary return.

We can see this policy reflected in the conception of 'multiculturalism' which has arisen for migrants who are denied access to citizenship—a conception which is very different from that in immigrant countries like Canada or Australia. In some German provinces (*Länder*), for example, until the 1980s, the government kept Turkish children out of German classes, and instead set up separate classes for Turks, often taught in Turkish by teachers imported from Turkey, with a curriculum focused on preparing the children for life in Turkey. This was called 'multiculturalism', but, unlike multiculturalism for immigrants in the USA, Canada, or Australia, it was not seen as a way of enriching or supplementing German citizenship. Rather, it was adopted precisely because these children were not seen as German citizens. It was a way of saying that these children do not really belong here, that their true 'home' is in Turkey. It was a way of reaffirming that they are aliens, not citizens. Multiculturalism without the offer of citizenship is almost invariably a recipe for, and rationalization of, exclusion.[34]

In short, the hope was that if metics were denied citizenship, so that they only had a precarious legal status within the country, and if they were told repeatedly that their real home was in their country of origin, and that they were not wanted as members of the society, then they would eventually go home.

But it is increasingly recognized that this approach to metics is not viable, and is both morally and empirically flawed. Empirically, it has become clear that metics who have lived in a country for several years are highly unlikely to go home, even if they have only a precarious legal status. This is particularly true if the metics have married and had children in the country. At this point, it is their new country, not their country of origin, which has become their 'home'. Indeed, it may be the only home that the metics' children and grand-children know. Once they have settled, founded a family, and started raising their children, nothing short of expulsion is likely to get metics to return to their country of origin.

So a policy based on the hope of voluntary return is simply unrealistic. Moreover, it endangers the larger society. For the likely result of such a policy is to create a permanently disenfranchised, alienated, and racially defined underclass. Metics may develop an oppositional subculture in which the very idea of pursuing success in mainstream institutions is viewed with suspicion. The predictable consequences can involve some mixture of political aliena-tion, criminality, and religious fundamentalism amongst the immigrants, particularly the second generation, which in turn leads to increased racial tensions, even violence, throughout the society.

To avoid this, there is an increasing trend in Western democracies, even in non-immigrant countries, towards adopting amnesty programmes for illegal immigrants, and granting citizenship to guest-workers and their children. In effect, long-settled metics are increasingly viewed as if they were legal immi-grants, and are allowed and encouraged to follow the immigrant path to integration.

This is not only prudent, but morally required. For it violates the very idea of a liberal democracy to have groups of long-term residents who have no right to become citizens. A liberal-democratic system is a system in which those people who are subject to political authority have a right to participate in determining that authority. To have permanent residents who are subject to the state, but unable to vote, is to create a kind of caste system which under-mines the democratic credentials of the state (Bauböck 1994; Carens 1989; Walzer 1983; Rubio-Marin 2000).

To be sure, these people arrived without any expectation or entitlement of becoming citizens, and may indeed have come illegally. But at some point, the original terms of admission become irrelevant. For all practical intents and purposes, this is now the metics' home, and they are *de facto* members of society who need the rights of citizenship.

(e) African-Americans

One final group which has been very important in recent American theorizing about multiculturalism is the blacks (African-Americans) who are descended from the African slaves brought to the United States between the seventeenth and nineteenth centuries. Under slavery, blacks were not seen as citizens, or even as 'persons', but simply as the property of the slave-owner, alongside his buildings and livestock. Although slavery was abolished in the 1860s, and blacks were granted citizenship, they were still subject to segregation laws which required that they attend separate schools, serve in separate army units, sit in separate train cars, etc., until the 1950s and 1960s. And while such discriminatory laws have now been struck down, the evidence suggests that blacks remain subject to pervasive informal discrimination in hiring and housing, and they remain disproportionately concentrated in the lower class, and in poor neighbourhoods.

African-Americans have a unique relationship to American nation-building. Like metics, they were historically excluded from becoming members of the nation. But unlike metics, the justification for this was not that they were citizens of some other nation to which they should return. Blacks in America can hardly be seen as 'foreigners' or 'aliens', since they have been in the USA as long as the whites, and have no foreign citizenship. Instead, they were effectively denationalized—they were denied membership in the American nation, but nor were they viewed as belonging to some other nation.

African-Americans are unlike other ethnocultural groups in the West. They do not fit the voluntary immigrant pattern, not only because they were brought to America involuntarily as slaves, but also because they were prevented (rather than encouraged) from integrating into the institutions of the majority culture (through racial segregation, and laws against miscegenation and the teaching of literacy). Nor do they fit the national minority pattern, since they do not have a homeland in America or a common historical language. They came from a variety of African cultures, with different languages, and no attempt was made to keep together those with a common ethnic background. On the contrary, people from the same culture (even from the same family) were typically split up once in America. Moreover, before emancipation, they were legally prohibited from trying to recreate their own cultural structure (e.g. all forms of black association, except churches, were illegal). The situation of African-Americans, therefore, is virtually unique.

In light of these complex circumstances and tragic history, African-Americans have raised a complex, unique, and evolving set of demands. The civil rights movement in the United States in the 1950s and 1960s was seen by many of its proponents as enabling blacks to follow the immigrant path of integration, through a more rigorous enforcement of anti-discrimination laws. Those African-Americans who were sceptical about the possibility of following the immigrant path to integration, however, have pursued the opposite tack of redefining blacks as a 'nation', and promoting a form of black nationalism. Much of the recent history of African-American political mobilization can be seen as a struggle between these two competing projects.

But neither of these is realistic. The legacy of centuries of slavery and segregation has created barriers to integration which immigrants simply do not face. As a result, despite the legal victories of the civil rights movement, blacks remain disproportionately at the bottom of the economic ladder, even as more recent (non-white) immigrants have integrated (e.g. Asian-Americans). But the territorial dispersion of blacks has made the option of national separatism equally unrealistic. Even if they shared a common black national identity, which they do not, there is no region of the United States where blacks form a majority.

As a result, it is increasingly recognized that a *sui generis* approach will have to be worked out for African-Americans, involving a variety of measures. These may include historical compensation for past injustice, special assistance in integration (e.g. affirmative action), guaranteed political representation (e.g. redrawing electoral boundaries to create black-majority districts), and support for various forms of black self-organization (e.g. subsidies for historical black colleges, and for black-focused education). These different demands may seem to pull in different directions, since some promote integration while others seem to reinforce segregation, but each responds to a different part of the complex and contradictory reality which African-Americans find themselves in. The long-term aim is to promote the integration of African-Americans into the American nation, but it is recognized that this is a long-term process that can only work if existing black communities and institutions are strengthened. A degree of short-term separateness and colour-consciousness is needed to achieve the long-term goal of an integrated and colour-blind society.[35]

It is difficult to specify precisely which principles should be used to evaluate these demands, all of which are controversial. As with most other groups, there are both moral and prudential factors to be considered. African-Americans suffer perhaps the greatest injustices of all ethnocultural groups, both in terms of their historical mistreatment and their current plight. Morally speaking, then, the American government has an urgent obligation to remedy these injustices. Moreover, as with metics, the result of this ongoing exclusion has been the development of a separatist and oppositional subculture in which the very idea of pursuing success in 'white' institutions is viewed by many blacks with suspicion. The costs of allowing such a subculture to arise are enormous, both for the blacks themselves, who are increasingly condemned to lives of poverty, marginalization, and violence, and for society at large, in terms of the waste of human potential, and the escalation of racial conflict. Given these costs, it would seem both prudent and moral to adopt whatever reforms are needed to prevent such a situation.

Much more could be said about the claims of each of these groups, or of other types of groups around the world. But enough has been said, I hope, to illustrate the importance of seeing how particular minority rights claims are related to, and a response to, state nation-building policies. In this third stage of the debate, we would look to see how each group's claims can be seen as specifying the injustices which majority nation-building has imposed or might impose on them, and as identifying the conditions under which majority nation-building would cease to be unjust. It is important to note that in all five of the cases I have examined, minorities are not saying that nation-building programmes are inherently impermissible. But they do insist that nation-building programmes be subject to certain conditions and limitations. If we try to combine these different demands into a larger conception of ethnocultural justice, we can say that majority nation-building in a liberal democracy is legitimate under the following conditions:

(a) no groups of long-term residents are permanently excluded from membership in the nation, such as metics or racial caste groups. Everyone living on the territory must be able to gain citizenship, and become an equal member of the nation if they wish to do so;

(b) insofar as immigrants and other ethnocultural minorities are pressured to integrate into the nation, the sort of socio-cultural integration which is required for membership in the nation should be understood in a 'thin' sense, primarily involving institutional and linguistic integration, not the adoption of any particular set of customs, religious beliefs, or lifestyles. Integration into common institutions operating in a common language should still leave maximal room for the expression of individual and collective differences, both in public and private, and public institutions should be adapted to accommodate the identity and practices of ethnocultural minorities. Put another way, the conception of national identity, and national integration, should be a pluralist and tolerant one;

(c) national minorities are allowed to engage in their own nation-building, to enable them to maintain themselves as distinct societal cultures.

These three conditions have rarely been met historically within Western democracies, but we can see a clear trend within most democracies towards greater acceptance of them. This trend partly reflects prudential reasons: earlier policies to exclude metics, assimilate immigrants, and suppress minority nationalisms have simply failed to achieve their aims, and so new patterns of ethnic relations are being tested. But it also reflects a recognition that previous policies were morally illegitimate.

The patterns I have been discussing in this section are of course generalizations, not iron laws. Some metics, immigrant groups, and national minorities have not mobilized to demand minority rights, and even when they have, some Western democracies continue to resist these demands.[36] Even in the United States, the usual tendencies toward immigrant integration have sometimes been deflected, particularly if the newcomers were expected to return quickly to their country of origin (as with the original Cuban exiles in Miami).

The extent to which national minorities have been able to maintain a separate societal culture also varies considerably. In some countries, national minorities have been almost completely integrated (e.g. Bretons in France). Even in the United States, the extent (and success) of nationalist mobilization varies. For example, compare the Chicanos in the south-west with the Puerto Ricans. The Chicanos were unable to preserve their own Spanish-speaking judicial, educational, or political institutions after being involuntarily incorporated into the United States in 1848, and they have not mobilized along nationalist lines to try to recreate these institutions. By contrast, Puerto Ricans mobilized very successfully to defend their Spanish-language institutions and self-government rights when they were involuntarily incorporated into the United States in 1898, and continue to exhibit a strong nationalist consciousness. The extent of nationalist mobilization also differs amongst the various Indian tribes in America.[37]

And even where these demands have been accepted, they often remain controversial, vulnerable to changes in popular opinion or governing party.[38] Still, the general trend is clear: Western states today exhibit a complex pattern of nation-building constrained by minority rights. On the one hand, Western states remain 'nation-building' states. All Western states continue to adopt the sorts of nation-building policies I discussed earlier, and no Western states have relinquished the right to adopt such policies. On the other hand, these policies are increasingly qualified and limited to accommodate the demands of minorities who feel threatened. Minorities have demanded, and increasingly been accorded, various rights which help ensure that nation-building does not exclude metics and racial caste groups, or coercively assimilate immigrants, or undermine the self-government of national minorities.

What we see in the 'real world of liberal democracies', therefore, is a complex dialectic of state nation-building (state demands on minorities) and minority rights (minority demands on the state). We can represent it as in Fig. 4.

Tools of state nation-building

- citizenship policy
- language laws
- education policy
- public service employment

- centralizing power
- national media, symbols, holidays
- military service

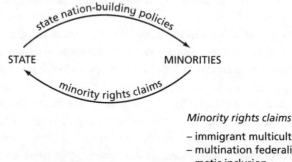

Minority rights claims

- immigrant multiculturalism
- multination federalism
- metic inclusion
- religious exemptions

Figure 4 The dialectic of nation-building and minority rights

In my view, it is essential to view both halves of this circle together. Too often in debates about minority rights, people simply look at the bottom half of the picture, and ask why pushy and aggressive minorities are asking for 'special status' or 'privileges'. What gives minorities the right to make such demands on the state? But if we look at the top half of the picture, it becomes clear that demands for minority rights must be seen in the context of, and as a response to, state nation-building. While minorities do make claims against the state, these are a response to the claims that the state makes against minorities. Moreover, many of these minority rights claims are, I believe, legitimate. That is, the rights being claimed by metics, racial groups, immigrants, and national minorities really do serve to protect them from real or potential injustices that would otherwise result from state nation-building.

If the presence of state nation-building policies helps to justify minority rights, one could also turn the equation around, and say that the adoption of minority rights has helped to justify state nation-building. After all, we cannot simply take for granted that it is legitimate for a liberal-democratic state to pressure minorities to integrate into institutions operating in the majority language. What gives the state the right to insist on common national languages, education systems, citizenship tests, and so on, and to impose such things on minorities? As I discussed in Chapters 6 and 7, liberal nationalists argue that there are certain valid purposes that are promoted by these nation-building policies, such as distributive justice and deliberative democracy, and I agree. But it is not legitimate to pursue these goals by assimilating, excluding, or disempowering minorities, or by imposing costs and burdens on groups that are often already disadvantaged. Unless supplemented and constrained by minority rights, state nation-building is likely to be oppressive and unjust. On the other hand, where these minority rights are in place, then state nation-building can serve a number of legitimate and important functions.

What we see, then, in the Western democracies, is a complex package of robust forms of nation-building combined and constrained by robust forms of minority rights. I believe that we could extend this method to look at other types of ethnocultural groups which do not fit into any of the categories discussed so far, such as the Roma in Slovakia, or Russian settlers in the Baltics. In each case, I think it is possible to view their claims to multiculturalism as a response to perceived injustices that arise out of nation-building policies.[39] Each group's claims can be seen as specifying the injustices that majority nation-building has imposed on them, and as identifying the conditions under which majority nation-building would cease to be unjust. A major task facing any liberal theory of multiculturalism is to better understand and articulate these conditions of ethnocultural justice.[40]

5. A NEW FRONT IN THE MULTICULTURALISM WARS?

So far, I have focused on the significant shifts in the recent multiculturalism debate. However, there has been an important assumption which is common to all three stages of the debate: namely, that the goal is to assess the *justice* of minority claims. This focus on justice reflects the fact that opposition to multiculturalism has traditionally been stated in the language of justice. Critics of multiculturalism had long argued that justice required state institutions to be 'colour-blind'. To ascribe rights on the basis of membership in ascriptive groups was seen as inherently morally arbitrary and discriminatory, necessarily creating first and second-class citizens.

The first task confronting any defender of multiculturalism, therefore, was to try to overcome this presumption, and to show that deviations from difference-blind rules which are adopted in order to accommodate ethnocultural differences are not inherently unjust. As we have seen, this has been done in two main ways: (*a*) by identifying the many ways that mainstream institutions are not indiffferent to people's ethnocultural identities, but rather are implicitly or explicitly tilted towards the interests and identities of the majority group; and (*b*) by emphasizing the importance of certain interests which have typically been ignored by liberal theories of justice—e.g. interests in recognition, identity, language, and cultural membership. If we accept either or both of these points, then we can see multiculturalism not as unfair privileges or invidious forms of discrimination, but as compensation for unfair disadvantages, and so as consistent with, and even required by, justice.

In my view, this debate over justice has subsided. As I noted earlier, much work remains to be done in assessing the justice of particular forms of multiculturalism or minority rights. But the older view that multiculturalism is *inherently* unjust is now widely discredited. I do not mean that defenders of multiculturalism have been successful in getting all or most of their claims implemented, although there is a clear trend throughout the Western democracies towards the greater recognition of minority rights.[41] Rather I mean that the terms of the public debate have been redefined in two profound ways: (*a*) few people continue to think that justice can simply be *defined* in terms of difference-blind rules or institutions. Instead, it is now recognized that difference-blind rules can cause disadvantages for particular groups. Whether justice requires common rules for all, or differential rules for diverse groups, is something to be assessed case by case in particular contexts, not assumed in advance; (*b*) as a result, the burden of proof has shifted. The burden of proof no longer falls solely on defenders of multiculturalism to show that their proposed reforms would not create injustices; the burden of proof equally falls on defenders of difference-blind institutions to show that the status quo does not create injustices for minority groups.

So the original justice-based grounds for blanket opposition to multiculturalism have faded. This has not meant that opposition to multiculturalism has disappeared. But it now takes a new form: critics have shifted the focus away from justice towards issues of social unity, focusing not on the justice or injustice of particular policies, but rather on the way that the general trend towards multiculturalism threatens to erode the sorts of civic virtues, identities, and practices which sustain a healthy democracy.

This focus on civic virtue and political stability represents the opening of a second front in the 'multiculturalism wars'. Many critics claim that multicultural policies are misguided, not because they are unjust in themselves, but because they are corrosive of long-term political unity and social stability. Why are they seen as destabilizing? The underlying worry is that multiculturalism involves the 'politicization of ethnicity', and that any measures which heighten the salience of ethnicity in public life are divisive. Over time they create a spiral of competition, mistrust, and antagonism between ethnic groups. Policies which increase the salience of ethnic identities act 'like a corrosive on metal, eating away at the ties of connectedness that bind us together as a nation' (Ward 1991: 598; cf. Schlesinger 1992; Schmidt 1997).

This is a serious concern. As I discussed in Chapter 7, there is growing fear that the public-spiritedness of citizens of liberal democracies may be in decline, and if group-based claims would further erode the sense of shared civic purpose and solidarity, then that would be a powerful reason not to adopt multiculturalism policies.

Another version of the same concern is the argument that too much emphasis on the 'politics of recognition' could undermine our capacity as a society to achieve a 'politics of redistribution'. The more we emphasize our cultural differences, the less likely we are to work together to fight economic inequality. On this view, we need to choose between struggling against the status hierarchy or struggling against the economic hierarchy. And the implicit assumption is that faced with this choice, the struggle against economic injustice should take precedence.[42]

It is an interesting question whether we should care more about economic inequalities than about status inequalities. If you were a black parent, would you care more about ensuring your child achieve an average income or about ensuring your child was not subject to racial epithets? If you were the parent of a gay teenager, would you choose a school that would maximize the child's economic prospects, or a school that would minimize his stigmization and persecution? It is far from clear that material inequalities are more important to the success of people's lives than status inequalities.

But do we really face a choice between these goals? Is it in fact true that multiculturalism erodes support for the welfare state and the politics of redistribution? There has been much armchair speculation on this question, but remarkably little evidence.[43] Reliable evidence is needed here, because one could quite plausibly argue the reverse: namely, that it is the *absence* of multiculturalism which erodes the bonds of civic solidarity. After all, if we accept the two central claims made by defenders of multiculturalism—namely, that mainstream institutions are biased in favour of the majority, and that the effect of this bias is to harm important interests related to personal agency and identity—then we might expect minorities to feel excluded from 'difference-blind' mainstream institutions, and to feel alienated from, and distrustful of, the political process. We could predict, then, that recognizing multiculturalism would actually strengthen solidarity and promote political stability, by removing the barriers and exclusions which prevent minorities from whole-heartedly embracing political institutions. This hypothesis is surely at least as plausible as the contrary hypothesis that multiculturalism erodes social unity.

We do not have the sort of systematic evidence needed to decisively confirm or refute these competing hypotheses. There is fragmentary evidence suggesting that multiculturalism often enhances, rather than erodes, social unity. For example, the evidence from Canada and Australia—the two countries which first adopted official multiculturalism policies—strongly disputes the claim that immigrant multiculturalism promotes political apathy or instability, or the mutual hostility of ethnic groups. On the contrary, these two countries do a better job integrating immigrants into common civic and political institutions than any other country in the world. Moreover, both have witnessed dramatic reductions in the level of prejudice, and dramatic increases in the levels of interethnic friendships and intermarriage. There is no evidence that the pursuit of fairer terms of integration for immigrants has eroded democratic stability (Kymlicka 1998: ch. 1).

The situation regarding the self-government claims of national minorities is more complicated, since these claims involve building separate institutions, and reinforcing a distinct national identity, and hence create the phenomenon of competing nationalisms within a single state. Learning how to manage this phenomenon is a profoundly difficult task for any state. However, even here there is significant evidence that recognizing self-government for national minorities assists, rather than threatens, political stability. Surveys of ethnic conflict around the world repeatedly confirm that 'early, generous devolution is far more likely to avert than to abet ethnic separatism' (Horowitz 1991: 224). It is the refusal to grant autonomy to national minorities, or, even worse, the decision to retract an already existing autonomy (as in Kosovo), which leads to instability, not the recognizing of their minority rights (Gurr 1993; Lapidoth 1996; Weinstock 1999).

Much more work needs to be done concerning the impact of multiculturalism on social unity and political stability. This relationship will undoubtedly vary from case to case, and so requires fine-grained empirical investigation. It is not clear that philosophical speculation can contribute much here: we need to wait for more and better evidence.[44] But as with concerns about justice, it is clear that concerns about social unity cannot provide any grounds for rejecting multiculturalism *in general*: there is no reason to assume in advance that there is any inherent contradiction between multiculturalism and democratic stability.

6. THE POLITICS OF MULTICULTURALISM

As with communitarianism and civic republicanism, multiculturalism is Janus faced: it has both a forward-looking or progressive side and a backward-looking or conservative side. The idea of multiculturalism has at times been invoked by conservatives who fear that liberalism and individual autonomy are eroding the traditional customs and practices of thick cultural communities, and undermining their capacity to pursue a communitarian politics of the common good. Multiculturalist rhetoric of this sort is invoked by traditionalist elites to prevent change within their group, to limit exposure to the larger world, and to defend some essentialized notion of their 'authentic' culture or tradition. To a large extent, this is just old-fashioned cultural conservatism dressed up in the new language of multiculturalism, and manifests the familiar conservative fear of the openness, mobility, diversity, and autonomy that modernization and globalization entail. It is 'multicultural' in the sense that it accepts that there is a diversity of groups within the larger society, but rejects any notion of diversity or dissent within each group.

But this is not the only, or most common, form of multiculturalist politics in the West. More frequently, multiculturalism has been invoked by progressive forces who endorse liberal values, and who want to fight practices of exclusion and stigmatization that prevent members of minority groups from fully enjoying their liberal rights and fair shares of resources. Multiculturalist rhetoric of this form is invoked by marginalized groups to challenge traditional status hierarchies, and to attack the privileged position of a particular gender, religion, skin colour, lifestyle, or sexual orientation in society. Viewed this way, multiculturalism is the enemy of cultural conservatism, and both reflects and embraces the openness, pluralism, and autonomy that modernization and globalization entail.

Multiculturalism takes these divergent political forms because modernization is a challenge not only for the mainstream society but also for minority groups. Multiculturalism can be invoked by minority groups to attack the conformism and conservatism of the larger society, and to pressure it to accept the new realities of openness and pluralism. But some members of the minority groups themselves fear this new openness, and invoke multiculturalism precisely to justify suppressing the freedom and changes it brings. As a result, multiculturalism is sometimes invoked by liberals against a narrow and conformist conception of the national culture, and sometimes invoked by conservatives to defend a narrow and conformist conception of a minority culture.

As with communitarianism and civic republicanism, the political implications of multiculturalism depend in part on whether the people invoking multiculturalism accept the liberal premiss about the revisability and plurality of our ends. If they do, then we are likely to see a liberal form of multiculturalism which seeks to challenge status inequalities while preserving individual freedom. If not, then we are likely to see a conservative form of multiculturalism that seeks to replace liberal principles with a communitarian politics of the common good, at least at the local or group level.

In this respect, multiculturalism bears the same political ambiguities as the nationalism to which it is a response. Just as nationalism can be invoked to construct either a thick and exclusive conservative form of national identity or a thin and inclusive liberal form, so too multiculturalist responses to nation-building can take a liberal or conservative form. Indeed, these two dynamics are probably related. Liberal forms of nation-building tend to generate liberal forms of multiculturalist responses, while conservative forms of nation-building generate conservative forms of multiculturalist responses. Here again, we can only understand the politics of multiculturalism by seeing it in relation to the politics of nation-building.

GUIDE TO FURTHER READING

There are several good anthologies of writings on multiculturalism, including Cynthia Willet, *Theorizing Multiculturalism: A Guide to the Current Debate* (Blackwell, 1998); Will Kymlicka (ed.), *The Rights of Minority Cultures* (Oxford University Press, 1995); and David Theo Goldberg (ed.), *Multiculturalism: A Critical Reader* (Blackwell, 1995).

As discussed in the chapter, the term 'multiculturalism' in fact encompasses a range of very different issues, which should be kept separate. One major area of controversy concerns *immigration*, including the right of states to restrict migration, and the terms under which immigrants should become citizens. The most sustained discussions to date are in Rainer Bauböck, *Transnational Citizenship: Membership and Rights in International Migration* (Edward Elgar, 1994), and Phillip Cole, *Philosophies of Exclusion: Liberal Political Theory and Immigration* (Edinburgh University Press, 2000). Other relevant discussions include David Jacobson, *Rights across Borders: Immigration and the Decline of Citizenship* (Johns Hopkins University Press, 1996); Veit-Michael Bader (ed.), *Citizenship and Exclusion* (St Martin's Press, 1997); Warren Schwartz (ed.), *Justice in Immigration* (Cambridge University Press, 1995); William Barbieri, *Ethics of Citizenship: Immigrants and Group Rights in Germany* (Duke University Press, 1998); Ruth Rubio-Marin, *Immigration as a Democratic Challenge: Citizenship and Inclusion in Germany and the US* (Cambridge University Press, 2000); and Brian Barry and Robert Goodin (eds.), *Free Movement: Ethical Issues in the Transnational Migration of People and of Money* (Pennsylvania State University Press, 1992).

A second set of issues concerns the legitimacy of *minority nationalism*. I listed several studies of the morality of nationalism in Chapter 6, although most of those focus on the legitimacy of state nationalism, rather than minority nationalism. For books which pay particular attention to the claims of national minorities, see Yael Tamir, *Liberal Nationalism* (Princeton University Press, 1993); Nenad Miscevic (ed.), *Nationalism and Ethnic Conflict: Philosophical Perspectives* (Open Court, 2000); Jocelyne Couture, Kai Nielsen, and Michel Seymour (eds.), *Rethinking Nationalism* (University of Calgary Press, 1998); Desmond Clarke and Charles Jones (eds.), *The Rights of Nations: Nations and Nationalism in a Changing World* (Palgrave, 1999). A related question concerns the legitimacy of *secession* by national minorities. This debate was initiated by Allen Buchanan, *Secession: The Legitimacy of Political Divorce* (Westview Press, 1991). More recent studies include Percy Lehning (ed.), *Theories of Secession* (Routledge, 1998); Margaret Moore (ed.), *National Self-Determination and Secession* (Oxford University Press, 1998).

A third area of debate concerns *racism*. See Charles Mills, *The Racial Contract* (Cornell University Press, 1997); Bob Brecher et al. (eds.), *Nationalism and Racism in the Liberal Order* (Ashgate, 1998); David Carroll Cochran, *The Color of Freedom: Race and Contemporary American Liberalism* (State University of New York Press, 1999); Clive J. Christie, *Race and Nation: A Reader* (St Martin's Press, 1998); Susan Babbitt and Sue Campbell (eds.), *Racism and Philosophy* (Cornell University Press, 1999); Les Back and John Solomos (eds.), *Theories of Race and Racism* (Routledge, 2000); Amy Gutmann and K. A. Appiah, *Color Conscious: The Political Morality of Race* (Princeton University Press, 1996). A related issue concerns the issue of historic injustice, including that of slavery and segregation. For interesting discussions, see Elazar Barkan, *The Guilt of Nations: Restitution and Negotiating Historical Injustices* (Norton, 2000); Roy L. Brooks (ed.), *When Sorry Isn't Enough: The Controversy over Apologies and Reparations for Human Injustice* (New York University Press, 1999).

A fourth area concerns *indigenous peoples*—see the special issue on 'Indigenous Rights' in *Australasian Journal of Philosophy*, 78/3 (2000); Duncan Ivison, Will Sanders, and Paul Patton (eds.), *Political Theory and the Rights of Indigenous Peoples* (Cambridge University Press, 2000); Curtis Cook and Juan Lindau (eds.), *Aboriginal Rights and Self-Government* (McGill-Queen's University Press, 2000).

A fifth area concerns *group representation*: see Anne Phillips, *The Politics of Presence* (Oxford University Press, 1995); Melissa Williams, *Voice, Trust and Memory: Marginalized Groups and the Failings of Liberal Representation* (Princeton University Press, 1998); Iris Marion Young, *Inclusion and Democracy* (Oxford University Press, 2000).

A sixth area concerns *religious groups*: see Robert Audi, *Religious Commitment and Secular Reason* (Cambridge University Press, 2000); Nancy L. Rosenblum (ed.), *Obligations of Citizenship and Demands of Faith: Religious Accommodation in Pluralist Democracies* (Princeton University Press, 2000); Meira Levinson, *The Demands of Liberal Education* (Oxford University Press, 1999); Stephen Macedo, *Diversity and Distrust: Civic Education in a Multicultural Democracy* (Harvard University Press, 2000); Jeff Spinner-Halev, *Surviving Diversity: Religion and Democratic Citizenship* (Johns Hopkins University Press, 2000).

A seventh concerns the relationship between multiculturalism and *gender equality*: see Uma Narayan and Sandra Harding (eds.), *Decentering the Center: Philosophy for a Multicultural, Postcolonial, and Feminist World* (Indiana University Press, 2000); Susan Okin, *Is Multiculturalism Bad for Women?* (Princeton University Press, 1999); Ayelet Shachar, *Multicultural Jurisdictions: Preserving Cultural Differences and Women's Rights in a Liberal State* (Cambridge University Press, 2001); Nira Yuval-Davis, *Gender and Nation* (Sage, 1997); Lois West (ed.), *Feminist Nationalism* (Routledge, 1997); Nira Yuval-Davis and P. Werbner (eds.), *Women, Citizenship, and Difference* (Zed Books, 1999); Monique Deveaux, *Cultural Pluralism and Dilemmas of Justice* (Cornell University Press, 2001).

While much of the writing on multiculturalism has focused on one of these topics, some people have tried to develop a more general theory that would cover some or all of these disputes. See, in particular, Joseph Carens, *Culture, Citizenship and Community* (Oxford University Press, 2000); Jacob Levy, *The Multiculturalism of Fear* (Oxford University Press, 2000); Bhikhu Parekh, *Rethinking Multiculturalism: Cultural Diversity and Political Theory* (Harvard University Press, 2000); James Tully, *Strange Multiplicity: Constitutionalism in an Age of Diversity* (Cambridge University Press, 1995); Jeff Spinner, *The Boundaries of Citizenship: Race, Ethnicity and Nationality in the Liberal State* (Johns Hopkins University Press, 1994); Charles Taylor, 'The Politics of Recognition', in Amy Gutmann (ed.), *Multiculturalism and the 'Politics of Recognition'*

(Princeton University Press, 1992); Michael Walzer, *On Toleration* (Yale University Press, 1997); Andrew Kernohan, *Liberalism, Equality and Cultural Oppression* (Cambridge University Press, 1998); David Ingram, *Group Rights: Reconciling Equality and Difference* (University Press of Kansas, 2000); Andrea Baumeister, *Liberalism and the Politics of Difference* (Edinburgh University Press, 2000); Paul Gilbert, *Peoples, Cultures, and Nations in Political Philosophy* (Georgetown University Press, 2000). I have tackled these issues myself in *Multicultural Citizenship* (Oxford University Press, 1995) and *Politics in the Vernacular: Nationalism, Multiculturalism and Citizenship* (Oxford University Press, 2001). Most of these books offer at least a qualified defence of multiculturalism and minority rights. For a critique, see Brian Barry, *Culture and Equality: An Egalitarian Critique of Multiculturalism* (Polity, 2001).

For collections which cover some or all of these topics, see Judith Baker (ed.), *Group Rights* (University of Toronto Press, 1994); Will Kymlicka and Wayne Norman (eds.), *Citizenship in Diverse Societies* (Oxford University Press, 2000); Ian Shapiro and Will Kymlicka (eds.), *Ethnicity and Group Rights: NOMOS 39* (New York University Press, 1997); Juha Raikka (ed.), *Do We Need Minority Rights: Conceptual Issues* (Kluwer, 1996); Christian Joppke and Steven Lukes (eds.), *Multicultural Questions* (Oxford University Press, 1999); John Horton and Susan Mendus (eds.), *Toleration, Identity and Difference* (St Martin's Press, 1999).

There are no political theory journals specifically devoted to issues of multiculturalism, but there are several interdisciplinary journals in the area of ethnic relations which frequently include debates about normative political theories of multiculturalism. These include: *Ethnicities; International Journal of Minority and Group Rights; Nations and Nationalism; Ethnic and Racial Studies; Journal of Ethnic and Migration Studies.*

In terms of websites, Lawrence Hinman's Ethics Homepage, mentioned in the guide to further reading in the Introduction, contains several resources related to multiculturalism, including sections on Race and Ethnicity, and Diversity and Moral Theory. Each section includes links to related Internet resources, summaries of recent articles, and a short survey of philosophical works on the topic (**www.ethics.acusd.edu/index.html**).

Also, the website for the Minorities at Risk Project, headed by Dr Ted Robert Gurr, is helpful. It is an independent, university-based research project that monitors and analyses the status and conflicts of 268 politically active communal groups in the larger countries of the world. It is designed to provide information in standardized form that will contribute to the understanding and peaceful accommodation of conflicts involving communal groups. Material relating to all 268 groups included in the project is available on the website. Information available includes the group's name and estimated population, a background account of the group's characteristics and political setting, a chronology of events initiated by or affecting the group from 1990 to 1995, and an assessment of prospects for change in the group's status in the near future (**www.bsos.umd.edu/cidcm/mar**).

Finally, my own website contains some resources for theorists studying issues of multiculturalism, including back-issues of an electronic newsletter on 'Citizenship, Democracy and Ethnocultural Diversity' that I edit. See **http://qsilver.queensu.ca/~philform/**.

NOTES

1. For a classic statement of this shift, see J. Cohen 1985; cf. Larana, Johnston, and Gusfield 1994.

2. See the discussion of citizenship's 'integrative function' in Barbalet 1988: 93.

3. It also provided a rationale for elites to channel public funds to support their culture, on the grounds that this culture was now the 'national' culture, available to all citizens regardless of class.

4. As we saw in Chapter 4, this link between social rights and national integration has also been challenged in another direction, from the right. Libertarians argue that social rights actually inhibit national integration by creating poverty traps and a culture of dependency that worsen the marginalization of the poor. In this chapter, however, I will focus on the claim that the traditional model of common citizenship rights fail to accommodate cultural difference.

5. By national minorities, I mean groups that formed complete and functioning societies on their historic homeland prior to being incorporated into a larger state. The incorporation of such national minorities has typically been involuntary, due to colonization, conquest, or the ceding of territory from one imperial power to another, but may also arise voluntarily, as a result of federation. See pp. 349–52.

6. For evidence about these oppressive aspects of the status inequality of homosexuals in North America, see B. Walker 1998; C. Cohen 1997: 582–8.

7. As Fraser notes, the relationship between recognition and redistribution in these 'mixed' cases can be quite complicated. For example, affirmative action programmes for women or blacks may be effective means for promoting redistribution in relation to the economic marketplace, but may actually worsen the stigmatization of these groups, who are singled out as needing 'special' help because they can not 'make it on their own'.

8. For a helpful typology, see Levy 1997. The term 'multiculturalism' is potentially mis-leading, since in some countries (like Canada or Australia) it is typically used to refer only to the accommodation of immigrant groups, not for other ethnocultural groups, like Aboriginals. Conversely, in some other countries (like the United States) 'multiculturalism' is often used to refer to all forms of 'identity politics', including not only ethnocultural groups, but also women, gays and lesbians, people with disabilities, and so on. In this chapter, however, I am using multiculturalism (and 'minority rights') to refer to the claims of ethnocultural groups.

9. Bauböck 1994; Buchanan 1991; Canovan 1996; Kymlicka 1995*a*; Miller 1995; Phillips 1995; Spinner 1994; Tamir 1993; Taylor 1992; Tully 1995; Walzer 1997; Young 1990. I am not aware of full-length books written by philosophers in English on any of these topics pre-dating 1990, with the exception of Plamenatz 1960. There have also been many edited collections of philosophical articles on these issues (Baker 1994; Kymlicka 1995*b*; Lehning 1998; Couture, Nielsen, and Seymour 1998; Shapiro and Kymlicka 1997; Schwartz 1995; Raikka 1996). For a comprehensive bibliography, see Kymlicka and Norman 2000.

10. For representatives of the 'individualist' camp, see Narveson 1991; Hartney 1991. For the 'communitarian' camp, see Garet 1983; Van Dyke 1977; 1982: Addis 1992; Johnston 1989; McDonald 1991*a*; 1991*b*; Svensson 1979; Karmis 1993.

11. Galenkamp 1993: 20–5. The belief in such a 'striking parallel' is partly the result of a linguistic sleight of hand. Because minority rights are claimed by groups, and tend to be group specific, they are often described as 'collective rights'. The fact that the majority seeks only 'individual' rights while the minority seeks 'collective' rights is then taken as evidence that the

minority is somehow more 'collectivist' than the majority. This chain of reasoning contains several non sequiturs. Not all group-specific minority rights are 'collective' rights, and even those which are 'collective' rights in one or other sense of that term are not necessarily evidence of 'collectivism'. See Kymlicka 1995a: ch. 3.

12. On the similarity in political views between native-born citizens and immigrants in North America, see Frideres 1997; Harles 1993. On the convergence in political values between anglophones and francophones in Canada, see Dion 1991.

13. For a pithy statement of these three objections, see Waldron 1995; cf. Johnson 2000.

14. Or so I argue in Kymlicka 1995a: ch. 6.

15. It is an interesting question why this liberal culturalist view—which is a clear departure from the dominant liberal view for several decades—has become so popular. I address this in Kymlicka 2001: ch. 2.

16. For discussions of the potential conflicts between multiculturalism and women's equality, see Deveaux 2001; Okin 1999; Shachar 2001.

17. As we saw in Chapter 6 (pp. 237–9), these internal restrictions can take the form of legally restricting certain civil liberties, or of attaching such costs to the exercise of these liberties that it becomes *de facto* impossible for individuals to exercise their (formal) legal rights.

18. Other liberal culturalists, however, argue that some limited forms of internal restrictions can be accepted, so long as group members have an effective right of exit from the group. This is likely to be the view of those who endorse a 'political' conception of liberalism, rooted in the value of tolerance, rather than a 'comprehensive' conception, rooted in the value of autonomy (e.g. Galston 1995; Kukathas 1997—see my discussion of these political liberals in Ch. 6, s. 7 above). For a discussion of the complications in determining what constitutes an 'effective' right of exit, see Okin 1998; Green 1995.

19. For a more detailed defence of this empirical claim, see Kymlicka 1998: ch. 4.

20. Unless, of course, they use gender-biased or other inegalitarian rules for selecting such representatives. This does not apply to most (any?) of the cases of group representation in the Western democracies, several of which are discussed in Phillips 1995.

21. In many of these cases, the appropriate solution may not be to exempt a minority from the law or rule, but rather to abandon the law entirely (Barry 2001: ch. 2; Kymlicka 1995a: 114–15, but cf. Modood 1994). I think this is the best response, for example, to sabbatarian laws. But note that this is not an objection to the minority's claim; it is an objection to the majority which passed the law for their own convenience, and if the majority is unable or unwilling to make this change, then the minority should be able to claim an exemption.

22. Indeed, my use of the term 'societal culture' is in conflict with the way the term culture is used in most academic disciplines, where it is defined in a very thick, ethnographic sense, referring to the sharing of specific folk customs, habits, and rituals. Citizens of a modern liberal state do not share a common culture in such a thick, ethnographic sense—indeed, the lack of a common thick ethnographic culture is part of the very definition of a liberal society. But it is equally essential to modern liberal forms of governance that citizens share a common culture in a very different, and thinner, sense, focusing on a common language and societal institutions.

23. To my knowledge, Switzerland is the only exception: it never made any serious attempt to pressure its French- and Italian-speaking minorities to integrate into the German-speaking majority. All of the other Western multination states have at one time or another made a concerted effort to assimilate their minorities, and only reluctantly gave up this ideal.

24. Of course, this sort of nation-building can also be used to promote illiberal goals. As Margaret Canovan puts it, nationhood is like a 'battery' which makes states run—the existence

of a common national identity motivates and mobilizes citizens to act for common political goals—and these goals can be liberal or illiberal (Canovan 1996: 80). Liberal reformers invoke the battery of nationhood to mobilize citizens behind projects of democratization, economic development, and social justice; illiberal authoritarians invoke nationhood to mobilize citizens behind attacks on alleged enemies of the nation, be they foreign countries or internal dissidents. This is why nation-building is just as common in authoritarian regimes as in democracies (e.g. Spain under Franco, or Latin America under the military dictators). Authoritarian regimes also need a 'battery' to help achieve public objectives in complex modern societies. What distinguishes liberal from illiberal states is not the presence or absence of nation-building, but rather the ends to which nation-building is put, and the means used to achieve them.

25. A fifth option would be to seek a military overthrow of the state, and to establish a minority-run dictatorship. This is not on the cards in the West, but we can see examples in Africa (e.g. Rwanda) or Asia (e.g. Fiji).

26. On the distinction between indigenous peoples and other national minorities, and its relevance for rights claims, see Anaya 1996; Kymlicka 2001: ch. 6.

27. On the need (and justification) for Aboriginal 'nation-building', see RCAP 1996; Alfred 1995.

28. This raises the question captured nicely in the title of Walker Connor's famous article: are nation-states 'Nation-Building or Nation-Destroying?' (Connor 1972). In truth, they are both. Nation-states have typically sought to build a common nationhood by destroying any pre-existing sense of distinct nationhood on the part of national minorities.

29. As Norman notes, these questions about the morality of nation-building have been ignored even by philosophers working on nationalism. They tend to ask about the morality of nation-states, not about the morality of *nation-building* states. In other words, philosophers of nationalism typically take the existence of nation-states as a given, and ask whether it is a good thing to have a world of nation-states. They do not explore the processes by which such nation-states are created in the first place (i.e. what methods of nation-building are permissible). Norman 1999: 60.

30. I make a preliminary attempt to develop criteria for distinguishing liberal from illiberal forms of nation-building in Kymlicka and Opalski 2001. For another recent discussion of the ethics of nation-building, see Norman 2001.

31. It is worth noting that in the major immigrant countries, refugees granted asylum are included in this category of immigrants who have a right to become citizens. Indeed, government policy towards the resettlement and naturalization of refugees is virtually identical to the policy for immigrants, and historically refugees have followed the same pattern of integration as other more voluntary immigrants.

32. They do of course accept strong responsibilities for attending to whatever problems arise within their own communities. But justice requires that we attend to problems beyond our immediate environment, even when we are not causally responsible for these wider problems. See Ch. 7, n. 31 and accompanying text.

33. For the contrast between liberal and communitarian conceptions of freedom of religion, see Ch. 6, pp. 230–2.

34. This earlier model has now been abandoned, and Germany is moving closer to what I called the immigrant model of multiculturalism.

35. For helpful discussions of the status and claims of African-Americans, and their connection to liberal-democratic norms, see Spinner 1994; Gutmann and Appiah 1996; Brooks 1996; Cochran 1999; and Kymlicka 2001: ch. 9.

36. In particular, France and Greece continue to resist any official recognition of either

immigrant multiculturalism or multination federalism, and Switzerland and Austria continue to resist any serious move to integrate metics. But these countries are now the clear exceptions to the norms in the West. And France is *de facto* liberalizing its approach to both autonomy for Corsica and multiculturalism for immigrants.

37. For a survey of the claims of national minorities in the US, see O'Brien 1987. Given these variations and hard cases, some theorists suggest that we should do away with the categories of 'immigrants' and 'national minorities', and simply think of ethnic groups as falling on a continuum with varying levels of cohesiveness, mobilization, concentration, size, historical rootedness, and so on. See, e.g. Young 1997a; Carens 2000: ch. 3; Barry 2001: 308–17; Favell 1999. I defend the typology in Kymlicka 2001: ch. 3.

38. It is worth noting, however, that no Western country has in fact reversed any of these major policy shifts—i.e. no country which adopted multiculturalism has subsequently repudiated it; no country which federalized has subsequently recentralized; and so on.

39. I discuss the claims of these other types of groups in Kymlicka and Opalski 2001.

40. The relationship between political practice and political theory is interestingly different in this case, I think, from other topics we have looked at. In most chapters, political theorists are developing normative theories to guide us in changing the status quo, and bring about models of justice or democracy which do not yet exist. In this chapter, many theorists have simply been trying to make normative sense out of the practices of multiculturalism which already exist in the Western democracies, but which have been ignored by previous political theorists. Theories of multiculturalism sometimes have an 'owl of Minerva' feel to them.

41. There is also a trend towards codifying minority rights at the international level. See Anaya 1996; De Varennes 1996; Kymlicka and Opalski 2001: Part 3.

42. Authors who say that the politics of recognition erodes the basis for a politics of redistribution (and who assume that the latter should take precedence) include Gitlin 1995; Barry 2001; Harvey 1996: ch. 12; Wolfe and Lausen 1997. For the opposite view that recognition supplements redistribution, see Fraser 1998; 2000; Young 2000a; Phillips 2000; Banting 2000; Tully 2000: 470.

43. Barry says that the negative impact of multiculturalism on redistribution is a major reason for rejecting multiculturalism (Barry 2001: p. 321) but he gives no evidence that there is a negative impact.

44. Philosophers' claims about the relationship between minority rights and social unity are often doubly speculative: first we speculate about the sources of social unity (the 'ties that bind'), and then we speculate about how minority rights affect these ties. Neither sort of speculation is grounded in reliable evidence. For example, some political philosophers have suggested (*a*) that it is shared values which form the bonds of social unity in modern liberal states, and (*b*) that immigrant multiculturalism and/or multination federalism reduce the level of shared values. There is no good evidence for either of these speculations. I seriously doubt that minority rights have reduced shared values, but I equally doubt that it is shared values which hold societies together. (See pp. 253–7 above) Other philosophers suggest that it is shared experiences, shared identities, shared history, shared projects, or shared conversations which hold countries together. We have little evidence to support such claims about the source of social unity (and even less evidence about how minority rights affect these factors). We simply do not know what are the sources of social unity in multiethnic and multination states. To argue against minority rights on the grounds that they erode the bonds of social unity is therefore doubly speculative: we do not know what the real bonds of social unity are, and we do not know how minority rights affect them.

9

FEMINISM

Contemporary feminist political theory is extremely diverse, in both premisses and conclusions. This is also true to some degree of the other theories I have examined. But this diversity is multiplied within feminism, for each of these other theories is represented within feminism. Thus we have liberal feminism, Marxist feminism, even libertarian feminism. Moreover, there is a significant movement within feminism towards forms of theorizing, such as psychoanalytic or poststructuralist theory, which lie outside the bounds of mainstream Anglo-American political philosophy. Alison Jaggar says that a commitment to eliminating the subordination of women unifies the diverse strands of feminist theory (Jaggar 1983: 5). But (as Jaggar notes) this agreement soon dissolves into radically different accounts of that subordination, and of the measures required to eliminate it.

It would require a separate book to discuss each of these strands of feminist theory.[1] I will instead focus on three feminist criticisms of the way mainstream political theories attend, or fail to attend, to the interests and concerns of women. I have argued that a wide range of contemporary political theories share an 'egalitarian plateau', a commitment to the idea that all members of the community should be treated as equals. Yet, until very recently, most mainstream political philosophy has defended, or at least accepted, sexual discrimination. And while traditional views about sexual discrimination have been progressively abandoned, many feminists believe that the principles which were developed with men's experience and interests in mind are incapable of adequately recognizing women's needs, or incorporating women's experiences. I will consider three such arguments. The first focuses on the 'gender-neutral' account of sexual discrimination; the second focuses on the public–private distinction. These two arguments claim that important aspects of the liberal-democratic conception of justice are male biased. The third argument, on the other hand, claims that the very emphasis on justice is itself reflective of a male bias, and that any theory which is responsive to the interests and experiences of women will replace the emphasis on justice with an emphasis on caring. These three arguments give only a limited idea of the scope of recent feminist theory, but they raise important issues which any account of sexual equality must address, and they represent three of the most sustained points of contact between feminism and mainstream political philosophy.

1. SEXUAL EQUALITY AND SEXUAL DISCRIMINATION

Until well into this century, most male theorists on all points of the political spectrum accepted the belief that there was a 'foundation in nature' for the confinement of women to the family, and for the 'legal and customary subjection of women to their husbands' within the family (Okin 1979: 200).[2] Restrictions on women's civil and political rights were said to be justified by the fact that women are, by nature, unsuited for political and economic activities outside the home. Contemporary theorists have progressively abandoned this assumption of women's natural inferiority. They have accepted that women, like men, should be viewed as 'free and equal beings', capable of self-determination and a sense of justice, and hence free to enter the public realm. And liberal democracies have progressively adopted anti-discrimination statutes intended to ensure that women have equal access to education, employment, political office, etc.

But these anti-discrimination statutes have not brought about sexual equality. In the United States and Canada, the extent of job segregation in the lowest-paying occupations is increasing, and there are concerns about the 'feminization' of poverty (Weitzman 1985: 350). Within the family, women do the vast majority of the domestic labour, even when they have full-time jobs—this is the famous 'second shift' or 'double day' that is still expected of working women (Hochschild 1989). Indeed, studies show that even unemployed husbands do much less housework than wives who work a forty-hour week (Okin 1989b: 153–4). Moreover, domestic violence and sexual assault have increased. Catherine MacKinnon summarizes her survey of the effects of equal rights in the United States by saying that 'sex equality law has been utterly ineffective at getting women what we need and are socially prevented from having on the basis of a condition of birth: a chance at productive lives of reasonable physical security, self-expression, individuation, and minimal respect and dignity' (MacKinnon 1987: 32).[3]

Why is this? Sex discrimination, as commonly interpreted, involves the arbitrary or irrational use of gender in the awarding of benefits or positions. On this view, the most blatant forms of sex discrimination are those where, for example, someone refuses to hire a woman for a job even though gender has no rational relationship to the task being performed. MacKinnon calls this the 'difference approach' to sexual discrimination, for it views as discriminatory unequal treatment that cannot be justified by reference to some sexual difference.

Sex discrimination law of this sort was modelled on race discrimination law. And just as race equality legislation aims at a 'colour-blind' society, so sex equality law aims at a sex-blind society. A society would be non-discriminatory if race or gender never entered into the awarding of benefits. Of course, while it is conceivable that political and economic decisions could entirely disregard race, it is difficult to see how a society could be entirely sex blind. A society which provides for pregnancy benefits, or for sexually segregated sports, is taking sex into account, but this does not seem unjust. And while racially segregated washrooms are clearly discriminatory, most people do not feel that way about sex-segregated washrooms. So the 'difference approach' accepts that there are legitimate instances of differential treatment of the sexes. These are not discriminatory, however, so long as there is a genuine sexual difference which explains and justifies the differential treatment. Opponents of equal rights for women often invoked the spectre of sexually integrated sports (or washrooms) as evidence that sex equality is misguided. But defenders of the difference approach respond that the cases of legitimate differentiation are sufficiently rare, and the cases of arbitrary differentation so common, that the burden of proof rests on those who claim that sex is a relevant grounds for assigning benefits or positions.

This difference approach, as the standard interpretation of sex equality law in most Western countries, has had some successes. Its 'moral thrust' is to 'grant women access to what men have access to', and it has indeed 'gotten women some access to employment and education, the public pursuits, including academic, professional, and blue-collar work, the military, and more than nominal access to athletics' (MacKinnon 1987: 33, 35). The difference approach has helped create gender-neutral access to, or competition for, existing social benefits and positions.

But its successes are limited, for it ignores the gender inequalities which are built into the very definition of these positions. The difference approach sees sex equality in terms of the ability of women to compete under gender-neutral rules for the roles that men have defined. But equality cannot be achieved by allowing men to build social institutions according to their interests, and then ignoring the gender of the candidates when deciding who fills the roles in these institutions. The problem is that the roles may be defined in such a way as to make men more suited to the role, even under gender-neutral competition.

Consider two examples. The first concerns the use of minimum height and weight rules for access to certain jobs, such as firefighters, police, and the army. These rules are officially gender neutral, but since men are on average taller and heavier than women, these rules operate to screen out most women from being able to apply for the positions. The use of these rules is typically justified on the grounds that the equipment used in the job requires a certain height or strength, and hence these are valid requirements for the job. But we need to ask why the equipment was designed for people who are, say, 5′ 9″, rather than 5′ 5″. The answer, of course, was that the people designing the equipment assumed that it would be used by men, and so they designed it for the average male height and build. This was not inevitable. It is quite possible to make the same equipment for smaller and lighter people. For example, in Japan, where men have traditionally been considerably shorter than in the West, military and firefighting equipment has been designed for shorter and lighter people. And no one familiar with the Second World War could argue that this undermined the efficiency of the Japanese military.

The problem here is not old-fashioned prejudice or chauvinism: the employer using these height and weight restrictions may pay no attention to the gender of the applicants. He may simply want people who can fulfil the job requirements. The problem, rather, is that the job requirements were initially designed by men, on the assumption that men would fill the job. And therefore sexual equality requires redesigning the job on the assumption that women should also be able to fill the job. And indeed this is currently taking place. Many jobs with height and weight restrictions are being re-examined to see if they can be redesigned to provide greater opportunities for women.[4]

A more serious example concerns the fact that most jobs 'require that the person, gender neutral, who is qualified for them will be someone who is not the primary caretaker of a preschool child' (MacKinnon 1987: 37). Given that women are still expected to take care of children in our society, men will tend to do better than women in competing for such jobs. This is not because women applicants are discriminated against. Employers may pay no attention to the gender of the applicants, or may in fact wish to hire more women. The problem is that many women lack a relevant qualification for the job—i.e. being free from childcare responsibilities. There is gender-neutrality, in that employers do not attend to the gender of applicants, but there is no sexual equality, for the job was defined under the assumption that it would be filled by men who had wives at home taking care of the children. The difference approach insists that gender not be taken into account in deciding who should have a job, but it ignores the fact 'that day one of taking gender into account was the day the job was structured with the expectation that its occupant would have no child care responsibilities' (MacKinnon 1987: 37).

Whether or not gender-neutrality yields sexual equality depends on whether and how gender was taken into account earlier. As Janet Radcliffe-Richards says, if a group is kept out of something for long enough, it is overwhelmingly likely that activities of that sort will develop in a way unsuited to the excluded group. We know for certain that women have been kept out of many kinds of work, and this means that the work is quite likely to be unsuited to them. The most obvious example of this is the incompatibility of most work with the bearing and raising of children; I am firmly convinced that if women had been fully involved in the running of society from the start they would have *found* a way of arranging work and children to fit each other. Men have had no such motivations, and we can see the results. (Radcliffe-Richards 1980: 113–14)

This incompatibility that men have created between child-rearing and paid labour has profoundly unequal results for women. The result is not only that the most valued positions in society are filled by men, while women are disproportionately concentrated into lower-paying part-time work, but also that many women become economically dependent on men. Where most of the 'household income' comes from the man's paid work, the woman who does the unpaid domestic work is rendered dependent on him for access to resources. The consequences of this dependence have become more apparent with the rising divorce rate. While married couples may share the same stand-ard of living during marriage, regardless of who earns the income, the effects of divorce in the US are seriously unequal: men's average standard of living goes up 10 per cent after divorce, while women's goes down 27 per cent—a disparity of close to 40 per cent.[5] However, none of these unequal con-sequences of the incompatibility of childcare and paid work are discrimin-atory, according to the difference approach, for they do not involve arbitrary discrimination. The fact is that freedom from childcare responsibilities is relevant to most existing jobs, and employers are not being arbitrary in insist-ing on it. Because freedom from childcare responsibilities is a relevant qualifi-cation, the difference approach says that it is not discriminatory to insist upon it, regardless of the disadvantages it creates for women. Indeed, the difference approach sees the concern with childcare responsibilities, rather than irrele-vant criteria like gender, as evidence that sex discrimination has been elimin-ated. It cannot see that the relevance of childcare responsibilities is itself a profound source of sexual inequality, one that has arisen from the way men have historically structured jobs to suit their interests.

So before we decide whether gender should be taken into account, we need to know how gender has *already* been taken into account. And the fact is that almost all important roles and positions have been structured in gender-biased ways:

virtually every quality that distinguishes men from women is affirmatively compen-sated in this society. Men's physiology defines most sports, their needs define auto and health insurance coverage, their socially-designed biographies define workplace expectations and successful career patterns, their perspectives and concerns define quality in scholarship, their experiences and obsessions define merit, their objectification of life defines art, their military service defines citizenship, their presence defines family, their inability to get along with each other—their wars and rulerships—define history, their image defines god, and their genitals define sex. For each of their differences from women, what amounts to an affirmative action plan is in effect, otherwise known as the structure and values of American society. (MacKinnon 1987: 36)

All of this is 'gender neutral', in the sense that women are not arbitrarily excluded from pursuing the things society defines as valuable. But it is sexist, because the things being pursued in a gender-neutral way are based on men's interests and values. Women are disadvantaged, not because chauvinists arbitrarily favour men in the awarding of jobs, but because the entire society systematically favours men in the defining of jobs, merit, etc.

Indeed, the more society defines positions in a gendered way, the less the difference approach is able to detect an inequality. Consider a society which restricts access to contraception and abortion, which defines paying jobs in such a way as to make them incompatible with childbearing and child-rearing, and which does not provide economic compensation for domestic labour. Women in such a society lack the legal means to guarantee that they will not have children, yet are unable to both raise children and work for wages. As a result, they are rendered economically dependent on someone who is a stable income-earner (i.e. a man). In order to ensure that they acquire this support, women must become sexually attractive to men. Knowing that this is their likely fate, many girls do not try as hard as boys to acquire employment skills which can only be exercised by those who avoid pregnancy. Where boys pursue personal security by increasing their employment skills, girls pursue security by increasing their attractiveness to men. This, in turn, results in a system of cultural identifications in which masculinity is associated with income-earning, and femininity is defined in terms of sexual and domestic service for men, and the nurturing of children. So men and women enter marriage with different income-earning potential, and this disparity widens during marriage, as the man acquires valuable job experience. Since the woman faces greater difficulty supporting herself outside the marriage, she is more dependent on maintaining the marriage, which allows the man to exercise greater control within it.

In such a society, men as a group exercise control over women's general life-chances (through political decisions about abortion, and economic decisions concerning job requirements), and individual men exercise control over economically vulnerable women within marriages. Yet there need be no arbitrary discrimination. All of this is gender neutral, in that one's gender does not necessarily affect how one is treated by those in charge of distributing contraception, jobs, or domestic pay. But whereas the difference approach takes the absence of arbitrary discrimination as evidence of the absence of sexual inequality, it may in fact be evidence of its pervasiveness. It is precisely because women are dominated in this society that there is no need for them to be discriminated against. Arbitrary discrimination in employment is not only unnecessary for the maintenance of male privilege, it is unlikely to occur, for most women will never be in a position to be arbitrarily discriminated against in employment. Perhaps the occasional woman can overcome the social pressures supporting traditional sex roles. But the greater the domination, the less the likelihood that any women will be in a position to compete for employment, and hence the less room for arbitrary discrimination. The more sexual inequality there is in society, the more that social institutions reflect male interests, the less arbitrary discrimination there will be.

None of the contemporary Western democracies corresponds exactly to this model of a patriarchal society, but they all share some of its essential features. And if we are to confront these forms of injustice, we need to reconceptualize sexual inequality as a problem, not of arbitrary discrimination, but of domination. As MacKinnon puts it,

to require that one be the same as those who set the standard—those which one is already socially defined as different from—simply means that sex equality is conceptually designed never to be achieved. Those who most need equal treatment will be the least similar, socially, to those whose situation sets the standard as against which one's entitlement to be equally treated is measured. Doctrinally speaking, the deepest problems of sex inequality will not find women 'similarly situated' to men. Far less will practices of sex inequality require that acts be intentionally discriminatory. (MacKinnon 1987: 44; cf. Taub and Schneider 1982: 134)

The subordination of women is not fundamentally a matter of irrational differentiation on the basis of sex, but of male domination, under which gender differences are made relevant to the distribution of benefits, to the systematic disadvantage of women. To remedy this problem, MacKinnon proposes the 'dominance approach' to sex equality, which aims to ensure that gender differences are not a source of disadvantage (MacKinnon 1987: 42; Frye 1983: 38). Whereas the difference approach says that sex inequality is only justified if there are real differences between men and women, the dominance approach says that sex differences (real or imagined) must never be used as a source of, or justification for, inequality and male domination.[6]

Since the problem is domination, the solution is not only the absence of discrimination, but the presence of power. Equality requires not only equal opportunity to pursue male-defined roles, but also equal power to create female-defined roles, or to create non-gendered roles that men and women have an equal interest in filling. The result of such empowerment could be very different from the 'equal opportunity to enter male-defined institutions' model that is favoured by contemporary sex-discrimination theory. From a position of equal power, we would not have created a system of social roles that defines 'male' jobs as superior to 'female' jobs. For example, the roles of male and female health practitioners were redefined by men against the will of women in the field. With the professionalization of medicine, women were squeezed out of their traditional health care roles as midwives and healers, and relegated to the role of nurse—a position which is subservient to, and financially less rewarding than, the role of doctor. That redefinition would not have happened had women been in a position of equality, and will have to be rethought now if women are to achieve equality.

Acceptance of the dominance approach would require many changes in gender relations. But what changes would it require in our theories of justice? Most of the theorists discussed in previous chapters implicitly or explicitly accept the difference approach. But does that reflect a flaw in their principles, or a flaw in the way those principles have been applied to issues of gender? Many feminists argue that the flaw lies in the principles themselves, that 'malestream' theorists (as Mary O'Brien calls them) on both the right and left interpret equality in ways that are incapable of recognizing women's sub-ordination. Indeed, some feminists argue that the struggle against sexual subordination requires us to abandon the very idea of interpreting justice in terms of equality. Elizabeth Gross argues that since women must be free to redefine social roles, their aims are best described as a politics of 'autonomy' rather than a politics of 'equality':

Autonomy implies the right to see oneself in whatever terms one chooses—which may imply an integration or alliance with other groups and individuals or may not. Equality, on the other hand, implies a measurement according to a given standard. Equality is the equivalence of two (or more) terms, one of which takes the role of norm or model in unquestionable ways. Autonomy, by contrast, implies the right to accept or reject such norms or standards according to their appropriateness to one's self-definition. Struggles for equality . . . imply an acceptance of given standards and a conformity to their expectations and requirements. Struggles for autonomy, on the other hand, imply the right to reject such standards and create new ones. (Gross 1986: 193)

Gross assumes that sex equality must be interpreted in terms of eliminating arbitrary discrimination. But the dominance approach is also an interpret-ation of equality, and if we accept it, then autonomy becomes a part of the best theory of sexual equality, not a competing value. The argument for women's autonomy appeals to, rather than conflicts with, the deeper idea of moral equality, for it asserts that women's interests and experiences should be equally important in shaping social life. As Zillah Eisenstein puts it, 'equality in this sense means individuals' having equal value as human beings. In this vision equality does not mean to be like men, as they are today, or to have equality with one's oppressors' (Eisenstein 1984: 253).

So the dominance approach shares with mainstream theorists the commitment to equality. But is it consistent with the way mainstream theorists interpret that commitment? Is there anything which prevents the theorists we have examined in previous chapters from adopting the dominance approach to sex equality? It is possible that both communitarianism and libertarianism would reject the dominance approach. Communitarians might object to this approach since it supposes that people can put in question their social roles in a way that some communitarians deny or disapprove of (Ch. 6, s. 6).[7] And since libertarians reject even the formal principle of non-discrimination underlying the difference approach, they are hardly going to accept the dominance approach. For libertarians, employers should be free to design their jobs however they see fit, and indeed to engage in old-fashioned discrimination if they want: if an employer says he will not hire any women, that is a legitimate exercise of his private property rights.[8]

Can liberal theories adopt the dominance approach? MacKinnon argues that the dominance approach takes us beyond the basic principles of liberalism. And it is certainly true that liberal theorists, like other malestream theorists, have historically accepted the difference approach to sex equality, and, as a result, have not seriously attacked women's subordination. But one can argue that liberals are betraying their own principles in adopting the difference approach.[9] Indeed the disjunction between the difference approach and liberal principles seems obvious. Liberalism's commitment to autonomy and equal opportunity, and to an ambition-sensitive, endowment-insensitive distribution of resources, would seem to rule out traditional gender divisions. There seems to be no reason why the gender bias of existing social roles would not be recognized by the contractors in Rawls's original position as a source of injustice. While Rawls himself says nothing about how his contractors would interpret sex equality, others have argued that the logic of Rawls's construction—i.e. the commitment to eliminating undeserved inequalities, and to the freedom to choose our ends—requires radical reform. For example, Karen Green argues that the contractors' interest in equal liberty requires redistributing domestic labour (Green 1986: 31–5). And Susan Okin argues that Rawls's contractors would insist on a more complete attack on the system of gender differentiation, eliminating both the unequal domestic division of labour and sexual objectification (Okin 1987: 67–8; 1989b: 173–86; cf. Kittay 1995).[10] Similar conclusions about the injustice of traditional gender roles can be reached if we ask whether these roles pass Dworkin's test of fairness (cf. Ch. 3, s. 5 above).

However, this is not to say that it will be easy for liberals to incorporate this stronger account of sexual equality. The dominance approach may require liberals to revise or abandon traditional assumptions about the relationship between public and private, and between justice and care. I will explore these challenges in the next two sections.

2. THE PUBLIC AND THE PRIVATE

If we employ the dominance approach to sex equality, one of the central issues concerns the unequal distribution of domestic labour, and the relationship between family and workplace responsibilities. But mainstream theorists have been wary of confronting family relations and judging them in the light of standards of justice. Classical liberals, for example, assumed that the (male-headed) family is a biologically determined unit, and that justice only refers to the conventionally determined relations between families (Pateman 1980: 22–4). Hence the natural equality they discuss is of fathers as representatives of families, and the social contract they discuss governs relations between families. Justice refers to the 'public' realm, where adult men deal with other adult men in accordance with mutually agreed upon conventions. Familial relationships, on the other hand, are 'private', governed by natural instinct or sympathy.

Contemporary theorists deny that only men are capable of acting within the public realm. But while sexual equality is now affirmed, this equality is still assumed, as in classical liberal theory, to apply to relations outside the family. Theorists of justice continue to ignore relations within the family, which is assumed to be an essentially natural realm. And it is still assumed, implicitly or explicitly, that the natural family unit is the traditional male-headed family, with women performing the unpaid domestic and reproductive work. For example, while J. S. Mill emphasized that women were equally capable of achievement in all spheres of endeavour, he assumed that women would continue to do the domestic work. He says that the sexual division of labour within the family is 'already made by consent, or at all events not by law, but by general custom', and he defends this as 'the most suitable division of labour between the two persons':

Like a man when he chooses a profession, so, when a woman marries, it may in general be understood that she makes choice of the management of a household, and the bringing up of a family, as the first call upon her exertions, during as many years of her life as may be required for the purpose; and that she renounces, not all other objects and occupations, but all which are not consistent with the requirements of this. (Mill and Mill 1970: 179; cf. Donner 1993)

While contemporary theorists are rarely as explicit as Mill, they implicitly share his assumption about women's role in the family (or if they don't, they say nothing about how domestic labour should be rewarded or distributed).

For example, while Rawls says that the family is one of the social institutions to be evaluated by a theory of justice, he simply assumes that the traditional family is just, and goes on to measure just distributions in terms of the 'household income' which accrues to 'heads of households', so that questions of justice within the family are ruled out of court.[11] The neglect of the family has even been present in much of liberal feminism, which 'accepted the division between the public and private sphere, and chose to seek equality primarily in the public sphere' (Evans 1979: 19).

The limits of any approach to sex equality that neglects the family have become increasingly clear. As we've seen, the result of women's 'double-day' of work is that women are disproportionately concentrated in low-paying, part-time work, which in turn makes them economically dependent. But even if this economic vulnerability were removed—for example, by guaranteeing an annual income to everyone—there is still an injustice because women are presented with a choice between family and career that men do not face.[12] Mill's claim that a woman who enters a marriage accepts a full-time occupation, just like a man entering a profession, is strikingly unfair. After all, men also enter marriage—why should marriage have such different and unequal consequences for men and women? The desire to be a part of a family should not preclude one's having a career, and in so far as it does have unavoidable consequences for careers, they should be borne equally by men and women.

Moreover, there remains the question of why domestic labour is not given greater public recognition. Even if men and women share the unpaid domestic labour, this would hardly count as genuine sexual equality if the reason why it was devalued was that our culture devalues 'women's work', or anything 'feminine'. Sexism can be present not only in the distribution of domestic labour, but also in its evaluation. And since the devaluation of housework is tied to the broader devaluation of women's work, then part of the struggle for increased respect for women will involve increased respect for their contribution to the family. The family is therefore at the centre of both the cultural devaluation and economic dependence which attach to women's traditional roles. And the predictable result is that men have unequal power in most marriages, power which is exercised in decisions concerning work, leisure, sex, consumption, etc., and which is also exercised, in a significant minority of marriages, in acts or threats of domestic violence (Okin 1989b: 128–30).[13]

The family is therefore an important locus of the struggle for sexual equality. There is an increasing consensus amongst feminists that the fight for sex equality must go beyond public discrimination to the patterns of domestic labour and women's devaluation in the private sphere. In fact, Carole Pateman says that the 'dichotomy between the public and the private . . . is, ultimately, what feminism is all about' (Pateman 1987: 103).

Confronting the injustice of the private sphere requires substantial changes in family life. But what changes does it require of theories of justice? As we have seen, the failure to confront gender inequalities in the family can be seen as a betrayal of liberal principles of autonomy and equal opportunity. According to some feminist critics, however, liberals refuse to intervene in the family, even to advance liberal goals of autonomy and equal opportunity, because they are committed to a public–private distinction, and because they see the family as the centre of the private sphere. Thus Jaggar argues that because the liberal right to privacy 'encompasses and protects the personal intimacies of the home, the family, marriage, motherhood, procreation, and child rearing', any liberal proposals to intervene in the family in the name of justice 'represent a clear departure from this traditional liberal conception of the family as the center of private life . . . as the liberal feminist emphasis on justice comes increasingly to overshadow its respect for so-called private life, one may begin to wonder whether the basic values of liberalism are ultimately consistent with one another' (Jaggar 1983: 199). In other words, liberals must give up either their commitment to sexual equality, or their commitment to the public–private distinction.

However, it is not clear that 'the traditional liberal conception' views the family 'as the center of private life'. There are in fact two different conceptions of the public–private distinction in liberalism: the first, which originated in Locke, is the distinction between the political and the social; the second, which arose with Romantic-influenced liberals, is the distinction between the social and the personal. Neither explains or justifies giving the family immunity from legal reform. Indeed, each distinction, if applied to the family, provides grounds for criticizing the traditional patriarchal family.

(a) State and civil society

The first version of liberalism's public–private distinction concerns the relationship between civil society and the state, or between the social sphere and the political sphere. As we discussed in Chapter 7, Aristotle and other ancient political thinkers assumed that freedom and the good life consisted in active participation in the exercise of political power, rather than in 'merely social' activities (Arendt 1959: 24). For liberals, by contrast, freedom and the good life are to be found primarily in the pursuit of our personal occupations and attachments in civil society, and the main function of politics is to protect our personal freedoms in civil society.

This is the first form of liberalism's public–private distinction—we can call it the 'state–society' distinction, since it equates the public with the state, and the private with civil society. It is important to recall that liberals privilege the private sphere of civil society: liberalism involves a 'glorification of society', since it supposes that the private (non-state) associations which individuals freely form and maintain in civil society are more meaningful and satisfying than the coerced unity of political association (Wolin 1960: 363). By contrast, contemporary Aristotelian civic republicans would like to return to the older model where political participation was seen as the privileged locus of the good life, and social life was seen as just a means to sustain political life.

Where does the family fit into this state–society distinction? One might think that it falls naturally into the private realm of civil society, since families are one of the associations that people freely form. But as many feminists have noted, most liberal descriptions of the social realm make it sound as if it contains only adult (and able-bodied) men, neglecting the labour needed to raise and nourish these participants, labour performed mainly by women, mainly in the family. As Pateman notes, 'liberalism conceptualizes civil society in abstraction from ascriptive domestic life', and so 'the latter remains "forgotten" in theoretical discussion. The separation between private and public is thus [presented] as a division *within* . . . the world of men. The separation is then expressed in a number of different ways, not only private and public but also, for example, "society" and "state"; or "economy" and "politics"; or "freedom" and "coercion"; or "social" and "political"' (Pateman 1987: 107), all of which are divisions 'within the world of men'.

Domestic life, in other words, has tended to fall outside both state and civil society. Why is the family excluded from civil society? The answer cannot be that it is excluded because it falls into the private realm, for the problem here is precisely that it is *not* viewed as part of the private (social) realm, which is the realm of liberal freedom. This exclusion of the family is surprising, in one sense, for the family seems a paradigmatically social institution, potentially based on just the sort of voluntary cooperation that liberals admired in the rest of society, yet traditionally mired in just the sort of ascriptive restrictions which liberals abhorred in feudalism. Yet liberals who were concerned with protecting men's ability to participate freely in social life have not been concerned with ensuring either that domestic life is organized along principles of equality and consent, or that domestic arrangements do not impede women's access to other forms of social life.

Why did liberals, who opposed ascriptive hierarchy in the realm of science, religion, culture, and economics, show no interest in doing the same for the domestic sphere?[14] Part of the answer, no doubt, is that male philosophers had no interest in questioning a sexual division of labour from which they benefited. This was rationalized at the level of theory through the assumption that domestic roles are 'natural' and biologically fixed, an assumption grounded either in claims of women's inferiority, or in the more recent ideology of the sentimental family, which says that the sentimental tie which naturally arises between mother and child is incompatible with the character traits needed for social or political life (Okin 1981).

Most liberal theorists historically have invoked one or other of these assumptions to justify excluding the family from the liberal conception of civil society. On this basis, liberals have accepted a sharp separation between the female domestic sphere and the male public sphere (including both civil society and politics). We can call this the traditional patriarchal 'domestic/ public' distinction, and liberals took this distinction for granted when developing their accounts of the distinction between the state and civil society. As Pateman rightly notes, liberal accounts of the state–society distinction describe it as a distinction 'within the world of men', with women assumed to be at home in the domestic sphere, where they 'naturally' belong.

However, it is important to note that these assumptions about women's roles or capacities were not invented by liberals—on the contrary, they predate the rise of liberalism by several centuries or even millennia. They are essentially pre-liberal views, and there is no logical or historical connection between them and acceptance of the liberal state–society distinction. The sad fact of the matter is that almost all political theorists in the Western tradition, whatever their views on the state–society distinction, have accepted one or other of these justifications for separating domestic life from the rest of society, and for relegating women to it. As Kennedy and Mendus note, 'In almost all respects the theories of Adam Smith and Hegel, of Kant and Mill, of Rousseau and Nietzsche are poles apart, but in their treatment of women, these otherwise diverse philosophers present a surprisingly united front.' Male theorists on all points of the political spectrum have accepted that 'the confinement of women to the [domestic] sphere is justified by reference to women's particularistic, emotional, non-universal nature. Since she knows only the bonds of love and friendship, she will be a dangerous person in political life, prepared, perhaps, to sacrifice the wider public interest to some personal tie or private preference' (Kennedy and Mendus 1987: 3–4, 10).

In other words, liberals inherited this sharp separation between the (female) domestic world and the (male) public world, and endorsed it for the same reasons that earlier non-liberals endorsed it—i.e. assumptions about women's natural role. The fact that liberals emphasized the importance of a non-political realm of civil society, and rejected the Aristotelian privileging of politics over society, was not the cause or explanation of their views about the family.[15] In fact, those civic republican theorists who reject the liberal state–society distinction have, if anything, tended to sharpen the traditional distinction between the female domestic world and the male public world. For example, while the ancient Greeks had no conception of the sort of free social realm which liberals favour, they did have a sharp distinction between the domestic household and the public realm which condemned women to public invisibility (Elshtain 1981: 22; Arendt 1959: 24; Kennedy and Mendus 1987: 6). Far from denying the domestic–public split, 'at the root of Greek political consciousness we find an unequalled clarity and articulateness in drawing this distinction' (Arendt 1959: 37). Similarly, while Rousseau opposed the liberal glorification of society over the state, he presented his vision of a politically integrated society 'as though it were and should be entirely male, supported by the private female familial structure' (Eisenstein 1981: 77; cf. Elshtain 1981: 165; Pateman 1975: 464). Indeed, he endorsed the Greek view that when women married, 'they disappeared from public life; within the four walls of their home they devoted themselves to the care of their household and family. This is the mode of life prescribed for women alike by nature and reason' (Rousseau, quoted in Eisenstein 1981: 66). And while Hegel rejected liberalism's 'radical separation' between state and society, his theory 'provides the most graphic example of the way the sentimental domestic family has been used to define women's capacities, and to justify their subordination, lack of education, and exclusion from the public realms of the market, citizenship, and intellectual life' (Elshtain 1981: 176; Okin 1981: 85).

So the liberal state–society distinction is different from the traditional domestic–public distinction. Aristotelian republican theorists who reject the former often support the latter. Conversely, accepting the former is consistent with rejecting the latter. Indeed, as we have seen, the reasons liberals give for valuing civil society also seem to argue for reconceptualizing the family on the basis of personal autonomy rather than ascriptive hierarchy, and for ensuring that it allows rather than precludes participation in wider social life.

Are there any feminist grounds for rejecting the liberal state–society distinction, once we distinguish it from the traditional domestic–public distinction? I believe that most contemporary feminists accept the essential features of the liberal view of the relationship between state and society, and reject the Aristotelian republican attempt to privilege politics over society.[16] For one thing, the Aristotelian glorification of the political sphere is based on a nature–culture dualism of just the sort that many feminists have argued is at the root of the cultural devaluation of women in our society. One important strand in the devaluation of women's work, particularly in bearing and rearing children, is the idea that it is merely natural, a matter of biological instinct rather than conscious intentions or cultural knowledge (V. Held 1993: 112–37). Thus women are associated with the merely animal functions of domestic labour, whereas men achieve truly human lives and true freedom by separating themselves as much as possible from the domestic sphere of 'natural' functions or instincts.

The Aristotelian claim that politics is a higher form of life often rests on a similar view—i.e. that social life, like domestic life, is mired in merely natural activities. According to Greek thought, social life remains 'in nature's prescribed cycle, toiling and resting, laboring and consuming, with the same happy and purposeless regularity with which day and night and life and death follow each other' (Arendt 1959: 106). This 'purposeless regularity' of everyday life is ultimately insignificant, destined to pass into the dust from which it came. Only politics is citizens' 'guarantee against the futility of life' (Arendt 1959: 56). Because Aristotelian politics attempts to transcend nature's cycles, 'it was a matter of course that the mastering of the necessities of life in the household was the condition for freedom of the polis . . . household life exists for the sake of the "good life" in the polis' (Arendt 1959: 30–1, 37). Indeed, 'no activity that served only the purpose of making a living, of sustaining only the life process, was permitted to enter the political realm' (Arendt 1959: 37; cf. Young 1989: 253).

It is difficult to imagine a conception of the purpose and value of public life in sharper opposition to Adrienne Rich's account of women's commitment to 'world-protection, world-preservation, world-repair . . . the invisible weaving of a frayed and threadbare family life' (Rich 1979: 205–6).[17] Indeed, as Anne Phillips puts it, 'there seem few traditions worse suited to an alliance with feminism than one [republicanism] that has viewed freedom as a matter of what goes on in the public rather than the private realm, and has regarded the homely activities of the domestic sphere as a drain on the manly heroisms of public life' (Phillips 2000: 279).

Moreover, since the priority of politics over society often rests on its alleged universality or commonality, protection of this universality requires separating politics from the realm of particularity, and that has invariably meant separating it from domestic concerns. As Iris Young notes,

in extolling the virtues of citizenship as participation in a universal public realm, [civic republicans] expressed a flight from sexual difference . . . Extolling a public realm of manly virtue and citizenship as independence, generality, and dispassionate reason entailed creating the private sphere of the family as the place in which emotion, sentiment, and bodily needs must be confined. The generality of the public thus depends on excluding women. (Young 1989: 253–4; cf. Phillips 2000: 285–6)

Unlike the Aristotelian republicans who value politics as the transcendence of nature and particularity, feminists and liberals share a basic commitment to viewing public power as a means for the protection of particular interests, needs, and social relationships.

This does not show that feminists and liberals agree on all aspects of the relationship between state and society. Even if we agree that political power should be justified in terms of the promotion of private interests in civil society, there are many areas of potential disagreement. For example, as I noted in Chapter 6 (pp. 246–52), liberals tend to view civil society as stable and self-adjusting: so long as individuals' rights to form and maintain associations are adequately safeguarded, we can safely assume that a vibrant and flourishing civil society will exist. But we might think this is overly optimistic, and that individuals will not, by themselves, maintain the web of social relationships passed down to them. Perhaps people will opt in and out of all social ties with such dizzying rapidity that society will distintegrate unless the state actively intervenes to encourage social groups. This concern was raised by some communitarian theorists (see Ch. 6, s. 8), and, in so far as feminists share it, they may want government to encourage the maintenance of certain social ties, including familial ones, and make exit from those ties more difficult.

Relatedly, feminists may not share the typical liberal faith that freedom of speech and the press will counteract prejudice and stereotypes, including traditional gender stereotypes, and so may endorse stronger government policies to fight demeaning cultural images of women. Liberals tend to think that if everyone has free and fair access to the means of expression and association, then truth will win out over falsity, and understanding over prejudice, without governments having to monitor these cultural developments (see Ch. 6, s. 8). Put another way, liberals tend to believe that cultural oppression cannot survive under conditions of civil freedom and material equality. So once women have achieved effective protection of their civil and political liberties, and gained equal material resources, then demeaning stereotypes and images of women will inevitably be contested and fade away.

But feminists may view this as overly optimistic. There may be some false and pernicious cultural representations that survive and even flourish in a free and fair fight with truth. Pornography and sexist advertising are cases in point. Liberals typically say that while pornography and sexist advertising may offer a false representation of women's sexuality, this is not sufficient grounds for legally restricting it, not because ideas are powerless, but because freedom of speech and association in civil society is a better testing ground for ideas than the coercive apparatus of the state. To some people, this will seem an unwarranted naivety about the power of free speech in civil society to weed out cultural oppression. As MacKinnon puts it, if free speech helps discover truth, 'why are we now—with more pornography available than ever before—buried in all these lies?' (MacKinnon 1987: 155). She argues that this faith in free speech shows that 'liberal morality cannot deal with illusions that *constitute* reality' (MacKinnon 1987: 162).

As a result, the problem of 'adaptive preferences' may be more serious than liberals suppose. As discussed in Chapter 2, there is strong evidence that people adapt their preferences to conform to what social and cultural norms define as normal or acceptable (pp. 15–16 above). If the prevailing cultural images define women's role as primarily to serve men, then women may adapt their preferences to fit this image. This is one reason why we cannot take the existence of 'contented housewives' (or 'contented slaves') as proof that there is no injustice. Liberals and feminists agree that it is important that people form their preferences and goals under conditions of non-oppression, free from fear or ignorance or prejudice. But whereas liberals tend to think that these conditions of non-oppression can be secured through firmer protection of individual rights and distributive justice, some feminists believe that active state policies are needed to challenge and overcome the long history of negative stereotyping of women in the schools, media, advertising, and so on.[18]

While these areas of possible dispute between liberals and feminists are of the first importance (and involve some of the empirical questions about state and culture that I raised at the end of Chapter 6), they are located within a shared commitment to the priority of social life over politics.

(b) The personal and the social: the right to privacy

The original liberal public–private split has been supplemented in the last hundred years by a second distinction, one which separates the personal or the intimate from the public, where the 'public' includes both state and civil society. This second distinction arose primarily amongst Romantics, not liberals, and indeed arose partly in opposition to the liberal glorification of society. Whereas classical liberals emphasized society as the basic realm of personal freedom, Romantics emphasized the effects of social conformity on individuality. Individuality was threatened not only by political coercion, but also by the seemingly omnipresent pressure of social expectations. For Romantics, 'private' means

detachment from mundane existence, [and] is associated with self-development, self-expression, and artistic creation . . . In classical liberal thought, by contrast, 'private' refers to society, not personal retreat, and society is a domain of free rational activity rather than expressive licence. Liberalism protects this sphere by restricting the exercise of governmental power and by enumerating rival liberties. Pure romanticism and conventional liberalism are separated not only by their notions of private life, but also by their motivations for designating a privileged private sphere. (Rosenblum 1987: 59)

Romantics included social life in the public realm because the bonds of civil society, while non-political, still subject individuals to the judgement and possible censure of others. The presence of others can be distracting, disconcerting, or simply tiring. Individuals need time for themselves, away from public life, to contemplate, experiment with unpopular ideas, regenerate strength, and nurture intimate relationships.[19] In these matters, social life can be just as demanding as political life. In fact, 'modern privacy in its most relevant functions, to shelter the intimate, was discovered as the opposite not of the political sphere but of the social' (Arendt 1959: 38; cf. Benn and Gaus 1983: 53). Hence Romantics viewed 'every formal association with others except for intimate relations like friendship or love' as public (Rosenblum 1987: 67).

While this second public–private distinction arose in opposition to liberalism, modern liberals have accepted much of the Romantic view, and have tried to integrate its emphasis on social pressures with the classical liberal emphasis on social freedom. The Romantic emphasis on privacy in fact coincided with liberal fears about the coercive power groups exercised over their own members in professional associations, labour unions, educational institutions, etc., and about the more generalized pressure for social uniformity, against which the plurality of associations and the marketplace of ideas provided inadequate protection for individuality. As a result, modern liberalism is concerned not only to protect the private sphere of social life, but also to carve out a realm *within the private sphere* where individuals can have *privacy*. Private life, for liberals, now means both active involvement in the institutions of civil society, as classical liberals emphasized, and personal retreat from that ordered social life, as Romantics emphasized.[20]

This second form of liberalism's public–private distinction is often discussed under its legal guise of a 'right to privacy'. Like the first public–private distinction, it has become the target of feminist criticism. The decision which gave the right to privacy constitutional status in the United States, *Griswold* v. *Connecticut* (381 US 479 [1965]), was initially seen as a victory for women, since it ruled that laws which denied access to contraception to married women violated the right of privacy. But it has since become clear that this right, as interpreted by the American Supreme Court, can also be a hindrance to further reform of women's domestic oppression. The idea of a right to privacy has been interpreted to mean that any outside interference in the family is a violation of privacy. As a result, it has served to immunize the family from reforms designed to protect women's interests—for example, state intervention which would protect women against domestic violence and marital rape, or empower women to sue for non-support, or officially recognize the value of domestic labour (Taub and Schneider 1982: 122; Seigal 1996: 2157–74; Gavison 1992: 35–7). According to MacKinnon, the right to privacy 'reinforces the division between public and private that . . . keeps the private beyond public redress and depoliticizes women's subjection within it' (MacKinnon 1987: 102). Indeed, she says that 'the doctrine of privacy has become the triumph of the state's abdication of women' (MacKinnon 1991: 1311).

Hence this second public–private distinction has reinforced the tendency to exempt family relations from the test of public justice. But there is something unusual about the Supreme Court's interpretation of the right to privacy, for it defines individual privacy in terms of the collective privacy of the family. The right to privacy has been held to attach to families as units, not to their individual members. As a result, individuals have no claim to privacy within the family. If two people enter a marriage, the right to privacy guarantees that the state will not interfere with the couple's domestic decisions. But if the woman has no privacy within her marriage to begin with, and no power in the making of those decisions, then this right of family privacy will not provide her with any individual privacy, and indeed it precludes the state from taking action to protect her privacy.

Indeed, this family-based conception of privacy fails women in two ways. On the one hand, it has failed to protect women's desire for privacy when threatened by abusive husbands or fathers. On the other hand, it has condoned the *involuntary* privacy of women—i.e. it has condoned the unwanted isolation, seclusion, or forced modesty of mothers and daughters who desired to escape from confinement of domestic roles to participate in public life. As Anita Allen puts it, women's 'privacy problem' is both 'the problem of getting rid of unwanted forms of privacy' and 'acquiring the privacy they do not have' (Allen 1988: 180–1; cf. Allen 1999: 743–4; McClain 1999a: 770–1). For women to get the right kind of privacy requires applying the right of privacy to individuals, not just to collective units like the family.

There are some cases where the Court has explicitly appealed to the woman's individual privacy, even within the family. But they seem to be the exception to the rule (Eichbaum 1979). Why haven't family relations been subjected to the test of individual privacy? The answer cannot be that the family is viewed as the heart of private life, because the problem here is precisely that the notion of privacy which is applied elsewhere is not applied to family relations. As June Eichbaum puts it, the idea of family-based privacy contradicts the whole point of a right to privacy: 'a right of privacy which protects the interests of a collective unit, the family, at the expense of individual autonomy, ignores the human necessity for privacy altogether and necessarily obfuscates privacy's deeper meaning' (Eichbaum 1979: 368). Protecting the family from state intervention does not necessarily guarantee women (or children) a sphere for personal retreat from the presence of others, or from the pressure to conform to others' expectations.

Why has the Supreme Court interpreted privacy as family-based? The answer seems to lie in the lingering influence of pre-liberal ideas about the naturalness of the traditional family. This is evident in the long tradition of judicial defences of the sanctity of the family, of which the 'right to privacy' is just the latest instalment. The first defence of family-based privacy was the paterfamilias doctrine, under which 'the family household was conceived as an extension of the personality of the pater familias', so that 'intervening in a man's family affairs was an invasion of his personal private sphere . . . in essence no different from requiring him to take baths more often' (Benn and Gaus 1983: 38). Under this doctrine, women became the husband's property on marriage, and so ceased to be persons under the law, their interests defined by, and submerged in, the family, which was taken to be their natural position. With the gradual recognition of the rights of other members of the household, there were challenges to the father's authority. But the legitimization of the traditional family provided by the paterfamilias doctrine was reaffirmed by conservative courts through a doctrine of 'family autonomy' in the 1920s. While the household was not the father's property, the basic structure of the traditional family remained immune to judicial reform because it was seen as a bastion of civilization, and a precondition for social stability (e.g. *Meyer* v. *Nebraska*, 262 US 390 [1923]).

With the changing view of the family in the 1960s, the family autonomy doctrine in turn was challenged, and the Court needed a new justification for leaving the family alone. The emerging emphasis on privacy was a tempting replacement, for the liberal concern with individual intimacy partially overlapped with the conservative concern with family autonomy, and provided some modern legitimacy for that old policy. But the change is more cosmetic than real, for what the Court means by privacy is remarkably similar to what was previously meant by paterfamilias or family autonomy.[21] Indeed, the American Supreme Court has not denied that its family-based right to privacy is a continuation of the old family autonomy doctrine. The Court has justified its emphasis on marital privacy by stressing 'the ancient and sacred character of marriage as the basis of their decisions' (Grey 1980: 84–5; cf. Eichbaum 1979: 372). Conversely, the Court has denied even the most basic components of a liberal conception of individual privacy if they are not tied to the traditional family structure—for example, the Supreme Court continues to uphold laws criminalizing homosexual relations between consenting adults in their own homes, and to deny that these laws are a violation of anyone's right to privacy (*Bowers* v. *Hardwick*, 478 US 186 [1986]).

Thus the Romantic ideal of individual privacy came into the law fused with the conservative ideal of the heterosexual, officially organized family as a bastion of society. While the Court invokes the language of a liberal public–private distinction, it is in fact invoking the traditional pre-liberal domestic–public distinction, one which subordinates individual privacy to family autonomy. MacKinnon notes that

it is probably not coincidental that the very things feminism regards as central to the subjection of women—the very place, the body; the very relations, heterosexual; the very activities, intercourse and reproduction; and the very feelings, intimate—form the core of what is covered by privacy doctrine. From this perspective, the legal concept of privacy can and has shielded the place of battery, marital rape, and women's exploited labour; has preserved the central institutions whereby women are *deprived* of identity, autonomy, control and self-definition . . . this right to privacy is a right of men 'to be let alone' to oppress women one at a time . . . It keeps some men out of the bedrooms of other men. (MacKinnon 1987: 101–2)

The reason it is not coincidental that the right to privacy has immunized the domestic sphere is not that liberal privacy entails protecting domesticity, but rather that the conservative protectors of domesticity have adopted the language of liberal privacy.

Once it is detached from patriarchal ideas of family autonomy, I believe that most feminists share the basic liberal motivations for respecting privacy—i.e. the value of having some freedom from distraction and from the incessant demands of others, and the value of having room to experiment with unpopular ideas and to nourish intimate relationships. (Consider Virginia Woolf's well-known claim that every woman should have 'a room of her own'.) As Allen puts it, 'feminist critiques of privacy leave the liberal conceptions of privacy of private choice very much alive. The longing for personal time and personal decisionmaking can linger long after the grip of patriarchy over women's bodies and lives is loosened' (Allen 1999: 750).[22]

In any event, liberalism's conception of privacy, like its state–society distinction, is not a defence of the traditional domestic–public split. For intimacy needs defending outside the traditional family, and solitude needs to be defended within the family. The line between privacy and non-private, therefore, cuts across the traditional domestic–public distinction. While we hope that the family forms a 'realm of privacy and personal retreat', for many people the family is itself an institution from which they desire privacy, and state action may be needed within the domestic sphere to protect privacy and prevent abuse. And nothing in either the liberal state–society distinction or the liberal right to privacy doctrine prevents such action. As Rawls puts it, 'if the private sphere is alleged to be a space exempt from justice, then there is no such thing', for the 'equal rights of women and the basic rights of their children as future citizens are inalienable and protect them wherever they are' (Rawls 1997: 791).[23]

Given the centrality of the family to the system of sexual inequality, it is crucially important that theories of justice pay attention to the effects of family organization on women's lives. The refusal of mainstream theories to do this is often explained by saying that the family has been relegated to the private realm. But in a sense this underestimates the problem. The family has not so much been relegated to the private realm, as simply ignored entirely.[24] And women's interests are harmed by the failure of political theory to examine the family in either its public or private components. For the gender roles associated with the traditional family are in conflict not only with public ideals of equal rights and resources, but also with the liberal understanding of the conditions and values of private life.

3. AN ETHIC OF CARE

One consequence of the traditional patriarchal public–domestic distinction, and of the relegation of women to the domestic sphere, is that men and women have become associated with different modes of thought and feeling.

Throughout the history of Western philosophy, we find political theorists distinguishing the intuitive, emotional, particularistic dispositions said to be required for women's domestic life from the rational, impartial, and dispassionate thought said to be required for men's public life. Morality

is fragmented into a 'division of moral labour' along the lines of gender . . . The tasks of governing, regulating social order, and managing other 'public' institutions have been monopolized by men as their privileged domain, and the tasks of sustaining privatized personal relationships have been imposed on, or left to, women. The genders have thus been conceived in terms of special and distinctive moral projects. Justice and rights have structured male norms, values, and virtues, while care and responsiveness have defined female moral norms, values, and virtues. (Friedman 1987a: 94)

These two 'moral projects' have been viewed as fundamentally different, indeed conflicting, such that women's particularistic dispositions, while functional for family life, are seen as subversive of the impartial justice required for public life. Hence the health of the public has been said to depend on the exclusion of women (Okin 1990; Pateman 1980, 1989).

Because this contrast has historically been used to justify patriarchy, early feminists like Mary Wollstonecraft argued that women's particularistic emotional nature was simply the result of the fact that women were denied the opportunity to fully develop their rational capacities. If women thought only of the needs of the people around them, ignoring the needs of the general public, it was because they were forcibly prevented from accepting public responsibilities (Pateman 1980: 31). Some contemporary feminists argue that the whole tradition of distinguishing 'masculine' and 'feminine' morality is a cultural myth that has no empirical basis. But there is a significant strand of contemporary feminism which argues that we should take seriously women's different morality—we should view it as a mode of moral reasoning, not simply intuitive feeling, and as a source of moral insight, not simply the artificial result of sexual inequality. Where male theorists claimed that women's dispositions were intuitive in nature and private in scope, some feminists argue that they are rational and potentially public in scope. The particularistic thought women employ is a better morality than the impartial thought men employ in the public sphere, or at least a necessary complement to it, especially once we recognize that sex equality requires a breaking down of the traditional public–domestic dichotomy.

The renewed feminist interest in women's modes of moral reasoning largely stems from Carol Gilligan's studies of women's moral development. According to Gilligan, men's and women's moral sensibilities do in fact tend to develop differently. Women tend to reason in a 'different voice', which she summarizes this way:

In this conception, the moral problem arises from conflicting responsibilities rather than from competing rights, and requires for its resolution a mode of thinking that is contextual and narrative rather than formal and abstract. This conception of morality as concerned with the activity of care centers moral development around the under-standing of responsibility and relationships, just as the conception of morality as fairness ties moral development to the understanding of rights and rules. (Gilligan 1982: 19)

These two 'voices' have been characterized in terms of an 'ethic of care' and an 'ethic of justice', which, Gilligan claims, are 'fundamentally incompatible' (Gilligan 1986: 238).

There is some controversy as to whether this different voice really exists, and, if it does, whether it is significantly correlated with gender. Some people argue that while there are two distinct moral voices of care and justice, men and women tend to employ both with roughly equal regularity. Others argue that while men and women often talk with a different voice, this obscures an underlying commonality: 'The moralization of gender is more a matter of how we *think* we reason than of how we actually reason.' We '*expect* women and men to exhibit this moral dichotomy', and, as a result, '*whatever* moral matters men concern themselves with are categorized, estimably, as matters of "justice and rights", whereas the moral concerns of women are assigned to the devalued categories of "care and personal relationships"' (Friedman 1987a: 96; cf. Baier 1987a: 48; Rooney 1991: 341). Perhaps men and women speak in a different voice, not because their actual thoughts differ, but because men feel they should be concerned with justice and rights, and women feel they should be concerned with preserving social relations.[25]

Whatever the empirical findings about gender differences, there remains the philosophical question of whether we can identify a care-based approach to political questions that competes with justice, and if there is, whether it is a superior approach. Some people have responded to Gilligan's findings by saying that the ethic of care, while a valid moral perspective, is not applicable outside the 'private' realm of friendship and family. It deals with the responsi-bilities we take on in virtue of participating in particular private relationships, rather than the obligations we owe to each other as members of the public (Kohlberg 1984: 358; Nunner-Winkler 1984). But many feminists argue that the care ethic, while initially developed in the context of private relationships, has public significance, and should be extended to public affairs.

What is the ethic of care? As is apparent in Gilligan's summary, there is more than one difference between the two moral voices. The differences can be looked at under three headings:[26]

(a) moral capacities: learning moral principles (justice) versus developing moral dispositions (care);

(b) moral reasoning: solving problems by seeking principles that have universal applicability (justice) versus seeking responses that are appropriate to the particular case (care);

(c) moral concepts: attending to rights and fairness (justice) versus attending to responsibilities and relationships (care).

I will look briefly at (a) and (b), before concentrating on (c), which I believe is the heart of the care–justice debate.

(a) Moral capacities

Joan Tronto says that the ethic of care 'involves a shift of the essential moral questions away from the question, What are the best principles? to the question, How will individuals best be equipped to act morally?' (Tronto 1987: 657). Being a moral person is less a matter of knowing correct principles, and more a matter of having the right dispositions—for example, the disposition to accurately perceive people's needs, and to imaginatively come up with ways of meeting them.

It is true that most contemporary theorists of justice concentrate more on determining correct principles than on explaining how individuals become 'equipped to act morally'. But the former leads naturally to the latter, for the justice ethic also requires these moral dispositions. While justice involves applying correct principles, 'what it takes to bring such principles to bear on individual situations involves qualities of character and sensibilities which are themselves moral and which go beyond the straightforward process of consulting a principle and then conforming one's will and action to it' (Blum 1988: 485). Consider, for example, the dispositions required for jurors to decide whether someone used 'reasonable precautions' in negligence cases, or to decide when pay differentials between traditionally male and female jobs are 'discriminatory'. To act justly in these circumstances, sensitivity to historical factors and current possibilities is as important as 'the intellectual task of generating or discovering the principle' (Blum 1988: 486; cf. Stocker 1987: 60). As we will see, there are some circumstances where it is important that principles of justice be easily interpreted, and their results easily predicted. But in many circumstances, moral sensitivities are required to see whether principles of justice are relevant to a situation, and to determine what those principles require. Hence justice theorists should join Gilligan in challenging the assumption that we need not worry about people's sensibilities or qualities other than their capacity for abstract reasoning (cf. Baier 1987b: 55). Even if justice involves applying abstract principles, people will only develop an effective 'sense of justice' if they learn a broad range of moral capacities, including the capacity for sympathetic and imaginative perception of the requirements of the particular situation (Nussbaum 1986: 304–6).

Why have justice theorists neglected the development of the affective capacities underlying our sense of justice? Perhaps because the sense of justice grows out of a sense of care which is initially learned within the family. It would be impossible to teach children about fairness unless they already learned within the family 'certain things about kindness and sensitivity to the aims and interests of others' (Flanagan and Jackson 1987: 635; cf. Baier 1987a: 42). Many justice theorists do recognize the role of the family in developing the sense of justice. Rawls, for example, has a lengthy discussion of how the sense of justice grows out of the moral environment of the family (Rawls 1971: 465–75). But this creates a contradiction within the justice tradition. As Okin puts it, 'in line with a long tradition of political philosophers', Rawls 'regards the family as a school of morality, a primary socializer of just citizens. At the same time, along with others in the tradition, he neglects the issue of the justice or injustice of the gendered family itself. The result is a central tension within the theory, which can be resolved only by opening up the question of justice within the family' (Okin 1989a: 231). Rawls begins his account of moral development by saying 'given that family institutions are just . . .' (Rawls 1971: 490). But, as we have seen, he does nothing to show that they are just. And 'if gendered family institutions are *not* just but are, rather, a relic of caste or feudal societies in which responsibilities, roles, and resources are distributed, not in accordance with the two principles of justice but in accordance with innate differences that are imbued with enormous social significance, then Rawls's whole structure of moral development seems to be built on uncertain ground' (Okin 1989a: 237; cf. Kearns 1983: 34–40). For example, what ensures that children are learning about equality rather than despotism, or reciprocity rather than exploitation? Investigating the justice of the family is important, therefore, not only as a potential site of inequality between adult men and women, but also as a school for the sense of justice in boys and girls.

Rather than confront these questions, most theorists of justice have been content to simply assume that people have somehow developed the requisite capacities. But while they say little about this, they do recognize that 'to have failed to develop in oneself the capacity to be considerate of others is to have failed morally, if only because many duties simply cannot be carried out by a cold and unfeeling moral agent' (Sommers 1987: 78).

(b) Moral reasoning

So moral agents need 'the broader moral capacities' which Tronto discusses. But can these capacities take the place of principles? According to Tronto, the care ethic says that, *rather than* 'asserting moral principles', one's 'moral imagination, character, and actions must respond to the complexity of a given situation' (Tronto 1987: 657–8; cf. Baier 1987a: 40). In other words, these broader moral dispositions do not simply help individuals apply universal principles, they render such principles unnecessary, and perhaps counter-productive. We should construe morality in terms of attending to a particular situation, not in terms of applying universal principles. 'The idea of a just and loving gaze directed upon an individual reality . . . is the characteristic and proper mark of the moral agent', and this sort of 'ethical caring' does not depend 'on rule or principle' (Iris Murdoch quoted in Grimshaw 1986: 234).[27]

But what does it mean to simply attend to the situation? After all, not all contextual features are relevant to moral decisions. In making moral decisions, we do not simply attend to the different features of the situation, we also judge their relative significance. And while we want people to be good at attending to the complexity of the situation, we also want them to be good at identifying which features of the situation are the morally significant ones. And this seems to raise questions of principle rather than sensitivity: 'We have been told nothing about [the care ethic] until we are told what features of situations context-sensitive people pick out as morally salient, what weight-ings they put on these different features, and so on . . . we simply need to know more, in a detailed way, about to what and to whom women feel respon-sible, and about exactly what it is they care about?' (Flanagan and Adler 1983: 592; Sher 1987: 180).

Ruddick claims that while we do distinguish salient and irrelevant features of moral situations, these distinctions come from the very process of attend-ing to the situation, rather than from external principles. Someone who attends closely to a particular situation will come to see it as making *demands* on us. But while some moral considerations may be readily observable to anyone who has developed the capacity for sympathetic attention to a particu-lar situation, there are other relevant considerations which are less obvious. For example, when are job qualifications discriminatory? As we have seen, the existing job situation may 'demand' someone who is free of childcare responsibilities, or who has a certain height or strength. Since these are genu-inely relevant criteria for the job, it is only within a broader social perspective that we can see how their combined effect is to create a system of sexual inequality. In these circumstances, knowing when relevant criteria are none-theless discriminatory, or when reverse discrimination is nonetheless legitim-ate, requires more than sympathetic attention to the particular situation. In order to know when there is a legitimate moral demand for affirmative action, we need to place the particular situation within a broader theory of social and economic equality (Tronto 1993: 167–70; Bowden 1996: 163).

Moreover, even if we have perceived all the relevant demands, these demands can conflict, and so detailed attention may lead to indecision in the absence of higher-level principles. If one is faced with a conflict between the demands of current male candidates and those of future generations of women, patient attention to the situation may just bring out how painful the conflict over affirmative action is. As Virginia Held notes, 'we have limited resources for caring. We cannot care for everyone or do everything a caring approach suggests. We need moral guidelines for ordering our priorities' (Held 1987: 119; Bubeck 1995: 199–214; Grimshaw 1986: 219).

Ruddick and Gilligan write as if appealing to principles involves abstracting from the particularity of the situation. But as Grimshaw notes, principles are not instructions to avoid examining the particulars, but rather are instructions about what to look for. Unlike 'rules', such as the ten commandments, which are intended as guides that can be applied without much reflection, a principle 'functions quite differently. It serves precisely to *invite* rather than block reflection', for it is 'a general consideration which one deems important to take into account when deciding what is the right thing to do' (Grimshaw 1986: 207–8; cf. O'Neill 1993). Every moral theory must have some account of such general considerations, and the sorts of considerations appealed to by theorists of justice often require, rather than conflict with, attention to particular details (Friedman 1987*b*: 203).[28]

Some care theorists claim that the tendency to appeal to principles to adjudicate conflicts pre-empts the more valuable tendency to work out solutions in which the conflicts are overcome. For example, Gilligan claims that when constructing moral problems in terms of justice or care, her subjects either 'stood back from the situation and appealed to a rule or principle for adjudicating the conflicting claims or they entered the situation in an effort to discover or create a way of responding to all of the needs' (Gilligan 1987: 27). And indeed she cites many cases where girls were able to find a solution that responds to all of the needs in the particular situation, a solution which boys missed in their haste to find a principled adjudication of the conflict. But there will not always be a way to accommodate conflicting demands, and it is not clear that we should always try to accommodate all demands. Consider the demands of racist or sexist codes of honour. These are clear 'demands', but many of them are illegitimate. The fact that white men expect to be treated in a deferential way is no reason to accommodate such expectations. Even if we could accommodate them, we might provoke a conflict in order to make clear our disapproval. If we are to question these demands, then 'attention cannot always be focused on the details and nuances of the particular situation', but rather must situate those details within some larger framework of normative principles (Grimshaw 1986: 238; Wilson 1988: 18–19).

(c) Moral concepts

The question, then, is not whether we need principles, but rather what sort of principles. As I noted earlier, some writers have suggested that we face a basic choice between principles of 'rights and fairness' (in the justice approach), or principles of 'responsibilities and relationships' (in the care approach). It seems to me that this basic distinction has been construed in at least three different ways in the literature:

(i) universality versus concern for particular relationships;
(ii) respect for common humanity versus respect for distinct individuality;
(iii) claiming rights versus accepting responsibilities.

I will look at these in turn.

(i) Universality versus preserving relationships

One common way of distinguishing care and justice is to say that justice aims at universality or impartiality, whereas care aims at preserving the 'web of ongoing relationships' (Blum 1988: 473; Tronto 1987: 660). As Gilligan puts it, 'From a justice perspective, the self as moral agent stands as the figure against a ground of social relationships, judging the conflicting claims of self and others against a standard of equality or equal respect (the Categorical Imperative, the Golden Rule). From a care perspective, the relationship becomes the figure, defining self and others. Within the context of relationship, the self as a moral agent perceives and responds to the perception of need' (Gilligan 1987: 23). Hence, for Gilligan, 'morality is founded in a sense of concrete connection between persons, a direct sense of connection which exists prior to moral beliefs about what is right and wrong or which principles to accept. Moral action is meant to express and sustain those connections to particular other people' (Blum 1988: 476–7).

There is some ambiguity in the notion of the 'existing web of relationships'. On one view, this refers to historically rooted relationships with particular others. If interpreted this way, however, the care ethic runs the danger of excluding the most needy, since they are most likely to be outside the web of relationships. Many care theorists recognize this danger.[29] Tronto says that 'in focusing on the preservation of existing relationships, the perspective of care has a conservative quality', and that how to ensure 'that the web of relationships is spun widely enough so that some are not beyond its reach remains a central question. Whatever the weaknesses of Kantian universalism, its premise of the equal moral worth and dignity of all humans is attractive because it avoids this problem' (Tronto 1987: 660–1). But the question is not simply to explain *how* 'social institutions might be arranged to expand these conventional understandings of the boundaries of care', but *why* they should be rearranged, unless we accept a universalistic principle of equal moral worth. As Deveaux notes, care theories 'have tremendous difficulty in explaining how, or why, we should be motivated to aid strangers' (Deveaux 1995*b*: 94). Tronto's surprisingly tentative answer is that 'it may be possible to avoid the need for special pleading while at the same time stopping short of universal moral principles; if so, an ethic of care might be viable' (Tronto 1987: 661, 660).[30]

Other care theorists, however, construe the 'existing web of relationships' in a more expansive way. Like Tronto, Gilligan says that 'each person is embedded within a web of ongoing relationships, and morality importantly if not exclusively consists in attention to, understanding of, and emotional responsiveness toward the individuals with whom one stands in these relationships' (Blum 1988: 473). But as Blum notes, 'Gilligan means this web to encompass all human beings and not only one's circle of acquaintances' (Blum 1988: 473). As one of the women in Gilligan's study puts it, we are responsible to 'that giant collection of everybody', so that 'the stranger is still another person belonging to that group, people you are connected to *by virtue of being another person*' (Gilligan 1982: 57, my emphasis; cf. Gilligan 1982: 74, 90, 160). For Gilligan, what joins people in this giant web of relationships is not necessarily any direct interaction, but rather a shared humanity. Since Gilligan's conception of the web of relationships *already* includes everyone, her commitment to preserving the web of relationships entails, rather than conflicts with, her claim that the motivation of the care ethic is 'that everyone will be responded to and included, that no one will be left alone or hurt' (Gilligan 1982: 63).

Of course, once care theorists say that each person is connected to us 'by virtue of being another person', then it seems that they too are committed to a principle of universality. As soon as care and concern 'are detached from the demands of unique and historically rooted relationships—as soon as they are said to be elicited merely by the affected parties' common humanity, or by the fact that those parties all have interests, or all can suffer', then 'we completely lose the contrast between the particularity of relationship and the generality of principle. Having lost it, we seem to be left with an approach that seeks to resolve moral dilemmas through sympathetic identification with all the affected parties.' And this sort of universality 'is at least closely related to that of the familiar impartial and benevolent observer' we find in Kantian and utilitarian theories (Sher 1987: 184). While Gilligan avoids the language of universality, her studies 'indicate that women's care and sense of responsibility for others are frequently universalized' (Okin 1990: 27; cf. Bubeck 1995: 193–4; Broughton 1983: 606; Kohlberg 1984: 356).

So the commitment to 'preserving the web of relationships' may or may not conflict with the commitment to universality, depending on how we interpret it. Much of the ethic of care literature has centred on the 'conflicted but creative tension' between the universalistic and more localized conceptions of our connection to others (Ruddick 1984*b*: 239). On the one hand, there is the impulse towards universalization: care theorists argue that we 'make moral progress . . . by expanding the scope of the injunctions to give care and to maintain connections' (Meyers 1987: 142), even if this requires 'transforming' and 'generalizing' existing practices for caring for the particular people in one's local setting (Ruddick 1984a: 222, 226). On the other hand, there is the impulse to defend existing connections from the requirements of universality: care theorists emphasize that 'the sense of responsibility at the core of the care perspective' tries to avoid 'imposing impartiality at the expense of ongoing attachment' (Meyers 1987: 142).

It seems then that most care theorists accept Gilligan's commitment to a universalistic web of relations, but prefer to emphasize its continuity with Tronto's more localized web of relations. However, as Blum notes, 'how this extension to all persons is to be accomplished is not made clear' (Blum 1988: 473).[31] As Okin notes, Gilligan's studies do not confront the question of 'how women think when confronted with a moral dilemma involving a conflict between the needs or interests of family and close friends and the needs or interests of more distant others' (Okin 1990: 158), and so it is difficult to judge how these dilemmas are to be managed within the care perspective.[32]

(ii) Respect for humanity and respect for individuality

According to some care theorists, the problem with justice is not that it responds universally to all those who share our common humanity, but that it responds solely to people's common humanity, rather than to people's distinct individuality. Care theorists claim that for justice-based theorists, 'the moral significance of persons as the objects of moral concern is solely as bearers of morally significant but entirely general and repeatable characteristics' (Blum 1988: 475). Justice is concerned with the 'generalized other', and neglects the 'concrete other':

The standpoint of the generalized other requires us to view each and every individual as a rational being entitled to the same rights and duties we would want to ascribe to ourselves. In assuming this standpoint, we abstract from the individuality and concrete identity of the other. We assume that the other, like ourselves, is a being who has concrete needs, desires and affects, but that what constitutes his or her moral dignity is not what differentiates us from each other, but rather what we, as speaking and acting rational agents, have in common . . . The standpoint of the concrete other, by contrast, requires us to view each and every rational being as an individual with a concrete history, identity and affective-emotional constitution. In assuming this standpoint, we abstract from what constitutes our commonality . . . In treating you in accordance with the norms of friendship, love and care, I confirm not only your *humanity* but your human *individuality*. (Benhabib 1987: 87; cf. Bowden 1996: 164–74; Meyers 1987: 146–7; Friedman 1987a: 105–10)

As Benhabib stresses, the standpoints of the general and concrete other are both fully universalized (indeed, she calls them 'substitutionalist universalism' and 'interactive universalism', respectively). But care, unlike justice, responds to our concrete differences, rather than our abstract humanity.

This contrast seems overdrawn in both directions. First the ethic of care, once universalized, also appeals to common humanity. As Sher notes, as soon as care and concern are 'said to be elicited merely by the affected parties' common humanity, or by the fact that those parties all have interests, or all can suffer', then they are 'viewed as appropriate responses to shared and repeatable characteristics' (Sher 1987: 184).

Secondly, theories of justice are not limited to respect for the generalized other. This is clear in the case of utilitarianism, which must attend to particularity in order to know whether a policy will promote people's various preferences. It may seem less clear in the case of Rawls's theory, and, not surprisingly, many feminists point to his original position as a paradigm of justice-thinking. Because the original position requires individuals to abstract from their particular selves, it is said to exemplify a tradition in which 'the moral self is viewed as a *disembedded* and *disembodied* being' (Benhabib 1987: 81). But this misrepresents the original position. As Okin notes,

> The original position requires that, as moral subjects, we consider the identities, aims, and attachments of every other person, however different they may be from ourselves, as of equal concern with our own. If we, who *do* know who we are, are to think *as if* we were in the original position, we must develop considerable capacities for empathy and powers of communicating with others about what different human lives are like. But these alone are not enough to maintain in us a sense of justice. Since we know who we are, and what are our particular interests and conceptions of the good, we need as well a great commitment to benevolence; to *caring* about each and every other as much as about ourselves. (Okin 1989a: 246)

Therefore, 'Rawls's theory of justice is itself centrally dependent upon the capacity of moral persons to be concerned about and to demonstrate care for others, especially others who are most different from themselves' (Okin 1989a: 247). Care theorists often say that conflict resolutions 'should be arrived at through the contextual and inductive thinking characteristic of taking the role of the particular other' (Harding 1987: 297). But this is precisely what the original position requires of us.

Benhabib questions whether 'taking the viewpoint of others' is truly compatible with reasoning behind a veil of ignorance, because justice is 'thereby identified with the perspective of the disembedded and disembodied generalized other ... The problem can be stated as follows: according to Kohlberg and Rawls, moral reciprocity involves the capacity to take the standpoint of the other, to put oneself imaginatively in the place of other, but under conditions of the "veil of ignorance", the *other as different from the self*, disappears' (Benhabib 1987: 88–9; cf. Blum 1988: 475; Gilligan 1986: 240; 1987: 31). But this misrepresents how the original position operates. The fact that people are asked to reason in abstraction from their own social position, natural talents, and personal preferences when thinking about others does not mean that they must ignore the particular preferences, talents, and social position of others. And, as we have seen, Rawls insists that parties behind the original position must take these things into account (Ch. 3, s. 3 above). Benhabib assumes that the original position works by requiring contractors to consider the interests of the other contractors (who all become 'generalized others' behind the veil of ignorance). But in fact the effect of the veil is that 'it no longer matters to the [contractor] in the original position who, if anyone, occupies the position with him or what its occupants' interests are. What matters to him are the desires of every actual member of his society, because the veil forces him to reason *as if he were any one of them*' (Hampton 1980: 335). As we have seen, Hare's ideal sympathizer imposes the same requirement (Ch. 2, s. 5). Both devices, impartial contractors and ideal sympathizers, work by requiring people to consider concrete others (cf. Broughton 1983: 610; Sher 1987: 184).[33]

(iii) Accepting responsibility and claiming rights

Since both ethics are universal, and both respect commonality as well as individuality, the difference (if there is one) lies elsewhere. One final distinction offered by Gilligan is that justice reasoning thinks of concern for others in terms of respecting rights-claims, whereas care reasoning thinks of concern for others in terms of accepting responsibilities. What is the difference between respecting rights and accepting responsibilities? The central difference, according to Gilligan, is that accepting responsibility for others requires some positive concern for their welfare, whereas rights are essentially self-protection mechanisms that can be respected by simply leaving other people alone. Thus she equates talk about rights with individualism and selfishness, and says that rights-based duties to others are limited to reciprocal non-interference (Gilligan 1982: 22, 136, 147; cf. Meyers 1987: 146).

This may be true of libertarian theories of rights, but all of the other theories I have examined recognize positive duties concerning the welfare of others.[34] So while the justice framework emphasizes people's rights, one could say that these rights impose responsibilities on others. And indeed that is how some of Gilligan's respondents describe their ethic of care. For example, one woman says that 'People suffer, and that gives them certain rights, and that gives you a certain responsibility' (quoted in Broughton 1983: 605). It is true that some women 'think less about what they are entitled to than about what they are responsible for providing'. But they may regard themselves as responsible for providing care to others precisely because they regard others as being entitled to it—'To suppose otherwise would be to conflate the well supported claim that women are less concerned than men with the protection of *their* rights with the quite different claim that women are less inclined to think that people have *rights* (or to hold views that are functionally equivalent to this)' (Sher 1987: 187).

Once we abandon the libertarian construal of rights as non-interference, the whole contrast between responsibilities and rights threatens to collapse (Okin 1990: 157). As Broughton puts it, 'Gilligan and her subjects seem to presuppose something like "the right of all to respect as a person", "the right to be treated sympathetically and as an equal", and "the duty to respect and not to hurt others"'. Hence 'it is difficult to see in what way she is not here recommending more or less binding rights and duties or perhaps even "principles" of personal welfare and benevolent concern' (Broughton 1983: 612). Indeed, many care theorists accept that rights must play an essential role within a care theory (Tronto 1993: 147–8; Held 1993: 75).

And while Gilligan insists that the two ethics are fundamentally different, she herself seems undecided about their relationship. She 'shifts between the ideas that the two ethics are incompatible alternatives to each other but are both adequate from a normative point of view; that they are complements of one another involved in some sort of tense interplay; and that each is deficient without the other and thus ought to be integrated' (Flanagan and Jackson 1987: 628). These shifts should not be surprising if, as I have argued, the key concepts Gilligan uses to distinguish the two ethics do not define genuine contrasts.[35]

While rights and responsibilities are not contrasting moral concepts, there may be a difference in the kind of responsibility each ethic imposes on us. According to Sandra Harding, Gilligan's research shows that 'subjectively-felt hurt appears immoral to women whether or not it is fair', whereas men 'tend to evaluate as immoral only objective unfairness—regardless of whether an act creates subjective hurt' (Harding 1982: 237–8; cf. Harding 1987: 297). For example, men are less inclined to recognize any moral obligation to ameliorate subjective hurts that arise from someone's own negligence, since they are her own fault. Here there is a subjective hurt, but no objective unfairness, and so men tend to recognize no moral obligation. For women, on the other hand, the moral obligation to respond to subjective hurts does not depend on the presence of objective unfairness.

There is a genuine contrast between taking subjective hurts or objective unfairness as the grounds for moral claims. Is this the fundamental difference between care and justice? It is certainly true that most justice theorists tie moral claims to objective unfairness rather than subjective hurt. As we have seen, this underlies the liberal idea that people are responsible for their own choices (Ch. 3, s. 3).[36] It is less clear whether the care ethic says that subjective hurts form the basis for moral claims, whether all subjective hurts, and only such hurts, ground moral claims. To care for somebody does not necessarily mean that one feels a moral obligation to attend to their every wish, or to spare them from all subjective hurts or disappointments. Care theorists have not in fact said much, so far, about how they understand the connection between subjective hurt, objective unfairness, and moral claims, and it is likely that different conceptions of ethical caring would arrive at different conclusions. So it is premature to assume that care and justice have fundamentally opposed views on this matter.

However, while the exact points of disagreement are unclear, it seems true that care theorists are more likely to emphasize subjective hurt rather than objective unfairness as the basis for moral claims.[37] Before considering some of the reasons care theorists have for emphasizing subjective hurt, I will examine some of the reasons justice theorists have for preferring objective unfairness as the basis for moral claims. I will argue that the emphasis on objective unfairness, while initially plausible, is only legitimate in certain contexts— namely, interactions between competent adults. Indeed, it may be legitimate only when our interactions with competent adults are sharply separated from our interactions with dependants. If so, then the debate between care and justice reasoning becomes inextricably linked to the debate over the domestic–public distinction.

Why do justice theorists think it is important to limit our responsibility for others to the claims of fairness? If subjective hurts always give rise to moral claims, then I can legitimately expect, as a matter of ethical caring, that others attend to all of my interests. But for justice theorists, this ignores the fact that I should accept full responsibility for some of my own interests. In the justice perspective, I can legitimately expect, as a matter of fairness, that others attend to *some* of my interests, even if it limits the pursuit of their own good. But I cannot legitimately expect people to attend to *all* of my interests, for there are some interests which remain my own responsibility, and it would be wrong to expect others to forgo their good to attend to things which are my responsibility.

Consider someone who is generous with his time and money when his friends are in need, but is also exceedingly careless in his expenditures. As a result, he is often (unnecessarily) in need of help, and he relies on others to spare him the consequences of his imprudence. Does he have a legitimate expectation that others help him—should we feel morally bound to spare him the results of his carelessness? The subjective hurt approach says that we are irresponsible if we do not attend to his suffering. If he feels a subjective hurt, then we are required to attend to him, even though the hurt is the result of his own careless planning or extravagance. The justice ethic, however, says that he is irresponsible in expecting us to spare him any suffering. His actions are his own responsibility, and it is immoral to make others pay for the costs of his carelessness.

Viewed this way, the debate between subjective hurts and objective unfairness is a genuine one, for there are importantly different positions we can take on the issue of responsibility for our own well-being. For some care theorists, the emphasis on objective unfairness sanctions an abdication of moral responsibility, because it limits our responsibility for others to claims of unfairness, and thereby allows people to ignore avoidable suffering. For justice theorists, the emphasis on subjective hurts sanctions an abdication of moral responsibility, because it denies that the imprudent should pay for the costs of their choices, and thereby rewards those who are irresponsible, while penalizing those who act responsibly.

The debate between care and justice, therefore, is not between responsibility and rights. On the contrary, responsibility is central to the justice ethic. The reason why my claim on other people is limited to fairness is not that they have rights, but that I have responsibilities—part of my responsibility for others involves accepting responsibility for my own desires, and for the costs of my choices. As Rawls puts it, his theory 'relies on a capacity to assume responsibility for our ends' (Rawls 1982b: 169). Conversely, those who tie moral obligations to subjective hurts rather than objective unfairness must deny that we are responsible agents: they 'must argue that it is unreasonable, if not unjust, to hold people responsible for their preferences and to require them to make out as best they can' (Rawls 1982b: 168). Since Rawls thinks we have the capacity to assume this responsibility, his theory requires people to live within their means, to adjust their plans to the fair share of resources they can rightfully expect. As a result, a careless and extravagant person cannot expect those who have been more responsible to pay for the costs of his imprudence: 'it is regarded as unfair that they now should have less in order to spare [him] from the consequences of [his] lack of foresight or self-discipline' (Rawls 1982b: 169). If we are obligated to spare people all subjective hurts, then those who have responsibly attended to their own well-being will be asked to make continual sacrifices to aid those who have been irresponsibly careless or extravagant, and that is unfair.[38]

The view that subjective hurts always give rise to moral claims is not only unfair, it can hide oppression. Subjective hurts are tied to expectations, and unjust societies create unjust expectations. Consider traditional marital relationships, in which 'men do not serve women as women serve men' (Frye 1983: 9, 10; cf. Friedman 1987a: 100–1; Grimshaw 1986: 216–19). Men expect women to attend to their needs, and so they feel subjective hurt whenever they are required to share the burdens of domestic life. Indeed, 'in all attempts to change exploitative or oppressive relations, someone is going to be deprived of something. They may be deprived of some attention, service or amenity to which they are accustomed. They may undergo some hardship or difficulty and experience this as lack of care' (Grimshaw 1986: 218). The oppressors will keenly feel any loss of privilege. Conversely, the oppressed are often socialized not to feel subjective hurt at their oppression: they adapt their preferences so as not to desire things they know they cannot get.

Wherever this process of adaptive preferences takes place, focusing on subjective hurts as the grounds for moral claims makes oppression harder to see. Within the justice perspective, on the other hand, the oppressors' subjective hurts have no moral weight, since they arise from unfair and selfish expectations (see Ch. 2, s. 5 above). Claims of justice are determined by people's rightful expectations, not their actual expectations. This explains why justice theorists say not only that subjective hurts lack moral significance in the absence of objective unfairness, but also that objective unfairness is immoral even when unaccompanied by subjective hurt, as when people are socialized to accept their oppression (cf. Harding 1987: 297). In this sense, 'morally valid forms of caring and community presuppose prior conditions and judgments of justice' (Kohlberg 1984: 305).[39]

There is another problem with using subjective hurt as the basis of moral claims. While it imposes too little responsibility for our own well-being, it imposes too great a responsibility for others. If subjective hurt always calls forth a caring response, there seems to be nothing which limits our obligation to attend to others. There is always something more that we can do for others, if we attend closely enough to their desires—there is always some frustrated desire we can help fulfil. And this becomes self-reinforcing, for once someone knows that we are attending to them, they will come to expect attention, and then be even more hurt if our attention is withdrawn.[40] As a result, the agent always faces moral claims on her time and energy, claims which leave no room for the free pursuit of her own attachments (Dancy 1992).

So the idea that subjective hurts give rise to moral claims threatens both fairness and autonomy. Care theorists are well aware of this problem of overload. After all, the idea that women should always sacrifice their own interests and projects for those of their husbands and children is part of the ideology of male dominance, which has been used to justify the exploitation of women for centuries. Care theorists obviously do not want to endorse that ideology, or perpetuate women's exploitation. So they emphasize that their conception of ethical caring is very different from the traditional sexist stereotype of the self-sacrificing woman who puts everyone else's interests ahead of her own. According to Gilligan, we need to distinguish a 'self-less' conception of caring, where women always subordinate their interests to others, from a 'self-inclusive' conception of caring, where women learn to care for themselves, not just for others (e.g. Gilligan 1982: 149; Bubeck 1995: 194).

Indeed, this shift towards a 'self-inclusive' conception of caring is often said to be what distinguishes a 'feminist' ethic of care from a 'feminine' ethic of self-sacrifice (West 1997; Gilligan 1995: 122; Tong 1993). To qualify as a feminist ethic, it is not enough for the ethic of care to value women's caring activities, it must also ensure that these activities do not come at the price of women's freedom and equality. The ethic of care must ensure that women are not isolated, disadvantaged, or exploited for undertaking caring activities, that being care-givers does not prevent women from participating fully and equally in public and political life, and that women have equal control over the terms and conditions under which care is provided.[41] In the traditional feminine ethic of self-sacrifice, women had a limitless responsibility to provide care, but had little power over the conditions under which it was provided or rewarded (Sevenhuijsen 1998: 84). In a feminist ethic of care, the responsibility for care is shared more fairly with men, as is the power to shape the social conditions under which it is provided.

So care theorists recognize the need to put limits on what others can legitimately expect of care-givers. Some theorists say that care-givers should attend to their own need for autonomy, or that genuine caring involves some kind of reciprocity or mutuality, so that there are limits on how much others can expect of us without helping us in return (Ruddick 1984b: 238; Gilligan 1982: 149; Noddings 1984: 12, 98–100, 105, 181–2). In these and other ways, care theorists distance themselves from any simple equation of subjective hurt and moral claims.[42]

But how much autonomy can we claim for ourselves, and how much reciprocity can we demand from others, without irresponsibly neglecting the subjective hurt of others? In line with their general methodology, care theorists say that the conflict between autonomy and responsibility for others must be decided contextually. Unlike one of Gilligan's male respondents, who said that we should treat this conflict as a 'mathematical problem' whose solution lies in a formula like 'one quarter for others, three quarters for me' (Gilligan 1982: 35, 37), care theorists say we should judge the appropriateness of any demand for autonomy or reciprocity 'on the grounds of what is reasonable to expect from the individual being cared-for, along with what should be expected from such an individual given the nature of the caring relationship at hand' (Wilson 1988: 20). Care theorists, unlike justice theorists, do not try to resolve these issues by developing a comprehensive system of abstract rules that runs roughshod over the particularity of persons and their relationships. As Monique Deveaux puts it, to expect care theory to come up with a formula or principle for resolving this conflict is to assume that it seeks to provide a 'grand theory' on a par with other moral theories, when the whole point is to question the need or utility of such theories (Deveaux 1995a: 117).[43]

There is obviously much wisdom in avoiding simplistic formulas like 'one quarter for others, three quarters for me'. For one thing, as care theorists emphasize, there are in fact many different forms of care, each with its own moral logic. A mother's care for her children is different from the care shown amongst friends, which is different yet again from ethical caring by a nurse or social worker.[44] As Peta Bowden notes, 'Varying shifts from relatively non-voluntarist to more freely chosen relations, from informal to formally organized contexts, from intimacy to public accessibility, bring with them significantly different liberties, responsibilities and constraints on the possibilities of caring' (Bowden 1996: 144). Since there is no 'essentialist' or 'unitary' conception of care (Bubeck 1995: 222–36), so there cannot be any abstract rule about how to balance autonomy and responsibility within an ethic of care.

However, this is one of the places where abstract rules may be important. If our aim is to ensure that the free pursuit of one's projects is not entirely submerged by the requirements of ethical caring, then we do not simply need limits on our moral responsibilities, we also need *predictable* limits. We need to know *in advance* what we can rely on, and what we are responsible for, if we are to make long-term plans. It is not much good being told at the last minute that no one needs your moral help today, and that you are free to take a moral holiday, as it were. We can only take advantage of holidays if we can plan them, and that requires that we can determine *now* which interests we will be held responsible for *later*. And that, in turn, requires that when deciding at that later date who is responsible for attending to others, we do not make a fully context-sensitive decision.

For example, when my vacation day comes up at work, we do not ask who is least needed in the office. We ask whose turn is it under the system of rules. The result may be that some people will suffer the frustration of desires that a more contextual decision-making process would have fulfilled (other people in the office really would be less missed). But if we want to be able to make genuine commitments to our projects, then our claims must be insulated, to some extent, from the contingent desires of those around us. Abstract rules provide some security in the face of the shifting desires of others.

Of course, care theorists are right to say that some kinds of relationships must invoke different standards for balancing autonomy and responsibility. For example, we can't expect children to have the same respect for autonomy and reciprocity as adults (I'll return to this below). But for interactions between competent adults, an important way to reconcile responsibility and autonomy is to codify some of our responsibilities in advance of particular situations, rather than determining them through constant assessment and reassessment of particular situations.

Does this appeal to abstract rules mean that justice ignores our 'distinct individuality'? It's true that justice, in this context, doesn't require us to adjust our notion of 'what is reasonable to expect' to the particular needs of those around us. Our rights and obligations in these contexts are fixed in advance by abstract rules, not by context-sensitive assessments of the needs of those around us. But this shouldn't be seen as evidence of an insensitivity to those particular needs. For the net result of this abstraction from particularity is to more fully protect particularity. The more our claims are dependent on context-sensitive calculations of everyone's particular desires, the more vulnerable our personal projects are to the shifting desires of others, and so the less we will be able to make long-term commitments. Meaningful autonomy requires predictability, and predictability requires some insulation from context-sensitivity.

This still leaves the possibility that some people will have strong desires that are frustrated by the application of abstract rules. But, as we've seen, the justice ethic assumes that competent adults are capable of adjusting their ends in the light of public standards. Assuming that the rules are publicly known, and confining our attention to competent adults for the moment, then the people who will suffer from the application of abstract rules are those who, through extravagance or carelessness, have formed desires which cannot be met within their rightfully allotted means. There may be such people in any particular situation, and their suffering may receive less notice in a society that appeals to abstract rules rather than context-sensitive assessments of particular needs. But this is their own responsibility, and it is unfair to ask others to make sacrifices to spare them from their irresponsibility.

The difficulty of staking out ground for personal autonomy within the care ethic is reminiscent of a similar problem within utilitarianism (Ch. 2, pp. 25–6). In both cases, the moral agent faces a seemingly 'unlimited responsibility' to 'act for the best in a causal framework formed to a considerable extent by the projects [of others]'. The agent's decisions become 'a function of all the satisfactions which he can affect from where he is: and this means that the projects of others, to an indeterminably great extent, determines his decision', leaving little room for the independent pursuit of his own desires and convictions (Williams 1973: 115).[45] This parallel should not be surprising, for while care theorists reject the utilitarian commitment to maximization, both theories tend to ground moral claims in subjective hurt and happiness, rather than objective unfairness. As a result, both theories interpret concern for others primarily as a matter of responding to their already given needs. But we can only protect fairness and autonomy if we view concern for others not solely in terms of responding to pre-existing preferences, but as something that should enter into the very formation of our preferences. Rather than taking into account people's specific aims in deciding on just distributions, people should take principles of justice into account in deciding on their aims and ambitions. As Rawls puts it, within the justice ethic, individuals are responsible for forming 'their aims and ambitions in the light of what they can reasonably expect'. Those who fail to do so may suffer the frustration of strong desires, but people know that 'the weight of their claims is not given by the strength or intensity of their wants and desires' (Rawls 1980: 545). Thus we shift from subjective hurt or happiness to objective unfairness as the basis for moral claims.

We can now see the kernel of truth underlying the two previous contrasts between care and justice. According to Tronto, justice emphasizes the learning of rules over the learning of moral sensitivities, and the applying of abstract principles over the making of context-sensitive assessments of particular needs. This debate over abstraction and context-sensitivity in our moral capacities and moral reasoning is often presented as distinct from the debate over rights and responsibilities as moral concepts. It is often viewed as an epistemological debate, as if justice theorists think that abstract principles are more 'objective' or 'rational', whereas care theorists reject notions of objectivity as epistemologically unsound (e.g. Jaggar 1983: 357; Young 1987: 60).[46] I earlier argued that the entire contrast is overdrawn, since the sort of abstraction involved in justice reasoning does not necessarily compete with context-sensitivity (e.g. moral sensitivity is required to be a good juror). But we can now see that even where justice is less context-sensitive, the explanation is moral not epistemological. The reason why justice emphasizes learning and applying rules is that this is required for fairness and autonomy. If we are to have genuine autonomy, we must know in advance what our responsibilities are, and these assignments of responsibility must be insulated to some extent from context-sensitive assessments of particular desires. As a result, some subjective hurts must be discounted. And if some subjective hurts do not give rise to moral claims, then people need to know in advance which these are, so that they can adjust their aims accordingly. For both these reasons, we need rules which are more abstract and less context-sensitive.[47] So any differences that do exist between justice theorists and care theorists concerning the importance of context-sensitivity in our moral capacities and moral reasoning are derived from more fundamental differences concerning the importance of fairness and personal responsibility as moral concepts. The first two contrasts are by-products of the third.

So if the world were solely composed of able-bodied adults, there might be strong reasons for endorsing the justice approach, with its public rules for balancing autonomy and responsibility. And as we have seen throughout this book, many justice theorists have written as if the world were solely composed of able-bodied adults, ignoring issues of how such adults were raised, and how the needs of dependants are met.[48] Justice theorists often implicitly follow Hobbes's suggestion that, in developing our theories, we should 'consider men as if but even now sprung up out of the earth, and suddenly, like mushrooms, come to full maturity, without all kind of engagement to each other'.[49] The nurturing of children and caring for dependants are either ignored, or assumed to be somehow 'naturally' dealt with in the family, which is seen as falling outside the scope of a theory of justice.

If adults did just pop out of the earth like mushrooms, then there would perhaps be no difficulty with the assumption that we are responsible for our ends, and that we should only be concerned with objective unfairness. But once we include care for dependants within the scope of justice, things become more complicated. Rawls rejects the view that subjective hurt is the standard of moral claims on the grounds that 'to argue this seems to presuppose that citizens' preferences are beyond their control as propensities or cravings which simply happen' (Rawls 1982b: 168–9). But this presupposition is of course quite true of many people. Rawls's rejection of subjective hurt as the basis for moral claims is plausible as long as we think only of (able-bodied and mentally competent) adults interacting in public life, while the sick, the helpless, and the young are kept safely out of view.[50] Rawls says that interactions between able-bodied adults are the 'fundamental case' of justice. But once we look beyond the public sphere, then the 'fundamental case' shifts, for as Willard Gaylin puts it, 'All of us inevitably spend our lives evolving from an initial to a final stage of dependence. If we are fortunate enough to achieve power and relative independence along the way it is a transient and passing glory' (quoted in Zaretsky 1982: 193).

On the other hand, the assumption that subjective hurts give rise to moral claims is plausible to the extent that we generalize from the caring relationships involved in child-rearing. A baby is not at all responsible for its needs, and cannot be expected to attend to its parent's welfare: 'Children cannot reciprocate care equally, they require a degree of selflessness and attention that is specific to them' (Grimshaw 1986: 251). But precisely for this reason, caring for infants is not a good model for interaction with adults. As Grimshaw notes, a parent's role 'may often require one to tolerate, accept, and try not to be hurt by, behaviour that would be quite intolerable or a cause for anger in most adult relationships . . . To see female "virtues" or priorities as arising mainly out of relationships with children may lead to a tendency to gloss over the ways in which resilience has become resignation and acceptance, attention has become chronic anxiety, and care and responsiveness chronic self-denial' (Grimshaw 1986: 251, 253).

In short, the justice and care models have been developed with different sorts of cases in mind, and neither seems well suited to deal with the full range of our moral obligations. Should we say then that the ethics of care applies to our relations with dependants, while the ethics of justice applies to relations amongst autonomous adults?[51] One problem is that the distribution of care is itself an issue of justice. Justice theorists have tended to assume that some people (women) will 'naturally' desire to care for others, as part of their plan of life, so that the work of caring for dependants is not something that imposes moral obligations on all persons. But as Baier argues, we cannot view caring as simply one possible life-plan, rather than a moral constraint on every life-plan, for 'the encouragement of some to cultivate [the disposition to care] while others do not could easily lead to exploitation of those who do. It obviously has suited some in most societies well enough that others take on the responsibilities of care (for the sick, the helpless, the young) leaving them free to pursue their own less altruistic goods.' And, of course, 'the long unnoticed moral proletarians were the domestic workers, mostly female' (Baier 1987*b*: 49–50). If we want to ensure that 'free affectivity' for some people does not 'rely on and exploit the usually unfree affectivity' of those who care for dependants, then our political theory 'cannot regard concern for new and future persons as an optional charity left for those with a taste for it. If the morality the theory endorses is to sustain itself, it must provide for its own continuers, not just take out a loan on a carefully encouraged maternal instinct' (Baier 1987*b*: 53–4; 1988: 328).

This suggests that certain activities or practices of care should be seen as an obligation of citizenship—as important as the obligation to pay taxes or serve in the military—and one which applies to men as much as women.[52] More-over, as we have seen, the elimination of sexual inequality not only requires the redistribution of domestic labour, but also a breakdown in the sharp distinction between public and domestic. We need to find ways to make it easier for people to integrate public life and parenting. But while this is required for sexual justice, it threatens to undermine the presuppositions of justice reasoning. For justice reasoning not only presupposes that we are autonomous adults, it seems to presuppose that we are adults *who are not care-givers for dependants*. Once people are responsible for attending to the (unpredictable) demands of dependants, they are no longer capable of guaranteeing their own predictability. Perhaps the whole picture of autonomy as the free pursuit of projects formed in the light of abstract standards presupposes that care for dependent others can be delegated to someone else, or to the state. It is interesting to note how little care theorists talk about the sort of autonomy that male justice theorists discuss at length—the setting of personal goals, the commitment to personal projects. According to Baier, the care perspective 'makes autonomy not even an ideal . . . A certain sort of freedom is an ideal, namely freedom of thought and expression, but to "live one's life in one's own way" is not likely to be among the aims of persons' (Baier 1987*a*: 46). Likewise Ruddick says that maternal thinking involves 'a fundamental metaphysical attitude' which she calls 'holding', 'governed by the priority of keeping over acquiring', in which preserving existing ties takes precedence over the pursuit of new ambitions (Ruddick 1984*a*: 217; 1987: 242). Other feminists have argued that we need to replace liberal 'autonomy' with 'agency' or 'integrity' as the relevant goal (Card 1996; Abrams 1999; Higgins 1997).[53] On these views, the commitment to women's freedom is not a commitment to staking out ground for the pursuit of personal projects, free from the shifting needs of particular others, but is rather a commitment to meeting those needs in a courageous and imaginative way, rather than a servile or deferential way. Any more expansive notion of autonomy can only come at the price of abandoning our responsibilities.[54]

Can we meet our responsibilities for dependent others without giving up the more robust picture of autonomy, and the notions of responsibility and justice that make it possible? It is too early to tell.[55] Justice theorists have constructed impressive edifices by refining traditional notions of fairness and responsibility. However, by continuing the centuries-old neglect of the basic issues of child-rearing and care for dependants, these intellectual achievements are resting on unexamined and perilously shaky ground. Any adequate theory of sexual equality must confront these issues, and the traditional conceptions of discrimination and privacy that have hidden them from view.

GUIDE TO FURTHER READING

For helpful overviews of contemporary feminist moral and political theory, see Alison Jaggar and Iris Marion Young (eds.), *A Companion to Feminist Philosophy* (Blackwell, 1998); Claudia Card (ed.), *On Feminist Ethics and Politics* (University Press of Kansas, 1999); Card (ed.), *Feminist Ethics* (University Press of Kansas, 1991); Alison Jaggar, *Feminist Politics and Human Nature* (Rowman and Allanheld, 1983); Rosemary Tong, *Feminist Thought: A More Comprehensive Introduction*, 2nd edn. (Westview, 1998); Judith Butler and J. W. Scott (eds.), *Feminists Theorize the Political* (Routledge, 1992); and Anne Phillips (ed.), *Feminism and Politics* (Oxford University Press, 1998).

For feminist critiques and reinterpretations of the history of political thought, see Mary Lyndon Shanley and Uma Narayan (eds.), *Reconstructing Political Theory: Feminist Perspectives* (Pennsylvania State University Press, 1997); Ellen Kennedy and Susan Mendus, *Women in Western Political Philosophy* (Wheatsheaf, 1987); Mary Lyndon Shanley and Carole Pateman (eds.), *Feminist Interpretations and Political Theory* (Pennsylvania State University Press, 1991); Susan Okin, *Women in Western Political Thought* (Princeton University Press, 1979); Arlene Saxonhouse, *Women in the History of Political Thought* (Praeger, 1981); Carole Pateman, *The Sexual Contract* (Polity, 1988); Nancy Hirschman and C. DiStefano (eds.), *Revisioning the Political: Feminist Revisions of Traditional Concepts in Western Political Theory* (Westview, 1996); Jean Bethke Elshtain, *Public Man, Private Woman: Women in Social and Political Thought* (Princeton University Press, 1981).

For the purposes of this chapter, I have organized feminist concerns about mainstream political philosophy under three headings. The first is the so-called *equality/ difference* debate, about the ways in which allegedly sex-blind laws or policies can disadvantage women. For important contributions to this debate, see Catherine MacKinnon, *Feminism Unmodified: Discourses on Life and Law* (Harvard University Press, 1987); Deborah Rhode, *Speaking of Sex: The Denial of Gender Inequality* (Harvard University Press, 1997); Susan Okin, *Justice, Gender, and the Family* (Basic Books,

1989); Eva Feder Kittay, *Equality, Rawls and the Inclusion of Women* (Routledge, 1995); Martha Nussbaum, *Sex and Social Justice* (Oxford University Press, 1999); Anne Phillips (ed.), *Feminism and Equality* (Blackwell, 1987); and Deborah Rhode (ed.), *Theoretical Perspectives on Sexual Difference* (Yale University Press, 1990).

A second area of debate concerns the *public/private* distinction, and the way it has been used historically to disadvantage or marginalize women. For a helpful overview of the debate, see Ruth Gavison, 'Feminism and the Public/Private Distinction', *Stanford Law Review*, 45/1 (1992): 1–45; Susan Okin, 'Gender, the Public and the Private', in David Held (ed.), *Political Theory Today* (Polity, 1991); Joan Landes (ed.), *Feminism, the Public and the Private* (Oxford University Press, 1998), Susan Boyd (ed.) *Challenging The Public/Private Divide: Feminism, Law and Public Policy* (University of Toronto Press, 1997); Anita Allen, *Uneasy Access: Privacy for Women in a Free Society* (Rowman and Allanheld, 1988); and the symposium in *William and Mary Law Review*, 40/3 (1999): 723–804. For more general discussions of the public/private sphere, see Maurizio Passerin and Ursula Vogel (eds.), *Public and Private: Legal, Political and Philosophical Perspectives* (Routledge, 2000); and S. I. Benn and G. F. Gaus (eds.), *Public and Private in Social Life* (Croom Helm, 1983).

On issues of the *ethic of care*, the starting point of the debate is Carol Gilligan, *In a Different Voice: Psychological Theory and Women's Development* (Harvard University Press, 1982), followed quickly by Nel Noddings's *Caring: A Feminine Approach to Ethics and Moral Education* (University of California Press, 1984). These two books initiated a voluminous debate amongst moral philosophers on the ethic of care, and its relationship to justice. Important contributions to this debate include Peta Bowden, *Caring: Gender-Sensitive Ethics* (Routledge, 1996); Daryl Koehn, *Rethinking Feminist Ethics: Care, Trust and Empathy* (Routledge, 1998); Susan Hekman, *Moral Voices, Moral Selves: Carol Gilligan and Feminist Moral Theory* (Polity Press, 1995); Eva Feder Kittay, *Love's Labor: Essays on Women, Equality and Dependency* (Routledge, 1998); Marilyn Friedman, *What Are Friends For? Feminist Perspectives on Personal Relationships and Moral Theory* (Cornell University Press, 1993); Diemut Bubeck, *Care, Gender, and Justice* (Oxford University Press, 1995), Grace Clement, *Care, Autonomy and Justice: Feminism and the Ethic of Care* (Westview, 1996); and the symposium on Noddings's book in *Hypatia* (1990), 5/1. For collections of readings in this debate, see Virginia Held (ed.), *Justice and Care: Essential Readings in Feminist Ethics* (Westview, 1995); Eva Kittay and Diana Meyers (eds.), *Women and Moral Theory* (Rowman and Littlefield, 1987); M. J. Larabee (ed.), *An Ethic of Care: Feminist and Interdisciplinary Perspectives* (Routledge, 1993). Much of the literature is more focused on personal ethics than political theory, but for attempts to develop the political implications of an ethic of care, see Selma Sevenhuijsen, *Citizenship and the Ethics of Care: Feminist Considerations on Justice, Morality and Politics* (Routledge, 1998); Joan Tronto, *Moral Boundaries: A Political Argument for an Ethic of Care* (Routledge, 1993); Virginia Held, *Feminist Morality: Transforming Culture, Society, and Politics* (University of Chicago Press, 1993).

The two most important journals of feminist theory are *Hypatia* and *Signs*.

For helpful websites, see (*a*) the 'Feminist Theory Website', with sections on various subfields of feminist theory, feminisms in different national/ethnic groups, and biographical information on individual feminists (**www.cddc.vt.edu/feminism/**

enin.html); (b) the 'Society for Women in Philosophy' (SWIP) website, with course syllabuses, bibliography, and a discussion listserv (www.uh.edu/~cfreelan/SWIP/index.html). The Canadian branch of SWIP also has a good website (www.sbrennan.philosophy.arts.uwo.ca/cswip/)

NOTES

1. For introductions to these diverse strands of feminist thought, see Tong 1998; Jaggar 1983; Nye 1988; Charvet 1982.

2. In accepting this prevailing view that there is 'a Foundation in Nature' for the rule of the husband 'as the abler and the stronger' (Locke, in Okin 1979: 200), classical liberals created a serious contradiction for themselves. For they also argued that all humans are by nature equal, that nature provides no grounds for an inequality of rights. This, as we have seen, was the point of their state of nature theories (Ch. 3, s. 3). Why should the supposed fact that men are 'abler and stronger' justify unequal rights for women when, as Locke himself says, 'differences in excellence of parts or ability' do not justify unequal rights? One cannot both maintain equality amongst men as a class, on the grounds that differences in ability do not justify different rights, and also exclude women as a class, on the grounds that they are less able. If women are excluded on the grounds that the average woman is less able than the average man, then all men who are less able than the average man must also be excluded. As Okin puts it, 'If the basis of his individualism was to be firm, he needed to argue that individual women were equal with individual men, just as weaker men were with stronger men' (Okin 1979: 199).

3. My focus in this chapter will be on feminism in the Western democracies, but it should be noted that the condition of women elsewhere is often much worse. In its recent declaration of the 'Decade of Women', the United Nations noted that:

> women constitute half of the world's population;
> perform nearly two-thirds of its work hours;
> receive one-tenth of the world's income;
> and own less than one-hundredth of the world's property

(quoted in Bubeck 1995: 2). For a philosophically informed discussion of the issues facing women in non-Western contexts, see Nussbaum 2000; Okin 1994.

4. A similar issue has arisen regarding the accommodation of people with disabilities. For example, many office jobs require that people be able to go from one floor to another, to attend meetings or get supplies. Unless there are elevators or ramps, which many small office buildings lack, this means that people in a wheelchair are unable to compete for the job. This inequality need not be a matter of prejudice against people with disabilities: it is simply a matter of the requirements of the job. But again, we need to ask why was the job designed to require moving between floors, and why was the building built with only stairs, not elevators or ramps? The answer is that the both the job and the building were designed by able-bodied people on the assumption that the employees would be able-bodied. And so true equality requires redesigning buildings and jobs where possible on the assumption that people with disabilities should also be able to work. And indeed employers and public agencies have a legal obligation to undertake this sort of job and building redesigning in both Canada and the United States.

5. The precise numbers regarding the economic consequences of divorce are a matter of dispute. In her 1985 book, Lenore Weitzman suggested that the disparity was even worse: she calculated a 42% rise in men's standard of living after divorce in California, and a 73% decline in women's standard of living (Weitzman 1985). Richard Peterson has shown that this was a

miscalculation, and I have cited his more conservative—but still distressing—estimate of the gender inequality involved in divorce (Peterson 1996).

6. As Littleton puts it, the goal of equality should be to make gender differences 'socially costless'. Women should not have to 'pay' for the fact that men and women differ: 'Differences should not be permitted to make a difference in the lived-out equality of those persons' (Littleton 1987: 206; cf. Minow 1991).

7. For more thorough discussions of the tension between feminism and communitarianism, see Frazer and Lacey 1993; Frazer 1999; Greschner 1989; Okin 1989b: 41–62; Friedman 1989; 1991; Weiss and Friedman 1995; V. Held 1993: 188–91.

8. For a libertarian critique of anti-discrimination laws, see Epstein 1995a. For the conflict between libertarianism and feminism, see Okin 1989b: ch. 4.

9. Indeed, Littleton's idea that difference should be 'costless' (see n. 6 above) is just another way of stating liberal equality's commitment to endowment-insensitivity (see ch. 3, s. 2–3). MacKinnon argues that the dominance approach is beyond the ken of liberalism because liberals aim at 'formal' or 'abstract' law that is 'transparent of substance'. I do not understand her contrast of 'form' and 'substance', or how it relates to liberal principles of equality and freedom. MacKinnon often seems to equate liberalism with a particular stream of American constitutional interpretation. For the relationship between MacKinnon's view and liberalism, see Langton 1990; Schaefer 2001; Nussbaum 1999: ch. 2; Bassham 1992.

10. Okin offers two broad strategies for achieving gender equality. The short-term response is to 'protect the vulnerable'. The marriage contract must be modified to protect those who subordinate their careers to perform the unpaid work of the family. One way to do this is to ensure that 'both partners have equal entitlement to all earnings coming into the household', and, in cases of divorce, 'both postdivorce households should enjoy the same standard of living' (Okin 1989b: 180–3). The long-term response aims at the creation of a gender-free society: 'A just future would be one without gender. In its social structures and practices, one's sex would have no more relevance than one's eye color or the length of one's toes. No assumptions would be made about "male" and "female" roles; childbearing would be so conceptually separated from child rearing and other family responsibilities that it would be a cause for surprise, and no little concern, if men and women were not equally responsible for domestic life or if children were to spend much more time with one parent than the other.' This would require fathers to take more responsibility for childcare, mothers to have more sustained labour-force attachment, the provision of high-quality day care, and the redesigning of workplace and school schedules so as to accommodate parenting. The ultimate goal is a gender-free society, and so we 'must encourage and facilitate the equal sharing by men and women of paid and unpaid work, or productive and reproductive labor. We must work toward a future in which all will be likely to choose this mode of life' (Okin 1989b: 171). For discussions of Okin's suggestions, see Kleingeld 1998; Sehon 1996; Russell 1995; Kymlicka 1991; Greene 1996.

11. See Rawls 1971: 128, 146. Rawls's account of the family is discussed in Okin 1987; Green 1986; English 1977; Kearns 1983; Kittay 1995. The 'Aristotelian hangover' of treating individuals as 'heads of households' remains common in both political science and political theory (Stiehm 1983).

12. Van Parijs argues that one of the central advantages of the basic income scheme I discussed in Chapter 3 (p. 83) is that it would lessen women's economic dependence (Van Parijs 2000, 2001).

13. Defenders of the traditional family often argue that the gendered division of domestic labour is rational, since it works to the overall good of the household, and fully consensual. But, as Okin notes, studies indicate that women do not like the existing distribution of domestic labour. Women know that they do more hours of work (paid and unpaid combined)

than men, and that their work has less intrinsic interest (as judged by both men and women), and they resent their economic dependence on men, and the fact that men do so little of the domestic work (Okin 1989b: 151–4). The domestic division of labour, therefore, is not consensual. Rather, 'the major reason that husbands and other heterosexual men living with wage-working women are not doing more housework is that they do not want to, and are able, to a large extent, to enforce their wills' (Okin 1989b: 153).

14. One explanation is that liberals maintained the same dismissive attitude towards the domestic realm as the ancients. Just as the ancients viewed the domestic sphere as something to be transcended in order to free men to participate in political life, so liberals viewed domestic life as something to be mastered in order to be free for social life. This seems to be part of the explanation for why Mill and Marx did not consider reproduction to be a realm of freedom and justice. They viewed the traditional woman's role as a merely 'natural' one, incapable of cultural development (cf. Jaggar 1983: ch. 4; Okin 1979: ch. 9; Donner 1993).

15. Many feminists say that the domestic–public distinction arose with, or was reflected in, liberalism's separation of public and private spheres (e.g. Nicholson 1986: 201; Kennedy and Mendus 1987: 6–7; Coltheart 1986: 112). But this is historically inaccurate, for 'the assignment of public space to men and [domestic] space to women is continuous in Western history' (Eisenstein 1981: 22). Liberalism inherited, rather than created, this public–domestic distinction. It may be true that by emphasizing the distinction between public and private within civil society, liberals obscure the more fundamental distinction between public and domestic (Pateman 1987: 109). But if so, it is a pre-liberal distinction between male and female domains which is being obscured (Eisenstein 1981: 223; cf. Green 1986: 34; Nicholson 1986: 161).

Why has this original liberal understanding of the private sphere been lost, so that 'to talk of an ideal of the private world within the context of contemporary American society is to talk about the family' (Elshtain 1981: 322; cf. Benn and Gaus 1983: 54)? Perhaps because people assume that 'public' and 'private' must mark a division in space. If so, then the most plausible location of private space is the family household. But the liberal public–private distinction is not a distinction between two physical areas, since society and polity are essentially coterminous. It is a distinction between two different aims and responsibilities. To act publicly is to accept responsibility for promoting the common good, defined in terms of the impartial concern for each person's interests. When acting privately, one is not required to act impartially, but is free to pursue one's own ends, consistent with the rights of others, and to join with others in the pursuit of shared ends. Both of these activities can occur anywhere in society. The fact that one goes out in public does not mean that one is responsible for acting impartially or obliged to account for one's actions. The fact that one is at home does not absolve one from respecting other people's rights.

16. There are feminist critics of the liberal state–society divide, even when it is distinguished from the patriarchal domestic–public divide. Pateman, for example, says that unlike republican critics who seek only to 'reinstate the political in public life', feminist critics 'insist that an alternative to the liberal conception must also encompass the relationship between public and domestic life' (Pateman 1987: 108). But she does not explain why feminists who reject the public–domestic distinction should also be concerned with the liberal state–society distinction. Her own comments suggest that we have no clear idea why collapsing the distinction between the state and civil society would benefit women (Pateman 1987: 120). Fran Olsen gives a feminist critique of the state–society distinction, drawing on Marx's comments on alienation (Olsen 1983: 1561–4).

17. Similarly, the Aristotelian republican conception of politics is in contradiction with feminist conceptions of politics based on an ethic of care, which I will discuss in the next section. Classical republican politics would have no room for Joan Tronto's conception of a

politics of care, which she defines as 'a species activity that includes everything that we do to maintain, continue, and repair our "world" so that we can live in it as well as possible. That world includes our bodies, our selves, and our environment, all of which we seek to interweave in a complex, life-sustaining web' (Tronto 1995: 142).

18. For discussions of how liberals have failed to deal adequately with the problem of adaptive preferences amongst women due to oppressive cultural norms and representations in civil society, see Kernohan 1998; Hampton 1997: 191–209; Sunstein 1996; 1999; Okin 1994; 1999; Nussbaum 2000: ch. 5. For Rawls's recognition of the problem of adaptive preferences, see Rawls 1971: 259–60.

19. For the importance to self-development of being able to occasionally seclude onself from society—to make oneself inaccessible to others—see Hefferman 1995; Allen 1999.

20. This Romantic view of privacy has become so integrated into modern liberalism that some people take it as the original liberal conception (e.g. Benn and Gaus 1983: 57–8). However, while the idea of retreating from society can be found in classic liberals (e.g. Locke's *Letter of Toleration*), it is primarily an adopted liberal position. Viewing privacy in terms of a retreat from all roles of civil society, far from being the original liberal position, means that 'the personal and private have been dissociated from virtually every institutional setting. The result is a dramatic collapse of the traditional liberal distinction between public and private as between government and society' (Rosenblum 1987: 66).

21. It is remarkable how policies that were justified on the grounds that the family was the man's private property are now justified on the grounds that men and women have an equal right to privacy (see, e.g., Benn and Gaus 1983: 38). As Taub and Schneider note, 'The state's failure to regulate the domestic sphere is now often justified on the ground that the law should not interfere with emotional relationships involved in the family realm because it is too heavy-handed ... The importance of this concern, however, is undercut by the fact that the same result was previously justified by legal fictions, such as the woman's civil death on marriage' (Taub and Schnieder 1982: 122; cf. Seigal 1996: 2142–70).

22. For feminist defences of the importance of privacy, once separated from patriarchal notions of paterfamilias or family autonomy, see Allen 1988; 1997; 1999; McClain 1995; 1999*a*; Stein 1993.

23. Some liberal feminists have started to challenge the traditional family. The characterization of liberal feminism as concerned only with access to the public sphere 'has become increasingly problematic. Liberal feminists, like many others, have steadily focussed their attention on women's personal lives' (Nicholson 1986: 22–3; cf. Wendell 1987). Paradoxically, when liberals endorse reforming the family, they are often accused of the 'devaluation of the private sphere' (Elshtain 1981: 243; cf. Nicholson 1986: 24). Jean Elshtain claims that the 'liberal imperative' is 'to thoroughly politicize or publicize the private sphere' (Elshtain 1981: 248). By making issues of child-rearing a public responsibility, liberalism would 'denude the private sphere of its central raison d'etre and chief source of human emotion and value. Similarly, to externalize all housekeeping activities, to make them public activities, would vitiate the private realm further. "All persons would, so far as possible, be transformed into public persons, and the sundering of the forms of social life begun by industrialization would be carried to completion by the absorption of the private as completely as possible into the public". This is the completion of the liberal imperative' (Elshtain 1981: 248, quoting R. P. Wolff). For a discussion of recent feminist concerns about 'liberalizing the family' (e.g. the extension of contractual thinking to marriage and the family), see Kymlicka 1991.

24. We have seen this repeatedly in earlier chapters: issues about reproduction and child-rearing are ignored in Nozick's account of self-ownership (Chapter 4), or Marx's account of the primacy of labour (Chapter 5); or the civic republican account of the good life (Chapter 7).

25. There is also some debate over the explanation for any gender difference in moral reasoning. Proposals range from sex-role socialization (Meyers 1987: 142–6) to our early infant experience of being mothered (Gilligan 1987: 20). There are also less gender-specific explanations. Powerless groups often learn empathy because they are dependent on others for protection, and 'as subordinates in a male-dominated society, [women] are required to develop psychological characteristics that please the dominant group and fulfill its needs' (Okin 1990: 154). For example, 'a woman who is dependent on a man may develop great skill in attending to and caring for him, in "reading" his behaviour and learning how to interpret his moods and gratify his desires before he needs to ask' (Grimshaw 1986: 252). This may explain why the male members of oppressed classes or races also exhibit some manifestations of a caring ethic (Tronto 1987: 649–51; Harding 1987: 307).

26. My typology of contrasts is adapted from Tronto 1987: 648. For other typologies, see Sher 1987 (who draws five contrasts); and Dancy 1992 (who draws eleven contrasts). Bubeck notes, correctly I believe, that these typologies tend to focus too much on alleged differences in the formal properties of the two ethics, rather than on the differences in their substantive values (Bubeck 1995: ch. 5).

27. Other care theorists who dispute the need for principles include Ruddick 1984a: 223–4; Noddings 1984: 81–94; Hekman 1995; Deveaux 1995a: 115; 1995b: 87.

28. Bubeck argues that the women in Gilligan's own studies are appealing to principles, and indeed to principles of justice, particularly principles of minimizing harm, and of equality (Bubeck 1995: 199–214).

29. For the need to integrate concern for distant others into a theory of care, see Hoagland 1991; Card 1990: 102, both of whom criticize Noddings's claim that the ethic of care privileges 'proximity' in caring relationships (Noddings 1984: 7, 86, 152).

30. In her later work, Tronto suggests that principles of justice might be needed, as a supplement to the care ethic, to avoid the problem of 'parochialism' (Tronto 1993: 170–1).

31. Ruddick's answer to this question is to say that 'mothers can . . . come to realize that the good of their own children is entwined with the good of all children' (Ruddick 1984b: 239; cf. Held 1993: 53). But it is doubtful whether the good of one child is connected with the good of all children, however distant. And even where it is 'entwined', the connection can be competitive rather than complementary. Their good can be entwined in such a way that resources spent on one child must be denied to another. If the mechanism for expanding the web of relationships is the realization that one's good is entwined with that of others, then it may be a very limited expansion. It seems hopelessly optimistic to say that attending to distant others imposes no costs on ongoing attachments, or that 'inequity adversely affects both parties in an unequal relationship' (Gilligan 1982: 174). These claims by Ruddick and Gilligan are, in effect, an attempt to say that the problems which theories of justice are intended to resolve simply do not exist. It is a feminist version of the Marxist/communitarian claim that we can transcend the circumstances of justice. Once we drop this naive assumption, only an explicit commitment to impartial concern, and not simply to preserving existing connections, could sustain the sort of generalization that Gilligan and Ruddick desire (Deveaux 1995b: 93).

32. For one attempt to grapple with this problem in the specific context of immigration policy, see Baier 1996. She contrasts a care perspective, which would admit immigrants based on whether they belong to 'a network of affiliative relationships that is already in place', with a liberal perspective which would admit immigrants based on need. Her conclusion is that the latter is more humane, and that the former runs the risk of endorsing exclusionary immigration policies, such as the former 'White Australia' policy, in which Australia recruited only (white) people with whom they felt some sense of kinship and common culture. See also

Hutchings 1999 and Robinson 1999 for discussions of the relevance of care theory to issues in international relations.

33. Iris Young offers a more general argument for the claim that 'the impartial point of view' denies differences: 'Impartial reason must judge from a point of view outside the particular perspectives of persons involved in interaction, able to totalize these perspectives into a whole, or general will . . . The impartial subject need acknowledge no other subjects whose perspective should be taken into account and with whom discussion might occur . . . From this impartial point of view one need not consult with any other, because the impartial point of view already takes into account all possible perspectives' (Young 1987: 62). But, as we have seen, Rawlsian impartiality consists precisely in the requirement that we attend to all the possible viewpoints. It seems that Young is confusing the moral requirement of impartiality with an epistemological requirement of impersonality or objectivity: 'As a characteristic of reason, impartiality means something different from the pragmatic attitude of being fair, considering other people's needs and desires as well as one's own. Impartiality names a point of view of reason that stands apart from any interests of desires. Not to be partial means being able to see the whole, how all the particular perspectives and interests in a given moral situation relate to one another in a way that, because of its partiality, each perspective cannot see itself. The impartial moral reasoner thus stands outside of and above the situation about which he or she reasons, with no stake in it, or is supposed to adopt an attitude toward a situation as though he or she were outside or above it' (Young 1987: 60). However, one can accept the moral claims of the original position as a mechanism for considering other people's distinct interests without accepting the epistemological ideal of standing above the situation. (Conversely, rejecting that ideal of impersonality does not guarantee that people will attend to other people's interests.)

34. And even libertarian theories need not deny the existence of positive moral duties to care, although they would deny these are legally enforceable.

35. According to some commentators, the difficulty in reconciling the two ethics is not conceptual, but developmental. According to Gilligan, different components of moral development are rooted in different childhood experiences—i.e. the child's experience of inequality/powerlessness gives rise to the search for independence and equality; whereas the experience of deep attachment and connection gives rise to compassion and love (Gilligan 1987: 20; 1995: 124). If so, then differences in infant experiences of being parented may affect their ability to learn different components of morality (Flanagan and Jackson 1987: 629).

36. However, most justice theorists recognize Good Samaritan obligations which are unrelated to objective unfairness (Ch. 2, n. 17 above).

37. Consider the following passage from Gilligan: 'a justice perspective draws attention to problems of inequality and oppression and holds up an ideal of reciprocity and equal respect. A care perspective draws attention to problems of detachment or abandonment and holds up an ideal of attention and response to need. Two moral injunctions—not to treat others unfairly and not to turn away from someone in need—capture these different concerns' (Gilligan and Attanuci 1988: 73).

38. A related concern is that the ethic of care could license paternalistic intervention to save people from what the care-giver regards as foolish or imprudent choices, or as likely subjective hurts. This is perfectly appropriate in the case of children, but worrisome in relations with competent adults. To avoid this, some care theorists emphasize that caring for others involves acknowledging and respecting their capacity for responsible self-direction. But if so, this pushes us back towards the view that our obligations to others are more a matter of objective unfairness than subjective hurts, at least in the case of competent adults. Narayan suggests that this potential for paternalism is present in care discourse, not only in terms of relations with individual members of one's society, but also in terms of relations with entire groups of

people around the world. She suggests that European colonization of Africa and Asia was typically justified in a care-based discourse about the white man's responsibility to care for the welfare of backward races (Narayan 1995: 133–5).

39. Some commentators argue that Gilligan, by neglecting the issue of oppressive relationships, runs the danger of 'moral essentialism'. She 'separates the qualities of care and connection from their context of inequality and oppression and demands that they be considered in their own right, according to their intrinsic merit' (Houston 1988: 176). As Tronto notes, 'If the preservation of a web of relationships is the starting premise of an ethic of care, then there is little basis for critical reflection on whether those relationships are good, healthy, or worthy of preservation' (Tronto 1987: 660; cf. Wilson 1988: 17–18).

40. See Bubeck's discussion of the problem of the 'egoist king'. In a community of carers, she notes, an egoist can not only free-ride on the care-giving of others, knowing he will always be taken care of, but will actually come to possess power over the care-givers (Bubeck 1995: 176).

41. On the danger of women being exploited by societal norms of caring, see West 1997; Bubeck 1995: 174–85, 245–9; Card 1990; 1996; Hoagland 1991; Houston 1987; 1990; Bowden 1996: 180.

42. Some authors worry that the traditional doctrine of maternal self-sacrifice is so deeply embedded in our notions of 'care' that it is better to base feminist ethics on a different concept, such as 'trust' (Baier 1986; 1994; Govier 1997; 1999), 'empathy' (Meyers 1987), or 'vulnerability' (Mendus 1993). All of these share the same starting point as the ethic of care—i.e. that mainstream ethics and political theory reflect a typically 'male' way of approaching moral problems, and that we can learn important insights by attending to the way that women deal with these issues. And they all share the same emphasis on a more 'relational' conception of persons, a more 'contextual' approach to ethics, and a more realistic attention to human dependency. For this reason, as Koehn notes, these alternative accounts of feminist ethics tend to share the same basic strengths and weaknesses. In particular, they all face the difficulty of protecting those people who are trusting/caring/empathic from being exploited or manipulated (Koehn 1998).

43. 'Liberals continue to treat the care perspective as a grand moral theory and raise criticisms accordingly. In response, care proponents say that their approach is antithetical to grand moral theorizing, that it's about seeing the world in terms of context, attachment, and actual, not hypothetical, experience. They reject the suggestion that they need to match liberalism concept for concept, and suggest that this very expectation obfuscates the broader critique of moral philosophy and ethical practice made by feminist care writers' (Deveaux 1995a: 117).

44. For a helpful exploration of the logic of these three different forms of caring, see Bowden 1996. While many care theorists have looked to mothering as the paradigm of ethical caring (e.g. Noddings 1984; Ruddick 1984a; Held 1993), Marilyn Friedman suggests that women's intimate friendships might be a more promising (and less dangerous) model for a feminist ethics (Friedman 1993).

45. Hence it is quite misleading to say that Gilligan shares Williams's belief that impartiality is 'too demanding', or his hope that by emphasizing the importance of 'the personal point of view' we can free personal projects from the constraints of morality (contra Adler 1987: 226, 205; Kittay and Meyers 1987: 8). As Blum notes, personal concerns are seen by Williams 'as legitimate not so much from the point of view of *morality*, but from the broader standpoint of practical reason. By contrast Gilligan argues . . . that care and responsibility within personal relationships constitute an important element of morality itself, genuinely distinct from impartiality. For Gilligan each person is embedded within a web of ongoing relationships, and morality importantly if not exclusively consists in attention to, understanding of, and emotional responsiveness towards the individuals with whom one stands in these relationships . . .

Nagel's and Williams's notions of the personal domain do not capture or encompass (though Nagel and Williams sometimes imply that they are meant to) the phenomenon of care and responsibility within personal relationships and do not explain why care and responsibility in relationships are distinctively moral phenomena' (Blum 1988: 473). Blum concludes that Gilligan's critique is 'importantly different' from Williams's critique of impartiality, but 'is not at odds' with it (Blum 1988: 473). But this still understates the problem, since Williams clearly wants to emphasize the *non-moral* value of personal projects, and wants to contain morality so as to protect these non-moral values. Gilligan wants to moralize the very attachments which Williams says have non-moral importance.

46. This is related to the widespread tendency to distinguish care and justice in terms of their formal properties rather than substantive values—a tendency noted and criticized in Bubeck 1995: ch. 5.

47. The argument for public standards is also relevant to democracy. The care ethic's claim that moral problems should be solved, not by appeal to public rules or principles, but through the exercise of moral sensitivities by the morally mature agent, has a strong similarity to conservative arguments that political leaders must not be held too accountable to the democratic process (e.g. Oakeshott 1984). Wise political leaders must be trusted, rather than scrutinized, for their reasoning is often tacit, and impossible to present systematically. As with rules of justice, we may want political leaders to employ clear public standards of justification, not because they are more objective, but because they are more democratic. See Dietz 1985 for a critique of maternal thinking for ignoring political values like democracy.

48. One explanation for this, mentioned earlier, is that male philosophers had a self-interested reason for not questioning a gendered division of labour they benefited from. But Annette Baier suggests another reason as well: she notes that the great moral theorists in the Western tradition 'not only are all men, they are mostly men who had minimal adult dealings with (and so were then minimally influenced by) women'. They were mostly 'clerics, misogynists and puritan bachelors', whose philosophy reflected the fact that their own adult lives involved 'cool, distanced relations between more or less free and equal adult strangers' (Baier 1986: 247–8). She suggests that had more of these theorists been husbands and fathers, even in traditional patriarchal marriages, they would have paid more attention to issues of the family, dependency, and the sorts of virtues and relationships needed to sustain an intergenerational human community.

49. Hobbes, 'Philosophical Rudiments Concerning Government and Society', quoted in Pateman 1991: 54. In her 1989 book, Okin has shown in detail how communitarians, libertarians, and liberal egalitarians all assume the existence of the 'gendered family', yet treat it as outside the scope of justice. In each case, theorists 'take mature, independent human beings as the subjects of their theories without any mention of how they got to be that way. We know, of course, that human beings develop and mature only as a result of a great deal of attention and hard work, by far the greater part of it done by women. But when theorists of justice talk about "work" they mean paid work performed in the marketplace. They must be assuming that women, in the gender-structured family, continue to do their unpaid work of nurturing and socializing the young and providing a haven of intimate relations—otherwise there would be no moral subjects for them to theorize about. But these activities apparently take place outside the scope of their theories. Typically, the family itself is not examined in the light of whatever standard of justice the theorist arrives at.' Hence, Okin concludes, 'the "individual" who is the basic subject of their theories is the male head of a fairly traditional household . . . to a large extent, contemporary theories of justice, like those of the past, are about men with wives at home' (Okin 1989*b*: 9, 10, 13).

50. While most liberal theories recognize that we have obligations towards dependent

others (Ch. 3, s. 4*b* above), they write as if these obligations are a matter of ensuring that a fair share of resources is allocated to children and the infirm. They do not discuss our obligation to provide *care* for dependants (V. Held 1995*b*: 130).

51. Tronto calls this the 'containment' strategy, used by mainstream theorists to contain or diminish the challenge that care theory poses to traditional political theory (Tronto 1993).

52. For the idea that care for dependants or the vulnerable should be seen as an obligation of citizenship, see Held 1993; Tronto 1993; Bowden 1996: 154; Bubeck 1995. This is obviously a dramatic revision to the traditional conception of citizenship which assumed that a good citizen was 'independent', meaning neither a primary care-giver nor in need of care (Young 1995*b*). A stronger claim is that citizenship in general should be defined as a relationship or practice of care, and should be informed by the same values and virtues as are found in more traditionally caring relationships, such as mothering or friendship (e.g. Sevenhuijsen 1998: 66; Bowden 1996: ch. 4). This claim is often associated with 'maternalist' accounts of citizenship, mentioned in Chapter 7, which suggest that mothering provides a model for citizenship in general (e.g. Nedelsky 2000; Held 1993; Ruddick 1987). Other feminists argue that, while citizenship may include as one component an obligation of care, it also includes virtues and practices which are distinct from, and even in conflict with, those found in mothering or other relations of care (e.g. Dietz 1985; 1992; Nauta 1992; Mendus 1993; Mouffe 1992*a*).

53. This preference for a more modest notion of 'agency' (or even 'partial agency') is partly rooted in care-based thinking about our obligation to sustain relationships, but also in post-modernist critiques of the very idea of a coherent self or choosing subject. For attempts to link care theory with postmodernism, see Hekman 1995; Sevenhuijsen 1998; White 1991; Flax 1993. For the view that feminists should maintain a (revised) conception of autonomy, see Nedelsky 1989; Friedman 1997, and the essays in MacKenzie and Stoljar 1999.

54. For example, Leslie Wilson says that the reason why the 'ethical self of a person requires a certain sort of autonomy' is that it enables us 'to become the sort of person who can be genuinely one-caring'. Hence an autonomous person exercises her autonomy 'trying to determine ways in which one could become a better caring individual' (Wilson 1988: 21–2). Likewise, Ruddick says that the reason why attentive love requires 'realistic self-preservation', rather than 'chronic self-denial', is that we can become better caring individuals that way (Ruddick 1984*b*: 238). This is some distance from the traditional picture of autonomy as the free pursuit of projects that matter to one for their own sake, and which occasionally compete for time and energy with one's moral obligations.

55. For tentative suggestions about what such an integration would look like, see V. Held 1995*b*: 130–1; Narayan 1995: 138–40; Bubeck 1995; Clement 1996. As Narayan emphasizes, in many real-world circumstances, justice and care are mutually reinforcing, rather than com-petitors. Improved care can be seen as an 'enabling condition' for more adequate forms of justice; and greater justice can be seen as the enabling condition for more adequate forms of care. Hence the two can be seen 'less as contenders for theoretical primary or moral and political adequacy and more as collaborators and allies in our practical and political efforts to make our world more conducive to human flourishing' (Narayan 1995: 139–40).

BIBLIOGRAPHY

ABBEY, RUTH (2001). *Charles Taylor* (Princeton University Press, Princeton).

ABRAMS, KATHYRN (1999). 'From Autonomy to Agency: Feminist Perspectives on Self-Direction', *William and Mary Law Review*, 40/3: 805–46.

ACKERMAN, BRUCE (1980). *Social Justice in the Liberal State* (Yale University Press, New Haven).

—— (1991). *We the People: Foundations* (Harvard University Press, Cambridge, Mass.).

—— and ALSTOTT, ANNE (1999). *The Stakeholder Society* (Yale University Press, New Haven).

ADAMS, ROBERT (1970). 'Motive Utilitarianism', *Journal of Philosophy*, 71: 476–82.

ADDIS, ADENO (1992). 'Individualism, Communitarianism and the Rights of Ethnic Minorities', *Notre Dame Law Review*, 67/3: 615–76.

ADLER, J. (1987). 'Moral Development and the Personal Point of View', in Kittay and Meyers 1987, 205–34.

ALEXANDER, LARRY, and SCHWARZSCHILD, MAIMON (1987). 'Liberalism, Neutrality, and Equality of Welfare vs. Equality of Resources', *Philosophy and Public Affairs*, 16/1: 85–110.

ALFRED, GERALD (1995). *Heeding the Voices of our Ancestors: Kahnawake Mohawk Politics and the Rise of Native Nationalism* (Oxford University Press, Oxford).

ALLEN, ANITA (1988). *Uneasy Access: Privacy for Women in a Free Society* (Rowman and Allanheld, Totowa, NJ).

—— (1997). 'The Jurispolitics of Privacy', in Shanley and Narayan 1997, 68–83.

—— (1999). 'Coercing Privacy', *William and Mary Law Review*, 40/3: 723–58.

—— and REGAN, MILTON (eds.) (1998). *Debating Democracy's Discontent: Essays on American Politics, Law, and Public Philosophy* (Oxford University Press, Oxford).

ALLEN, D. (1973). 'The Utilitarianism of Marx and Engels', *American Philosophical Quarterly*, 10/3: 189–99.

ALLISON, LINCOLN (ed.) (1990). *The Utilitarian Response: The Contemporary Viability of Utilitarian Political Philosophy* (Sage, London).

ANAYA, S. JAMES (1996). *Indigenous Peoples in International Law* (Oxford University Press, New York).

ANDERSON, BENEDICT (1983). *Imagined Communities: Reflections on the Origin and Spread of Nationalism* (New Left Books, London).

ANDERSON, ELIZABETH (1999). 'What is the Point of Equality?', *Ethics*, 99/2: 287–337.

ANDREWS, GEOFF (1991). *Citizenship* (Lawrence and Wishart, London).

ARCHIBUGI, DANIELLE (1995). 'From the United Nations to Cosmopolitan Democracy', in Archibugi and Held 1995, 121–62.

—— and HELD, DAVID (1995). *Cosmopolitan Democracy: An Agenda for a New World Order* (Polity Press, London).

ARENDT, HANNAH (1959). *The Human Condition* (Anchor, New York).

ARNESON, RICHARD (1981). 'What's Wrong with Exploitation?', *Ethics*, 91/2: 202–27.

ARNESON, RICHARD (1985). 'Freedom and Desire', *Canadian Journal of Philosophy*, 15/3: 425–48.

ARNESON, RICHARD (1987). 'Meaningful Work and Market Socialism', *Ethics*, 97/3: 517–45.

—— (1989). 'Equality and Equal Opportunity for Welfare', *Philosophical Studies*, 56: 77–93.

—— (1990). 'Liberalism, Distributive Subjectivism, and Equal Opportunity for Welfare', *Philosophy and Public Affairs*, 19: 159–94.

—— (1991). 'Lockean Self-Ownership: Towards a Demolition', *Political Studies*, 39/1: 36–54.

—— (1993*a*). 'Market Socialism and Egalitarian Ethics', in Bardhan and Roemer 1993, 218–47.

—— (1993*b*). 'Equality', in Goodin and Pettit 1993, 489–507.

—— (1997*a*). 'Egalitarianism and the Undeserving Poor', *Journal of Political Philosophy*, 5/4: 327–50.

—— (1997*b*). 'Feminism and Family Justice', *Public Affairs Quarterly*, 11/4: 313–30.

—— (2000*a*). 'Egalitarian Justice versus the Right to Privacy', *Social Philosophy and Policy*, 17/2: 91–119.

—— (2000*b*). 'Luck Egalitarianism and Prioritarianism', *Ethics*, 110/2: 339–49.

—— and SHAPIRO, IAN (1996). 'Democracy and Religious Freedom: A Critique of Wisconsin vs. Yoder', in Ian Shapiro and Russell Hardin (eds.), *Political Order: NOMOS 38* (New York University Press, New York), 356–411.

ARNSPERGER, CHRISTIAN (1994). 'Envy-Freeness and Distributive Justice', *Journal of Economic Surveys*, 8: 155–86

ARTHUR, JOHN (1987). 'Resource Acquisition and Harm', *Canadian Journal of Philosophy*, 17/2: 337–47.

ATKINSON, TONY (1996). 'The Case for Participation Income', *Political Quarterly*, 67: 67–70.

AUDI, ROBERT (2000). *Religious Commitment and Secular Reason* (Cambridge University Press, Cambridge).

AVINERI, SHLOMO, and DE-SHALIT, AVNER (eds.) (1992). *Communitarianism and Individualism* (Oxford University Press, Oxford).

BABBITT, SUSAN, and CAMPBELL, SUE (eds.) (1999). *Racism and Philosophy* (Cornell University Press, Ithaca, NY).

BACK, LES, and SOLOMOS, JOHN (eds.) (2000). *Theories of Race and Racism* (Routledge, London).

BADER, VEIT (1995). 'Citizenship and Exclusion', *Political Theory*, 23/2: 211–46.

—— (ed.) (1997). *Citizenship and Exclusion* (St Martin's Press, New York).

BAIER, ANNETTE (1986). 'Trust and Anti-Trust', *Ethics*, 96: 231–60.

—— (1987*a*). 'Hume, the Women's Moral Theorist?', in Kittay and Meyers 1987, 37–55.

—— (1987*b*). 'The Need for More than Justice', *Canadian Journal of Philosophy*, supplementary vol. 13: 41–56.

—— (1988). 'Pilgrim's Progress', *Canadian Journal of Philosophy*, 18/2: 315–30.

—— (1994). *Moral Prejudices* (Harvard University Press, Cambridge, Mass.).

—— (1996). 'A Note on Justice, Care and Immigration', *Hypatia*, 10/2: 150–2.

BAILEY, JAMES (1997). *Utilitarianism, Institutions, and Justice* (Oxford University Press, Oxford).

BAKER, C. EDWIN (1985). 'Sandel on Rawls', *University of Pennsylvania Law Review*, 133/4: 895–928.

BAKER, JUDITH (ed.) (1994). *Group Rights* (University of Toronto Press, Toronto).

BALL, STEPHEN (1990). 'Uncertainty in Moral Theory: An Epistemic Defense of Rule-Utilitarian Liberties', *Theory and Decision*, 29: 133–60.

BANTING, KEITH (2000). 'Social Citizenship and the Multicultural Welfare State', in Alan Cairns et al. (eds.), *Citizenship, Diversity and Pluralism* (McGill-Queen's University Press, Montreal), 108–36.

BARBALET, J. M. (1988). *Citizenship: Rights, Struggle and Class Inequality* (University of Minnesota Press, Minneapolis).

BARBER, BENJAMIN (1984). *Strong Democracy: Participatory Politics for a New Age* (University of California Press, Berkeley and Los Angeles).

—— (1999). 'The Discourse of Civility', in Stephen Elkin and Karol Soltan (eds.) *Citizen Competence and Democratic Institutions* (Pennsylvania State University Press, University Park), 39–47.

BARBIERI, WILLIAM (1998). *Ethics of Citizenship: Immigrants and Group Rights in Germany* (Duke University Press, Durham, NC).

BARDHAN, PRANAB, and ROEMER, JOHN (eds.) (1993). *Market Socialism: The Current Debate* (Oxford University Press, New York).

BARKAN, ELAZAR (2000). *The Guilt of Nations: Restitution and Negotiating Historical Injustices* (Norton, New York).

BARKER, E. (1960). *Social Contract: Essays by Locke, Hume and Rousseau* (Oxford University Press, London).

BARRY, BRIAN (1973). *The Liberal Theory of Justice* (Oxford University Press, Oxford).

—— (1989*a*). *Theories of Justice* (University of California Press, Berkeley and Los Angeles).

—— (1989*b*). 'Utilitarianism and Preference Change', *Utilitas*, 1: 278–82.

—— (1989*c*). 'Humanity and Justice in Global Perspective', in B. Barry, *Democracy, Power, and Justice: Essays in Political Theory* (Oxford University Press, Oxford).

—— (1994). 'In Defense of Political Liberalism', *Ratio Juris*, 7/3: 325–30.

—— (1995). *Justice as Impartiality* (Oxford University Press, Oxford).

—— (1997). 'Political Theory: Old and New', in Robert Goodin and Hans-Dieter Klingeman (eds.) *A New Handbook of Political Science* (Oxford University Press, Oxford), 531–48

—— (1999). 'Statism and Nationalism: A Cosmopolitan Critique', in Brilmayer and Shapiro 1999, 12–66.

—— (2001). *Culture and Equality: An Egalitarian Critique of Multiculturalism* (Polity, Cambridge).

—— and GOODIN, ROBERT (eds.) (1992). *Free Movement: Ethical Issues in the Transnational Migration of People and of Money* (Pennsylvania State University Press, University Park).

BARRY, NORMAN (1986). *On Classical Liberalism and Libertarianism* (Macmillan, London).

—— (1990). 'Markets, Citizenship, and the Welfare State', in Raymond Plant and Norman Barry, *Citizenship and Rights in Thatcher's Britain: Two Views* (IEA Health and Welfare Unit, London).

BARRY, NORMAN (1991). *Libertarianism in Philosophy and Politics* (Cambridge University Press, New York).

BASSHAM, GREGORY (1992). 'Feminist Legal Theory: A Liberal Response', *Notre Dame Journal of Law, Ethics and Public Policy*, 6/2: 293–308.

BATSTONE, DAVID, and MENDIETA, EDUARDO (eds.) (1999). *The Good Citizen* (Routledge, London).

BAUBÖCK, RAINER (1994). *Transnational Citizenship: Membership and Rights in International Migration* (Edward Elgar, Aldershot).

BAUMEISTER, ANDREA (2000). *Liberalism and the Politics of Difference* (Edinburgh University Press, Edinburgh).

BEARS (Brown Electronic Article Review Service) (1999). 'Symposium on Elizabeth Anderson's "What is the Point of Equality?"' (**www.brown.edu/Departments/ Philosophy/bears/9904sobe.html**).

BEINER, RONALD (1983). *Political Judgment* (Methuen, London).

—— (1989). 'What's the Matter with Liberalism', in Allan Hutchinson and Leslie Green (eds.) *Law and Community* (Carswell, Toronto), 37–56.

—— (1992). 'Citizenship', in R. Beiner, *What's the Matter with Liberalism* (University of California Press, Berkeley and Los Angeles), 98–141.

—— (ed.) (1995). *Theorizing Citizenship* (State University of New York Press, Albany).

—— (ed.) (1999). *Theorizing Nationalism* (State University of New York Press, Albany).

BEITZ, CHARLES (1979). *Political Theory and International Relations* (Princeton University Press, Princeton).

—— (1989). *Political Equality: An Essay in Democratic Theory* (Princeton University Press, Princeton).

—— (1999). 'International Liberalism and Distributive Justice: A Survey of Recent Thought', *World Politics*, 51: 269–96.

BELL, DANIEL A. (1993). *Communitarianism and its Critics* (Oxford University Press, Oxford).

—— (2000). *East Meets West* (Princeton University Press, Princeton).

BELLAH, ROBERT, et al. (1985). *Habits of the Heart: Individualism and Commitment in American Life* (University of California Press, Berkeley and Los Angeles).

BENHABIB, SEYLA (1986). *Critique, Norm, and Utopia* (Columbia University Press, New York).

—— (1987). 'The Generalized and the Concrete Other: The Kohlberg–Gilligan Controversy and Feminist Theory', in S. Benhabib and D. Cornell (eds.), *Feminism as Critique* (University of Minnesota Press, Minneapolis), 77–95.

—— (1992). *Situating the Self: Gender, Community and Postmodernism in Contemporary Ethics* (Routledge, London).

—— (1996). 'Toward a Deliberative Model of Democratic Legitimacy', in S. Benhabib (ed.), *Democracy and Difference: Contesting the Boundaries of the Political* (Princeton University Press, Princeton), 67–94.

BENN, STANLEY, and GAUS, GERALD (1983). *Public and Private in Social Life* (Croom Helm, London).

BENTHAM, JEREMY (1970). *An Introduction to the Principles of Morals and Legislation*, ed. J. H. Burns and H. L. A. Hart (Athlone Press, London; 1st pub. 1823).

BERKOWITZ, PETER (1999). *Virtue and the Making of Modern Liberalism* (Princeton University Press, Princeton).

BERLIN, ISAIAH (1969). *Four Essays on Liberty* (Oxford University Press, London).

—— (1981). 'Does Political Philosophy Still Exist?', in H. Hardy (ed.), *Concepts and Categories: Philosophical Essays* (Penguin, Harmondsworth), 143–72.

BERTRAM, CHRISTOPHER (1988). 'A Critique of John Roemer's Theory of Exploitation', *Political Studies*, 36/1: 123–30.

BICKFORD, SUSAN (1996). *The Dissonance of Democracy: Listening, Conflict and Citizenship* (Cornell University Press, Ithaca, NY).

BLACK, SAMUEL (1991). 'Individualism at an Impasse', *Canadian Journal of Philosophy*, 21/3: 347–77.

BLATTBERG, CHARLES (2000). *From Pluralist to Patriotic Politics: Putting Practices First* (Oxford University Press, Oxford).

BLAUG, RICARDO (1996). 'New Theories of Discursive Democracy: A User's Guide', *Philosophy and Social Criticism*, 22/1: 49–80.

BLUM, LAWRENCE (1988). 'Gilligan and Kohlberg: Implications for Moral Theory', *Ethics*, 98/3: 472–91.

BOAZ, DAVID (ed.) (1997). *The Libertarian Reader: Classic and Contemporary Writings from Lao-tzu to Milton Friedman* (Free Press, New York).

BOBBIO, NORBERTO (1995). 'Democracy and the International System', in Archibugi and Held 1995, 17–41.

BOGART, J. H. (1985). 'Lockean Provisos and State of Nature Theories', *Ethics*, 95/4: 828–36.

BOHMAN, JAMES (1996). *Public Deliberation: Pluralism, Complexity and Democracy* (MIT Press, Cambridge, Mass.).

—— (1998a). 'The Coming of Age of Deliberative Democracy', *Journal of Political Philosophy*, 6/4: 399–423.

—— (1998b). 'The Globalization of the Public Sphere: Cosmopolitan Publicity and the Problem of Cultural Pluralism', *Philosophy and Social Criticism*, 24: 199–216.

—— and REHG, WILLIAM (eds.) (1997). *Deliberative Democracy: Essays on Reason and Politics* (MIT Press, Cambridge, Mass.).

BOSNIAK, LINDA (2000). 'Citizenship Denationalized', *Indiana Journal of Global Legal Studies*, 7/2: 447–509.

BOWDEN, PETA (1996). *Caring: Gender-Sensitive Ethics* (Routledge, London).

BOWLES, SAMUEL and GINTIS, HERBERT (1998). 'Is Equality Passé? Homo Reciprocans and the Future of Egalitarian Politics', *Boston Review*, 23/6: 4–10.

—— (1999). *Recasting Egalitarianism: New Rules for Markets, States, and Communities* (Verso, London).

BOYD, SUSAN (ed.) (1977). *Challenging the Public/Private Divide: Feminism, Law and Public Policy* (University of Toronto Press, Toronto.)

BRANDT, R. B. (1959). *Ethical Theory* (Prentice-Hall, Englewood Cliffs, NJ).

—— (1979). *A Theory of the Right and the Good* (Oxford University Press, Oxford).

BRAVERMAN, HARRY (1974). *Labor and Monopoly Capital* (Monthly Review Press, New York).

BRECHER, BOB, et al. (eds.) (1998). *Nationalism and Racism in the Liberal Order* (Ashgate, Aldershot).

BRENKERT, GEORGE (1981). 'Marx's Critique of Utilitarianism', *Canadian Journal of Philosophy* 7: 193–220.

—— (1983). *Marx's Ethics of Freedom* (Routledge and Kegan Paul, London).

BRENKERT, GEORGE (1998). 'Self-Ownership, Freedom, and Autonomy', *Journal of Ethics*, 2/1: 27–55.

BRIDGES, DAVID (ed.) (1997). *Education, Autonomy and Democratic Citizenship: Philosophy in a Changing World* (Routledge, London).

BRIGHOUSE, HARRY (1998). 'Against Nationalism', in Couture, Nielsen, and Seymour 1998, 365–406.

—— (2000). *School Choice and Social Justice* (Oxford University Press, Oxford).

BRILMAYER, LEA, and SHAPIRO, IAN (eds.) (1999). *Global Justice* (New York University Press, New York).

BRINK, DAVID (1986). 'Utilitarian Morality and the Personal Point of View', *Journal of Philosophy*, 83/8: 417–38.

BRITTAN, SAMUEL (1988). *A Restatement of Economic Liberalism* (Macmillan, London).

BROMWICH, DAVID (1995). 'Culturalism: The Euthanasia of Liberalism', *Dissent*, Winter: 89–102.

BROOKS, ROY (1996). *Separation or Integration: A Strategy for Racial Equality* (Harvard University Press, Cambridge, Mass.).

—— (ed.) (1999). *When Sorry Isn't Enough: The Controversy over Apologies and Reparations for Human Injustice* (New York University Press, New York).

BROOME, JOHN (1989). 'Fairness and the Random Distribution of Goods', in Jon Elster (ed.), *Justice and the Lottery* (Cambridge University Press, Cambridge).

—— (1991). *Weighing Goods* (Blackwell, Oxford).

BROUGHTON, J. (1983). 'Women's Rationality and Men's Virtues', *Social Research*, 50/3: 597–642.

BROWN, ALAN (1986). *Modern Political Philosophy: Theories of the Just Society* (Penguin, Harmondsworth).

BROWN, JONATHAN (2001). 'Genetic Manipulation in Humans as a Matter of Rawlsian Justice', *Social Theory and Practice*, 27/1: 83–110.

BRUGGER, BILL (1999). *Republican Theory in Political Thought: Virtuous or Virtual?* (St Martin's Press, New York).

BUBECK, DIEMUT (1995). *Care, Gender, and Justice* (Oxford University Press, Oxford).

—— (1999). 'A Feminist Approach to Citizenship', in O. Huftan and Y. Jravaritou (eds.) *Gender and the Uses of Time* (Kluwer, Dordrecht).

BUCHANAN, ALLEN (1975). 'Revisability and Rational Choice', *Canadian Journal of Philosophy*, 5: 395–408.

—— (1982). *Marx and Justice: The Radical Critique of Liberalism* (Methuen, London).

—— (1989). 'Assessing the Communitarian Critique of Liberalism', *Ethics*, 99/4: 852–82.

—— (1990). 'Justice as Reciprocity versus Subject-Centred Justice', *Philosophy and Public Affairs*, 19/3: 227–52.

—— (1991). *Secession: The Legitimacy of Political Divorce* (Westview Press, Boulder, Colo.).

BUCHANAN, JAMES (1975). *The Limits of Liberty: Between Anarchy and Leviathan* (University of Chicago Press, Chicago).

BUCHANAN, JAMES and CONGLETON, RICHARD (1998). *Politics by Principle, Not Interest* (Cambridge University Press, Cambridge).

—— and TULLOCK, GORDON (1962). *The Calculus of Consent* (University of Michigan Press, Ann Arbor).

BULMER, MARTIN, and REES, ANTHONY (eds.) (1996). *Citizenship Today: The Contemporary Relevance of T. H. Marshall* (University College London Press, London).

BURTT, SHELLEY (1993). 'The Politics of Virtue Today: A Critique and a Proposal', *American Political Science Review*, 87: 360–8.

BUTLER, JUDITH, and SCOTT, JOAN W. (eds.) (1992). *Feminists Theorize the Political* (Routledge, London).

CAIRNS, ALAN (1995). 'Aboriginal Canadians, Citizenship, and the Constitution', in A. Cairns, *Reconfigurations: Canadian Citizenship and Constitutional Change* (McClelland and Stewart, Toronto), 238–60.

—— and WILLIAMS, CYNTHIA (1985). *Constitutionalism, Citizenship and Society in Canada* (University of Toronto Press, Toronto).

CALHOUN, CHESHIRE (2000). 'The Virtue of Civility', *Philosophy and Public Affairs*, 29/3: 251–75.

CALLAN, EAMONN (1994). 'Beyond Sentimental Civic Education', *American Journal of Education*, 102: 190–221.

—— (1995). 'Common Schools for Common Education', *Canadian Journal of Education*, 20: 251–71.

—— (1996). 'Political Liberalism and Political Education', *Review of Politics*, 58: 5–33.

—— (1997). *Creating Citizens: Political Education and Liberal Democracy* (Oxford University Press, Oxford).

CAMPBELL, RICHMOND, and SOWDEN, LANNING (eds.) (1985). *Paradoxes of Rationality and Cooperation* (UBC Press, Vancouver).

CAMPBELL, TOM (1983). *The Left and Rights: A Conceptual Analysis of the Idea of Socialist Rights* (Routledge and Kegan Paul, London).

—— (1988). *Justice* (Macmillan, Basingstoke).

—— (2000). *Justice*, 2nd edn. (Palgrave, New York).

CANEY, SIMON (1991). 'Consequentialist Defenses of Liberal Neutrality', *Philosophical Quarterly*, 41/165: 457–77.

—— (1995). 'Anti-perfectionism and Rawlsian Liberalism', *Political Studies*, 43/2: 248–64.

—— GEORGE, DAVID, and JONES, PETER (eds.) (1996). *National Rights, International Obligations* (Westview, Boulder, Colo.).

CANOVAN, MARGARET (1996). *Nationhood and Political Theory* (Edward Elgar, Cheltenham).

CARD, CLAUDIA (1990). 'Caring and Evil', *Hypatia*, 5/1: 101–8.

—— (1991). *Feminist Ethics* (University Press of Kansas, Lawrence).

—— (1996). *The Unnatural Lottery: Character and Moral Luck* (Temple University Press, Philadelphia).

—— (ed.) (1999). *On Feminist Ethics and Politics* (University of Kansas Press, Lawrence).

CARENS, JOSEPH (1985). 'Compensatory Justice and Social Institutions', *Economics and Philosophy* 1/1: 39–67.

—— (1986). 'Rights and Duties in an Egalitarian Society', *Political Theory*, 14/1: 31–49.

CARENS, JOSEPH (1987). 'Aliens and Citizens: The Case for Open Borders', *Review of Politics*, 49/3: 251–73.

—— (1989). 'Membership and Morality: Admission to Citizenship in Liberal Democratic States', in W. R. Brubaker (ed.), *Immigration and the Politics of Citizenship in Europe and North America* (University Press of America, Lanham, Md.), 31–50.

—— (2000). *Culture, Citizenship, and Community: A Contextual Exploration of Justice as Evenhandedness* (Oxford University Press, Oxford).

CARENS, JOSEPH (ed.) (1995). *Is Quebec Nationalism Just? Perspectives from Anglophone Canada* (McGill-Queen's University Press, Montreal).

CAREY, GEORGE (1984). *Freedom and Virtue: The Conservative/Libertarian Debate* (University Press of America, Lanham, Md.).

CARTER, APRIL (2001). *The Political Theory of Global Citizenship* (Routledge, London).

CARTER, IAN (1992). 'The Measurement of Pure Negative Freedom', *Political Studies*, 40/1: 38–50.

—— (1995*a*). 'Interpersonal Comparisons of Freedom', *Economics and Philosophy*, 11: 1–23.

—— (1995*b*). 'The Independent Value of Freedom', *Ethics*, 105/4: 819–45.

—— (1999). *A Measure of Freedom* (Oxford University Press, Oxford).

CARVER, TERRELL (ed.) (1991). *The Cambridge Companion to Marx* (Cambridge University Press, Cambridge).

—— and THOMAS, PAUL (eds.) (1995). *Rational Choice Marxism* (Pennsylvania State University Press, University Park).

CASTLES, STEPHEN, and MILLER, MARK (1993). *The Age of Migration: International Population Movements in the Modern Age* (Macmillan, Basingstoke).

CAVALIERI, PAOLA, and SINGER, PETER (eds.) (1993). *The Great Ape Project: Equality beyond Humanity* (Fourth Estate, London).

CHAMBERS, SIMONE (1996). *Reasonable Democracy: Jürgen Habermas and the Politics of Discourse* (Cornell University Press, Ithaca, NY).

—— (1998). 'Contract or Conversation? Theoretical Lessons from the Canadian Constitutional Crises', *Politics and Society*, 26/1: 143–79.

—— (2001). 'Critical Theory and Civil Society', in Simone Chambers and Will Kymlicka (eds.), *Alternative Conceptions of Civil Society* (Princeton University Press, Princeton).

CHAN, JOSEPH (2000). 'Legitimacy, Unanimity, and Perfectionism', *Philosophy and Public Affairs*, 29/1: 5–42.

CHARVET, JOHN (1982). *Feminism* (J. M. Dent and Sons, London).

CHILD, JAMES (1994). 'Can Libertarianism Sustain a Fraud Standard?', *Ethics*, 104/4: 722–38.

CHRISTIANO, THOMAS (1996). *The Rule of the Many* (Westview Press, Boulder, Colo.).

CHRISTIE, CLIVE, J. (1998). *Race and Nation: A Reader* (St Martin's Press, New York).

CHRISTMAN, JOHN (1986). 'Can Ownership be Justified by Natural Rights?', *Philosophy and Public Affairs*, 15/2: 156–77.

—— (1991). 'Self-Ownership, Equality and the Structure of Property Rights', *Political Theory*, 19/1: 28–46.

CHRISTODOULIS, EMILIOS (ed.) (1998). *Communitarianism and Citizenship* (Ashgate, Aldershot).

CLARK, B., and GINTIS, HERBERT (1978). 'Rawlsian Justice and Economic Systems', *Philosophy and Public Affairs*, 7/4: 302–25.

CLARKE, DESMOND, and JONES, CHARLES (eds.) (1999). *The Rights of Nations: Nations and Nationalism in a Changing World* (Palgrave, New York).

CLARKE, PAUL BARRY (ed.) (1994). *Citizenship* (Pluto Press, London).

CLEMENT, GRACE (1996). *Care, Autonomy and Justice: Feminism and the Ethic of Care* (Westview, Boulder, Colo.).

COCHRAN, DAVID CARROLL (1999). *The Color of Freedom: Race and Contemporary American Liberalism* (State University of New York Press, Albany).

COHEN, ANDREW (1998). 'A Defense of Strong Voluntarism', *American Philosophical Quarterly*, 35/3: 251–65.

COHEN, CATHY (1997). 'Straight Gay Politics: The Limits of an Ethnic Model of Inclusion', in Shapiro and Kymlicka 1997, 572–616.

COHEN, G. A. (1978). *Karl Marx's Theory of History: A Defense* (Princeton University Press, Princeton).

—— (1979). 'Capitalism, Freedom and the Proletariat', in A. Ryan (ed.), *The Idea of Freedom* (Oxford University Press, Oxford).

—— (1981). 'Illusions about Private Property and Freedom', in J. Mepham and D. H. Ruben (eds.) *Issues in Marxist Philosophy*, vol. iv (Harvester, Hassocks), 223–39.

—— (1986a). 'Self-Ownership, World-Ownership, and Equality', in F. Lucash (ed.), *Justice and Equality: Here and Now* (Cornell University Press, Ithaca, NY), 108–35.

—— (1986b). 'Self-Ownership, World-Ownership and Equality: Part 2', *Social Philosophy and Policy*, 3/2: 77–96.

—— (1988). *History, Labour, and Freedom: Themes from Marx* (Oxford University Press, Oxford).

—— (1989). 'On the Currency of Egalitarian Justice', *Ethics*, 99/4: 906–44.

—— (1990a). 'Marxism and Contemporary Political Philosophy, or Why Nozick Exercises Some Marxists More Than He Does Any Egalitarian Liberal', *Canadian Journal of Philosophy*, supplementary vol. 16: 363–87.

—— (1990b). 'Self-Ownership, Communism, and Equality', *Proceedings of the Aristotelian Society*, supplementary vol. 64: 25–44.

—— (1992). 'Incentives, Inequality and Community', in G. B. Peterson (ed.), *The Tanner Lectures on Human Values*, vol. xiii (University of Utah Press, Salt Lake City), 261–329.

—— (1993). 'Equality of What? On Welfare, Goods, and Capabilities', in Nussbaum and Sen 1993, 9–29.

—— (1995a). *Self-Ownership, Freedom and Equality* (Cambridge University Press, Cambridge).

—— (1995b). 'The Pareto Argument for Inequality', *Social Philosophy and Policy*, 12/1: 160–85.

—— (1997). 'Where the Action Is: On the Site of Distributive Justice', *Philosophy and Public Affairs*, 26/1: 3–30.

—— (1998). 'Once More into the Breach of Self-Ownership', *Journal of Ethics*, 2/1: 57–96.

—— (2000). *If You're an Egalitarian, How Come You're So Rich?* (Harvard University Press, Cambridge, Mass.).

COHEN, JEAN (1985). 'Strategy or Identity: New Theoretical Paradigms and Contemporary Social Movements', *Social Research*, 54/4: 663–716.

COHEN, JOSHUA (1996). 'Procedure and Substance in Deliberative Democracy', in Seyla Benhabib (ed.), *Democracy and Difference: Contesting the Boundaries of the Political* (Princeton University Press, Princeton), 95–119.

—— (1997a). 'Deliberation and Democratic Legitimacy', in Goodin and Pettit 1997, 143–55.

COHEN, JOSHUA (1997b). 'The Arc of the Moral Universe', *Philosophy and Public Affairs*, 26/2: 91–134.

COHEN, MARSHAL (1985). 'Moral Skepticism and International Relations', in Charles Beitz (ed.), *International Ethics* (Princeton University Press, Princeton), 3–50.

COLE, EVE BROWNING, and COULTRAP-McQUIN, SUSAN, (eds.) (1992). *Explorations in Feminist Ethics: Theory and Practice* (Indiana University Press, Bloomington).

COLE, PHILLIP (2000). *Philosophies of Exclusion: Liberal Political Theory and Immigration* (Edinburgh University Press, Edinburgh).

COLTHEART, D. (1986). 'Desire, Consent and Liberal Theory', in Carole Pateman and E. Gross (eds.), *Feminist Challenges: Social and Political Theory* (Northeastern University Press, Boston), 112–22.

CONNOLLY, WILLIAM (1984). 'The Dilemma of Legitimacy', in William Connolly (ed.), *Legitimacy and the State* (Blackwell, Oxford), 222–49.

—— (1991). *Identity/Difference: Democratic Negotiations of Political Paradox* (Cornell University Press, Ithaca, NY).

—— (1993). *The Terms of Political Discourse* (Princeton University Press, Princeton).

—— (1995). *The Ethos of Pluralization* (University of Minnesota Press, Minneapolis).

CONNOR, WALKER (1972). 'Nation-Building or Nation-Destroying', *World Politics*, 24: 319–55.

—— (1984). *The National Question in Marxist-Leninist Theory and Strategy* (Princeton University Press, Princeton).

—— (1999). 'National Self-Determination and Tomorrow's Political Map', in Alan Cairns et al. (eds.), *Citizenship, Diversity and Pluralism: Canadian and Comparative Perspectives* (McGill-Queen's University Press, Montreal), 163–76.

CONOVER, PAMELA, CREWE, IVOR, and SEARING, DONALD (1991). 'The Nature of Citizenship in the United States and Great Britain: Empirical Comments on Theoretical Themes', *Journal of Politics*, 53/3: 800–32.

COOK, CURTIS, and LINDAU, JUAN (eds.) (2000). *Aboriginal Rights and Self-Government* (McGill-Queen's University Press, Montreal).

COOKE, MAEVE (2000). 'Five Arguments for Deliberative Democracy', *Political Studies*, 48: 947–69.

COPP, DAVID (1991). 'Contractarianism and Moral Skepticism', in Vallentyne 1991, 196–228.

COSER, ROSE LAMB (1991). *In Defense of Modernity: Role Complexity and Individual Autonomy* (Stanford University Press, Stanford, Calif.).

COUTURE, JOCELYNE, NIELSEN, KAI, and SEYMOUR, MICHEL (eds.) (1998). *Rethinking Nationalism* (University of Calgary Press, Calgary).

CRAGG, WESLEY (1986). 'Two Concepts of Community or Moral Theory and Canadian Culture', *Dialogue*, 25/1: 31–52.

CRISP, ROGER (ed.) (1997). *Routledge Philosophy Guidebook to Mill on Utilitarianism* (Routledge, London).

CROCKER, LAWRENCE (1977). 'Equality, Solidarity, and Rawls' Maximin', *Philosophy and Public Affairs*, 6/3: 262–6.

CROSLAND, C. A. R. (1964). *The Future of Socialism* (Cape, London).

CROSSLEY, DAVID (1990). 'Utilitarianism, Rights and Equality', *Utilitas*, 2/1: 40–54.

CROWLEY, BRIAN (1987). *The Self, the Individual and the Community: Liberalism in the Political Thought of F. A. Hayek and Sidney and Beatrice Webb* (Oxford University Press, Oxford).

CUDDIHY, JOHN MURRAY (1978). *No Offense: Civil Religion and Protestant Taste* (Seabury Press, New York).

CUMMINSKY, DAVID (1990). 'Kantian Consequentalism', *Ethics*, 100: 586–630.

DAGGER, RICHARD (1997). *Civic Virtues: Rights, Citizenship and Republican Liberalism* (Oxford University Press, Oxford).

D'AGOSTINO, FRED (1996). *Free Public Reason: Making it Up as We Go Along* (Oxford University Press, Oxford).

DANCY, JONATHAN (1992). 'Caring about Justice', *Philosophy*, 67/262: 447–66.

DANIELS, NORMAN (1975a). 'Equal Liberty and Unequal Worth of Liberty', in Daniels 1975b, 258–81.

—— (ed.) (1975b). *Reading Rawls* (Basic Books, New York).

—— (1979). 'Wide Reflective Equilibrium and Theory Acceptance in Ethics', *Journal of Philosophy* 76: 256–82.

—— (1985). *Just Health Care* (Cambridge University Press, Cambridge).

—— (1990). 'Equality of What? Welfare, Resources, or Capabilities?', *Philosophy and Phenomenological Research*, supplementary vol. 50: 273–96.

DARWALL, STEPHEN (ed.) (1995). *Equal Freedom: Selected Tanner Lectures on Human Values* (University of Michigan Press, Ann Arbor).

—— (1998). *Philosophical Ethics* (Westview, Boulder, Colo.).

DAVIDSON, BASIL (1993). *Black Man's Burden: Africa and the Curse of the Nation-State* (Times Books, New York).

DAVION, VICTORIA, and WOLF, CLARK (eds.) (2000). *The Idea of a Political Liberalism: Essays on Rawls* (Rowman and Littlefield, Totowa, NJ).

DAVIS, BOB (1994). 'Global Paradox: Growth of Trade Binds Nations, But It Also Can Spur Separatism', *Wall Street Journal*, 30 June 1994: A1.

DEGRAZIA, DAVID (1995). *Taking Animals Seriously: Mental Life and Moral Status* (Cambridge University Press, Cambridge).

DE GREIFF, PABLO (2000). 'Deliberative Democracy and Group Representation', *Social Theory and Practice*, 26/3: 397–416.

DELANEY, C. F. (ed.) (1994). *The Liberal-Communitarian Debate: Liberty and Community Values* (Rowman and Littlefield, Savage, Md.).

DEN UYL, DOUGLAS (1993). 'The Right to Welfare and the Virtue of Charity', in E. F. Paul, F. D. Miller, and J. Paul (eds.), *Altruism* (Cambridge University Press, Cambridge), 192–224.

DE-SHALIT, AVNER (2000). *The Environment: Between Theory and Practice* (Oxford University Press, Oxford).

DE VARENNES, FERNAND (1996). *Language, Minorities and Human Rights* (Kluwer, The Hague).

DEVEAUX, MONIQUE (1995a). 'Shifting Paradigms: Theorizing Care and Justice in Political Theory', *Hypatia*, 10/2: 115–19.

—— (1995b). 'New Directions in Feminist Ethics', *European Journal of Moral Philosophy*, 3/1: 86–96.

—— (2001). *Cultural Pluralism and Dilemmas of Justice* (Cornell University Press, Ithaca, NY).

DICK, JAMES (1975). 'How to Justify a Distribution of Earnings', *Philosophy and Public Affairs*, 4/3: 248–72.

DIETZ, MARY (1985). 'Citizenship with a Feminist Face: The Problem with Maternal Thinking', *Political Theory* 13/1: 19–37.

—— (1992). 'Context is All: Feminism and Theories of Citizenship', in Mouffe 1992b, 63–85.

DIGGS, B. J. (1981). 'A Contractarian View of Respect for Persons', *American Philosophical Quarterly*, 18/4: 273–83.

—— (1982). 'Utilitarianism and Contractarianism' in H. B. Miller and W. H. Williams (eds.), *The Limits of Utilitarianism* (University of Minnesota Press, Minneapolis), 101–14.

DION, STÉPHANE (1991). 'Le Nationalisme dans la convergence culturelle', in R. Hudon and R. Pelletier (eds.), *L'Engagement intellectuel: mélanges en l'honneur de Léon Dion* (Les Presses de l'Université Laval, Sainte-Foy), 291–311.

DIQUATTRO, ARTHUR (1983). 'Rawls and Left Criticism', *Political Theory*, 11/1: 53–78.

DOBSON, ANDREW (1990). *Green Political Thought* (Unwin Hyman, London).

—— (1991). *The Green Reader* (Mercury House, San Francisco).

DONNER, WENDY (1993). 'John Stuart Mill's Liberal Feminism', *Philosophical Studies*, 69: 155–66.

DOPPELT, GERALD (1981). 'Rawls' System of Justice: A Critique from the Left', *Nous*, 15/3: 259–307.

DRYZEK, JOHN (1990). *Discursive Democracy* (Cambridge University Press, Cambridge).

—— (2000). *Deliberative Democracy and Beyond: Liberals, Critics, Contestations* (Oxford University Press, Oxford).

DWORKIN, RONALD (1977). *Taking Rights Seriously* (Duckworth, London).

—— (1978). 'Liberalism', in S. Hampshire (ed.) *Public and Private Morality* (Cambridge University Press, Cambridge), 113–43.

—— (1981). 'What is Equality? Part I: Equality of Welfare; Part II: Equality of Resources', *Philosophy and Public Affairs*, 10 3/4: 185–246, 283–345.

—— (1983). 'In Defense of Equality', *Social Philosophy and Policy*, 1/1: 24–40.

—— (1985). *A Matter of Principle* (Harvard University Press, London).

—— (1986). *Law's Empire* (Harvard University Press, Cambridge, Mass.).

—— (1987). 'What is Equality? Part 3: The Place of Liberty', *Iowa Law Review*, 73/1: 1–54.

—— (1988). 'What is Equality? Part 4: Political Equality', *University of San Francisco Law Review*, 22/1: 1–30.

—— (1989). 'Liberal Community', *California Law Review*, 77/3: 479–504.

DWORKIN, RONALD (1992). 'Deux conceptions de la démocratie', in Jacques Lenoble and Nicole Dewandre (eds.), *L'Europe au soir de la siècle: identité et démocratie* (Éditions Esprit, Paris), 111–35.

—— (1993). 'Justice in the Distribution of Health Care', *McGill Law Journal*, 38/4: 883–98.

—— (2000). *Sovereign Virtue: The Theory and Practice of Equality* (Harvard University Press, Cambridge, Mass.).

DYZENHAUS, DAVID (1992). 'Liberalism, Autonomy and Neutrality', *University of Toronto Law Journal*, 42: 354–75.

ECKERSLEY, ROBYN (1992). *Environmentalism and Political Theory* (State University of New York Press, Albany).

EHRENREICH, BARBARA, AND ENGLISH, DEIRDRE (1973) *Witches, Midwives, and Nurses: A History of Women Healers* (Feminist Press, Old Westbury, NY).

EICHBAUM, JUNE (1979). 'Towards an Autonomy-Based Theory of Constitutional Privacy: Beyond the Ideology of Familial Privacy', *Harvard Civil Rights–Civil Liberties Law Review*, 14/2: 361–84.

EISENBERG, AVIGAIL (1995). *Reconstructing Political Pluralism* (State University of New York Press, Albany).

EISENSTEIN, ZILLAH (1981). *The Radical Future of Liberal Femininsm* (Longman, New York).

—— (1984). *Feminism and Sexual Equality: Crisis in Liberal America* (Monthly Review Press, New York).

ELKIN, STEPHEN, and SOLTAN, KAROL (eds.) (1999). *Citizen Competence and Democratic Institutions* (Pennsylvania State University Press, University Park).

ELSHTAIN, JEAN BETHKE (1981). *Public Man, Private Woman: Women in Social and Political Thought* (Princeton University Press, Princeton).

ELSTER, JON (1982a). 'Roemer vs. Roemer', *Politics and Society*, 11/3: 363–73.

—— (1982b). 'Utilitarianism and the Genesis of Wants', in Sen and Williams 1982, 219–38.

—— (1983a). 'Exploitation, Freedom, and Justice', in J. R. Pennock and J. W. Chapman (eds.), *Marxism: NOMOS 26* (New York University Press, New York), 277–304.

—— (1983b). *Sour Grapes* (Cambridge University Press, Cambridge).

—— (1985). *Making Sense of Marx* (Cambridge University Press, Cambridge).

—— (1986). 'Self-Realization in Work and Politics: The Marxist Conception of the Good Life', *Social Philosophy and Policy*, 3/2: 97–126.

—— (1987). 'The Possibility of Rational Politics', *Archives européennes de sociologie*, 28: 67–103.

—— (1992). *Local Justice* (Russell Sage, New York).

—— (1995). 'Strategic Uses of Argument', in Kenneth Arrow (ed.), *Barriers to Conflict Resolution* (Norton, New York), 236–57.

—— (1998a). 'Introduction', in J. Elster (ed.), *Deliberative Democracy* (Cambridge University Press, New York), 1–18.

—— (1998b). 'Deliberation and Constitution Making', in J. Elster (ed.), *Deliberative Democracy* (Cambridge University Press, New York), 97–122.

—— and ROEMER, JOHN (eds.) (1991). *Interpersonal Comparisons of Well-Being* (Cambridge University Press, Cambridge).

ENGELS, FRIEDRICH (1972). *The Origin of the Family, Private Property, and the State* (International Publishers, New York).

ENGLISH, JANE (1977). 'Justice between Generations', *Philosophical Studies*, 31/2: 91–104.

EPSTEIN, RICHARD (1985). *Takings* (Harvard University Press, Cambridge, Mass.).

—— (1995a). *Forbidden Grounds: The Case against Employment Discrimination Laws* (Harvard University Press, Cambridge, Mass.).

—— (1995b). *Bargaining with the State* (Princeton University Press, Princeton).

—— (1995c). *Simple Rules for a Complex World* (Harvard University Press, Cambridge, Mass.).

—— (1998). 'The Right Set of Simple Rules', *Critical Review*, 12/3: 305–18.

ESTLUND, DAVID (1998). 'Liberalism, Equality and Fraternity in Cohen's Critique of Rawls', *Journal of Political Philosophy*, 6/1: 99–112.

ETZIONI, AMITAI (1993). *The Spirit of Community: Rights, Responsibilities and the Communitarian Agenda* (Crown Publishers, New York).

—— (1999). 'The Good Society', *Journal of Political Philosophy*, 7/1: 88–103.

—— (2001). *Next: The Road to the Good Society* (Basic Books, New York).

EVANS, SARA (1979). *Personal Politics: The Roots of Women's Liberation in the Civil Rights Movement and the New Left* (Knopf, New York).

EXDELL, JOHN (1977). 'Distributive Justice: Nozick on Property Rights', *Ethics*, 87/2: 142–9.

—— (1994). 'Feminism, Fundamentalism, and Liberal Legitimacy', *Canadian Journal of Philosophy*, 24/3: 441–64.

FAVELL, ADRIAN (1999). 'Applied Political Philosophy at the Rubicon', *Ethical Theory and Moral Practice*, 1/2: 255–78.

FEALLSANACH, AM (1998). 'Locke and Libertarian Property Rights', *Critical Review*, 12/3: 319–23.

FEINBERG, JOEL (1980). *Rights, Justice, and the Bounds of Liberty* (Princeton University Press, Princeton).

—— (1988). *Harmless Wrongdoing: The Moral Limits of the Criminal Law*, vol. iv (Oxford University Press, Oxford).

FEINBERG, WALTER (1998). *Common Schools/Uncommon Identities: National Unity and Cultural Difference* (Yale University Press, New Haven).

FEMIA, JOSEPH (1996). 'Complexity and Deliberative Democracy', *Inquiry*, 39: 359–97.

FEREJOHN, JOHN (2000). 'Instituting Deliberative Democracy', in Ian Shapiro and Stephen Macedo (eds.), *Designing Democratic Institutions: NOMOS 42* (New York University Press, New York), 75–104.

FIERLBECK, KATHERINE (1991). 'Redefining Responsibilities: The Politics of Citizenship in the United Kingdom', *Canadian Journal of Political Science*, 24/3: 575–83.

FINNIS, JOHN (1981). *Natural Law and Natural Rights* (Oxford University Press, Oxford).

—— (1983). *Fundamentals of Ethics* (Oxford University Press, Oxford).

FISHKIN, JAMES (1983). *Justice, Equal Opportunity and the Family* (Yale University Press, New Haven).

—— (1991). *Democracy and Deliberation: New Directions for Democratic Reform* (Yale University Press, New Haven).

—— (1995). *The Voice of the People* (Yale University Press, New Haven).

FISHKIN, JAMES (1996). *The Dialogue of Justice: Toward a Self-Reflective Society* (Yale University Press, New Haven).

FLANAGAN, OWEN, and ADLER, JONATHAN (1983). 'Impartiality and Particularity', *Social Research*, 50/3: 576–96.

—— and JACKSON, KATHRYN (1987). 'Justice, Care, and Gender: The Kohlberg–Gilligan Debate Revisited', *Ethics*, 97/3: 622–37.

FLAX, JANE (1993). *Disputed Subjects: Essays on Psychoanalysis, Politics and Philosophy* (Routledge, New York).

FLEURBAEY, MARC (1994). 'L'Absence d'envie dans une problématique post-welfariste', *Recherches économiques de Louvain*, 60: 9–42.

FLEW, ANTHONY (1979). *A Dictionary of Philosophy* (Fontana, London).

—— (1989). *Equality in Liberty and Justice* (Routledge, London).

FOX-DECENT, EVAN (1998). 'Why Self-Ownership is Prescriptively Impotent', *Journal of Value Inquiry*, 32/4: 489–506.

FRANCK, THOMAS (1997). 'Tribe, Nation, World: Self-Identification in the Evolving International System', *Ethics and International Affairs*, 11: 151–69.

FRANKLIN, JANE (ed.) (1997). *Equality* (Institute for Public Policy Research, London).

FRASER, NANCY (1989). 'Talking about Needs: Interpretive Contests as Political Conflicts in Welfare State Societies', *Ethics*, 99: 291–313.

—— (1992). 'Rethinking the Public Sphere: A Contribution to the Critique of Actually Existing Democracy', in Craig Calhoun (ed.), *Habermas and the Public Sphere* (MIT Press, Cambridge, Mass.), 109–42.

—— (1995). 'From Redistribution to Recognition? Dilemmas of Justice in a 'Post-Socialist' Age', *New Left Review*, 212: 68–93.

—— (1996). 'Multiculturalism and Gender Equity: The U.S. "Difference" Debates Revisited', *Constellations*, 3/1: 61–72.

—— (1997). *Justice Interruptus: Critical Reflections on the 'Post-Socialist' Condition* (Routledge, New York).

—— (1998). 'Social Justice in the Age of Identity Politics: Redistribution, Recognition and Participation', in Grethe Peterson (ed.) *The Tanner Lectures on Human Values*, vol. xix (University of Utah Press, Salt Lake City), 1–67.

—— (2000). 'Rethinking Recognition', *New Left Review* 3: 107–20.

FRAZER, ELIZABETH (1999). *The Problems of Communitarian Politics: Unity and Conflict* (Oxford University Press, Oxford).

—— and LACEY, NICOLA (1993). *The Politics of Community: A Feminist Critique of the Liberal-Communitarian Debate* (Harvester Wheatsheaf, London).

FREEMAN, SAMUEL (1994). 'Utilitarianism, Deontology and the Priority of Right', *Philosophy and Public Affairs*, 23/4: 313–49.

FREY, RAYMOND (ed.) (1984). *Utility and Rights* (University of Minnesota Press, Minneapolis).

FRIDERES, JAMES (1997). 'Edging into the Mainstream: Immigrant Adults and their Children', in Wsevolod Isajiw (ed.), *Comparative Perspectives on Interethnic Relations and Social Incorporation in Europe and North America* (Canadian Scholar's Press, Toronto), 537–62.

FRIED, CHARLES (1978). *Right and Wrong* (Harvard University Press, Cambridge, Mass.).

FRIED, CHARLES (1983). 'DISTRIBUTIVE JUSTICE', *Social Philosophy and Policy*, 1/1: 45–59.

FRIEDMAN, MARILYN (1987a). 'Beyond Caring: The De-moralization of Gender', *Canadian Journal of Philosophy*, supplementary vol. 13: 87–110.

—— (1987b). 'Care and Context in Moral Reasoning', in Kittay and Meyers 1987, 190–204.

—— (1989). 'Feminism and Modern Friendship: Dislocating the Community', *Ethics*, 99/2: 275–90.

—— (1991). 'The Social Self and the Partiality Debates', in Card 1991, 161 79.

—— (1993). *What Are Friends For? Feminist Perspectives on Personal Relationships and Moral Theory* (Cornell University Press, Ithaca, NY).

—— (1997). 'Autonomy and Social Relationships: Rethinking the Feminist Critique', in Meyers 1997, 40–61.

FROLICH, NORMAN, and OPPENHEIMER, JOE (1992). *Choosing Justice: An Experimental Approach to Ethical Theory* (University of California Press, Berkeley and Los Angeles).

FRYE, MARILYN (1983). *The Politics of Reality: Essays in Feminist Theory* (Crossing Press, Trumansburg, NY).

FULLINWIDER, ROBERT (ed.) (1995). *Public Education in a Multicultural Society* (Cambridge University Press, Cambridge).

—— (ed.) (1999). *Civil Society, Democracy and Civic Renewal* (Rowman and Littlefield, Savage, Md.).

FUNK, NANETTE (1988). 'Habermas and the Social Goods', *Social Text*, 18: 19–37.

GALENKAMP, MARLIES (1993). *Individualism and Collectivism: The Concept of Collective Rights* (Rotterdamse Filosofische Studies, Rotterdam).

GALLOWAY, DONALD (1993). 'Liberalism, Globalism and Immigration', *Queen's Law Journal*, 18: 266–305.

GALSTON, WILLIAM (1980). *Justice and the Human Good* (University of Chicago Press, Chicago).

—— (1986). 'Equality of Opportunity and Liberal Theory', in F. Lucash (ed.), *Justice and Equality Here and Now* (Cornell University Press, Ithaca, NY), 89–107.

—— (1989). 'Community, Democracy, Philosophy: The Political Thought of Michael Walzer', *Political Theory*, 17/1: 119–30.

—— (1991). *Liberal Purposes: Goods, Virtues, and Duties in the Liberal State* (Cambridge University Press, Cambridge).

—— (1993a). 'Cosmopolitan Altruism', *Social Philosophy and Policy*, 10: 118–34.

—— (1993b). 'Political Theory in the 1980s', in Ada Finifter (ed.), *Political Science: The State of the Discipline 2* (American Political Science Association, Washington), 27–53.

—— (1995). 'Two Concepts of Liberalism', *Ethics*, 105/3: 516–34.

GANS, CHAIM (1998). 'Nationalism and Immigration', *Ethical Theory and Moral Practice*, 1/2: 159–80.

GARET, RONALD (1983). 'Communality and Existence: The Rights of Groups', *Southern California Law Review*, 56/5: 1001–75.

GAUTHIER, DAVID (1986). *Morals by Agreement* (Oxford University Press, Oxford).

—— (1991). 'Why Contractarianism?', in Vallentyne 1991, 15–30.

GAVISON, RUTH (1992). 'Feminism and the Public/Private Distinction', *Stanford Law Review*, 45/1: 1–45.

GELLNER, ERNEST (1983). *Nations and Nationalism* (Blackwell, Oxford).

GEORGE, ROBERT (1993). *Making Men Moral: Civil Liberties and Public Morality* (Oxford University Press, Oxford).

GERAS, NORMAN (1989). 'The Controversy about Marx and Justice', in A. Callinicos (ed.), *Marxist Theory* (Oxford University Press, Oxford), 211–67.

—— (1993). 'Bringing Marx to Justice: An Addendum and Rejoinder', *New Left Review*, 195: 37–69.

GIBBARD, ALLAN (1985). 'What's Morally Special about Free Exchange?', *Social Philosophy and Policy*, 2/2: 20–8.

GIDDENS, ANTHONY (1998). *The Third Way* (Polity, Oxford).

GILBERT, ALAN (1980). *Marx's Politics: Communists and Citizens* (Rutgers University Press, New Brunswick, NJ).

—— (1991). 'Political Philosophy: Marx and Radical Democracy', in Carver 1991, 168–95.

GILBERT, PAUL (1998). *Philosophy of Nationalism* (Westview, Boulder, Colo.).

—— (2000). *Peoples, Cultures, and Nations in Political Philosophy* (Georgetown University Press, Washington).

GILENS, MARTIN (1996). '"Race Coding" and White Opposition to Welfare', *American Political Science Review*, 90: 593–604.

—— (1999). *Why Americans Hate Welfare* (University of Chicago Press, Chicago).

GILLIGAN, CAROL (1982). *In a Different Voice: Psychological Theory and Women's Development* (Harvard University Press, Cambridge, Mass.).

—— (1986). 'Remapping the Moral Domain', in Thomas Heller and Morton Sosna (eds.), *Reconstructing Individualism: Autonomy, Individuality, and the Self in Western Thought* (Stanford University Press, Stanford, Calif.), 237–50.

—— (1987). 'Moral Orientation and Moral Development', in Kittay and Meyers 1987, 19–36.

—— (1995). 'Hearing the Difference: Theorizing Connection', *Hypatia*, 10/2: 120–7.

—— and ATTANUCI, J. (1988). 'Two Moral Orientations', in C. Gilligan, J. Ward, and J. Taylor (eds.), *Mapping The Moral Domain: A Contribution of Women's Thinking to Psychology and Education* (Harvard University Graduate School of Education, Cambridge, Mass.), 73–86.

GITLIN, TODD (1995). *The Twilight of Common Dreams: Why America is Wracked by Culture Wars* (Henry Holt, New York).

GLAZER, NATHAN (1983). *Ethnic Dilemmas: 1964–1982* (Harvard University Press, Cambridge, Mass.).

—— (1988). *The Limits of Social Policy* (Harvard University Press, Cambridge, Mass.).

—— (1997). *We Are All Multiculturalists Now* (Harvard University Press, Cambridge, Mass.).

GLENDON, MARY-ANN (1991). *Rights Talk: The Impoverishment of Political Discourse* (Free Press, New York).

—— and BLANKENHORN, DAVID (eds.) (1995). *Seedbeds of Virtue: Sources of Competence, Character and Citizenship in American Society* (Madison Books, Lanham, Md.).

GLOVER, JONATHAN (ed.) (1990). *Utilitarianism and its Critics* (Macmillan, New York).

GOLDBERG, DAVID THEO (ed.) (1995). *Multiculturalism: A Critical Reader* (Blackwell, Oxford).

GOODIN, ROBERT (1982). *Political Theory and Public Policy* (University of Chicago Press, Chicago).

—— (1988). *Reasons for Welfare* (Princeton University Press, Princeton).

—— (1990). 'International Ethics and the Environmental Crisis', *Ethics and International Affairs*, 4: 91–105.

—— (1990). 'Liberalism and the Best-Judge Principle', *Political Studies*, 38: 181–5.

—— (1992a). *Green Political Theory* (Polity, Oxford).

—— (1992b). 'If People Were Money' in Barry and Goodin 1992, 6–22.

—— (1995). *Utilitarianism as a Public Philosophy* (Cambridge University Press, Cambridge).

—— (1998). 'Public Service Utilitarianism as a Role Responsibility', *Utilitas*, 10/3: 320–36.

—— and PETTIT, PHILIP (eds.) (1993). *A Companion to Contemporary Political Philosophy* (Blackwell, Oxford).

—— —— (eds.) (1997). *Contemporary Political Philosophy: An Anthology* (Blackwell, Oxford).

—— and REEVE, ANDREW (eds.) (1989). *Liberal Neutrality* (Routledge, London).

GORDON, SCOTT (1980). *Welfare, Justice, and Freedom* (Columbia University Press, New York).

GORR, MICHAEL (1995). 'Justice, Self-Ownership, and Natural Assets', *Social Philosophy and Policy*, 12/2: 267–91.

GOUGH, J. W. (1957). *The Social Contract*, 2nd edn. (Oxford University Press, London).

GOULD, CAROL (1978). *Marx's Social Ontology* (MIT Press, Cambridge, Mass.).

GOVIER, TRUDY (1997). *Social Trust and Human Communities* (McGill-Queen's University Press, Montreal).

—— (1999). *Dilemmas of Trust* (McGill-Queen's University Press, Montreal).

GRAHAM, KEITH (1990). 'Self-Ownership, Communism and Equality II', *Proceedings of the Aristotelian Society*, supplementary vol. 64: 45–61.

GRANT, GEORGE (1974). *English-Speaking Justice* (Mount Allison University Press, Sackville).

GRAY, JOHN (1986a). *Liberalism* (University of Minnesota Press, Minneapolis).

—— (1986b). 'Marxian Freedom, Individual Liberty, and the End of Alienation', *Social Philosophy and Policy*, 3/2: 160–87.

—— (1989). *Liberalism: Essays in Political Philosophy* (Routledge, London).

GREEN, KAREN (1986). 'Rawls, Women and the Priority of Liberty', *Australasian Journal of Philosophy*, supplementary vol. 64: 26–36.

GREEN, LESLIE (1995). 'Internal Minorities and Their Rights', in Kymlicka 1995b: 256–72

GREENE, STEPHEN (1996). 'Rethinking Kymlicka's Critique of Humanist Liberalism', *International Journal of Applied Philosophy*, 10/2: 51–7.

GREENFELD, LIAH (1992). *Nationalism: Five Roads to Modernity* (Harvard University Press, Cambridge, Mass.).

GRESCHNER, DONNA (1989). 'Feminist Concerns with the New Communitarians', in A. Hutchinson and L. Green (eds.), *Law and the Community* (Carswell, Toronto), 119–50.

GREY, THOMAS (1980). 'Eros, Civilization, and the Burger Court', *Law and Contemporary Problems*, 43/3: 83–100.

GRICE, GEOFFREY (1967). *The Grounds of Moral Judgement* (Cambridge University Press, Cambridge).

GRIFFIN, JAMES (1986). *Well-Being: Its Meaning, Measurement, and Moral Importance* (Oxford University Press, Oxford).

GRIMM, DIETER (1995). 'Does Europe Need a Constitution?', *European Law Journal*, 1/3: 282–302.

GRIMSHAW, JEAN (1986). *Philosophy and Feminist Thinking* (University of Minnesota Press, Minneapolis).

GROOT, LOEK, and VAN DER VEEN, ROBERT JAN (eds.) (2000). *Basic Income on the Agenda: Policy Objectives and Political Chances* (University of Amsterdam Press, Amsterdam).

GROSS, ELIZABETH (1986). 'What is Feminist Theory?', in Carole Pateman and E. Gross (eds.), *Feminist Challenges: Social and Political Theory* (Northeastern University Press, Boston), 125–43.

GUÉHENNO, JEAN-MARIE (1995). *The End of the Nation-State* (University of Minnesota Press, Minneapolis).

GURR, TED (1993). *Minorities at Risk: A Global View of Ethnopolitical Conflict* (Institute of Peace Press, Washington).

—— (2000). 'Ethnic Warfare on the Wane', *Foreign Affairs*, 79/3: 52–64.

GUTMANN, AMY (1980). *Liberal Equality* (Cambridge University Press, Cambridge).

—— (1985). 'Communitarian Critics of Liberalism', *Philosophy and Public Affairs*, 14/3: 308–22.

—— (1987). *Democratic Education* (Princeton University Press, Princeton).

—— (1993). 'The Challenge of Multiculturalism to Political Ethics', *Philosophy and Public Affairs* 22/3: 171–206.

—— and APPIAH, KWAME ANTHONY (1996). *Color Conscious: The Political Morality of Race* (Princeton University Press, Princeton).

—— and THOMPSON, DENNIS (1996). *Democracy and Disagreement* (Harvard University Press, Cambridge, Mass.).

HABERMAS, JÜRGEN (1979). *Communication and the Evolution of Society*, trans. T. McCarthy (Beacon, Boston).

—— (1985). 'Questions and Counter Questions', in R. Bernstein (ed.), *Habermas and Modernity* (MIT Press, Cambridge, Mass.), 192–216.

—— (1992). 'Citizenship and National Identity: Some Reflections on the Future of Europe', *Praxis International*, 12/1: 1–19.

—— (1996). *Between Facts and Norms: Contributions to a Discourse Theory of Law and Democracy* (MIT Press, Cambridge, Mass.).

HALSTEAD, MARK (1990). 'Muslim Schools and the Ideal of Autonomy', *Ethics in Education*, 9/4: 4–6.

—— (1991). 'Radical Feminism, Islam and the Single-Sex School Debate', *Gender and Education*, 3/1: 263–78.

HAMILTON, ALEXANDER, MADISON, JAMES, and JAY, JOHN (1982). *The Federalist Papers* (Bantam, New York).

HAMPTON, JEAN (1980). 'Contracts and Choices: Does Rawls Have a Social Contract Theory?', *Journal of Philosophy*, 77/6: 315–38.

—— (1986). *Hobbes and the Social Contract Tradition* (Cambridge University Press, Cambridge).

—— (1997). *Political Philosophy* (Westview Press, Boulder, Colo.).

HANNUM, HURST (1990). *Autonomy, Sovereignty, and Self-Determination: The Adjudication of Conflicting Rights* (University of Pennsylvania Press, Philadelphia).

HANSER, MATTHEW (1990). 'Harming Future People', *Philosophy and Public Affairs*, 19/1: 47–70.

HARDIMON, MICHAEL (1992). 'The Project of Reconciliation: Hegel's Social Philosophy', *Philosophy and Public Affairs*, 23/2: 165–95.

—— (1994). *Hegel's Social Philosophy: The Project of Reconciliation* (Cambridge University Press, Cambridge).

HARDIN, GARRETT (1968). 'The Tragedy of the Commons', *Science*, 162: 1243–8.

HARDIN, RUSSELL (1988). *Morality within the Limits of Reason* (University of Chicago Press, Chicago).

—— (1995). *One for All: The Logic of Group Conflict* (Princeton University Press, Princeton).

HARDING, SANDRA (1982). 'Is Gender a Variable in Conceptions of Rationality? A Survey of Issues', *Dialectica*, 36/2: 225–42.

—— (1987). 'The Curious Coincidence of Feminine and African Moralities', in Kittay and Meyers 1987, 296–316.

HARDWIG, JOHN (1990). 'Should Women Think in Terms of Rights?', in Cass Sunstein (ed.), *Feminism and Political Theory* (University of Chicago Press, Chicago), 53–67.

HARE, R. M. (1963). *Freedom and Reason* (Oxford University Press, London).

—— (1971). *Essays on Philosophical Method* (Macmillan, London).

—— (1975). 'Rawls' Theory of Justice', in Daniels 1975*b*, 81–107.

—— (1978). 'Justice and Equality', in J. Arthur and W. Shaw (eds.), *Justice and Economic Distribution* (Prentice-Hall, Englewood Cliffs, NJ), 118–32.

—— (1981). *Moral Thinking* (Oxford University Press, Oxford).

—— (1982). 'Ethical Theory and Utilitarianism', in Sen and Williams 1982, 23–38.

—— (1984). 'Rights, Utility, and Universalization: Reply to J. L. Mackie', in Frey 1984, 106–21.

HARLES, JOHN (1993). *Politics in the Lifeboat: Immigrants and the American Democratic Order* (Westview Press, Boulder, Colo.).

HARMAN, GILBERT (1983). 'Human Flourishing, Ethics, and Liberty', *Philosophy and Public Affairs*, 12/4: 307–22.

HARRIS, JOHN (1975). 'The Survival Lottery', *Philosophy*, 50: 81–7.

HARRISON, ROSS (ed.) (1999). *Bentham* (Routledge, London).

HARSANYI, JOHN (1976). *Essays on Ethics, Social Behavior and Scientific Explanation* (Reidel, Dordrecht).

—— (1977*a*). *Rational Behavior and Bargaining Equilibrium in Games and Social Situations* (Cambridge University Press, Cambridge).

—— (1977*b*). 'Rule Utilitarianism and Decision Theory', *Erkenntnis*, 11: 25–53.

—— (1985). 'Rule Utilitarianism, Equality, and Justice', *Social Philosophy and Policy*, 2/2: 115–27.

HART, H. L. A. (1975). 'Rawls on Liberty and its Priority', in Daniels 1975*b*, 230–52.

—— (1979). 'Between Utility and Rights', in Alan Ryan (ed.), *The Idea of Freedom* (Oxford University Press, Oxford), 77–98.

HARTNEY, MICHAEL (1991). 'Some Confusions Concerning Collective Rights', *Canadian Journal of Law and Jurisprudence*, 4/2: 293–314.

HARVEY, DAVID (1996). *Justice, Nature and the Geography of Difference* (Blackwell, Oxford).

HASLETT, D. W. (1987). *Equal Consideration: A Theory of Moral Justification* (University of Delaware, Newark).

HAVEMAN, ROBERT (1988). *Starting Even* (Simon and Schuster, New York).

HAWORTH, ALAN (1994). *Anti-libertarianism: Markets, Philosophy and Myth* (Routledge, London).

HAYEK, FRIEDRICH (1944). *The Road to Serfdom* (University of Chicago Press, Chicago).

—— (1960). *The Constitution of Liberty* (Routledge and Kegan Paul, London).

HEATER, DEREK (1990). *Citizenship: The Civic Ideal in World History, Politics and Education* (Longman, London).

—— (1996). *World Citizenship and Government: Cosmopolitan Ideas in the History of Western Political Thought* (St Martin's Press, New York).

—— (2000). *What is Citizenship* (Blackwell, Oxford).

HEFFERMAN, WILLIAM (1995). 'Privacy Rights', *Suffolk University Law Review*, 29: 737–808.

HEFNER, ROBERT (ed.) (1998). *Democratic Civility: The History and Cross-cultural Possibility of a Modern Political Ideal* (Transaction Publishers, New Brunswick, NJ).

HEGEL, G. W. F. (1949). *Philosophy of Right*, trans. T. M. Knox (Oxford University Press, London).

HEKMAN, SUSAN (1995). *Moral Voices, Moral Selves: Carol Gilligan and Feminist Moral Theory* (Polity Press, Cambridge).

HELD, DAVID (1989). 'Citizenship and Autonomy', in *Political Theory and the Modern State* (Stanford University Press, Stanford, Calif.), 189–213.

—— (1995). *Democracy and the Global Order: From the Modern State to Cosmopolitan Governance* (Polity Press, London).

—— (1999). 'The Transformation in Political Community: Rethinking Democracy in the Context of Globalization', in Ian Shapiro and Casiano Hacker-Cordon (eds.), *Democracy's Edges* (Cambridge University Press, Cambridge), 84–111.

HELD, VIRGINIA (1987). 'Feminism and Moral Theory', in Kittay and Meyers 1987, 111–28.

—— (1988). 'The Non-contractual Society', in M. Hanen and K. Nielsen (eds.), *Science, Morality and Feminist Theory* (University of Calgary Press, Calgary), 111–37.

—— (1993). *Feminist Morality: Transforming Culture, Society, and Politics* (University of Chicago Press, Chicago).

—— (ed.) (1995a). *Justice and Care: Essential Readings in Feminist Ethics* (Westview, Boulder, Colo.).

—— (1995b). 'The Meshing of Care and Justice', *Hypatia*, 10/2: 128–32.

HERZOG, DON (1986). 'Some Questions for Republicans', *Political Theory*, 14/3: 473–93.

HILL, GREG (1993). 'Citizenship and Ontology in the Liberal State', *Review of Politics*, 55: 67–84.

HIGGINS, TRACY (1997). 'Democracy and Feminism', *Harvard Law Review*, 110: 1657–703.

HIRSCH, H. N. (1986). 'The Threnody of Liberalism: Constitutional Liberty and the Renewal of Community', *Political Theory* 14/3: 423–49.

HIRSCHMANN, NANCY (1999). 'Difference as an Occasion for Rights: A Feminist Rethinking of Rights, Liberalism and Difference', *Critical Review of International Social and Political Philosophy*, 2/1: 27–55.

—— and DiSTEFANO, CHRISTINE (eds.) (1996). *Revisioning the Political: Feminist Revisions of Traditional Concepts in Western Political Theory* (Westview, Boulder, Colo.).

HIRST, PAUL (1994). *Associative Democracy: New Forms of Economic and Social Governance* (Polity, Cambridge).

HOAGLAND, SARAH (1991). 'Some Thoughts About "Caring"', in Card 1991, 246–86.

HOBSBAWM, ERIC J. (1990). *Nations and Nationalism since 1780: Programme, Myth and Reality* (Cambridge University Press, Cambridge).

HOCHSCHILD, ARLIE (1989). *The Second Shift: Working Parents and the Revolution at Home* (Viking, New York).

HOLLINGER, DAVID (1995). *Postethnic America: Beyond Multiculturalism* (Basic Books, New York).

HOLMES, STEPHEN (1989). 'The Permanent Structure of Antiliberal Thought', in N. Rosenblum (ed.) *Liberalism and the Moral Life* (Harvard University Press, Cambridge, Mass.), 227–53.

HOLMSTROM, NANCY (1977). 'Exploitation', *Canadian Journal of Philosophy*, 7/2: 353–69.

HOOKER, BRAD (1993). 'Political Philosophy', in Leemon McHenry and Frederick Adams (eds.), *Reflection on Philosophy* (St Martin's Press, London), 87–102.

HOROWITZ, DONALD (1985). *Ethnic Groups in Conflict* (University of California Press, Berkeley and Los Angeles).

—— (1991). *A Democratic South Africa: Constitutional Engineering in a Divided Society* (University of California Press, Berkeley and Los Angeles).

—— (1997). 'Self-Determination: Politics, Philosophy and Law', in Shapiro and Kymlicka 1997, 421–63.

HORTON, JOHN, and MENDUS, SUSAN (eds.) (1994). *After MacIntyre: Critical Perspectives on the Work of Alisdair MacIntyre* (Polity, Cambridge).

—— —— (eds.) (1999). *Toleration, Identity and Difference* (St Martin's Press, New York).

HOSPERS, JOHN (1961). *Human Conduct: An Introduction to the Problems of Ethics* (Harcourt, Brace and World, New York).

HOUSTON, BARBARA (1987). 'Rescuing Womanly Virtues: Some Dangers of Moral Reclamation', *Canadian Journal of Philosophy*, supplementary vol. 13: 237–62.

—— (1988). 'Gilligan and the Politics of a Distinctive Women's Morality', in L. Code, S. Mullett, and C. Overall (eds.), *Feminist Perspectives: Philosophical Essays on Method and Morals* (University of Toronto Press, Toronto), 168–89.

—— (1990). 'Caring and Exploitation', *Hypatia*, 5/1: 115–19.

HURKA, THOMAS (1993). *Perfectionism* (Oxford University Press, Oxford).

—— (1995). 'Indirect Perfectionism: Kymlicka on Liberal Neutrality', *Journal of Political Philosophy*, 3/1: 36–57.

HURLEY, SUSAN (2001). 'Luck and Equality', Proceedings of the Aristotelian Society.

HUTCHINGS, KIMBERLY (1999). 'Feminism, Universalism and the Ethics of International

Politics', in Vivienne Jabri and Eleanor O'Gorman (eds.) *Women, Culture and International Relations* (Lynne Rienner, Boulder, Colo.), 17–38.

—— and DANNREUTHER, RONALD (eds.) (1999). *Cosmopolitan Citizenship* (St Martin's Press, New York).

IGNATIEFF, MICHAEL (1989). 'Citizenship and Moral Narcissism', *Political Quarterly*, 60: 63–74.

—— (1993). *Blood and Belonging: Journeys into the New Nationalism* (Farrar, Straus and Giroux, New York).

—— (2000). *The Rights Revolution* (Anansi Press, Toronto).

INGRAM, ATTRACTA (1993). 'Self-Ownership and Worldly Resources', *International Journal of Moral and Social Studies*, 8/1: 3–20.

INGRAM, DAVID (2000). *Group Rights: Reconciling Equality and Difference* (University Press of Kansas, Lawrence).

ISIN, ENGIN, and WOOD, PATRICIA (1999). *Citizenship and Identity* (Sage, Beverly Hills, Calif.).

IVISON, DUNCAN, SANDERS, WILL, and PATTON, PAUL (eds.) (2000). *Political Theory and the Rights of Indigenous Peoples* (Cambridge University Press, Cambridge).

JACKSON, FRANK (1991). 'Decision-Theoretic Consequentialism and the Nearest and Dearest Objection', *Ethics*, 101: 462–83.

JACOBS, LESLEY (1996). 'The Second Wave of Analytical Marxism', *Philosophy of Social Sciences*, 26/2: 279–92.

—— (1997). *An Introduction to Modern Political Philosophy: The Democratic Vision of Politics* (Prentice-Hall, Upper Saddle River, NJ).

JACOBSON, DAVID (1996). *Rights across Borders: Immigration and the Decline of Citizenship* (Johns Hopkins University Press, Baltimore).

JAGGAR, ALISON (1983). *Feminist Politics and Human Nature* (Rowman and Allanheld, Totowa, NJ).

—— and YOUNG, IRIS MARION (eds.) (1998). *A Companion to Feminist Philosophy* (Blackwell, Cambridge).

JANOSKI, THOMAS (1998). *Citizenship and Civil Society: Obligations in Liberal, Traditional and Social Democratic Regimes* (Cambridge University Press, Cambridge).

JANZEN, WILLIAM (1990). *Limits of Liberty: The Experiences of Mennonite, Hutterite and Doukhobour Communities in Canada* (University of Toronto Press, Toronto).

JESKE, DIANE (1996). 'Libertarianism, Self-Ownership, and Motherhood', *Social Theory and Practice*, 22/2: 137–60.

JOHNSON, JAMES (1998). 'Arguing for Deliberation: Some Skeptical Considerations', in Jon Elster (ed.), *Deliberative Democracy* (Cambridge University Press, Cambridge), 161–84.

—— (2000). 'Why Respect Culture?', *American Journal of Political Science*, 44/3: 405–18.

JOHNSTON, DARLENE (1989). 'Native Rights as Collective Rights: A Question of Group Self-Preservation', *Canadian Journal of Law and Jurisprudence*, 2/1: 19–34.

JONES, CHARLES (1999). *Global Justice: Defending Cosmopolitanism* (Oxford University Press, Oxford).

JONES, PETER (1982). 'Freedom and the Redistribution of Resources', *Journal of Social Policy*, 11/2: 217–38.

JOPPKE, CHRISTIAN, and LUKES, STEVEN (eds.) (1999). *Multicultural Questions* (Oxford University Press, Oxford).

KAGAN, SHELLEY (1989). *The Limits of Morality* (Oxford University Press, Oxford).

—— (1994). 'The Argument from Liberty', in J. Coleman and A. Buchanan (eds.), *In Harm's Way* (Cambridge University Press, Cambridge), 16–41.

KAHANE, DAVID (2000). 'Pluralism, Deliberation and Citizen Competence: Recent Developments in Democratic Theory', *Social Theory and Practice*, 26/3: 509–35.

KAHNEMAN, DANIEL, et al. (1986). 'Fairness as a Constraint on Profit-Seeking', *American Economic Review*, 76/4: 728–41.

KAMENKA, EUGENE (ed.) (1982). *Community as a Social Ideal* (Edward Arnold, London).

KARMIS, DIMITRIOS (1993). 'Cultures Autochtones et libéralisme au Canada: les vertus médiatrices du communautarisme libéral de Charles Taylor', *Canadian Journal of Political Science*, 26/1: 69–96.

KATZ, LEO (1999). 'Responsibility and Consent: The Libertarian's Problems with Freedom of Contract', *Social Philosophy and Policy*, 16/2: 94–117.

KAUS, MICKEY (1992). *The End of Equality* (Basic Books, New York).

KAVKA, GREGORY (1986). *Hobbesian Moral and Political Theory* (Princeton University Press, Princeton).

KEARNS, D. (1983). 'A Theory of Justice–and Love: Rawls on the Family', *Politics*, 18/2: 36–42.

KEAT, RUSSELL (1982). 'Liberal Rights and Socialism', in Keith Graham (ed.), *Contemporary Political Philosophy: Radical Perspectives* (Cambridge University Press, Cambridge), 59–82.

KEATING, MICHAEL, and McGARRY, JOHN (eds.) (2001) Minority Nationalism and the Changing International Order (Oxford University Press, Oxford.)

KENNEDY, ELLEN, and MENDUS, SUSAN (1987). *Women in Western Political Philosophy* (Wheatsheaf Books, Brighton).

KERNOHAN, ANDREW (1988). 'Capitalism and Self-Ownership', *Social Philosophy and Policy*, 6/1: 60–76.

—— (1990). 'Rawls and the Collective Ownership of Natural Abilities', *Canadian Journal of Philosophy*, 20/1: 19–28.

—— (1993). 'Desert and Self-Ownership', *Journal of Value Inquiry*, 27/2: 197–202.

—— (1998). *Liberalism, Equality and Cultural Oppression* (Cambridge University Press, Cambridge).

KERSHNAR, STEPHEN (2000). 'There is No Moral Right to Immigrate to the United States', *Public Affairs Quarterly*, 14/2: 141–58.

KING, DESMOND (1999). *In the Name of Liberalism: Illiberal Social Policy in the U.S. and Britain* (Oxford University Press, Oxford).

—— and WALDRON, JEREMY (1988). 'Citizenship, Social Citizenship and the Defence of the Welfare State', *British Journal of Political Science*, 18: 415–43.

KITTAY, EVA FEDER (1995). *Equality, Rawls and the Inclusion of Women* (Routledge, New York).

—— (1998). *Love's Labor: Essays on Women, Equality and Dependency* (Routledge, New York).

KITTAY, EVA FEDER and MEYERS, DIANA (eds.) (1987). *Women and Moral Theory* (Rowman and Littlefield, Savage, Md.).

KLEINGELD, PAULINE (1998). 'Just Love: Marriage and the Question of Justice', *Social Theory and Practice*, 24/2: 261–81.

KLEY, ROLAND (1994). *Hayek's Social and Political Thought* (Oxford University Press, Oxford).

KLOSS, HEINZ (1977). *The American Bilingual Tradition* (Newbury House, Rowley, Mass.).

KNIGHT, KELVIN (ed.) (1998). *The MacIntyre Reader* (University of Notre Dame Press, Notre Dame, Ind.).

KNOWLES, DUDLEY (2001). *Political Philosophy* (McGill-Queen's University Press, Montreal).

KOEHN, DARYL (1998). *Rethinking Feminist Ethics: Care, Trust and Empathy* (Routledge, London).

KOHLBERG, LAWRENCE (1984). *Essays on Moral Development*, vol. ii (Harper and Row, San Francisco).

KORSGAARD, CHRISTINE (1993). 'Commentary on Cohen and Sen', in Nussbaum and Sen 1993, 54–61.

KRISTJANSSON, KRISTJAN (1992*a*). 'For a Concept of Negative Liberty—But Which Conception?', *Journal of Applied Philosophy*, 9/2: 221–32.

—— (1992*b*). 'What is Wrong with Positive Liberty', *Social Theory and Practice*, 18/3: 289–310.

—— (1992*c*). 'Social Freedom and the Test of Moral Responsibility', *Ethics*, 103: 104–16.

KROUSE, RICHARD, and MCPHERSON, MICHAEL (1988). 'Capitalism, "Property-Owning Democracy", and the Welfare State', in Amy Gutmann (ed.), *Democracy and the Welfare State* (Princeton University Press, Princeton), 79–106.

KUKATHAS, CHANDRAN (1989). *Hayek and Modern Liberalism* (Oxford University Press, Oxford).

—— (1992). 'Are There any Cultural Rights', *Political Theory*, 20/1: 105–39.

—— (1997). 'Cultural Toleration', in Shapiro and Kymlicka 1997, 69–104.

—— and PETTIT, PHILIP (1990). *Rawls: A Theory of Justice and its Critics* (Polity, Oxford).

KYMLICKA, WILL (1988*a*). 'Liberalism and Communitarianism', *Canadian Journal of Philosophy*, 18/2: 181–203.

—— (1988*b*). 'Rawls on Teleology and Deontology', *Philosophy and Public Affairs*, 17/3: 173–90.

—— (1989*a*). *Liberalism, Community, and Culture* (Oxford University Press, Oxford).

—— (1989*b*). 'Liberal Individualism and Liberal Neutrality', *Ethics*, 99/4: 883–905.

—— (1990). 'Two Theories of Justice', *Inquiry*, 33/1: 99–119.

—— (1991). 'Rethinking the Family', *Philosophy and Public Affairs*, 20/1: 77–97.

—— (ed.) (1992). *Justice in Political Philosophy* (Edward Elgar, Aldershot).

—— (1995*a*). *Multicultural Citizenship: A Liberal Theory of Minority Rights* (Oxford University Press, Oxford).

—— (ed.) (1995*b*). *The Rights of Minority Cultures* (Oxford University Press, Oxford).

—— (1998). *Finding our Way: Rethinking Ethnocultural Relations in Canada* (Oxford University Press, Toronto).

KYMLICKA, WILL (2001). *Politics in the Vernacular: Nationalism, Multiculturalism and Citizenship* (Oxford University Press, Oxford).

—— (2002). 'Nation-Building and Minority Rights: Comparing Africa and the West', in Bruce Berman, Dickson Eyoh, and Will Kymlicka (eds.), *Ethnicity and Democracy in Africa* (James Currey, Oxford).

—— and NORMAN, WAYNE (1994). 'Return of the Citizen', *Ethics*, 104/2: 352–81.

—— —— (eds.) (2000). *Citizenship in Diverse Societies* (Oxford University Press, Oxford).

—— and OPALSKI, MAGDA (eds.) (2001). *Can Liberal Pluralism be Exported? Western Political Theory and Ethnic Relations in Eastern Europe* (Oxford University Press, Oxford).

LADENSON, ROBERT (1983). *A Philosophy of Free Expression and its Constitutional Applications* (Rowman and Littlefield, Totowa, NJ).

LAITIN, DAVID (1992). *Language Repertoires and State Construction in Africa* (Cambridge University Press, Cambridge).

LAMONT, JULIAN (1997). 'Incentive Income, Deserved Income and Economic Rents', *Journal of Political Philosophy*, 5/1: 26–46.

LANDES, JOAN (1988). *Women and the Public Sphere in the Age of the French Revolution* (Cornell University Press, Ithaca, NY).

—— (ed.) (1998). *Feminism, the Public and the Private* (Oxford University Press, Oxford).

LANGTON, RAE (1990). 'Whose Right? Ronald Dworkin, Women and Pornography', *Philosophy and Public Policy*, 19/4: 311–59.

LAPIDOTH, RUTH (1996). *Autonomy: Flexible Solutions to Ethnic Conflict* (Institute for Peace Press, Washington).

LARABEE, MARY JEAN (ed.) (1993). *An Ethic of Care: Feminist and Interdisciplinary Perspectives* (Routledge, London).

LARANA, ENRIQUE, JOHNSTON, HANK, and GUSFIELD, JOSEPH (eds.) (1994). *New Social Movements: From Ideology to Identity* (Temple University Press, Philadelphia).

LARMORE, CHARLES (1987). *Patterns of Moral Complexity* (Cambridge University Press, Cambridge).

LeGRAND, JULIAN, and ESTRIN, SAUL (eds.) (1989). *Market Socialism* (Oxford University Press, Oxford).

LEHMAN, EDWARD W. (ed.) (2000). *Autonomy and Order: A Communitarian Anthology* (Rowman and Littlefield, Savage, Md.).

LEHNING, PERCY (ed.) (1998). *Theories of Secession* (Routledge, London).

—— and WEALE, ALBERT (eds.) (1997). *Citizenship, Democracy and Justice in the New Europe* (Routledge, London).

LESSNOFF, MICHAEL (1986). *Social Contract* (Macmillan, London).

LEVINE, ANDREW (1988). 'Capitalist Persons', *Social Philosophy and Policy*, 6/1: 39–59.

—— (1989). 'What is a Marxist Today?', *Canadian Journal of Philosophy*, supplementary vol. 15: 29–58.

—— (1998). *Rethinking Liberal Equality from a 'Utopian' Point of View* (Cornell University Press, Ithaca, NY).

—— (1999). 'Rewarding Effort', *Journal of Political Philosophy*, 7/4: 404–18.

LEVINSON, MEIRA (1999). *The Demands of Liberal Education* (Oxford University Press, Oxford),

LEVY, JACOB (1997). 'Classifying Cultural Rights', in Shapiro and Kymlicka 1997, 22–66.

—— (2000). *The Multiculturalism of Fear* (Oxford University Press, Oxford).

LICHTENBERG, JUDITH (1999). 'How Liberal Can Nationalism Be?', in Beiner 1999, 167–88.

LINDBLOM, CHARLES (1977). *Politics and Markets* (Basic Books, New York).

LINKLATER, ANDREW (1998). *The Transformation of Political Community: Ethical Foundations of the Post-Westphalian Era* (University of South Carolina Press, Columbia).

LIPPERT-RASMUSSEN, KASPER (1999). 'Arneson on Equality of Opportunity', *Journal of Political Philosophy*, 7/4: 478–87.

LISTER, RUTH (ed.) (1998). *Citizenship: Feminist Perspectives* (New York University Press, New York).

LITTLETON, CHRISTINE (1987). 'Reconstructing Sexual Equality', *California Law Review*, 75: 201–59.

LLOYD, SHARON (1992). 'Stepping Back', *Analyse & Kritik*, 14/1: 72–85.

—— (1994). 'Family Justice and Social Justice', *Pacific Philosophical Quarterly*, 755: 353–71.

LLOYD THOMAS, DAVID (1988). *In Defense of Liberalism* (Blackwell, Oxford).

LOEVINSOHN, ERNEST (1977). 'Liberty and the Redistribution of Property', *Philosophy and Public Affairs*, 6/3: 226–39.

LOMASKY, LOREN (1987). *Persons, Rights, and the Moral Community* (Oxford University Press, Oxford).

—— (1998). 'Libertarianism as if (the Other 99 Percent of) People Mattered', *Social Philosophy and Policy*, 15/2: 350–71.

LUKES, STEVEN (1985). *Marxism and Morality* (Oxford University Press, Oxford).

—— (1995). 'Marxism, Liberalism and the Left' (paper presented at Universidad Internacional Menéndez y Pelayo, Santander, 1995).

LYONS, DAVID (1965). *Forms and Limits of Utilitarianism* (Oxford University Press, London).

—— (1981). 'The New Indian Claims and Original Rights to Land', in Paul 1981, 355–79.

—— (ed.) (1997). *Mill's Utilitarianism: Critical Essays* (Rowman and Littlefield, Savage, Md.).

MacCALLUM, GERALD (1967). 'Negative and Positive Freedom', *Philosophical Review*, 76/3: 312–34.

McCABE, DAVID (1996). 'New Journals in Political Philosophy and Related Fields', *Ethics*, 106/4: 800–16.

McCLAIN, LINDA (1994). 'Rights and Irresponsibility', *Duke Law Journal*, 43: 989–1088.

—— (1995). 'Inviolability and Privacy: The Castle, the Sanctuary, and the Body', *Yale Journal of Law and the Humanities*, 7/1: 195–242.

—— (1999a). 'Reconstructive Tasks for a Liberal Feminist Conception of Privacy', *William and Mary Law Review*, 40/2: 759–94.

—— (1999b). 'The Liberal Future of Relational Feminism: Robin West's Caring for Justice', *Law and Social Inquiry*, 24/2: 477–516.

McDONALD, MICHAEL (1991a). 'Questions about Collective Rights', in D. Schneiderman (ed.), *Language and the State: The Law and Politics of Identity* (Les Éditions Yvon Blais, Cowansville), 3–25.

McDONALD, MICHAEL (1991*b*). 'Should Communities Have Rights? Reflections on Liberal Individualism', *Canadian Journal of Law and Jurisprudence*, 4/2: 217–37.

MACEDO, STEPHEN (1988). 'Capitalism, Citizenship and Community', *Social Philosophy and Policy*, 6/1: 113–39.

—— (1990). *Liberal Virtues: Citizenship, Virtue and Community* (Oxford University Press, Oxford).

—— (1995). 'Liberal Civic Education and Religious Fundamentalism', *Ethics*, 105/3: 468–96.

—— (ed) (1999). *Deliberative Politics: Essays on Democracy and Disagreement* (Oxford University Press, Oxford).

—— (2000). *Diversity and Distrust: Civic Education in a Multicultural Democracy* (Harvard University Press, Cambridge, Mass.).

MACHAN, TIBOR, and RASMUSSEN, DOUGLAS (eds.) (1995). *Liberty for the Twenty-First Century: Contemporary Libertarian Thought* (Rowman and Littlefield, Lanham, Md.).

MACINTYRE, ALISDAIR (1981). *After Virtue: A Study in Moral Theory* (Duckworth, London).

—— (1988). *Whose Justice? Which Rationality?* (University of Notre Dame Press, Notre Dame, Ind.).

—— (1994). 'A Partial Response to my Critics', in Horton and Mendus 1994, 283–304.

MACINTYRE, ALISDAIR (1999). *Dependent Rational Beings: Why Human Beings Need the Virtues* (Open Court Publishing, La Salle, Ill.).

MACK, ERIC (1990). 'Self-Ownership and the Right of Property', *Monist*, 73/4: 519–43.

—— (1995). 'The Self-Ownership Proviso: A New and Improved Lockean Proviso', in Ellen Frankel Paul (ed.), *Contemporary Political and Social Philosophy* (Needham Heights, Cambridge), 186–216.

MACKENZIE, CATRIONA, and STOLJAR, NATALIE (eds.) (1999). *Relational Autonomy in Context: Feminist Perspectives on Autonomy, Agency and the Social Self* (Oxford University Press, New York).

McKERLIE, DENNIS (1994). 'Equality and Priority', *Utilitas*, 6/1: 25–42.

—— (1996). 'Equality', *Ethics*, 106/2: 274–96.

MACKIE, J. L. (1984). 'Rights, Utility, and Universalization', in Frey 1984, 86–105.

McKIM, ROBERT, and McMAHAN, JEFF (eds.) (1997). *The Morality of Nationalism* (Oxford University Press, Oxford).

MACKINNON, CATHERINE (1987). *Feminism Unmodified: Discourses on Life and Law* (Harvard University Press, Cambridge, Mass.).

—— (1991). 'Reflections on Sex Equality under the Law', *Yale Law Journal*, 100: 1281–328.

McLAUGHLIN, T. H. (1992*a*). 'Citizenship, Diversity and Education', *Journal of Moral Education*, 21/3: 235–50.

—— (1992*b*). 'The Ethics of Separate Schools', in Mal Leicester and Monica Taylor (eds.), *Ethics, Ethnicity and Education* (Kogan Page, London), 114–36.

MACLEOD, COLIN (1998). *Liberalism, Justice and Markets: A Critique of Liberal Equality* (Oxford University Press, Oxford).

MACPHERSON, C. B. (1973). *Democratic Theory: Essays in Retrieval* (Oxford University Press, Oxford).

MALLON, RON (1999). 'Political Liberalism, Cultural Membership and the Family', *Social Theory and Practice*, 25/2: 271–97.

MANENT, PIERRE (2000). 'The Return of Political Philosophy', *First Things*, 103: 15–22.

MAPEL, DAVID (1989). *Social Justice Reconsidered* (University of Illinois Press, Urbana).

MARGALIT, AVISHAI (1996). *The Decent Society* (Harvard University Press, Cambridge, Mass.).

—— and RAZ, JOSEPH (1990). 'National Self-Determination', *Journal of Philosophy*, 87/9: 439–61.

MARSHALL, T. H. (1965). *Class, Citizenship and Social Development* (Anchor, New York).

MARTIN, REX (1985). *Rawls and Rights* (University Press of Kansas, Lawrence).

MARX, KARL (1973). *Grundrisse*, ed. M. Nicolaus (Penguin, Harmondsworth).

—— (1977a). *Economic and Philosophic Manuscripts of 1844* (Lawrence and Wishart, London).

—— (1977b). *Karl Marx: Selected Writings*, ed. D. McLellan (Oxford University Press, Oxford).

—— (1977c). *Capital: A Critique of Political Economy*, vol. i (Penguin, Harmondsworth).

—— (1981). *Capital: A Critique of Political Economy*, vol. iii (Penguin, Harmondsworth).

—— and ENGELS, FRIEDRICH (1968). *Marx/Engels: Selected Works in One Volume* (Lawrence and Wishart, London).

—— (1970). *The German Ideology* (Lawrence and Wishart, London).

MASON, ANDREW (1993). 'Liberalism and the Value of Community', *Canadian Journal of Philosophy*, 23/2: 215–40.

MEAD, LAWRENCE (1986). *Beyond Entitlement: The Social Obligations of Citizenship* (Free Press, New York).

MENDUS, SUSAN (1989). *Toleration and the Limits of Liberalism* (Humanities Press, Atlantic Highlands, NJ).

—— (1993). 'Eve and the Poisoned Chalice: Feminist Morality and the Claims of Politics', in M. Brügmann (ed.), *Who's Afraid of Femininity? Questions of Identity* (Rodopi, Amsterdam), 95–104.

MEYER, MICHAEL (1997). 'When Not to Claim Your Rights: The Abuse and the Virtuous Use of Rights', *Journal of Political Philosophy*, 5/2: 149–62.

MEYERS, DIANA (1987). 'The Socialized Individual and Individual Autonomy', in Kittay and Meyers 1987, 139–53.

—— (1994). *Subjection and Subjectivity: Psychoanalytic Feminism and Moral Theory* (Routledge, London).

—— (ed.) (1997). *Feminists Rethink the Self* (Westview, Boulder, Colo.).

MICHAEL, MARK (1997). 'Redistributive Taxation, Self-Ownership and the Fruit of Labour', *Journal of Applied Philosophy*, 14/2: 137–46.

MICHELMAN, FRANK (1975). 'Constitutional Welfare Rights and *A Theory of Justice*', in Daniels 1975b, 319–46.

—— (1996). 'Socio-Political Functions of Constitutional Protections of Private Property Holdings in Liberal Political Thought', in G. E. van Maanen (ed.) *Property Law on the Threshold of the 21st Century* (Maklv, Apeldorn).

MIDGLEY, MARY (1978). *Beast and Man: The Roots of Human Nature* (New American Library, New York).

MILDE, MICHAEL (1999). 'Unreasonable Foundations: David Gauthier on Property Rights, Rationality and the Social Contract', *Social Theory and Practice*, 25/1: 93–125.

MILL, J. S. (1962). *Mill on Bentham and Coleridge*, ed. F. Leavis (Chatto and Windus, London).

—— (1965). 'Principles of Political Economy', in *Collected Works*, vol. iii (University of Toronto Press, Toronto)

—— (1967). 'Chapters on Socialism', in *Collected Works*, vol. v (University of Toronto Press, Toronto).

—— (1968). *Utilitarianism, Liberty, Representative Government*, ed. A. D. Lindsay (J. M. Dent and Sons, London).

—— (1982). *On Liberty*, ed. G. Himmelfarb (Penguin, Harmondsworth).

—— and MILL, H. T. (1970). *Essays on Sex Equality*, ed. A. Rossi (University of Chicago Press, Chicago).

MILLER, DAVID (1976). *Social Justice* (Oxford University Press, Oxford).

—— (1989). 'In What Sense must Socialism be Communitarian?', *Social Philosophy and Policy*, 6/2: 51–73.

—— (1992). 'Distributive Justice: What the People Think', *Ethics*, 102/3: 555–93.

—— (1993). 'Equality and Market Socialism', in Bardhan and Roemer 1993, 298–314.

MILLER, DAVID (1995). *On Nationality* (Oxford University Press, Oxford).

—— (1997). 'What Kind of Equality Should the Left Pursue', in Franklin 1997, 83–100.

—— (1998). 'Secession and the Principle of Nationality', in Couture, Nielsen, and Seymour 1998, 261–82.

—— (1999). *Principles of Social Justice* (Harvard University Press, Cambridge, Mass.).

—— (2000). *Citizenship and National Identity* (Polity Press, Cambridge).

—— and WALZER, MICHAEL (eds.) (1995). *Pluralism, Justice and Equality* (Oxford University Press, Oxford).

—— et al. (1996). 'Symposium on David Miller's On Nationality', *Nations and Nationalism*, 2/3: 407–51.

MILLER, RICARD (1984). *Analyzing Marx* (Princeton University Press, Princeton).

MILLS, CHARLES (1997). *The Racial Contract* (Cornell University Press, Ithaca, NY).

MINOW, MARTHA (1990). *Making all the Difference: Inclusion, Exclusion and American Law* (Cornell University Press, Ithaca, NY).

—— (1991). 'Equalities', *Journal of Philosophy*, 88/11: 633–44.

MISCEVIC, NENAD (1999). 'Close Strangers: Nationalism, Proximity and Cosmopolitanism', *Studies in East European Thought*, 51: 109–25.

—— (ed.) (2000). *Nationalism and Ethnic Conflict: Philosophical Perspectives* (Open Court, La Salle, Ill.).

MODOOD, TARIQ (1994). 'Establishment, Multiculturalism, and British Citizenship', *Political Quarterly*, 65/1: 53–73.

MOON, DONALD (1988). 'The Moral Basis of the Democratic Welfare State', in Amy Gutmann (ed.), *Democracy and the Welfare State* (Princeton University Press, Princeton), 27–52.

MOON, DONALD (1993). *Constructing Community: Moral Pluralism and Tragic Conflicts* (Princeton University Press, Princeton).

MOORE, G. E. (1912). *Ethics* (Oxford University Press, London).

MOORE, MARGARET (ed.) (1998). *National Self-Determination and Secession* (Oxford University Press, Oxford).

MORRIS, CHRISTOPHER (1988). 'The Relation between Self-Interest and Justice in Contractarian Ethics', *Social Philosophy and Policy*, 5/2: 119–53.

—— (ed.) (1999). *The Social Contract Theorists* (Rowman and Littlefield, Lanham, Md.).

MOUFFE, CHANTAL (1992*a*). 'Feminism, Citizenship and Radical Democratic Politics', in Butler and Scott 1992, 369–84.

—— (ed.) (1992*b*). *Dimensions of Radical Democracy: Pluralism, Citizenship and Community* (Routledge, London).

—— (1992*c*). 'Democratic Citizenship and the Political Community', in Mouffe 1992*b*, 225–39.

—— (2000). *The Democratic Paradox* (Verso, London).

MULGAN, GEOFF (1991). 'Citizens and Responsibilities', in Andrews 1991, 37–49.

MULHALL, STEPHEN, and SWIFT, ADAM (1996). *Liberals and Communitarians*, 2nd edn. (Blackwell, Oxford).

MURPHY, JEFFRIE (1973). 'Marxism and Retribution', *Philosophy and Public Affairs*, 2/3: 214–41.

MURPHY, LIAM (1999). 'Institutions and the Demands of Justice', *Philosophy and Public Affairs*, 27/4: 251–91.

NAGEL, THOMAS (1973). 'Rawls on Justice', *Philosophical Review*, 82: 220–34.

—— (1979). *Mortal Questions* (Cambridge University Press, Cambridge).

—— (1980). 'The Limits of Objectivity', in S. McMurrin (ed.), *The Tanner Lectures on Human Values*, vol. i (University of Utah Press, Salt Lake City), 75–140.

—— (1981). 'Libertarianism without Foundations', in Paul 1981, 191–205.

—— (1986). *The View from Nowhere* (Oxford University Press, New York).

—— (1991). *Equality and Partiality* (Oxford University Press, New York).

NARAYAN, UMA (1995). 'Colonialism and its Others: Considerations on Rights and Care Discourses', *Hypatia*, 10/2: 133–40.

—— and HARDING, SANDRA (eds.) (2000). *Decentering the Center: Philosophy for a Multicultural, Postcolonial, and Feminist World* (Indiana University Press, Bloomington).

NARVESON, JAN (1983). 'On Dworkinian Equality', *Social Philosophy and Policy*, 1/1: 1–23.

—— (1988). *The Libertarian Idea* (Temple University Press, Philadelphia).

—— (1991). 'Collective Rights?', *Canadian Journal of Law and Jurisprudence*, 4/2: 329–45.

—— (1995). 'Contracting for Liberty', in Machan and Rasmussen 1995, 19–40.

—— (1998). 'Libertarianism versus Marxism: Reflections on G. A. Cohen's *Self-Ownership, Freedom and Equality*', *Journal of Ethics*, 2/1: 1–26.

NAUTA, LOLLE (1992). 'Changing Conceptions of Citizenship', *Praxis International*, 12/1: 20–34.

NEAL, PATRICK (1994). 'Perfectionism with a Liberal Face? Nervous Liberals and Raz's Political Theory', *Social Theory and Practice*, 20/1: 25–58.

NEDELSKY, JENNIFER (1989). 'Reconceiving Autonomy: Sources, Thoughts, and

Possibilities', in Allan Hutchinson and Leslie Green (eds.), *Law and the Community: The End of Individualism?* (Carswell, Toronto), 219–52.

NEDELSKY, JENNIFER (1993). 'Reconceiving Rights as Relationship', *Review of Constitutional Studies*, 1/1: 1–26.

—— (2000). 'Citizenship and Relational Feminism', in Ronald Beiner and Wayne Norman (eds.), *Canadian Political Philosophy: Contemporary Reflections* (Oxford University Press, Toronto), 131–46.

NENTWICH, MICHAEL, and WEALE, ALBERT (eds.) (1998). *Political Theory and the European Union: Legitimacy, Constitutional Choice and Citizenship* (Routledge, London).

NEWMAN, SAUL (1996). *Ethnoregional Conflicts in Democracies: Mostly Ballots, Rarely Bullets* (Greenwood, London).

NICHOLSON, LINDA (1986). *Gender and History: The Limits of Social Theory in the Age of the Family* (Columbia University Press, New York).

NICKEL, JAMES (1990). 'Rawls on Political Community and Principles of Justice', *Law and Philosophy*, 9: 205–16.

—— (1995). 'The Value of Cultural Belonging', *Dialogue*, 33/4: 635–42.

NIELSEN, KAI (1978). 'Class and Justice', in J. Arthur and W. Shaw (eds.), *Justice and Economic Distributions* (Prentice-Hall, Englewood Cliffs, NJ).

—— (1985). *Equality and Liberty: A Defense of Radical Egalitarianism* (Rowman and Allanheld, Totowa, NJ).

—— (1987). 'Rejecting Egalitarianism: On Miller's Nonegalitarian Marx', *Political Theory*, 15/3: 411–23.

—— (1989). *Marxism and the Moral Point of View* (Westview Press, Boulder, Colo.).

—— (1993). 'Relativism and Wide Reflective Equilibrium', *Monist*, 76/3: 316–32.

NODDINGS, NEL (1984). *Caring: A Feminine Approach to Ethics and Moral Education* (University of California Press, Berkeley and Los Angeles).

NORMAN, RICHARD (1981). 'Liberty, Equality, Property', *Proceedings of the Aristotelian Society*, supplementary vol. 55: 192–209.

—— (1987). *Free and Equal* (Oxford University Press, Oxford).

—— (1989). 'What is Living and What is Dead in Marxism?', *Canadian Journal of Philosophy*, supplementary vol. 15: 59–80.

NORMAN, WAYNE (1991a). *Taking Freedom Too Seriously? An Essay on Analytic and Post-analytic Political Philosophy* (Garland, New York).

—— (1991b). 'Taking "Free Action" Too Seriously', *Ethics*, 101/3: 505–20.

—— (1994). 'Towards a Normative Theory of Federalism', in Baker 1994, 79–100.

—— (1995). 'The Ideology of Shared Values', in Carens 1995, 137–59.

—— (1996). 'Prelude to a Liberal Morality of Nationalism', in S. Brennan, T. Isaacs, and M. Milde (eds.), *A Question of Values* (Rodopi Press, Amsterdam), 189–208.

—— (1998). 'Inevitable and Unacceptable? Methodological Rawlsianism in Contemporary Anglo-American Political Philosophy', *Political Studies*, 46/2: 276–94.

—— (1999). 'Theorizing Nationalism (Normatively): The First Steps', in Beiner 1999, 51–66.

—— (2001). 'Ética y la construcción de la nación', in R. M. Suárez and J. M. Rivera Otero (eds.), *Europa Mundi: democracia, globalización y europeización* (Prensa de la Universidad de Santiago de Compostela, Santiago).

NOVE, ALEC (1983). *The Economics of Feasible Socialism* (George Allen and Unwin, London).

NOZICK, ROBERT (1974). *Anarchy, State, and Utopia* (Basic Books, New York).

—— (1981). *Philosophical Explanations* (Harvard University Press, Cambridge, Mass.).

NUNNER-WINKLER, GERTRUD (1984). 'Two Moralities?', in W. Kurtines and J. Gewirtz (eds.), *Morality, Moral Behavior and Moral Development* (John Wiley, New York), 348–61.

NUSSBAUM, MARTHA (1986). *The Fragility of Goodness* (Cambridge University Press, Cambridge).

—— (1999). *Sex and Social Justice* (Oxford University Press, New York).

—— (2000). *Women and Human Development: The Capabilities Approach* (Cambridge University Press, Cambridge).

—— and SEN, AMARTYA (eds.) (1993). *The Quality of Life* (Oxford University Press, Oxford).

NYE, ANDREA (1988). *Feminist Theory and the Philosophies of Man* (Croom Helm, London).

OAKESHOTT, MICHAEL (1984). 'Political Education', in Michael Sandel (ed.), *Liberalism and its Critics* (Blackwell, Oxford), 219–38.

O'BRIEN, MARY (1981). *The Politics of Reproduction* (Routledge and Kegan Paul, London).

O'BRIEN, SHARON (1987). 'Cultural Rights in the United States: A Conflict of Values', *Law and Inequality Journal*, 5: 267–358.

OKIN, SUSAN (1979). *Women in Western Political Thought* (Princeton University Press, Princeton).

—— (1981). 'Women and the Making of the Sentimental Family', *Philosophy and Public Affairs* 11/1: 65–88.

—— (1987). 'Justice and Gender', *Philosophy and Public Affairs*, 16/1: 42–72.

—— (1989a). 'Reason and Feeling in Thinking about Justice', *Ethics*, 99/2: 229–49.

—— (1989b). *Justice, Gender, and the Family* (Basic Books, New York).

—— (1990). 'Thinking Like a Woman', in Rhode 1990, 145–59.

—— (1991). 'Gender, the Public and the Private', in David Held (ed.), *Political Theory Today* (Polity, Cambridge), 67–90.

—— (1992). 'Women, Equality and Citizenship', *Queen's Quarterly*, 99/1: 56–71.

—— (1994). 'Gender Inequality and Cultural Differences', *Political Theory*, 22/1: 5–24.

—— (1998). 'Mistresses of their Own Destiny? Group Rights, Gender, and Realistic Rights of Exit' (presented at the American Political Science Association annual meeting, Sept.).

—— (1999). *Is Multiculturalism Bad for Women?* (Princeton University Press, Princeton).

OLDFIELD, ADRIAN (1990a). 'Citizenship: An Unnatural Practice?', *Political Quarterly*, 61: 177–87.

—— (1990b). *Citizenship and Community: Civic Republicanism and the Modern World* (Routledge, London).

OLLMAN, BERTELL (ed.) (1998). *Market Socialism: The Debate among Socialists* (Routledge, London).

OLSEN, FRANCES (1983). 'The Family and the Market: A Study of Ideology and Legal Reform', *Harvard Law Review*, 96/7: 1497–578.

O'NEILL, ONORA (1980). 'The Most Extensive Liberty', *Proceedings of the Aristotelian Society*, 85: 45–59.

O'NEILL, ONORA (1993). 'Justice, Gender and Interational Relations', in Nussbaum and Sen 1993.

—— (1996). *Toward Justice and Virtue* (Cambridge University Press, Cambridge), 303–23.

OREND, BRIAN (2001). *Michael Walzer on War and Justice* (McGill-Queen's University Press, Montreal).

ORWIN, CLIFFORD (1998). 'The Encumbered American Self', in Allen and Kegan 1988: 86–91.

OTSUKA, MICHAEL (1998a). 'Making the Unjust Provide for the Least Well Off', *Journal of Ethics*, 2/3: 247–59.

—— (1998b). 'Self-Ownership and Equality: A Lockean Reconciliation', *Philosophy and Public Affairs*, 27/1: 65–92.

PALMER, TOM G. (1998). 'G. A. Cohen on Self-Ownership, Property, and Equality', *Critical Review*, 12/3: 225–51.

PAREKH, BHIKHU (1982). *Contemporary Political Thinkers* (Martin Robertson, Oxford).

—— (1994). 'Decolonizing Liberalism', in Alexsandras Shiromas (ed.), *The End of 'Isms'? Reflections on the Fate of Ideological Politics after Communism's Collapse* (Blackwell, Oxford), 85–103.

—— (1997). 'Political Theory: Traditions in Political Philosophy', in Robert Goodin and Hans-Dieter Klingeman (eds.), *A New Handbook of Political Science* (Oxford University Press, Oxford), 503–18.

—— (2000). *Rethinking Multiculturalism: Cultural Diversity and Political Theory* (Harvard University Press, Cambridge, Mass.).

PARFIT, DEREK (1984). *Reasons and Persons* (Oxford University Press, Oxford).

—— (1998). 'Equality and Priority', in Andrew Mason (ed.), *Ideals of Equality* (Blackwell, Oxford), 1–20.

PARIS, DAVID (1991). 'Moral Education and the "Tie that Binds" in Liberal Political Theory', *American Political Science Review*, 85/3: 875–901.

PARRY, GERAINT (1991). 'Paths to Citizenship', in Vogel and Moran 1991, 167–96.

PASSERIN, MAURIZIO, and VOGEL, URSULA (eds.) (2000). *Public and Private: Legal, Political and Philosophical Perspectives* (Routledge, London).

PATEMAN, CAROLE (1975). 'Sublimation and Reification: Locke, Wolin and the Liberal Democratic Conception of the Political', *Politics and Society*, 5/4: 441–67.

—— (1980). ' "The Disorder of Women": Women, Love and the Sense of Justice', *Ethics*, 91/1: 20–34.

—— (1987). 'Feminist Critiques of the Public/Private Dichotomy', in A. Phillips (ed.), *Feminism and Equality* (Blackwell, Oxford), 103–26.

—— (1988). *The Sexual Contract* (Polity Press, Oxford).

—— (1989). *The Disorder of Women: Democracy, Feminism and Political Theory* (Stanford University Press, Stanford, Calif.).

—— (1991). ' "God Hath Ordained to Man a Helper": Hobbes, Patriarchy and Conjugal Right', in Shanley and Pateman 1991, 53–73.

PATTEN, ALAN (1996). 'The Republican Critique of Liberalism', *British Journal of Political Science*, 26: 25–44.

PAUL, ELLEN FRANKEL, MILLER, FRED, and PAUL, JEFFREY (eds.) (1996). *The Communitarian Challenge to Liberalism* (Cambridge University Press, Cambridge).

PAUL, JEFFREY (ed.) (1981). *Reading Nozick* (Rowman and Littlefield, Totowa, NJ).

PEFFER, RODNEY (1990). *Marx, Morality and Social Justice* (Princeton University Press, Princeton).

PETERSON, RICHARD (1996). 'A Re-evaluation of the Economic Consequences of Divorce', *American Sociological Review*, 61: 528–36.

PETTIT, PHILIP (1980). *Judging Justice: An Introduction to Contemporary Political Philosophy* (Routledge and Kegan Paul, London).

—— (1989). 'The Freedom of the City: A Republican Ideal', in A. Hamlin and P. Pettit (eds.), *The Good Polity* (Blackwell, Oxford).

—— (1997). *Republicanism* (Oxford University Press, Oxford).

—— (2000). 'Democracy, Electoral and Contestatory', in Ian Shapiro and Stephen Macedo (eds.), *Designing Democratic Institutions: NOMOS 42* (New York University Press, New York), 105–44.

PFAFF, WILLIAM (1993). *The Wrath of Nations: Civilization and the Furies of Nationalism* (Simon and Schuster, New York).

PHILLIPS, ANNE (1991). *Engendering Democracy* (Pennsylvania State University Press, University Park).

—— (1995). *The Politics of Presence* (Oxford University Press, Oxford).

—— (ed.) (1998). *Feminism and Politics* (Oxford University Press, Oxford).

—— (1999). *Which Equalities Matter?* (Polity Press, Cambridge).

—— (2000). 'Feminism and Republicanism: Is This a Plausible Alliance', *Journal of Political Philosophy*, 8/2: 279–93.

PHILLIPS, DAVID (1999). 'Contractualism and Moral Status', *Social Theory and Practice*, 24/2: 183–204.

PHILLIPS, DEREK (1993). *Looking Backward: A Critical Appraisal of Communitarian Thought* (Princeton University Press, Princeton).

PLAMENATZ, JOHN (1960). *On Alien Rule and Self-Government* (Longman, London).

PLANT, RAYMOND (1974). *Community and Ideology* (Routledge and Kegan Paul, London).

—— (1991). *Modern Political Thought* (Blackwell, Cambridge).

PLUHAR, EVELYN (1995). *Beyond Prejudice: The Moral Significance of Human and Nonhuman Animals* (Duke University Press, Durham, NC).

POCOCK, J. G. A (1992). 'The Ideal of Citizenship since Classical Times', *Queen's Quarterly*, 99/1: 33–55.

POGGE, THOMAS (1989). *Realizing Rawls* (Cornell University Press, Ithaca, NY).

—— (1994). 'An Egalitarian Law of Peoples', *Philosophy and Public Affairs*, 23/3: 195–224.

—— (1995). 'How Should Human Rights Be Conceived', *Jahrbuch für Recht und Ethik*, 3: 103–20.

—— (1997a). 'A Global Resources Dividend', in David Crocker and Toby Linden (eds.), *Ethics of Consumption: The Good Life, Justice, and Global Stewardship* (Rowman and Littlefield, Lanham, Md.), 501–36.

—— (1997b). 'Migration and Poverty', in Bader 1997, 12–27.

—— (1998). 'The Bounds of Nationalism', in Couture, Nielsen, and Seymour 1998, 463–504.

—— (2000). 'On the Site of Distributive Justice: Reflections on Cohen and Murphy', *Philosophy and Public Affairs*, 29/2: 138–69.

POOLE, ROSS (1999). *Nation and Identity* (Routledge, London).

PORTER, JOHN (1987). *The Measure of Canadian Society* (Carleton University Press, Ottawa).

POSNER, RICHARD (1983). *The Economics of Justice* (Harvard University Press, Cambridge, Mass.).

—— (1996). *Overcoming Law* (Harvard University Press, Cambridge, Mass.).

PUTNAM, ROBERT (1993). *Making Democracy Work: Civic Traditions in Modern Italy* (Princeton University Press, Princeton).

QUINN, MICHAEL (1993). 'Liberal Egalitarianism, Utility and Social Justice', *Utilitas*, 5/2: 311–16.

RADCLIFFE-RICHARDS, JANET (1980). *The Sceptical Feminist: A Philosophical Enquiry* (Routledge and Kegan Paul, London).

RAIKKA, JUHA (ed.) (1996). *Do We Need Minority Rights?* (Kluwer, Dordrecht).

—— (1998). 'The Feasibility Condition in Political Theory', *Journal of Political Philosophy*, 6/1: 27–40.

RAILTON, PETER (1984). 'Alienation, Consequentialism, and the Demands of Morality', *Philosophy and Public Affairs*, 13/2: 134–71.

RAKOWSKI, ERIC (1993). *Equal Justice* (Oxford University Press, Oxford).

—— (2000). 'Can Wealth Taxes Be Justified?', *Tax Law Review*, 53/3: 263–375.

RAPHAEL, D. D. (1970). *Problems of Political Philosophy* (Pall Mall, London).

—— (1981). *Moral Philosophy* (Oxford University Press, Oxford).

RAWLS, JOHN (1971) *A Theory of Justice* (Oxford University Press, London).

—— (1974). 'Reply to Alexander & Musgrave', *Quarterly Journal of Economics*, 88: 633–55.

—— (1975). 'Fairness to Goodness', *Philosophical Review*, 84: 536–54.

RAWLS, JOHN (1978). 'The Basic Structure as Subject', in A. Goldman and J. Kim (eds.), *Values and Morals* (Reidel, Dordrecht), 47–61.

—— (1979). 'A Well-Ordered Society', in P. Laslett and J. Fishkin (eds.), *Philosophy, Politics, and Society* (Yale University Press, New Haven), 6–20.

—— (1980). 'Kantian Constructivism in Moral Theory', *Journal of Philosophy*, 77/9: 515–72.

—— (1982a). 'The Basic Liberties and their Priority', in S. McMurrin (ed.), *The Tanner Lectures on Human Values*, vol. iii (University of Utah Press, Salt Lake City), 1–89.

—— (1982b). 'Social Unity and Primary Goods', in Sen and Williams 1982, 159–86.

—— (1985). 'Justice as Fairness: Political not Metaphysical', *Philosophy and Public Affairs*, 14/3: 223–51.

—— (1987). 'The Idea of an Overlapping Consensus', *Oxford Journal of Legal Studies*, 7/1: 1–25.

—— (1988). 'The Priority of Right and Ideas of the Good', *Philosophy and Public Affairs*, 17/4: 251–76.

—— (1989). 'The Domain of the Political and Overlapping Consensus', *New York University Law Review*, 64/2: 233–55.

—— (1993a). *Political Liberalism* (Columbia University Press, New York).

—— (1993b). 'The Law of Peoples', in S. Shute and S. Hurley (eds.), *On Human Rights: The Oxford Amnesty Lectures 1993* (Oxford University Press, Oxford), 41–82.

—— (1997). 'The Idea of Public Reason Revisited', *University of Chicago Law Review*, 64: 765–807.

RAWLS, JOHN (1999a). *Collected Papers*, ed. Samuel Freeman (Harvard University Press, Cambridge, Mass.).

—— (1999b). *The Law of Peoples* (Harvard University Press, Cambridge, Mass.).

RAZ, JOSEPH (1986). *The Morality of Freedom* (Oxford University Press, Oxford).

—— (1994). 'Multiculturalism: A Liberal Perspective', *Dissent*, Winter: 67–79.

—— (1998). 'Multiculturalism', *Ratio Juris*, 11/3: 193–205.

RCAP (1996). *Report of the Royal Commission on Aboriginal Peoples*, ii: *Restructuring the Relationship* (Ottawa).

RÉAUME, DENISE (1991). 'The Constitutional Protection of Language: Security or Survival?', in D. Schneiderman (ed.), *Language and the State: The Law and Politics of Identity* (Les Éditions Yvon Blais, Cowansville), 37–57.

—— (1995). 'Justice between Cultures: Autonomy and the Protection of Cultural Affiliation', *UBC Law Review* 29/1: 117–41.

REGAN, TOM (2001). *Defending Animal Rights* (University of Illinois Press, Champaign).

REIMAN, JEFFREY (1981). 'The Possibility of a Marxian Theory of Justice', *Canadian Journal of Philosophy*, supplementary vol. 7: 307–22.

—— (1983). 'The Labor Theory of the Difference Principle', *Philosophy and Public Affairs*, 12/2: 133–59.

—— (1987). 'Exploitation, Force, and the Moral Assessment of Capitalism: Thoughts on Roemer and Cohen', *Philosophy and Public Affairs*, 16/1: 3–41.

—— (1989). 'An Alternative to "Distributive" Marxism: Further Thoughts on Roemer, Cohen, and Exploitation', *Canadian Journal of Philosophy*, supplementary vol. 15: 299–331.

—— (1991). 'Moral Philosophy: The Critique of Capitalism and the Problem of Ideology', in Carver 1991, 143–67.

REINDERS, HANS (2000). *The Future of the Disabled in Liberal Society* (University of Notre Dame Press, Notre Dame, Ind.).

RESCHER, N. (1966). *Distributive Justice: A Constructive Critique of the Utilitarian Theory of Distribution* (Bobbs-Merrill, Indianapolis).

RHODE, DEBORAH (ed.) (1990). *Theoretical Perspectives on Sexual Difference* (Yale University Press, New Haven).

—— (1997). *Speaking of Sex: The Denial of Gender Inequality* (Harvard University Press, Cambridge, Mass.).

RICH, ADRIENNE (1979). *On Lies, Secrets and Silence: Selected Prose, 1966–1978* (Norton, New York).

RICHARDSON, HENRY, and WEITHMAN, PAUL (eds.) (1999). *The Philosophy of Rawls* (Garland, New York).

RIEBER, STEVEN (1996). 'Freedom and Redistributive Taxation', *Public Affairs Quarterly*, 10/1: 63–74.

RILEY, PATRICK (1982). *Will and Political Legitimacy: A Critical Exposition of Social Contract Theory in Hobbes, Locke, Rousseau, Kant, and Hegel* (Harvard University Press, Cambridge, Mass.).

RIPSTEIN, ARTHUR (1987). 'Foundationalism in Political Theory', *Philosophy and Public Affairs*, 16: 114–37.

—— (1989). 'Gauthier's Liberal Individual', *Dialogue*, 28: 63–76.

Ripstein, Arthur (1994). 'Equality, Luck and Responsibility', *Philosophy and Public Affairs*, 23/1: 3–23.

Robbins, Bruce (ed.) (1998). *Cosmopolitics: Thinking and Feeling beyond the Nation* (University of Minnesota Press, Minneapolis).

Roberts, Marcus (1996). *Analytical Marxism: A Critique* (Verso, London).

—— (1997). 'Analytical Marxism: An Ex-Paradigm? The Odyssey of G. A. Cohen', *Radical Philosophy*, 82: 17–28.

Robinson, Fiona (1999). *Globalizing Care: Ethics, Feminist Theory and International Relations* (Westview, Boulder, Colo.).

Roemer, John (1982a). *A General Theory of Exploitation and Class* (Harvard University Press, Cambridge, Mass.).

—— (1982b). 'Property Relations vs. Surplus Value in Marxian Exploitation', *Philosophy and Public Affairs*, 11/4: 281–313.

—— (1982c). 'New Directions in the Marxian Theory of Exploitation and Class', *Politics and Society*, 11/3: 253–87.

—— (1985a). 'Equality of Talent', *Economics and Philosophy*, 1/2: 151–87.

—— (1985b). 'Should Marxists Be Interested in Exploitation?', *Philosophy and Public Affairs*, 14/1: 30–65.

—— (1986a). 'The Mismarriage of Bargaining Theory and Distributive Justice', *Ethics*, 97/1: 88–110.

—— (ed.) (1986b). *Analytical Marxism* (Cambridge University Press, Cambridge).

—— (1988). *Free to Lose: An Introduction to Marxist Economic Philosophy* (Harvard University Press, Cambridge, Mass.).

Roemer, John (1989). 'Second Thoughts on Property Relations and Exploitation', *Canadian Journal of Philosophy*, supplementary vol. 15: 257–66.

—— (1993a). 'A Pragmatic Theory of Responsibility for the Egalitarian Planner', *Philosophy and Public Affairs*, 22: 146–66.

—— (1993b). 'Can There be Socialism after Communism?', in Bardhan and Roemer 1993, 89–107.

—— (1994). *A Future for Socialism* (Verso, London).

—— (1995). 'Equality and Responsibility', *Boston Review*, 20/2: 3–7.

—— (1996). *Theories of Distributive Justice* (Harvard University Press, Cambridge, Mass.).

—— (1999). 'Egalitarian Strategies', *Dissent*, 64–74.

Rooney, Phyllis (1991). 'A Different Different Voice: On the Feminist Challenge in Moral Theory', *Philosophical Forum*, 22/4: 335–61.

Rorty, Richard (1985). 'Postmodernist Bourgeois Liberalism', in R. Hollinger (ed.), *Hermeneutics and Praxis* (University of Notre Dame Press, Notre Dame, Ind.), 214–21.

Rosenblum, Nancy (1987). *Another Liberalism: Romanticism and the Reconstruction of Liberal Thought* (Harvard University Press, Cambridge, Mass.).

—— (1998). *Membership and Morals: The Personal Uses of Pluralism in America* (Princeton University Press, Princeton).

—— (2000). *Obligations of Citizenship and Demands of Faith: Religious Accommodation in Pluralist Democracies* (Princeton University Press, Princeton).

Ross, W. D. (1930). *The Right and the Good* (Oxford University Press, London).

ROTHBARD, MURRAY (1982). *The Ethics of Liberty* (Humanities Press, Atlantic Highlands, NJ).

ROTHSTEIN, BO (1992). 'Social Justice and State Capacity', *Politics and Society*, 20/1: 101–26.

—— (1998). *Just Institutions Matter: The Moral and Political Logic of the Universal Welfare State* (Cambridge University Press, Cambridge).

RUBIO-MARIN, RUTH (2000). *Immigration as a Democratic Challenge: Citizenship and Inclusion in Germany and the US* (Cambridge University Press, Cambridge).

RUDDICK, SARAH (1984*a*). 'Maternal Thinking', in J. Trebilcot (ed.), *Mothering: Essays in Feminist Theory* (Rowman and Allanheld, Totowa, NJ), 213–30.

—— (1984*b*). 'Preservative Love and Military Destruction', in J. Trebilcot (ed.), *Mothering: Essays in Feminist Theory* (Rowman and Allanheld, Totowa, NJ), 231–62.

—— (1987). 'Remarks on the Sexual Politics of Reason', in Kittay and Meyers 1987, 237–60.

RUSSELL, J. S. (1995). 'Okin's Rawlsian Feminism', *Social Theory and Practice*, 21/3: 397–426.

RYAN, ALAN (1994). 'Self-Ownership, Autonomy, and Property Rights', *Social Philosophy and Policy*, 11/2: 241–58.

SABETTI, F. (1996). 'Path Dependency and Civic Culture: Some Lessons from Italy about Interpreting Social Experiments', *Politics and Society*, 24/1: 19–44.

SANDEL, MICHAEL (1982). *Liberalism and the Limits of Justice* (Cambridge University Press, Cambridge).

—— (1984*a*). 'The Procedural Republic and the Unencumbered Self', *Political Theory*, 12/1: 81–96.

—— (1984*b*). 'Morality and the Liberal Ideal', *New Republic*, 190: 15–17.

—— (ed.) (1984*c*). *Liberalism and its Critics* (Blackwell, Oxford).

—— (1989). 'Moral Argument and Liberal Toleration: Abortion and Homosexuality', *California Law Review*, 77/3: 521–38.

—— (1990). 'Freedom of Conscience or Freedom of Choice?', in James Hunter and O. Guinness (eds.), *Articles of Faith, Articles of Peace* (Brookings Institute, Washington), 74–92.

—— (1996). *Democracy's Discontent: America in Search of a Public Philosophy* (Harvard University Press, Cambridge, Mass.).

—— (1998). 'Reply to critics', in Allen and Regan 1988: 319–35.

SANDERS, JOHN (1987). 'Justice and the Initial Acquisition of Property', *Harvard Journal of Law and Public Policy*, 10: 369–87.

SARTORIUS, ROLF (1969). 'Utilitarianism and Obligation', *Journal of Philosophy*, 66/3: 67–81.

SAXONHOUSE, ARLENE (1981). *Women in the History of Political Thought* (Praeger, Westport, Conn.).

SAYRE-McCORD, GEOFFREY (1994). 'On Why Hume's "General Point of View" Isn't Ideal—and Shouldn't Be', *Social Philosophy and Policy*, 11: 202–28.

SCALES, ANN (1993). 'The Emergence of Feminist Jurisprudence', in Patricia Smith (ed.) *Feminist Jurisprudence* (Oxford University Press, Oxford), 94–109.

SCANLON, THOMAS (1982). 'Contractualism and Utilitarianism', in Sen and Williams 1982, 103–28.

—— (1983). 'Freedom of Expression and Categories of Expression', in D. Copp and S. Wendell (eds.), *Pornography and Censorship* (Prometheus, Buffalo), 139–66.

SCANLON, THOMAS (1988). 'The Significance of Choice', in S. McMurrin (ed.), *The Tanner Lectures on Human Value*, vol. viii (University of Utah Press, Salt Lake City), 151–216.

—— (1991). 'The Moral Basis of Interpersonal Comparisons', in Elster and Roemer 1991, 17–44.

—— (1993). 'Value, Desire and Quality of Life', in Nussbaum and Sen 1993: 187–207.

—— (1998). *What We Owe to Each Other* (Harvard University Press, Cambridge, Mass.).

SCARRE, GEOFFREY (1996). *Utilitarianism* (Routledge, London).

SCHAEFER, DENISE (2001). 'Feminism and Liberalism Reconsidered: The Case of Catherine MacKinnon', *American Political Science Review*, 95/3.

SCHALLER, WALTER (1997). 'Expensive Preferences and the Priority of Right: A Critique of Welfare Egalitarianism', *Journal of Political Philosophy*, 5/3: 254–73.

SCHLERETH, THOMAS (1977). *The Cosmopolitan Ideal in Enlightenment Thought* (University of Notre Dame Press, Notre Dame, Ind,).

SCHLESINGER, ARTHUR (1992). *The Disuniting of America* (Norton, New York).

SCHMIDT, ALVIN (1997). *The Menace of Multiculturalism: Trojan Horse in America* (Praeger, Westport, Conn.).

SCHMIDTZ, DAVID (1990*a*). 'When is Original Appropriation *Required*?', *Monist*, 73/4: 504–18.

—— (1990*b*). 'Justifying the State', *Ethics*, 101/1: 89–102.

—— (1994). 'The Institution of Property', *Social Philosophy and Policy*, 11/1: 42–62.

SCHULTZ, BART (ed.) (1992). *Essays on Sidgwick* (Cambridge University Press, Cambridge).

SCHWARTZ, ADINA (1973). 'Moral Neutrality and Primary Goods', *Ethics*, 83: 294–307.

—— (1982). 'Meaningful Work', *Ethics*, 92/4: 634–46.

SCHWARTZ, JUSTIN (1992). 'From Libertarianism to Egalitarianism', *Social Theory and Practice*, 18/3: 259–88.

SCHWARTZ, NANCY (1979). 'Distinction between Public and Private Life: Marx on the Zoon Politikon', *Political Theory*, 7/2: 245–66.

SCHWARTZ, WARREN (ed.) (1995). *Justice in Immigration* (Cambridge University Press, Cambridge).

SCHWEICKART, DAVID (1978). 'Should Rawls Be a Socialist?', *Social Theory and Practice*, 5/1: 1–27.

SEHON, SCOTT (1996). 'Okin on Feminism and Rawls', *Philosophical Forum*, 27/4: 321–32.

SEIGAL, REVA (1996) '"The Rule of Love": Wife Beating as Prerogative and Privacy', *Yale Law Journal*, 105/8: 2117–208.

SEN, AMARTYA (1980). 'Equality of What?', in S. McMurrin (ed.), *The Tanner Lectures on Human Values*, vol. i (University of Utah Press, Salt Lake City), 353–69.

—— (1985). 'Rights and Capabilities', in T. Honderich (ed.), *Morality and Objectivity* (Routledge and Kegan Paul, London), 130–48.

—— (1990*a*). 'Justice: Means versus Freedom', *Philosophy and Public Affairs*, 19/2: 111–21.

—— (1990*b*). 'Welfare, Freedom and Social Choice', *Recherches économiques de Louvain*, 56/3: 451–86.

—— (1991). 'Welfare, Preference and Freedom', *Journal of Econometrics*, 50: 15–29.

—— and WILLIAMS, BERNARD (eds.) (1982). *Utilitarianism and Beyond* (Cambridge University Press, Cambridge).

Sevenhuijsen, Selma (1998). *Citizenship and the Ethics of Care: Feminist Considerations on Justice, Morality and Politics* (Routledge, London).

Shachar, Ayelet (1998). 'Group Identity and Women's Rights: The Perils of Multicultural Accommodation', *Journal of Political Philosophy*, 6: 285–305.

—— (1999). 'The Paradox of Multicultural Vulnerability', in Joppke and Lukes 1999, 87–111.

—— (2001). *Multicultural Jurisdictions: Preserving Cultural Differences and Women's Rights in a Liberal State* (Cambridge University Press, Cambridge).

Shafir, Gershon (ed.) (1998). *The Citizenship Debates: A Reader* (University of Minnesota Press, Minneapolis).

Shanley, Mary Lyndon, and Narayan, Uma (eds.) (1997). *Reconstructing Political Theory: Feminist Perspectives* (Pennsylvania University Press, Philadelphia).

—— and Pateman, Carole (eds.) (1991). *Feminist Interpretations and Political Theory* (Pennsylvania State University Press, University Park).

Shapiro, Daniel (1993). 'Liberal Egalitarianism, Basic Rights, and Free Market Capitalism', *Reason Papers* 18: 169–88.

—— (1997). 'Can Old-Age Social Insurance be Justified?', *Social Philosophy and Policy*, 14/2: 116–44.

—— (1998). 'Why Even Egalitarians Should Favour Market Health Insurance', *Social Philosophy and Policy*, 15/2: 84–132.

Shapiro, Ian (1991). 'Resources, Capacities, and Ownership: The Workmanship Ideal and Distributive Justice', *Political Theory*, 19/1: 47–72.

—— (1999). *Democratic Justice* (Yale University Press, New Haven).

—— and Kymlicka, Will (eds.) (1997). *Ethnicity and Group Rights* (New York University Press, New York).

Shaw, William (1998). *Contemporary Ethics: Taking Account of Utilitarianism* (Blackwell, Oxford).

Sher, George (1975). 'Justifying Reverse Discrimination in Employment', *Philosophy and Public Affairs*, 4/2: 159–70.

—— (1987). 'Other Voices, Other Rooms? Women's Psychology and Moral Theory', in Kittay and Meyers 1987, 178–89.

—— (1997). *Beyond Neutrality: Perfectionism and Politics* (Cambridge University Press, Cambridge).

—— and Brody, Baruch (eds.) (1999). *Social and Political Philosophy: Contemporary Readings* (Harcourt Brace, New York).

Shklar, Judith (1991). 'American Citizenship: The Quest for Inclusion', in *The Tanner Lectures on Human Values*, vol. x (University of Utah Press, Salt Lake City), 386–439.

Shrage, Laurie (1998). 'Equal Opportunity', in Jaggar and Young 1998, 559–68.

Shue, Henry (1988). 'Mediating Duties', *Ethics*, 98/4: 687–704.

Sidgwick, Henry (1981). *The Methods of Ethics* (Hackett, Indianapolis; 1st pub. 1874).

Silvers, Anita, Wasserman, David, and Mahowald, Mary (1998). *Disability, Difference, Discrimination: Perspectives on Justice in Bioethics and Public Policy* (Rowman and Littlefield, Lanham, Md.).

Singer, Peter (1977). 'Utility and the Survival Lottery', *Philosophy*, 52: 218–22.

—— (ed.) (1991). *A Companion to Ethics* (Blackwell, Oxford).

SINGER, PETER (1993). *Practical Ethics* (Cambridge University Press, Cambridge).

SINOPLI, RICHARD (1992). *The Foundations of American Citizenship: Liberalism, the Constitution and Civic Virtue* (Oxford University Press, New York).

SKINNER, QUENTIN (1990). 'The Republican Ideal of Political Liberty', in Gisela Bock et al. (eds.) *Machiavelli and Republicanism* (Cambridge University Press, Cambridge), 293–309.

—— (1992). 'On Justice, the Common Good and the Priority of Liberty', in Mouffe 1992*b*, 211–24.

—— (1998). *Liberty before Liberalism* (Cambridge University Press, Cambridge).

SKITKA, L. J., and TETLOCK, P. E. (1993). 'Of Ants and Grasshoppers: The Political Psychology of Allocating Public Assistance', in B. A. Mellers and J. Baron (eds.), *Psychological Perspectives on Justice: Theory and Applications* (Cambridge University Press, New York), 205–33.

SMART, J. J. C. (1973). 'An Outline of a System of Utilitarian Ethics', in J. J. C. Smart and B. Williams (eds.), *Utilitarianism: For and Against* (Cambridge University Press, Cambridge), 1–75.

SMITH, MICHAEL (1988). 'Consequentialism and Moral Character' (unpublished manuscript, Philosophy Department at Monash University).

SMITH, PAUL (1998). 'Incentives and Justice: G. A. Cohen's Egalitarian Critique of Rawls', *Social Theory and Practice*, 24/2: 205–35.

SMITH, ROGERS (1985). *Liberalism and American Constitutional Law* (Harvard University Press, Cambridge, Mass.).

—— (1997). *Civic Ideals: Conflicting Visions of Citizenship in American History* (Yale University Press, New Haven).

SMITH, STEVEN (1989). *Hegel's Critique of Liberalism: Rights in Context* (University of Chicago Press, Chicago).

SOMMERS, CHRISTINA (1987). 'Filial Morality', in Kittay and Meyers 1987, 69–84.

SPINNER, JEFF (1994). *The Boundaries of Citizenship: Race, Ethnicity and Nationality in the Liberal State* (Johns Hopkins University Press, Baltimore).

—— (2000). *Surviving Diversity: Religion and Democratic Citizenship* (Johns Hopkins University Press, Baltimore).

SPRAGENS, THOMAS (1999). *Civic Liberalism: Reflections on our Democratic Ideals* (Rowman and Littlefield, Lanham, Md.).

STEIN, LAURA (1993). 'Living with the Risk of Backfire: A Response to the Feminist Critiques of Privacy and Equality', *Minnesota Law Review*, 77/5: 1153–92.

STEINER, HILLEL (1977). 'The Natural Right to the Means of Production', *Philosophical Quarterly*, 27/106: 41–9.

—— (1981). 'Liberty and Equality', *Political Studies*, 29/4: 555–69.

—— (1983). 'How Free? Computing Personal Liberty', in A. P. Griffiths (ed.), *On Liberty* (Cambridge University Press, Cambridge), 73–89.

—— (1994). *An Essay on Rights* (Blackwell, Oxford).

—— (1998). 'Choice and Circumstance', in Andrew Mason (ed.), *Ideals of Equality* (Blackwell, Oxford), 95–112.

STERBA, JAMES (1988). *How to Make People Just: A Practical Reconciliation of Alternative Conceptions of Justice* (Rowman and Littlefield, Totowa, NJ).

STERBA, JAMES (2000). 'Fom Liberty to Welfare: An Update', *Social Theory and Practice*, 26/3: 465–78.

STIEHM, JUDITH (1983). 'The Unit of Political Analysis: Our Aristotelian Hangover', in S. Harding and M. Hintikka (eds.), *Discovering Reality* (Reidel, Dordrecht), 31–44.

STOCKER, MICHAEL (1987). 'Duty and Friendship: Toward a Synthesis of Gilligan's Contrastive Moral Concepts', in Kittay and Meyers 1987, 56–68.

STOUT, JEFFREY (1986). 'Liberal Society and the Languages of Morals', *Soundings*, 69/1: 32–59.

STRIKE, KENNETH (1994). 'On the Construction of Public Speech: Pluralism and Public Reason', *Educational Theory*, 44/1: 1–26.

SULLIVAN, WILLIAM (1982). *Reconstructing Public Philosophy* (University of California Press, Berkeley and Los Angeles).

SUMNER, L. W. (1987). *The Moral Foundation of Rights* (Oxford University Press, Oxford).

SUNSTEIN, CASS (1986). 'Legal Interference with Private Preferences', *University of Chicago Law Review*, 53/4: 1129–74.

—— (1991). 'Preferences and Politics', *Philosophy and Public Affairs*, 20/1: 3–34.

—— (1996). 'Social Roles and Social Norms', *Columbia Law Review*, 96: 903–68.

—— (1997). *Free Markets and Social Justice* (Oxford University Press, Oxford).

—— (1999). 'Should Sex Equality Law Apply to Religious Institutions', in Okin 1999, 85–94.

SVENSSON, FRANCES (1979). 'Liberal Democracy and Group Rights: The Legacy of Individualism and its Impact on American Indian Tribes', *Political Studies*, 27/3: 421–39.

SWIFT, ADAM, MARSHALL, GORDON, BURGOYNE, CAROLE, and ROUTH, DAVID (1995). 'Distributive Justice: Does it Matter What the People Think', in J. R. Kluegel, D. S. Mason and B. Wegener (eds.), *Social Justice and Political Change: Public Opinion in Capitalist and Post-communist States* (Aldine de Gruyter, New York), 15–47.

TALISSE, ROBERT (2000). *On Rawls* (Wadsworth, Belmont, Calif.).

TAM, HENRY (1998). *Communitarianism: A New Agenda for Politics and Citizenship* (New York University Press, New York).

TAMIR, YAEL (1993). *Liberal Nationalism* (Princeton University Press, Princeton).

TAN, KOK-CHOR (2000). *Toleration, Diversity, and Global Justice* (Pennsylvania State University Press, University Park).

TAUB, NADINE, and SCHNEIDER, ELIZABETH (1982). 'Perspectives on Women's Subordination and the Role of Law', in D. Kairys (ed.) *The Politics of Law* (Pantheon, New York), 152–76.

TAWNEY, R. H. (1964). *Equality*, 4th edn. (Allen and Unwin, London).

TAYLOR, CHARLES (1979). *Hegel and Modern Society* (Cambridge University Press, Cambridge).

—— (1985a). *Philosophy and the Human Sciences: Philosophical Papers*, vol. ii (Cambridge University Press, Cambridge).

—— (1985b). 'Alternative Futures: Legitimacy, Identity and Alienation in Late Twentieth Century Canada', in Cairns and Williams 1985, 183–229.

—— (1989a). 'Cross-Purposes: The Liberal-Communitarian Debate', in Nancy Rosenblum (ed.) *Liberalism and the Moral Life* (Harvard University Press, Cambridge, Mass.), 159–82.

—— (1989b). *Sources of the Self: The Making of the Modern Identity* (Cambridge University Press, Cambridge).

TAYLOR CHARLES (1991). 'Shared and Divergent Values', in Ronald Watts and D. Brown (eds.), *Options for a New Canada* (University of Toronto Press, Toronto), 53–76.

—— (1992). 'The Politics of Recognition', in Amy Gutmann (ed.), *Multiculturalism and the 'Politics of Recognition'* (Princeton University Press, Princeton), 25–73.

—— (1997). 'Nationalism and Modernity', in McKim and McMahan 1997, 31–55.

—— (1999). *A Catholic Modernity* (Oxford University Press, Oxford).

TEMKIN, LARRY (1993). *Inequality* (Oxford University Press, New York).

THOMPSON, DENNIS (1999). 'Democratic Theory and Global Society', *Journal of Political Philosophy*, 7/2: 111–25.

TILMAN, RICK (2001). *Ideology and Utopia in the Social Philosophy of the Libertarian Economists* (Greenwood, New York).

TOMASI, JOHN (1991). 'Individual Rights, and Community Virtues', *Ethics*, 101/3: 521–36.

—— (2001). *Liberalism beyond Justice: Citizens, Society, and the Boundaries of Political Theory* (Princeton University Press, Princeton).

TONG, ROSEMARY (1993). *Feminine and Feminist Ethics* (Wadsworth, Belmont, Calif.).

—— (1998). *Feminist Thought: A More Comprehensive Introduction*, 2nd edn. (Westview, Boulder, Colo.).

TREMAIN, SHELLEY (1996). 'Dworkin on Disablement and Resources', *Canadian Journal of Law and Jurisprudence*, 9/2: 343–59.

TRONTO, JOAN (1987). 'Beyond Gender Difference to a Theory of Care', *Signs*, 12/4: 644–63.

—— (1993). *Moral Boundaries: A Political Argument for an Ethic of Care* (Routledge, New York).

—— (1995). 'Care as a Basis for Radical Political Judgements', *Hypatia*, 10/2: 141–9.

TULLY, JAMES (1995). *Strange Multiplicity: Constitutionalism in an Age of Diversity* (Cambridge University Press, Cambridge).

—— (2000). 'Struggles over Recognition and Distribution', *Constellations*, 7/4: 469–82.

—— and WEINSTOCK, DANIEL (eds.) (1994). *Philosophy in an Age of Pluralism: The Philosophy of Charles Taylor in Question* (Cambridge University Press, Cambridge)

TYLER, TOM, et al. (1997). *Social Justice in a Diverse Society* (Westview, Boulder, Colo.).

UNGER, ROBERTO (1984). *Knowledge and Politics* (Macmillan, New York).

VALLENTYNE, PETER (ed.) (1991). *Contractarianism and Rational Choice: Essays on Gauthier* (Cambridge University Press, New York).

—— (1997). 'Self-Ownership and Equality: Brute Luck, Gifts, Universal Dominance, and Leximin', *Ethics*, 107/2: 321–43.

—— (1998). 'Critical Notice of G. A Cohen *Self-Ownership, Freedom, and Equality*', *Canadian Journal of Philosophy*, 28/4: 609–26.

—— and STEINER, HILLEL (eds.) (2000a). *The Origins of Left-Libertarianism: An Anthology of Historical Writings* (Palgrave, London).

—— —— (eds.) (2000b). *Left-Libertarianism and its Critics: The Contemporary Debate* (Palgrave, London).

VALLS, ANDREW (1999). 'The Libertarian Case for Affirmative Action', *Social Theory and Practice*, 25/2: 299–323.

VAN DER VEEN, ROBERT, and VAN PARIJS, PHILIPPE (1985). 'Entitlement Theories of Justice', *Economics and Philosophy*, 1/1: 69–81.

VAN DYKE, VERNON (1975). 'Justice as Fairness: For Groups?', *American Political Science Review* 69: 607–14.

VAN DYKE, VERNON (1977). 'The Individual, the State, and Ethnic Communities in Political Theory', World Politics, 29/3: 343–69.

—— (1982). 'Collective Rights and Moral Rights: Problems in Liberal-Democratic Thought', Journal of Politics, 44: 21–40.

—— (1985). Human Rights, Ethnicity and Discrimination (Greenwood, Westport, Conn.).

VAN GUNSTEREN, HERMAN (1978). 'Notes towards a Theory of Citizenship', in P. Birnbaum et al. (eds.), Democracy, Consensus and Social Contract (Sage, London), 9–35.

—— (1998). A Theory of Citizenship: Organizing Plurality in Contemporary Democracies (Westview, Boulder, Colo.).

VAN PARIJS, PHILIPPE (1991). 'Why Surfers Should Be Fed: The Liberal Case for an Unconditional Basic Income', Philosophy and Public Affairs, 20/2: 101–31.

—— (ed) (1992). Arguing for Basic Income (Verso, London).

—— (1993). Marxism Recycled (Cambridge University Press, Cambridge).

—— (1995). Real Freedom for All (Oxford University Press, Oxford).

—— (2000). 'A Basic Income for All', Boston Review, 25/5, 4–8.

—— (2001). What's Wrong with a Free Lunch: A New Democracy Forum on Universal Basic Income (Beacon Press, Boston).

VARIAN, HAL (1985). 'Dworkin on Equality of Resources', Economics and Philosophy, 1/1: 110–25.

VINCENT, ANDREW, and PLANT, RAYMOND (1984). Philosophy, Politics and Citizenship: The Life and Thought of the British Idealists (Blackwell, Oxford).

VOET, MARIA CHRISTINE BERNADETTA, and VOET, RIAN (1998). Feminism and Citizenship (Sage, London).

VOGEL, URSULA (1988). 'When the Earth Belonged to All: The Land Question in Eighteenth-Century Justifications of Private Property', Political Studies, 36/1: 102–22.

—— (1991). 'Is Citizenship Gender-Specific?', in Vogel and Moran 1991, 58–85.

—— and MORAN, MICHAEL (1991). The Frontiers of Citizenship (St Martin's Press, New York).

VOICE, PAUL (1993). 'What Do Children Deserve?', South African Journal of Philosophy, 12/4: 122–5.

WALDRON, JEREMY (1986). 'Welfare and the Images of Charity', Philosophical Quarterly, 36/145: 463–82.

—— (1987). 'Theoretical Foundations of Liberalism', Philosophical Quarterly, 37/147: 127–50.

—— (1989). 'Autonomy and Perfectionism in Raz's Morality of Freedom', Southern California Law Review, 62/3: 1097–152.

—— (1991). The Right to Private Property (Oxford University Press, Oxford)

—— (1992). 'Superseding Historic Injustice', Ethics, 103/1: 4–28.

—— (1993). Liberal Rights: Collected Papers 1981–1991 (Cambridge University Press, Cambridge).

—— (1995). 'Minority Cultures and the Cosmopolitan Alternative', in Kymlicka 1995b, 93–121.

—— (1999). Law and Disagreement (Oxford University Press, Oxford).

WALKER, BRIAN (1998). 'Social Movements as Nationalisms', in Couture, Nielsen, and Seymour 1998, 505–47.

WALKER, SAMUEL (1998). *The Rights Revolution: Rights and Community in Modern America* (Oxford University Press, New York).

WALL, STEVEN (1998). *Liberalism, Perfectionism and Restraint* (Cambridge University Press, Cambridge).

WALLACH, JOHN (2000). 'Can Liberalism be Virtuous?', *Polity*, 33/1: 163–74.

WALZER, MICHAEL (1981). 'Liberalism and the Art of Separation', *Political Theory*, 12: 315–30.

—— (1983). *Spheres of Justice: A Defence of Pluralism and Equality* (Blackwell, Oxford).

—— (1989). 'Citizenship', in T. Ball and J. Farr (eds.), *Political Innovation and Conceptual Change* (Cambridge University Press, Cambridge), 211–19.

—— (1990). 'The Communitarian Critique of Liberalism', *Political Theory*, 18/1: 6–23.

—— (1992*a*) 'The Civil Society Argument', in Mouffe 1992*b*, 89–107.

—— (1992*b*). *What it Means to be an American* (Marsilio, New York).

—— (1992*c*). 'The New Tribalism', *Dissent*, Spring: 164–71.

—— (1992*d*). 'Comment', in Amy Gutmann (ed.), *Multiculturalism and the 'Politics of Recognition'* (Princeton University Press, Princeton), 99–103.

—— (1994). *Thick and Thin: Moral Argument at Home and Abroad* (Harvard University Press, Cambridge, Mass.).

—— (1995*a*). 'Pluralism in Political Perspective', in Kymlicka 1995*b*, 139–54.

—— (1995*b*). 'Response', in Miller and Walzer 1995, 281–98.

—— (ed.) (1995*c*). *Toward a Global Civil Society* (Berhahn Books, (Oxford).

—— (1997). *On Toleration* (Yale University Press, New Haven).

WARD, CYNTHIA (1991). 'The Limits of "Liberal Republicanism": Why Group-Based Remedies and Republican Citizenship Don't Mix', *Columbia Law Review*, 91/3: 581–607.

WARE, ROBERT (1989). 'How Marxism is Analyzed: An Introduction', *Canadian Journal of Philosophy*, supplementary vol. 15: 1–26.

WARREN, MARK (ed.) (1999). *Democracy and Trust* (Cambridge University Press, Cambridge).

WARREN, PAUL (1994). 'Self-Ownership, Reciprocity, and Exploitation, or Why Marxists Shouldn't Be Afraid of Robert Nozick', *Canadian Journal of Philosophy*, 24/1: 33–56.

—— (1997). 'Should Marxists be Liberal Egalitarians?', *Journal of Political Philosophy*, 5/1: 47–68.

WEALE, ALBERT (1982). *Political Theory and Social Policy* (Macmillan, London).

WEINBERG, JUSTIN (1997). 'Freedom, Self-Ownership, and Libertarian Philosophical Diaspora', *Critical Review*, 11/3: 323–44.

—— (1998). 'Self- and World-Ownership: Rejoinder to Epstein, Palmer, and Feallsanach', *Critical Review*, 12/3: 325–36.

WEINSTOCK, DANIEL (1998). 'Neutralizing Perfection: Hurka on Liberal Neutrality', *Dialogue*, 38/1: 45–62.

—— (1999). 'Building Trust in Divided Societies', *Journal of Political Philosophy*, 7/3: 287–307.

—— (2000). 'Saving Democracy from Deliberation', in Ronald Beiner and Wayne Norman (eds.), *Canadian Political Philosophy: Contemporary Reflections* (Oxford University Press, Toronto), 78–91.

WEINSTOCK, DANIEL (2001). 'Citizenship and Pluralism', forthcoming in Robert L. Simon (ed.), *Blackwell Guide to Social and Political Philosophy* (Blackwell, Oxford).

WEISS, PENNY, and FRIEDMAN, MARILYN (eds.) (1995). *Feminism and Community* (Temple University Press, Philadelphia).

WEITZMAN, LENORE (1985). *The Divorce Revolution: The Unexpected Social and Economic Consequences for Women and Children in America* (Free Press, New York).

WENAR, LEIF (1998). 'Original Acquisition of Private Property', *Mind*, 107: 799–819.

WENDELL, SUSAN (1987). 'A (Qualified) Defense of Liberal Feminism', *Hypatia*, 2/2: 65–93.

WEST, LOIS (ed.) (1997). *Feminist Nationalism* (Routledge, London).

WEST, ROBIN (1997). *Caring for Justice* (New York University Press, New York).

WHEWELL, WILLIAM (1845) *The Elements of Morality* (Harper and Brothers, New York).

WHITE, PATRICIA (1992). 'Decency and Education for Citizenship', *Journal of Moral Education*, 21/3: 207–16.

WHITE, STEVEN (1991). *Political Theory and Postmodernism* (Cambridge University Press, Cambridge).

WHITE, STUART (1998). 'Interpreting the "Third Way"', *Renewal*, 6/2: 17–30.

—— (2000). 'Review Article: Social Rights and the Social Contract—Political Theory and the New Welfare Politics', *British Journal of Political Science*, 30: 507–32.

WILLET, CYNTHIA (1998). *Theorizing Multiculturalism: A Guide to the Current Debate* (Blackwell, Oxford).

WILLIAMS, ANDREW (1998). 'Incentives, Inequality, and Publicity', *Philosophy and Public Affairs*, 27/3: 225–47.

WILLIAMS, BERNARD (1971). 'The Idea of Equality', in H. Bedau (ed.), *Justice and Equality* (Prentice-Hall, Englewood Cliffs, NJ), 116–37.

—— (1972). *Morality: An Introduction to Ethics* (Harper and Row, New York).

—— (1973). 'A Critique of Utilitarianism', in J. J. C. Smart and B. Williams (eds.) *Utilitarianism: For and Against* (Cambridge University Press, Cambridge), 75–150.

—— (1981). *Moral Luck* (Cambridge University Press, Cambridge).

—— (1985). *Ethics and the Limits of Philosophy* (Fontana Press, London).

—— and SEN, AMARTYA (1982). 'Introduction' in Sen and Williams (eds.), *Utilitarianism and Beyond* (Cambridge University Press, Cambridge), 1–21.

WILLIAMS, MELISSA (1998). *Voice, Trust and Memory: Marginalized Groups and the Failings of Liberal Representation* (Princeton University Press, Princeton).

—— (2000). 'The Uneasy Alliance of Group Representation and Deliberative Democracy', in Kymlicka and Norman 2000, 124–52.

WILSON, LOIS (1988). 'Is a "Feminine" Ethic Enough?', *Atlantis*, 13/2: 15–23.

WOLFE, ALAN, and LAUSEN, JYETTE (1997). 'Identity Politics and the Welfare State', *Social Philosophy and Politics*, 14/2: 231–55.

WOLFF, JONATHAN (1991). *Robert Nozick: Property, Justice, and the Minimal State* (Stanford University Press, Stanford, Calif.).

—— (1992). 'Not Bargaining for the Welfare State', *Analysis*, 52/2: 118–25.

—— (1996a). *An Introduction to Political Philosophy* (Oxford University Press, Oxford).

—— (1996b). 'Rational, Fair, and Reasonable', *Utilitas*, 8/3: 263–71.

—— (1998). 'Fairness, Respect, and the Egalitarian Ethos', *Philosophy and Public Affairs*, 27/2: 97–122.

WOLFF, ROBERT P. (1977). *Understanding Rawls* (Princeton University Press, Princeton).

WOLGAST, ELIZABETH (1987). *The Grammar of Justice* (Cornell University Press, Ithaca, NY).

WOLIN, SHELDON (1960). *Politics and Vision* (Little Brown, Boston).

WOOD, ALLEN (1972). 'The Marxian Critique of Justice', *Philosophy and Public Affairs*, 1/3: 244–82.

—— (1979). 'Marx on Right and Justice', *Philosophy and Public Affairs*, 8/3: 267–95.

—— (1981). 'Marx and Equality', in J. Mepham and D. H. Ruben (eds.), *Issues in Marxist Philosophy*, vol. iv (Harvester Press, Brighton), 195–220.

—— (1984). 'Justice and Class Interests', *Philosophica*, 33/1: 9–32.

WRIGHT, SUE (2000). *Community and Communication* (Multilingual Matters, Clevedon).

YOUNG, IRIS MARION (1981). 'Toward a Critical Theory of Justice', *Social Theory and Practice*, 7/3: 279–302.

—— (1987). 'Impartiality and the Civic Public', in S. Benhabib and D. Cornell (eds.) *Feminism as Critique* (University of Minnesota Press, Minneapolis), 56–77.

—— (1989). 'Polity and Group Difference: A Critique of the Ideal of Universal Citizenship', *Ethics*, 99/2: 250–74.

—— (1990). *Justice and the Politics of Difference* (Princeton University Press, Princeton).

—— (1993). 'Justice and Communicative Democracy', in Roger Gottlieb (ed.), *Radical Philosophy: Tradition, Counter-Tradition, Politics* (Temple University Press, Philadelphia), 123–43.

—— (1995a). 'Together in Difference: Transforming the Logic of Group Political Conflict', in Kymlicka 1995b, 155–76.

—— (1995b). 'Mothers, Citizenship and Independence: A Critique of Pure Family Values', *Ethics*, 105/3: 535–56.

—— (1996). 'Communication and the Other: Beyond Deliberative Democracy', in Seyla Benhabib (ed.), *Democracy and Difference: Contesting the Boundaries of the Political* (Princeton University Press, Princeton), 120–35.

YOUNG, IRIS MARION (1997a). 'A Multicultural Continuum: A Critique of Will Kymlicka's Ethnic-Nation Dichotomy', *Constellations*, 4/1: 48–53.

—— (1997b). 'Political Theory: An Overview', in Robert Goodin and Hans-Dieter Klingeman (eds.), *A New Handbook of Political Science* (Oxford University Press, Oxford), 479–502.

—— (2000a). *Inclusion and Democracy* (Oxford University Press, Oxford).

—— (2000b). 'Self-Determination and Global Democracy: A Critique of Liberal Nationalism', in Ian Shapiro and Stephen Macedo (eds.), *Designing Democratic Institutions* (New York University Press, New York), 147–83.

YUVAL-DAVIS, NIRA (1997). *Gender and Nation* (Sage, London).

—— and WERBNER, P. (eds.) (1999). *Women, Citizenship, and Difference* (Zed Books, London).

ZARETSKY, ELI (1982). 'The Place of the Family in the Origins of the Welfare State', in B. Thorne and M. Yalom (eds.), *Rethinking the Family: Some Feminist Questions* (Longman, New York), 184–224.

ZIMMERMAN, MICHAEL (ed.) (1993). *Environmental Philosophy: From Animal Rights to Radical Ecology* (Prentice-Hall, Englewood Cliffs, NJ).

INDEX

abortion 161n.2

Abrams, K. 419

abstraction 44–45, 52n.18, 62, 404, 406–409, 414–417

abundance 170, 172, 187, 189

accountability
European Union (EU) 313–314
national governments 314

Ackerman, B. 83, 95, 100n.13, 164n.42, 277n.8, 324n.23

adaptive preferences 15–17, 50n.2, 393, 425n.18

Addis, A. 373n.10

Adler, J. 403, 428n.45

adultery 17

advertising, sexist 393

aesthetics 11–12, 36

affirmative action 58, 89, 205n.18, 382, 403

African Americans 47, 360–362, 375n.35
education 84
integration 361

aggregative democracy 290–291, 323n.11, n.13

Albania 143–144, 162–163n.26

Alexander, L. 99n.9

Alfred, G. 375n.27

alienation 163, 190–195, 199–201, 213, 424n.16

Allen, A. 396, 398, 425n.18, n.22

Allen, D. 206n.20

Alstott, A. 83, 100n.13

ambition-sensitivity (Dworkin) 74–76, 80–87, 94, 99n.9, 100n.18, 154–155, 166, 185–186, 189, 206n.19, 385

American Supreme Court 238–239, 281n.34, 288, 325n.31

Amish 238–239, 240, 243, 278n.18, 338, 348–349, 355
education 308, 309–310, 325n.31, n.32

anarchism 62

Anaya, J. 375n.26, 376n.41

Anderson, B. 198, 282n.38, 374n.23

Anderson, E. 94, 100n.17, 101n.21

androgyny 3

apostasy 231, 233–234, 236–237, 238

Appiah, K. 375n.35

Archibugi, D. 326n.34

Arendt, H. 296, 297, 388, 390, 391–392, 394

Aristotle 294, 296, 388

Arneson, R. 66, 80, 92n.9, 93, 100n.12, 100n.17, 101n.21, 144, 146, 162n.11, 162n.25, 163n.27, 164n.27, 164n.42, 170, 171, 181, 183–186,

188–189, 192, 193–195, 197, 204n.9, n.14, 205n.18, 206n.21, 325n.31

Arnsperger, C. 99n.8

Arthur, J. 120, 162n.11

artifice 129

assimilation, cultural 353–354

associations see attachments; social unions

Athens, self-government 295

Atkinson, T. 100n.15

atomism 245, 248, 251–252, 271, 280n.26
private life as 295–296

attachments 25–26, 30, 43, 192–193, 194, 222–228, 392–393, 394–395, 398–400, 405–407, 426n.31, 428n.45
see also conceptions of the good

Attanuci, J. 427n.37

auction scheme (Dworkin) 75–79, 87–89, 95, 189

Australia
immigration 353, 426n.32
multicultural policies 367–368

Austria
immigration 375–376n.36
migrants 358

authority, questioning of 308, 309, 356

autonomy, individual 116–118, 119, 147, 162n.9, 245–246, 248–249, 251, 279n.20, 280n.24, 280n.26, 384, 388, 396–398
and communitarianism 240, 336–337
development of 245–246
of individuals 336–337, 339
and internal restrictions 342
and multiculturalism 339
rejection of 229, 243
social exercise of 245–246
and tolerance 229–230
within care perspective 413–420, 430n.54
see also self-determination

Bader, V. 282n.45

Baier, A. 302, 400, 401, 402, 418–419, 426n.32, 428n.42, 48

Bailey, J. 18, 28, 51n.12, n.13, 52n.19, 66

Baker, C. 173, 373n.9

Ball, S. 51n.11

Banting, K. 376n.42

Barbalet, J. M. 373n.2

Barber, B. 292, 323n.7

Bardhan, P. 203n.3